WILLIAM
SHAKESPEARE'S

Hamlet

THE
Tragicall Hiſtorie of
HAMLET,

Prince of Denmarke.

By William Shakeſpeare.

Newly imprinted and enlarged to almoſt as much
againe as it was, according to the true and perfect
Coppie.

AT LONDON,
Printed by I. R. for N. L. and are to be ſold at his
ſhoppe vnder Saint Dunſtons Church in
Fleetſtreet. 1604.

Title page of the 1604 quarto edition
of William Shakespeare's *Hamlet* (Q2).

WILLIAM SHAKESPEARE'S

Hamlet

Edited and Annotated by

GIDEON
RAPPAPORT

ONE MIND GOOD PRESS
San Diego, California

Cover image: Adam Vogler,
Hamlet and the Ghost of His Father (1789),
pen and gray ink drawing on graphite
(from a painting by Henry Fuseli),
Metropolitan Museum of Art open access.

Frontispiece image: Title page of William Shakespeare's
Tragical History of Hamlet, Prince of Denmark,
Second Quarto (1604),
Wikimedia Commons (CC-PD-US).

One Mind Good Press
San Diego, CA 92117

ISBN 979-8-218-34591-4

Typeset in Bennet Text

Designed by P D Burgess

Contents

Preface — vii

✳

Acknowledgements — x

✳

A Note on the Text — xi

✳

Abbreviations Used in the Annotation — xii

✳

List of Bibliographical References — xiii

✳

Introduction
Divine Shaping:
The Moral Drama of *Hamlet* — 1

✳

The Tragedy of Hamlet,
Prince of Denmark — 19

Preface

This edition of William Shakespeare's *Hamlet*, the work of a lifelong teacher and theatrical dramaturge, is intended to provide what is needed to get from the play itself what Shakespeare essentially means by *Hamlet*. It aims to help general readers, students, teachers, actors, directors, playwrights, literary critics, and scholars to appreciate this famous but much misunderstood play by grasping not only the meanings of particular words and phrases that can be glossed in footnotes but the essential dramatic structure of the play as a whole.

In our time there have been two main obstacles to experiencing the dramatic meaning of *Hamlet*: a) the assumptions about the nature of the world and the nature of man that modern readers and audiences bring to the play; and b) the false and distracting pre-existing interpretations of the play that have become part of the culture and of our minds.

Despite the implication of many modern discussions, Shakespeare would not have intended to make this or any other play obscure. In fact, he made the meaning of *Hamlet* quite clear to his own audience. We encounter obscurities in it partly because the language is four hundred years old, but more importantly because what Shakespeare's audience believed when they walked into their theaters was in many ways different from what we believe when we walk into ours. This edition is intended to clarify what the play meant in its time and thereby what it can still mean in ours. It will do so by assuming about man, the world, and God what Shakespeare and his audience assumed. When we start by knowing where Shakespeare's audience started, the meaning of the whole will become clear and will resist being supplanted by the variety of often contradictory modern interpretations.

Those erroneous interpretations have been legion. Though "To be or not to be" is probably the best-known phrase in Shakespeare, the speech it begins is not the most important in the play, whose center lies elsewhere. Neither is *Hamlet* about "a man who could not make up his mind," as the voice-over pronounces at the beginning of the 1948 Laurence Olivier film version of the play. Nor is the play about a man who thinks too much to be able to act, or is too melancholy to act, or wants to commit suicide, or is secretly in love with his mother, or can't decide whether to be a scholar or a soldier, or is so profound and mysterious that no one can figure him out at all. Nor is the play to be relegated into the interpretive dead end called the "problem play," by which epithet Hamlet's actual moral dilemma is turned into a hypothetical dramaturgical failure of Shakespeare's. Nor is it about many another notion that has been projected onto it by critics, directors, and other interpreters over the years.

Certainly many students of *Hamlet* have offered valid insights about the play, and the scholarly contribution to our knowledge has been vast. But too many interpreters in modern times have missed the mark by substituting their own ideas for the meanings that Shakespeare has actually given us. To recover those meanings, this edition will apply the following principles:

1 "The players cannot keep counsel: they'll tell all" (III. ii.141–42), the corollary being that if no player tells it, it probably isn't there—Shakespeare did not write this play to keep secrets from us.
2 When Shakespeare uses the words "Heaven," "Hell," "damn," "divinity," and "soul," he means them not only metaphorically but literally, as his audience would have understood them.
3 Stage and film productions and scholarly commentaries in which the character of Hamlet is pre-defined as essentially indecisive, melancholy, confused, hyper-conscious, Oedipal, existentialist, unfathomable, or modern, and which then color the play's general atmosphere and all its lines to fit that "mood" or "state of mind" without regard to any precise psychological, moral, or spiritual development, or even to the explicit meaning of the play's actual lines, are at best misleading and at worst deadly to the actual drama of the play, nor are they consistent with the way Shakespeare's plays work.

4   The play uses the revenge play formula to put revenge itself on trial and locates all human action in the context of the moral-spiritual givens of reality as Shakespeare and his audience saw them: God exists, the human soul is immortal, death brings the soul to judgment, and either salvation or damnation is the soul's actual future. These givens are not merely conjectures: they are explicitly stated in the text. As J. V. Cunningham said, "In Shakespeare's plays, foreground is background."[1] If only we will take him at his word, Shakespeare tells us what we need to know to understand the context of his drama.

5   As in *Othello*, *King Lear*, and *Macbeth*, the development of the inner life of the main character is the center of the drama. In *Hamlet*, the climax and turning point in the life of the main character and in the play's dramatic movement come in Act III, Scene iii. My inspiration for this understanding comes from the poet Philip Thompson's observation about the scene that "At his one 'ready' moment, in terms of the success of his cause, Hamlet is (literally) damnably unready," demanding "the eternal damnation of Claudius as the only possible means of relief for his personal shame and suffering" and thereby revealing to Shakespeare's Christian audience that his own "guilt is at this moment greater than that of Claudius."[2]

Following these principles, we will find that, though in Hamlet's case the particulars are extreme, *Hamlet* is a play about a man who, like every man, is given a paradoxical assignment: to do the right thing in response to a complex situation not of his own making. Despite a small but dangerous flaw in his character, Hamlet behaves rightly through the first half of the play. At the climax, however, his one flaw pitches him into a fatal moral error. By the consequences of that error, both disastrous and providential, Hamlet is corrected before it is too late. In worldly terms, the play is a tragedy, in particular a revenge-style tragedy. In spiritual terms, it is a morality play, a spiritual pilgrimage, the image of a fall and a redemption. In short, the comical existentialist condensation of the play by "The Reduced Shakespeare Company" to "To be or not to be ... the rest is silence" is seriously misleading. A more authentic condensation would read "No ... the readiness is all," or, more briefly, "No ... Let be." Why this is so will be seen in the introductory essay, "Divine Shaping: The Moral Drama of *Hamlet*," and in the course of the annotation.

My reading of the play rests upon the extraordinary contributions of the great scholars of the last two centuries, as will be seen in the references in the annotation. Beyond my own development of the insight of Philip Thompson quoted above, I believe I may take credit for two points that I have not found written about elsewhere: a) that Hamlet's artful pretense of madness takes the forms of two specific kinds of insanity familiar to Shakespeare's audience and described in Burton's *Anatomy of Melancholy* and other works of the time: the form of madness thought to arise from thwarted love and the form of madness thought to arise from thwarted ambition, both of which Hamlet pretends to exhibit at different times depending on who his onstage audience is; and b) that in the matter of Osric's hat, thematically speaking, Hamlet is to Osric a comical version (a foil) of what the Ghost is to Hamlet. This also may be the first edition in which the details of the fencing wager in Act V, Scene ii, are correctly articulated.

The introductory essay, "Divine Shaping: The Moral Drama of *Hamlet*," gives an overall view of the play's structure, meaning, and drama. In attempting to articulate the thematic unity of the play, it also refutes the long-prevalent idea that the play is a "problem" play, that the main character "cannot make up his mind," that Shakespeare has written a work so far ahead of its time that it expresses the kinds of existential doubt, angst, and confusion that modern thinkers have characteristically brought to ultimate questions. This is not to say that thinkers in Shakespeare's age did not suffer from doubts and confusion. But their fundamental questions differed from ours to the degree that their underlying assumptions about life and the world differed. Neither do those differences mean that Shakespeare's work is irrelevant to us. Part of its greatness lies in its universality. But to appreciate this universality requires that we begin by understanding the play in its own terms. Otherwise we are likely to obscure what Shakespeare is revealing and to put our own, often narrower, concerns in its place. The arguments in the introduction will be supported with specifics in the course of the annotation.

---

1   J. V. Cunningham, in a graduate seminar on *Shakespeare* at Brandeis University, 1974.

2   Philip Thompson, *Dusk and Dawn: Poems and Prose of Philip Thompson*, edited by Gideon Rappaport (San Diego, California: One Mind Good Press, 2005), pages 186–87.

The annotation is intended to serve several purposes: a) to explain the meanings of words and phrases and illuminate the import of longer speeches; b) to provide essential textual information; c) to provide essential background information; d) to offer some practical guidance to directors and actors in making meaningful choices in stage and film productions of the play; and e) most importantly, to put the specific meaning of any word or line of the play into the context of the whole and thereby to provide, detail by detail, an overall sense of the coherence, depth, and significance of the play.

To serve these purposes, the annotation offers

1 The relevant quotation from the text in boldface and then the following kinds of notes:

- the source of a particular reading in the early editions where it seems called for;
- a clarifying explanation or rephrasing of a word or phrase, with a brief indication of the editorial source where it seems relevant;
- background sufficient to recovering what the word or phrase meant to Shakespeare's audience;
- clarification of an unfamiliar grammatical usage with reference to Abbott's *Shakespearian Grammar*;
- some attention to figures of speech;
- references to Shakespeare's educational background in the classics;

2 After a bullet point [•], comments on the meaning of a word, phrase, passage, or dramatic moment and of its relation to the larger context, themes, and meaning of the play;

3 An occasional Note to Actors or Directors with specific suggestions on how to pronounce a word or to bring out the meaning of a line or lines or a point of staging;

4 An occasional longer Speech Note or Scene Note.

Line numbers run down the center between the text and the notes in five-line increments. They refer both to the text on the left and to the annotations on the right, and they correspond to the line numbering of the Riverside Edition. The List of Bibliographical References includes all those works to which short references are made in the annotation. (It is not an exhaustive list of the works consulted.) Unless otherwise noted, all quotations from the Bible are from the Geneva edition, the one that Shakespeare most probably read. Quotations from other works of Shakespeare are taken from the Riverside Edition, and their line indications refer to that edition.

Acknowledgements

Like all present-day commentaries on Shakespeare's work, this edition of *Hamlet* builds upon the previous contributions of the great nineteenth-century scholars H. H. Furness, editor of the New Variorum, E. A. Abbott, cataloguer of Shakespearean grammar, and others, and of the twentieth-century masters of Shakespeare scholarship, E. K. Chambers, W. W. Greg, T. W. Baldwin, G. Blakemore Evans, editor of the *Riverside Shakespeare*, and many others. I have found specific inspiration from the work of G. Wilson Knight, C. S. Lewis, E. M. W. Tillyard, and J. V. Cunningham, among many other commentators. And I have made extensive use of the facsimile editions of the first and second quarto and first folio editions of the play.

I am especially indebted to the prodigious accomplishment of Harold Jenkins in his Arden Shakespeare edition of *Hamlet*. Though my interpretation of the central themes and through-line of the play differ from his, my annotations would not have been possible without his exhaustive scholarship, as frequent references in the notes will show. I am also indebted to the late fencing master Charles Selberg for the clarification of fencing terms in Act V, Scene ii.

Sister Miriam Joseph requires a special note. After my doctoral dissertation was completed, I discovered the existence of her essay called "*Hamlet*: A Christian Tragedy" but did not then have access to it. Even when a chapter of my dissertation was modified and published in 1987 as "Hamlet: Revenge and Readiness," I had not yet found a copy of her essay. When, already in the age of the computer, I began to do the research for this annotation of the play, I was able to secure a copy of the essay, but I did not read it before completing my own work. Knowing that her viewpoint would be similar to mine, I wanted to avoid the unconscious influence of her ideas by working independently, and only at the last to compare our respective readings of the play. When the present work was substantially completed, I did read her essay, wherein I found—much to my joy and astonishment—an almost complete and thorough agreement between us. Her view focuses more on a theological analysis, mine more on a moral. What I call Hamlet's pride or willfulness in Act III, Scene iii, she calls a failure of charity. But we both find in that moment the moral and spiritual fall of Hamlet and the turning point of the play. Everything else stems from that, and we were in agreement about almost all of it. Had I read her essay before doing my own work on the play, I might have felt my contribution to be unnecessary were it not for the fact that her work has been almost entirely ignored by nearly all scholarly professors, drama critics, directors, and dramaturges since its publication in 1962, relegated to dusty libraries as the wishful thinking of a credulous nun. But Sister Miriam Joseph was one of the most astute of Shakespeare's readers of this play, and I would be honored to know that this work had sent even one student of *Hamlet* to the library to take her essay seriously.

Specific personal gratitude goes to my teachers, the late Mary Holmes, perennial inspiration; the late Philip Thompson, whose short paragraphs on Hamlet articulated the kernel of my understanding of the play; the late John Hazel Smith, my mentor in Shakespeare studies; Professor Michael Warren; and Professor Alan Levitan. I am also grateful to my friend Jonathan Saville for illuminating conversation and critical comments, to Jane Bradford, Anna Roseboro, Watson Branch, the late Robert Mulgrew, the late Joyce Sparling, and Deborah Shaul, encouraging and supportive chairmen of the two high-school English departments in which I have taught, and Rachel Malkin for fruitful suggestions. I want to thank the actor and director Joe Sofranko for challenging me to respond in the book to seven pages of questions about the play. Thanks are also due to many friends and students for particular insights and inspirations. My gratitude goes to copyeditor Tom Feltham and to proofreader Penny Silva. Special thanks go to Peter Burgess for his talented book and cover design, his unflagging commitment to the project, and his exemplary patience with the author. Errors of fact and limits of vision, those things of darkness, I acknowledge mine.

There are not words enough in the dictionary or time enough in a life to express the gratitude I owe to my parents, to my sisters, and to Bruce Cantz, Christopher Maron, and Stan Bui.

A Note on the Text

There are three early editions of Hamlet: The First Quarto (Q1), the Second Quarto (Q2), and the First Folio (F). A quarto edition was a small edition of a single play. It is called "quarto" because the large sheets of paper on which the play was printed were folded in four before being bound together. A folio was printed on sheets that were folded in half. Q1 was probably a pirated edition. Q2 and F were editions authorized by Shakespeare's acting company, who owned the rights to the play. The latter was the first collected edition of the plays of Shakespeare, printed by his colleagues a few years after his death.

Quarto 1 has the least authority, though it does shed light in places. It is called a "bad quarto" because it is significantly inferior to the other two texts, probably because it was typeset from a version of the play reconstructed from memory by a small group of actors who had performed in it rather than from a manuscript deriving from Shakespeare's hand. Some believe (though I do not) that it is derived from some form of early draft. According to most editors, Q2 has the greatest degree of authority, meaning that it derives, either directly or via a scribal copy, from a manuscript in Shakespeare's own hand. It is the longest version of the play. F is also authoritative, and much of it is identical to Q2. However, there are lines in Q2 that do not appear in F, and lines in F that do not appear in Q2, and both are apparently corrupt in some places. Neither Q2 nor F has lines or cuts that substantially alter the essential meaning of the play, the core concern of this edition.

The text of this edition, presented on the left, uses Q2 as copy text. It takes some readings from F and very occasionally from Q1. There are also some editorial emendations I have felt to be necessary for sense and clarity. In editing the text I have relied heavily on the editions of previous editors, principally G. Blakemore Evans in the 1997 (Second) Riverside edition, Willard Farnham in the 1970 Pelican edition, and Harold Jenkins in the 1982 Arden edition, and have often consulted the editions of Braunmuller, Mack and Boynton, Hoy, Greenblatt, Craig, Ribner and Kittredge, Bevington, Mowat and Werstine, and Raffel.

In recent years it has been fashionable to argue that the three early editions represent three different versions of the play, or three stages of its development, and two- and three-text editions have consequently multiplied. The emphasis of this edition is the opposite. Its goal is to show the unity of the play and its through-line of dramatic meaning, which I take to be essentially unaffected by the variations between the Second Quarto and First Folio texts. Many of the differences between Q2 and F may be a result of playhouse accretions and cuts preserved in F, as Jenkins argues. Some of those differences offer the editor maddeningly unresolvable dilemmas. But none of them impairs the unity or clarity of the play's essential dramatic conflict and resolution.

My purpose is to foster a deep and satisfactory understanding of the play as a whole. Hence, where textual matters significantly impinge on the general meaning of the play, I have chosen to give my own best guess about difficult readings, including brief justifications for my choices. However, this edition is not meant to exhaust the textual arguments but rather to keep them in perspective. "The play's the thing," as actors and directors are fond of saying, quoting Hamlet out of context. Arguments about particular textual cruxes should not obscure the play's essential dramatic meaning. Readers interested in a complete textual apparatus should consult either the Arden or the Riverside edition.

As much as possible, the spelling and punctuation have been modernized and regularized. Where Shakespeare intends "-ed" to form a syllable completing the meter of a verse line, I have indicated it thus: "-èd". Where he would have stressed a syllable that modern speech would not normally stress, I have indicated it thus: "cómplete," "sécure," "canónized." Line numbering is consistent with the Riverside edition. The few discrepancies are acknowledged in the annotation.

Abbreviations Used in the Annotation

[An open bracket in the text of the play indicates a word or phrase that completes the verse line above it.

§   This symbol indicates a section number in E. A. Abbott's *Shakespearian Grammar*.

cf.   *confer*, Latin for "compare," meaning compare with the following, is also used here in the Latin sense "bear together" to note the relation between the word or phrase under discussion and other passages relevant to its meaning or usage.

F   indicates a reading from *Hamlet* as printed in the First Folio of the plays of Shakespeare (see F in the List of Bibliographical References), the first collected edition of Shakespeare's plays.

ff.   and following, referring to lines following the line number given

LN   indicates a long note by Harold Jenkins in his Arden edition.

ME   Middle English

OE   Old English, Anglo-Saxon

OED   Oxford English Dictionary

Q1   indicates a reading from the memorially reconstructed First Quarto edition of *Hamlet* (see Q1 in the List of Bibliographical References), the so-called "bad" quarto.

Q2   indicates a reading from the Second Quarto edition of *Hamlet* (see Q2 in the List of Bibliographical References), the so-called "good" quarto.

s.d.   Stage Direction

s.h.   Speech Heading

List of Bibliographical References

The following works are those referred to in the annotation by author or short title.

Abbott E. A. Abbott, *A Shakespearian Grammar: An Attempt to Illustrate Some of the Differences between Elizabethan and Modern English*, New Edition (London: Macmillan and Company, 1874) ● a complete and subtle handbook to Shakespearean grammar, with many examples quoted, one of the most useful works of Shakespeare scholarship of the nineteenth century.

Andrews John Andrews, editor, *Hamlet*, The Guild Shakespeare (Garden City, New York: Doubleday, 1989).

Aristotle, *Ethics* Aristotle, *The Ethics of Aristotle: The Nicomachean Ethics*, translated by J. A. K. Thomson, revised by Hugh Tredennick (London: Penguin, 1976).

Aristotle, *Poetics* Aristotle, *The Poetics*, in *Aristotle in 23 Volumes*, Volume 23, translated by W. H. Fyfe (Cambridge, Massachusetts: Harvard University Press; London: William Heinemann Ltd., 1932), reproduced online by Perseus at http://www.perseus.tufts.edu/hopper/text?doc=Perseus%3A-text%3A1999.01.0056%3Asection%3D1447a.

Bacon, Francis Francis Bacon, *Essays, Civil and Moral*, Volume III, Part 1, The Harvard Classics (New York: P. F. Collier & Son, 1909–14), www.bartleby.com/3/1/.

Baldwin T. W. Baldwin, *William Shakspere's Small Latine & Lesse Greeke*, two volumes (Urbana, Illinois: University of Illinois Press, 1944) ● a thorough study of the content of Shakespeare's grammar-school education.

Baldwin *Five-Act* T. W. Baldwin, *Shakspere's Five-Act Structure* (Urbana, Illinois: University of Illinois Press, 1947).

Barb A. A. Barb, "Cain's Murder-Weapon and Samson's Jawbone of an Ass," *Journal of the Warburg and Courtauld Institutes*, Volume 35 [1972], pages 386–89, www.jstor.org/stable/750938 [login required].

Borthwick, E. K. E. Kerr Borthwick, "'So Capital a Calf': The Pun in Hamlet, III.ii.105" in *Shakespeare Quarterly*, Volume 35, Number 2 (Summer, 1984), pages 203–204 ● see III.ii.105 note.

Braunmuller A. R. Braunmuller, editor, *Hamlet*, The Pelican Shakespeare (New York: Penguin Books, 2001).

Bright Timothy Bright, *A Treatise of Melancholy* (London: Vautrollier, 1586, Reprinted Facsimile Text Society, 1940).

Bullough Geoffrey Bullough, *Narrative and Dramatic Sources of Shakespeare*, Volume 7 (New York: Columbia University Press, 1973).

Burton Robert Burton, *The Anatomy of Melancholy*, edited by Floyd Dell and Paul Jordan-Smith (New York: Tudor Publishing Company, 1955).

Caldecott Thomas Caldecott, *Hamlet and As You Like It: A Specimen of a New Edition of Shakespeare* (London: John Murray, 1819), cited in Furness.

Certain Sermons *Certain Sermons or Homilies Appointed to be Read in Churches*, First Book (1547), I.ix, online at https://books.google.co.uk/books?id=JDSnBa84t-KoC&printsec=frontcover#v=onepage&q&f=false.

Chambers, *El.St.* E. K. Chambers, *The Elizabethan Stage* (Oxford: Clarendon Press, 1923), 4 volumes.

Chambers, *WS* E. K. Chambers, *William Shakespeare: A Study of Facts and Problems* (Oxford: Clarendon Press, 1930), 2 volumes.

Child Francis James Child, editor, *The English and Scottish Popular Ballads* (Boston: Houghton Mifflin, 1880), https://archive.org/details/englishandscopt203chiluoft.

Cicero, *De Officiis* M. Tullius Cicero, *De Officiis*, translated by Walter Miller, Loeb Classical Library (London: Heinemann and New York: Macmillan, 1913), http://www.perseus.tufts.edu/hopper/text?doc=Perseus%3Atext%3A2007.01.0048%3Abook%3D1%3Asection%3D11.

Cicero, *Topica* Cicero, *Topica*, §§63–64, http://www.thelatinlibrary.com/cicero/topica. shtml ● see V.i.12 note.

City of God St. Augustine, *City of God*, translated by Marcus Dods, Great Books of the Western World, Volume 18. Augustine (Chicago: Encyclopaedia Britannica, 1952).

Clarke Charles and Mary Cowden Clarke, editors, *The Plays of William Shakespeare*, illustrated by H. C. Selous, 3 volumes. (London: Cassell & Company, 1875); reissued as *Cassell's Illustrated Shakespeare* (London: Cassell, Petter & Galpin, 1886), cited in Furness.

Coleridge Samuel Taylor Coleridge, *Shakespearean Criticism*, edited by T. M. Raysor, Everyman's Library edition, 2 volumes, 1960 (references in Jenkins).

Colaianni Louis Colaianni, *Shakespeare's Names: A New Pronouncing Dictionary* (New York: Drama Publishers, 1999).

Corson Hiram Corson, *Jottings on the Text of Hamlet*, 1874 (quoted in Furness and in Jenkins).

Cotgrave Randle Cotgrave, *A Dictionary of the French and English Tongues*, 1611, Second Edition, 1632, online at http://www.pbm.com/~lindahl/cotgrave/.

Crystal David Crystal and Ben Crystal, *Shakespeare's Words: A Glossary and Language Companion* (London: Penguin, 2002).

Cunningham Sem. J. V. Cunningham, Graduate Seminars on Shakespeare and on *Hamlet*, Brandeis University, 1974 and 1975 respectively.

Cunningham *W/W* J. V. Cunningham, *Woe or Wonder: The Emotional Effect of Shakespearean Tragedy* (Chicago: The Swallow Press, second printing, 1969) ● a concise and piercing correction to much that is wrong with modern *Hamlet* criticism.

Dollerup Cay Dollerup, *Denmark, 'Hamlet', and Shakespeare: A Study of Englishmen's Knowledge of Denmark ... with Special Reference to Hamlet*, Salzburg Studies in English Literature, 1975 (reference in Jenkins).

Donne John Donne, "Metempsychosis: The Progresse of the Soule" in John T. Shawcross, editor, *The Complete Poetry of John Donne* (Garden City, New York: Doubleday, Anchor Books, 1967).

Donnelly Donnelly, Marian C. (December 1984), "Theaters in the Courts of Denmark and Sweden from Frederik II to Gustav III," *Journal of the Society of Architectural Historians* (University of California Press on behalf of the Society of Architectural Historians) 43 (4): 328–340, cited at https://en.wikipedia.org/wiki/Kronborg_Castle.

Dover Wilson John Dover Wilson, editor, *Hamlet*, The New Cambridge Shakespeare (Cambridge: Cambridge University Press, 1934, 1954); and John Dover Wilson, *What Happens in 'Hamlet'* (Cambridge: Cambridge University Press, 1935, 1937, 1951).

Enc. Brit. *Encyclopaedia Britannica* (Chicago: Encyclopaedia Britannica, Inc., 1948).

F (or F1) The First Folio edition of "The Tragedie of Hamlet, Prince of Denmarke," from *Mr. William Shakespeare's Comedies, Histories, & Tragedies. Published according to the True Originall Copies* (London: Isaac Iaggard, and Edward Blount, 1623), reproduced in *The First Folio of Shakespeare* (The Norton Facsimile), editor Charlton Hinman (New York: W. W. Norton and London: Paul Hamlyn, 1968), pages 760–90.

Florio *WW* John [Giovanni] Florio, *A World of Words: A Most Copious and Exact Dictionarie in Italian and English*, 1598, http://www.pbm.com/~lindahl/florio1598/.

Fergusson Francis Fergusson, *Shakespeare: The Pattern in His Carpet* (New York: Delacorte/Dell, 1958, reprinted 1970).

Furness Horace Howard Furness, editor, *A New Variorum Edition of Shakespeare: Hamlet*, Volume 1 (New York: Dover Publications, 1963, republication of tenth edition, 1877).

Geneva The Geneva Bible, 1560/1599, reproduced online by Steve Zychal at http://www.genevabible.org/Geneva.html. ● All quotations from the Bible are from this edition unless otherwise noted.

Greenblatt Stephen Greenblatt, General Editor, *The Norton Shakespeare Based on the Oxford Edition* (New York: W. W. Norton, 1997).

Greene Robert Greene, *The Life and Complete Works in Prose and Verse of Robert Greene*, editor A. B. Grosart, 15 volumes. (1881–86) (quoted in Furness and in Jenkins).

Greene *GW* Robert Greene, *Groats-worth of Wit*, 1592, modern spelling transcript copyright © 1996 Nina Green www.oxford-shakespeare.com, http://www.oxford-shakespeare.com/Greene/Greenes_Groatsworth.pdf.

Greene *Mamillia* Robert Greene, *Mamillia: A Mirror or Looking-glass for the Ladies of England*, 1583, transcript http://www.oxford-shakespeare.com/Greene/Mamillia_1583.pdf.

Greene *Quip* Robert Greene, *A Quip for an Upstart Courtier*, 1592, modern spelling transcript copyright © 1996 Nina Green www.oxford-shakespeare.com, http://www.oxford-shakespeare.com/Greene/Quip%20For%20An%20Upstart%20Courtier.pdf ● see Speech Note before IV.v.175 and IV.v.180 note.

Grose Francis Grose, *A Provincial Glossary, with a Collection of Local Proverbs, and Popular Superstitions* (London: S. Hooper, 1787, Second Edition. 1790), https://archive.org/details/aprovincialglosoounkngoog (reference in Jenkins).

Gummere Richard M. Gummere, translator, Lucius Annaeus Seneca, *Moral Epistles*, Loeb Classical Library (Cambridge, Massachusetts: Harvard University Press, 1917–25), Volume V, pages 54–55, reproduced at http://www.brainfly.net/html/books/seneco04.pdf ● see V.ii.223–24 note.

Halliday F. E. Halliday, *A Shakespeare Companion 1564–1964* (Baltimore, Maryland: Penguin Books, 1964).

Harmon Alice Harmon, "How Great Was Shakespeare's Debt to Montaigne?" *PMLA*, Volume 57, Number 4 (Dec. 1942), pages 988–1008, http://www.jstor.org/stable/458873 [login required].

Henning Standish Henning, "Branding Harlots on the Brow," *Shakespeare Quarterly*, Volume 51, Number 1 (Spring, 2000), pages 86–89, https://www.jstor.org/stable/2902324 [login required] ● see III.iv.43–44 note.

Hogen Paige Hogen, in-class student discussion (2013).

Holmes Professor Mary Holmes (1910–2002), Professor Emerita of Art at the University of California at Santa Cruz, lectures (see www.mary-holmesart5a.com, www.maryholmes.org, and www.maryholmesbook.com).

Homily on Matr. The Elizabethan Homily of the State of Matrimony (1563–71), reproduced online at https://onesearch.library.utoronto.ca/sites/default/files/ret/homilies/bk2hom18.html.

Horace Horace, *The Second Book of the Satires of Horace*, translated and reproduced online at http://www.authorama.com/works-of-horace-7.html (no copyright) ● see V.ii.272 note.

Hough Graham Hough, *A Preface to "The Faerie Queene"* (New York: W. W. Norton, 1963).

Hoy Cyrus Hoy, editor, *Hamlet* (New York: W. W. Norton, second edition, 1992).

Hulme Hilda M. Hulme, *Explorations in Shakespeare's Language: Some Problems of Lexical Meaning in the Dramatic Text* (London: Longmans, 1962).

Irvine Theodora Ursula Irvine, *The Names in Shakespeare* (New York, Philadelphia, Chicago: Hinds, Hayden & Eldredge, 1919), reprinted as *How to Pronounce the Names in Shakespeare* (London: Forgotten Books, trademark of FB &c Ltd., 2015).

Jenkins Harold Jenkins, editor, *Hamlet*, The Arden Shakespeare (London and New York: Methuen, 1982) ● a complete scholarly edition with invaluable research and notes, without which this edition would not have been possible.

Jenkins *Stud. Bib.* Harold Jenkins, "Playhouse Interpolations in the Folio Text of Hamlet," *Studies in Bibliography* 13 (1960).

Kennedy Riley Kennedy, in-class student discussion (2015).

Kermode *SL* Frank Kermode, *Shakespeare's Language* (New York: Farrar Straus and Giroux, 2000).

Kittredge Irving Ribner and George Lyman Kittredge, *The Complete Works of Shakespeare* (Waltham, Massachusetts: Ginn and Company, 1971), based on Kittredge, *Complete Works of Shakespeare* (1936).

KJV King James Version of the Bible (1611).

Landry Hilton Landry, "The Leaven of Wickedness: *Hamlet* I.iv.1–38," in *Pacific Coast Studies in Shakespeare*, edited by Waldo F. McNeir and Thelma N. Greenfield (Eugene, Oregon: University of Oregon Books, 1966), pages 122–33.

Lanham Richard A. Lanham, *A Handlist of Rhetorical Terms* (Berkeley, California: University of California Press, 1968, paper-bound 1969).

Leavis F. R. Leavis, "The Greatness of 'Measure for Measure,'" *Scrutiny* 10 (January 1942).

Lewis "P/P" C. S. Lewis, "Hamlet: The Prince or the Poem," in *Selected Literary Essays*, edited by Walter Hooper (Cambridge: Cambridge University Press, 1969, paperback reprinted 1980), pages 88–105.

Lewis *Studies* C. S. Lewis, *Studies in Words*, Second Edition (Cambridge: Cambridge University Press, 1967, paperback reprinted 1988).

Lewis "Variation" C. S. Lewis, "Variation in Shakespeare and Others," in *Selected Literary Essays*, edited by Walter Hooper (Cambridge: Cambridge University Press, 1969, paperback reprinted 1980), pages 74–87.

Lincolniana Letter to James Hackett, August 17, 1863, https://www.loc.gov/resource/lprbscsm.scsmo853/?sp=3.

Linthicum Mary Channing Linthicum, *Costume in the Drama of Shakespeare and his Contemporaries* (Oxford: Clarendon Press, 1936).

Lyly John Lyly, *Euphues: The Anatomy of Wit* (1578, 1580), edited by Morris William Croll and Harry Clemons (London: George Routledge & Sons; New York: E. P. Dutton & Company, 1916) transcribed and https://archive.org/stream/cu31924013122084/cu31924013122084_djvu.txt.

Maddox Diana Maddox, dramaturge, private conversations (1982).

Mason John Monck Mason, *Comments on the Several Editions of Shakespeare's Plays* (Dublin: Graisberry and Campbell, 1807), https://books.google.com/books?id=VCdMAAAAcAAJ.

Matthews Dakin Matthews, "Sheltering with Shakespeare," (podcast) Episode 16, 6/6/20, https://www.youtube.com/watch?v=IMs9_CJNg7o.

Montaigne *Essays of Michel de Montaigne*, translated by Charles Cotton, edited by William Carew Hazlitt, 1877, http://www.gutenberg.org/files/3600/3600-h/3600-h.htm#link2HCH0040. See also the Florio translation online at http://www.luminarium.org/renascence-editions/montaigne/ ● References to Montaigne in Harmon are to the Tudor Translations edition (London 1892), to which I have not found access for cross-referencing.

MSR Malone Society Reprint

Mulgrew Robert Mulgrew, late Chairman of English at The Bishop's School, private conversations (2007).

Nares Robert Nares, *A Glossary ... of Words, Phrases, Names and Allusions*, 1822, revised by J. O. Halliwell[-Phillipps] and T. Wright, 2 volumes, 1859, cited in Jenkins.

Nashe Thomas Nashe, Preface to Sidney's *Astrophel and Stella* (1591), Q1, printed at London by Thomas Newman (from copy in the British Museum), http://www.bartleby.com/359/23.html and quoted in Tilley at M254 from Nashe, *Works* III.332 ● see next entry.

Nashe *W* Thomas Nashe, *The Works of Thomas Nashe*, edited by Ronald B. McKerrow, 5 volumes, 1904–10; revised by F. P. Wilson, 1958 (cited in Jenkins).

OED *Oxford English Dictionary*, Compact Edition (Oxford: Oxford University Press, 1971).

Onions C. T. Onions, *A Shakespeare Glossary* (Oxford: Clarendon Press, 1925).

Ovid *Fasti* Ovid, *Fasti*, translated by James George Frazer, Loeb Classical Library, edited by Page *et. al.* (London: Heinemann and Cambridge, Massachusetts: Harvard University Press, 1959), https://archive.org/stream/ovidsfastioooviduoft/ovidsfastioooviduoft_djvu.txt ● see IV.v.122 note.

Pliny Pliny the Elder, *The Natural History*, edited by John Bostock, IX.56, 58, 59, reproduced online at http://www.perseus.tufts.edu/hopper/text?doc=Perseus%3Atext%3A1999.02.0137%3Abook%3D9%3Achapter%3D56, http://www.perseus.tufts.edu/hopper/text?doc=Perseus:text:1999.02.0137:book:9:chapter=58, and http://www.perseus.tufts.edu/hopper/text?doc=Perseus%3Atext%3A1999.02.0137%3Abook%3D9%3Achapter%3D59 ● see V.ii.272 note.

Plowden Edmund Plowden, *The Commentaries, or Reports of Edmund Plowden ... : Containing Divers Cases Upon Matters of Law, Argued and Adjudged in the Several Reigns of King Edward VI, Queen Mary, King and Queen Philip and Mary, and Queen Elizabeth [1548–1579]: to which are Added, The Quaeries of Mr. Plowden*. [London: S. Brooke, 1816], https://archive.org/details/commentariesorrooplowgoog.

Power Malik Power, unpublished letter (2017).

Q1 The First Quarto of "The Tragicall Historie of Hamlet Prince of Denmarke By William Shakespeare (London, 1603)," the "bad" quarto, probably memorially reconstructed, reproduced in facsimile in Maxwell E. Foster, *The Play Behind the Play: Hamlet and Quarto One*, edited by Anne Shiras (Pittsburgh, Pennsylvania: Foster Executors, 1991), pages 131–95, and in Michael J. B. Allen and Kenneth Muir, *Shakespeare's Plays in Quarto: A Facsimile Edition of Copies Primarily from the Henry E. Huntington Library* (Berkeley and Los Angeles: University of California Press, 1981).

Q2 The Second Quarto of "The Tragicall Historie of Hamlet, Prince of Denmarke. By William Shakespeare" (London, 1604), the "good" quarto, probably set from Shakespeare's "foul papers" (i.e., his own manuscript), reproduced in *Shakespeare's Hamlet: The Second Quarto 1604, Reproduced in facsimile from the* [so-called "Devonshire"] *copy in the Huntington Library* (San Marino, California: 1964), and in Michael J. B. Allen and Kenneth Muir, *Shakespeare's Plays in Quarto: A Facsimile Edition of Copies Primarily from the Henry E. Huntington Library* (Berkeley and Los Angeles: University of California Press, 1981).

Quint. Quintilian (Marcus Fabius Quintilianus), *Institutio Oratoria*, translated by H. E. Butler, 1920–22, Loeb Classical Library, http://penelope.uchicago.edu/Thayer/E/Roman/Texts/Quintilian/Institutio_Oratoria/home.html, photographic reproduction at https://archive.org/details/institutooratorio2quinuoft.

Raffel Burton Raffel, editor, *Hamlet* (The Annotated Shakespeare) (New Haven, Connecticut: Yale University Press, 2003).

Rappaport *N&Q* Gideon Rappaport, "Another Sonnet in *Romeo and Juliet*," *Notes and Queries* XXV, Number 2 (April 1978) ● see IV.v.23 note.

Rappaport "R&R" Gideon Rappaport, "*Hamlet*: Revenge and Readiness," *Upstart Crow* VII (1987), pages 80–95.

Rappaport "Soliloquy" Gideon Rappaport, "Some Special Uses of the Soliloquy in Shakespeare," Ph.D. dissertation, Brandeis University, 1979.

Riverside *Hamlet* in *The Riverside Shakespeare: The Complete Works*, Second Edition, edited by G. Blakemore Evans (text) and Frank Kermode (commentary) (Boston: Houghton Mifflin Company, 1997).

Saven Adam Saven, "Strength of Will," unpublished student essay (November 26, 2007).

Sayers Dorothy Sayers, Introduction to *The Comedy of Dante Alighieri the Florentine, Cantica II: Purgatory (Il Purgatorio)* (London and New York: Penguin, 1955).

Schmidt Alexander Schmidt, *Shakespeare Lexicon*, 2 volumes, 1874–75, Third Edition. Revised and Enlarged by Gregor Sarrazin (Berlin: Georg Reimer, 1902; republication New York: Dover Publications, 1971, 2015).

Seneca *Epist.* Seneca, *Moral Letters to Lucilius (Epistulae morales ad Lucilium)*, translated by Richard Mott Gummere, Loeb Classical Library, Volume 2 (1920), https://en.wikisource.org/wiki/Moral_letters_to_Lucilius/Letter_70.

Sidney Sir Philip Sidney, *Defense of Poesy* in *English Essays: Sidney to Macaulay*. Volume XXVII, The Harvard Classics (New York: P. F. Collier & Son, 1909–14); Bartleby.com, 2001, www.bartleby.com/27/.

Smith Introduction to D. Nichol Smith, editor, *Shakespeare Criticism: A Selection 1623–1840* (London: Oxford University Press, 1916, reset 1946, reprint 1963), pages v–xxi.

SMJ "CT" Sister Miriam Joseph, C.S.C., "*Hamlet*, a Christian Tragedy," in *Studies in Philology*, Volume 59, Number 2, Part 1 (University of North Carolina Press, April 1962), pages 119–140, http://www.jstor.org/stable/4173378 [login required].

SMJ "Ghost" Sister Miriam Joseph, C.S.C., "Discerning the Ghost in *Hamlet*," *PMLA*, LXXVI (1961), pages 493–502.

SMJ *Lang.* Sister Miriam Joseph, C.S.C., *Shakespeare's Use of the Arts of Language* (Philadelphia, Pennsylvania: Paul Dry Books), 2005.

Spencer Tanah Spencer, unpublished student essay (2007).

Spenser Edmund Spenser, *The Faerie Queene* (1596), in *Edmund Spenser's Poetry*, Second Edition, edited by Hugh Maclean (New York: W. W. Norton, 1982).

Steer Alex Steer, Assistant Editor of the OED, private email (2007).

STM *Sir Thomas More*, Addition II, ll. 162–63, https://archive.org/stream/bookofsirthomasmoobritu-oft/bookofsirthomasmoobrituoft_djvu.txt ● see IV.v.100 note.

Stoll *Hamlet* E. E. Stoll, *Hamlet: an Historical and Comparative Study* in *Research Publications of the University of Minnesota*, Volume VIII, Number 5, Studies in Language and Literature, Number 7 (Sept. 1919), https://archive.org/stream/hamletanhistoricoostoluoft/hamletanhistoric-oostoluoft_djvu.txt.

Stoll *SS* E. E. Stoll, *Shakespeare Studies: Historical and Comparative in Method* (New York: Frederick Ungar, 1942, 1960).

"Tables" Peter Stallybrass, Roger Chartier, J. Franklin Mowery, Heather Wolfe, "Hamlet's Tables and the Technologies of Writing in Renaissance England," *Shakespeare Quarterly*, 55:4, pages 379–419.

Taverner Richard Taverner, *Proverbes or Adagies gathered out of the Chiliades of Erasmus* (1552, one of six editions), a translation of Erasmus's *Adagiorum Chiliades*, a compendium of adages that itself went through many editions ● see III.iv.23 note.

Thompson Philip Thompson, *Dusk and Dawn: Poems and Prose of Philip Thompson*, edited by Gideon Rappaport (San Diego: One Mind Good Press, 2005).

Tilley Morris Palmer Tilley, *A Dictionary of the Proverbs in England in the Sixteenth and Seventeenth Centuries: A Collection of the Proverbs Found in English Literature and the Dictionaries of the Period* (Ann Arbor: University of Michigan Press, 1950), https://babel.hathitrust.org/cgi/pt?id=mdp.39015016495585;view=1up;seq=1.

Tillyard E. M. W. Tillyard, *The Elizabethan World Picture* (New York: Random House, Vintage Books, [1959]).

Turberville *Epitaphs* George Turberville (Turbervile), *Epitaphes, Epigrams, Songs and Sonets* (London: Henry Denham, 1567, 1570), http://quod.lib.umich.edu/e/eebo/A14019.0001.001/1:47?rgn=div1;view=fulltext and http://quod.lib.umich.edu/e/eebo/A14019.0001.001/1:48?rgn=div1;view=fulltext ● see IV.v.180 note.

Virgil *Georgics* Virgil, *Georgics*, translated by H. R. Fairclough, Loeb Classical Library, Vols. 63 & 64. (Cambridge, Massachusetts: Harvard University Press, 1916), http://www.theoi.com/Text/VirgilGeorgics1.html.

Walker William Sidney Walker, *A Critical Examination of the Text of Shakespeare*, 3 volumes. (London: John Russell Smith, 1860) (reference in Jenkins).

Webster's 2nd *Webster's New International Dictionary of the English Language*, Second Edition, Unabridged (Springfield, Massachusetts: G. & C. Merriam Company, 1946).

Williams Gordon I. Williams, "Ophelia's 'Show'," *Trivium*, IV (Lampeter, Wales: St. David's College, 1969).

Wright George T. Wright, "Hendiadys and Hamlet" *PMLA*, Volume 96, Number 2 (March 1981), pages 168–93, http://www.jstor.org/stable/461987?seq=1#page_scan_tab_contents [login required]. ● Table 1 lists the instances of hendiadys in *Hamlet*; Table 2 lists instances of "phrases that, if not hendiadys, are close" and illustrates "the curious ways in which Shakespeare ... especially in this play, doubled his nouns and adjectives" (page 189).

INTRODUCTION
Divine Shaping: The Moral Drama of *Hamlet*

Problem Play?

The poet and scholar J. V. Cunningham wryly observed that "There is less to be said about *Hamlet* than has been said."[1] His statement is true because for about two centuries interpreters of the play have labored to make the play fit beliefs about reality that were not those of Shakespeare or his audience. The results have been confusion, the burdening of this great work with the misleading epithet "problem play," and many unnecessary words.

But what if we did not inject our own themes into the play but instead discerned Shakespeare's? We would find no insoluble problem but instead a work of masterful integrity, showing the same unity of thought and intention that we see in Shakespeare's other great plays. We would find the play to be not a problematic mirror of our own conflicted opinions but an illuminating revelation of Shakespeare's singularly deep vision and of its universal implications. There would be a little more truth to be said about the play and many fewer misguided readers and audiences.

Hamlet is not a man who thinks too much to be able to act, or one "who could not make up his mind," as the voiceover at the start of Laurence Olivier's film version (1948) tells us, or one who is too melancholy, or too passionate, or too rational, or too cowardly, or existentialist, or nihilistic, or in love with his mother, or conflicted about whether he is a scholar or a soldier, or clinically suicidal. Nor is Hamlet ever actually mad, though he can be melancholy, fly into a passion, play at madness, and sometimes do all three at once.

No one trying to find a unity in all the play's lines can be content with any of these interpretations or any combination of them. Though each has been embraced as the essence of the play by virtue of the interpreter's own predispositions, Shakespeare could not have meant any of them to be the essence of Hamlet *and* written the play that we have. Least of all did he make

Hamlet so profound and mysterious that no one can ever understand him at all. No serious playwright, certainly no successful one, sits down to write plays that cannot be comprehended, and Shakespeare knew what he was doing in this play as in his others.

In the moral clarity of a paragraph by the poet Philip Thompson lies the key to a unified vision of *Hamlet*, a key that unlocks the resolution of the apparent contradictions that for two centuries have distracted us from the play's essential meanings. In light of Thompson's insight about Hamlet's moral error in Act III, Scene iii, we find that in fact the play is a coherent and profound spiritual drama. Once we leave aside our un-Shakespearean modern assumptions about reality and accept Shakespeare's own assumptions and those of his time, the meaning of the play springs forth from every part with clarity, unity, and magnificence. Seen in its true context—that of belief in divine providence and in God's judgment of souls, reality as any believing Christian of the Elizabethan period would see it—the play reveals a man discovering the human being's right relation to the divine and to the morally complex world we all inhabit.

At the same time, though it descends from the medieval morality play, as it does from the Senecan revenge play, *Hamlet* is neither an allegory nor a dogmatic tract. A central quality of the genius of Shakespeare is his ability to unite two kinds of audience experience in one set of words: specificity and universality. One kind of experience is seeing characters as real people like us, living real lives in time and space, with names, personal characteristics, and painful choices to make. The other is seeing universal significance, the applicability of a play's insights or truths to our own and everyone else's lives. Living at perhaps the only time in the history of Western drama in which it was possible, Shakespeare invents and masters a technique for blending these two kinds of experience into one, or suffusing the former with the latter. His arrangement of plot, character, and word is such that his plays become both convincingly realistic and profoundly

---

1 J. V. Cunningham, in a graduate course on *Hamlet* at Brandeis University, Spring 1975.

meaningful—not successively or alternately but at once in every moment. As Graham Hough wrote, in Shakespeare,

> theme and image are completely fused and the relation between them is only implicit, never open or enforced. We have not yet found a name for this. For want of a better I shall call it incarnation (without any theological implication). Incarnational literature is that in which any 'abstract' content is completely absorbed in character and action and completely expressed by them.[2]

And so it is in *Hamlet*. The meaning of the play is *in* the characters, actions, and words. But neither is it hidden in them, nor is it so deeply latent that it cannot be discerned. Rather, through them the play's meaning is made sublimely visible, if only we take those characters, actions, and words as they were meant to be taken by the audience for whom they were written.

Test Case: Revenge

An early version of the revenge story that we know from Shakespeare's *Hamlet*, though it was not a source for Shakespeare's play, appeared in the *Historiae Danicae* of Saxo Grammaticus, written in the twelfth century and published in 1514. (The German *Tragoedia der Bestrafte Brudermord oder Prinz Hamlet aus Dännemark* is a later "version of *Hamlet* in a very degenerate form,"[3] hence also not a source for Shakespeare.) Shakespeare's own immediate sources probably included the third story of the fifth series of the *Histoires Tragiques* of the Frenchman Belleforest and the so-called *Ur-Hamlet*. That play, presumably based on Belleforest, was never printed and so is lost to us, though there are early references that suggest it existed. Thus we can only speculate about what it might have contained. It is this lost revenge tragedy that Shakespeare is thought to have reworked into the play we know as *Hamlet*. The *Ur-Hamlet* may or may not have been written by Thomas Kyd, but "the probability that the *Ur-Hamlet* was by Kyd, though not an essential premise, makes it easier to regard Kyd's *Spanish Tragedy* as in some sort a companion-piece."[4]

In any case, in the late 1580s theatrical dynamite exploded upon the Elizabethan stage in the form of Kyd's *Spanish Tragedy*. The story of a secret murder and a long-delayed revenge, it was spectacularly popular by Elizabethan standards, going through many revivals and four printed editions by 1602. There were even some lines written to be added to it at about the time Shakespeare was working on *Hamlet* (about 1601–2). Heavily influenced by the closet dramas of the Roman tragedian Seneca, *The Spanish Tragedy* in turn greatly influenced two generations of playwrights, including Shakespeare, whose *Titus Andronicus*, *Richard III*, *Macbeth*, and other plays show the influence of Kyd's play and of its popularity.

The most profound influence of *The Spanish Tragedy* is to be seen in *Hamlet*. Among the many elements in the earlier play that appear in the later are a central father-son relationship, a ghost returned from the underworld seeking revenge, a play-within-the-play, pretended madness in the avenger, real madness in the avenger's beloved, the wooing of a dead man's beloved, and the name Horatio. There are, of course, the usual differences that distinguish Shakespeare from predecessors and contemporaries alike: the verisimilitude, the fluidity and vitality of the verse (Kyd's end-stopped lines, common in the 1580s, having yielded to Shakespeare's mature enjambments), the subtle psychology, the complex and interrelated plot, the elaboration of foils, and above all, that wedding of realism and universality in the "incarnational" style mentioned above.

However, in one particular respect Shakespeare can almost be heard saying to his audience, "If you thought *The Spanish Tragedy* was dramatic, watch this!" In *Hamlet* he makes the single most radical transformation in the history of the revenge-play tradition, assuring that his play would far transcend its forebears and descendants.

Following the model of Seneca, Kyd had set his revenge play in the context of the classical afterlife. In Kyd's underworld, the dead cross the river Styx into Hades, they are judged by Aeacus, Minos, and Rhadamanthus, they descend to Tartarus for eternal suffering or walk pleasantly in the Elysian Fields, and it is Pluto and Proserpine who return the ghost to the world to seek his revenge. In this context taking vengeance is a self-evident value and a point of honor, delay in effecting it is emotionally agonizing, and its accomplishment, even at the cost of the avenger's own life, is a consummation.

By contrast, Shakespeare challenges himself to set *Hamlet* in the context of the Christian afterlife—the

---

2 Graham Hough, *A Preface to The Faerie Queene* (New York: W.W. Norton, 1963), page 107.
3 Jenkins, Introduction, page 112.
4 Jenkins, Introduction, page 97.

real and true afterlife in which Shakespeare and nearly everyone in his audience believed. At death the soul of every human being goes to the judgment of God and reaps eternal reward in heaven (perhaps after a time in the purgatory that the Ghost in *Hamlet* refrains from describing) or punishment in hell for its choices made in life.[5] In an essay called "What Chaucer Really Did To '*Il Filostrato*,'" C. S. Lewis argues that "the process which [Boccaccio's work] underwent at Chaucer's hands was first and foremost a process of *medievalization*."[6] Similarly, Shakespeare took Kyd's secularized idea of revenge and Christianized it.

The implications of this change in metaphysical context are enormous. The Elizabethan audience took the ancients' belief in the classical myths to be a fictional shadow of truth, an image of reality labored under by people deprived of Christian revelation. Stories unfolding in front of that metaphysical backdrop might be morally instructive, but the context itself was not to be taken for reality. By contrast, the afterlife assumed in *Hamlet*, being (despite conflict over details) the true one believed in by all Christians, brings home the formerly theoretical problem of revenge. In this context, "Vengeance is mine: I will repay, saith the Lord"[7] must be taken utterly seriously. Hence the central question of revenge is not upon whom or when to be revenged, but whether and how one may take revenge at all: If one is instructed to take revenge by a spirit, is that charge a commandment of God or a temptation of the Devil? Can an avenger take revenge without risking the eternal damnation of his soul?

The question of revenge in a Christian world was a live issue for Shakespeare's age. Francis Bacon's well-known essay "On Revenge" (1625), which (unlike *Hamlet*) is not explicitly Christian, contains contradictory observations on the subject: Revenge is "a kind of wild justice"; it "putteth the law out of office"; "it is a prince's part to pardon"; "the most tolerable sort of revenge is for those wrongs which there is no law to remedy"; the "delight [of revenge] seemeth to be not so much in doing the hurt as in making the party repent"; "a man that studieth revenge keeps his own wounds green, which otherwise would heal and do well"; "public revenges are for the most part fortunate ... But in private revenges it is not so"; "vindictive persons ... as they are mischievous, so end they infortunate."[8] For believing Christians the question of revenge was more pointed: How could the traditional aristocratic honor code, which commanded victims of unpunished crimes to seek revenge, be squared with revealed Christian doctrine, which proclaims that vengeance belongs only to God and commands any who desires salvation to love his enemies? In setting *Hamlet* in the context of Christian reality, Shakespeare writes the most serious of all revenge plays by putting revenge itself on trial.

But in addressing this question directly, *Hamlet* examines not only revenge. The test case for revenge, arising in an age of burgeoning scientific and intellectual exploration of man's increasing power over his world, becomes also a test case for all human action. What is the relation between freedom and necessity? How is a man to serve God with his free will when he is subject also to the influence of circumstances and of the givens of his own fallen nature? In other words, given my nature with its powers and limitations, and given particular external circumstances, how am I to be good in the eyes of God? This universalizing of the problem of revenge into that of the human free will—caught between worldly facts and divine commandment—transforms the play from merely the best of revenge plays into one of the most universally relevant plays ever written. And it is relevant not only to Christians, or indeed only to religious believers. It

---

5   The spiritual concerns of *Hamlet* applied equally to Catholics, who believed in Purgatory, and Protestants, who did not. Those who seek to label Shakespeare a crypto-Catholic, and those who oppose them, distract us from the greater point—that for political, artistic, and perhaps also moral reasons, Shakespeare in his plays avoids taking sides in the sectarian conflicts that divided Christians and might at any moment lead to bloodshed, focusing instead on questions of universal spiritual import that united them. That his play is set in a foreign land and a past time allows him to use for dramatic purposes some beliefs that were not shared by the religious establishment of his day.

6   C. S. Lewis, "What Chaucer Really Did to '*Il Filostrato*,'" in Walter Hooper, editor, *Selected Literary Essays by C. S. Lewis* (Cambridge: Cambridge University Press, 1969, paper 1979, reprinted 1980), page 27.

7   Romans 12:19 (Geneva Bible). Almost always in Shakespeare's other plays, revenge is a sign of error if not outright villainy. Cf., *Taming of the Shrew* II.i.29,36, *Twelfth Night* V.i.378, *Merchant of Venice* III.i.54, 66–73, *Othello* II.i.294, etc.

8   Francis Bacon, "On Revenge," from *Essays, Civil and Moral*, in *The Harvard Classics* (1909–14), http://www.bartleby.com/3/1/4.html.

speaks powerfully and profoundly to all human beings, who know that the life of the self inevitably ends but cannot know what lies in store for that self in death.

In the Christian context of the play and of Shakespeare's time, the question of salvation or damnation becomes specific and crucial when a spirit, apparently the ghost of Hamlet's father, instructs Hamlet to "Revenge his foul and most unnatural murder" (I.v.25) and at the same time to "taint not thy mind" (I.v.85).[9] Hamlet is thereby confronted with two apparently insoluble dilemmas. The first is this: Is this a ghost come from God, bearing divine commandment, or is it a spirit from the Devil, bearing temptation to sin? Hamlet finds an effective method of resolving this dilemma, namely the play-within-the-play, "The Murder of Gonzago." The King's reaction to the performance of this play proves that the Ghost spoke truly.

The second dilemma is more profound and more difficult: If the Ghost is of God, how may one obey the order to take revenge when the order not to do so is also of God? Is God speaking through the Ghost or through scripture? Through personal experience or through traditional dogma? If through both, how may one fulfill the former charge without being damned for breaking the latter? How may one take revenge without tainting the mind with sin? Or, in more general terms, how is a man to harmonize his life in a particular time, place, and situation with universal principles? The resolution of this dilemma is revealed to Hamlet by the events of his life, and to us by the play in which they unfold.

Parallel dilemmas exist for the other characters as well: Fortinbras must determine how to achieve honor without betraying his nation, his uncle-king, and his father, whose agreement with Denmark was "well ratified by law and heraldry" (I.i.87). Laertes must choose whether to fulfill the King's will and his own desire for revenge or to forgive a perceived enemy who has asked his pardon. Gertrude must choose between her second husband's version of her future life and her son's. Ophelia must choose whether to deceive her beloved in order to obey her father. The priest must choose between church law and royal decree. Osric is comically caught between the demand of court etiquette

that he take off his hat in politeness to the prince and the apparently mad prince's own demand that he put it on. For an instant even the rational Horatio is caught between his passion to die with his friend and his duty to live on and tell the hidden story.

In *Hamlet*, in the guise of a revenge play, Shakespeare has taken for his real subject the whole paradoxical condition of man. How can we do the right thing when the right is not clear, when our passions and our reason move us in contrary directions, and when one wrong move, arising from a mere "dram of evil" (I.iv.36), could land us in hell?

The Moral Drama

Hamlet, in C. S. Lewis's words, has been "given a task by a ghost."[10] His first impulse is to "sweep to my revenge" (I.v.31). Then he has second thoughts—good ones. The spirit he has seen may indeed be a devil, as both Hamlet (I.iv.40) and his friend, the rational Horatio (I.iv.69–74), have pointed out. Hamlet must engage in a test to see whether Claudius is in fact guilty. This, as Hamlet says, is because if the spirit is a devil in disguise and Claudius is not guilty, to kill Claudius means to risk his own damnation. Hamlet accomplishes this test with the play-within-the-play, which proves the Ghost has told the truth. We conclude that Hamlet has been chosen by God as his instrument to execute the fratricidal, regicidal, and adulterous king.

There being, in Bacon's phrase, "no law to remedy" the murder of the former king, Hamlet is the right and only man for the job for two reasons. First, Hamlet is a man of intense emotion balanced by superior reason. Though he responds to external pressures with passionate outbursts, these are generally succeeded by clear rationality. His own pre-existing distaste for the King does not lead him to act rashly ("But break, my heart, for I must hold my tongue"—I.ii.159). Only when he shows that he is both passionately willing to follow the Ghost ("Go on, I'll follow thee"—I.iv.86) and unwilling to follow beyond limit ("Whither wilt thou lead me? Speak, I'll go no further"—I.v.1) does the Ghost finally speak. Hamlet then subjects the Ghost's charge to the judgment of reason, his own and Horatio's. This pattern of passion brought under the government of reason continues in Hamlet throughout: "Never make known what

9   Line references in this edition correspond to the line numbering in G. Blakemore Evans, editor, *The Riverside Shakespeare*, Second Edition (Boston: Houghton Mifflin, 1997).

10 C. S. Lewis, "Hamlet: The Prince or the Poem?" in *Selected Literary Essays*, page 97.

you have seen tonight" (I.v.144); "About, my brains" (II.ii.588); "What is the reason that you use me thus?" (V.i.289).[11]

Second, because Hamlet, not the fratricidal usurper Claudius, is the rightful heir to his father's throne, he is, under God, the only rightful executor of justice in the kingdom. The knowledge that he is so depends upon the revelation of the Ghost. When that is confirmed, we and Hamlet know that the execution of the King is within Hamlet's proper authority. Hence, the givens both of Hamlet's nature and of his circumstances make him the perfect and appropriate instrument of divinity in overcoming that "divinity [that] doth hedge a king" (IV.v.124). Whether he executed Claudius in a fit of rage or in rational obedience—passion or reason— Hamlet would be acting as the instrument of divine justice.

After the performance of "The Murder of Gonzago," Hamlet is convinced that the King is guilty. He is ready to "drink hot blood / And do such bitter business as the day / Would quake to look on" (III.ii.390–92). In the next scene Hamlet's conviction about the guilt of Claudius is reinforced by our own knowledge when Claudius confirms in soliloquy that the guilt he has previously revealed to us ("How smart a lash that speech doth give my conscience ... O heavy burden"— III.i.48–53) is in fact over "a brother's murder" (III.iii.38). We now know for certain a) that the Ghost was honest and not a demonic tempter; b) that Claudius is not the rightful king of Denmark, being an adulterous and murderous usurper; and c) that Hamlet, as rightful heir to the throne and hence true steward of justice in Denmark, is duty-bound to execute the King. As a result, we expect that when Hamlet next finds Claudius he will, in a single action, accomplish the revenge that both he and Heaven desire, whether he does it by lashing out in a rage or by soberly performing his duty.

When Hamlet next enters, what he does instead of killing Claudius is remarkable: He approaches the kneeling King with drawn sword, stops, and stands doing nothing—like the "painted tyrant" of the First Player's speech about Pyrrhus (II.ii.480–82). Then, unlike the "hellish Pyrrhus" (II.ii.463), he sheaths his sword and exits. Why didn't he kill the King? What has got in the way of his execution of the divinely ordained

vengeance? To our *eyes* Hamlet's restraint looks like mercy. But in the second of the scene's two soliloquies, our *ears* hear otherwise. We hear Hamlet's inner thoughts, and they reveal a "will most incorrect to heaven" (I.ii.95). Hamlet, in this moment of hubris, is bent on a vicious personal revenge that the Ghost was never intended to inspire, namely the intent to make sure that Claudius will be damned. Here is the key observation of Philip Thompson mentioned above:

> At his one "ready" moment, in terms of the success of his cause, Hamlet is (literally) damnably unready. In explicit renunciation of that "readiness" he later espouses, he declares himself unsatisfied by the mere "hire and salary" of killing the body and leaving the soul to God, and demands the eternal damnation of Claudius as the only possible means of relief for his personal shame and suffering. This is the Hamlet that must be transformed (rather than the one of "To be or not to be"); a Christian audience would certainly have recognized that Hamlet's guilt is at this moment greater than that of Claudius, who, though he killed an "unhouseled" victim, did so only for his own benefit and not for the sake of sending his brother's soul to Hell. The opportunity is perfect and the lack of readiness is complete: since the entire castle had just seen Claudius betray himself (or at least raise serious suspicion), Hamlet's defense of the killing would have had convincing force.[12]

Seeing the King on his knees in apparent prayer, Hamlet ignores his own wise observation that "how his audit stands who knows save heaven?" (III.iii.82) and reasons his way into justifying a literally damnable choice: the choice to play God—and a vengeful God at that—in willing the eternal damnation of a fellow and apparently penitent mortal. He refrains from killing Claudius now so that he can kill him later in some act of sin and so be sure he is damned. The Ghost had described as "most horrible" his own being sent to purgatory, even to hear of which would "harrow up thy soul" (I.v.16). Hamlet now wants his uncle's soul in hell (III.iii.94–95).

The tone of Hamlet's speech is far from that of the passionate outbursts we have seen in him. It sounds like reason. But it is not true reason. It is reason pandering to will, the very sin of which Hamlet will accuse his mother in the next scene. In the service of his per-

---

11 This pattern, most visible in the soliloquies, is discussed more fully in the next section.

12 Philip Thompson, "Hamlet," in Gideon Rappaport, editor, *Dusk and Dawn: Poems and Prose of Philip Thompson* (San Diego: One Mind Good Press, 2005), pages 186–87.

verse will, rather than of either royal or divine justice, Hamlet's reason has conceived the most villainous plot in the play—the damnation of a soul. Polonius had advised Laertes: "This above all, to thine own self be true / And it must follow as the night the day / Thou canst not then be false to any man" (I.iii.78–80). Here Hamlet, being false to himself, has failed himself, Denmark, and God, and has put his own soul in jeopardy of damnation.

It is important to note that Hamlet's decision here is not a result of cowardice, or of too much thought, or of uncertainty about his role in life, or of humane kindness, or of anything else but what he says it is. In the theater there is no time to come up with our own explanations for characters' actions.[13] Nor does Shakespeare assume in his audience a Freudian awareness of unconscious ulterior motives. Shakespearean drama works by telling us what we are to think as we are to think it. In particular, the meaning of any soliloquy depends upon our accepting the convention by which the speaker is assumed to be telling the truth about his inner life as he sees it. If we do not take Hamlet at his word—if we assume he is rationalizing the postponement of a deed that he resists doing for other unstated reasons—we open the play up to an infinity of interpretations that rush in to fill the void we have invented, and no conclusion is possible.[14] If we do take Hamlet at his word, everything else in the play falls into place, unified meaning is the result, and the epithet "problem play" dissolves.

Hamlet's words express his mind. But he is wrong about Claudius's spiritual state, as is dramatized by

the terrible irony of the final couplet of the scene, which completes the soliloquy of Claudius that silent prayer and Hamlet's soliloquy have interrupted. Claudius has not in fact repented, is not engaged "in the purging of his soul." Rather, "My words fly up, my thoughts remain below. / Words without thoughts never to heaven go" (III.iii.97–98). Hence, if Hamlet had killed Claudius now, Claudius might well have been damned, though not by Hamlet's own will. Instead, pretending to know what he cannot know, serving his own desire for ultimate revenge, Hamlet gets in the way both of his passion and of his duty, either of which would have served here as the instrument of divine justice. Having set his will in place of God's, Hamlet has lost the opportunity to fulfill both. As a result, Hamlet opens the door to further depravity on the part of Claudius and to the ultimate destruction of the court and himself along with it.

How could our witty and beloved hero have gone so wrong? The first hint of that "particular fault" (I.iv.36) which has grown into this "scandal" (I.iv.38) was revealed in Act I, Scene ii, in an apparently throwaway line. When Horatio agrees that the marriage of Claudius and Gertrude took place rather soon after Hamlet Senior's death, Hamlet says, "Would I had met my dearest foe in heaven, / Or [= before] ever I had seen that day, Horatio!" (I.ii.182–83). In Hamlet's mind, the worst thing that could have happened to him was that marriage. But the next-to-worst thing would be to meet his enemy in heaven. To find oneself in heaven is good. But to Hamlet's mind, to find oneself in heaven and

13 As D. Nichol Smith wrote in his Introduction to *Shakespeare Criticism: A Selection 1623–1840* (London: Oxford University Press, 1916, reset 1946, reprinted 1963), page xx, "Shakespeare expects us to think of his characters as they are shown within the limits of the plays. We gain nothing by asking what was Hamlet's history before we first meet him; and when we trouble ourselves with the problem of his exact age we forget that, if the matter were of any importance, we should not have been left in doubt. Such inquiries are irrelevant to the impression derived from the drama, and in the drama, as Morgann said, 'the impression is the fact'."

14 The same idea is expressed by F. R. Leavis in "The Greatness of 'Measure for Measure'" (*Scrutiny* 10 [January 1942]: 237): "Taking advantage of the distraction caused by the problems that propose themselves if one doesn't accept what *Measure for Measure* does offer, [the bad prepotent tradition] naturally tends to smuggle its irrelevancies into the

vacancies one has created." The same "bad prepotent tradition" of critical misreading of *Hamlet* is represented in the irresolution of Francis Fergusson (*Shakespeare: The Pattern in His Carpet*, pages 196–97): About Hamlet's words in III.iii he writes, "This rationalization sounds far-fetched, and few commentators accept it. Some think that Hamlet's delay proves that he is pathologically incapable of action. Others point out that we should hardly expect a fine, sensitive young man to stab the King in the back while he was praying. But few, if any believe that Hamlet has given the real reason for his delay." As a result of not taking Hamlet at his word and assuming he is rationalizing, Fergusson is forced to conclude, "*Hamlet* is, even among great tragedies, one of the most mysterious of plays" and "every reader will form his own opinion of Hamlet and his own notion of the meaning of the play as a whole." It is unimaginable that Shakespeare could have intended us to come to such a conclusion.

there to meet one's worst enemy is unbearable, only less unbearable than his mother's hasty marriage to the uncle he mistrusts.

Modern readers who may not believe in heaven and hell find this line merely metaphorical and hyperbolical, the expression of an understandable emotion, and leave it at that. But Shakespeare's audience, who mostly did believe in heaven and hell, would have recognized in it a very un-Christian attitude. Ideally, every Christian wishes his enemy to see the error of his ways, to repent, and to be forgiven. Hate the sin; forgive the (repentant) sinner. But Hamlet's statement reveals a form of pride that would have heaven exist to please the self rather than the self exist to serve heaven.

In Act I, Scene iv, Hamlet expresses the idea that however great a man's virtues may be, he nevertheless may "in the general censure take corruption" from a "particular fault," a mere "dram of evil" destroying all his "noble substance" (lines 35–37). "General censure" can mean the judgment made by the general population, but the same words can also mean the Last Judgment. As did J. V. Cunningham,[15] I argue that it means both. In the eyes of the public, the good reputation of a generally good man, like that of a nation, might be ruined for a single fault. Equally, for a single unrepented fault, a good man for all we know might be damned. Hamlet's tendency to think of the heavenly salvation of his enemy in a negative light is his own "dram of evil." That particular fault, not of nature or of fortune but of the free will, grows into the pride, hideous in a Christian context, of Hamlet's motive for not killing Claudius in Act III, Scene iii.

The essence of Hamlet's fall appears in his utterance of the single word "No" at III.iii.87, the climax and turning point of the play (punctuated by Shakespeare with four and a half empty feet). Everything has been set up by Providence to allow Hamlet with clear conscience to effect the just punishment of the unrepentant Claudius, to explain his action to a shocked court (with the help of Horatio, Marcellus, and Barnardo, and potentially of Gertrude), to win election to the throne, and to do all this without disaster to the commonwealth—in short, to fulfill God's will. It was the job of the princely instrument of heaven's revenge, and (to quote Fabian in the comic context of *Twelfth*

15   Cunningham, graduate seminar on *Hamlet*, 1975.

Night III.ii.24) it "was balk'd." The failure arises neither from wild passion nor from excess reason but from false reasoning pressed into the service of a corrupt will. Philip Thompson adds that Hamlet

"knows" as much about death ... as any Christian does, knows that it sends the soul to Judgment and if to an undiscovered country yet to one whose laws are published. His bad purpose depends on revealed truth...

As a legitimate ruler in "This World," he should have felt that his duty was better fulfilled in executing a repentant murderer than it would have been in killing one rejoicing in his crime. On one level, his sin lies in breaking the law made especially for kings; on another, it lies in his truly damnable desire for a soul's damnation, in the identification of his hatred (not his mission) with the divine justice.[16]

As a result of Hamlet's moral error here, in the very next scene the wages of sin begin to be paid. Thinking he is killing the King in just such a moment as he had hoped for and sending him to hell ("I took thee for thy better"—III.iv.32), Hamlet flies into a passion and kills Polonius. Having failed in the previous scene to see into a man's soul, as God does, through his gesture, here he fails to see even through an arras.[17] Where in the previous scene this passionate thrust of the sword was called for as the instrument of divine vengeance, here, in the service of the pride of human vengeance, it opens the door to tragedy. When Hamlet then chastises his mother by naming her sins, effecting her repentance and loyalty, he fails to see that his accusations against her have a reflexive application. In the previous scene Hamlet too had allowed his reason to pander his will (III.iv.88).

Seeing Fortinbras and his army on the way to Poland, Hamlet asks himself why he has not acted to accomplish his revenge when the "Excitements of my reason and my blood [i.e., passion, impulse]" (IV.iv.58) have justified his doing so. His speech, which retains the rational-sounding pseudo-logic of the previous soliloquy, is motivated by frustration and revulsion with himself because he has not yet killed the King. It is this speech that is most responsible for the belief

16   Thompson, "Notes on Shakespeare," *Dusk and Dawn*, page 223.

17   An arras of the same sort as that behind which, before his moral fall, Hamlet was able to detect Polonius in hiding in Act III, Scene i, when the latter and Claudius used Ophelia as bait in the attempt to catch Hamlet's thoughts.

that Hamlet "cannot make up his mind," having sent any number of interpreters back through the play looking for general psychological reasons why Hamlet cannot act.

But Hamlet is here revealing not a general quality of his character but a particular blindness to what the audience already knows. He is certainly stuck when he says, "I do not know / Why yet I live to say, 'This thing's to do,' / Sith I have cause, and will, and strength, and means / To do't" (lines 43–46). But *we* know why. We have seen precisely when and precisely why he chose *not* to do "this thing" at the one perfect moment in which all of reality had conspired for him to do it. The cause of the delay is not "bestial oblivion," nor "craven scruple," nor "thinking too precisely on th' event [= outcome]" in a general way, except the "event" of Claudius's eternal fate. Nor was cowardice the cause, for in fact Hamlet did act to kill the King. But it was at the wrong moment with the wrong motive, and it was the wrong man he killed. The reason Hamlet did not act when he might have killed the right man, as we know from the climactic scene, was his pride, his choice to substitute the satisfaction of his own vengeance for the accomplishment of God's. (Sister Miriam Joseph calls it a failure of Christian charity.[18]) Now, ashamed of his failure to act but blind to the cause of that failure, he comes to a conclusion both unworthy of himself and, under the circumstances, futile: "My thoughts be bloody or be nothing worth" (IV.iv.66), a phrase that only confirms his moral blindness. His reason still panders his will.

When we next see Hamlet, he is a changed man. Back from the highly eventful sea voyage, we find him in the graveyard, contemplating the skull of Yorick. The scene is a visual *memento mori* ("remember that you die"). Medieval and Renaissance saints and monks, in art and in life, often kept a human skull on their desks to humble them with the prospect of their own mortality and inevitable divine judgment. Hamlet's musing here is to the same effect: Why should a man be proud when his end, like that of even Alexander and Caesar—history's most triumphant leaders—is dust? Hamlet has been chastened by experience, though we find out how only in the following scene. But first he must endure learning of the death of his beloved Ophelia and hear-

ing the proud boasting and the misguided and vengeful threats of Laertes. In response to his own grief and to Laertes' anger, he flies into a rage and the two young men grapple.

Once again Hamlet suppresses his passion and becomes reasonable ("Hear you, sir, / What is the reason that you use me thus? / I loved you ever. But it is no matter"—V.i.288–90), and the fact is significant. Whatever happened on the sea voyage did *not* alter Hamlet's nature or fundamental personality. With spiritual conversion we do not change into someone else but grow into better versions of ourselves. Hamlet remains a rational man who, under the pressure of external stimulus, still flies into passions and then regains rationality again.

Then how *is* Hamlet changed, if not in personality? Significantly, the answer comes not in a soliloquy but in dialogue with Horatio, the rational man, the friend whom Hamlet holds in his "heart's core" (III.ii.73). Thanks to the providential events of the sea voyage (Hamlet's inability to sleep, his impulse to read the King's commission, his possession of his father's seal ring, the exchange of letters, the attack by pirates, his impulse to leap aboard the pirate ship—proving he is not in fact a coward—the separation of the vessels, the mercy of the pirates), Hamlet has learned that "there's a divinity that shapes our ends, / Rough-hew them how we will" (V.ii.10–11), and that even human rashness may be put to use by it. He has learned that "we defy augury"—"defy" in the sense in which we say something "defies description" (*not* Romeo's sense in "I defy you, stars!"—*Romeo and Juliet* V.i.24); in other words, the fate of a human being, whether in this life or in the next, cannot be predicted by men. He has learned that "the readiness is all" (V.ii.222). Our wills are to be used to make us ready for the divine shaping, in which we may trust, for even the fall of a sparrow is providential. How much more so is the appearance of a ghost or of pirates. The readiness to die, to be like the sparrow, to leave the judging of souls to God, is all. Hamlet has learned to "let be" (V.ii.224).

"Let be," Cunningham argued, means "drop the subject; people are coming." This is true. But it also means "let be what will be; outcomes are not in our hands." As so often in moments pregnant with spiritual import, Shakespeare here unites two worlds of meaning in a single phrase, the mundane world of the senses and the invisible world of deepest truth dramatically

---

18 Sister Miriam Joseph, "*Hamlet*: A Christian Tragedy," in *Studies in Philology*, Volume 59, Number 2, Part 1 (University of North Carolina Press, April 1962), page 131.

incarnated in the moment. (Compare "Pray you undo this button" in *King Lear*, V.iii.310.) Thanks to the providential events of his sea voyage and to the chastening of the graveyard scene, Hamlet is now a man ready for the assignment of the moment, for whatever "the divinity that shapes our ends" has in store.[19]

Some readers find that Hamlet's enlightenment is vitiated by his apparently cavalier dismissal of the deaths of Rosencrantz and Guildenstern ("They are not near my conscience"—V.ii.58). How can he be so unfeeling? Once again, we must hear his words within the context of both the age and the events of the drama. First of all, Hamlet, who is not only the prince and heir to the throne but by rights the true king, bears responsibility for the well-being of all Denmark and the right to execute traitors, including those loyal to the state's actual enemy, Claudius. Second, Hamlet now knows that he has not sent the souls of Rosencrantz and Guildenstern to hell, as he tried to do with Claudius. In going to death they go to the judgment of God, who will infallibly discern what they deserve and will reward them accordingly. Third, Hamlet has no reason to believe that the "friends" who have spied upon him for the king are not in on the king's plot to have him killed. He has earlier said he will trust them as he will "adders fanged" (III.iv.203). Finally, and most important to remember, when Hamlet is actually writing the commission that will cause the king of England to put the bearers to death, he believes that both he and they will soon be appearing before that king and that Hamlet himself is meant to die by the commission they carry. He can only imagine that their private testimony about him will second Claudius's murderous intention. He cannot then know that a pirate ship will attack them, that he will leap aboard to lead a counter-assault, that the ships will drift apart and sail in opposite directions, leaving him prisoner to the uncharacteristically merciful pirates. The deaths of Rosencrantz and Guildenstern result from Hamlet's attempt to save his life, the life of the rightful king of Denmark. Hence his words to Horatio are a sign neither of depravity nor of callousness. They arise out of the recognition that Rosencrantz and Guildenstern, like Hamlet himself, are subject to the shaping of a power that human rough-hewing cannot control.

In the final scene, though for the sake of the court Hamlet maintains the fiction that it was because of madness that he killed Polonius, we know, because we have heard his words of humility spoken to Horatio, that his penitence expressed to Laertes ("Give me your pardon, sir"—V.ii.226) is genuine. The spiritually transformed Hamlet, under the immediate stimulus of his mother's sudden and his own imminent death, now kills the King in precisely the kind of passionate rage he might have flown into after the play-within-the-play, when false reason got in the way. He has finally fulfilled his mission, and just in time. His death, arising from his having killed Polonius, is punishment not for that physical action but for the moral fall that led to it, namely the proud choice in III.iii not to kill Claudius because he wanted him damned. The grace in the same events lies in Hamlet's having been given a second chance after a successful education in humility by providential reality in the form of all the heaven-ordained events of the sea voyage and the *memento mori* of the graveyard scene.

But before Hamlet dies, one more remarkable thing happens to confirm the transformation of his soul. Hamlet, who once had expressed the unchristian feeling that seeing his worst enemy in heaven was nearly the last thing he would desire, forgives his own murderer. In exchanging forgiveness with Laertes, Hamlet demonstrates the total integration of his soul: the absence of any vengefulness or pride and the presence of magnanimity and humility. His dram of evil is entirely "burnt and purged away" (I.v.13). And though all we can surely know of his ultimate reward is "silence" (V.ii.358), we share Horatio's hope for him, which recalls Laertes' for Ophelia (V.i.241): May "flights of angels sing thee to thy rest" (V.ii.360).

We have the analogy of the foil character Fortinbras to suggest that such will indeed be Hamlet's reward. Fortinbras is also given a second chance to serve rightly. Having given up his unjust desire to conquer a piece of Denmark and having used his army instead to serve his uncle-king's purposes instead of his own, he reaps the unimagined honor of having all Denmark fall into his lap. Analogously, Hamlet, having renounced his will in favor of God's, inherits the unimaginable kingdom of heaven.

---

19 In "a witty but serious fifty-word interpretation of *Hamlet*" Philip Thompson writes, "In choosing to effect the damnation of a soul while momentarily sparing a body, Hamlet sets out to write the ultimate revenge play; this choice is ultimately revenged upon Hamlet's body but not upon his soul, which has rested in choosing the revenge of the Ultimate." Thompson, "Notes on Shakespeare," *Dusk and Dawn*, page 222.

At the beginning of the play, in answer to Marcellus's famous line "Something is rotten in the state of Denmark," Horatio says a line far more important though less often quoted: "Heaven will direct it" (I.iv.90–91). At the end of the play, Hamlet himself, in retelling his adventures to Horatio, says about the seal ring in his possession, "Why, even in that was heaven ordinant" (V.ii.48). He sees at last that all his choices have been woven into the fabric of reality according to a will not his own. At his death, we see that he has been preserved alive long enough, and given just those experiences necessary, to enter that silence with a will altogether reformed (cf., III.ii.38) and at last correct to heaven (cf., I.ii.95).

Thus has Providence accomplished in the realm of the soul what Polonius only imagined he could accomplish in the realm of politics. Polonius says to Reynaldo,

> thus do we of wisdom and of reach,
> With windlasses and with assays of bias,
> By indirections find directions out. (II.i.61–63)

His proud imaginary control of political reality is a foil for Hamlet's proud imaginary control of spiritual reality. But the indirections he mentions are evident not only in the machinations of men—of Fortinbras in seeking to regain his father's lost honor, of Claudius in taking the throne and later plotting against Hamlet, of Polonius in analyzing Hamlet's madness, of Hamlet in seeking revenge through pretended madness and the play-within-the-play, of Rosencrantz and Guildenstern in seeking to pluck out the heart of Hamlet's "mystery," of Laertes in plotting Hamlet's death, and so on. Indirections are also apparent in the operations of Providence itself. Through madness Ophelia's injured innocence finds voice. Through Hamlet's mediation between Gertrude and her fighting soul her own repentance is effected. Most centrally, when Hamlet fails to perform his proper role in III.iii, Heaven is "ordinant" in providing sleeplessness and rashness in him, the possession of the king's seal ring, a pirate ship peopled by "thieves of mercy," the death of Ophelia, the exchange of weapons in the fencing bout, and all the other events that get Hamlet back into position to fulfill his calling. Though the deepest plots of wiser men than Polonius do pall (V.ii.9), shaping divinity, with wisdom and reach that are infallible, by indirections finds directions out.

Pattern in the Soliloquies

By stage convention, in a soliloquy the speaker speaks honestly about something in his or her inner life. In his mature works, Shakespeare subtly molds the soliloquy form to the speaker's character and to the dramatic and thematic purposes of the particular situation and of the play as a whole.[20]

A significant pattern in Hamlet's soliloquies is that in each, with two exceptions, Hamlet responds to an external stimulus with extreme passion which is soon displaced by calm and clarifying reason. This pattern, not entirely limited to the soliloquies but clearest in them, continues through the play until Hamlet's experience leads to the resolution of the moral conflict that the play exists to dramatize. That resolution is then expressed not in soliloquy but in dialogue with Horatio, the friend Hamlet holds most dear. (The tone of the two exceptions—"To be or not to be" [III.i.55ff.] and "Now might I do it pat" [III.iii.73ff.]—is calmly reasonable throughout, though the reason in the former is sound, in the latter tainted.) It is fruitful to watch this pattern unfolding from soliloquy to soliloquy.

In the soliloquy beginning "O that this too too solid flesh would melt" (I.ii.129–59), Hamlet is in a passion of misery over the hasty marriage of his mother with his despised uncle. His passion gives way to reason in the last line: "But break my heart, for I must hold my tongue." The conflict is between his feeling that his mother's remarriage is a depravity and the inappropriateness of speaking out against it. Given what he knows at this point, he lacks sufficient rational grounds for acting upon his feelings of dismay and disgust. The suppression of his feeling by his reason here shows wisdom and virtue.

At I.ii.254–57, in the soliloquy beginning "My father's spirit—in arms! All is not well," having heard of the appearance of a ghost looking like his father, Hamlet rightly suspects foul play. But he properly seeks a meeting with the ghost before acting on those suspicions. Once again, his reason has command over his passions.

In the soliloquy beginning "O all you host of heaven! O earth! What else?" (I.v.92–112), Hamlet begins in passionate determination to fulfill the command of the Ghost that he revenge the king's murder. By the end

20 See Gideon Rappaport, "Some Special Uses of the Soliloquy in Shakespeare" (Ph.D. dissertation, Brandeis University, 1979).

of the scene, Hamlet has mastered his emotions and conceived the rational plan to "put an antic disposition on." The plan will allow him to expose the King's guilt without himself coming under suspicion of plotting revenge. (Following Kyd's *Spanish Tragedy*, playing at madness became a conventional revenge-play method of surreptitiously exposing the villain.) Again Hamlet's passion has been brought under the government of reason.

Responding to the Player's speech about Pyrrhus, Priam, and Hecuba, Hamlet cries, "O what a rogue and peasant slave am I!" (II.ii.550). His rage against himself for not already having taken revenge soon directs itself toward the King. In the midst of it, Hamlet once again waxes reasonable ("Why, what an ass am I! ... About, my brains."—lines 582–88). He then reveals why he has not yet killed the King: namely, the fear that the Ghost may be a devil who "abuses [= deceives] me to damn me" (line 603). His conclusion is the wise plan to use a play to confirm whether the King is guilty in fact. In this expedient, we may also see Shakespeare asserting the value of drama in general and punctuating the seriousness of the play *we* are watching. The play *Hamlet* is the thing wherein our own consciences too may be caught. We may not be murderers like Claudius; are we like Hamlet in being tempted to play God, allowing our own fallen reason to corrupt our will where passionate desires are concerned?

The first of the two exceptions mentioned above, the "To be or not to be" (III.i.55–89) soliloquy, breaks the pattern of the others. It does not begin in a passion at all but is characterized by clear reason throughout. Hamlet is still in just that condition of resolution in which we left him at the end of the previous soliloquy (II.ii.605). As a student of philosophy and theology at Wittenberg, Hamlet now applies his training to the problem at hand, revisiting with philosophical detachment his decision to avoid his own damnation by not acting against the King until he can be sure of the King's guilt. As Philip Thompson writes, in this speech Hamlet

> elegantly phrases a conventional (Renaissance-graduate-student) explanation of the general human preference for quotidian misery over death, leaving Christianity completely out of the matter as the assignment dictated (impersonal, selfless). The speech is sweet-tempered and without personal urgency, and this mood continues into his conversation with Ophelia,

up to the moment when he notices the court in hiding. Compare this music of generalities—the mind, outrageous fortune, this mortal coil, the will, resolution, thought, great enterprises, etc.—with the several blood-and-guts outbursts and "the readiness is all" (personal, selfless).[21]

Reason here appears, as Cunningham discerned,[22] in the form of the traditional *quaestio* of medieval and Renaissance scholastic education: A philosophical question is proposed, pro and contra responses are given and refuted, and a conclusion is reached. The question at hand is whether it is better to be alive or dead, a general statement of Hamlet's particular question—whether it is better to risk death by killing the King immediately. For many reasons it would be better to be dead. But if one dies in a state of sin one might be damned. That is the concern that makes people prefer the misery they know to doing something that might get them killed and possibly damned. This soliloquy reinforces with formal reason the rational conclusion of the previous one. Exhibiting Hamlet's rational capacity, it also confirms that though he may fly into passions for cause, he is very far from madness.

In the dialogue following this soliloquy (III.i.89–149), Hamlet again flies into a passion in response to the sudden observation that Ophelia has been putting on a false show of virtuous prayer while in fact serving as Polonius's "bait of falsehood" meant to take the "carp" of Hamlet's truth (II.i.60). Practically speaking, the actor playing Hamlet must be directed just before line 102 ("Ha, ha! Are you honest?") to see some visible sign that Polonius and Claudius are eavesdropping. Hamlet suddenly shifts from the calm pretense of detachment about Ophelia into an outburst of actual rage that he pretends to direct against the abstract idea of women's frailty and men's abuse of it. The real source of the rage is that these willful plotters won't leave his women alone. They will be taking advantage of women's frailty to corrupt first his mother and now his beloved. In this scene Hamlet is entirely reasonable and calm until moved to passion by external circumstances. The order is reversed, but the pattern is intact.

In the soliloquy beginning "'Tis now the very witching time of night" (III.ii.388–99) Hamlet is prepared to "drink hot blood." But having most immediately on

21 Thompson, "Notes on Shakespeare," *Dusk and Dawn*, page 221.
22 Cunningham, graduate seminar on *Hamlet*, 1975.

his mind his mother, who has called him to her rooms, he reasonably determines to "speak daggers to her, but use none" (line 396). Everything seems to point to Hamlet's readiness to fulfill the Ghost's charge by killing the King and by refraining from doing harm to Gertrude.

Then comes the double-soliloquy climax of the play (III.iii.36–99). We have seen how Hamlet's soliloquy here, in tones sounding very like reason, in fact reveals that Hamlet's will has fallen shockingly into self-indulgence and depravity, and how the last two lines of the soliloquy of Claudius punctuate Hamlet's error.

Hamlet's next soliloquy, which comes a few scenes later and begins "How all occasions do inform against me" (IV.iv.32–66), has also been discussed above. It is his last soliloquy in the play, though the deepest things said in the play remain to be said. But when Hamlet says them, it is not in soliloquy but in dialogue with the friend of his soul. He has learned them in dialogue with his own providentially prepared experience. They include the humility of the *memento mori* in the graveyard (V.i), and (borrowing Thompson's phrasing) the personal and selfless profundity of Hamlet's enlightenment: "There's a divinity that shapes our ends, / Rough-hew them how we will" (V.ii.10–11) and "the readiness is all ... Let be" (V.ii.222–24).

The soliloquies are over because Hamlet has been chastened. Because he is no longer in conflict with himself, the soliloquy form previously used to show him so is no longer needed. He retains his double natural bent, flying into passions for cause (as against Laertes at the grave of Ophelia and at the King in the last scene) and then growing reasonable again. Conversion does not mean the alteration of one's given nature or the expunging of passion. But Hamlet's mind is no longer tainted, his reason no longer a pander to his will. His words to and about Laertes are confirmation: "But I am very sorry, good Horatio, / That to Laertes I forgot myself" (V.ii.75–76), "Give me your pardon, sir. I have done you wrong" (V.ii.226), "Heaven make thee free of it!" (V.ii.332).

Madness

Interpreters who follow two rules on the subject of Hamlet's madness will not go wrong. Rule 1: Hamlet is never actually mad. Rule 2: In cases where Hamlet seems to be mad, see Rule 1. Corollary: The only true madness depicted in the play is that of Ophelia.

These rules hold because Shakespeare distinguishes between extreme emotion and madness. As we have seen, Hamlet flies into passions and then in the midst of them suddenly brings reason to bear. The passions are not functions of interior illness but responses to specific external stimuli in a man who by nature is capable of intense emotion. The reason that supplants them is a function of the rationality that is also Hamlet's by nature. Wherever Hamlet *seems* to be mad, either he is playing at being mad or he is in a passion (of the sort that a sane man may fall into temporarily for cause) or both. It is one of the superb characteristics of this play that Shakespeare's art distinguishes clearly among Hamlet's highly artful pretense of madness, his genuine rages, and those rages into which he flies when he is also aware that he must keep up the pretense of being mad. We will see those clear distinctions so long as we do not assume that every moment of apparent irrationality or emotional intensity is a sign of real madness.

There are many explicit confirmations to the audience that what looks like madness is in fact the playacting for which Hamlet prepares us with the warning that "I perchance hereafter shall think meet / To put an antic disposition on" (I.v.170–72). They include "These tedious old fools" (II.ii.219); "Nay then I have an eye of you" (II.ii.290); Hamlet's perfectly rational advice to the Players (III.ii.1–45); "That's wormwood" (III.ii.181); Hamlet's pleasure at the success of his plan (III.ii.275–80); "They fool me to the top of my bent" (III.ii.384); Hamlet's proof to Gertrude that he is not mad (III.iv.140–46) and its reiteration, "That I essentially am not in madness, / But mad in craft" (III.iv.187–88); and Hamlet's perfectly rational conversations with Horatio (V.ii.1–80, 82–88, 183–94).

Hamlet's moments of passion are evoked by external stimuli: his mother's hasty marriage to his uncle (I.ii.129ff.); the appearance of the Ghost (I.iv.81ff.); the Ghost's story and the charge to revenge (I.v.92ff.); the Player's speech and emotion about Priam and Hecuba (II.ii.550ff., climaxing at "kindless villain!" in line 581); the erroneous belief that the King is hiding behind the arras in Gertrude's room (III.iv.24); his own litany of accusations against Gertrude and Claudius, in which he becomes swept up (III.iv.91ff.); Ophelia's death (V.i.242); Laertes' passionate cursing of him and bragging (V.i.266ff.); the death of the Queen (V.ii.310); the revelation of the King's last plot (V.ii.320); and Horatio's attempted suicide (V.ii.342–43).

In contrast, Hamlet's "antic disposition" involves the pretense of madness acted with total self-control. To complicate matters, however, depending upon his audience of the moment, Hamlet imitates at least two different forms of madness as conventionally understood at the time: that of heart-broken love[23] and that of disappointed ambition.[24] (It is not accidental that these two causes of Hamlet's playacted madness are parallel to the two motives for the crimes of Claudius, love and ambition). The opportunity to enact the former is provided by Polonius's order that Ophelia reject Hamlet's attentions. It appears in Ophelia's description of Hamlet at II.i.74ff., Hamlet's focus on Polonius's daughter at II.ii.172ff. (until the entrance of the Players), and his pretended detachment from Ophelia at III.i.91–95. The opportunity to enact the latter is provided by the conclusion Rosencrantz and Guildenstern jump to ("Why then your ambition makes it one" etc.—II.ii.252–62). It appears then in "I am most dreadfully attended" (II.ii.267ff.); "I eat the air, promise-crammed" (Hamlet knows Rosencrantz and Guildenstern have been reporting to the King) (III.ii.93ff.); the verbal changes worked upon the word "king" in IV.ii, whose import Rosencrantz and Guildenstern cannot fathom as we do; Hamlet's humiliating words to the King in IV.iii; and the exchange about the hat in which Osric is posed the problem of how to honor the apparently mad prince while disobeying him (V.ii.91ff.).

Lastly, at times Hamlet is *both* in a passion *and* pretending to be mad. Examples of this subtle accomplishment of Shakespeare's art appear where Hamlet, still in wild passion in response to the words of the Ghost, begins to play at speaking nonsense in words Horatio calls "wild and whirling" (I.v.118–32); where Hamlet suddenly discovers the eavesdroppers and flies into a rage at the abuse of Ophelia (associated in Hamlet's mind with the abuse of Gertrude), while keeping up the pretense of madness, in this case the mania of thwarted love (of which we will later see a real example in the madness of Ophelia) (III.i.102–149); and where real passion over the death of Ophelia and the extremity of Laertes' response is expressed in

23 Cf., Burton, page 721 and passim (Third Partition, Section 2, Member 3: "Symptoms or Signs of Love-Melancholy").

24 Cf., Burton, page 244 (First Partition, Section 2, Member 3, Subsection 11: "Concupiscible Appetite, as Desires, Ambition, Causes"): "[I]f he cannot satisfy his [ambitious] desire . . . he runs mad," and Francis Bacon, Essay XXXVI: "Of Ambition."

Hamlet's own apparently mad but self-consciously performed exaggerations (V.i.266–83).

Hence, madness in Hamlet is never itself the issue. All the variations in Hamlet's tone—reason, passion, and madness acted either calmly or passionately in craft (in keeping with the convention begun by Kyd and elaborated with unsurpassed realism here)—serve to clothe and heighten the essential drama played out in Hamlet's soul: his moral fall and spiritual regeneration.

Imperatives

Hamlet is filled with imperatives—tasks given by one character to another, almost always with some stipulation about how the task is to be accomplished. The central example, which initiates the through-line of the play, is the Ghost's charge to Hamlet: "Revenge [my] foul and most unnatural murder / ... But howsomever thou pursues this act, / Taint not thy mind, nor let thy soul contrive / Against thy mother aught" (I.v.25, 84–86). Take revenge, do it virtuously, don't do it by harming your mother. All other imperatives in the play may be considered foils for this one.

An earlier example sets the terms in which all the others may be understood. It is that of Claudius to Cornelius and Voltemand:

> we here dispatch
> You, good Cornelius, and you, Voltemand,
> For bearers of this greeting to old Norway,
> Giving to you no further personal power
> To business with the King, more than the scope
> Of these delated articles allow. (I.ii.33–38)

Here is your task; do it in a certain way; do not overdo it. A comic version of the pattern is that of Polonius to Reynaldo to put "forgeries" but not "scandal" on Laertes, with the qualification "as you may season it in the charge" (II.i.28).

Some of the many imperatives in the play are ceremonially formal, like that of Claudius to the ambassadors above *about* Fortinbras, Horatio's *to* Fortinbras at the end, "give order that these bodies / High on a stage be placèd to the view" (V.ii.377ff.), and the final orders *by* Fortinbras, "Let four captains / Bear Hamlet" (V.ii.395ff.). Some carry a universal application, like Polonius's instructions to Laertes (I.iii.58ff.) and Hamlet's to the Players (III.ii.1ff.). Some are more immediate and passionate, like Hamlet's charge to Horatio to live on and tell his story (V.ii.346ff.).

Some are light and only thematically connected, like the First Gravedigger's to the Second to answer his riddle (V.i.37ff.) or Hamlet's to Osric to put on his hat (V.ii.92ff.). After an initial question ("Who's there?"—I.i.1—and interrogatives in the play, too, bear examining), imperatives begin the play ("Nay, answer me. Stand and unfold yourself"—I.i.2) and another ends it ("Go bid the soldiers shoot"—V.ii.403).

Other significant imperatives: Polonius charges Ophelia to be a decoy; Hamlet instructs the Players to play "The Murder of Gonzago"; he instructs Horatio to observe the King's response to the play; he charges Gertrude not to reveal his craft to the King; Claudius commissions England's king and later Laertes to kill Hamlet; Hamlet charges Horatio to tell Fortinbras of Hamlet's "dying voice [= vote]" for Fortinbras to be the next king of Denmark along with "th' occurrents more and less / Which have solicited" (V.ii.357–58); and Fortinbras orders the final rites. The language of Hamlet's charge to Osric comically articulates the central theme in all the examples: deliver your message "after what flourish your nature will" (V.ii.180–81).

Once one begins noticing them, imperatives are everywhere: "Stay, illusion! ... Speak to me" (I.i.127–39); "Let us impart what we have seen tonight / Unto young Hamlet" (I.i.169–70); "Take thy fair hour, Laertes" (I.ii.62); "bend you to remain / Here" (I.ii.115); "But break my heart" (I.ii.159); "Give it an understanding but no tongue" (I.ii.249); "Think it no more" (I.iii.10); "Do not ... / Show me the steep and thorny way to heaven" (I.iii.47ff.); "these few precepts in thy memory / Look thou character," followed by the series of charges to aim for Aristotle's golden mean (I.iii.58–80); "But do not go with it" (I.iv.62); "Go on, I'll follow thee" (I.iv.86); "Speak, I'll go no further" (I.v.1); "If thou hast nature in thee, bear it not" (I.v.81); "remember me" (I.v.91); "Swear by my sword" (I.v.154); "Swear" (I.v.155); "Inquire me first what Danskers are in Paris" (II.i.7); "Come, go we to the King" (II.i.114); Hamlet's appearance to Ophelia, described by her (II.i.74–97), is a veiled charge to her to carry to Polonius the news that he is mad; "I entreat you both / ... to gather / So much as from occasion you may glean" (II.ii.10–16); "O, speak of that" (II.ii.50); "Give first admittance to th'ambassadors" (II.ii.51); Voltemand reports that Old Norway "sends out arrests / On Fortinbras, which he, in brief, obeys" (II.ii.67–68) and "Gives ... his commission to employ those soldiers / ... against the Polack" (II.ii.73–75); "Be

you and I behind an arras then" (II.ii.163); "mock him not" (II.ii.545–46); "Get thee to a nunnery" (III.i.120); "Will you play upon this pipe?" (III.ii.350–51); "Help, angels!" (III.iii.69); "Up, sword, and know thou a more horrid hent" (III.iii.88); "Look here upon this picture, and on this" (III.iv.53); "Do not forget" (III.iv.110); "go not to my uncle's bed—/ Assume a virtue if you have it not" (III.iv.159–60); "Seek him i' th' other place yourself" (IV.iii.34–35); "Do it, England" (IV.iii.65); "Give me my father" (IV.v.117); "Repair thou to me with as much speed as thou wouldest fly death" (IV.vi.23–24); "But, good Laertes, ... keep close within your chamber" (IV.vii.128–29); "when you are asked this question next, say 'a gravemaker'" (V.i.58–59); "take thy fingers from my throat" (V.i.260); "Let be" (V.ii.224); "Give me your pardon, sir" (V.ii.226); "drink off this potion" (V.ii.326); "Report me and my cause aright" (V.ii.339); "Take up the bodies" (V.ii.401). An exhaustive list would be far longer.

The point of these imperatives is that every situation in the play is a variation on Hamlet's situation, pregnant with the same universal theme that is carried to us by the story arising from the Ghost's imperative to Hamlet.

Foils

Shakespeare makes every character a foil for Hamlet, developing in myriad ways reflections of the paramount human concern centrally depicted in Hamlet himself: how to turn one's free will to the proper fulfillment of a charge rightfully laid on when one's knowledge of the future or of the ultimate context of the choice is limited. How is one to strike the golden mean when life presents contradictory temptations and both context and outcomes are hidden? The answer lies in the arc of Hamlet's spiritual transformation from revenge to readiness, which is recapitulated in the lesser, parallel arcs in the lives of his foils.

Whereas Hamlet does not go wrong until Act III, Fortinbras begins by getting his own mission wrong. Rather than serving his uncle's true authority, he takes upon himself the job of winning back the honor lost by his father, thereby risking all of Norway, as Hamlet later will risk all of Denmark. When his uncle recalls him, he "receives rebuke" (II.ii.69), that is, repents. In reward for his new obedience, he is given money and the same soldiers he had already levied and is sent off to Poland. Winning there, he finds, passing back through Denmark on his return, that all of Denmark (not merely the small parcel his father had lost) has fallen into his hands. His political journey depicts an early version of the moral transformation depicted later in Hamlet's spiritual journey.

Laertes is more explicitly a foil, for Hamlet says "by the image of my cause I see / The portraiture of his" (V.ii.77–78), and later "I'll be your foil, Laertes" (V.ii.255). Both have fathers slain, both want revenge, both are tempted by malevolence, voiced to Laertes by the King and to Hamlet by his own imagination. Both go wrong. Both are awakened to reality by mortality—Hamlet by the palling of his plots (the experience of heaven's ordination of events) and by the increasing nearness of death (Alexander and Caesar, Yorick, Ophelia), and Laertes by his own imminent death. Both repent and then are able to forgive. Both in different ways love Ophelia. Both are moved by passions and derailed by false reason. Laertes "dare[s] damnation" (IV.v.134) in vengeful passion by plotting to kill Hamlet; Hamlet "dare[s] damnation" in vengefully perverse reason by plotting to damn Claudius. In the end, converted by providential experience, each goes to death having fulfilled the words of the Paternoster, forgiving his enemy as he himself wishes to be forgiven. The difference that these similarities exist to emphasize is in degree of profundity. As the political and emotional qualities of the Gloucester plot in *King Lear* make way for the Lear plot to reach otherwise inaccessible spiritual depths, so here Laertes plays out at the level of emotion and action what is happening in the depths of Hamlet's soul.

Horatio's equanimity is a foil to Hamlet's extremes of passion and reason. Yet like Fortinbras early in the play, Horatio late in the play has a moment in which he too gets things wrong and must be recalled by a power greater than himself. Seeing his friend and prince dying and the collapse of all his hopes, Horatio wishes to die with him like an "antique Roman" (V.ii.341). Once again, Shakespeare reminds us that the context of this play is not classical but Christian. Hamlet first prevents Horatio from risking damnation for the self-slaughter against which the Everlasting has fixed his canon (I.ii.131–32). Then Hamlet charges Horatio for love of him to live on and report his cause aright. In response, Horatio "receives rebuke" from his prince (as Fortinbras from his king, Laertes from his imminent death, and Hamlet from divine providence itself) and goes on to fulfill Hamlet's charge.

Pyrrhus, as described in Hamlet's and the Player's speeches (II.ii.450–518), is also a foil for Hamlet. The reason Hamlet asks to hear the speech of Aeneas' tale to Dido describing Pyrrhus' vicious murder of Priam and the anguish of Hecuba is that he wishes to be inspired to take revenge. He sees Pyrrhus, from the traditional English point of view that sides with Troy against the Achaeans, as like the villain Claudius, Hamlet Senior as like the defenselessly murdered Priam, and Gertrude as *unlike* Hecuba in not showing much grief at her husband's death. But when Hamlet's own sword (at III.iii.75–87) seems "i' th' air to stick" as Pyrrhus's did (II.ii.479), we find that Pyrrhus has also become a foil for Hamlet's own pride and cruelty—the avenger has temporarily become the villain, desiring to accomplish not the King's death but his damnation.

Claudius is a foil for Hamlet in another sense. Where Hamlet "receives rebuke" from Providence, Claudius does not, but only reconfirms his decline toward hell. After "The Murder of Gonzago" has evoked his passion of guilt and put the fear of God in him, he has the choice to give up his crown, his ambition, and his queen, to repent, to die (if necessary) reconciled (like the first Thane of Cawdor in *Macbeth*). Instead he heaps upon himself damnation by twice plotting Hamlet's murder. His refusal to repent contrasts with Hamlet's conversion to "readiness." He enacts morally the part of the impenitent Herod of the morality plays (cf., III.ii.14) whereas Hamlet succeeds in reforming altogether his own interior version of Herod's strutting and bellowing (cf., III.ii.28–38).

The First Player is an explicit foil for Hamlet in appearing to feel the ancient wrongs done to Priam and Hecuba as deeply as Hamlet actually feels the wrongs done to his father and mother (II.ii.551–62). The parallel reinforces again that as the actor has cues for passion and fulfills his function by responding appropriately to them, so every man too has a similar role to play in life. In the playhouse called the Globe, Shakespeare explicitly as well as implicitly makes theater an image of the world.

Lucianus, "nephew to the king" (III.ii.244) in "The Murder of Gonzago," is a double foil like Pyrrhus. He is an image of Claudius, killing the king to steal his crown and his wife. But he is also an image of Hamlet, who stalks his own uncle for the villainous satisfaction of his desire for personal revenge. Hence Shakespeare makes (or has Hamlet make) him a nephew instead of a brother.

Polonius, like Hamlet, jumps to conclusions and trusts his own judgment even as he articulates good reasons for not doing so. "By heaven, it is as proper to our age / To cast beyond ourselves in our opinions, / As it is common for the younger sort / To lack discretion" (II.i.111–14), he says, whereupon he proceeds to demonstrate the truth of the platitude in his certainty about the cause of Hamlet's madness. This is exactly like Hamlet's saying "And how his audit stands who knows save heaven?" (III.iii.82). In both cases, the men articulate the very truth that ought to give them pause, and in both cases they ignore that truth and forge ahead in the service of their own pride. When Polonius says, "take this from this if this be otherwise" (II.ii.156)—meaning his head from his shoulder if Hamlet's madness be not caused by Ophelia's rejection of Hamlet's love—he stands before us self-condemned for pride, for we know it is otherwise, and his hasty offer ironically is fulfilled. Likewise, Hamlet's certainty that he can will Claudius into hell leads to his killing the wrong man. In both, "Pride goeth before destruction,"[25] and Polonius' death blow is, morally speaking, Hamlet's as well.

Gertrude's frailty in succumbing to the blandishments of Claudius is a foil for Hamlet's in succumbing to his own temptation to personal revenge. And Hamlet's accusations against her in III.iv, as we have seen, are equally applicable to himself, though he does not then know it. Like Fortinbras earlier, Gertrude "receives rebuke" from Hamlet and from then on remains true to him, never revealing to Claudius that Hamlet's madness is in fact crafty (IV.i.7–8, V.i.284). She is contrite (III.iv.156) and remains so (IV.v.17–20), and her death is her penance.

Ophelia is a foil for Hamlet, as she is for Gertrude. Like Gertrude she is frail and subject to the wills of unscrupulous men. Unlike Hamlet, she is driven literally mad by the insolubility of the dilemma with which, like Osric, Fortinbras, Laertes, Horatio, and the others, she is faced. Her experience is this: Her brother is gone to France, to protect her from the threat of unchastity her father tells her to drop her ideal lover, and her lover thereupon goes mad and kills her father. She now has her chastity but neither father nor lover

nor brother. What is virtue if it leads to this end? Yet how could she have behaved otherwise? Her condition, which is not her fault, is an embodiment of the condition of man. Our frailty is expected to rise to the occasion of dilemmas that our minds cannot comprehend how to resolve. Her actual madness is of course a foil for Hamlet's pretend madness and exists in part to dramatize the difference. In particular, the lewd songs and phrasing of her mad scenes enact the feminine version of the very thwarted-love mania from which Hamlet pretends to be suffering when playing at madness to Ophelia and Polonius (II.i.72–97, II.ii.174–86, III.i.102–149, and III.ii.112–21). In her innocent guiltiness (for she cannot help betraying either Hamlet or her father), she represents the tragic condition of man, whose fate depends on forces more powerful than his. But about her as about Gertrude we feel that, as Prince Hal says, "the end of life cancels all bands" (*I Henry IV* III.ii.157).

In all the above foils except Ophelia, pride is the downfall, whether in the end the guilty party repents or not. In the case of the Gravedigger, the thematic parallel is comically drawn. The Gravedigger imitates the language of the court out of a bumpkin's pride, and yet he cannot handle the real logic involved, just as Hamlet cannot really handle responsibility for the damnation or salvation of souls. The Gravedigger's hilarious attempt to anatomize "an act" as "to act, to do, to perform" (V.i.12) reveals he has "only got the tune of the time," like Osric, but blown to his trial, "the bubble [is] out" (V.ii.189–94). That is, he imitates the form of logical dialectic, as Hamlet the judgment of souls, without comprehending the substance.

On the other hand, the Gravedigger does know about dead bodies, and so he becomes the literally down-to-earth reminder of our mortality, hence of the spiritual necessity of humility. In foolish terms he and his fellow debate the state of Ophelia's soul, blundering in their language with no hope of getting to the heart of the question whether Ophelia is damned or not. But they are not alone. Laertes and the Priest debate the same question and perfectly understandably come down on opposite sides (V.i.223–42). In fact, Ophelia goes to judgment, so far as we know, with no greater sin than human frailty to answer for, and the judgment of her soul, now beyond the arrogant certainties of the living, is left to the mercy of God. In the meantime, both these debates about the state of her soul after death are foils

25 Proverbs, 16:18 (Geneva Bible).

for Hamlet's interior debate about the King's fate and his own. All of them must lead in one of two directions: either toward the pride of pretending to know what one does not and cannot know, or toward the humility of surrendering one's own will to that of the only possible Knower of all things.

Osric is another comical foil for Hamlet, and one may wonder why, at such a point of high tension (V.ii.80), Shakespeare felt the need to inject what is usually called "comic relief." But Shakespeare's comic relief is always also comic reiteration of the central themes of the play in which it appears. Placed where it is, Osric's scene becomes a precise metaphor for Hamlet's own situation. Court etiquette dictated that one remove one's hat in the presence of the prince. Hamlet asks Osric to put his hat on. Osric is thus faced with a painful dilemma. Is he to obey the form of civility made to honor the prince or to obey the prince himself? It is not an easy problem, for the "prince himself" is known to be mad. To dishonor him by humoring him Osric would put his lifetime's investment in court etiquette on the line. On the other hand, how is it possible to fulfill one's duty by disobeying a direct request of the prince? Osric is stuck. He tries to wriggle out of it with excuses, but he is incapable of rising to the occasion and ends by betraying substance (the prince's request) for form.

Osric's dilemma is an exact reflection of Hamlet's about the Ghost: How is it possible for a man to take revenge without tainting his mind, to obey God without disobeying God's law? Though, like Fortinbras (in Act I), Laertes (in Act IV), and Horatio (in Act V), Hamlet at first gets it wrong (in III.iii), later, like them but unlike Osric and Claudius, he gets it right. In the humbling of the sea voyage and the graveyard scene, Hamlet, in a deeper sense than Fortinbras, "receives rebuke" from Heaven and makes the equivalent of a vow never more to act out of mere self-will as if a higher power were not in charge. He has given up concerning himself about the disposition of souls after death, leaving it to that "special providence" which takes care even of a sparrow. He surrenders his will and undertakes nothing but readiness for whatever the "divinity that shapes our ends" will ask of him. In the end, he kills the King in the right frame of mind—that is, exactly the sort of passionate rage in which earlier he might have served the purposes of Heaven by killing the King, had

his false reason, pandering his perverse will, not got in the way.

"The readiness is all."

The Ghost's charge is the fundamental imperative of the play. But the play's philosophical heart is Hamlet's imperatives to the Players (III.ii.1–45). In these speeches Hamlet is of course voicing Shakespeare's own golden-mean advice on the subject of acting, akin to the life precepts of Polonius (I.iii.58–80). For Shakespeare, Aristotle remains the philosopher he was held to be in the high Middle Ages. But once again, treading the well-worn path of St. Thomas Aquinas, who as it were converted Aristotle to Christianity, Shakespeare is using the classical ideal as a window on a deeper spiritual principle than the golden mean. So far from being a diversion from the central theme of the play, the instructions to the Players in fact articulate its essence.

In the "torrent, tempest, and, as I may say, whirlwind of your passion"—in Hamlet's case, the passionate desire for revenge—"you must acquire and beget a temperance that may give it smoothness"—a temperance Hamlet himself lacks at the climax of the play but finds by its end. In wanting to damn Claudius, Hamlet morally "out-Herods Herod" (line 14). As the Players are not to "o'erstep ... the modesty of nature" (line 19) lest they distract "from the purpose of playing" (line 20), so must Hamlet not overstep the bounds of his commission lest he be distracted from the purpose of his own role, which is to put an end to Denmark's corrupting usurper without causing the fall of the state and its royal family.

"Now this overdone" (lines 24–25)—wanting Claudius not merely dead but damned—"or come tardy off" (line 25)—the postponement to assure that damnation —"cannot but make the judicious grieve" (line 26)—the judge of Hamlet's performance in life being that One whose censure (cf., "general censure" at I.iv.35) o'erweighs that "whole theatre of others" (line 28) that is the world. Hamlet has let himself "speak ... more than is set down" (line 39) for him by the Ghost, "though in the mean time some necessary question of the play be then to be considered" (lines 42–43), namely getting rid of Claudius without causing the deaths of Ophelia, Polonius, Gertrude, Laertes, Rosencrantz, Guildenstern, and himself. "That's villainous, and shows a most pitiful ambition in the fool that uses it" (lines 43–45). The worldly ambition Rosencrantz and Guildenstern are fooled into thinking Hamlet harbors is illusion; the ambition of spiritual pride we have seen in him in Act III, Scene iii, is deadly real.

But between Hamlet's fall and his death, Providence has spoken to him as clearly as Hamlet is speaking to the Players here. It has invited him to "reform it altogether" (line 38) in the discovery of the "divinity that shapes our ends, / Rough-hew them how we will" (V.ii.10). When Hamlet is able to say to Horatio that "the readiness is all" (V.ii.222)—and more, to forgive his own murderer (V.ii.332)—we see evidence of that reform and can well believe in Horatio's "flights of angels" (V.ii.360) singing the soul of Hamlet to its heavenly rest.

This redemptive reformation of Hamlet does not make of the play any less a tragedy. As Morton Bloomfield cautioned, the joy of the next world implied in Christian tragedy differs significantly from the joy of the happy ending in this world in comedy.[26] And tragedy in the Renaissance consists not in the damnation of souls but in the violent ending of lives onstage.[27] But *Hamlet* is a *Christian* tragedy,[28] and this tragedy of man's free will held up to the judgment of God is also the story of man's chastening by the incarnations of God's mercy. As the Players have been instructed by him, so is Hamlet instructed by ordinant heaven. Hamlet's last imperative to the players, "Go make you ready" (III.ii.45), is the play's imperative to us, for "the readiness is all."

---

26 Morton Bloomfield, in a lecture series entitled "Medieval and Renaissance Tragedy and Notions of Tragedy," delivered at Brandeis University, Spring 1978.
27 Cf., J. V. Cunningham, *Woe or Wonder: The Emotional Effect of Shakespearean Tragedy* (Chicago: The Swallow Press, 1969), pages 52, 56–59.
28 For another thorough discussion of what this means, see Sister Miriam Joseph, op.cit.

THE TRAGEDY OF HAMLET,
PRINCE OF DENMARK

Act I, Scene i

Enter Barnardo and Francisco, two sentinels.

BARNARDO
Who's there?

FRANCISCO
        Nay, answer me. Stand and unfold
Yourself.

BARNARDO
    Long live the King!
FRANCISCO
             Barnardo?
BARNARDO
                  He.   5

FRANCISCO
You come most carefully upon your hour.

BARNARDO
'Tis now struck twelve. Get thee to bed, Francisco.

Act I, Scene i ● The guards' platform of Elsinore Castle.

S.D. *sentinels*: guards, upon the platform where cannon are placed in a fortress (cf., I.ii.213 and note).

Who's there?: The phrase may be a separate line outside the normal pentameter verse (Abbott §512), as at lines 129, 132, and 135 below and in many places which will not usually be noted. That F puts "your selfe" on the next line may suggest that lines 1–5 here are in fact two verse lines. While it is true, as Jenkins argues (LN), that this opening scene emphasizes "short colloquial exchanges," it is their pressure against the expectation of blank verse that adds tension to the exchange. The typography indicating pentameter lines keeps us aware of that pressure and instructs the actors to convey it in performance.
● The question and response set a mood of uncertainty and open the theme of not knowing someone's identity and needing to find it out. That theme will be developed in the efforts of others and in particular Hamlet to determine who or what the Ghost is, whether Claudius is guilty, what is going on in the souls of the apparently mad Hamlet and actually mad Ophelia, and "who is there" when one has died.

me: "Emphatic. It is the sentry on guard who has the right to challenge" (Jenkins). **Stand:** stop. **unfold:** identify, reveal. ● Through the play, Hamlet and others will be "unfolded" to one another in varying degrees and to us thoroughly. Francisco voices the first of the many major and minor imperatives imposed by one character upon another in the play. Almost every imperative will involve the imposition of a task and instruction about how it is to be done, often with a warning not to overstep bounds (see Introduction, page 13ff.).

Long live the king!: ● Whether or not this is the official password, loyalty to the king identifies the speaker, "dramatically ironical in view of all that follows" (Dover Wilson in Jenkins), who also then *acknowledges* his identity. Cf., other questions of identity: Polonius illustrates "if't be he I mean" (II.i.18). Is it the King whom Hamlet stabs through the arras (III.iv.26)? Whose skulls are contemplated by Hamlet (V.i.75ff.)? "This is I, / Hamlet the Dane" (V.i.257–58). Above all, who or what is the Ghost?

carefully: attentively and promptly. **upon:** at, immediately after (Abbott §191). ● The impression is given that Barnardo is trustworthy.

twelve: midnight. ● The hour of the shift in guards is also the witching hour.

FRANCISCO
For this relief much thanks. 'Tis bitter cold,

And I am sick at heart.

BARNARDO
Have you had quiet guard?
FRANCISCO
                          Not a mouse stirring.   10
BARNARDO
Well, good night.
If you do meet Horatio and Marcellus,
The rivals of my watch, bid them make haste.

                    Enter Horatio and Marcellus.

FRANCISCO
I think I hear them. Stand, ho! Who is there?

HORATIO
Friends to this ground.
MARCELLUS
                          And liegemen to the Dane.   15
FRANCISCO
Give you good night.
MARCELLUS
                          O, farewell, honest soldier.
Who hath relieved you?
FRANCISCO
                          Barnardo hath my place.
Give you good night.
                                            Exit Francisco.
MARCELLUS
                          Holla, Barnardo!
BARNARDO
                                Say,
What, is Horatio there?

---

thanks: "often singular" (Jenkins), cf., II.ii.25.
cold: It may be a natural cold, but the devil is traditionally believed to be cold and to make those experiencing his appearance feel cold, so that a kind of spiritual suspense is being set up.

sick at heart: miserable. • We are never told specifically why Francisco is sick at heart, and after this scene we never meet him again by name. His lines imply not only cold, dark, and unpleasant physical conditions, but internal discomfort. This is both dramatic foreshadowing and also premonition (cf., V.ii.212–16 and note), implying that something undesirable is coming. Is it war, death, or some other disruption of the natural or social order? Why are they on guard? What is going on?

Have you … guard?: • A normal question (from Francisco's viewpoint), but in a few minutes we will realize it is weighted by what Barnardo has seen the previous two nights.

rivals of my watch: partners (as in Q1), fellow guards for the late shift. **make haste:** • Because it is nearing the time, as we'll hear, that the apparition has appeared previously.

Stand, ho!: see line 2 note • Francisco is doing his duty, continuing the opening theme of identity questioned and established through loyalty to the king.
this ground: Denmark.

the Dane: the king of Denmark.

Give … : short for "May God give…"

honest soldier: • Unlike Barnardo, Marcellus does not know Francisco's name, but the phrase repeats the impression that the soldiers and guards are honest and that the threat does not come from them.

Give you good night: • Francisco's repetition of his parting phrase suggests he is anxious to depart.

What: a sign of interrogation rather than itself the question, as at line 21 and II.i.104 (OED A. 21.).
Horatio: The name reminds us of the Roman poet Horace and of a character in *The Spanish Tragedy* (see Introduction, page 2) but also contains the Latin word *ratio*, reason, rationality. • Balanced reason is the quality for which Hamlet will especially love Horatio. Is it fanciful to hear in his name "Ho, ratio," behold reason?

HORATIO

        A piece of him.

BARNARDO

  Welcome, Horatio. Welcome, good Marcellus.   20

HORATIO

  What, has this thing appeared again tonight?

BARNARDO

  I have seen nothing.

MARCELLUS

  Horatio says 'tis but our fantasy,

  And will not let belief take hold of him

  Touching this dreaded sight twice seen of us.   25

  Therefore I have entreated him along,

  With us to watch the minutes of this night,

  That, if again this apparition come,

  He may approve our eyes and speak to it.

HORATIO

  Tush, tush, 'twill not appear.

BARNARDO

        Sit down awhile,   30

A piece: He is only partly here. ● Horatio is present in body by request but not especially wanting to be here.

good: ● A further impression of their upright character.

What: see line 19 note. **thing:** ● The first mention of the Ghost uses the most general possible noun. Note how the terms for the Ghost develop in the next several lines.

nothing: ● The second noun used of the Ghost. Is it nothing or something?

fantasy: ● The third noun for the Ghost, the initial judgment of the rational man, Horatio.

dreaded sight: ● The fourth phrase for the Ghost, preparing us to believe the characters are frightened by it.

along,: i.e., to come along with us, both the verb of motion and the prepositional phrase being commonly omitted with "along" (Abbott §30). The comma (as in Q2) indicates that "With us" in the next line belongs with "to watch" (= to stay awake during, as well as to be on guard duty) rather than with "along," though "the word order permits us to take it with both" (Jenkins).

apparition: ● The fifth noun for the Ghost, each more precise than the former. Now the more general Anglo-Saxon monosyllabic "sight" has become the more specific Latin polysyllabic "apparition."

approve our eyes: confirm what we have seen.

speak to it: ● By tradition, "A ghost has not the power to speak till it has been first spoken to; so that, notwithstanding the urgency of the business on which it may come, everything must stand still till the person visited can find sufficient courage to speak to it" (Grose, *A Provincial Glossary*; Brand, *Popular Antiquities*, ed. Hazlitt, cited in Jenkins, with examples from Fielding's *Tom Jones* and Boswell's *Johnson*). Ghosts must also be spoken to in proper form, and four witnesses were required to confirm the reality of a ghost. Here two soldiers seek the confirmation of a third witness, and one who, having studied philosophy and divinity (cf., "scholar" at line 42 below), has more knowledge about such things. Only the reasonable man can confirm that a ghost has been seen, and only the scholarly man can address it in proper form and therefore without risking "offense and consequent danger" to himself (Jenkins substantially).

Tush, tush: a common Shakespearean expletive expressing disdain or disapproval, the vowel is pronounced as in "brush" not "bush." **'twill not appear:** ● Precisely because Horatio is skeptical, he will be trusted when he does see the Ghost for himself. This skepticism is why only "a piece of him" is here. At the same time, Horatio is wrong that the thing will not appear, the first example among many in the play of the error of being too sure of one's own picture of things.

Sit down awhile: A minor imperative. Not all imperatives will be noted, but they are everywhere (see Introduction, pages 13ff.).

And let us once again assail your ears,

That are so fortified against our story,

What we have two nights seen.

HORATIO

                          Well, sit we down,
And let us hear Barnardo speak of this.

BARNARDO

Last night of all,

When yond same star that's westward from the pole
Had made his course t'illume that part of heaven
Where now it burns, Marcellus and myself,

The bell then beating one—

                Enter Ghost.

MARCELLUS

Peace, break thee off. Look where it comes again!

BARNARDO

In the same figure like the King that's dead.

MARCELLUS

Thou art a scholar; speak to it, Horatio.

BARNARDO

Looks a not like the King? Mark it, Horatio.

HORATIO

Most like. It harrows me with fear and wonder.

---

assail: attack with argument in order to persuade or convince (OED 5.).

fortified: ● Horatio is metaphorically "fortified" by skepticism against too easy a credulity, as Denmark is fortified against the yet unknown threat.

What: that which (see Abbott §252). **two nights:** The guards have seen the Ghost twice already.

sit we down …: Let us sit down (first-person plural imperative, Abbott §361). ● The reasonable Horatio is willing to listen.

35 **Last night of all:** i.e., last night, emphatic, as in "last of all" (Jenkins).

When yond … now it burns: i.e., at exactly this time (when that star was just where it is now). **pole:** pole-star, i.e., the North Star, Polaris. **his:** its, "the ordinary form of the neuter, as well as masculine, possessive. The Elizabethan alternative was *it*" (Jenkins, Abbott §228, cf., I.ii.216, I.iii.60, I.iv.26, III.iii.62, IV.vii.15, V.i.221 etc.). **illume:** illuminate.

beating: striking. ● The sentence increases suspense, as does the pause after it (Abbott §511).

40 **Peace:** imperative for be quiet, do not speak. **break thee off:** imperative for stop talking. Abbott (§513) calls the phrase amphibious, forming the end of one pentameter verse line ("The bell then beating one … Peace, break thee off") and the beginning of another ("Peace, break thee off. Look where it comes again!").

same: i.e., same as we have seen before, with the overtone of how like the image is to the former king. **like:** in the likeness of. ● The audience sees the apparition, as the guards and Horatio do. It looks like the former king, now dead, our first news of him. But every former king is now dead. Why should this one appear as a ghost? And is it the ghost of the dead king or only similar to him, a spirit in disguise?

scholar: student of the seven liberal arts: the trivium (grammar, logic, and rhetoric) and quadrivium (arithmetic, geometry, music, astronomy) followed by philosophy (classical) and divinity (Christian), the crown of the arts, the study of which means that Horatio would know how to speak to a ghost in proper form (cf., line 29 note above). **Horatio:** "polysyllabic names often receive but one accent at the end of the line" (Abbott §469), so that the word is pronounced as only three syllables, of which only "ra" gets the stress. So in the next and later lines.

a: he (OED A *pron.* 1.), a common usage throughout this play. **Mark:** note, pay attention to. **Horatio:** given only one stress (see line 42 note).

Most like: very much like (the dead king). ● The rational, skeptical man now confirms the impression of the other two. **harrows:** lacerates, wounds (metaphorically breaking one up as one breaks up soil with a harrow, a rake-like machine dragged by horses or oxen) (OED *v.*¹ 4.). **fear and wonder:** fearful awe and amazement, echoing Aristotle's two terms (often translated "pity and fear") for the effects of tragedy on the soul (cf., V.ii.363 and note and Cunningham *W/W*, page 35). • Horatio experiences the universal human awe in the face of the supernatural, and we believe what Horatio says about it, partly because of his established rationality and partly because in a sense we the audience are the fourth observer, confirming the reality of the apparition (cf., line 29 note).

would be spoke to: wishes (Abbott §329) to be spoken to.

BARNARDO
It would be spoke to.

MARCELLUS
Speak to it, Horatio.   45

Speak to it: Q2 (F, Q1 Question it = hold discourse with it, cf., I.iv.43). • The common soldier can see that the apparition needs to communicate, that it cannot speak until spoken to, and that only the scholar can address it in proper form. And now Horatio the scholar will so address it.

HORATIO
What art thou that usurp'st this time of night

usurp'st: take over what does not normally and naturally belong to you.

Together with that fair and warlike form
In which the majesty of buried Denmark

fair: handsome, impressive. **warlike:** armored.
majesty of buried Denmark: i.e., the dead king of Denmark (cf., "your majesty" used in addressing a king).

Did sometimes march? By heaven I charge thee, speak.

sometimes: in the past, formerly (OED 2.). • Asking what the apparition is, Horatio uses the idea of usurpation, setting up a possible offense to the spirit, if it is in fact the ghost of Hamlet Senior, though the spirit has indeed taken over both the time of night and the form of the dead king as he used to appear armed for battle, a form that ought properly to remain entombed. Usurpation is an important concept through the play. Claudius is a political usurper. Hamlet will become a spiritual usurper for a time. Polonius, Laertes, and Fortinbras are in their respective ways foils for those two usurpations. But is the usurper of the king's form in fact the soul of the king or a demon in disguise? **By heaven:** an oath. • Another imperative, this one made in the name of heaven, a necessary appeal for one speaking to the ghost of a king who could hardly be exhorted "In the name of the king."

MARCELLUS
It is offended.
BARNARDO
See, it stalks away.   50

offended: • The spirit is not, in fact, offended. As we will see, it never intended to speak to these men, but its appearance to them will accomplish what *was* intended (cf., line 171 below), that Hamlet be brought to speak with him.

HORATIO
Stay. Speak, speak. I charge thee, speak.
                                        Exit Ghost.

MARCELLUS
'Tis gone and will not answer.

will not answer: "Ghosts, even when questioned, will speak only to those for whom they have a message" (Jenkins). • Horatio's imperative ("I charge thee") cannot make it speak. Cf., Hamlet's words to Rosencranz and Guildenstern, "there is much music … in this little organ, yet cannot you make it speak" (III.ii.353–55). Throughout the scene there is more going on than Horatio's human reason

BARNARDO

How now, Horatio? You tremble and look pale.
Is not this something more than fantasy?

What think you on't?   55

HORATIO

Before my God, I might not this believe

Without the sensible and true avouch
Of mine own eyes.

MARCELLUS

                    Is it not like the King?

HORATIO

As thou art to thyself.
Such was the very armor he had on   60

When he the ambitious Norway combated.

So frowned he once when in an angry parle

---

can master, just as later there is more to Hamlet than Rosencrantz and Guildenstern are permitted to know. **Horatio:** one stress on the second syllable, keeping the line to five stresses (cf., Abbott §458, 467, 468), and the "io" may even be elided into the *Y* of "You." **tremble and look pale:** ● NOTE TO ACTORS: Whether or not the actor playing Horatio in Shakespeare's day felt the need to pretend to tremble or try to make himself look pale, the text does the job for him. The audience knows that he is trembling and looking pale with fear because Barnardo says so. "Shakespeare's characters are created not only out of everything they say themselves but out of everything said about them by other characters" (Maddox). Shakespeare's audience went to hear (rather than see) a play; it is primarily the words that form the reality in our minds, however realistic or stylized the performance.

on't: of it (Abbott §181).

Before my God: ● Like everyone else in the play and most in Shakespeare's audience, Horatio believes in God, and here the rational man is explicitly swearing by him. **might:** could (Abbott §312).

sensible and true avouch: the first of the 66 instances of hendiadys found in the play by George Wright. Hendiadys (pronounced *hen-DYE-a-dis*) is a figure of speech that turns a noun and its modifier into a pair of nouns joined by the coordinate conjunction "and," *cf.*, "gross and scope" (line 68), "book and volume" (line 103), "form and pressure" (III.ii.24), etc. See Wright and Kermode *SL*. **sensible:** feeling, the passive sense "being felt" rather than the active sense "capable of feeling" (Abbott §3). **avouch:** testimony, an example of a verb used as a noun (cf., *inquire* II.i.4, *disclose* III.i.166, *supervise* V.ii.23, Abbott §451). ● This seeing of the apparition was not a fantasy. Seeing is believing.

Is it not like the King: i.e., similar to the previous king. The line metrically completes a regular pentameter line but also begins a "trimeter couplet" (Abbott §513). ● Horatio and Marcellus are used to thinking of the dead king, not the living one, as their king.

As thou art to: as you are similar to.

armor he had on / When: ● We are not meant to focus on chronology here. Doing so would throw us into confusion about Horatio's age, especially if we try to link this passage with the Clown's words at V.i.144 and 162. The emphasis is on how much the Ghost resembles the dead king, cf., line 79 note (and see Introduction, page 6 note 13 and Jenkins V.i.139–57 LN).

Norway: the king of Norway. **combated:** cf., lines 84ff. below.

So frowned he … parle: either literally frowning during a parley (verbal confrontation) or metaphorically with warlike anger during battle "as befitted a martial hero" (Jenkins), cf., I.ii.231 and note (Jenkins LN).

He smote the sledded Polacks on the ice.

sledded: riding on sleds. **Polacks:** the normal Elizabethan term for Poles (Jenkins LN), against whom Fortinbras will first pretend to be marshaling troops (II.ii.62–63) and whom he then will actually fight (II.ii.74–75, IV.iv.12) and defeat (V.ii.350).

'Tis strange.

'Tis strange: ● The rational man confesses that his reason is defeated in this matter.

MARCELLUS
Thus twice before, and jump at this dead hour,   65

jump: just, precisely (cf., V.ii.375, and *Othello* II.iii.386). **dead hour:** midnight (cf., line 7), "when the normal activities of life are suspended" (Jenkins) and the witching hour, associated with darkness, silence, death, and ghosts.

With martial stalk hath he gone by our watch.

martial stalk: in the stately walk of a soldier in arms ● The spirit appears in armor partly to be recognized and partly to mislead the guards about his real purpose, which we will learn only later. We soon see that he succeeds in the deception when they come to a wrong conclusion.

HORATIO
In what particular thought to work I know not,

In what particular thought to work: In order to accomplish (OED Work *v.* 24. and 25.) what specific intention (OED Thought¹ 4.d.).

But in the gross and scope of my opinion,

gross and scope: the general overall range (OED gross *a.* and *sb.⁴* B.2.a.), contrasting with "particular" in the previous line, a hendiadys (see line 57 note).

This bodes some strange eruption to our state.

bodes: forbodes. **strange:** unusual, unwonted, foreign. **eruption:** outbreak or upheaval (cf., *Julius Caesar* I.iii.78, where the same phrase refers to the happenings described in lines 115–20 below). **state:** Denmark as place, nation, and government, as well as condition. ● It is a sign of Horatio's wisdom that he recognizes that he does not know exactly what the apparition's purpose is though he is willing to guess that at least it is a bad omen for Denmark, and he turns out to be right. Jenkins finds authority for Horatio's "orthodox" conclusion in Lewes Lavater, *Of Ghosts and Spirits Walking by Night*, translated into English by Robert Harrison 1572 (in Latin 1570): "If they be not vain persuasions, or natural things, then are they forewarnings of God."

MARCELLUS
Good now, sit down, and tell me, he that knows,   70

Good: for "Good sirs" or "Good friends," the strength of the vocative adjective allowing the omission of the noun (cf., *Comedy of Errors* IV.vi.21 and Abbott §13). **tell me … knows:** let him who knows tell me, subjunctive used as imperative (Abbott §364). ● This line introduces the subplot of the threatened war. Why is there all the preparation described in the next several lines?

Why this same strict and most observant watch

watch: guard, with a secondary sense of staying awake.

So nightly toils the subject of the land,

toils: causes toil to, i.e., causes to toil ("any noun could be converted into a verb … generally in an active signification," Abbott §290). **subject:** the subjects of the king, the people, used as a collective noun (cf., I.ii.33 and *Measure for Measure* II.iv.27).

And why such daily cast of brazen cannon,

why such: why is there such. **cast of brazen cannon:** casting of brass cannons.

And foreign mart for implements of war,

foreign mart ... war: purchase (mart = market) of arms abroad.

Why such impress of shipwrights, whose sore task   75

impress: draft, conscription, as of soldiers (cf., *Troilus and Cressida* II.i.97). **sore:** severe, involving hardship.

Does not divide the Sunday from the week.

divide ... week: the shipwrights work even on the Sabbath.

What might be toward that this sweaty haste

might: could (Abbott §312). **toward:** coming toward us, impending, imminent (cf., V.ii.365 and *As You Like It* V.iv.35), pronounced (*TOE-ward*) with stress on the first syllable to preserve the meter, cf., *froward*.

Doth make the night joint-laborer with the day?
Who is't that can inform me?

joint-laborer: co-worker (night and day imaged as workers).

HORATIO

　　　　　That can I.
At least the whisper goes so. Our last king,   80

That can I ... whisper: ● Here we are to take it that Horatio has access to court history and gossip. That he is a Dane is established here, below at line 125 ("our climatures and countrymen"), and at V.ii.341. Many apparent contradictions in Horatio can be dispensed with. The seeming contradiction between I.ii.184 ("I saw him once") and I.ii.210 ("I knew your father") is resolved if we take "knew" in the latter line to mean "recognized" based on having seen him. Horatio's unfamiliarity with the drinking custom at I.iv.12 may be a result of his being a Dane but not familiar with the court at Elsinore. And Hamlet's surprise at seeing Horatio at I.ii.165ff. may arise not because Horatio is in Denmark but because he is away from school and at Elsinore instead. The major contradiction in Horatio lies in his claim at lines 60–63 above ("Such was the very armor ..."), which suggests that he has seen Hamlet Senior long ago, seeming to raise the question of Horatio's age. But there is no question about Horatio's age. Like Hamlet he is a mature young man, and that is what matters. Such technical contradictions, which trouble some scholars, are entirely irrelevant to audiences during a performance, where the impression of the moment, not absolute consistency of plot details, is paramount. Cf., the discussion of Hamlet's own age at V.i.143 note (and see Introduction, page 6 note 13).

Whose image even but now appeared to us,
Was, as you know, by Fortinbras of Norway,
Thereto pricked on by a most emulate pride,

even but now: even now (for the redundant use of "but" see Abbott §130).

Thereto pricked on: goaded to it (as a horse by spurs). **emulate:** emulous, implying not merely imitation and rivalry, but self-aggrandizement, aspiration to a place above one's proper rank in the hierarchy of all things, associated with envy and destructive factionalism (cf., *1 Henry VI* IV.i.113, *Richard III* II.iii.25, *Julius Caesar* II.iii.14, etc.). **pride:** one of the seven capital sins (called mortal or deadly sins), traditionally understood to be the root sources of all other sins.

Dared to the combat; in which our valiant Hamlet

the combat: "the combat that ends all dispute" ("*the* used to denote notoriety," Abbott §92).

(For so this side of our known world esteemed him)   85

so: i.e., valiant. **this side ... world:** Christendom and the West (as opposed to the side of the world belonging to the infidels, the Orient).

Did slay this Fortinbras; who, by a sealed compact

Did slay … compact: The line is probably stressed as a pentameter ("Did sláy this Fórtinbras; whó by a séaled compáct," Abbott §469 [stressing *by* instead of *who*]), less likely as a hexameter ("Did sláy this Fórtinbrás; who bý a séaled compáct"); the stress on the second syllable of *compact* is the normal one in Shakespeare (Abbott §490).

Well ratified by law and heraldry,

Well ratified … heraldry: *heraldry* (Heraldrie F, Q1; heraldy Q2) refers to "the recognized usages of chivalry, of which the heralds were arbiters. Elsewhere Shakespeare employs the word in its more usual sense of the lore of armorial bearings or, by synecdoche, for the coat-of-arms itself" (Jenkins), cf., II.ii.456 and *All's Well* II.iii.262. ● Whether "law and heraldry" are a hendiadys (see above line 68 note and I.v.101 note) for "heraldic law" or actual parallel systems of law (cf., "sealed compact" at line 86 above), the agreement between Hamlet Senior, former King of Denmark, and Fortinbras Senior, former King of Norway, to engage in single combat was "well ratified," i.e., confirmed by standard procedure to be fair, equal, legal, ceremonial, and unexceptionable, involving no crime or injustice. They put up equal parcels of land ("moiety competent"), and Hamlet Senior won the parcel from Fortinbras Senior fair and square. Hence Young Fortinbras, in his effort to overturn the consequences of that compact, is acting illegally and so overstepping his bounds.

Did forfeit (with his life) all those his lands
Which he stood seized of to the conqueror;

Did forfeit … to the conqueror: Fortinbras Senior, the loser, forfeited to Hamlet Senior, the winner, the specified lands in his possession.

Against the which a moiety competent   90
Was gagèd by our king, which had returned
To the inheritance of Fortinbras

Against the which … gagèd: Hamlet Senior had engaged to risk a "moiety competent," i.e., a parcel sufficient (to equal the parcel that Fortinbras Senior was risking). **had returned:** would have been transferred, "a loose use, not to be taken as implying that Fortinbras would have got *back* possessions originally his" (Jenkins).

Had he been vanquisher; as, by the same comart

as: stressed after the pause (Abbott §453). **comart:** Q2, bargain or, by another possible derivation, single combat (from "mart" = battle, the only time the word appears, OED). F's "Cou'nant" (i.e., "covenant"), preferred by Jenkins, if the true reading, would throw the stress from "same" back to "by" (Abbott §494).

And carriage of the article designed,

carriage … designed: a phrase requiring emendation in both Q2 (desseigne) and F (designe) and having several possible meanings: the carrying out or bearing (*carriage*) of the terms, or a clause (*article*) purposed, designated, or aforementioned (*designed*). ● "Whatever construction is placed on the individual words, the legal terminology emphasizes the justice of King Hamlet's taking possession of Fortinbras's lands in contrast to young Fortinbras's lawless attempt to recover them" (Jenkins).

His fell to Hamlet. Now, sir, young Fortinbras,   95

young Fortinbras: introduced here to become a foil for Hamlet. He is the son of the previous king of Norway and nephew of the present king.

Of unimprovèd mettle hot and full,

unimprovèd: a) not yet fulfilling its function or made the most of (cf., *Julius Caesar* II.i.159), b) undisciplined, ill-regulated, and c) not reproved, not corrected. **mettle:** substance, what he's made of, or (loosely) courage, spiritedness, cf., III.ii.109.

Hath in the skirts of Norway here and there
Sharked up a list of lawless resolutes

skirts: outskirts.

Sharked up: quickly snatched, outside proper government, with the "predatory connotations of the noun" (Jenkins). **list:** troop roster (OED *sb.*⁶).

lawless resolutes: willful outlaws, desperadoes (participial noun, Abbott §433). ● Jenkins' conjecture that Shakespeare "changed his design in the course of composition" because later they appear as a well-disciplined army misses the point: Here they are led by a renegade, later by an obedient and rightfully commissioned prince paying them under the king's auspices. The difference in language about the army reflects the change in its leader. The point about Fortinbras is important because he becomes an exact foil, in different circumstances, for the Hamlet situation to be revealed later. As Fortinbras here goes lawlessly beyond his commission, so Hamlet goes beyond his in III.iii, and as Fortinbras will be recalled and corrected by his uncle-king, so Hamlet's will will be corrected by the providential experiences of the sea voyage (reported in the letter in IV.vi and in V.ii) and by his contemplation of death in the graveyard scene (V.i).

For food and diet to some enterprise

For food and diet to: i.e., to feed, possibly a hendiadys. **enterprise:** cf., Hamlet's use of the word at III.i.85.

That hath a stomach in't; which is no other,   100

stomach: the seat of hunger both for food and for the satisfaction of a desire or passion, hence of courage, resolution, resentment, anger, temper, etc. (cf., *Shrew* IV.i.158, which plays on both senses, and *Julius Caesar* V.i.66). ● Fortinbras, needing men to feed his hunger for avenging his father by reconquest of the lost lands but lacking legal justification and Old Norway's permission, has gathered up a troop of desperadoes. **which:** i.e., the enterprise.

As it doth well appear unto our state,
But to recover of us by strong hand

our state: i.e., the government of Denmark.

But: than (Abbott §127). **strong hand:** the name *Fortinbras* (pronounced "*FORT-in-brass*") means "strong (in) arm" (Fr. *fort* from Latin *fortis*, strong, French *bras* from Latin *bracchium*, arm).

And terms compulsatory those foresaid lands
So by his father lost; and this, I take it,
Is the main motive of our preparations,   105
The source of this our watch, and the chief head

compulsatory: compulsory, by compulsion.

So: in that manner (cf., line 88).

head: source (cf., *headwaters, fountainhead*, and II.ii.55).

Of this post-haste and romage in the land.

post-haste: speed and activity (cf., "sweaty haste" line 77 above). **romage:** rummage, bustle, from the word for rearranging a ship's cargo. ● As we will see in the following scene, Horatio is right that the actions of Fortinbras account for the Danish preparations for war. Dramatically, the elaborate description of the past conflict between two dead

BARNARDO
I think it be no other but e'en so.

Well may it sort that this portentous figure
Comes armèd through our watch so like the King   110

That was and is the question of these wars.

HORATIO
A mote it is to trouble the mind's eye.

In the most high and palmy state of Rome,

A little ere the mightiest Julius fell,

---

kings and the present actions of the son of one of them sets up the political situation and character of Fortinbras as an elaborate foil to the unfolding of the moral drama of Hamlet's own situation and character and incidentally prepares the ground for the ultimate inheritance of Denmark.

I think it ... and countrymen: Lines 108–125, like I.iv.17–38, are not in F or Q1. **be:** used instead of "is" with "some notion of doubt, question, thought, etc." (Abbott §299). **but:** than (as at line 102 above, Abbott §127).

sort: fit. **that this ... wars:** that this ominous apparition would appear, armed, looking like the former king, who was and is the subject of the threatened conflict.

question: subject, issue ● Barnardo's reasonable interpretation of the appropriateness of the Ghost's appearance given the threatened war is pondered by Horatio, who offers another interpretation (cf., line 113ff.), which turns out to be closer to the truth.

mote: speck (spelled *moth* in Q2, but pronounced *mote*). **mind's eye:** an ancient metaphor (see I.ii.185 note). ● The mind of the rational Horatio is troubled by this question of the Ghost as the eye would be by a speck or cinder; he remains temporarily mystified. "Hugh of St. Cher, commenting on Psalm iv.4 ['Tremble, and sin not: examine your own heart upon your bed, and be still' (Geneva)], distinguishes between the sinful anger which blinds, and the zealous anger which merely troubles (*turbat*) the eye for a time, like a collyrium [i.e., eyewash], so that it may later see more clearly. So the mind, now troubled by the Ghost, may later see what it betokens, as happened with the Roman portents Horatio now cites. The emphasis, however, is on present perplexity rather than on future clarification" (Jenkins).

palmy: flush with victory, which is symbolized by palm branches. **state of Rome:** the land, nation, and government (as at line 69 above) of ancient Rome. ● Horatio now introduces a parallel situation to the portents they have just been discussing.

the mightiest Julius: the most mighty Julius, that is, Caesar, the *ie* and *iu* being elided so that each word is a disyllable (Abbott §468). ● Though Abbott says that the superlative is "sometimes used to signify 'very'" (§8), Shakespeare is emphasizing that Julius Caesar was superlative among men, thought of by his function, even if not in his person (as in *Julius Caesar*), as the mightiest and most exalted ruler of the ancient world and founder of its greatest Empire (cf., V.i.213–14), whose fall to his assassins was an archetypal image of the overturning of the political and social order of the world (cf., Dante's placement of Caesar's assassins in *Inferno* 34). Thus the parallel is made to the overturning of the rightful political and social order of Denmark, felt by Hamlet and later confirmed by the Ghost.

The graves stood tenantless, and the sheeted dead   115

The graves ... with eclipse: Shakespeare took the description of the ominous events surrounding Caesar's death, both here and (except for the sunspots and eclipse) in *Julius Caesar* I.iii and II.ii, from Plutarch's *Lives*, Ovid's *Metamorphoses*, Virgil's *Georgics*, and Lucan's *Pharsalia* (Jenkins). **sheeted dead:** i.e., ghosts appearing in their winding sheets or shrouds (cf., *Julius Caesar* I.iii.74, II.ii.18).

Did squeak and gibber in the Roman streets.

Did: "commonly used in excited narrative [in place of the simple past tense]" (Abbott §304). **squeak and gibber:** cf., *Julius Caesar* II.ii.24, "Ghosts traditionally spoke in a thin shrill voice" (Jenkins, referring to *Odyssey* 24.5, *Aeneid* 6.492–92, and the Elizabethan play *Locrine* III.vi.19).

As stars with trains of fire, and dews of blood,

As stars ...: There is probably a line missing before this one. **As:** such as (depending on what came before it, Abbott §113). **stars with trains of fire:** comets (cf., *Julius Caesar* II.ii.30–31). **dews of blood:** (cf., *Julius Caesar* II.ii.21).

Disasters in the sun, and the moist star,

Disasters in the sun: ominous conditions in the sun, possibly sunspots, having a negative influence on the world, from the root meaning of *disaster*: the unfavorable astrological influence of a star. **moist star:** the moon, "often called 'watery' with reference not simply to its pallid light but to the belief that it drew up moisture from the sea. It has power over 'Neptune's empire' through its control of the tides" (Jenkins).

Upon whose influence Neptune's empire stands,

influence: in astrology, the effect, positive or negative, that a heavenly body sheds upon the world, from Latin *influĕre*, to flow into, the flowing in of ethereal fluid, later of power or virtue, from the stars, whence French *influence* and Italian *influenza*, from which we get the English *influenza* and *flu*, indicating a disease ascribed to astrological causes when no earthly medical cause was known. **stands:** depends, perhaps based on an inversion of the idiomatic phrase "to stand (one) upon" (see Abbott §204).

Was sick almost to doomsday with eclipse.   120

sick ... eclipse: the moon is in eclipse, as if it were the complete darkness prophesied for the Day of Judgment ("doomsday"), based on Matthew 24:29 ("And immediately after the tribulations of those days, shall the sun be darkened, and the moon shall not give her light, and the stars shall fall from heaven, and the powers of heaven shall be shaken"). "The solar and lunar eclipses which in fact occurred during 1598–1601 may have intensified for the populace the terror of this passage" (Jenkins).

And even the like precurse of feared events,

even the like: just the same (emphasis on "like"). **precurse:** precursors, "that which precedes (and foretokens)" (Jenkins), with a possible play on *curse*. **feared:** Collier's conjecture for Q2's "feare" based on sense and the ease with which *d* could be mistaken for *e* in Elizabethan handwriting (Jenkins substantially).

As harbingers preceding still the fates

still: always (as almost always in Shakespeare, Abbott §69). **fates:** both the powers that determine the future and the events determined, hinting

And prologue to the omen coming on,
Have heaven and earth together demonstrated
Unto our climatures and countrymen.   125

Enter Ghost.

But soft, behold! lo where it comes again!
I'll cross it though it blast me. Stay, illusion!

[Ghost] spreads its arms.

If thou hast any sound or use of voice,
Speak to me.

If there be any good thing to be done   130
That may to thee do ease and grace to me,
Speak to me.

If thou art privy to thy country's fate,
Which happily foreknowing may avoid,
O speak!   135
Or if thou hast uphoarded in thy life
Extorted treasure in the womb of earth,

For which, they say, your spirits oft walk in death,
Speak of it. Stay and speak!

---

at Horatio's tendency toward a stoical Roman philosophy (cf., I.v.167 and V.ii.341) that will be modified by Hamlet's enlightened view (V.ii.10–11 and 219–20). Because Horatio clearly expresses Christian convictions at I.iv.91 and V.ii.11, we may take this attitude as only a tendency, his own "dram of evil" that burgeons into sin at V.ii.341–42 and is parallel to Hamlet's dram of evil at I.ii.182–83 that burgeons into sin at III.iii.87.

omen: "strictly, that which foreshadows an event, but here the event foretold" (Jenkins).

our: emphasized, following "like" in line 121 above. **climatures:** climes, climates, areas of the world (Denmark representing a northern one, Rome a southern one, cf., *Julius Caesar* I.iii.31–32). ● Horatio is offering an alternative reading of events to Barnardo's and, as it turns out, a better one: the very same omens the Danes have observed presented by heaven and earth were seen in ancient Rome and foretold a leader's assassination. These two different interpretations of the meaning of the phenomena open the theme of what human beings can know of the divine purposes. The rational scholar's is the better guess, but it can only be a guess without further revelation, which will be granted to Hamlet and only later to Horatio.

soft: hush, stop talking. **lo:** behold.

cross: confront. **blast:** to blow on perniciously, shrivel, blight, used of baleful planetary influence (OED *v.* 7). ● Horatio's determination shows his courage in the face of the danger of evil influence, as also in the series of imperatives to the Ghost to "Stay" (= stop, stand still, wait) and to "Speak."

If thou hast … Speak of it: ● Horatio exhorts the Ghost to speak based on a list of what educated people of the time believed might cause a ghost to appear. "If you want to know what Shakespeare's audience believed about ghosts," said J. V. Cunningham, "read everything said about ghosts in *Hamlet* and believe it" (Cunningham Sem.). **use of voice:** cf., line 116 note.

good thing … grace to me: The first possibility is that a ghost may need a good deed done that would ease its conscience or condition while offering spiritual benefit ("grace") to the living person doing it. An example would be saying prayers for the dead.

privy … avoid: A ghost might come with a message about how to protect the country from impending disaster (hinted at in lines 109–111 and 113–125).

uphoarded: hoarded up (an adverbial compound not uncommon, Abbott §429); a ghost might hang about a place where secretly buried treasure lies hidden (cf., *Jew of Malta* II.i.26–27).

your: one's, a colloquial indefinite use, not yours personally, cf., I.v.167, III.ii.3 (F, Q1), IV.iii.21, 23, V.i.57, 171–72, *Measure for Measure* IV. ii. 43–47, etc., and Abbott §221. It is still heard, e.g., "Your copper pipe will last longer than your steel."

The cock crows.

Stop it, Marcellus.

MARCELLUS

Shall I strike at it with my partisan?   140

HORATIO

Do, if it will not stand.

BARNARDO

'Tis here!

HORATIO

'Tis here!

Exit Ghost.

MARCELLUS

'Tis gone.

We do it wrong, being so majestical,
To offer it the show of violence,

For it is as the air, invulnerable,   145

And our vain blows malicious mockery.

BARNARDO

It was about to speak when the cock crew.

HORATIO

And then it started like a guilty thing

Upon a fearful summons. I have heard,

---

s.d. *cock crows*: Later we are told that the Ghost appears about to speak but at the sound of the cock crow turns to depart (lines 147 and 157 below and I.ii.215–20).

partisan: "a military weapon ... consisting of a long-handled spear, the blade having one or more lateral cutting projections, variously shaped" (OED *sb.*² 1.), "borne by officers of the guard" (Jenkins, based on *Shakespeare's England*, i.137–38, and Cotgrave's *Dictionary of the French and English Tongue*, 1611).

Do ... here!: These three speeches form a single pentameter line.

'Tis gone.: This speech begins a new pentameter with, however, four empty feet, Shakespeare's way of indicating a significant pause, cf., the profoundly significant pause at the climax of the play, III.iii.87.

being so majestical: referring to the Ghost, not to "We" ("being" is contracted to fit the meter, as is common when "a light vowel is preceded by a heavy vowel or diphthong" Abbott §470). ● We are to think of the Ghost as majestic.

air: In the *Divine Comedy* Dante explains that the substantial form of a human being, his soul, which survives death, may appear to the living by organizing the surrounding air into a body bearing his likeness (cf., also Le Loyer and Taillepied, quoted in Jenkins). **invulnerable:** "Some others, when spirits appear unto them, will by and by set on them, and drive them away with naked swords ... not considering ... that spirits are nothing hurt with weapons" (Lavater, *Of Ghosts and Spirits*, III.xi, quoted in Jenkins, and cf., *Tempest* III.iii.61–65).

vain: useless, empty. **malicious mockery:** a mere imitation of the power to harm that cannot harm in fact (cf., OED malice 2., "power to harm," and mockery 2., "imitation," "counterfeit," "unreal appearance," and 3., "futile action," "insultingly unfitting" quoting this use).

crew: past tense of "to crow". ● Later we will hear that the Ghost has come from purgatory; the cock crow, heralding the sunrise, reminds the ghost of light, the image of God's grace, and thereupon of his own as yet unpurged sins.

it: the Ghost. **started:** moved with sudden impulse (OED start *v.* 2.) and hastily (cf., I.ii.219).

I have heard ... to his confine: "The tradition is of great antiquity, being already recorded in Prudentius' hymn *Ad Galli Cantum*, lines 37–40" (Jenkins).

The cock, that is the trumpet to the morn, 150

trumpet: common for trumpeter (cf., *3 Henry VI* V.i.16, *Troilus and Cressida* IV.v.6). The image of the cock as trumpeter of sunrise and the new day appears in Drayton, *Endimion and Phoebe* (1595), line 387, "the cock, the morning's trumpeter" (Jenkins substantially).

Doth with his lofty and shrill-sounding throat

lofty: "Suggesting both the cock's upstretched throat and the trumpeter's proud, majestic sound" (Jenkins).

Awake the god of day, and at his warning,
Whether in sea or fire, in earth or air,

god of day: the sun.

in sea or fire, in earth or air: modifying "confine" in line 155. ● From Empedocles through the Renaissance, earth, air, fire, and water were taken to be the four fundamental elements of the natural world (to which Aristotle added a fifth element or quintessence, sometimes called ether, cf., II.ii.308 and note, and which modern science has now increased to 118), every natural thing being made up of the combination of these elements. Each of the four elements was imagined to have its native spiritual inhabitants (like the "airy spirit" Ariel in *Tempest*), a classical idea promoted by Paracelsus, developed by the Rosicrucians, mentioned in Milton's *Il Penseroso*, lines 93–96, and affectionately satirized in "The Rape of the Lock," in the Dedicatory Letter to which, Pope writes that "According to [the Rosicrucians], the four elements are inhabited by spirits, which they call Sylphs, Gnomes, Nymphs, and Salamanders." The Ghost seems to have returned to its own confining element, which we learn at I.v.11 is fire.

Th' extravagant and erring spirit hies

extravagant and erring: "extravagant" = wandering around outside of bounds (of their respective elements) and "erring" = wandering, both words being used in their strict Latin senses (see Abbott Introduction, page 13, for discussion of such use of Latin-derived words). **hies:** hastens. **his:** its (see above line 37 note).

To his confine; and of the truth herein 155

confine: place of confinement, i.e., the relevant one of the four elements mentioned two lines above (cf., II.ii.245–46, *Tempest* IV.i.121).

This present object made probation.
MARCELLUS
It faded on the crowing of the cock.

object: "A word often applied to a spectacle which excites a strong emotional reaction (of horror, dread, admiration, etc.). See OED 3 b." (Jenkins, who refers to *Othello* V.ii.364, *Titus Andronicus* III.i.64, *Cymbeline* I.vi.102, *Merchant of Venice* I.i.20, and *King Lear* V.iii.239). **made probation:** gave evidence or proof. ● Horatio has heard that ghosts go back where they belong on the crowing of the cock, and this experience of the Ghost is evidence of the truth of that belief.

Some say that ever 'gainst that season comes
Wherein our Saviour's birth is celebrated,

Some say ... that time: "For the legend of the cock's crowing all night for Christmas no other authority is known. But there are various stories in which the cock crows all night to signal a victory or a famous birth ..., and as the announcer of light the cock is emblematically the herald of Christ" (Jenkins LN). **'gainst:** just before, in expectation of (Abbott §142, cf., II.ii.483, III.iv.50), i.e., the period just preceding Christmas.

This bird of dawning singeth all night long,   160

And then they say no spirit dare stir abroad,

The nights are wholesome, then no planets strike,

No fairy takes, nor witch hath power to charm,

So hallowed and so gracious is that time.

HORATIO

So have I heard and do in part believe it.   165

But look, the morn in russet mantle clad

Walks o'er the dew of yon high eastward hill.

Break we our watch up, and by my advice

Let us impart what we have seen tonight

Unto young Hamlet, for, upon my life,   170

This spirit, dumb to us, will speak to him.

Do you consent we shall acquaint him with it,

As needful in our loves, fitting our duty?

MARCELLUS

Let's do't, I pray, and I this morning know

Where we shall find him most convenient.   175

Exeunt.

bird of dawning: the cock.

spirit: pronounced almost as a single syllable ("[The letter] R frequently softens or destroys a following vowel" Abbott §463).

strike: "destroy by evil [astrological] influence, blast.... Cf. *moonstruck*" (Jenkins, who refers to *Coriolanus* II.ii.113–14, *Titus Andronicus* II.iv.14, and *Winter's Tale* I.ii.201; cf., line 119 note).

takes: magically causes harm, particularly disease (cf., *Merry Wives* IV.iv. 32, *King Lear* II.iv.164, *Gammer Gurton's Needle* I.ii.26).

gracious: graced, blessed (cf., V.ii.84).

So have I heard … believe it: ● The line expresses the essence of Horatio, "in part" being the rational man's way of relating to things that may or may not be true as stated. He is skeptical not about fundamental religious truths but about superstitions and old wives' tales, which may or may not have substance.

morn … hill: "conventional poetic images" about dawn, *russet mantle* being "traditional, and in Gavin Douglas [c. 1474–1522] (*The Palice of Honour*, Prol. line 2) … belonged to 'Aurora'" (Jenkins).

Break we: "Subjunctive used optatively or imperatively" (Abbott §364). ● The scene ends with imperatives, cf., line 30 note.

young Hamlet: the first mention of the protagonist ● He is called "young Hamlet," making a parallel to "young Fortinbras," each being the son of a dead king and living under the reign of an uncle. Horatio believes the Ghost will speak to him, Hamlet being a prince, the Ghost's son (if indeed the Ghost is the spirit of the dead king), and perhaps more of a scholar even than Horatio.

dumb: not speaking. **will speak to him:** ● Horatio is correct; the Ghost will speak to Hamlet at I.v.2.

loves: "Elizabethan idiom permits the plural of an abstract noun which refers to a quality as possessed by more than one person" (Jenkins, who refers to *loves* I.ii.250, 253, III.ii.201; *wisdoms*, I.ii.15; *companies*, II.ii.14; *modesties*, II.ii.280). **loves … duty:** ● Love and duty express proper relations to one's rightful superiors in the hierarchical world Shakespeare and his audience inherited from the medieval age.

convenient: conveniently (for the use of adjectives as adverbs see Abbott §1).

Act I, Scene ii

Flourish. Enter Claudius, King of Denmark, Gertrude the Queen, Counsaile, Polonius, his son Laertes, Hamlet, cum aliis [including Voltemand and Cornelius, possibly Ophelia, Lords, and Attendants].

KING

Though yet of Hamlet our dear brother's death

The memory be green, and that it us befitted
To bear our hearts in grief, and our whole kingdom

To be contracted in one brow of woe,

Yet so far hath discretion fought with nature   5
That we with wisest sorrow think on him
Together with remembrance of ourselves.

Therefore our sometime sister, now our queen,
Th' imperial jointress to this warlike state,

Have we, as 'twere with a defeated joy,   10

With an auspicious and a dropping eye,
With mirth in funeral and with dirge in marriage,

In equal scale weighing delight and dole,

Act I, Scene ii. • The main audience room of the castle.
Flourish: Trumpet fanfare (Riverside).
Claudius: This name appears only here in F and only here and in the first speech heading of this scene in Q2. Elsewhere, "King." ***Counsaile:*** councilors.
cum aliis: with others (Latin); the characters are named "in the order in which the ensuing scene takes notice of them" (Jenkins); Ophelia does not speak in this scene but appears in the F stage direction.

our: • In formal speech, Shakespearean kings use the royal plural, indicating the king's double nature, both individual man and embodiment of the office and state, cf., wordplay on the two bodies of the king at IV.ii.27 and note.

green: fresh, new. ***that:*** "used (like French *que*) as a substitute instead of repeating a previous conjunction (OED that *conj.* 8.)" (Jenkins, cf., Abbott §287). ***it us befitted:*** it was appropriate for us. • Here "us" and "our," modifying the plural "hearts," refer to the court and kingdom, but Claudius continues in the royal plural, implying that he and the kingdom are one.

contracted: used in four senses: formally agreed upon, drawn together, condensed, and (in a common idiom) knitted like a forehead in shared grief.

discretion fought with nature: judgment, which looks out for one's interests (his desire to marry Gertrude), contended against the natural feeling of grief (for his brother), an antithesis continued in the oxymorons that follow.

sometime: former.

jointress: possibly co-ruler, more probably inheritor of a royal estate.

as 'twere: as [if] it were. ***defeated:*** undone, ruined (cf., II.ii.571, V.ii.58). ***defeated joy:*** an oxymoron.

an auspicious and a dropping eye: one eye looking up in happiness, one eye downcast as in grief • This was a familiar trope (cf., *Winter's Tale* V.ii.74–76) indicating mixed emotions, but there may be an implied undertone of falsehood, not detected by the court, because "It was proverbially said of the false man that he looks up with one eye and down with the other (e.g. Fergusson's *Scottish Proverbs*, ed. Beveridge, Scot. Text Soc., page 56). This was a variant of the ancient proverb ["To cry (look up) with one eye and laugh (down) with the other"] (Tilley E 248), which was traditionally applied to Fortune (as in Chaucer, *Book of the Duchess*, lines 633–4) in indication of her fickleness" (Jenkins LN).

equal scale: weighing equally in the two pans of a balance scale. ***dole:*** grief, sorrow • The series of oxymorons ("wisest sorrow," "defeated joy," "auspicious ... dropping," "mirth in funeral," "dirge in marriage," "delight and dole"), in formal, ceremonial, and orderly speech, both embody and try to smooth over the conflict that, as we soon see, troubles Hamlet. The funeral of the dead king has been hastily followed

by the wedding between his brother and his wife. The new king presents the marriage as lending stability to the government.
● NOTE TO ACTORS: The parallelism of the four successive oxymorons (lines 10–13) diplomatically interrupt the main clause "Have we ... Taken to wife."

Taken to wife; nor have we herein barred

to wife: as my wife, for a wife (Abbott §189).
barred: excluded from consideration (OED bar *v.* I.8).

Your better wisdoms, which have freely gone 15
With this affair along. For all, our thanks.

Your better wisdoms: the wisdom of you who are of noble rank, cf., III.iv.32. **freely ... along:** The courtiers have supported the marriage ("this affair"), and by implication the accession of Claudius to the throne (which Jenkins thinks may be implied by "For all"). Denmark had an elective monarchy, and Shakespeare portrays the Danish kings as being chosen by electors (i.e. the court nobility) from among members of the royal family, cf., V.ii.65 and note ("Popped in between the election and my hopes") and V.ii.355–56 ("I do prophesy th' election lights / On Fortinbras, he has my dying voice").

Now follows that you know young Fortinbras,

Now follows that you know: "Walker's attempted improvement (*know:*) is adopted by many editors, who thus make the Council already acquainted with the matter that 'now follows'. But I agree with Sisson (*NR*) that the sense is not 'follows what you already know, namely' but 'the next point is, you must be told that'. It may be objected that Fortinbras's warlike preparations are in fact known (I.i.98–107); but it is his formal demands (*message*, line 22) that the Council are now to be told" (Jenkins). Abbott (§244) seems to agree with Walker, but I find Jenkins' reading more persuasive: "the next thing is that you be told that young Fortinbras." **young Fortinbras:** hinting that Fortinbras will be a foil for Hamlet (cf., "young Hamlet" at I.i.170).

Holding a weak supposal of our worth,
Or thinking by our late dear brother's death
Our state to be disjoint and out of frame, 20

Holding ... worth: supposing us to be weak.

disjoint: disjointed (*-ed* is often omitted in "verbs ending in *-te, -t,* and *-d* ... resembling participles in their terminations," Abbott §342, cf., *deject* III.i.155, *bloat* III.iv.182, *hoist* III.iv.207). ● cf., the echoes "jointress" (line 9 above) and "The time is out of joint" (I.v.188). **out of frame:** disordered, the order or *frame* of the kingdom being a microcosm corresponding to the macrocosmic *frame* of God's created world (cf., II.ii.298, *1 Henry IV* III.i.16, and *Macbeth* III.ii.16, "let the frame of things disjoint," which recombines the ideas here, Macbeth being a later and more evil version of Claudius.)

Colleaguèd with this dream of his advantage,

Colleaguèd: allied, joined, modifying Fortinbras (line 17) or "He" (line 22). **this dream of his advantage:** referring to the previous three lines.
● Claudius stresses that Fortinbras's supposition that Denmark's weakness (as expressed in lines 18–20) gives him an advantage is a mere dream.

He hath not failed to pester us with message

He: "When a proper name [here Fortinbras] is separated by an intervening clause from its verb, then for clearness the redundant pronoun is often inserted" (Abbott §242); "pester us with message": annoy me with messages (cf., Abbott §471).

Importing the surrender of those lands
Lost by his father, with all bands of law,

Importing: signifying, carrying as its intent.
with all bands of law: Fortinbras has no just or legal claim to the lands lost by his father by formal agreement.

To our most valiant brother. So much for him. 25
Now for ourself and for this time of meeting,

So much for him. / Now for ourself: "'so much' for what he has done and 'now' for my reaction to it" (Jenkins). **and for … meeting:** and for the reason we now meet.

Thus much the business is: we have here writ
To Norway, uncle of young Fortinbras—

writ: written (the inflection -en in past participles was often dropped, Abbott §343). • Even as he announces the demand of Fortinbras, Claudius has already taken steps to deal with it. The ruler's being already on top of things at the opening of the action is a common trope in European literature, cf., the beginning of *Oedipus Rex*. Everything in this speech makes it appear that Claudius is a responsible and savvy king. That Norway (= the king of Norway) is the uncle of Fortinbras further establishes the parallel to Hamlet and reinforces the appearance that Claudius has been legitimately elected to inherit the throne from his dead brother despite the previous king's having a son.

Who, impotent and bedrid, scarcely hears
Of this his nephew's purpose—to suppress 30

impotent and bedrid: without physical strength and bedridden, possibly a hendiadys meaning "feeble to the point of being confined to bed" (Wright, page 189).

His further gait herein, in that the levies,

gait: going, proceeding (OED gate *sb.*² II.6.d.). **levies:** troops raised by enlistment or conscription.

The lists, and full proportions are all made
Out of his subject; and we here dispatch
You, good Cornelius, and you, Voltemand,

lists: rosters of troops (cf., I.i.98). **proportions:** numbers of troops (cf., *Henry V* I.ii.137, 304). **made / Out of his subject:** collected from among his subjects (cf., I.i.72 note).

For bearers of this greeting to old Norway, 35
Giving to you no further personal power
To business with the King, more than the scope

For: to serve as, to be (Abbott §148). **old Norway:** the king of Norway.

To business: for the purpose of business (Abbott §186; though the OED cites no examples of *business* as a verb, it is tempting to make this an infinitive as Kittredge and Folger do, and it is not beyond Shakespeare to be inventing it here).

Of these delated articles allow.

[Gives them a paper.]

delated: variant of *dilated*, set down at length, expanded on. **allow:** This error in agreement of subject and verb, as we would call it, ("scope … allow" for *allows*) because of the proximity of a plural noun ("articles") is not uncommon in Shakespeare (Abbott §412). • The passage is a representative and characteristic example of the theme of imperatives: do this (carry this letter), do it in a certain way (following these written articles), do not overdo it ("no further personal power / To business with the King"), a parallel to the Ghost's instructions to Hamlet to "revenge" but "taint not thy mind." As we see at II.ii.60–80, Cornelius and Voltemand will successfully fulfill these instructions, becoming contrasting foils for Hamlet's failure in III.iii and ultimate success in V.ii.

Farewell, and let your haste commend your duty.

CORNELIUS, VOLTEMAND
In that and all things will we show our duty.   40

KING
We doubt it nothing; heartily farewell.
                    [*Exeunt Voltemand and Cornelius.*]
And now, Laertes, what's the news with you?

You told us of some suit; what is't, Laertes?
You cannot speak of reason to the Dane
And lose your voice. What wouldst thou beg, Laertes,   45
That shall not be my offer, not thy asking?

The head is not more native to the heart,
The hand more instrumental to the mouth,
Than is the throne of Denmark to thy father.
What wouldst thou have, Laertes?

---

let your haste commend your duty: let your speed, instead of the conventional curtsy and words, indicate your obedience (cf., line 253 below, V.ii.182, and *Love's Labor's Lost* IV.ii.143).

In that and all things ... duty: Cornelius and Voltemand will show their duty *both* by their haste *and* conventionally.

nothing: used adverbially, in no way (Abbott §55).

And now, Laertes: ● The king, while "Caressing [Laertes] with his name four times in nine lines" (Dover Wilson) and spotlighting Hamlet's foil (Jenkins), is following proper court etiquette: He deals first with the stability of the government, next with foreign affairs and their threats, next with his courtiers' needs, and only lastly with family and personal matters, i.e. with Hamlet. This order is no slight to Hamlet. In every respect as yet visible Claudius appears to the court and to us to be a reasonable and competent ruler, and a magnanimous one, for he shifts from the formal "you" (lines 42–45) to the informal and personal "thou" (lines 45–50) as a sign of kindness to Laertes. When he shifts back (line 57 below), it is because he has returned to formality in preparing to give public permission (cf., Abbott §235).

suit: request.

of reason: reasonably.   **the Dane:** the king of Denmark

lose your voice: waste your breath.

That shall ... thy asking: that shall not be my own willing offer rather than the granting of your request ("not ... not" = not ... rather than).

native: naturally joined.   **instrumental to:** at the service of.   ● This is flattering courtly magnanimity expressed in terms of "the traditional correspondence between the human organism ... and the body politic. The king is naturally the *head*, and the councilors are often referred to as the *heart* ... cf. *Cor*[*iolanus*] I.i.113–14 ... In the next line the king as the *hand* is the provider for his subjects" (Jenkins). In fact, it is Polonius who is instrumental to the throne, not the throne to Polonius, but with this show of magnanimous condescension, Claudius publicly honors him, as he does Laertes with the familiar *thou*. "Note that the first reference to Polonius is to him as the father of Laertes, stressing what is to be a determining factor of the plot" (Jenkins). The play gives us no evidence to determine whether Polonius has been newly appointed or had served the previous king in similar capacity, and hence we can conclude that the question is not relevant to the play. We know that Hamlet has respected Laertes (cf., V.i.224) and loves Ophelia (I.iii etc.), and that the Queen had intended a marriage between Ophelia and Hamlet (V.i.244). Any efforts at the invention of biographical details not provided by the play (as at III. ii.99–104) would be a distraction from what the play does offer (see Introduction, page 6 and note 13).

LAERTES

                      My dread lord,   50

Your leave and favor to return to France,
From whence though willingly I came to Denmark

To show my duty in your coronation,
Yet now I must confess, that duty done,

My thoughts and wishes bend again toward France   55
And bow them to your gracious leave and pardon.

KING

Have you your father's leave? What says Polonius?

POLONIUS

He hath, my lord, wrung from me my slow leave

By laborsome petition, and at last
Upon his will I sealed my hard consent.   60

I do beseech you give him leave to go.

KING

Take thy fair hour, Laertes; time be thine,

---

dread: to be dreaded, awe-evoking (cf., II.ii.28, III.iv.108).

leave: permission. **favor:** approval. • In the age of kings, nobles could not come and go between home and foreign countries without the express permission of the sovereign. Since every lord had subordinates loyal to him, including military liegemen, the king must be aware of who is where at all times to prevent conspiracy and even the appearance of it. Our passports and visas are modern versions of similar governmental permission.

To show ... coronation: • It is worth comparing Laertes' formal public statement that he has returned to show his duty in the coronation of Claudius to Horatio's personal and intimate statement in private that he has returned "to see your father's funeral" (line 176). Both Laertes and Horatio must have been present at both ceremonies, and the two statements are in courtly manner tailored to the person addressed, expressing etiquette rather than implying mere cynical self-interest, but see line 176 note.

bend: turn, lean.

bow them: metaphorically submit themselves.

leave and pardon: permission and indulgence (cf., IV.vii.46).

Polonius: • The name of the king's chief counselor, as Jenkins suggests, is related to Poland. The reason will be clear if we keep in mind that Fortinbras is a foil for Hamlet. What Poland is to the political journey of Fortinbras, Polonius is to the spiritual journey of Hamlet. In relation to Claudius, the aim of Fortinbras is honor, that of Hamlet, revenge. Old Norway uses Poland to focus the ambition of Fortinbras; Hamlet uses Polonius to report his madness to the court. From his defeat of Poland Fortinbras returns to inherit Denmark, winning more honor than he had imagined; from his mistaken defeat of Polonius by killing him (which sends Hamlet to sea) Hamlet returns to accomplish God's revenge and inherit the kingdom of heaven.

He hath, my lord: Where Q2 has only "Hath" (possibly an elision, "H'ath" in Riverside), F has "He hath". • In either case, Polonius could have stopped after "my Lord" and the question would be answered; that he goes on hints at his enjoyment of prolixity, a tendency that will be expanded on later.

laborsome: laborious. **petition:** requesting.

Upon his will: with a play on *will* in the sense of a written testament (Jenkins). **sealed:** as a document with wax and stamp "to give it authority" (Jenkins). **hard:** reluctant, hard-won.

beseech: beg, entreat, stronger than merely to request (cf., III.ii.355).

fair hour: "opportunity (while you are young)" (Greenblatt). **time be thine:** you are free to use your time (i.e., to leave for France when you wish).

And thy best graces spend it at thy will.

But now, my cousin Hamlet, and my son—
HAMLET [*aside*]
A little more than kin, and less than kind.   65

KING
How is it that the clouds still hang on you?
HAMLET
Not so, my lord, I am too much in the sun.

QUEEN
Good Hamlet, cast thy nighted color off,
And let thine eye look like a friend on Denmark.

Do not for ever with thy vailèd lids   70
Seek for thy noble father in the dust.

Thou know'st 'tis common, all that lives must die,
Passing through nature to eternity.
HAMLET
Ay, madam, it is common.
QUEEN
                        If it be,

Why seems it so particular with thee?   75

HAMLET
Seems, madam? nay it is; I know not "seems."

And thy best ... at thy will: And may your best qualities or endowments make use of the time as you please.
cousin: relative, here nephew. **son:** by marriage.

kin: as a noun, relative; as an adjective, related by nature (of the same clan or family). **kind:** as a noun, nature, family, lineage, naturalnes; as an adjective, loving, affectionate, natural. • In a multi-layered play on words, Hamlet says that in calling Hamlet his cousin and his son, the King is more than kin (i.e., doubly kin, not only uncle but now stepfather) but less than kind (i.e. unnatural, incestuous in Hamlet's view at line 157 below, and not truly loving). Hamlet is also playing on the spelling of the words. How is it possible for a word to be more than k-i-n (three letters) and less than k-i-n-d (four letters)? There is paradox and therefore mystery here, to which Hamlet is responding with bitter irony.
clouds: implying Hamlet's melancholy demeanor.

too much in the sun: • With more bitter irony, Hamlet contradicts Claudius by implying a) that he spends too much time not under clouds but in the sun, b) that he is too much in the presence of the King, who corresponds in the microcosm of the court and the nation to the sun in the macrocosm of the heavens (cf., *Richard III* I.i.1–2, *Richard II* III.ii.37ff., esp. line 50, *1 Henry IV* I.ii.197ff., etc.), and c) with a pun on *son*, objecting to being so often called his son by Claudius.

nighted color: "night-like color" (Abbott §294). • Hamlet is wearing black in mourning. **Denmark:** the King.
for ever: "Ironical in view of lines 145–51" (Jenkins), where Hamlet complains about the brevity of the Queen's own grief. **vailèd lids:** lowered eyelids (OED vailed and vail *v.*²).
common: universal. • The Queen uses a "traditional commonplace of consolation" (Jenkins, citing Ovid's *Metamorphoses*, tr. Golding, xv.550, Seneca's *Ad Polybium*, *Works*, tr. Lodge, 1614, page 692, and for other instances B. Boyce, *PMLA*, LXIV, 771–80).
all that lives: cf., Abbott §333 for the singular form of the verb with a plural subject, which here enlarges the meaning of "all" from "all persons" through "all living beings" to perhaps "everything that is."
particular: out of the ordinary, special (OED a. 7.), rather than personal, which requires *to* rather than *with* (OED a. 2.b.) • The Queen asks why Hamlet seems to take as so extraordinary or unusual what is common.

Seems, madam, ... "seems.": • The contrast is between *seems* (on the outside) and *is* (on the inside), the show of grief and the true grief within. This is an explicit introduction of the familiar Shakespearean theme of appearance vs. reality. In one sense the entire play is a revelation of "that within," both within Hamlet and within the condition of man. Here what is visible ("trappings" and "suits") is contrasted with what is by its nature invisible, "that within which passeth [= surpasses] show" (line 85), punctuating the main theme of what cannot be seen or known by human beings. Cf., Hamlet's assumption of divine sight and the irony of his error at III.iii.73–98 and the later debates about Ophelia's demise at V.i.1–29 and 225–42.

'Tis not alone my inky cloak, good mother,

'Tis not alone: "Implying a contrast with the [superficial] character of his mother's own mourning" (Jenkins). **inky:** black.

Nor customary suits of solemn black,

solemn: a) ceremonial, b) dark, gloomy, somber, mournful, all metaphorically applied to the color of his clothing.

Nor windy suspiration of forced breath,

windy … breath: i.e., heavy sighs.

No, nor the fruitful river in the eye,   80

fruitful: abundant (OED 3.), i.e., copious tears.

Nor the dejected havior of the visage,

havior: expression, demeanor (for the dropped prefix of *behavior*, cf., Abbott §460, with influence from the earlier root in French *avoir* OED).

Together with all forms, moods, shapes of grief,
That can denote me truly. These indeed seem,

moods: literally frames of mind, states of feeling, tempers, dispositions (OED *sb.*¹ 3), but coming to mean the outward expressions of them (cf., Sonnet 93:8 and "A Lover's Complaint," lines 200–203) (Jenkins substantially). **shapes:** Q3 correction of Q2 "chapes," outward appearances, often false (as at IV.vii.89, *Midsummer Night's Dream* V.i.16, and *Timon of Athens* IV.iii.427), and specifically outward signs of grief (*Much Ado* V.i.14, *Love's Labor's Lost* V.ii.763, and *Richard II* II.ii.22).

For they are actions that a man might play,

play: playact, pretend.

But I have that within which passes show,   85

passes: (Q2, passeth F) surpasses. **show:** the outwardly visible ● "It was a commonplace that the greatest griefs were inexpressible, Cf. Seneca, *Hippolytus*, 607" (Jenkins).

These but the trappings and the suits of woe.

trappings and the suits: outward covering, clothes.

KING
'Tis sweet and commendable in your nature, Hamlet,
To give these mourning duties to your father.
But you must know your father lost a father,

commendable: Though Jenkins is right that the stress on the first syllable was not uncommon, Abbott places the stress on the second syllable (§490): "'Tis swéet and comméndable in your náture, Hámlet." Either way, the extra unstressed syllables in the word and feminine ending (i.e., unstressed final syllable) of the line give the effect of kindly softness in the initial lines of the King's address to Hamlet, which will grow in the strictness of its pentameters as in its severity.

That father lost, lost his, and the survivor bound   90

father lost: father (who was) lost (the relative omitted before the participle, Abbott §246). ● On the death of fathers, cf., Seneca, *Epistles*, 77 (Jenkins). **the survivor bound:** "Grammar and Kittredge suggest '(that father) bound the survivor', sense 'the survivor (was) bound'" (Jenkins). I think the sense taken by the audience is not only that every past survivor was bound but that every survivor successively is (always) bound.

In filial obligation for some term

term: limited period of time, cf., "forever" in line 70 above, *All's Well*, I.i.51–56, Ecclesiasticus 38:17, Seneca (Lodge, page 706), and Plutarch (tr. Holland, 1603, page 510) (Jenkins substantially).

To do obsequious sorrow. But to perséver

obsequious: having to do with obsequies, funeral rites, cf., *Titus Andronicus* V.iii.152, *3 Henry VI* II.v.118, *Richard III* I.ii.3, and see Abbott §3 for adjectives with both active and passive senses. **perséver:** stress is on the second syllable (Abbott §492, *perséver*).

In obstinate condolement is a course
Of impious stubbornness; 'tis unmanly grief;
It shows a will most incorrect to heaven,   95

condolement: grieving, from Latin *condolere*, to feel pain or grief. **course:** way of acting (OED 21).

will: the free will, the choice-making function of the human mind. **incorrect:** uncorrected, hence unsubmissive. **to:** toward, in relation to, as in lines 99 and 103 below (Abbott §188a). ● Despite the hypocrisy we will later discover to be present in this speech, the concept is essential to the play's drama. A will correct in relation to, and corrected by, heaven is precisely what Hamlet must and will achieve by the end of the play. Evil characters can say true things. Though the words do not in fact apply to Hamlet here, they will apply to him later, though Claudius cannot know it. Cf., Regan's true though maliciously meant line in *King Lear* II.iv.302–304.

A heart unfortified, a mind impatient,

unfortified: vulnerable to the assaults of temptation. **impatient:** unwilling to bear affliction, patience being the virtue of the willingness to suffer if one's suffering is God's will, from the Latin *patior* (to bear, to suffer).

An understanding simple and unschooled.
For what we know must be, and is as common
As any the most vulgar thing to sense,

simple: untaught, ignorant.
what: that which (a relative pronoun, Abbott §252). **any the most ... thing:** anything the most (Abbott 419a), cf., *Cymbeline* I.iv.61 ("any the rarest of our ladies"). **vulgar:** commonly perceived or known (cf., *King Lear* IV.vi.210). **sense:** Many senses of the word *sense* are possible here, including physical sensation, perception generally, and rational understanding, and are complicated by the nearness of the word *common*, implying an appeal to *common sense*, itself a phrase of several possible meanings, among them universal human reason, normal thinking, and one of the five inner wits that Burton calls "the judge or moderator of the rest" (see Lewis *Studies*, Ch. 6). The essential point is that we ought not to take so to heart the death of a father, which is as common and obvious a fact of life as anything that we feel/experience/observe.

Why should we in our peevish opposition   100
Take it to heart? Fie, 'tis a fault to heaven,
A fault against the dead, a fault to nature,

peevish: refractory, self-willed, obstinate.
it: referring back to "what" in line 98, a supplementary pronoun (Abbott §243, 249). **Fie:** an expression of "disgust or indignant reproach ... said to children to excite shame for some unbecoming action" (OED). **fault to heaven ... to nature:** offense against God; against the natural created order (Abbott §188a).

To reason most absurd, whose common theme
Is death of fathers, and who still hath cried,

From the first corse till he that died today,   105
"This must be so." We pray you throw to earth

This unprevailing woe, and think of us

As of a father, for let the world take note
You are the most immediate to our throne,

And with no less nobility of love   110
Than that which dearest father bears his son

Do I impart toward you. For your intent

In going back to school in Wittenberg,

It is most retrograde to our desire,
And we beseech you bend you to remain   115

To: in relation to, as in line 95 above. **whose ... who:** referring to reason, or perhaps to both reason and nature, though reason is likelier to be crying "This must be so" *about* nature (Abbott §264). **still:** always.

corse: corpse, i.e., that of Abel in Genesis 4, "with the irony of an analogy [that] goes beyond what the speaker intends" (Jenkins), cf., III.iii.37–38. **till:** a preposition (Abbott §184). **he:** him (Abbott §206).

unprevailing: unavailing, not helpful (cf., *Romeo and Juliet* III.iii.60). **us:** the royal plural. ● The uncle/king tells his nephew/heir to get over his father's death, as in I.v the father/king/ghost will tell him to kill his uncle/king; both imperatives sound reasonable, hence the need for the "Mousetrap" play, cf., II.ii.603–605, and III.ii.75–84.

let the world take note: indicating a formal public announcement. **immediate:** next in line of succession, pending election by the nobility when the time comes, cf., lines 15–16 note and V.ii.356. ● "The King's statement need not be inconsistent with an elective monarchy ... [i]ndeed in a [merely] hereditary monarchy there would be no occasion for it" (Jenkins). In later scenes, Laertes (I.iii.24), Ophelia (III.i.152), and Rosencrantz (III.ii.341–42) all reaffirm the expectation of Hamlet's succession to the throne.

no less nobility of love ... dearest father: equal in the admirable quality of paternal love (Jenkins substantially) to that of the most loving and beloved actual father. **dearest father:** the article ["the"] is omitted when "the whole class is expressed" and often "before superlatives" (Abbott §82).

impart: either a uniquely intransitive use of the word, meaning "relate or deal with," or else, with a shift away from the "with" construction in line 110, implying a direct object and meaning "communicate (the above information)" (Raffel), or "share (myself)" (Kittredge in Jenkins), or "bestow (love)" (Johnson in Jenkins and Riverside), or "parcel out (my favors)" (my own conjecture). **For:** as regards (Abbott §149).

Wittenberg: "[T]o note with Dover Wilson that Hamlet's university was Protestant is less important than to learn from Brandes that it was the favourite university of Danes studying abroad.... In the decade 1586–95 it had two students named Rosenkrantz and one Gyldenstjerne.... Its name was well known to the Elizabethans and had been familiarized in the theatre by [Christopher Marlowe's] *Dr Faustus*" (Jenkins, LN). **retrograde:** contrary.

we beseech you bend you: that is, I beseech you to bend yourself (i.e., turn your will) toward remaining in Denmark. ● So far as we can tell from appearances, the King asks Hamlet to remain in Denmark for Hamlet's own sake, i.e., within the "cheer and comfort" of the King's eye, rather than *to be* that cheer and comfort of the King's eye, though the phrasing could easily be taken in that flattering sense, perhaps

Here in the cheer and comfort of our eye,

Our chiefest courtier, cousin, and our son.

QUEEN

Let not thy mother lose her prayers, Hamlet;

I pray thee stay with us; go not to Wittenberg.

HAMLET

I shall in all my best obey you, madam.   120

KING

Why, 'tis a loving and a fair reply.

Be as ourself in Denmark. Madam, come.

This gentle and unforced accord of Hamlet
Sits smiling to my heart, in grace whereof,

No jocund health that Denmark drinks today,   125

---

a hint of the King's subtly double nature. In the light of later developments, it may be a sign of the King's astuteness that he recognizes in Hamlet's position and mood a potential threat from Hamlet's being out of sight that he did not find in Laertes, whom he happily allows to leave for France (lines 62–63 above). **eye:** "a frequent metonymy for the royal presence, as in *Macbeth* IV.iii.186" (Jenkins), cf., IV.iv.6, IV.vii.45, and *Troilus and Cressida* I.iii.219.

cousin ... son: again Claudius unites *cousin* (= relative, nephew) to *son* (cf., line 64 above). ● Kittredge points out that the Queen again intervenes in response to the same phrases, perhaps to forestall bad feeling.

I pray thee ... Wittenberg: Stress thus: "I práy thee stáy with ús; go nót to Wíttenberg" (Abbott §469 and §456), though the line may be an intentional hexameter (or what Abbott calls a trimeter couplet, §501).

I shall ... madam: Thanks to the older meaning of "shall" (= owe, ought, must), here "perhaps there is a mixture of 'I am bound to' [= must] and 'I am sure to' [= destined] ... often used [thus] in the replies of inferiors to superiors" (Abbott §315). **in all my best:** as best I can. ● NOTE TO ACTORS: Hamlet may say this line with normal iambic stresses, making *you* plural and intending courtly obedience with a nod to both his mother and the King. Or he may go counter to the meter by stressing the word *you*, making it singular and directed to the Queen only, intending a slight to the King. Or he may say it with neutral stress ambiguously in between the two.

Why ... reply: ● The King's apparent intention is to defuse any negative implication in Hamlet's reply with outward courtliness akin to that directed at Laertes and Polonius above (lines 44–50), a gesture that would hardly be necessary if there were no barb in Hamlet's previous line, whether pointed or surreptitious. If it is the latter, the King recognizes as much, demonstrating to us his astuteness. In any case, the public royal interpretation of Hamlet's words is that they are without offense, indicating at least outward magnanimity in the King.

Be as ourself: ● You may be as free to do as you please in Denmark as if you were ourself (= the King, the royal plural), perhaps an ambiguous phrase matching Hamlet's previous ambiguity and implying that Hamlet may do as he pleases so long as he remains in Denmark (where he can be watched).

accord: agreement to the royal request.

to: near (Abbott §188); "'Sits *at* my heart' would be normal, but the preposition is influenced by 'smiling'" (Jenkins). **in grace whereof:** in thanksgiving for which.

jocund health: happy toast. **Denmark:** the King.

But the great cannon to the clouds shall tell,

And the King's rouse the heavens shall bruit again,
Respeaking earthly thunder. Come away.
                    Flourish. Exeunt all but Hamlet.

But: = that not, i.e., there will be no toast that the King drinks today that the cannons will not tell (retell, with the additional sense of count, as a teller counts money) to the clouds, *but* acting as both a conjunction and a negative relative pronoun, object of "tell" (see OED 12. b.), expelling the normal object *it* (Abbott §123).

rouse: an act or bout of drinking, probably from *carouse* (OED rouse *sb³* 1.), possibly related to the Danish word *rus*, cf., I.iii.8, II.i.56, *Othello* II.iii.64, and Marlowe's *Doctor Faustus* IV.i.18. **bruit:** to noise, resound, from the French *bruit*. • Each drink and toast of the King will be announced by the cannon, whose sound will echo back from the heavens to earth (as happens at I.iv.6). The Danish custom of blowing trumpets and shooting off cannon when the king drinks ceremonially is introduced here, preparing us for Hamlet's commentary on it (I.iv.8ff.) and its significant reappearance in the final scene (V.ii.270ff.). It may be true that "The King's intemperance is very strongly impressed; everything that happens to him gives him occasion to drink" (Johnson in Jenkins, who refers us to I.ii.175, I.iv.8–22, II.ii.84, III.ii.302, III.iii.89, V.ii.267ff., and "for an appropriate nemesis" V.ii.326–28; note also that Hamlet *keeps* Horatio from drinking at V.ii.343), though some of the examples adduced suggest reasonable ceremony rather than excess (II.ii.84, V.ii.267). But the image of the cannon ("earthly thunder") celebrating the King's drinking and of the heavens echoing them back to earth hints at something worse than drunkenness, namely the King's pride, which reduces the heavens to a mere reflection of earthly self-indulgence.

• **SPEECH NOTE:** The following soliloquy is an excellent example of what C. S. Lewis calls the technique of variation (in Lewis, "Variation"), which, through successive versions of the same essential idea expressed in different ways, accomplishes two goals. It creates the illusion of actual speech or thought (because when we speak or think, we do not do so in finished polished sentences but try this way of making the point, then try that way, until we get it across); and it deepens our empathic response to the idea through varied poetic images until the aggregate impression is powerful and clear. Here, Hamlet is saying, essentially, that he is profoundly disturbed because his mother has rushed to marry his uncle, a far worse man than Hamlet's father. The variation produces both truth to life and empathy, making the thoughts, and thereby the character and condition of Hamlet, both believable and moving. This speech also provides the first example of the general pattern of Hamlet's soliloquies: passionate emotional outburst superseded by calm reason. Shakespeare sets up this pattern of passion yielding to reason in order to contrast it with the purely rational soliloquy at III.1.55ff., the will-pandering fall into false reason of the soliloquy at III.iii.73ff., the benighted reasoning of the soliloquy at IV.iv.32ff., and the true and enlightened reason of the dialogue at V.ii.1ff.

The speech begins with Hamlet's wanting not to be and later reveals why he feels this way. But Hamlet takes as a given that God has forbidden suicide. He is not atheistic or agnostic, nor is he what we might call clinically suicidal. Though he feels he would like to be dead, he has inherited and believes in the Christian world view and knows it wrong to commit suicide, echoing St. Paul (Philippians 1:21–24) and "An Exhortation against the Fear of Death" in *Certain Sermons* (1547), which speaks of "the desire of [St. Paul's] heart ... to bee dissolued and loosed from his body ... [although] ... it was more necessary that hee should liue, which he refused not" (I.ix.3-290–93). There is also in the classical philosophical tradition an opposition to suicide beginning with Plato's *Phaedo* (62 b–c) that counterbalances the later Stoic adoption of suicide as a way out of life's troubles, the latter opinion embodied in Seneca (cf., V.ii.341).

HAMLET

O that this too too solid flesh would melt,
Thaw, and resolve itself into a dew!   130

too too: a duplication for emphasis (OED too 4.).
solid: the F reading where Q2 has "sallied" (assailed, or perhaps a form of *sullied*, to which it is often emended). • A much debated textual crux. While "sallied" has the better textual authority, it is not Hamlet's body but his mind that is assailed, and it is his mother, not he, who is sullied; both *sallied* and *sullied* would obscure the antithesis with *melt* and *thaw*, and either would probably have been heard by the audience as a pun on *solid*, as "a dew" in the next line could be heard as "Adieu." In addition, Renaissance thought (Timothy Bright, Robert Burton) associated melancholy with solidity (Jenkins, LN).

Or that the Everlasting had not fixed
His canon 'gainst self-slaughter! O God, God,

the Everlasting: God. **fixed / His canon 'gainst self-slaughter:** established his law against suicide, as asserted by many including St. Augustine in *City of God*, Book I, Chapter 20, whose heading is "That Christians have no authority for committing suicide in any circumstances whatever" (cf., *Cymbeline*, III. iv.76–78).

How weary, stale, flat, and unprofitable
Seem to me all the uses of this world!

How weary ... this world!: "Cf. La Primaudaye, *The French Academy*, pt 2, 1594, page 254: 'When grief is in great measure, it bringeth withal a kind of loathing and tediousness, which causeth a man to hate and to be weary of all things.... Some grow so far as to hate themselves, and so fall to despair, yea many kill and destroy themselves'" (Jenkins). **uses:** common practices, usages, customs.

Fie on't! ah fie! 'tis an unweeded garden   135
That grows to seed; things rank and gross in nature
Possess it merely. That it should come to this!

Fie: expressing "disgust or indignant reproach" (OED). **unweeded garden ... merely:** Harmon (pages 992–93) shows that similar images were available to Shakespeare not only in Florio's translation of Montaigne (I.39) but also directly in classical writers (Seneca, *Epistle* 34, Cicero, *Tusculanae Disputationes* II.13) and indirectly in translations (e.g., North's translation of Plutarch's *Lives* under "Coriolanus")

But two months dead—nay, not so much, not two—
So excellent a king, that was to this,
Hyperion to a satyr, so loving to my mother   140

That he might not beteem the winds of heaven
Visit her face too roughly. Heaven and earth,

and in commonplace books like Francis Meres' *Wit's Commonwealth* under "Youth," Nicholas Ling's *Politeuphuia* under "Of Schools" (Ling was the printer of both Q1 and Q2 of *Hamlet*), Berners' *Golden Book of Marcus Aurelius*, and Cawdrey's *A Treasure or Storehouse of Similies* under "Idleness" (Harmon, pages 992–93). **rank and gross:** both adjectives have layered senses, *rank* implying overgrown, smelly, lustful, loathsome, and coarse, and *gross* implying large, excessively and unwholesomely bloated, and coarse. **merely:** entirely, from Latin *merus*, pure, unmixed, unadulterated (Abbott§15)

● Metaphorically the world is a garden entirely taken over by large, noxious weeds. Hamlet is in a state of natural grief (of the kind admitted at lines 87–92 to be reasonable by the King) compounded by a melancholy brought on by external circumstances, of which he will now speak and about which he can see nothing to be done, as he will indicate at the conclusion of the speech (line 159).

But: only. **not two:** not even two.

to this: compared to this (king), i.e., to Claudius.

A hexameter line (or trimeter couplet, Abbott §501). **Hyperion:** originally a titan, father of Helios (sun), Selene (moon), and Eos (dawn), deposed by Zeus, later conflated with Helios, the sun god, and perhaps meant by Shakespeare to refer to Apollo, the Olympian god of the sun. **satyr:** half-man, half-beast (usually goat) and characteristically lecherous (cf., "goatish disposition" in *King Lear* I.ii.127–28)

● The beauty of Apollo (Hyperion) is contrasted with the monstrosity and hence ugliness of the satyr, cf., "Hyperion's curls" at III.iv.56. Hamlet thus demotes the seemingly capable and magnanimous living king we have just seen to the level of a half-brute in comparison with Hamlet's (to him) godlike dead father, whose image we have just seen earlier as an apparition. Jenkins stresses that the Renaissance concept of "man as partaking of both god and beast," rational soul and brute sensuality, underlies the play. The two brothers, at least in Hamlet's mind, represent these two aspects of man, the lower now reigning after having destroyed the higher (LN). The conflict between Hamlet's father and Claudius serves as the external occasion of the profounder dramatic conflict within Hamlet himself between what Friar Lawrence calls "grace and rude will" (*Romeo and Juliet* II.iii.28).

he might not beteem ... roughly: ● A common expression (Jenkins) that Shakespeare intensifies to contrast how greatly Gertrude was beloved and loved in return with how quickly she recovered from her husband's death and turned to his brother. **might:** could (Abbott §312). **beteem:** suffer, allow, permit. **visit:** to visit (Abbott §349). **Heaven and earth:** ● An extension evoked by "winds of heaven" in the previous line and calling to mind again the friction between the higher and lower that Hamlet finds in his mother's behavior.

Must I remember? Why, she would hang on him

As if increase of appetite had grown
By what it fed on, and yet within a month—   145

Let me not think on't! Frailty, thy name is woman!—

A little month, or ere those shoes were old

With which she followed my poor father's body,
Like Niobe, all tears, why she—

O God, a beast, that wants discourse of reason   150

Why: interjection of mild surprise and protest (OED IV.7).

increase of appetite had grown: a duplication for emphasis, not literally the increase but her appetite itself for his love grew by feeding upon his love.

on't: on it. **Frailty … woman:** Frailty is a common term in Shakespeare for general human weakness, physical and moral, but the weakness of feminine resistance to masculine argument and force is a particular Renaissance cliché founded on the successful temptation of Eve in Genesis I:3 (cf., *Richard III* I.ii, *Twelfth Night* II.ii.29–32, *Measure for Measure* II.iv.124–30, etc.).

or ere: before, either a redundancy (both "or" and "ere" coming from the same Old English word) or a contraction of "or e'er" = before ever (cf., V.ii.30, Abbott §131).

followed … body: in the funeral procession.

Niobe: proud daughter of Tantalus who boasted that having fourteen children made her greater than the goddess Latona (Lena), who had only two, Apollo and Diana (Artemis), who punished Niobe by killing all her children (or all but two), whereupon, consumed with grief, she wept until she was turned to stone and continued weeping even then (see Ovid, *Metamorphoses*, VI.146–312). • NOTE TO ACTORS: The stress is on the first syllable (*NYE-o-bee*). **why she:** see line 143 note. • F adds "even she," which does fill out the meter but is probably an actor's interpolation (Jenkins).

wants: lacks. **discourse of reason:** • Based on Plato's idea of the three kinds of soul, the tradition taught that plants have a vegetable soul (they grow), animals have in addition a sensible soul (they grow and feel), men have in addition an intelligible or rational soul (they grow, feel, and reason), and angels have only an intelligible or rational soul (being pure intelligences). Men's reason is discursive, i.e., they reason by deduction and argumentation; angels' reason is intuitive, i.e., their reason is direct and instantaneous comprehension, cf., IV.iv.35–39. "The faculty of reason was traditionally recognized as the crucial difference between man and the beasts, for the classical statement of which see Cicero, *De Officiis*, I.iv.11" (Jenkins LN), "[T]he most marked difference between man and beast is this: the beast, just as far as it is moved by the senses and with very little perception of past or future, adapts itself to that alone which is present at the moment; while man—because he is endowed with reason, by which he comprehends the chain of consequences, perceives the causes of things, understands the relation of cause to effect and of effect to cause, draws analogies, and connects and associates the present and the future—easily surveys the course of his whole life and makes the necessary preparations

Would have mourned longer—married with my uncle,
My father's brother, but no more like my father
Than I to Hercules. Within a month,

Ere yet the salt of most unrighteous tears
Had left the flushing in her gallèd eyes,   155

She married—O most wicked speed, to post
With such dexterity to incestuous sheets!

It is not, nor it cannot come to good,

---

for its conduct." Here Hamlet asserts that even a beast, having sensation but lacking the discursive reason of man, would have mourned longer, cf., IV.iv.36 and note.

married with: married (Abbott §194).

Than I to: Than I am like to. **Hercules:** "who performed superhuman tasks" (Jenkins), foreshadowing the apparently superhuman task of Hamlet to come (at I.v.25 and 85), i.e., taking revenge without committing a wrong.

Ere yet ... eyes: before she had stopped weeping, a hyperbole characterizing her haste, as at lines 180-81. **unrighteous:** because (as he thinks) they are pretended. **flushing:** reddening (OED 2.).

gallèd: irritated.

post: rush.

dexterity: agility, nimbleness (cf., *1 Henry IV* II.iv.259). **incestuous:** ● In the Bible, sexual relations with the wife of one's brother were forbidden if the brother was alive (Leviticus 18:16, 20:21), though marriage to the wife of one's dead brother was biblically required if the brother had no son (Deut. 25:5). In the Table of Kindred and Affinity (#17) in the Book of Common Prayer, marriage was forbidden between a woman and her husband's brother and likewise in the Catholic Church by the Fourth Lateran Council (1215) in its rules of impediment by affinity, though in later years dispensations were available. It will become clear that this marriage of Claudius and Gertrude, however it contributes to the stability of the state, is not motivated only by politics. Gertrude is an "effect for which [Claudius] did the murder" (III.iii.54), his intent being therefore incestuous whether or not the two had sexual relations before the death of Hamlet Senior, which we never know explicitly, though the Ghost asserts that Claudius "won to his shameful lust / The will [= free will, desire, sexual lust] of my most seeming virtuous queen" (I.v.45–46). The lack of specificity is intentional on Shakespeare's part. The entire play is devoted to showing dramatically the reality and consequence of spiritual conditions and choices when the outward show of physical actions may hide them (cf., line 85 above). Is Claudius guilty of incest and murder and usurpation? Is Hamlet guilty of the wrong kind of revenge in *not* killing Claudius in III.iii? Was Ophelia's suicide forgivably unintentional or damnably intentional? Here it is the haste of the marriage that causes Hamlet to treat as fact his suspicion of the incestuous intentions of Claudius. The audience will not be certain about those intentions until III.iii when the truth is revealed in soliloquy.

It is not ... to good: It is not good nor can it come to good.

But break, my heart, for I must hold my tongue.

But break … tongue: Hamlet tells his heart to break, for his will has decided not to speak and "Silent griefs were said to make the heart break, Cf. *Mac*[*beth*] IV.iii.209–10" (Jenkins) and cf., *King Lear* V.iii.313. ● This is the first instance of Hamlet's passion surrendering to reason, establishing a pattern in his thought. He concludes the soliloquy as he does because, despite his feelings about the weak will of the queen, the hasty wedding, and the inferiority of the King to his own father, he has no evidence of any specific wrongdoing. To rebel against a rightful king, whatever one's feelings, would go against both the moral law and reason. Hence the importance of the accusation later provided by the Ghost and the response that the play within the play evokes from Claudius. **break:** let it break or go ahead and break, subjunctive used optatively or imperatively (Abbott §364).

Enter Horatio, Marcellus, and Barnardo.

s.d. *Enter Horatio:* ● As soon as Hamlet's reason suppresses his passion, his friend Horatio, the embodiment of reason, enters (cf., I.iv.86 and I.v.1–3 and note).

HORATIO

Hail to your lordship!

HAMLET

　　　　　I am glad to see you well.　　　　160

Horatio!—or I do forget myself.

Hail to … you well: a single pentameter line with "I am" elided, cf., Abbott §497. **I am … well:** ● NOTE TO ACTORS AND DIRECTORS: Hamlet says this before he sees who is addressing him, then recognizes his friend.

forget myself: with emphasis on "myself" rather than on "forget". ● Recognizing Horatio, Hamlet responds with a courtly phrase: to forget you is to forget myself, recalling the themes of identity and of appearance vs. reality and setting up Hamlet's expression of friendship to Horatio at III.ii.63–74.

HORATIO

The same, my lord, and your poor servant ever.

poor servant: Horatio is "poor," having neither title nor land, and he is Hamlet's servant in the sense that a courtier owes obedience and fealty to the prince. **ever:** asserts Horatio's loyalty, past and future.

HAMLET

Sir, my good friend—I'll change that name with you.

my good friend: the emphasis is on the word *friend*. **change:** exchange. ● In a gesture both magnanimous and earnest, Hamlet wishes to exchange the name *friend* with Horatio, meaning to assert that his relation to Horatio is not merely that of prince and servant but also of friend and friend (cf., lines 252–3). There is no reason to suppose that the friendship of the two at school implies that they would have been in personal communication in Denmark before this moment. The friendship is being cemented with a new level of intimacy as we watch. If further explanation is wanted, we may suppose that earlier, Hamlet would have been busy with ceremonial affairs not involving Horatio, and Horatio, without the good cause of having seen the Ghost, would not have presumed to intrude upon Hamlet at such a time.

And what make you from Wittenberg, Horatio?

what make you: what are you doing (OED make *v.*¹ 58.), cf., II.ii.270 and *As You Like It* I.i.29. **from:** away from, out of. **Wittenberg:** see line 113 note above. ● Hamlet and Horatio are school mates there in what we would call graduate school.

Marcellus.   165

MARCELLUS
My good lord.

HAMLET
I am very glad to see you.
                      [*To Barnardo*] Good even, sir.

But what, in faith, make you from Wittenberg?

HORATIO
A truant disposition, good my lord.

HAMLET
I would not hear your enemy say so,   170

Nor shall you do mine ear that violence
To make it truster of your own report
Against yourself. I know you are no truant.

But what is your affair in Elsinore?

We'll teach you to drink deep ere you depart.   175

Marcellus: • Hamlet knows Marcellus by name (some editors make Hamlet guess at the name by inserting a question mark that is not in Q2 or F). **My good lord:** • Marcellus' greeting confirms he is who Hamlet thinks he is.

Good even: good afternoon or evening (*even* = the latter part of the day). **sir:** • Hamlet does not know Barnardo by name. • Hamlet's different responses to the three men indicate their three degrees of familiarity with him and his princely magnanimity appropriate to each. Later we will hear of "the great love the general gender [the public] bear him" (IV.vii.18).

you: Horatio. **from:** away from, as above (line 164).

truant: adj. or noun, (of) one who avoids school, lazy. **disposition:** natural tendency (OED 6.) or temporary inclination (OED 7.). • Hamlet apparently takes him to mean the former. **good my:** a common transposition to make the adjective (*good*) modify the noun and possessive pronominal adjective together (*my lord*).

I would not ... say so: that is, I would not hear such an accusation against you without responding. • Being a friend, Hamlet would not let even a supposed enemy of Horatio get away with such an accusation (truancy) without challenging him, hinting at the idea that being a friend means taking revenge on a friend's enemy, an idea further hinted at below at lines 182–83 and coming to full expression in I.v. with the command of the Ghost to revenge his murder.

do mine ear that violence: wrench my ear out of its natural condition of wanting to hear about a friend only good and forcing it to hear something negative, with perhaps a secondary sense of forcing it to hear a paradox, it being assumed that a man would not wish to report against himself. **that violence / To make:** such violence as to make, cf., Abbott §277. **truster:** *-er* added to a noun to signify an agent (Abbott §443), cf., "enginer" at III.iv.206.

Elsinore: For purposes of the play, the capital of Denmark and seat of the king; historically, Helsingør, on the spit of land on the northeast coast of the island of Zealand, the spot nearest to Sweden across the Øresund strait, was the site of Kronborg castle, originally a medieval fortress "where Danes exacted tribute of passing ships" (Jenkins), rebuilt by Frederick II in 1574–85 into a great castle where "players performed . . , when [Frederick] held court there in 1579" (Donnelly).

to drink deep: in F, Q2 "for to drinke". • a reference to the Danish reputation for drinking and the king's custom introduced above (cf., lines 125–28 and note) and deplored by Hamlet at I.iv.13–22. **ere:** before.

HORATIO

My lord, I came to see your father's funeral.

My lord ... funeral: a pentameter, with the *e* in "funeral" elided, cf., Abbott §494. **father's funeral:** "Verity [ed. *Hamlet*, 1904] contrasts Laertes's reference to the 'coronation,' line 53" (Jenkins). • In comparison with Laertes' reason for returning, namely to attend the coronation of Claudius, Horatio's reason here hints that he, like Hamlet, valued the former king above the present one, but cf., line 53 note.

HAMLET

I pray thee, do not mock me, fellow student;

mock me: make a fool of me, put me on. • Hamlet means this sarcastically to introduce the next line.

I think it was to see my mother's wedding.

mother's wedding: • Hamlet alludes to how quickly the marriage followed the funeral.

HORATIO

Indeed, my lord, it followed hard upon.

hard upon: soon after, *upon* used adverbially like *on*, cf., Abbott §192. • That Horatio gets the point indicates the mutual understanding between the two friends.

HAMLET

Thrift, thrift, Horatio. The funeral baked meats   180

Thrift ... meats: a pentameter line with the unstressed syllables in "Horatio" elided, cf., Abbott §469. **Thrift:** saving expense. **baked meats:** pies ("bakemeats" in KJV).

Did coldly furnish forth the marriage tables.

coldly: when the hot food had cooled. • Hamlet ironically says that the court saved money by serving at the wedding party the cold leftovers of the hot food served after the funeral, implying by hyperbole how quickly the second ceremony followed the first. • NOTE TO ACTORS: Bring out the antitheses "funeral/marriage" and "baked/coldly" within the parallel "meats [=foods]/tables."

Would I had met my dearest foe in heaven

Would I had: I wish I had. **dearest foe:** worst enemy ("dearest" = direst, bitterest).

Or ever I had seen that day, Horatio!

Or ever: before ever (cf., line 147 note above, V.ii.30, Abbott §131). • These two lines are crucial to the main spiritual drama of the play. Continuing in the tone of hyperbole, Hamlet reveals a habit of mind which, though not sinful in itself, will later grow into the profound error of will that constitutes his fall in III.iii. He suggests here that the next-to-worst thing that could happen to him would be to meet his worst enemy in heaven, the worst thing being to see his mother marry his uncle. But a Christian audience would recognize that a good Christian would *want* to see his enemy in heaven, for it would mean that his enemy had repented before dying, and Christ enjoined his followers to love their enemies. What is here the mere hint of a flaw in thinking, a dram of evil, becomes in III.iii an outright crime of the will against God, for which Hamlet will pay with his life, though not before he is converted to a more Christ-like willingness to forgive his own murderer and wish him in heaven. This phrase initiates the through-line of Hamlet's spiritual transformation, whose implications for all men constitute the main business of the play.

My father—methinks I see my father.

My father ... my father: a pentameter line with a pause indicated by the dash standing in for the stress of the second iamb, cf., Abbott §506.

HORATIO
Where, my lord?
HAMLET
   In my mind's eye, Horatio.   185

HORATIO
I saw him once; a was a goodly king.

HAMLET
A was a man, take him for all in all:
I shall not look upon his like again.

HORATIO
My lord, I think I saw him yesternight.

Where, my lord?: ● NOTE TO ACTORS: Horatio says this with urgency, taking Hamlet to mean that he is seeing now the apparition that Horatio saw the previous night. **mind's eye:** "A traditional metaphor, going back to Plato (ψυχης ομμα, *Republic*, vii 533 D; cf. *Sophist*, 254 B). Cf. e.g. Aristotle, *Nichomachean Ethics*, VI.12 (1144a 30); Cicero, *De Oratore*, III.163 ('mentis oculi') and elsewhere; Chaucer, *Man of Law's Tale*, 552; Sidney, *Apology*, 6th para; Ephesians i.18 (Bishops' Bible, 'the eyes of your minds'). See *SQ*, VII, 351–4, For the phrase, cf. above I.i.[112], *Lucr.* 1426; and for the expansion of the idea, *Sonn.* XXVII and CXIII" (Jenkins).

once: Horatio implies earlier (I.i.60ff.) and later (lines 211 and 240) that he has seen Hamlet Senior and knows well what he looked like, whereas here he says he has seen him only once. This contradiction, apparent in the study, whether or not an oversight on Shakespeare's part, is irrelevant to the play. The point in each case is that Horatio has the authority of experience to authenticate his testimony (see Introduction, page 6, note 13). **a:** he, here and in the next line (cf., I.i.43 note).

A: see previous note. **a man:** the ideal of a man (as at III.iv.62 and *Julius Caesar* V.v.75). **take him for all in all:** were you to consider him the perfect instance, the summation of all good qualities, "take" being "subjunctive rather than imperative" (Jenkins). **all in all:** "Often taken to mean, as in modern use, 'all things considered', 'on the whole'. But when Shakespeare uses *all in all* adverbially, it implies not qualification but intensification (= 'entirely'), as in *H[enry] V* I.i.42 [and] *Oth[ello]* IV.i.88, 26[5]. The sense here is not that of weighing one thing against another but of accumulating them all [cf., III.iv.55–62] ... This sense of completeness or perfection is borne out by other Elizabethan instances: e.g. Stubbes, *Anatomy of Abuses* (New Shakspere Soc. i. 29) 'he is all in all; yea, so perfect ...'; R. Carew, *The Excellency of the English Tongue* (Smith, *Elizn Critical Essays*, ii.293), 'Will you have all in all for prose and verse? take the miracle of our age Sir Philip Sidney.' ... Cf. Tilley A133, "All in all and all in every part,' a proverb which T.W. Baldwin (*Literary Genetics of Shakspere's Poems*, pages 157ff.) shows to derive from the neo-platonic doctrine of the soul" (Jenkins LN) ● Hamlet's image of his father is that he was the complete man without negatives, an image that will be tempered by the Ghost's later implication (I.v.12–13) that the soul of Hamlet Senior is in purgatory. This idealizing of his father may be another hint of Hamlet's dram of evil, a taint of the spiritual self-exaltation that betrays him in III.iii when he will take it upon himself to play God.

yesternight: last night (cf., yesterday).

HAMLET

Saw, who?   190

HORATIO

My lord, the King your father.

HAMLET

The King my father?

HORATIO

Season your admiration for a while

With an attent ear, till I may deliver,
Upon the witness of these gentlemen,
This marvel to you.

HAMLET

For God's love let me hear!   195

HORATIO

Two nights together had these gentlemen,
Marcellus and Barnardo, on their watch,
In the dead waste and middle of the night,
Been thus encountered: A figure like your father,

Armèd at point exactly, cap-a-pe,   200

Appears before them, and with solemn march
Goes slow and stately by them; thrice he walked
By their oppressed and fear-surprisèd eyes

Within his truncheon's length, whilst they, distilled

Almost to jelly with the act of fear,   205

Stand dumb and speak not to him. This to me
In dreadful secrecy impart they did,
And I with them the third night kept the watch,

Where, as they had delivered, both in time,
Form of the thing, each word made true and good,   210

The apparition comes. I knew your father;

These hands are not more like.

HAMLET

But where was this?

Saw, who?: Q2, in F "Saw? Who?" Dyce thought the Q2 punctuation right, adding "nor do I recollect any performer of Ham. who understood the words but as a single question; no pause of astonishment was made between 'Saw' and 'who' by the two Kembles, Kean, and Young; none is made by Macready and the younger Kean" (New Variorum). **who:** common for *whom* (Abbott §274).

Season: temper, moderate (verb), cf., II.i.28, *Merchant of Venice* IV.i.197 and V.i.107. **admiration:** wonder, amazement, cf., III.ii.327, 330.

attent: attentive. **may:** am able to (Abbott §307). **deliver:** report.

had: previously to last night when I joined them.

dead waste and middle: a hendiadys (cf., Wright, page 185). **waste:** literally, an uninhabited or desert land, here metaphorically applied to night because it is normally empty of people, who are asleep, (cf., "dead hour" at I.i.65), with a possible pun on *waist* (as at II.ii.232–33) because of the link to "middle," implying midnight.

at point: precisely in every detail, cf., *King Lear* I.iv.324, *Macbeth* IV.iii.135. **cap-a-pe:** head to foot, referring to complete armor, cf., line 228, from Old French *cap-à-pied*, from Latin *caput*, head, and *pes*, foot.

march: regular forward motion (OED *sb.*⁴ 1.) or possibly the rhythm of that motion (OED *sb.*⁴ 5).

oppressed: burdened, crushed, troubled (OED oppress 2.). **fear-surprisèd:** overcome, overpowered by fear (OED surprise 1.b.), cf., *Winter's Tale* III.i.10.

truncheon: "a staff carried as a symbol of military command" (Jenkins). **distilled:** dissolved (OED distil *v.* 7.).

act: operation, working (OED act 4.), cf., *Othello* III.iii.328.

dumb: speechless.

dreadful: awed, solemn, from the passive sense (feeling dread) rather than the active (causing dread), cf., Abbott §3. **impart:** tell, relate.

delivered: reported. **both in time, / Form:** for the omission of *and*, cf., *King Lear* I.i.49–50 (Jenkins). **made true and good:** confirmed.

knew: was acquainted with him well enough to know what he looked like (see line 186 note above).

These hands: Horatio holds up his own two hands, which he says are not more like one another than the ghost was like Hamlet's father.

MARCELLUS
My lord, upon the platform where we watch.

HAMLET
Did you not speak to it?

HORATIO
              My lord, I did,
But answer made it none. Yet once methought   215

It lifted up it head and did address
Itself to motion like as it would speak;

But even then the morning cock crew loud,

And at the sound it shrunk in haste away
And vanished from our sight.

HAMLET
                          'Tis very strange.   220

HORATIO
As I do live, my honored lord, 'tis true,

And we did think it writ down in our duty
To let you know of it.

HAMLET
Indeed, sirs. But this troubles me.
Hold you the watch tonight?

MARCELLUS, BARNARDO
                    We do, my lord.   225

HAMLET
Armed, say you?

ALL
          Armed, my lord.

HAMLET
From top to toe?

ALL
          My lord, from head to foot.

HAMLET
Then saw you not his face.

HORATIO
O, yes, my lord, he wore his beaver up.   230

HAMLET
What looked he, frowningly?

---

platform: "A level place constructed for mounting guns in a fort or battery" (OED 6.a.).

speak to it: see I.i.29 note.

methought: it seemed to me, from an old sense of *think*, meaning to seem, appear, taking the pronoun *me* in the dative case (OED think $v.^1$ B.2.b.).

it: its, an old form of the neuter possessive (Abbott §228), cf., I.i.37 note, V.i.221, and *King Lear* I.iv.216.

address / Itself to motion: Prepare to make a gesture appropriate to speaking (OED address *v.* 3. and 10.).

like as it would: (approximately) as if it intended to, (literally) in the way it would if it were intending to, cf., Abbott §107.

even then: at that exact moment, cf., Abbott §38.

crew: a past tense form of *to crow*, crowed.

shrunk: withdrew furtively (OED shrink *v.* 6.); "Past indicative forms in *u* are very common in Shakespeare" (Abbott §339).

As I do live: an oath = I swear that it is as true as that I am alive, in pointed antithesis to the apparition of the dead king.

writ down in: written in, included in (the curtailed form of the past participle is common, cf., Abbott §343).

Indeed: a response to the previous phrase, not an emphasis of the following (Jenkins substantially).

s.h. **Marcellus, Barnardo:** Q2 has "All" here and at lines 226 and 227. Presumably only Marcellus and Barnardo serve as watchmen, but Horatio is included in the confirmation of how the Ghost looked. F has "Both," but "F's variation of the speech-headings [lines 225–238] shows no systematic purpose" (Jenkins).

s.h. **All:** see previous note.

from head to foot: cf., line 200 above.

beaver: hinged face-guard of a helmet that "could be pushed up entirely over the top of the helmet" (Planché, *Cyclopaedia of Costume*, i.39 in Jenkins), from Old French *bavière*, child's bib.

What looked he, frowningly?: Q2 "What look't he frowningly?" F "What, lookt he frowningly?" The sense is "How did he look, frowning?" (cf., OED what A. 20.) because "Hamlet is not taking up

HORATIO

                          A countenance more

In sorrow than in anger.

HAMLET

                Pale or red?

HORATIO

  Nay, very pale.

HAMLET

        And fixed his eyes upon you?

HORATIO

  Most constantly.

HAMLET

        I would I had been there.

HORATIO

  It would have much amazed you.

HAMLET

                Very like.   235

Stayed it long?

HORATIO

  While one with moderate haste might tell a hundred.

MARCELLUS, BARNARDO

  Longer, longer.

HORATIO

  Not when I saw't.

HAMLET

        His beard was grizzled, no?

HORATIO

  It was as I have seen it in his life,   240

A sable silvered.

HAMLET

        I will watch tonight.

Perchance 'twill walk again.

---

anything that has been said but introducing a new question" (Jenkins). **frowningly:** "i.e., with the mien appropriate to an armed warrior. See I.i.[62], and cf. *Mer*[*chant of*] *V*[*enice*] III.ii.85 [and] *Cym*[*beline*] II.iv.23" (Jenkins).

countenance: the middle syllable is elided, cf., Abbott §468.

sorrow ... anger: • NOTE TO ACTORS: Given I.i.62, Horatio is saying that of the two main kinds of frowning, that of the Ghost seemed to be more of sorrow than of the anger that might characterize a soldier. • The phrase not only gives a hint about how the Ghost should be played in the previous scene but suggests that the reason for the appearance of the Ghost was not military and that his appearance in armor to soldiers was intended both to show himself as they might have known him and to mislead about his secret purposes. At the same time, he will be inviting Hamlet to a kind of conflict as soldier in an inner war (cf., V.ii.396–99) for which he must be in the armor of virtue (cf., V.ii.395–400).

Pale or red ... very pale: • Hamlet seeks to confirm Horatio's interpretation of the Ghost's expression, in which paleness would imply melancholy and redness anger. Horatio asserts that the Ghost was pale, despite "angry parle" at I.i.62, perhaps suggesting that the speeches of the Ghost in I.v are to be delivered with somewhat more sadness than anger.

amazed: perplexed and bewildered (OED amaze *v.* 2.) and overwhelmed with wonder, astonished (OED 4.).

like: likely.

tell: count (to) (a bank teller is a counter of money).
S.H. **Marcelus, Barnardo:** Q2 has "Both" (cf., line 225 note).

Not when I saw't: • Horatio's resistance to the overestimation of the time the Ghost was visible illustrates that Horatio is the man of rational balance, trustworthy because not apt to misread even an extreme situation or to exaggerate the truth for dramatic effect.

grizzled: gray.

as I have seen it: cf., lines 186 and note and 211 and note.

sable silvered: dark mixed with gray or white.

watch: join you on the watch, with the secondary sense stay awake, not sleep.

'twill: it will.

HORATIO

        I war'nt it will.

HAMLET

If it assume my noble father's person,

I'll speak to it, though hell itself should gape

And bid me hold my peace. I pray you all,   245

If you have hitherto concealed this sight,

Let it be tenable in your silence still,

And whatsomever else shall hap tonight,
Give it an understanding but no tongue.
I will requite your loves. So fare you well.   250
Upon the platform 'twixt eleven and twelve
I'll visit you.

ALL

        Our duty to your honor.

HAMLET

  Your loves, as mine to you; farewell.
                  [Exeunt all but Hamlet.]

---

war'nt: contraction of *warrant*, guarantee, assure, "used *colloq.* as a mere expression of strong belief = 'I'll be bound'" (OED warrant *v.* 4.a.), probably pronounced as one syllable (cf., III.iv.6).

If it assume ... person: cf., line 254 below:
● "Hamlet alternates between regarding the Ghost as an unknown spirit in his father's shape and as his 'father's spirit' itself. There being no question of mere hallucination (cf. I.i.[23–24]), it must be one or the other" (Jenkins). In speaking to others, Hamlet hypothesizes the former; when alone, the latter. These are the two possibilities between which Hamlet must choose before acting on the Ghost's imperative because if it is the former and the spirit is a devil, Hamlet's soul would be in danger, not from the spirit itself (cf., I.iv.66–67) but from succumbing to its temptation (cf., I.iv.69–74, II.ii.598–603). The method of determining which alternative is the true one will be Hamlet's and Horatio's observation of the response of the King to the "Mousetrap" play.

I'll speak to it: cf., I.i.29 note. **though hell itself ... hold my peace:** ● Hamlet is determined to address the Ghost even if hell, in an attempt to silence him with the threat of damnation ("bid me"), should "gape," i.e., open its mouth wide "as ready to receive one who converses with a devil," an image the audience had seen "not only in pictures but as an actual stage-property" (Jenkins), cf., II.ii.598ff. and note.

hold my peace: keep quiet, say nothing. ● Compare Hamlet's determination here with Laertes' "I dare damnation" at IV.v.134. **I pray you:** a parenthetical phrase used to add deference to a request or entreaty (OED pray *v.* 8. a.).

hitherto: until now; **concealed this sight:** kept secret your experience of seeing the Ghost.

tenable in your silence: hold it in silence, keep it secret ("tenable" from French *tenir* from Latin *tenere*, to hold) **still:** always, constantly.

whatsomever: whatsoever. **hap:** happen.

no tongue: do not talk about it.

requite your loves: repay your devotion and loyalty. **loves:** for the plural, as at line 253, see I.i.173 note.

Our duty ... honor: The men properly pledge their service to Hamlet as is their duty, he being their prince; "The plain man's abbreviation of the more elaborate formula used by Osric at V.ii.[182]" (Jenkins).

Your loves ... to you: for the plural, as at line 251 see I.i.173 note. ● As above at lines 162–63, Hamlet here responds magnanimously by wishing not merely to receive their duty but to receive and give love, i.e., friendship, loyalty, devotion.

My father's spirit—in arms! All is not well.

My father's spirit: see line 243 note. ● "That ghosts were the spirits of the departed was the traditional view from classical times and reinforced by the Catholic doctrine of purgatory.... Shakespeare is aware of various beliefs and allows Hamlet to be the same" (Jenkins), or, as J. V. Cunningham put it, "If you want to know what Shakespeare's audience believed about ghosts, read everything said about ghosts in *Hamlet*, and believe it."

I doubt some foul play. Would the night were come.   255

doubt: suspect (OED 6.b.), cf., II.ii.56, III.i.166.
foul play: treacherous or violent action. ● Hamlet here adds to Horatio's list at I.i.130–39 another familiar reason why ghosts, and particularly ghosts in the revenge tragedies of the time, might appear, namely to report otherwise undetectable crimes. Hamlet's suspicion, adding to the suspense (Jenkins), turns out to be right.

Till then sit still, my soul. Foul deeds will rise,
Though all the earth o'erwhelm them, to men's eyes.

                                                    Exit.

sit still, my soul: ● Again Hamlet is attempting to subdue his emotion with reason, commanding himself to patience until he can meet the Ghost.
Foul deeds will rise ... to men's eyes: The truth, however hidden (with the hyperbolical image of burial under the entire earth), will be revealed to the eyes of men one way or another, even if it must be by supernatural means, like the appearance of the ghost of one buried, as Hamlet's father is, under a small portion of that earth. See Introduction, pages 2–4, for the implications of Shakespeare's radical transposition of the classical ghost tradition into a Christian context.

Act I, Scene iii

Enter Laertes and Ophelia, his sister.

Act I, Scene iii. ● A room in Polonius's apartment in the castle.

LAERTES

My necessaries are embarked. Farewell.

necessaries: needed belongings. **embarked:** put aboard ship ("bark" = ship). ● Laertes will travel to France by ship as later Hamlet will set sail for England.

And, sister, as the winds give benefit
And convoy is assistant, do not sleep,
But let me hear from you.

as: whenever, according as (Abbott §109).
convoy: conveyance, means of transport. **assistant:** available (from French *assister* = to attend upon, stand by to help). **sleep:** to be idle or remiss (OED sleep *v.* 5.).

OPHELIA

                    Do you doubt that?

that: i.e., that you will hear from me.

LAERTES

For Hamlet, and the trifling of his favor,   5

trifling: idleness, frivolity, lack of seriousness.
favor: approving attention and condescension of a superior and also particular affection or good will, partiality. **Hamlet, and the trifling of his favor:** possibly a hendiadys for "the trifling of Hamlet's favor" (Wright, page 185).

Hold it a fashion and a toy in blood,

fashion and a toy in blood: possibly a hendiadys (Wright, p. 185). **fashion:** mere outward form or ceremony, pretense (OED 7.) and also passing fad (OED 10.). **toy in blood:** "idle fancy of youthful passion" (Riverside). ● *toy* means an insignificant trifle, as in IV.v.18 and *1 Henry VI* IV.i.145 ("a toy, a thing of no regard"), or "a whim, a fancy, or a short-lived passion" (Jenkins) as in I.iv.75 and *Othello* III.iv.156, or an "idle diversion ... of an amorous kind" (Jenkins) as in *Othello* I.iii.268–69 and here; "in blood" implies that Hamlet's fancy is merely sexual and therefore transient, "The blood [being] popularly held to be the seat of the emotions, of passion as opposed to reason ... also associated with sensual appetite and in particular with sexual desire" (Jenkins LN), cf., I.iii.116, III.ii.69, and III.iv.69.

A violet in the youth of primy nature,

violet: representing short-lived beauty, as in Sonnet 12.3. **primy:** coined by Shakespeare, meaning in its prime, i.e., the first part or morning hour or springtime of its life, hence full of vigor and sap, here referring to Hamlet's affection for Ophelia as merely an aspect of his youthful *nature*, moved by sexual vigor but likely to fade as the violet past its prime withers.

Forward, not permanent, sweet, not lasting,

Forward: blossoming early (in the day or the spring). **sweet:** monosyllables with long vowels "are often so emphasized as to dispense with an unaccented syllable" (Abbott §484), which here would come before the word.

The perfume and suppliance of a minute—
No more.

perfume and suppliance: possibly a hendiadys (Wright, page 185). **perfume:** cf., III.i.98. **suppliance of a minute:** a mere pastime to fill up (OED supply *v*.1) no more than a minute's vacant time (OED suppliance[1] and cf., supply *sb*.).

OPHELIA

    No more but so?

so?: "so." in Q2 and F, the question mark here supplied by the early editor Rowe. Whatever the punctuation, Ophelia is not pleased with her brother's analysis of Hamlet's intention and requires more persuasion to accept it.

LAERTES

        Think it no more.   10

Think it no more:. ● Laertes wishes Ophelia to think of Hamlet's love for her as merely a passing fancy. Though it will appear to Ophelia later (III.i.92ff.) that Laertes has been right about this, we will find that he is not (V.i.269) and that in care for his sister, Laertes is overreaching himself in disparaging Hamlet's virtue, though not so much as Polonius will do later in the scene. Laertes advises Ophelia to beware (lines 33–34 and 43) whereas Polonius in self-assured certainty commands her to break off relations with Hamlet entirely (line 131ff.). ● NOTE TO ACTORS: The three phrases "No more. / No more but so? / Think it no more" make a single verse line, in which "Think it" is a trochee, rather than an iamb.

For nature crescent does not grow alone

crescent: growing, from Latin *crescere*. ● "The *ss* spelling (from French) in Q2 and F was normal until the 17th century re-formed the word according to the Latin" (Jenkins). **alone:** only, modifying the next phrase.

In thews and bulk, but as this temple waxes,

thews and bulk: *thews* is "bodily proportions, lineaments, or parts, as indicating physical strength" (OED *sb*.1 3.b.), *bulk* is the trunk of the body and the body itself (OED *sb*.1 2.), physical size (OED 4.), both as distinct from the mind or spirit. The two words are unlikely to form a hendiadys (Wright, page 185), cf., *2 Henry IV* III.ii.258 ("Care I for the limb, the thews, the stature, bulk, and big assemblance of a man? Give me the spirit, Master Shallow"). **temple:** the human body, a common New Testament image, cf., John 2:21, 1 Corinthians 3:16 and 6:19, etc., and cf., *Rape of Lucrece* lines 719 and 1172, *Macbeth* II.iii.68 and *Tempest* I.ii.458. **waxes:** increases, grows.

The inward service of the mind and soul

service: continuing the metaphor of the body as temple, the service performed by the mind and soul for the sake of the self, the body, and God, and also for the sake of Denmark and its king, the idea Laertes will develop in the following lines.

Grows wide withal. Perhaps he loves you now,

withal: with it, with which ("used for *with* after the object at the end of a sentence" Abbott §196).
● Laertes warns Ophelia that Hamlet not only has grown physically into a man but, as heir to the throne, will grow greater yet in mind and soul in service to the King, to the kingdom, and, with unintentional foreshadowing, to God. ● NOTE TO ACTORS: "thews and bulk" and "this temple" are parallel and contrast with "mind and soul"; "crescent," "waxes," and "Grows" are parallel; and "alone" and "withal" are antitheses. All these serve the general contrast between body and mind.

And now no soil nor cautel doth besmirch   15

soil nor cautel: possibly a hendiadys (Wright, page 186), *cautel* = deceit, wile, trickery (Fr. *cautèle*, Latin *cautela*, precaution), cf., *Coriolanus* IV.i.33, and *Julius Caesar* II.i.129 ("cautelous").

The virtue of his will, but you must fear,

will: a word of layered meanings including free choice, intentions, desires generally, and sexual desire specifically.

His greatness weighed, his will is not his own.

His greatness weighed: his rank and position as heir to the throne being considered, the participle with a nominative absolute (Abbott §376). **will:** again both free will and sexual desire.

For he himself is subject to his birth:

subject to his birth: subject (as we are to kings) to his own rank, to the present king, and to the fact of being likely heir to the throne, to which Claudius has proclaimed him the nearest heir (cf., I.ii.109 and note).

He may not, as unvalued persons do,
Carve for himself, for on his choice depends   20

unvalued: lower ranking.

Carve for himself: have his own way, control his own life, proverbial (Tilley C 110), cf., *Richard II* II.iii.144 ("carver") and probably *Othello* II.iii.173. **choice:** of a wife.

The safety and health of this whole state,

safety: Q2 has "safty," F has "sanctity," which scans but is probably a compositor's error, Q3 has "safety," correcting Q2's spelling but not the meter, and the editor Hanmer, based on a conjecture of Theobald that Jenkins accepts (LN), as does Abbott (§484), has "sanity," which, since it can mean general health as well as specifically mental health (OED 1.), is tempting for metrical reasons. But though Shakespeare does not elsewhere give "safety" three syllables (as Spenser does in *Faerie Queene*, V.iv.46.6), the word is common throughout his works, whereas he uses the word "sanity" only once, in the F version of *Hamlet* at II.ii.210, where it means specifically mental health, and the pairing of exact synonyms ("sanity [= general health] and health") seems less satisfactory in terms of sense. Hence I follow the authority of Q2 for the better sense rather than emending for the sake of the meter.

And therefore must his choice be circumscribed

circumscribed: bounded, limited (OED circumscribe 2.).

Unto the voice and yielding of that body
Whereof he is the head. Then if he says he loves you,
It fits your wisdom so far to believe it   25

voice and yielding: possibly a hendiadys for consenting voice (Wright, page 186), "voice" = approval, vote (OED 3. and 10.), cf., V.ii.356, and "yielding" = consent. **body / Whereof he is the head:** the body politic, the state, of which the king is the head, in a common analogy between the macrocosm of the state and the microcosm of an individual man. ● Hamlet cannot choose to marry whomever he pleases; his choice must be guided by political concerns and the good of Denmark, of which he will one day be the ruler. **Whereof ... loves you:** a pentameter if "he is" is elided to "he's" and "the" to "th'," cf., Abbott §497.

As he in his particular act and place

particular act and place: "acting as he must in his special circumstances and under the restrictions of his rank" (Kittredge).

May give his saying deed, which is no further

May give his saying deed: may actually perform what he has promised.

Than the main voice of Denmark goes withal.
Then weigh what loss your honor may sustain

the main voice: the principal, majority, general, or whole choice, will, or vote (OED main *a.* 7. b.; voice 3. and 10.), the general will of the nation. **withal:** with (see line 14 note above). ● Jenkins maintains that "There is no thought here of Hamlet's having or needing the King's 'voice.'" But while in one sense the opinion of the multitude constitutes the "main voice of Denmark," in practice that opinion is expressed by the will of the King, who speaks for the whole, and, assuming he marries before becoming king, Hamlet would probably not marry without the "voice" (= approval) of Claudius. Hence, the audience would not be wrong to hear "main voice of Denmark" as meaning the will of the King as well. In any case, Laertes is correct in asserting that whom Hamlet marries will depend not merely on his personal desire but on the national interest. His concern is therefore that even if Hamlet now intends to marry Ophelia, she cannot be certain he will actually do so.

If with too credent ear you list his songs,   30

credent: credulous, believing; **list:** listen to, hear; "The preposition is ... sometimes omitted before the *thing* heard after verbs of hearing" (Abbott §199).

Or lose your heart, or your chaste treasure open

chaste treasure: virginity, cf., *Measure for Measure* II.iv.96, *Cymbeline* II.ii.42.

To his unmastered importunity.
Fear it, Ophelia, fear it, my dear sister,
And keep you in the rear of your affection,

his unmastered importunity: Hamlet's (hypothetical) uncontrolled entreaty.

in the rear of: far back behind (see next note).

Out of the shot and danger of desire. 35	**shot and danger:** a hendiadys (Wright, page 186) for dangerous shot. • "In this military metaphor Ophelia's affection [for Hamlet] is figured as the forward troops, exposed to danger, while she herself is to stay behind out of reach of the enemy shot" (Jenkins).
The chariest maid is prodigal enough	**chariest:** most modest, chaste. **prodigal:** unthrifty, lavish, reckless.
If she unmask her beauty to the moon.	**to the moon:** i.e., *even* to the moon, let alone to a man. • Q2 places opening double quotation marks before lines 36, 38, and 39 (as at IV.v.17–20, where they are single) without closing quotation marks, an Elizabethan printing convention indicating sententious sayings (Jenkins substantially).
Virtue itself scapes not calumnious strokes.	**Virtue itself:** even a maid so chaste as to embody virtue itself. **scapes not:** does not escape. **calumnious strokes:** the blows of false accusation, cf., III.i.135–36, *Measure for Measure* III.ii.186–87, *Winter's Tale* II.i.73–74, and Tilley E 175.
The canker galls the infants of the spring	**canker:** the canker-worm (rose worm). **galls:** chafes, frets, injures. **infants of the spring:** i.e., the new flower buds, cf., *Love's Labor's Lost*, I.i.101.
Too oft before their buttons be disclosed, 40	**buttons:** "(French *bouton*), is, since the *Roman de la Rose*, poetic for 'bud' (cf., *2 Noble Kinsmen*, III.i.6)" (Jenkins). **disclosed:** opened, unfolded, cf., Sonnet 54.8, also used of eggs hatching, cf., III.i.166 and V.i.287 (Jenkins). • The idea of the invisible worm eating up the bud before it blossoms is commonplace, cf., *Venus and Adonis* 656, Sonnets 35.4, 70.7, 95.2–3, 99.13, *Romeo and Juliet* II.iii.30, *Two Gentlemen* I.i.42–43, 45–46, etc., and cf., William Blake, "The Sick Rose."
And in the morn and liquid dew of youth	**morn and liquid dew:** a hendiadys (Wright, page 186) for clear morning dew, or dewy morning brightness, one of the senses of the Latin *liquidus* being clear, bright, serene, pure (Jenkins substantially).
Contagious blastments are most imminent.	**Contagious blastments:** "disease-bringing blights, Cf. *blasting*, III.iv.65. This meaning of *blast* comes from the attribution of disease in plants to blasts of foul air. As these are associated with morning dampness, so the 'morn' of 'youth' is the time both of bright promise and of greatest susceptibility to corruption. Cf. *Meas[ure for Measure]* II.ii.11, 'falling in the flaws [= blasts] of her own youth'" (Jenkins); Riverside's gloss of "flaws" there as "sudden gusts (of passion)" is also relevant here. **imminent:** hanging over, threatening soon.
Be wary then; best safety lies in fear.	**best safety ... fear:** for the corollary "Cf. *Mac[beth]* III.v.32–3, 'Security [= freedom from fear] Is mortals' chiefest enemy'" (Jenkins). For the absent article see Abbott §82.
Youth to itself rebels, though none else near.	**Youth to itself rebels:** Youth succumbs to passion even when there is no external tempter, hence is in that much greater danger when there *is* another, like Hamlet, who may actively tempt. The rebellion is of the lower parts of the self against the higher, the body and will, in the sense of desires, including sexual desire, against the government of reason and conscience, cf., III.iv.82–85, Sonnet 146.2, *Merchant of Venice* III.i.34–36, *1 Henry IV* V.ii.17 about the rebel Hotspur, *All's Well* IV.iii.19–20 and V.iii.6, *Antony and Cleopatra* I.iii.31–33, etc.

OPHELIA

I shall the effect of this good lesson keep   45
As watchman to my heart. But, good my brother,
Do not, as some ungracious pastors do,
Show me the steep and thorny way to heaven,

Whiles like a puffed and reckless libertine

Himself the primrose path of dalliance treads   50

And recks not his own rede.

shall: am sure to (Abbott §315). **effect:** essence, substance.

ungracious: lacking divine grace, cf., *Richard II* II.iii.89, *1 Henry IV* II.iv.445, probably *Twelfth Night* IV.i.47, etc.

Whiles: while. **puffed:** bloated, physically with self-indulgence and spiritually with pride, cf., IV.iv.49, *Merry Wives* V.v.152, and *Timon of Athens* IV.iii.180. **reckless:** not reckoning on the consequences, particularly of divine judgment. **libertine:** one unrestrained by moral law, esp. in relation to women (OED *sb.* 3, citing this passage).

pastors ... Himself: Shakespeare occasionally plays loose with grammatical agreement in number to shift focus, cf., I.iv.30–33 ("men ... His"), and III.ii.188–92 ("Purpose ... they") (Jenkins substantially), cf., Abbott §415. **primrose path of dalliance:** the way decorated (as a path with primroses) with self-indulgence, especially frivolous amorous play (cf., *1 Henry VI* V.i.23) that leads to destruction and hell, *cf.*, Matthew 7:13 ("for it is the wide gate, and broad way that leadeth to destruction"), *Macbeth* II.iii.19 ("the primrose way to th' everlasting bonfire"), and *All's Well* IV.v.54–55 ("the flow'ry way that leads to the broad gate and the great fire").

recks: heeds (cf., *reckons*). **rede:** advice, counsel, related to older meanings of *read*. ● Ophelia is voicing a central concern of the play, the failure to follow the advice one gives others. It will apply to her father, who counsels the golden mean to Laertes but oversteps in relation to Hamlet and his apparent madness; to Claudius, who has the nerve to claim that "There's such divinity doth hedge a king" (IV.v.124); and most importantly to Hamlet, by the principle of whose advice to the players in III.ii he fails to be guided in III.iii, and whose accusations against his mother in III.iv apply to him more than to Gertrude though he cannot then see it.

LAERTES
                    O fear me not.
I stay too long.

Enter Polonius.

                    But here my father comes.
A double blessing is a double grace;
Occasion smiles upon a second leave.

fear me not: fear not for me (Abbott §200), do not worry about me on that score.

double blessing ... grace: see line 57.
Occasion smiles upon: "It is a happy circumstance which gives opportunity for" (Jenkins), circumstances (personified) are smiling. **leave:** leave-taking, saying goodbye. ● I am in luck in being able to say goodbye to Polonius a second time.

POLONIUS

Yet here, Laertes? Aboard, aboard, for shame!   55
The wind sits in the shoulder of your sail,

Aboard: get aboard your ship.
The wind ... sail: the winds are favorable for sailing.

And you are stayed for. There— my blessing with thee.

[Laying his hand on Laertes' head.]

And these few precepts in thy memory
Look thou character. Give thy thoughts no tongue,

stayed for: awaited. **There:** referring to his bestowing a second blessing for a second farewell, the "double grace" Laertes mentions above (line 53), perhaps with a physical gesture, as in the s.d. added by Theobald.

these few precepts:. ● The following precepts are not to be taken as empty rhetoric, though the speech is often played so. However garrulous Polonius may be, the advice is made up of standard platitudes, common in the period in the advice of fathers to sons. Cf., the many examples cited in Jenkins LN, who emphasizes the importance of the scene in establishing the father-son relationship of Polonius and Laertes and the latter as a foil for Hamlet in his role as filial avenger. "The tradition goes back ultimately to Isocrates, *Ad Demonicum,* which the 16th century knew well…. It owed much also to Cato, *Disticha de Moribus ad Filium,* a favourite in the Middle Ages, to Erasmus (*Adagia, Disticha Catonis*), and to their 16th-century popularizers" (Jenkins LN). The particular forms of Polonius's platitudes constitute well-accepted Aristotelian wisdom: the practice of the golden mean in all things, avoiding both excess and deficiency, and thereby echoing the theme of imperatives to do something and to do it in a certain manner without overdoing it, cf., I.ii.36–38 note. **in thy memory … character:** write them down in your memory, as if with characters = letters of the alphabet (for the absent *that* with the subjunctive, cf., Abbott §368). **character:** the stress is on the second syllable, cf., *Two Gentlemen* II.vii.4, *2 Henry VI* III.i.300, *Rape of Lucrece* line 807, *Richard III* III.i.81, *Troilus and Cressida* III.ii.188, probably *Julius Caesar* II.i.308, 125, and Abbott §400, though Shakespeare more often places it on the first. ● NOTE TO ACTORS: On the modern stage pronouncing *charácter* would distract from the meaning, so the actor should stress "Lóok thou" and "chárac-" (trochees) to both make sense and preserve the meter. And note the elaborate parallelism throughout the speech. **tongue:** speech.

Nor any unproportioned thought his act.   60

unproportioned: unfitting, intemperate, unnatural, cf., *Richard II* III.iv.41, *Henry V* II.ii.109, IV.i.146, *Troilus and Cressida* I.iii.87. **his:** its, cf., I.i.37 note. **act:** action, the potential of thought becoming actual in deed.

Be thou familiar, but by no means vulgar;

Those friends thou hast, and their adoption tried,

familiar: affable, sociable (Riverside). **vulgar:** equally familiar with everyone without distinction.

and their adoption tried: their worthiness for acceptance as friends having been tested and proven by experience, cf., OED try *v.* 13., citing *Romeo and Juliet* IV.iii.29, and see Abbott §95 for *and* with the participle indicating an emphatic addition, cf., "The effect of *and* [being] that of adding a further circumstance to what has already been said (almost 'moreover'). So too III.iii.62" (Jenkins). ● NOTE TO ACTORS: Hence "and their" is a trochee, and the line reads "Those friénds thou hást, ánd their adóption tríed."

Grapple them to thy soul with hoops of steel,

Grapple: attach closely and firmly (OED *v*. 1. c., citing this line and *Henry V* Prol. 18). **them:** for the redundant pronoun cf., Abbott §242. **hoops:** circular metal rings that tightly bind the wooden staves of a barrel.

But do not dull thy palm with entertainment

dull thy palm: make coarse or insensitive the palm of the hand, cf., V.i.69–70, or possibly weaken your grip (Raffel). **entertainment / Of:** engagement with, reception of.

Of each new-hatched, unfledged couráge. Beware   65

unfledged: of a bird (following "new-hatched") not yet feathered, still unfit to fly. **couráge:** a gallant, a young blood, swaggerer (cf., *Knight of the Burning Pestle*, Ind., "where 'a couraging part' is a noisy, swaggering role" Jenkins), with the stress on the short *a* of the second syllable as in French (F has "comrade").

Of entrance to a quarrel, but being in,

being: contracted to one syllable (Abbott §470), with the stresses falling on "but" and "in."

Bear't that th'opposèd may beware of thee.
Give every man thy ear, but few thy voice;

Bear't that: manage it in such a way that (Riverside). **th'opposèd:** the person quarreled with. **may beware of thee:** will respect or fear you. ● i.e., if you do get into a fight, win it.

Take each man's censure, but reserve thy judgment.

censure: opinion, judgment, possibly but not necessarily adverse (OED *sb*. 3. and 4.), cf., III.ii.27 and 87 for neutral senses and I.iv.35 note for the special case of "general censure". **reserve thy judgment:** either hold for a later time and further attention (OED *sb*. 1.b., citing this line) or more likely retain for oneself, not share (OED 2.). ● "Take" and "reserve" imply an antithesis, so that Laertes is told to listen to others' opinions but not to tell them his.

Costly thy habit as thy purse can buy,   70

habit: clothing, cf., III.iv.135. **as:** "The first *As* is sometimes omitted" (Abbott §276) as here before "Costly". **purse:** funds, assets, from the leather purses used to carry coin money (banknotes not having come into use in England until 1695). **fancy:** fantastical ornamentation.

But not expressed in fancy; rich, not gaudy;
For the apparel oft proclaims the man,
And they in France of the best rank and station

they in France: they (who are) in France, i.e., Frenchmen, the omission of the relative pronoun and verb is common "especially when *locality is predicated*" (Abbott §245). **station:** status, position in society.

Are of a most select and generous chief in that.
Neither a borrower nor a lender be,   75

Are of a most ... in that: The line is probably a pentameter and not a hexameter if "Are of a" and the *e* in "generous" are elided, cf., Abbott §497. **select:** superior, picked out, distinguished. **generous:** noble, from Latin *generosus*, of noble birth. **chief:** if "of a" is not a false intrusion and the line is not corrupt, "chief" may be a noun meaning something like "preeminence," but many emendations have been suggested. In any case, the point is that the most high-born Frenchmen are especially to be noted for exemplifying the golden mean in apparel.

For loan oft loses both itself and friend,

loan … friend: loaning often causes the amount loaned to be lost and the person given the loan to be turned from friend to enemy if the loan is not paid back, *cf., "Amico mutuam roganti me pecuniam si dedero, et amicum, et pecuniam perdo"* ascribed by Baldwin (II.610–11) to *sententiae* of Seneca as quoted in Domenico Nani Mirabelli's *Polyanthea (1503),* which Shakespeare would have studied in grammar school. A version (with "*ipsum*" for "*amicum*") ascribed to Demades appears in the fictional Pseudo-Caecilius Balbus's *De Nugis Philosophorum* (http://www.thelatinlibrary.com/caeciliusbalbus.html) of John of Salisbury's *Polycraticus* (c. 1159).

And borrowing dulleth th'edge of husbandry.

dulleth th'edge: Parrott-Craig conjecture for Q2 dulleth edge, F dulls the edge, and Q3 dulleth the edge.
husbandry: thrift, a householder's care (from *hus bonda*, master of a house), cf,. Sonnet 94.6, *Macbeth* II.i.4–5.

This above all: to thine own self be true,
And it must follow as the night the day
Thou canst not then be false to any man.   80

true: loyal. • By being true to oneself Polonius cannot mean "follow your desires" or "stick to your own opinions" as in modern speech. Nor is "constant" a sufficient gloss on Shakespeare's extension of the "tradition of the maxim" (Jenkins note and LN). It is not mere variability in oneself that leads to being false to others but rather varying from the ideal golden mean expressed throughout the speech. *True* here means both honest and faithful, and truth to oneself means not betraying one's own good by going to any of the extremes previously listed. This platitude of Polonius asserts that it is built in to the structure of creation that if one is faithful to one's own true good (rather than intemperately rebellious to oneself, as Laertes warned Ophelia not to be at line 44 above), then one will not betray any other person. In short, one who is virtuous in himself will not wrong others. This truth is central to the play, for it is precisely when Hamlet fails in truth to himself in III.iii that he will act in the following scene so as to harm others and indeed threaten all of Denmark by unintentionally killing the speaker of this line. And that failure in truth to himself lies not merely in variability or altering of opinion but in hubris, the extreme exaggeration of his own place and the substitution of his own personal mission for the divine imperative. Similar breaches of the principle can be seen in every main character of the play, from Claudius and Gertrude to Osric, including, ironically, Polonius himself and, in a moment of extremity, even the rationally exemplary Horatio.

Farewell. My blessing season this in thee.
LAERTES
Most humbly do I take my leave, my lord.

season this: ripen, mature, bring to fruition (not enhance its flavor), cf., III.ii.209 and *Merchant* V.i.107.
this: my advice.

POLONIUS

The time invites you; go, your servants tend.

LAERTES

Farewell, Ophelia, and remember well

What I have said to you.

OPHELIA

             'Tis in my memory locked,   85

And you yourself shall keep the key of it.

LAERTES

Farewell.   *Exit.*

POLONIUS

What is't, Ophelia, he hath said to you?

OPHELIA

So please you, something touching the Lord Hamlet.

POLONIUS

Marry, well bethought.   90

'Tis told me he hath very oft of late

Given private time to you, and you yourself

Have of your audience been most free and bounteous.

If it be so—as so 'tis put on me,

And that in way of caution—I must tell you,   95

You do not understand yourself so clearly

As it behooves my daughter and your honor.

What is between you? Give me up the truth.

OPHELIA

He hath, my lord, of late made many tenders

Of his affection to me.   100

POLONIUS

Affection, puh! You speak like a green girl,

---

invites: F, invests Q2, which in the sense of "presses upon" is defended by Theobald and Jenkins, but parallel uses of *invite* with abstract nouns support the F reading: e.g., V.ii.390, *Twelfth Night* II.ii.23, *Henry V* V. Prol. 37, *Macbeth* I.vii.62–63 and II.i.62, *Timon of Athens* V.i.206, and *Cymbeline* III.iv.105. **tend:** attend, wait (as at IV.iii.45).

What I have said ... locked: Possibly a hexameter line or a trimeter couplet (Abbott §501), though elision (or reading it as dactylic rather than iambic) would preserve it as a pentameter thus: "Whát I have sáid to you. 'Tís in my mémory lócked."

you ... keep the key: "She will remember it till he permits her to forget it" (Jenkins).

touching: touching on, regarding. **touching the Lord Hamlet:** Abbott puts a stress on "the" and gives other examples of the word *the* being "regarded as capable of more emphasis than with us" (§457), but
● NOTE TO ACTORS: on the modern stage we are better off reading "-ing the" as a pyrrhic foot and "Lord Ham-" as a spondee.

Marry: "indeed (originally the name of the Virgin Mary used as an oath)" (Riverside). **well bethought:** that calls for being thought about, consideration of it is called for.

audience: hearing, attention, pronounced as two syllables. **free:** liberal, generous. **bounteous:** pronounced as two syllables.

put on: told to, perhaps urgently, pressed upon, cf., *As You Like It* I.ii.93–94 and *Twelfth Night* V.i.67.

in way: "*The* was frequently omitted before a noun already defined by another noun" (Abbott §89). **in way of caution:** in the manner of a warning.

behooves: is proper to, advantageous for.

tenders: offers.

Affection , puh!: the phrase may be amphibious, completing a pentameter begun with the previous line as well as serving as the first part of this pentameter line (Abbott §513). **green:** inexperienced, immature, foolish, from "green sickness," the iron-anemia disease of adolescent girls called chlorosis and thought in the Renaissance to result from lack of sexual satisfaction or "want of a husband" (Greene *Mamillia*, page 13), and "Cf. Chapman, *All Fools*, IV.i.18, 127, 'You're green, you're credulous, easy to be blinded', 'young and green'" (Jenkins).

Unsifted in such perilous circumstance.

Unsifted: untried, inexperienced (OED 3. citing this use), from *sift*, to pass through a sieve, hence "inexperienced in resisting temptation. Cf. Luke XXII.31, 'Satan hath desired to have you, that he may sift you as wheat'" (Jenkins).

Do you believe his tenders, as you call them?

tenders: offers of affection, as above in line 99.

OPHELIA
I do not know, my lord, what I should think.
POLONIUS
Marry, I will teach you: think yourself a baby   105
That you have ta'en these tenders for true pay

tenders: Polonius now shifts the sense of the word from offerings of affection to payments of money (OED's first instance of *tender* meaning the money itself, as in *legal tender*, is from 1740), the antithesis being between valid ("true pay," "sterling") and invalid money ("not sterling"). ● Whereas Laertes above conceded about Hamlet that "perhaps he loves you now," and went on to warn Ophelia of possible or likely alteration in him toward her, Polonius here overconfidently asserts as a certainty that Hamlet does not mean what he says.

Which are not sterling. Tender yourself more dearly,

Tender yourself more dearly: means offer yourself at a higher price (OED Dearly 1.) and treat yourself more tenderly (OED tender *v.*2 3., "to feel tenderly toward," OED dearly 2. "affectionately").

Or—not to crack the wind of the poor phrase,

crack the wind: make breathless like an over-ridden horse.

Running it thus—you'll tender me a fool.

Running: Collier's emendation, Q2 Wrong, F Roaming, Q1 tendring. ● "In this generally accepted emendation *running* completes the metaphor of the broken-winded horse in the previous line" (Jenkins). **tender me a fool:** make yourself a fool, *me* being either an indirect object or, more likely, an ethical dative (Abbott §220). According to Jenkins, the senses some editors have found here—make a fool of me, and offer me an (illegitimate) child—strain the text: though the word *fool* is used as an endearment, cf., *Romeo and Juliet* I.iii.31 and 48 and *King Lear* V.iii.306, and "baby" has appeared five lines earlier in the same position in the line (line 105), "*fool* unqualified does not mean 'baby'" (Jenkins). The audience may nonetheless hear the overtone.

OPHELIA
My lord, he hath importuned me with love   110

importuned: solicited, pressed, plied (OED 3.), stressed on the second syllable.

In honorable fashion.

fashion: manner.

POLONIUS
Ay, fashion you may call it. Go to, go to.

Ay, fashion... call it: perhaps an amphibious phrase both completing a trimeter couplet and beginning a pentameter, with a stress on "you" as well as "call" (Abbott §513). **fashion:** punning on a) mere pretense and b) passing fad, as in line 6 above. **Go to:** an imperative expression equivalent to "come on" or "enough of this" (from "go to your work").

OPHELIA

And hath given countenance to his speech, my lord,

With almost all the holy vows of heaven.

POLONIUS

Ay, springes to catch woodcocks. I do know,   115

When the blood burns, how prodigal the soul

Lends the tongue vows. These blazes, daughter,

Giving more light than heat, extinct in both

Even in their promise as it is a-making,

You must not take for fire. From this time   120

Be somewhat scanter of your maiden presence;

Set your entreatments at a higher rate

Than a command to parley. For Lord Hamlet,

Believe so much in him that he is young,

And with a larger tether may he walk   125

---

countenance: authority, approval, sanction.

almost:. ● *All* the holy vows would include the official ones of the wedding ceremony.

springes: *springes* (the *g* is soft) = snares.
woodcocks: fools, simpletons, the woodcock *scolopax rusticola*, a woodland bird related to sandpipers and snipes, being proverbially known to be easily caught, cf., V.ii.306 and Tilley S 788.

blood: sexual heat, see line 6 note above.
prodigal: prodigally, intemperately, for adjectives used as adverbs see Abbott §1. ● Sexual heat causes one intemperately to speak vows of love.

Lends … daughter: Some have felt that the metrical problem with the line in both Q2 and F (which has "Gives" for "Lends") calls for emendation, but ● NOTE TO ACTORS: if "Lends" is sufficiently stressed, the missing unstressed syllable need not trouble the performer. **These blazes … take for fire:** These brief bursts of flame, i.e., Hamlet's vows, producing more superficial attractiveness ("light") than life-sustenance ("heat"), dying out in both even as the vows are being uttered, you must not mistake for lasting love. **blazes:** bursts of flame, "a sudden kindling up of passion as of a fire" (OED *sb.*1 3.), cf., *Richard II* II.i.33 ("His rash fierce blaze of riot cannot last").

extinct: extinguished, quenched. **in both:** providing neither light nor heat. **in:** For *in* with a noun see Abbott §164.

promise: the good (light and fire) portended by the blazes, with a secondary sense of the spoken promise itself connected with *vows* in line 117. **a-making:** in being made, i.e., even as the blaze is promising fire and heat = even as the lover is making his vow, cf., Abbott §24.

fire: lasting fire that can be trusted to provide both light and heat.

scanter: more sparing (OED scant *a.* 6). **maiden:** emphasizing again Ophelia's virginity (*maid* = unmarried woman, virgin).

entreatments: negotiations to discuss surrender.
higher rate: greater cost.

parley: (F) meeting to discuss terms (Q2 parle). ● "It was … traditional to represent courtship in terms of war. Ophelia, as defender of a citadel, is not to accept the besieger's call for a parley as a sufficient reason for her to … enter into negotiations with him" (Jenkins).

Believe so much in him: believe no more than this about him (Riverside substantially)

larger: longer. **tether:** F, leash or rope, from that used to tie a domestic animal to a stake to limit the radius of its range of movement, used also figuratively = scope, limit (OED 1. and 3.), Q2 tider = *ted(d)er*, "the commoner Elizabethan form" (Jenkins).

Than may be given you. In few, Ophelia,

In few: in a few words, idiomatic for "in short," cf., Abbott §5.

Do not believe his vows, for they are brokers,

brokers: go-betweens, hence panders, bawds, pimps, cf., *King John* II.i.582, *All's Well* III.v.71 ("brokes"), *Troilus and Cressida* III.ii.203–204 and V.x.33.

Not of that dye which their investments show

dye: ingrained color, the antithesis of "show," the mere outward appearance. **investments:** clothes, cf., *2 Henry IV* IV.i.45, where the word is used in a similar contrast between outward show and inner purpose. The possible secondary sense of a being surrounded by a hostile army, siege (OED invest *v.* 7, cited in Jenkins) may point back to lines 122–23 but would distract from the present point. • Polonius asserts that Hamlet's vows are not what they are dressed up to be.

But mere implorators of unholy suits,

implorators: implorers, entreaters (Fr. *implorateur*). **unholy suits:** sinful entreaties, contradicting the "holy vows" in line 114, with a pun on *investments* (*suits* = clothing). • NOTE TO ACTORS: For the meter two syllables may be elided, preferably "-ators" but possibly "of un-."

Breathing like sanctified and pious bawds   130

sanctified and pious bawds: an extreme oxymoron = holy pimps. The argument by Jenkins [LN] for accepting Theobald's conjecture "bawds" for Q2 and F "bonds" is thorough and persuasive.

The better to beguile. This is for all:
I would not, in plain terms, from this time forth

beguile: deceive into seduction. • Polonius here overreaches, breaking the principle of the golden mean that he recommended to Laertes earlier in the scene (lines 59–80), by asserting that Hamlet's vows *are*, not *may be*, brokers (= panders, bawds). Laertes had told Ophelia not to believe Hamlet's promises except as Hamlet might fulfill them with deeds (i.e., marriage). Presumably to enforce his point, Polonius claims to know that Hamlet's vows are intended only to seduce Ophelia. As a result, his warning goes further than Laertes' warning to be wary. Presuming to know what is in Hamlet's soul, he goes so far as to slander the Prince, and the error is emphasized by the irony of his own use of the word *slander* in line 133. As Hamlet in III.iv will accuse his mother of errors that he cannot yet see are in himself, so here Polonius does the same with Ophelia. **This:** what I am about to say. **for all:** once and for all, as we would say, cf., *Cymbeline* II.iii.106 and Abbott §57.

Have you so slander any moment leisure
As to give words or talk with the Lord Hamlet.

slander: disgrace, discredit. **moment leisure:** moment's leisure. For the noun used as a possessive, see Abbott §22 and 430, and cf., "region kites" II.ii.579 and "every minute while" *1 Henry VI* I.iv.54. • In another of the important imperatives of which the play is full, Polonius explicitly orders Ophelia not to see Hamlet at all. In this, again going further than Laertes, Polonius oversteps the bounds of moderation, assuming in the Prince the nefarious intent where Laertes only feared in him the pressures of youth and the exigencies of the kingdom's politics. Polonius's error in assuming what is going on in Hamlet's soul foreshadows Hamlet's assumption of what is going on in the soul of Claudius in III.iii.

Look to't, I charge you. Come your ways.   135

OPHELIA
I shall obey, my lord.

Exeunt.

Act I, Scene iv

Enter Hamlet, Horatio, and Marcellus.

HAMLET
The air bites shrewdly; it is very cold.

HORATIO
It is a nipping and an eager air.

HAMLET
What hour now?

HORATIO
                I think it lacks of twelve.

HAMLET
No, it is struck.

HORATIO
                Indeed? I heard it not.
It then draws near the season   5
Wherein the spirit held his wont to walk.

A flourish of trumpets, and two pieces go off.

What does this mean, my lord?

HAMLET
The King doth wake tonight and takes his rouse,

Look to't: See that you do what I say. **Come your ways:** come along, "A common idiom, in which *ways* shows an old adverbial use of the genitive. See *OED* way *sb.*I 23.[b.]" (Jenkins), cf., III.i.128–29.

I shall obey: ● Ophelia's acquiescence is consistent with the virtue of obedience to her father, but the mistrust of Hamlet that originates with her father places her between two mighty opposites, her father and her lover. Ultimately it is the corrupt king who is to blame for Hamlet's need later (II.i) to make use of this enforced rejection by his beloved as the supposed cause of Hamlet's madness, and Hamlet's role as the instrument of divine justice in the state necessitates his making Ophelia a victim of a deception of which neither Laertes, for all his concern for his sister, nor Polonius, for all his suspicion, could have any idea.

Act I, Scene iv. ● The guards' platform of Elsinore Castle.

s.d.: The absence of Barnardo, whose testimony to the existence of the Ghost was previously given, "receives no explanation, and needs none beyond dramatic convenience" (Jenkins); Hamlet will make the fourth witness of the witnesses needed to authenticate the Ghost's reality, see I.i.29 note.

shrewdly: F (Q2 shrouly, Q1 shrewd) woundingly, severely, sharply (OED 2., with influence from 1., maliciously, wickedly).

nipping: biting, sharp, blighting by stopping the growth as if pinching ("nipping") off buds.

eager: (Fr. *aigre*, sharp, keen, sour) bitter, biting, cf., vinegar = *vin* + *aigre* and I.v.69.

it lacks of: it is not yet (OED lack *v.*¹ 4., cf., OED want *v.* 1.c., 2.d.). On impersonal verbs see Abbott §297.

twelve ... is struck: ● The time and bitter cold are the same as on the previous night when the Ghost appeared, cf., I.i.7–8.

No, it is struck ... near the season: for the complex metrical analysis, amphibious line plus interjection, see Abbott §513. **season ... Wherein:** time (of night) in which (OED 13.).

held his wont: had as a custom, habit, in the sense that the Ghost has appeared on three successive nights at this time. *Wont* is used as a noun in Shakespeare only here and in 2 *Henry VI* III.i.2, cf., OED wont *sb.* and Abbott §5.

s.d. *pieces:* cannons, pieces of ordnance, cf., I.ii.126.

wake: stay awake. **takes his rouse:** takes his full draught or bumper of liquor (OED rouse *sb*³ 1.), i.e., carouses, cf., I.ii.127 and note, II.i.56.

Keeps wassail and the swaggering upspring reels;

Keeps: carries on, sponsors (OED keep *v*. 36), cf., *Twelfth Night* II.iii.72. **wassail:** drinking revels, usually pronounced to rhyme with *fossil*. **swaggering:** lurching, swaying (OED *ppl.a.*, whose first citation, however, is 1865; if it is a participial adjective, as I take it, it must derive from swagger *v*. 2., earliest citation 1724, or more directly from swag *v*. 1., to move unsteadily, cf., "swag-bellied" in *Othello*, II.iii.78, which, in the context of drunkenness, may imply swaying with drink). **upspring:** leaping, bouncing, from the verb (OED *v*. 2), though possibly from a kind of wild dance (OED *sb*. 3.). **reels:** reveling (OED *sb*.² 1.b., citing this line as first instance) or perhaps reelings, rollings, or staggerings (*sb*.² 1.a.). There is editorial debate over the syntax of the line. I take "reels" as a noun, the object, parallel to *wassail*, of the verb "Keeps" and modified by "swaggering" and "upspring" as adjectives. The King stays up late ("doth wake"), carouses, and entertains drunken revelry and wild dancing or leaping.

And as he drains his draughts of Rhenish down,   10
The kettle-drum and trumpet thus bray out
The triumph of his pledge.

Rhenish: Rhine wine, cf., V.i.180.

kettle-drum and trumpet ... his pledge: as at S.D. line 6, I.ii.125–26, and V.ii.275–77. **kettle-drum:** a drum of brass or copper and parchment tuned to a particular note (OED). "The kettle-drum, though familiar in England from the mid-16th century, again gives local colour as a traditional accompaniment of Danish rejoicings (cf., Cleveland, *Fuscara*, 'As Danes carouse by kettle-drums'). 'Like a Denmark drummer' became a common phrase" (Jenkins LN). **triumph:** festive elation or celebration (OED *sb*. 5., the feeling, or 4., the activity), cf., *Midsummer Night's Dream* I.i.19. **pledge:** toast (OED *sb*. 4.), "the 'jocund health' of I.ii.125" (Jenkins).

HORATIO

Is it a custom?

Is it a custom?: Evidence that it was is given by William Segar, Garter King at Arms, quoted in Stow's *Annals* (1605), pages 1433–7, as saying about the Danes in 1603, "It would make a man sick to hear of their drunken healths: use hath brought it into fashion, and fashion made it a habit," giving the example of King Christian on board the British ambassador's ship at which "every health reported six, eight, or ten shot of great Ordnance, so that during the King's abode, the ship discharged 160 shot" (Jenkins LN). ● That Horatio here seems to be a stranger to this custom, if a contradiction, is bothersome only in the study (see I.i.80 note).

marry: a mild oath (cf., I.iii.90 note).

HAMLET
  Ay marry is't,
  But to my mind, though I am native here
  And to the manner born, it is a custom   15
  More honored in the breach than the observance.

honored in the breach: honorable to be broken ● This phrase has been misunderstood here because it has been so often misapplied in popular speech. It means that it is more honorable ("honored" = to be honored) to break the custom than to keep it, *not* that it is honored only with lip service but not actually practiced. Hamlet disapproves of this custom because it ruins the reputation of the Danes in the opinion of other nations, despite the Danes' other good qualities.

This heavy-headed revel east and west

heavy-headed revel: dull or stupid (because exaggerated? overindulgent?) reveling (OED heavy-headed 2., and cf., heavyhead), or perhaps, over-drinking causes heavy-headedness in the revelers, a "transferred epithet" (Jenkins) from the revelers to the revelling. **east and west:** everywhere, referring to the next line: nations whether east or west of us, or perhaps more broadly Oriental and Occidental, censure us.

Makes us traduced and taxed of other nations.

traduced: falsely implicated in shame or crime. **taxed:** censured, accused. **of:** by, cf., IV.ii.12 and Abbott §170.

They clip us drunkards, and with swinish phrase

clip: clepe, call (cf., the archaic *yclept* = called). **swinish phrase:** "The name of Dane is regularly accompanied by an allusion to swine" (Jenkins).

Soil our addition; and indeed it takes   20

addition: what is added to one's mere name, attributes and honors, hence, reputation, cf., II.i.47.

From our achievements, though performed at height,

at height: most excellently (Riverside), for omission of *the* cf., Abbott §90.

The pith and marrow of our attribute.

pith and marrow: vital or essential essence, from *pith*, the center of the plant stalk, and *marrow*, the center of animal bones, apparently already idiomatic together before Shakespeare. **attribute:** reputation, what is attributed to us ● The over-indulgent custom of toasting, trumpet, cannon fire, and drunken reveling "causes our achievements, even when these attain the acme of possible performance, to lose the best and most vital part of the esteem we should enjoy" (Jenkins).

So, oft it chances in particular men

So … particular men: ● The rest of this crucial speech makes an analogy between the revel-marred assessment of Denmark's quality and the marred assessment of the lives of individual men. Jenkins cites Nashe's *Pierce Penniless* (i.205) on drunkenness: "Let him be indued with never so many virtues … : yet if he be thirsty after his own destruction, … that one beastly imperfection will utterly obscure all that is commendable in him"; Greene's *Pandosto* (Greene iv.250): "One mole staineth a whole face: and what is once spotted with infamy can hardly be worn out with time"; and Belleforest: Hamlet "showed himself admirable in everything, if one spot alone had not darkened a good part of his praises." See SPEECH NOTE after line 38 below. **particular:** individual.

That for some vicious mole of nature in them,

vicious: both corrupt, impure, defective and corrupting, noxious, vitiating (OED vicious 6., 7., 8.). **mole:** blemish, which, being a defect, causes corruption. **of nature:** inborn, as opposed to chosen by the free will, cf., "choose" in line 26.

As in their birth, wherein they are not guilty   25
(Since nature cannot choose his origin),

As: as for example. **his:** its, cf., I.i.37 note

By their o'ergrowth of some complexion,

their: Q2, giving a greater sense of the man's agency in the "o'ergrowth" than the commonly accepted emendation by Pope to "the". **o'ergrowth of some complexion:** excess of some quality or characteristic, see SPEECH NOTE after line 38 below.

Oft breaking down the pales and forts of reason,

pales: fences, an excess of one humor or another could drive one beyond the normal bounds of rational thought or action.

Or by some habit that too much o'erleavens

Or by some habit ... manners: • The habit may taint the pattern of praiseworthy behavior that would otherwise be characteristic of the person. **habit:** "settled practice, custom" • Onions cites only two other instances of this sense in Shakespeare, *Two Gentlemen* V.iv.1, and *Merchant of Venice* I.ii.59, the other senses being "dress, garb" and "bearing, demeanor." Jenkins finds the sense of dress latent here, "giving rise to 'Nature's livery' in line 32," and refers to III.iv.161–65 as tying "habit" to both "custom" and "livery," all to demonstrate that *habit* here may not be "an acquired characteristic merely" but possibly "a manifestation of nature." This is in keeping with Jenkins' reading of the syntax of lines 25–30 as illustrating line 24. But see note to line 35 and SPEECH NOTE below. **o'erleavens:** taints, ferments, sours throughout, cf. I Corinthians 5:4–8, *Cymbeline* III.iv.62, and Landry • It is the "leaven of maliciousness and wickedness" that is going to corrupt Hamlet in III.iii.

The form of plausive manners—that these men,   30

form: exemplary pattern, cf., "mold of form" = model for ideal behavior at III.i.153. **plausive:** praiseworthy, = worthy of applause as in *All's Well* I.ii.53, gracious, pleasing (Malone in Furness). For the passive use of the adjective see Abbott §3. **manners:** behavior.

Carrying, I say, the stamp of one defect,

stamp: imprint, certifying mark, according to Jenkins corresponding to the "mole" in line 24 above based on *Cymbeline* V.v.364–66.

Being nature's livery or fortune's star,

nature's livery: clothing given by nature, which, according to Jenkins, corresponds to the dress sense of "habit" in line 29 above. **star:** both the source of astrological influence and the blemish that may result from it • Both are distinct from "virtues" and "grace" in the next line, "virtues" being the good qualities a man exhibits in his free will choices, and "grace" the direct and unmediated good influence of God.

His virtues else be they as pure as grace,

His: for the shift in number see I.iii.50 note.
else: apart from (these defects), in other respects.
be they: subjunctive = even if they are, let them hypothetically be.

As infinite as man may undergo,

As infinite ... particular fault: Quoting this passage, Baldwin writes, "[Cicero] says that there are two types of questions, infinite, and definite. Shakespeare knew the distinction upon which the division between infinite and definite questions rests ... One particular fault breaks an infinity of virtue; one limiting circumstance makes a finite or definite question out of an indefinite or infinite one." A definite question, called a cause or hypothesis, "has definite persons, places, times, etc. for the most part," and an infinite

question, called a thesis, theme, or *propositum*, "for the most part has not." The source was in Cicero's *Topica* and *Ad Herennium*, which Shakespeare would have studied in grammar school (Baldwin II.124–25).
undergo: carry the weight of, sustain (Riverside and Jenkins), support (Dowden in Jenkins), bear the weight of (Onions), have accumulated upon him (Johnson in Furness).

Shall in the general censure take corruption	35

Shall: is certain to (Abbott §315). **general censure:** in the context of the words "vicious," "guilty," "virtue," "grace," "corruption," "evil," and "o'erleaven," this phrase carries a double implication, meaning *both* public opinion about a man (as about a nation in lines 17–22) *and* the Last Judgment, God's judgment of the soul of every human being on Doomsday, cf., "general" at II.ii.437, 563, III.iii.23, and IV.vii.18 ● Jenkins' opinion that "general censure" refers to either "public opinion" or "the appraisal of the man as a whole, the overall estimate, in contrast with the '*particular* fault'" fatally reduces Hamlet's human concerns and the thematic seriousness of the play to worldly "reputation, or 'image'." In reality, in the world of this play, so charged with questions of the afterlife, and in Shakespeare's world generally, so rife with spiritual debate, this speech reveals Hamlet's far more pressing concern about the eternal state of the human soul and the risks to it. Hamlet is observing with dread that a man replete with virtues may, for a single fault not of his own choosing, be not only condemned by other men but damned by God.

From that particular fault. The dram of evil

dram: a very small amount (1/16 of an ounce, 1/8 of a fluid ounce, earlier spelling *drachm*, from Latin *drachma*, Greek *drachmē*). **evil:** This likeliest emendation for the famous crux of Q2's "eale" is supported by two arguments: It is the word "most likely to have given rise to *eale*" and it "fully satisfies the sense requirement for a word which will stand in opposition to *noble substance*. Cf. Sir Rich[ar]d Barckley, *The Felicity of Man*, 1598, page 568, 'Evil is no substance ..., but an accident that cometh to the substance, when it is void of those good qualities that ought naturally to be in them, and supplieth the other's absence with his presence'" (Jenkins LN). The applicability of the quotation from Barckley, which uses "substance" (an independently existent being, an essence) and "accident" (a quality or characteristic inhering or happening to a substance) in their medieval scholastic senses, is reinforced by the sense of "of a [do out]" (see next note and SPEECH NOTE below).

Doth all the noble substance of a [do out]

Of a [do out]: J. V. Cunningham's superb emendation of Q2's "of a doubt," a notorious crux, cf., IV.vii.191 note. **a:** him, as often in the play, cf., I.i.43 note.
[do out]: dout = put out, expel, extinguish (OED do v.49 and cf., our colloquial "do in" as "she done him in") ● The small taint of evil ("accident") drives out or extinguishes all the noble or virtuous "substance" (essence) of the man.

To his own scandal.

Enter Ghost

HORATIO

Look, my lord, it comes!

To: "with the consequence of" (Jenkins), perhaps "even up to," "all the way to" (Abbott §187). **his own:** referring either (if "his" is masculine) to him whose virtues may otherwise be pure and infinite (line 33) and so back to the plural "these men" (line 30) and "particular men" (line 23), or (if "his" is neuter, cf., I.i.37 note) to what amounts to the same thing, "all the noble substance of a," meaning his otherwise virtuous essence, his soul (see SPEECH NOTE below). • Probably it is both. **scandal:** both disgrace and, by implication in this context, damnation, cf., OED under "scandal," sb. 1a, 1b, and 3 and v. 3, and Landry for a discussion of biblical allusions in the whole passage.

• SPEECH NOTE: Hamlet's speech establishes a central theme of the play. As Denmark's custom of blowing trumpets and shooting cannon when the king drinks ruins the nation's reputation in the opinion of other nations, so one defect in an individual person may corrupt his reputation in the eyes of society and his soul in the judgment of God.

The speech lists three causes of this possible corruption in "particular men" (lines 24–32). Jenkins treats them as three illustrations of the "mole of nature" in line 24, i.e., three effects of nature as the agent: "The 'mole' or 'defect' [line 24] may occur in men a) 'in their birth', b) 'by their o'ergrowth of some complexion', or c) 'by some habit'" (Jenkins).

I think rather that they are three *kinds* of defect: The first kind of defect, taking only lines 25–26 as illustrating "mole of nature" in line 24, is entirely a function of nature, what we would call the physical, of which the person is "not guilty" (line 25) "Since nature cannot choose his origin" (line 26). That is, the flaw is unwilled, like a birth defect or perhaps lowness or illegitimacy of birth.

The second kind of defect (lines 27–28) involves reciprocal natural and human influences, reason being affected by an excess of one of the four humors, which occupy a position somewhere between what we would call the physical body and the emotions or personality, like hormones, and therefore involving some influence by the will. According to medieval and Renaissance physiology, a person's "complexion" (= make-up, nature, complex of qualities) is a function of the particular proportion or temperament of the four humors, blood, phlegm, choler (yellow bile), and melancholy (black bile), and of the mental and emotional qualities and hues of skin associated with them. Excess of a humor shows itself in one's "complexion" in both the physical sense (skin color) and the mental/behavioral senses: Excess blood makes one sanguine, jolly, fat, and red-faced, like Falstaff or Santa Claus; excess phlegm makes one dull, phlegmatic, gray; excess yellow bile makes one quick-tempered, angry, choleric, like Hotspur in *1 Henry IV*; excess black bile makes one sad, depressed, dark-faced, brooding, melancholy, like Don John in *Much*

Ado or Jaques in *As You Like It*. This imbalance in the "complexion" can break down the "pales [= fences] and forts" (line 28) that protect reason from nature. The even-tempered man, by contrast, has the four humors in just or harmonious proportion, as Hamlet implies about Horatio (III.ii.54, 69) and about Hamlet Senior (III.iv.55ff.), and Mark Antony claims about Brutus (*Julius Caesar* V.v.73–75), cf., V.ii.99.

The third kind of defect (lines 29–30) is something over which, as Hamlet implies to his mother at III.iv.160–70, the mind can have some influence if it chooses ("For use almost can change the stamp of nature"). Here some habit, in its various possible senses, whether custom, metaphorical dress, or demeanor (see line 29 note), if one allows it to do so, may corrupt one's normally praiseworthy manners.

Once he has listed these three kinds of relation between a possible defect and man's will, Hamlet asserts that even if the origin of the defect is outside himself, i.e., nature or fortune (line 32, cf., *As You Like It* I.ii.40–42), that single fault may corrupt the whole man, whatever other virtues he may have. According to the scholastic philosophy Hamlet would have been studying at Wittenberg, all these kinds of defect are "accidents," that is, non-essential characteristics that happen to or in a "substance" (= essence) but are not part of the substance itself. The "substance" or "substantial form" of a human being is the human soul. Hamlet says that any of these accidents (in the scholastic sense), even if totally unwilled, may corrupt a man by driving out his other virtues, however great, and ruin his noble substance—in social terms his reputation, in spiritual terms his eternal soul.

This speech made in general terms invites us to see every character in the play in light of its implications.

Fittingly, it is precisely when Hamlet has uttered this fear that the Ghost appears, the vehicle by which "all the noble substance of" Hamlet will be tested. It is in response to *both* the thought of damnation and the sudden appearance of the Ghost that Hamlet utters his fervent prayer for grace (Cunningham Sem.), suggesting that only divine grace can both counteract the "scandal" of damnation and defend men from ghosts.

Angels ... defend us: a prayer in the form of an imperative (= may you defend). **Angels and ministers of grace:** possibly a hendiadys for "angels who minister grace" (Wright, page 186). Ministers may be of heaven, as here and *Measure for Measure* V.i.115, of hell, as *Macbeth* I.v.48, or mixed human instruments of divine justice, as III.iv.175.

Be thou: subjunctive = whether thou be. **spirit of health ... charitable:** ● Hamlet, like Horatio later, recognizes that a ghost, whether it is a spirit taking the form of one who has died or the actual soul of that person, may be either a divine or a demonic messenger. Here "Hamlet addresses the Ghost not

HAMLET
Angels and ministers of grace defend us!

Be thou a spirit of health or goblin damned,   40

Bring with thee airs from heaven or blasts from hell,

Be thy intents wicked or charitable,

Thou com'st in such a questionable shape
That I will speak to thee; I'll call thee Hamlet,

King, father, royal Dane—O answer me!   45

Let me not burst in ignorance, but tell

Why thy canónized bones, hearsèd in death,

---

as his father's spirit but as a spirit in his father's shape. … The question [at this moment] is not whether his father is saved or damned but whether this is a good spirit or an evil one. Cf. [*Julius*] *Caes*[*ar*] IV.iii.277, 'Art thou some god, some angel, or some devil …?'" (Jenkins), cf., I.ii.243 and note. **health:** healing, "wholesome, good" (Riverside), "salvation" (Jenkins). **goblin:** devil, demon.

Bring: subjunctive = whether thou bring. **airs:** pleasant breezes. **blasts:** strong gusts of wind, also infection, blight (OED 1., 6.) ● Noel Taillepied, in *Traité de l'Apparition des Esprits* (1588), Ch. 15, "records that those who have seen spirits often find their lips crack and faces swell as if they have been struck with an ill wind" (cited in Jenkins). ● NOTE TO ACTORS: "Bring with" may be spoken as either a trochee or an iamb, and "heaven" may be elided to "heav'n."

Be thy intents: subjunctive = whether thy intents be. **intents:** intentions. **wicked or charitable:** again acknowledging that the spirit may be demonic or heavenly ("charitable" from *charity*, Latin *caritas*, translating Greek *agape*, the New Testament word for selfless Christian love). ● NOTE TO ACTORS: Lines 40–42 are not merely a list but a series of parallel antitheses: "spirit/goblin," "health/damned," "airs/blasts," "heaven/hell," "wicked/charitable" building up a single contrast.

Thou: the familiar form is used through the speech, suggesting intimacy. **questionable:** able to be conversed with, rational, "to question with" meaning to discuss with, cf., "that is the question" at III.i.55 and note and *Macbeth* I.iii.43. **shape:** i.e., of a human being, implying the ability to be conversed with.

royal Dane: i.e., king of Denmark ● Having addressed the Ghost as hypothetically angel or devil, he now addresses it as what it appears to be; he thus first believes it is his father here, then wisely doubts (II.ii.598ff.), then cleverly proves its honesty with the Mousetrap play in III.ii.

burst: The same word appears two lines below, leading Jenkins to assert that "Shakespeare could use the same expressive word twice within three lines." True, but that is to avoid the point that it is a physical bursting, of the cerements (line 48), that threatens a mental or spiritual bursting of the mind or soul here. ● NOTE TO ACTORS: The line begins with a trochee, "Lét mě," which throws a heavy stress onto "burst."

Why thy canónized … up again: ● "A traditional motive of the classical ghost was to demand proper burial. The emphasis here upon the due formality, the finality … and the sanctity of the burial rites makes the appearance of *this* ghost the more unaccountable" (Jenkins LN). It also reinforces the dramatic preparation for the Ghost's appearance from a Christian rather than a classical afterlife (see Introduction, pages 2–4). **canónized:** buried with proper religious rites, the stress is on the second syllable (Abbott §491).

Have burst their cerements; why the sepulcher

burst: see line 46 note. **cerements:** shroud, burial clothes, two syllables, the first *e* is long and the first syllable is stressed (Fr. *cirement*, a waxing, from *cirer*, to wax, cf., *cerecloth*, waxed cloth, not related to *ceremony*).

Wherein we saw thee quietly interred

interred: buried, Q2 interr'd, F enurn'd. For the F reading see OED urn *sb.* 1., *v.*² b., *Henry V* I.ii.228–29, and *Coriolanus* V.vi.144. It is preferred by Jenkins and Riverside as "a word formed in Shakespeare's manner and ... much less easily explained as a corruption of *interr'd* (Q1, Q2) than the other way about" (Jenkins LN). Jenkins' argument is strong, but I have not been persuaded in this case to go against the generally greater authority of Q2, which is also followed by Q1, Q3, and Q4.

Hath oped his ponderous and marble jaws   50

oped: opened. **his:** its, cf., I.i.37 note. **ponderous and marble jaws:** heavy marble jaws, the tomb and its lid, a hendiadys (Wright, page 186), cf., *Romeo and Juliet* V.iii.47, and Battenhouse (PMLA XLVIII, 173), who "finds a reminiscence of Christ's emergence from the tomb and its prefiguring in Jonah's from the whale (Matthew xii.39–40)" (cited in Jenkins).

To cast thee up again. What may this mean,

may: can (Abbott §307).

That thou, dead corse, again in cómplete steel

corse: corpse. **in cómplete steel:** in full armor, cf., I.i.60, I.ii.200; "*Complete*, like many other disyllabic adjectives, takes the stress on either syllable. See Walker, *Sh[akespeare]'s Versification*, pages 291–95. Hence *cómplete* will be normal before a noun accented on the first syllable, *compléte* predicatively. Cf. *secure*, I.v.61; *absurd*, III.ii.60; *profound*, IV.i.1" (Jenkins), cf., Abbott §492.

Revisits thus the glimpses of the moon,

revisits: for "revisitest," -*test* becoming -*ts* for euphony (Abbott §340). **glimpses:** intermittent flashes or shinings (OED 1.) and intermittent glances upon the Ghost by the moon personified (OED 3.).

Making night hideous and we fools of nature

hideous: causing dread, frightening (OED 1.), cf., II.ii.476 and *Romeo and Juliet* IV.iii.50. **we:** the subjective pronoun (or possibly here the pronominal adjective) is often used in place of an objective pronoun after a conjunction and before an infinitive (Abbott §216). **fools of nature:** playthings or dupes of nature, subject to the limitations of the natural order and thus baffled or confounded by the supernatural, as in line 56 (Riverside, Jenkins substantially), cf., "Time's Fool" in Sonnet 116.9, "fortune's fool" in *Romeo and Juliet* III.i.136, "Death's fool" in *Measure for Measure* III.i.11. ● NOTE TO ACTORS: "Making" is a trochee, "hideous" is probably to be elided into "HID-yus," "and" is in the stressed position, and "we fools" may be a spondee, hence "Máking night hídeous ánd wé fóols of náture." The next line by contrast then has only three major stresses.

So horridly to shake our disposition   55
With thoughts beyond the reaches of our souls?

disposition: natural condition of our mental and physical faculties, cf., *Merry Wives* IV.v.109.

Say why is this? wherefore? what should we do?

Ghost beckons Hamlet.

HORATIO
It beckons you to go away with it

As if it some impartment did desire
To you alone.
MARCELLUS
                    Look with what courteous action   60
It waves you to a more removèd ground.
But do not go with it.
HORATIO
                    No, by no means.
HAMLET
It will not speak; then I will follow it.
HORATIO
Do not, my lord.
HAMLET
                    Why, what should be the fear?
I do not set my life at a pin's fee,   65
And for my soul, what can it do to that,
Being a thing immortal as itself?
It waves me forth again. I'll follow it.

HORATIO
What if it tempt you toward the flood, my lord,
Or to the dreadful summit of the cliff   70

why … wherefore?: why = what is the cause, wherefore = for what purpose (Abbott §75). **what should we do?:** • In keeping with common beliefs, Hamlet, like Horatio (I.i.130–39), assumes that the Ghost appears in order to assign them a task or call them to an action, and this turns out to be the case. The Ghost will charge Hamlet alone with the central imperative of the play.
impartment: communication, disclosure.

action: gesture.
waves: beckons with a wave of the hand or arm, as again at lines 68 and 78.

set: rate, value (OED *set* v. 89 b.), cf. IV.iii.62.
life … soul: • "It is one of these that the Ghost, if it were a devil, would be aiming at. Cf. James I, *Demonology*, III.2, where the devil is said to trouble men 'to obtain one of two things … The one is the tinsel of their life … The other … is the tinsel of their soul'" (Jenkins). **what can it do … itself?:** • Since a man's soul cannot be harmed except by what his free will chooses (cf., Plato *Apology*, 41d, Aquinas *Summa Theologica*, II.1.80.3), the danger to the soul if the Ghost were a demon would lie not in a direct attack, as would the danger to the life, but in the offer of a temptation to sin, a possibility that Hamlet does not consider either here or in lines 23–38 above, where he locates the source of corruption in the "stamp of one defect," man's free will remaining unaddressed. The play's answer to Hamlet's question here is twofold: The Ghost, being not a devil but a vehicle for the divine calling of Hamlet (as the Mousetrap play will confirm to Hamlet and the King's confession in III. iii will confirm to the audience), will not itself harm either Hamlet's life or his soul. The Ghost does offer, however, the occasion of a temptation, which will come in III.iii, not in the form of any imperative from the Ghost but from within Hamlet himself.

tempt: • It is the rational Horatio that recognizes the real danger as lying in temptation, here potentially offered by a devil "who aims at the lives of his victims 'by inducing them to … perilous places' (James I, [*Demonology*, III.2]. Dover Wilson compares [*King Lear*] IV.vi.67–72, where Edgar pretends that it was 'some fiend' that brought Gloucester to the [imaginary] cliff-top" (Jenkins). **flood:** the sea, overlooked, as Shakespeare implies, by tall cliffs.

That beetles o'er his base into the sea,

And there assume some other horrible form

Which might deprive your sovereignty of reason
And draw you into madness? Think of it.

The very place puts toys of desperation,   75
Without more motive, into every brain
That looks so many fathoms to the sea
And hears it roar beneath.

HAMLET
                    It waves me still.
  Go on, I'll follow thee.
MARCELLUS
  You shall not go, my lord.
HAMLET
                    Hold off your hands.   80
HORATIO
  Be ruled; you shall not go.
HAMLET
                    My fate cries out

beetles: Shakespeare's coining of a nonce word from beetle-browed, implying not (as now) merely projecting and overhanging but probably some reference to the eyebrows, and therefore either to scowling or, possibly, to the shrubbery that projects over the edge of the cliff as eyebrows do over the lower parts of the face and thus offer only illusory and precarious footing (see OED *v.*¹ 1. and *a.*).

horrible form: contrasted with the familiar and beloved form of Hamlet's father, cf., *King Lear* IV.vi.69–72.

deprive: remove, carry off (OED 5.), a sense in which "the direct object is the thing taken away, not, as in the more familiar construction (as at V.i.[249]), the person dispossessed," cf., *Rape of Lucrece* lines 1186 and 1752 and Abbott §200 (Jenkins LN). **your sovereignty of reason:** "your" modifies either "reason" (the sovereignty of your reason), cf., III.ii.[337–38] and Abbott §423, or the whole phrase "which refers to the proper condition of man in which reason is supreme," cf., III.i.157 and Milton, *Paradise Lost* IX.1130 (Jenkins LN) ● Reason, being the highest of man's faculties, properly rules the lesser faculties of emotion and sensation. Hence it is the sovereign power in the microcosmic kingdom that is a man and the power by which man is sovereign over himself. Horatio fears that the Ghost might be a demon taking the form of the dead king for the purpose of temptation, a devil in disguise, and that some shape such as that which a demon might take could remove the proper governor over Hamlet, his sovereign reason, and leave him prey to irrational fantasies, in which condition he might harm himself.

The very place ... beneath: the place itself, even without the presence of a ghost or demon, because of its height, could put into the mind fantasies or impulses of despair, and hence of leaping to one's death, cf., *King Lear* IV.vi.11–24. **toys:** fancies, whims, irrational impulses, false notions, cf., I.iii.6 note and *Romeo and Juliet* IV.i.119. **motive:** inducement or prompting (OED *sb.* 4.), possibly a supernatural one (OED 2.c.).

still: continuously, without stopping.

You shall not go, my lord: ● In this imperative, made by an inferior to a superior in extreme circumstances, Marcellus shows that there is a higher obedience than the merely hierarchical. He takes it upon himself to try to overrule the apparent extremity of the Prince's passion. Not seeing the whole picture, he is not right to do so. But his impulse, arising from care and obedience rather than from pride, is not either sinful or harmful. The same is true of Horatio at line 81. As throughout the play, one is charged to obey

And makes each petty artire in this body
As hardy as the Nemean lion's nerve.
Still am I called. Unhand me, gentlemen.

By heaven, I'll make a ghost of him that lets me.   85
I say away.—Go on, I'll follow thee.

Exeunt Ghost and Hamlet.

HORATIO
He waxes desperate with imagination.

MARCELLUS
Let's follow. 'Tis not fit thus to obey him.

HORATIO
Have after. To what issue will this come?

MARCELLUS
Something is rotten in the state of Denmark.   90

HORATIO
Heaven will direct it.

MARCELLUS
    Nay, let's follow him.

Exeunt.

---

an imperative not merely by doing it but by doing it rightly. ●NOTE TO ACTORS: "My fate cries out" may be read as two iambs, but perhaps should be an iamb and a spondee, making three heavy stresses in a row.

petty artire … nerve: ●NOTE TO ACTORS: See the following notes to these two lines for the intended pronunciation and antithesis. **artire:** Jenkins, Riverside artere, Q2 arture, F Artire, Q3 artyre, Q1 Artiue, Q5 artery, here meaning sinew (Kittredge, cf., OED artery 5., influenced by French *artère*). **Nemean lion:** killed by Hercules in the first of his nine labors, after which he wore its pelt. Shakespeare seems to intend *Nemean* to be stressed on the first syllable, as in *Love's Labor's Lost* IV.i.88 and Golding's translation of Ovid's *Metamorphoses* IV.242 (Jenkins substantially). **nerve:** sinew (Riverside), synonymous with "artire" in the previous line, making the antithesis between "this body" and "lion" (which therefore takes a heavy stress) rather than between "artire" and "nerve."

By heaven: i.e., I swear by heaven, a passionate oath. **lets:** obstructs, hinders (OED let *v.*² 1., and *sb.*¹, cf., a let ball in games like tennis or ping pong).

waxes: grows (OED *v.*¹ 1.). **desperate:** reckless, ready to run any risk, careless (OED 4.), cf., *Twelfth Night* V.i.64. **imagination:** fantasy, mental invention, as at III.ii.83, which may be associated with madness as in *Midsummer Night's Dream* V.i.10 and 14, where it is also associated with poetry and love, and *2 Henry IV* I.iii.31–32, or with "the work of spirits" as in *Merry Wives* III.iii.215–16. ●Jenkins suggests that "Horatio, still fearing for Hamlet's 'sovereignty of reason' (lines 73–74), sees him succumbing to the influence of the spirit," but Horatio, though aware that a spirit *could* be the cause of Hamlet's extreme passion to follow the Ghost, is nevertheless not explicit about that cause because, being the rational man, he does not leap to conclusions.

'Tis not fit … obey him: see above line 80 note

Have after: let us follow him. **issue:** outcome, eventuality.

in the state: two senses are present: in the condition of the nation and in the nation itself and the government identified with it. ●With perhaps a foreshadowing sense (not intended by Horatio) that something is rotten in the King, who is called Denmark.

Heaven will … follow him: "it" = the "issue" of line 89. ●The previous line of Marcellus has become famous through repeated quotation, but Horatio's response is the more important line. Horatio knows intellectually and on principle what Hamlet will learn more profoundly through tragic experience—that whatever human beings do, "There's a divinity that shapes our ends" (V.ii.10). At the same time, with his "Nay," Marcellus recognizes that the moment calls for action, not merely for philosophical acceptance, and Horatio, recognizing the justice of that call, joins him in following Hamlet. The two together are a picture of the two qualities Hamlet is about to reveal in the next line, the first of the next scene—passionate action and rational reflection. Only when Hamlet has revealed both a willingness to follow the Ghost and an ability to draw a line and to go no further is he ready to receive the crucial revelation and imperative from the other world.

Act I, Scene v

Enter Ghost and Hamlet.

Act I, Scene v ● A different area on the battlements of the castle.

HAMLET
Whither wilt thou lead me? Speak. I'll go no further.

Speak: A ghost cannot speak until spoken to, and by the one for whom he has a message, cf., I.i.29 note. **I'll go no further:** ● At the risk of his life and his mind Hamlet has been willing to follow the Ghost (I.iv.63ff.). But the Ghost does not speak until Hamlet says, "I'll go no further." This is a dramatic enactment of the advice Polonius has given to Laertes (I.iii.59–80) and Hamlet will give to the players (III.ii.1–45) and of the golden mean characteristic of all reasonable charges given in the play: go so far but no further; do but do not overdo. It will also characterize the Ghost's own charge to Hamlet (lines 81–86). Only when Hamlet exhibits this quality of moderation does the Ghost finally speak. Cf., I.ii.159, where Horatio, the embodiment of reason, enters only when Hamlet has reasonably decided not to act on his passionate antipathy to Claudius.

GHOST
Mark me.
HAMLET
    I will.

Mark: listen, pay attention, the Ghost's first spoken word.

GHOST
    My hour is almost come
When I to sulph'rous and tormenting flames
Must render up myself.
HAMLET
    Alas, poor ghost.

My hour: dawn, cf., I.i.147–57 and lines 58–59 below. **sulph'rous and tormenting flames:** a hendiadys (Wright, page 186) and a classical image: "'Sulphurish flame' is referred to in *Orpheus his Journey to Hell* (st. 45), by R.B., 1595, and, as a torment of the classical underworld, it is familiar to the stage ghost of the Senecan tradition (e.g. *Locrine*, III.vi.51, 'burning sulphur of the Limbo-lake')" (Jenkins).
● This reference, particularly after the talk of ghosts in relation to the Christmas season at I.i.158–64, raises the question whether the Ghost has come from classical Hades or from Christian Hell or Purgatory (see Introduction, pages 2–4).

GHOST
Pity me not, but lend thy serious hearing   5

To what I shall unfold.
HAMLET
                          Speak; I am bound to hear.

GHOST
So art thou to revenge when thou shalt hear.

HAMLET
  What?
GHOST
  I am thy father's spirit,

Doomed for a certain term to walk the night,   10

And for the day confined to fast in fires,

Pity me not: • That Hamlet is told not to pity the Ghost suggests that the Ghost is suffering God's just punishment and that Hamlet is to focus instead on the mission he is about to be given.

To what ... bound to hear: The apparent hexameter may be seen as a trimeter couplet (Abbott §500) or may be a pentameter if "I shall" and "I am" are elided. **bound:** both a) directed toward, prepared to undertake, intending, as at IV.vi.11 ("bound for England"), and b) under obligation, as at I.ii.90–91 ("bound / In filial obligation"). Both senses may also be present at III.iii.41 "to double business bound." • Whether Hamlet also means bound by "inescapable fate" (Jenkins, referring to I.iv.81) is questionable, and whether he *is* bound by fate remains to be seen. Hamlet seems to have chosen by free will to follow and hear the Ghost.

So art thou: i.e., bound, now in the sense of being under an obligation, cf., previous note.
revenge: • Hamlet's earlier suspicion of foul play is now fulfilled in the call to revenge. If it has not earlier, the audience now understands that it is watching a revenge play of the kind that they have likely seen before (especially in the popular *Spanish Tragedy*). But a new and profound question is raised. As a gesture of nobility, revenge may be acceptable for an ancient avenger in the context of a classical underworld. But Shakespeare's Christian audience knew that God said, "To me belongeth vengeance and recompence" (Deuteronomy 32:35), that St. Paul wrote, "avenge not yourselves, but rather give place unto wrath: for it is written, Vengeance is mine; I will repay, saith the Lord" (Romans 12:19). Is it proper for a Christian prince to take revenge when commanded to do so by a ghost when the context is the actual universe Christians believe in, as opposed to a fictional classical universe? Does this ghost have the authority to command it? Is the Ghost a messenger from heaven calling for justice or a demon from hell tempting to sin?

What?: i.e., bound to revenge what crime?

I am ... spirit: Hamlet will believe this statement at first (lines 137–38), then doubt it (II.ii.598–604), then confirm it (III.ii.286–87).

Doomed: sentenced, consigned. OED at doom *v.* 3., citing this line, implies an impersonal fate or destiny, but sense 2., "judged," "condemned," is more apt, the judge being God.

for the day: as regards the daytime (Abbott §149).
confined ... away: • NOTE TO ACTORS: Here the sound of the sentence incarnates its meaning. With alliteration on the letter *f*, antithesis between the *fi* sounds and the *ay* sounds, and the *ur-t* and *ur-d* sounds between them, the poet makes the *fi* sound imply sins, the *ur* sounds imply purging and the *way*

Till the foul crimes done in my days of nature

Are burnt and purged away. But that I am forbid
To tell the secrets of my prison-house,
I could a tale unfold whose lightest word   15

Would harrow up thy soul, freeze thy young blood,
Make thy two eyes like stars start from their spheres,

sound (echoing *day* and *nature*) imply disappearance of sin. Thus *ur* turns *fi* to *way* even as *confined, fast, fires, foul,* and *crimes* are *purged* to the open sound and freedom from sin of *away*. **to fast:** to be deprived of something in a spiritual discipline (OED fast $v.^2$ I.), cf., *As You Like It* III.v.58, but possibly also specifically of food and drink, one of the commonly imagined deprivations of hell, cf., Chaucer's "Parson's Tale," line 194, in a passage also mentioning fire.

foul crimes: sins, imperfections, cf., line 79 below and II.i.43, III.iii.81, not necessarily terrible ones but seen so from the point of view of the judged soul in the afterlife. **days of nature:** when alive in the world.

burnt and purged: possibly a hendiadys (Wright, page 186). ● At this point we know that if the Ghost is in fact the spirit of Hamlet's father and is telling the truth, his sufferings take place in a Christian, not a classical, afterlife, and that they are not eternal but temporary and purgatorial. The idea is confirmed by lines 76–79. Catholics believed in the doctrine of Purgatory, which "gained support from accounts of ghosts which claimed to come from there. But Protestants, who held that the dead went straight to heaven or hell, whence they did not return, saw in these only evidence of the deceits of diabolic spirits" (Jenkins LN). Shakespeare thus makes use of both beliefs at once, leaving us uncertain, at this point, about whether the Ghost is truthful or not. The tradition of the idea of purgatorial suffering in the afterlife is long, cf., Plato *Phaedo* (113d–114b), Virgil *Aeneid* (VI.742), Augustine *City of God* (XX.25, XXI.24), Thomas Aquinas, *Summa Theologica* (Suppl. III, Appendix II, Art. 1), Dante *Purgatorio*, More's *Supplication of Souls* (*Works*, 1557, page 321), and many others. Everyone in Shakespeare's audience would have been familiar with the doctrine and imagery of purgatory, whatever he or she believed. Because the play is set in a foreign land, Shakespeare could make dramatic use of that imagery without being thought to be promoting the doctrine. **But that:** except that, if I were not. **forbid:** for the curtailed past participle, see Abbott §343.

harrow: lacerate, see I.i.44 note.

Make ... start ... to part: for the omitted *to* before "start" and inserted before "part" see Abbott §350. **start from their spheres:** jump out of their sockets (OED start $v.$ 3.b.). ● In the old Ptolemaic astronomy, stars and planets (also called stars) were thought to revolve around the earth attached to invisible concentric crystalline spheres. Just as a meteor, a star that has left its sphere, signified disorder in the heavens and a bad omen for earth, so the disorder of terror in the human person was signified by the popping of the eyes (also sources of light in the old theory of optics) out of their proper spheres (the eye sockets or possibly the head).

Thy knotted and combinèd locks to part,

And each particular hair to stand an end

Like quills upon the fretful porpentine.   20

But this eternal blazon must not be
To ears of flesh and blood. List, list, O list!
If thou didst ever thy dear father love—

HAMLET
O God!

GHOST
Revenge his foul and most unnatural murder.   25
HAMLET
Murder!

knotted and combinèd: a hendiadys (Wright, page 186). **combinèd:** intertwined. **locks:** of hair.

an: "not just a variant spelling of *on* but the preposition *a*, the weakened form of O.E. *on* (cf., *afire, afoot,* II.ii.[488] *awork*) with *n* retained before a vowel. So at III.iv.122 ["stand an end"], *R[ichard] 3* I.iii.304 (F), *2H[enry] 6* III.ii.318 (F). See OED A *prep.*[1], An *prep.,* An-end *phr.*" (Jenkins). ● cf., also II.ii.387–88, V.i.23, and *an edge* in *1 Henry IV* III.i.131, *Winter's Tale* IV.iii.7, and Abbott §24.

fretful: F and Q1, frightened (Q2 "fearful"). **porpentine:** porcupine.

eternal blazon: detailed description of the spiritual ("eternal," OED 3.b.) world, the antithesis of "eternal" being "flesh and blood" in the next line (OED gives no evidence supporting Abbott's taking "eternal" to mean "infernal," page 16 note). ● A blazon was literally a heraldic coat-of-arms but came to mean a) a vivid description, b) a kind of poem, particularly a sonnet, describing the beloved's qualities part by part, and c) an unrestrained proclamation, cf., Sonnet 106.5, Sonnet 130 (an anti-blazon), and *Twelfth Night* I.v.293, *Othello* II.i.63, etc.. **List:** listen.

Revenge … murder: ● This, together with line 85, forms the central imperative of the play. It names what crime is to be revenged and adds to Horatio's list (I.ii.130ff.) one more familiar reason why ghosts may appear to the living, i.e., to seek revenge, an idea dating back to Plato (*Laws,* IX.865d), present among the common people, and dramatized in the tragedies of Seneca, where the Elizabethan and Jacobean revenge play tradition finds its source (cf., Kyd's popular *Spanish Tragedy* and Marston's *Antonio's Revenge,* which predate *Hamlet*). In the earlier plays in the revenge tradition, the supernatural machinery, the invisible world surrounding the action, was pictured in ancient classical terms. When gods were mentioned, they were the Greek and Roman gods, and any implied afterlife was more or less like that described in Book VI of Virgil's *Aeneid,* where shades of the dead live in a sort of limbo or netherworld of non-physical existence in which only memory or prophecy but not life was real. In *Hamlet* Shakespeare does something radically contrasting. He sets the revenge play within the Christian context, from his and his audience's point of view the real rather than fictional universe. And because in Christianity personal revenge is forbidden and love of one's enemies is commanded, *Hamlet* becomes a test case for revenge itself. Because the execution of justice by a just ruler, since St. Augustine's *City of God,* is not forbidden as personal vengeance is, the play raises a variety of questions: What does revenge mean? Who can enact it? When? With what motives? If vengeance belongs to God, what or who are his instruments? In addressing these questions, *Hamlet* also addresses the question of

GHOST
  Murder most foul, as in the best it is,
  But this most foul, strange, and unnatural.

HAMLET
  Haste me to know't, that I with wings as swift
  As meditation or the thoughts of love   30

  May sweep to my revenge.

GHOST
                               I find thee apt,

  And duller shouldst thou be than the fat weed
  That roots itself in ease on Lethe wharf,

  Wouldst thou not stir in this. Now, Hamlet, hear:

  'Tis given out that, sleeping in my orchard,   35

  A serpent stung me; so the whole ear of Denmark

  Is by a forgèd process of my death
  Rankly abused. But know, thou noble youth,
  The serpent that did sting thy father's life
  Now wears his crown.

---

what constitutes right action and right motives for any man alive in the morally complex universe we all inhabit (see Introduction, pages 2–5).

foul: wicked, detestable, treacherous (OED 7., 14.b.).

strange: aberrant, exceptional. **unnatural:** against nature, kin, and kind because fratricidal, hence especially vile, cf., I.ii.65 and note.

swift … thoughts of love: This hyperbole of the speed of thought, and particularly thoughts of love, often contrasted with the slowness and stupidity of stones and lead, is based on the ancient image of the mind's greater likeness to the elements of air and fire in its mobility, as opposed to the slower and heavier elements of water and earth, images that would have been learned by Shakespeare in grammar school in his study of the *Thesaurus* of Susenbrotus (1565, page 19) and the *Copia* (1566, pages 145, 402) of Erasmus (Baldwin II.148–49) and had become proverbial, cf., Tilley T 240. Thought itself being swift, uninterrupted thought ("meditation") and thought of love (driven by desire) must be even swifter, cf., *Love's Labor's Lost* IV.iii.327–30, V.ii.261, *Henry V* III.vii.21–23, *Romeo and Juliet* II.v.4–5.

sweep to my revenge: ● In the moment, Hamlet is indeed ready to rush to revenge. Later he will reconsider, and for good reasons (II.ii.598–603).

apt: suited, fit, prepared, ready (OED *a.* 2.b.) and also ready to learn, susceptible (OED *a.* 5.), cf., "readiness" at V.ii.222.

duller: more sleepy, less apt to act, more phlegmatic. **shouldst:** would, "*should* is frequently used to denote contingent futurity" (Abbott §322). **than the fat weed… Lethe wharf:** perhaps the poppy, which itself causes sleepy dullness (cf., *Othello* III.iii.330), that grows on the bank ("wharf") of Lethe, the river of forgetfulness in the classical underworld, the image derived from Virgil *Georgics* I.78 and *Aeneid* VI.713-15, 748-51, cf., Baldwin II.468-70. Jenkins does not concur and asserts that "Shakespeare need have had no particular plant in mind" (Jenkins LN). ● NOTE TO ACTORS: "than the" is a pyrrhic foot and "fat weed" a spondee. **roots:** Q2 and Q1, F has "rots," defended by Dover Wilson and Kittredge, citing *Antony and Cleopatra* I.iv.44-47 ("This common body…rot itself with motion") but rightly rejected by Jenkins because the point is not the mob's erratic motion, as there, but a fixed and unmoved dullness. **Lethe:** For the noun used as adjective, cf., Abbott §22.

Wouldst thou not: if you were not to. **stir:** move briskly, get busy (OED *v.* II.14)". **this:** this matter.

given out: announced, said publicly. **orchard:** enclosed garden for herbs and fruit trees.

stung: poisonously wounded (OED sting *v.*¹ 2.), cf., *2 Henry VI*, III.ii.266-67. **whole ear:** the hearing of everyone.

forgèd process: fabricated report of events.

Rankly: foully, flagrantly. **abused:** deceived.

HAMLET

                O my prophetic soul!   40
  My uncle!

GHOST

  Ay, that incestuous, that adulterate beast,

my prophetic soul: cf., Hamlet's "I doubt some foul play" at I.ii.255.

incestuous ... adulterate beast: ● In wishing to seduce Gertrude, Claudius is aiming at the wife of another man (adultery), who is also his brother (incest). He is bestial in permitting his lust to overrule the particularly human faculties of reason and moral responsibility. The beast in Plato's tripartite image of man represents sensual desire, which must be governed by the mind through the agency of the well-trained heart. Whether or not Claudius literally seduced the queen before his brother's death is not made explicit, and for good reason. Our attention is to be focused on the wills of the sinners more than on their specific actions. The will to incestuous and adulterous relations in Claudius and Gertrude is meant to seem vile whether or not it was sexually consummated before the murder. The same applies to the other evidence for their adultery (lines 45–57 and 105, III.iv.44–45, 66–71, and V.ii.64). The entire play is an unfolding of the drama of the will, of which the external action is the revelation and the vehicle, conveying that inner drama to our experience.

With witchcraft of his wits, with traitorous gifts—
O wicked wit and gifts that have the power
So to seduce!—won to his shameful lust   45

witchcraft: use of magic was a commonplace accusation against seducers, e.g., seriously in *Othello* I.ii.63–65, comically in *Midsummer Night's Dream* I.i.27ff., and cf., *Antonio's Revenge* III.v.8–9. **wits:** Q2, F, Riverside, Pope emends to "wit" based on the singular in the next line. **traitorous gifts:** either "gifts of mind and manner" (Kittredge) or physical presents, which would make an antithesis to "natural gifts" at line 51. ● The gifts are traitorous in pretending to offer value but will betray the receiver into sin and self-destruction.

The will of my most seeming-virtuous queen.

will: as often in the plays and sonnets (esp. 134, 135, 136), the word has multiple congruent layers of meaning: the free will, desire generally, any particular desire or intention, specifically sexual desire, and genitalia. ● Claudius has won over the free will and the sexual lust (and possibly the physical parts) of Gertrude.

O Hamlet, what a falling-off was there,

a falling-off: a fall, a decline, as in line 50. The "a" is missing in Q2, but "Meter favours the article, which F supplies. But cf. Q2 *What*, F *What a* at II.ii.303" (Jenkins), and cf., Abbott §86.

From me, whose love was of that dignity

that: that degree of, that much (Abbott §277). **dignity:** worth, worthiness (OED 1.), cf., *Midsummer Night's Dream* I.i.233, *Troilus and Cressida* I.iii.204, *Macbeth* V.i.56, etc.

That it went hand in hand even with the vow

hand in hand ... marriage: ● The love of Hamlet Senior was such that his actions corresponded perfectly with his marriage vows: he was loving and faithful as promised.

I made to her in marriage, and to decline   50

decline: fall, lower oneself, as in line 47.

Upon a wretch whose natural gifts were poor

To those of mine.

But virtue, as it never will be moved,

Though lewdness court it in a shape of heaven,

So lust, though to a radiant angel linked,   55
Will sate itself in a celestial bed
And prey on garbage.

But soft, methinks I scent the morning air;

Brief let me be. Sleeping within my orchard,
My custom always of the afternoon,   60
Upon my sécure hour thy uncle stole

With juice of cursèd hebona in a vial,

And in the porches of my ears did pour
The leperous distilment, whose effect

Holds such an enmity with blood of man   65

That swift as quicksilver it courses through
The natural gates and alleys of the body,

wretch: a combination of two senses (OED 2 and 3), both a miserable and hapless person, because of the poverty of his gifts, and a despicable and reprehensible one, because of his bad will and actions.

To: compared to. ● NOTE TO ACTORS: The empty feet indicate a pause, here and below at line 57.

virtue: "Sometimes a noun occurs in a prominent position at the beginning of a sentence, to express the subject of the thought, without the usual grammatical connection with a verb or preposition" (Abbott §417).

a shape of heaven: an angelic form, "The Bible says that 'Satan himself is transformed into an angel of light' (2 Corinthians xi.14), and in Christian legend he often tempted saints and ascetics by appearing to them in dreams in the likeness of another saint or a beautiful woman. See *Meas[ure for Measure]* II.ii.179–81. The word *shape*, denoting an assumed appearance or an acted role, often in itself implied deception" (Jenkins).

linked: as in marriage. **sate itself ... And prey on garbage:** become sated or fed up to the point of disgust with the good and turn away to go after the vile. **celestial:** heavenly.

soft: wait, enough of that. **methinks:** it seems to me, from an obsolete sense of *think* (OED *think v.*), meaning to seem, appear, *me* being in the dative case. **morning air:** Cf., I.i.149–56.

orchard: see line 35 note.

of: during (Abbott §176).

sécure: carefree, unsuspecting, unconcerned, from the Latin *securus*, with the stress on the first syllable, as in *Othello* IV.i.71, cf., I.iv.52 note and Abbott §492. To be secure in this sense means not to be free from danger but to *think* one is so. **stole:** crept quietly and secretly (OED steal *v.* 10.).

hebona: Q2 and Q1 Hebona, F Hebenon, from the Latin and Greek for ebony. ● "Juice of hebon" was a poison in Marlowe's earlier *Jew of Malta* (III.iv.98), but I agree with Jenkins that any identification of it with an actual poisonous plant, whether henbane or something else, involves mere conjecture and that Shakespeare "surely relied ... on a suggestion of the fabulous to intensify the horror" (Jenkins, LN).

porches: vestibule, outer approaches.

leperous: "creating scales on the body like leprosy" (Jenkins), cf., lines 71–73. **distilment:** distillation (of the plant), drops.

enmity: hostility, mutual natural antipathy. **with blood of man:** *the* is frequently omitted before a noun modified by a prepositional phrase (Abbott §89).

quicksilver: mercury, which at room temperature is liquid, mobile, and in Bacon's words "hard to hold or imprison" (OED *n.* 2.). **courses:** runs, rushes.

And with a sudden vigor it doth posset
And curd, like eager droppings into milk,

> **vigor:** active force or power, intensity of effect (OED vigour 3.b.). **posset:** as a noun, "a drink composed of hot milk curdled with ale, wine, or other liquor" (OED), here used as a verb, to curdle (OED *v.* a., quoting this passage). **curd:** curdle, coagulate. **eager:** sharp, sour, acidic (F has "Aygre"), from Latin *acer* (sharp, pungent) via French *aigre*, sharp, keen, sour, acidic (cf., *vin aigre*, vinegar and *eisel* V.i.276), i.e., the poison curdled his blood as vinegar or acidic alcohol curdles milk.

The thin and wholesome blood. So did it mine,   70

> **thin:** "The natural condition of the blood in health," whereas blood in a body suffering from the excess humor of black bile (melancholy) is "thick and gross" (Jenkins, quoting Bright's *Treatise of Melancholy*, p. 270). **thin and wholesome:** possibly a hendiadys (Wright, page 186).

And a most instant tetter barked about,

> **tetter:** scabby skin eruption. **barked:** covered with bark, like a tree.

Most lazar-like, with vile and loathsome crust
All my smooth body.
Thus was I, sleeping, by a brother's hand

> **lazar-like:** like a leper, from the parable of Lazarus (Luke 16:20ff.), the syntax being "a tetter wrapped my whole smooth body in bark with a vile and disgusting crust like that of a leper." **crust:** scab.

Of life, of crown, of queen, at once dispatched,   75

> **dispatched:** deprived, bereaved (OED dispatch *v.* 7.b., quoting this passage), cf., the sense of being rid of by putting to death (OED 4).

Cut off even in the blossoms of my sin,

> **Cut off:** ● NOTE TO ACTORS: The hard *c* and *t*, by their suddenness and contrast with the *s* and *n* sounds that follow, and the initial spondee, by its contrast with the unstressed syllables that follow, incarnate in sound the meaning of the line, the abruptness of the sudden end ("cut off") of a sinning life ("blossoms ... sin"), the *o* in "blossoms" echoing the *o* in "off" and the *n* sounds persisting in the next line.

Unhouseled, disappointed, unaneled,

> **Unhouseled ... unaneled:** not having received the last rites of the Church. **Unhouseled:** not having received the Eucharist, or *housel*, from an Old English word meaning sacrifice or offering. **disappointed:** improperly appointed, equipped, or fitted out, unfurnished, unprepared, i.e., by not having made confession to and been absolved by a priest, cf., *Measure for Measure* III.i.59. **unaneled:** unanointed with the holy oil of extreme unction. ● NOTE TO ACTORS: the repetition of the negating prefixes and "No" in the next line emphasize the spiritual absence consequent on the sudden and sharp "Cut off" in the previous line.

No reckoning made, but sent to my account
With all my imperfections on my head.
O horrible! O horrible! most horrible!   80

> **No reckoning ... head:** Dying by violence, Hamlet Senior has not had the time or opportunity to reckon up his sins in order to repent of them, do penance, and receive absolution. As a result he has gone to God's judgment of his soul ("account") with his sins still counting against him.

If thou hast nature in thee, bear it not;
Let not the royal bed of Denmark be

> **nature:** natural filial feeling, as at III.ii.393, III.iii.32, V.ii.231, 244, and 2 *Henry IV* IV.v.37–40 (Jenkins). **bear it not:** contrast with the opposite imperative of Claudius at I.ii.106–107 and note.

A couch for luxury and damnèd incest.

couch: bed, animal's lair (Raffel). **luxury:** lust.
incest: cf., line 42 note.

But howsomever thou pursues this act,

howsomever ... act: however you proceed, whatever
you do, cf., line 170.

Taint not thy mind, nor let thy soul contrive   85

Taint not thy mind: ● Together with line 25 above, this
is the most crucial imperative of the play, the one around
which all the others turn. Revenge my murder, but do not
stain ("taint") your mind. How is a mind tainted? With
sin, as those of Gertrude and Claudius have been tainted.
But how is it possible to take revenge without sin? If
"Vengeance is mine ... saith the Lord," how can Hamlet
rightly avenge his father's murder? Scripture says,
"Thou shalt not avenge" (Lev. 19:18), and "Vengeance
and recompense are mine ... for the Lord shall judge his
people" (Deut. 32:35), and "avenge not yourselves, but
give place unto wrath, for it is written, Vengeance is
mine, I will repay, saith the Lord" (Romans 12:19), but the
Ghost has told Hamlet to avenge his murder. This, then,
becomes the central trial of Hamlet's character.

In ignoring the general implication of this line
and linking it in implication only to the potential
mistreatment of Gertrude, Jenkins misreads the
essential theme and through-line of the play,
even as he acknowledges the more profound and, I
believe, truer reading of Sister Miriam Joseph (SMJ
"Ghost") that the intent of the Ghost is to challenge
Hamlet to act without falling into sin. See Introduction,
pages 1–10 and SMJ "CT."

Against thy mother aught. Leave her to heaven,

aught: anything. ● Hamlet is told not in any way
to take vengeance upon his mother (cf., Orestes in
Aeschylus's *Oresteia*).

And to those thorns that in her bosom lodge
To prick and sting her. Fare thee well at once.
The glow-worm shows the matin to be near

thorns ... sting her: the stings of conscience, which
Hamlet will awaken in III.iv.

glow-worm: firefly. **matin:** dawn, morning, from
"Matuta," the Roman goddess of morning = Aurora,
dawn, with an overtone of morning prayers, *matins*
being the name for the monastic service of daybreak, cf.,
I.i.147–56 and I.ii.218–20.

And 'gins to pale his uneffectual fire.   90

'gins: begins. **to pale:** to make pale, a transitive verb here,
"fire" being its direct object (Abbott §290). **his:** the glow-
worm's. **uneffectual:** ineffective in giving light because
of the greater light of dawn, cf., *Pericles* II.iii.43–44 and
Abbott §442.

Adieu, adieu, adieu. Remember me.

Exit.

Adieu: French farewell (lit., [go] toward God).
● The repetition emphasizes and the entire line
reiterates poetically the essential and paradoxical
imperative of the Ghost: go with God, implying taint not
thy mind, and remember me, implying do not neglect to
avenge my murder.

HAMLET

O all you host of heaven! O earth! What else?
And shall I couple hell? O fie! Hold, hold, my heart,

And shall I ... my heart: The line may be a hexameter or
a trimeter couplet, cf., Abbott §500, but more likely it is
a pentameter with "And shall I" elided and "coup-"
being the first stressed syllable, cf., Abbott §503.
couple hell: add hell to the list of the directions in
which Hamlet is exclaiming—the implication is that
the Ghost may be appearing on earth from heaven or
from hell and also perhaps that hell is represented by

And you, my sinews, grow not instant old

But bear me stiffly up. Remember thee?   95

Ay, thou poor ghost, whiles memory holds a seat

In this distracted globe. Remember thee?

Yea, from the table of my memory

I'll wipe away all trivial fond recórds,

All saws of books, all forms, all pressures past   100

what the Ghost has said of Claudius. **fie:** interjection expressing disgust (from the sound made in response to a disagreeable smell) or indignant reproach (OED). **Hold:** remain intact, i.e., do not burst from intensity of emotion (cf., e.g., *King Lear* V.iii.197–200, 217–18).

sinews: tendons, muscles, strength, and possibly nerves.

bear ... up: hold me upright physically and possibly keep me firm, resolute (Raffel).

whiles: while, so long as. **seat:** its proper place (OED *sb.* 14.), with some influence from the sense of its right to sit there (cf., OED *sb.* 6.b. and 8.), i.e., so long as memory, one of the five wits or inner senses, holds its proper place in my mind. (The other four are fancy, imagination, judgment, and common sense.)

distracted: troubled, perplexed (OED 4., quoting this use, and cf., the root meaning of drawn apart, divided, separated, and OED 1., 2., and 3. as at IV.iii.4). The sense of the full derangement of mind or madness does not apply here as it does to Hamlet's pretended madness at III.i.5 or to Ophelia's actual madness at IV.v.2. **globe:** his head, with the implication of the human mind being a microcosm of the world (Jenkins), with memory having a "seat" among its governing body. There is a possible but unlikely pun on the Globe theater, where the play was performed. **Remember thee?:** referring back to line 91.

table of my memory: "table" is a tablet on which to write, particularly a lasting inscription, cf., line 107 below, but the phrase is a metaphor for the kind of memory, like Shakespeare's, that would have been filled with grammar school learning, cf., Sonnet 122, Proverbs 3:3, 7:3, Aeschylus' *Prometheus Bound* line 789, Sir Philip Sidney's *Defense of Poetry* ¶ 50 ("Only let Æneas be worn in the tablet of your memory"), and Baldwin II.101.

wipe away: erase, as from a tablet or table-book (see line 107 and note). **trivial:** elementary, hence comparatively insignificant, from *trivium* (Latin, three ways), the three lower division subjects, grammar, dialectic or logic, and rhetoric, comprising what we would call "humanities," studied in the medieval schools and in the grammar schools of Shakespeare's day. They were followed in the upper division by the *quadrivium* (Latin, four ways), arithmetic, music, geometry, and astronomy, comprising what we would call "science." All together they formed the seven liberal arts, the curriculum that Hamlet would have completed before entering the university at Wittenberg and that Shakespeare probably did complete. With continued studies (as at Wittenberg) the seven would have been capped by philosophy and theology, "the queen of the sciences." **fond:** foolish, silly. **recórds:** stressed on the second syllable, as indicated.

saws: sayings, maxims. **forms:** drawings, shapes; "Shakespeare often uses *form* to refer to an exact image such as is given by a wax impression;

e.g. *M*[*idsummer*] *N*[*ight's*] *D*[*ream*] I.i.49, *Tw*[*elfth*]
N[*ight*] II.ii.[30]" (Jenkins). **pressures:** impressions,
as of writing or drawing on a tablet or a table- or
copy-book (see line 107 and note), cf., II.ii.305 note
and III.ii.24.

That youth and observation copied there,

youth and observation: observations made in
youth—a hendiadys like "book and volume" at
line 103 (see I.i.57 note). **there:** i.e., in his memory, for
which the copy-book is a metaphor, cf., "Youth and
observation were supposed to spend their time in
such enterprise" (Baldwin II.101).

And thy commandment all alone shall live

thy commandment: as stated at lines 25, 81–83, 85,
86, and 91, akin to the Ten Commandments copied by
Moses on the two stone tablets.

Within the book and volume of my brain,

book and volume: a hendiadys combining two
senses of "volume," *tome* and *largeness*, hence
"spacious book" (Wright, page 186), cf., line 101 and
note and I.i.57 note.

Unmixed with baser matter. Yes, by heaven!

baser: lower, less noble. **matter:** subjects, topics.
Yes: confirming his determination as just stated.
by heaven: a formal oath, cf., line 112.

O most pernicious woman!   105

O most ... woman: for the three-foot line in the midst
of passion, see Abbott §511. **woman:** Gertrude.

O villain, villain, smiling damnèd villain!

villain: Claudius.

My tables—meet it is I set it down

tables: table-book or copy-book, bound sheets,
surfaced with a combination of glue and gesso, that
could be written on and later erased (by wetting)
and used again, a Renaissance upgrade from the wax
tablets used in the ancient world and in medieval
monasteries. **meet:** adj., appropriate, fitting. **set it
down:** write it in my table-book for preservation.

That one may smile, and smile, and be a villain;

That one ... villain: ● An image of the central theme
of the contrast between appearance and reality. That
Claudius may both smile and be a villain is a lesson
in man's potential for hypocrisy. In exemplifying
the difference between an outer action and the
invisible motive behind it, the line also prepares
us for the drama of the alteration in the motives of
Hamlet reflected in his actions, from the vengeance
behind his not killing the King in III.iii and his killing
Polonius thinking Polonius is the King in III.iv, to the
surrender to divinity behind his final killing of the
King in V.ii.

At least I am sure it may be so in Denmark.

in Denmark: in one sense an ironic understatement,
since it is possible anywhere as well as in Denmark,
but also pointed at Claudius, who for the time
being *is* Denmark, as at I.ii.69 etc. ● Many editors
(including Jenkins) erroneously follow Rowe in
inserting the stage direction "Writes" after this line or
after line 107, though there is no authority for it in the
original texts. In doing so they mistake a metaphor
for a literal gesture. Hamlet has not brought his
writing tablets with him to the parapet and is not
literally writing down anything. He is *imagining* the
act of writing the Ghost's imperative in his tables, as
students and scholars wrote down a piece of wisdom
or information that they particularly wanted to

So, uncle, there you are. Now to my word: 110
It is "Adieu, adieu. Remember me."

I have sworn't.

Enter Horatio and Marcellus.

HORATIO
My lord, my lord!
MARCELLUS
            Lord Hamlet!
HORATIO
                     Heavens secure him.
HAMLET
So be it.
HORATIO
Illo, ho, ho, my lord!   115
HAMLET
Hillo, ho, ho, boy! Come, bird, come.

MARCELLUS
How is't, my noble lord?
HORATIO
             What news, my lord?
HAMLET
O, wonderful!
HORATIO
Good my lord, tell it.
HAMLET
            No, you will reveal it.

---

preserve for later copying into a more permanent medium. Hamlet is using writing in his tables as a metaphor to emphasize the significance of what he has heard and must keep in mind. The "emblem by Whitney [1586, page 100], on hypocrites [that] recommends testing the correspondence of a man's words and deeds by noting them on 'a table'" (cited by Jenkins quoting Evans) does not alter the fact that Hamlet is evoking the image of such recording only metaphorically.

there you are: referring not to any physical writing (see previous note) but to the Ghost's confirmation of Hamlet's previous suspicions (I.ii.157–58, 255, and above lines 40–41). **word:** order or command of a superior (OED 7.), which Hamlet has sworn to follow, though the idea of a motto or watchword may contribute to the sense, perhaps analogous to *King Lear* III.iv.183 and *Pericles* II.ii.21 (Jenkins).

I have sworn't: at line 104.

S.D. *Enter Horatio and Marcellus:* They do not yet see Hamlet in the dark.

secure him: keep him safe.

So be it.: Let it be so, amen. ● Although Horatio and Marcellus do not hear him, Hamlet responds to Horatio's prayer with his own confirmation of it, given the danger, both physical and spiritual, of the obligation laid on him by the Ghost.

Illo, ho, ho: a falconer's cry commonly used for any call to someone or something at a distance, to which Hamlet responds in the same vein with the jestingly literal extension "Come, bird, come." Jenkins cites analogues: *Birth of Merlin* II.i.61–63, Tyro's *Roaring Megge*, 1598 (cited by Steevens), Cutwode, *Caltha Poetarum*, st. 136, and Marston, *Dutch Courtesan*, I.ii.131. ● Highly energized, Hamlet here begins to interact with his comrades with forced merriment and play of wit as a way of keeping the Ghost's intent secret, as was standard for the avenger in the tradition.

How is't: What's the situation? What has happened?

wonderful: full of wonder, to be wondered at.

Good my lord: = My good lord (Abbott §13).

HORATIO
  Not I, my lord, by heaven.

MARCELLUS
             Nor I, my lord.   120

HAMLET
  How say you then, would heart of man once think it?
  —But you'll be secret?

HORATIO, MARCELLUS
          Ay, by heaven, my lord.

HAMLET
  There's never a villain dwelling in all Denmark
  But he's an arrant knave.

HORATIO
  There needs no ghost, my lord, come from the grave   125
  To tell us this.

HAMLET
        Why right, you are in the right,
  And so without more circumstance at all

  I hold it fit that we shake hands and part,
  You as your business and desire shall point you—
  For every man hath business and desire,   130
  Such as it is—and for my own poor part,
  I will go pray.

HORATIO
  These are but wild and whirling words, my lord.

HAMLET
  I'm sorry they offend you, heartily—
  Yes faith, heartily.

HORATIO
          There's no offense, my lord.   135

HAMLET
  Yes, by Saint Patrick, but there is, Horatio,

---

by heaven: an oath. ● Horatio swears now but will soon be asked to swear again.

How say you then: what do you say to this. **once:** even once, ever.

Ay, by heaven: Now both men swear.

There's never … arrant knave: there is not even one villain living in Denmark who is not an outrageous villain, an obvious and platitudinous tautology. ● Hamlet's jesting tautology is not newsworthy. He is testing them as the Ghost has tested him. The audience will hear in his truism a reference to Claudius, but Horatio and Marcellus do not since they have not heard the Ghost's words to Hamlet. **never … But:** not even one who is not. **arrant:** thoroughgoing, notorious. **knave:** villain.

There needs no ghost … come: no ghost need come, needs to come.

circumstance: ceremony (Riverside), elaboration of detail, cf., *King John* II.i.77, *2 Henry VI* I.i.105, and *Much Ado* III.ii.102–103 (Jenkins).
hold it: deem it to be. **fit:** fitting, proper, appropriate.
business: activity, duty, occupation, concern.
point: direct.

pray: Lewes Lavater, *Of Ghosts and Spirits Walking by Night* (translated into English by Robert Harrison, 1572, edited by J. Dover Wilson and May Yardley, 1929), III.vi: "it behoveth them which are vexed with spirits, to pray especially" (cited in Jenkins).
wild and whirling: possibly a hendiadys for wildly whirling (Wright, page 186).

heartily: earnestly, from the heart.
faith: short for "in faith," a relatively mild oath in this context, but cf., lines 145–46.

no offense: Hamlet's words have not offended him.

there is: there is an offense—not to Horatio in words, but by Claudius in deeds. **by Saint Patrick:** a witty oath based on the legend of St. Patrick's Purgatory, a cave on an island in Loch Derg, County Donegal, Ireland, in which, in order to aid St. Patrick in converting the Irish, God granted that the pains of Purgatory might be witnessed with the eyes. In the Middle Ages the cave became a popular pilgrimage spot. Hamlet's quip suggests that he believes the Ghost has indeed come from Purgatory and has in his words revealed something of it to Hamlet. Cf., Dekker,

And much offense too. Touching this vision here,
It is an honest ghost, that let me tell you.

For your desire to know what is between us,

O'ermaster't as you may. And now, good friends,   140
As you are friends, scholars, and soldiers,
Give me one poor request.

HORATIO
                              What is't, my lord? We will.

HAMLET
Never make known what you have seen tonight.

HORATIO, MARCELLUS
My lord, we will not.

HAMLET
                   Nay, but swear't.

HORATIO
                                    In faith,   145
My lord, not I.

MARCELLUS
Nor I, my lord, in faith.

HAMLET
                   Upon my sword.

MARCELLUS
We have sworn, my lord, already.

HAMLET
 Indeed, upon my sword, indeed.

             Ghost cries [from] under the stage.

GHOST
 Swear.

HAMLET
Ah ha, boy, say'st thou so? Art thou there, truepenny?   150

Come on. You hear this fellow in the cellarage.
Consent to swear.

HORATIO
                   Propose the oath, my lord.

HAMLET
Never to speak of this that you have seen,
Swear by my sword.

GHOST [*Beneath.*]
Swear.   155

Honest Whore, Part 2, I.i.42, Holinshed, *Chronicles*, 1587, ii.28, and D. P. Barton, *Ireland and Shakespeare*, 1919, pages 30ff. (Jenkins).

Touching: in regard to. **vision:** the Ghost.

honest: genuine, a true ghost (with a possible overtone of honest-speaking).

For: as regards (Abbott §149). **what is between us:** what has passed between us, what we "have to do with one another" (Jenkins).

O'ermaster't: overmaster it, control it. **as you may:** as best you can. ● Hamlet will later reveal all to Horatio, who, as we saw at I.ii.161–67, is more intimate with Hamlet than are Marcellus and Barnardo, see III.ii.76–77.

Nay: not an outright negation, but an expression that what they have said is insufficient to satisfy him, cf., I.iv.91. **In faith:** Both men swear the oath, which in this context becomes more serious than "faith" meaning in truth, verily, as at line 135. Here it has something like the sense "by my faith in God," "as I am a faithful Christian". **not I … Nor I:** "i.e. 'I will not make it known', not 'I will not swear'" (Jenkins).

Upon my sword: i.e., upon the hilt of the sword, which forms a cross; they now swear by the cross, cf., *Henry V* II.i.101 and Thomas Decker's *Old Fortunatus* III.i, in which Agripyne says of her "Spanish prisoner" "He has sworn to me by the cross of his pure Toledo [= Spanish sword] to be my servant."

s.d. *Ghost cries [from] under the stage:* Q2 and F, see line 151 note and cf., line 162.

Ah ha: F, Ha, ha Q2. **truepenny:** honest fellow, as in the early comedy *Ralph Roister Doister* and *2 Return from Parnassus*, line 654 (Jenkins).

cellarage: the space containing the scaffolding holding up the theater's stage, used for sound effects, graves, and sudden miraculous appearances. ● As the roof over the stage was called "the heavens," the cellarage often symbolized hell, though here it perhaps hints again at Saint Patrick's Purgatory (see line 136 note). The words of the Ghost have utterly persuaded Hamlet and us for the moment, but there remains the question, which will arise in the next act, of whether the Ghost is in fact sent from heaven to guide Hamlet or from hell to tempt him. Hamlet's use of the word for the literal space under the stage is an example of the interpenetration of the literal and the metaphorical in Shakespeare's art, there being no fear that the pun, as with the punning on "the Globe" (cf.,

[Horatio and Marcellus prepare to swear by Hamlet's sword.]

HAMLET

Hic et ubique? Then we'll shift our ground.
Come hither, gentlemen,
And lay your hands again upon my sword.
Swear by my sword
Never to speak of this that you have heard.   160
GHOST [*Beneath.*]
Swear by his sword.

[Horatio and Marcellus prepare to swear by Hamlet's sword.]

HAMLET
Well said, old mole. Canst work i' th' earth so fast?

A worthy pioner! Once more remove, good friends.

Tempest IV.i.153 and possibly though not probably line 95 above) would significantly interrupt the illusion.

S.D.: • There are no stage directions in either Q2 or F to indicate when Horatio and Marcellus actually do swear. While Jenkins is persuasive that Horatio and Marcellus are asked to swear three times to three different particulars at the three behests of the Ghost, "never to speak of this that you have *seen*" (line 153), "never to speak of this that you have *heard*" (line 160), and "never ... to note that you know aught of me" (lines 169–79), it is difficult to see how they can actually be swearing between the Ghost's "Swear" and Hamlet's commands that they "shift ... ground" (line 156) and "once more remove" (line 163). No doubt "Threefold oaths had a particularly binding force (sometimes explained by their invocation of the Trinity), and this one will have still further solemnity from seeming to be sworn at the behest not of Hamlet only but of a supernatural agent also" (Jenkins LN), yet I think what is actually happening is that the Ghost is evoking and testing their *intention* to swear each time until the last when they finally do swear. This mirrors the Ghost's leading Hamlet onward until at I.v.1 Hamlet, having shown his willingness to follow, calls a halt and commands the Ghost to speak (see line 1 note). Once again Shakespeare is demonstrating that inner intentions are the central concern, the outward action being but a reflection of them, and setting us up for the climactic dramatization of action vs. intention in III.iii. Horatio and Marcellus must actually swear at line 181.

Hic et ubique: Latin for "here and everywhere." • The Ghost is moving from place to place under the stage. Strictly, as commentators point out, only God can be "here and everywhere" at the same time, so the phrase is used both jocularly and with a possibly deeper implication that he is in fact a messenger from God, who can will apparitions to do whatever and to be wherever he wants. In any case, the movement of the Ghost, while comically playing on the actor's actual movements, also reinforces the supernatural element in the Ghost's appearance and demands.
S.D.: see note to S.D. at line 155.

old mole: • Hamlet's jocular familiarity with the Ghost expresses his "wild and whirling" intensity of emotion even as it contrasts with the supernatural solemnity of the moment. This tone "gives more than a touch of burlesque; and this 'comic relief' ... has, in a manner characteristically Shakespearean, serious ... overtones" (Jenkins LN). It is worth stressing that "comic relief" in Shakespeare is never just that but always also thematic reiteration or development.
pioner: digger, miner, with the accent on the first syllable (Abbott §492), a variant of *pioneer*, a foot soldier sent ahead to dig or prepare fortifications.

HORATIO

O day and night, but this is wondrous strange!

HAMLET

And therefore as a stranger give it welcome.   165

There are more things in heaven and earth, Horatio,
Than are dreamt of in your philosophy.

But come,

Here, as before, never, so help you mercy,

How strange or odd some'er I bear myself—   170

As I perchance hereafter shall think meet
To put an antic disposition on—

O day and night: ● In his outburst Horatio calls upon the most basic and familiar of earthly phenomena to contrast with the strangeness of this unearthly one, implying that even the most extreme natural opposites cannot contain it. **strange:** bizarre, supernatural.

as a stranger … welcome: ● Hamlet plays on Horatio's use of the word *strange*, charging him to follow the traditional precept to welcome the stranger in another sense, as in many places in the Old Testament, Matthew 25:35, and Middleton's *Women Beware Women* II.ii.225 (Jenkins substantially).

There are more … philosophy: ● Hamlet responds to Horatio's image of the rationally understood limits of reality ("day and night") with the assertion that reality contains more than rational philosophy comprehends. **your:** one's, the colloquial indefinite use, see I.i.138 note. **your philosophy:** not Horatio's personal philosophy but philosophy generally, particularly classical philosophy, and perhaps specifically natural philosophy, what we would call science, as opposed to Christian theology.

But come: "A phrase like this, calling attention to what follows, is often extra-metrical. Cf. II.i.[41], [59]; II.ii.105. Only the last of these is printed as a separate line in Q2 and none of them in F" (Jenkins).

Here, as before … this do swear: ● "The oath … begins with *never* … but then goes off into conditions and explanations, only to emerge … in an anacoluthon [shift in syntax within a sentence], the syntax reflecting Hamlet's excited state. The main construction is: 'swear … here, as before … that you … never shall … (to) note … that you know aught of me'" (Jenkins), and see line 178 note. ● In short, swear never to hint that you know anything about me. **so help you mercy:** i.e., swear to do the following as faithfully as you would wish for divine mercy to help you in your need, with the implication that failure to keep the oath would be tantamount to renouncing divine grace and mercy, cf., line 180.

How strange or odd some'er: however (howsoever) strange or odd (cf., line 84 and I.ii.248). **bear myself:** behave, act.

meet: adj., fitting, suitable, appropriate.

To put … on: to take upon oneself, adopt, assume (OED put $v.^1$ 46.b.), here with the intention of deceiving, cf., III.i.2 and *King Lear* I.iii.12.

an antic disposition: a fantastic attitude, crazy or grotesque behavior: "*antic*, grotesque = 'strange or odd' [line 170 above]. Cawdrey, *A Table Alphabetical*, 1604, defines 'anticke, disguised'. The word is particularly used of an actor with a false head or grotesque mask" (Jenkins). ● Hamlet is here hinting that he may in future appear to be odd or insane, a standard element of the revenge play tradition. The avenger pretends to be mad in order

That you, at such times seeing me, never shall,
With arms encumbered thus, or this head-shake,

Or by pronouncing of some doubtful phrase, 175

As "Well, well, we know," or "We could, and if we
[would,"
Or "If we list to speak," or "There be, and if they
[might,"

Or such ambiguous giving out, to note

That you know aught of me—this do swear,
So grace and mercy at your most need help you. 180
GHOST [*Beneath.*]
Swear.

[*They swear.*]

HAMLET
Rest, rest, perturbèd spirit. So, gentlemen,

With all my love I do commend me to you,
And what so poor a man as Hamlet is
May do t'express his love and friending to you, 185

God willing, shall not lack. Let us go in together.

And still your fingers on your lips, I pray.

---

to escape detection as he gathers information about the villain and pursues his plot against him.

seeing: contracted to one syllable (Abbott §470).

encumbered thus: folded in a knot, indicating brooding and sadness, cf., *Tempest*, I.ii.224.

by pronouncing of: for the *of* after the verbal see Abbott §178, and for the omitted *the* see Abbott §89.
doubtful: dubious, suspicious.

and if: if (= an if). **would:** wanted to. **We could ... would:** We could (tell) if we wanted to.

list: wished, desired. **There be, and if they might:** There are (those who could tell) if they might (be allowed to speak).

ambiguous: Quintilian's fourth form of obscurity "in words conjunct" is *ambiguitas* (Baldwin II.226).
giving out: letting on, intimation (Dowden), implying, revealing, publishing (OED give *v.* 62.a.), cf., *Measure for Measure* I.iv.54. **to note:** to indicate, to say publicly, the *to* "is often inserted before an infinitive, even one which would not normally require it, when the infinitive stands at a distance from its preceding verb (here *shall*, line [173]). Cf. lines 17–18, 'Make ... to part'. See Abbott [§]350, and, for instances of *shall ... to*, [*English Studies*], xxvi, 142–4" (Jenkins).

aught: anything.

So grace ... you: see line 169 note. **most:** greatest (Abbott §17).

s.d.: see note to s.d. at line 155. As we will see, they keep their oaths. From III.ii.76–77 we know that Hamlet later confides the details of the Ghost's speech to Horatio. But at this point he has not yet done so.

commend: entrust (OED 1.).

poor: modest, lowly, insignificant, used in a humble or self-deprecatory sense (OED 4.d., quoting line 131). ● Hamlet, with humility and kindness, promises to reward Horatio and Marcellus for their loyalty to him and to their oath. Because he is not the king, it can only be a promise for the future. Since he is the heir apparent to the throne, it is a valuable promise.
God willing ... in together: The hexameter can be read as a trimeter couplet (Abbott §501) or perhaps a pentameter if "shall not" is elided. **God willing:** God being willing, if God wills it. **shall not lack:** for the impersonal verb, see Abbott §297. **together:** another sign of humble magnanimity. Hamlet invites them to go together rather than bidding them follow behind him (see line 190 and note). ● NOTE TO ACTORS: "Let us" is doubtless a trochee.

still: always (Abbott §69). **fingers on your lips:** as today, keeping silent on some subject.

The time is out of joint. O cursed spite,
That ever I was born to set it right.

out of joint: disordered, lacking right government, cf., *disjoint* at I.ii.20, Tilley J 75, and Horsey, *Travels* (Hakluyt Society, page 262): "This turbulent time … all out of joint, not likely to be reduced a long time to any good form of peaceable government" (Jenkins substantially). ● Can the time be "set right" by means of revenge?

Nay, come, let's go together.   190

Exeunt.

together: see line 186 and note. ● Horatio and Marcellus, as is proper, stand aside to let their prince go first. Hamlet, with princely magnanimity, overrules their courtly manners and asks them to depart together with him as friends, as he wished to be called Horatio's friend at I.ii.163 and to receive the soldiers' loves rather than merely their duty at I.ii.253. Compare these exchanges to that with Osric in V.ii where Osric, incapable of any depth let alone friendship with Hamlet, obeys the custom rather than the prince. (In Browning's "My Last Duchess," the Duke of Ferrara makes an insincere version of Hamlet's sincere invitation here, then immediately negates it at lines 53–54.)

Act II, Scene i

Enter old Polonius with his man [Reynaldo].

POLONIUS
Give him this money and these notes, Reynaldo.
REYNALDO
I will, my lord.
POLONIUS
You shall do marvelous wisely, good Reynaldo,

Before you visit him, to make inquire
Of his behavior.
REYNALDO
                        My lord, I did intend it.   5
POLONIUS
Marry, well said, very well said. Look you, sir,

Inquire me first what Danskers are in Paris,

Act II, Scene i. ● A room in Polonius's apartment in the castle.

s.d. old: cf., the satire on "old men" at II.ii.196ff.. **his man:** his servant.

Give him … notes: There is no stage direction, but Polonius must be physically handing money and something written to Reynaldo.

shall: "expressing not mere futurity but inevitability (= cannot but, are certain to). Cf. *Mac[beth]* III. iv.5[6], *Oth[ello]* I.i.44 (Jenkins). **marvelous:** used adverbially (Abbott §1) and pronounced as two syllables (mar-vel's), Q2 meruiles, F maruels. **inquire:** inquiry, another example of a verb used as a noun, cf., *avouch* I.i.57, *disclose* III.i.166, *supervise* V.ii.23, Abbott §451 (Jenkins substantially).

Marry: a mild interjection whose source is the oath "by the Virgin Mary". **Look you, sir:** Listen here. ● "This manner of insisting on attention to what he is about to say is characteristic of Polonius," cf., lines 15, 41, 59 below and II.ii.105, 107 (Jenkins)— Polonius likes to hear himself talk and expects others to be equally interested, like the old men satirized in the book Hamlet reads at II.ii.196ff. as having "a plentiful lack of wit," and contrasting with the serious "Mark me" of the Ghost at I.v.2. Jenkins points out that such a phrase is often extra-metrical, though usually not given a separate line in Q2 or F, cf., I.v.168 note.

Danskers: Danes, perhaps confused by Shakespeare and others with Danzigers, i.e., people from Danzig, a confusion that one commentator (Sjögren, referred

And how, and who, what means, and where they keep,

What company, at what expense; and finding

By this encompassment and drift of question   10

That they do know my son, come you more nearer
Than your particular demands will touch it.
Take you, as 'twere, some distant knowledge of him,
As thus, "I know his father and his friends,
And in part him"—Do you mark this, Reynaldo?   15

REYNALDO
Ay, very well, my lord.

POLONIUS
"And in part him. But," you may say, "not well.
But if't be he I mean, he's very wild,
Addicted so and so"—and there put on him

What forgeries you please—marry, none so rank   20

As may dishonor him, take heed of that,
But, sir, such wanton, wild, and usual slips

As are companions noted and most known
To youth and liberty.

---

to by Jenkins) suggests may have led to the idea that Denmark and Poland shared a border, cf., I.i.63, II.ii.63, 75–78, IV.iv.12–16, V.ii.350.

And how: by what circumstances they come to be in Paris. **and who:** who they are. **what means:** what material means, i.e., how wealthy they are. **keep:** lodge or reside.

What company: what company they keep (object of "keep" in the previous line, now understood as transitive), with whom they hang out. **at what expense:** how much they spend. ● Polonius, as usual, extends his speech beyond what is necessary to making his point. **and finding ... touch it:** "When Reynaldo has first found out that Laertes is known, he is then to come nearer to the crucial matter than is possible by specific questions (*particular demands* [line 12]); and Polonius proceeds to instruct him how to do this (by talking about Laertes in such a way as to draw the others on [without revealing his intentions])" (Jenkins).

encompassment: roundabout approach. **drift of question:** direction of the conversation.

come you: an imperative. **more nearer:** a common doubling of the comparative (Abbott §11).

Take you: take upon yourself, pretend to have, assume.

mark: pay attention to.

Addicted: inclined, given to. **so and so:** in this way or that, the details to be supplied by Reynaldo's invention, as the next phrase indicates. **put on him:** accuse him of.

forgeries: false accusations, fabrications, cf., I.v.37 and *Midsummer Night's Dream* II.i.81 (Jenkins substantially). **marry:** see line 6 note. **rank:** foul, nasty.

take heed: beware.

wanton, wild, and usual slips: a hendiadys (Wright, page 186) for usual wanton and wild slips. **wanton:** self-indulgent, sportive, frolicsome. **slips:** errors, faults.

As are companions ... liberty: i.e., such moral lapses as are observed and well known to accompany youth and privilege or freedom from external restraint (parental, financial, etc.). ● Suggesting that Polonius, out of moral laxity or worldly wisdom, or both, thinks that common youthful indiscretions do not necessarily involve dishonor. **As are companions ... to:** as accompany. **noted and most known:** possibly a

REYNALDO

  As gaming, my lord.

POLONIUS

  Ay, or drinking, fencing, swearing,   25

  Quarrelling, drabbing—you may go so far.

REYNALDO

  My lord, that would dishonor him.

POLONIUS

  Faith no, as you may season it in the charge.

  You must not put another scandal on him,

---

hendiadys (Wright, page 186). **noted:** observed. **youth and liberty:** possibly a hendiadys for youthful liberty (Wright, page 186). **liberty:** freedom, privilege. **As:** as for example. **gaming:** gambling.

fencing: "this traditionally noble art … completes a common pattern of wild living" (Jenkins), fencing being associated with dancing and bear-baiting in *Twelfth Night* (I.iii.93), with plays, dancing, wrestling, "and a thousand other foolish sports" in Greene's *Debate between Folly and Love* (appended to *Card of Fancy*, in Greene iv.218), dancing and tennis in Nashe's *Piers Penniless* (i.209), quarreling in Gosson's *School of Abuse* (ed. Arber, page 46), and cony-catching (= swindling) in Dekker's *Gull's Hornbook* (*Non-Dramatic Works*, ed. Grosart, ii.213) (Jenkins LN substantially). **drabbing:** whoring.

As gaming … dishonor him: Line breaks follow Q2 and F (which make line 24 two lines, a trimeter followed by a dimeter, line 25 a tetrameter, line 26 a pentameter, and line 27 a tetrameter). Riverside sets line 24 as a pentameter (indenting at "As"), puts the break in line 25 after "quarreling" (making it a pentameter and line 26 a trimeter), and line 27 as here. Jenkins sets line 24 as here, indents line 25 to complete a pentameter (or hexameter if "Ay, or" is treated as stressed) with the break after "swearing," and lines 26 and 27 as here. • The empty feet in the two lines of Q2 and F that make line 24 here might indicate a pause before Reynaldo's line, suggesting his attempt to guess at Polonius's meaning, followed by Polonius's irregular (garrulous?) listing of examples and Reynaldo's following him in departing from the meter, whereupon Reynaldo's contradicting him sends Polonius back into pentameters at line 28. Alternatively, if we consider "Ay" a monosyllabic exclamation (Abbott §482), line 25 might include through "drabbing," making lines 26 and 27 a trimeter couplet (Abbott §500) or a pentameter with "My Lord" as an extra-metrical interjection.

Faith: in faith or by my faith, a mild oath. **no:** only in F. **season:** qualify, temper, adjust. **in the charge:** in making the accusation. • One of the central ideas of the play is reiterated in this partly comical sub-plot. The way any charge (= accusation) is leveled needs to be seasoned (moderated, fit to the circumstances), and the same is true of any charge in the other sense (= imperative, assignment), in which the *manner* of execution is essential to the fulfillment of the *matter*. How one performs a duty, in this case a dubious one, is as important as that one performs it.

put … on him: lay on him, to clothe him in (OED put *v.*¹ 46.). **another:** "Not implying that the things already mentioned are scandals, which Polonius has denied. In Elizabethan usage *other* may refer to an instance of a different kind instead of to a different instance of the same kind. See OED other *adj.* 7." (Jenkins), cf.,

Macbeth IV.iii.89–90: "All these [vices] are portable, / With other graces weighed". **scandal:** ● Compare the use of this word here in a social context with Hamlet's use of it at I.iv.38, where it has spiritual implications.

That he is open to incontinency—   30

incontinency: indulgence in lust. ● "The distinction between this and 'drabbing' is a question of how it is regarded—whether as confirmed libertinism or merely as the natural hot-bloodedness of youth" (Jenkins), cf., lines 22–24, 31–35. Is this distinction morally accurate or a form of self-serving moral relativism on the part of Polonius? Cf., II.ii.249–51 and note.

That's not my meaning; but breathe his faults so
                            [quaintly

quaintly: artfully, subtly.

That they may seem the taints of liberty,

taints: stains. ● Cf., the Ghost's imperative to Hamlet at I.v.85 ("Taint not thy mind").

The flash and outbreak of a fiery mind,

fiery: passionate, characterized by the fundamental element fire, the other three elements being earth, air, and water, see I.i.149–53 note.

A savageness in unreclaimèd blood,

savageness: animal wildness, instinct, sexual passion, whose seat was in the blood, cf., I.iii.6 note, Measure for Measure II.iv.15, etc. **unreclaimèd:** untamed.

Of general assault.
REYNALDO
  But, my good lord—   35

Of general assault: It is common, usual, universal ("general") that men (especially young men) are attacked ("assault") by such passions. ● Compare Polonius's words at I.iii.116, where he warns against the youthful fire in the blood of Hamlet, which is a threat to his daughter's chastity, and his words here, where he excuses the same in his own son. Is there a real difference between scandalous lust and the common lust of youth, between Hamlet's fiery blood and that of Laertes? Does the distinction really depend on manner and situation, or is it a function of Polonius's greater concern with his daughter's chastity than with his son's? In both cases Polonius is reaching beyond himself by assuming worse behavior and weaker character in the young men than there is evidence to justify. His questionable logic not only illustrates his tendency to overreach by applying generalities to particular cases. It also sets up the very serious distinction-making that the Ghost commands in saying "Revenge his foul and most unnatural murder" (I.v.25) "But ... / Taint not thy mind" (I.v.84–85) and that the unfolding plot demands of Hamlet, and the play of us, in III.iii and in V.ii.

POLONIUS
  Wherefore should you do this?

Wherefore: why, for what purpose. ● Polonius will answer why Reynaldo should put these "forgeries" upon Laertes, namely to find out from his acquaintances how Laertes is really behaving. But why is he assuming immoral behavior in Laertes and sending Reynaldo to spy on his own son, particularly when we have seen Laertes in I.iii show concern for his sister's chastity and promise not to be a libertine himself? Polonius trusts his own cleverness and methods of spying more than he trusts his son. As he will later use his daughter to gain important political information about the Prince, so he is importing into his relations with his son the habit of mind of a "politician," a derogatory term in Shakespeare, meaning someone who engages in secret and self-serving plotting. This compromise of family in the name of self-serving "policy" is a less serious but nonetheless tragic parallel to the betrayal by Claudius of his brother, sister-in-law, and nephew. In Polonius the spying arises ironically from his failing to heed his own advice about the golden mean given at I.ii.58ff. It serves also as a parallel and foil to the King's use of Rosencrantz and Guildenstern and of Ophelia to fathom Hamlet's mind, and to Hamlet's own use of playacted madness to ferret out the guilt of the King.

would: wish to, want to.

REYNALDO
  Ay, my lord, I would know that.

POLONIUS
  Marry, sir, here's my drift,

drift: intention, purpose, cf., IV.vii.151, where the word means *plot*. **Of general ... drift:** As at lines 24–27 above, line breaks here follow Q2 and F, the empty feet possibly indicating Reynaldo's hesitations and the interruption of his own discourse by Polonius to acknowledge them. Riverside regularizes these lines into pentameters.

  And I believe it is a fetch of warrant.

fetch of warrant: a stratagem, trick, or pretense that is warranted, justified, cf., *King Lear* II.iv.89 ("fetches"). For F "of warrant" Q2 has "of wit" which, "like its *wait* at III.iv.[6], appears to be a misreading of an abbreviation of *warrant*. Errors with this word in other texts ... suggest that Shakespeare was in the habit of contracting it. Cf. *warn't*, I.ii.243" (Jenkins).

  You laying these slight sullies on my son,

sullies: F, blemishes, Q2 has "sallies," which may mean "accusations against" or may be a variant of "sullies," cf., I.ii.129 note.

  As 'twere a thing a little soiled i'th' working,   40

As 'twere: as if it were. **soiled i'th' working:** dirtied in the course of being made, like a piece of embroidery—as though a young man's indulgences were the inevitable outcome of the maturing process, "sullied by that worldly contact through which he acquires his accomplishments" (Jenkins).

  Mark you,

Mark you: listen, pay attention, cf., line 6 note above and I.v.168 note.

  Your party in convérse, him you would sound,

convérse: conversation, stressed on the second syllable. **him:** for "him whom," (Abbott §208), or possibly for "he whom" making "He" in line 45 redundant. **sound:** measure the depth of, probe.

  Having ever seen in the prenominate crimes

prenominate: previously named. **crimes:** faults, lapses, not necessarily serious, but cf., I.v.12 and note.

  The youth you breathe of guilty, be assured
  He closes with you in this consequence: 45

breathe of: speak about.

closes with you in this consequence: necessarily must join with you (in conversing about the person in question) in the following way.

  "Good sir," or so, or "friend," or "gentleman,"
  According to the phrase or the addition

or so: or something of that kind (OED so 33.).

phrase or the addition: possibly a hendiadys. F has "and" for "or" (Wright, page 186). **phrase:** style of speech. **addition:** what is added to one's name, here rank and position, cf., I.iv.20, which will affect the way one speaks—another instance of the theme of the relation between the manner of doing something and the thing done.

man and country: possibly a hendiadys for man's country (Wright, page 186).

Of man and country.

REYNALDO

　　　　Very good, my lord.

POLONIUS

And then, sir, does a this—a does—what was I about to say? By the mass, I was about to say something.　　50

a: he, common throughout the play, cf., I.i.43, I.iv.37 note. **By the mass:** an oath, swearing by the liturgy of the Eucharist.

Where did I leave?

REYNALDO

　　　　At "closes in the consequence."

Where did I leave: i.e., leave off, where was I?
● Polonius loses the train of his thought in trying to cover all the possible variations he can think of and falls out of verse into prose again until he recovers the thought and returns to verse, cf., lines 24–27 and 35–37 above. That Polonius both takes pleasure in his own speech and loses its thread emphasizes his age and folly, and particularly the folly of absolute trust in his own judgment.

POLONIUS

At "closes in the consequence"—ay, marry,
He closes thus: "I know the gentleman.
I saw him yesterday," or "th'other day,"
Or then, or then, with such, or such, "and, as you say,　　55

marry: a mild oath, see line 6 note.

closes: see line 45 note.

Or then … or such: ● Polonius combines vagueness with his attempt to be exhaustive, as in lines 46 and 59.
a: he, see line 49 note, reinforced by F "he," but possibly also "There was ("he" understood) a-gaming" (Abbott §24, §400). **gaming:** gambling. **o'ertook:** overcome by drinking, drunk (OED overtake 9). **rouse:** drinking bout, carousing, from *carousal* (OED rouse *sb³* 2.), cf., I.ii.127, I.iv.8.

There was a gaming," "there o'ertook in's rouse,"

"There falling out at tennis," or perchance,

falling out: quarreling. **tennis:** "a favourite game of the aristocracy (*Sh*[akespeare's] *Eng*[land], ii.459–62), and notoriously popular in France. (Cf. *H*[enry]8 I.iii.30).… [I]t was said that there were more tennis-courts in Paris than drunkards in England. That tennis, like fencing, was a typical pastime of youthful roisterers one could infer from the habits of Poins (*2H*[enry]4 II.ii.[18–20]); the occupations that go with it here are exactly repeated in [Thomas] Tomkis, *Lingua*, III.iv.10–12…. See also Nashe [*W*], i.209" (Jenkins LN).

"I saw him enter such a house of sale"—

such a house of sale: this or that particular whorehouse.

Videlicet, a brothel, or so forth. See you now,

Videlicet: namely, that is to say, from the Latin "it is permitted to see," from Latin *videre*, to see, and *licere*, it is permitted, often abbreviated *Viz.* ● NOTE TO ACTORS: The stress is on the second syllable and the *c* is soft (*vi-DEL-i-set*). **or so forth:** cf., line 55 note. **See you now:** cf., line 6 note.

Your bait of falsehood takes this carp of truth;　　60

carp: the fish, with a possible pun on an old sense meaning talk, discourse, especially prating, chattering talk (OED carp *sb.²*, *v.¹* 4.). If the pun is meant, it is meant by the author, not by Polonius.

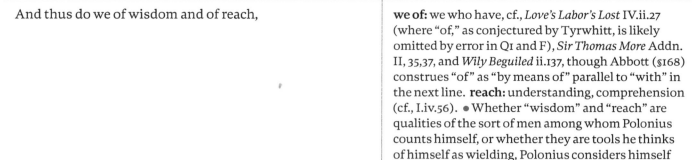

And thus do we of wisdom and of reach,

we of: we who have, cf., *Love's Labor's Lost* IV.ii.27 (where "of," as conjectured by Tyrwhitt, is likely omitted by error in Q1 and F), *Sir Thomas More* Addn. II, 35,37, and *Wily Beguiled* ii.137, though Abbott (§168) construes "of" as "by means of" parallel to "with" in the next line. **reach:** understanding, comprehension (cf., I.iv.56). ● Whether "wisdom" and "reach" are qualities of the sort of men among whom Polonius counts himself, or whether they are tools he thinks of himself as wielding, Polonius considers himself perceptive and wise.

With windlasses and with assays of bias,

windlasses: roundabout ways (OED sb.² 2., from "a circuit made to intercept game in hunting" OED sb.² 1.), cf., Golding's translation of Ovid's *Metamorphoses* II.891 and VII.1015. **assays of bias:** devious attempts, from the assessment of the curve the bowl must take in the game called "bowls" (from which we get "bowling") in order to reach the goal (called the "jack"). The bowl is weighted on one side or shaped so that it rolls not directly at the jack but with a "bias" in a lateral curve.

By indirections find directions out.

By indirections ... out: by indirect methods discover "the way things are going" (Riverside). ● This phrase is the key to the whole passage and to its relation to the Hamlet plot. Hamlet must also find out directions by indirections, just as the Ghost has already reached Hamlet through the indirect route of appearing first to the guards and Horatio. And to find out what he needs to know about Claudius, Hamlet will have to use two major indirections, his pretense of madness (in one way to Ophelia, which we will hear of in her report in this scene, and in another to Rosencrantz, Guildenstern, and the rest of the court) and the play within the play. Other examples include the King's use of Ambassadors to Old Norway, Old Norway's providential sending of Fortinbras to Poland, Polonius's use of Ophelia to spy on Hamlet, the King's use of Rosencrantz and Guildenstern to do the same and of Laertes to kill Hamlet, Hamlet's use of the sailor to carry word to Horatio, etc. By the end of the play, we will have discovered that Providence itself uses "indirections [to] find directions out," in its case infallibly, not only by the general laws of the world's operation and the specific graces shown toward men, but by the very use of our own "rough-hewing," that is, our free will choices, in its shaping of our ends (V.ii.10–11).

So by my former lecture and advice

former lecture: previous instruction. **lecture and advice:** possibly a hendiadys (Wright, page 186).

Shall you my son. You have me, have you not?   65
REYNALDO
My lord, I have.
POLONIUS
　　God buy ye, fare ye well.

Shall you my son: i.e., shall you find out (referring elliptically to the verb in line 63) my son, i.e., discover the truth about him. **have me:** understand what I am saying.

God buy ye: Originally a contraction of "May God be with you," with a serious pun, familiar to Shakespeare's audience, on "May God (i.e., Christ) buy (= redeem) you (from sin and death)," also at II.ii.549, IV.iv.30, and IV.v.200–201.

REYNALDO
Good my lord.

POLONIUS
Observe his inclination in yourself.

REYNALDO
I shall, my lord.

POLONIUS
And let him ply his music.

REYNALDO
Well, my lord.   70

                                        Exit.

                            Enter Ophelia.

POLONIUS
Farewell. How now, Ophelia, what's the matter?

OPHELIA
O my lord, my lord, I have been so affrighted!

POLONIUS
With what, i' the name of God?

OPHELIA
My lord, as I was sewing in my closet,

Lord Hamlet, with his doublet all unbraced,   75

No hat upon his head, his stockings fouled,

Good my lord: "Deferentially accepting his dismissal. Cf. II.ii.542" (Jenkins).

inclination: leaning, tendency. **in yourself:** in your own person, i.e., with your own eyes. ● This imperative is an ironically practical suggestion after all the subtle plotting and suggests that Polonius feels a last-minute need to trust the first-hand spying of Reynaldo on top of the second-hand spying of those Reynaldo is told to question, a comical conclusion because had Polonius given this instruction at the start he would have had no need for all the rest. He exhibits here a practical side that contrasts with his own "inclination" to use stratagems, but expresses no interest in questioning Laertes directly nor any expectation that he would get an honest answer from him.

ply: practice, music being "one of the essential accomplishments of the gentleman" (Jenkins). ● Like Polonius's previous imperative, this practical and common parental exhortation, in its simplicity and directness, also contrasts with the subtle plotting to find out what Laertes is up to.

s.d.: In Q2 and F Reynaldo's exit is here rather than after "Farewell" in the next line. Polonius "follows Reynaldo with his afterthoughts and is still talking as the latter leaves the stage, by which time Ophelia has entered from the other side, to confront her father as he turns" (Jenkins).

what's the matter: the response to Ophelia's rushing in obviously upset.

affrighted: frightened.

With what: by what, *with* expressing a relation of cause and effect (Abbott §193).

closet: private rooms, "the private apartment of a monarch or potentate" (OED *sb.* 2.), from French *clos*, Latin *clausum*, closed place, enclosure, not the small space for hanging clothes that the word has come to mean.

doublet: tight jacket. **unbraced:** "unfastened. Cf. [*Julius*] *Caes*[*ar*], I.iii.48, II.i.262. The doublet was fastened with buttons all down the front. To appear with it undone was very unseemly. Cf. Rowley, *A Match at Midnight*, IV (Hazzlitt's Dodsley, xiii.79), '*Widow*. You will not be so uncivil to unbrace you here?'" (Jenkins).

No hat … head: "Hats were normally worn in public, even indoors. See *Sh*[*akespeare*]'*s Eng*[*land*], ii.109" (Jenkins). ● cf., the ironic situation of Osric at V.ii.92ff., which depends upon the custom of removing one's hat in the presence of royalty.
fouled: dirty.

Ungartered, and down-gyvèd to his ankle,
Pale as his shirt, his knees knocking each other,

And with a look so piteous in purpórt

As if he had been loosèd out of hell   80

To speak of horrors, he comes before me.

Ungartered: without garters to hold them up.
down-gyvèd: fallen down around his ankles and hence looking like gyves, which are fetters or leg-irons, "A Shakespearean coinage" (Jenkins). The g is soft.

so piteous … As if: i.e., so piteous that it was as if (Abbott §275). **piteous:** pitiful, pronounced as two syllables rather than three. **purpórt:** meaning, implication, stressed on the second syllable.

As if … hell: "Perhaps a traditional simile for the madman's gaze. Cf. *Marriage of Wit and Science* (M[alone] S[ociety] R[eprint], line 1239), 'Thy look is like to one, that came out of hell'" (Jenkins). **loosèd out of:** released from.

To speak of horrors … before me: "The melancholic was thought liable to suffer from terrifying delusions of 'goblins' and other 'shapes'. See [Timothy] Bright [*A Treatise of Melancholy* (London: Vautrollier, 1586)], pages 103-4" (Jenkins). • The phrase is also a strong reminder of the Ghost's words to Hamlet at I.v.13-22.
horrors: Abbott sees "horrors" as having two stresses (§478), thus making up the pentameter;
• **SPEECH NOTE:** Hamlet has appeared to Ophelia accurately enacting the cliché melancholy of a hopeless rejected lover, cf., *Two Gentlemen* II.i.18-26, *Romeo and Juliet* I.i.131-224, and Burton III.2.3 ("Symptoms or Signs of Love-Melancholy, in Body, Mind …"). We the audience are not to fall for Hamlet's ruse, as many critics have done, imagining that Hamlet is truly anguished over Ophelia's rejection, or that he is bidding her a "despairing farewell" (Jenkins) before taking on the duties of an avenger. Hamlet has warned us that he might "put an antic disposition on" (I.v.171-72), and that is precisely what he is doing here, engaging in a somewhat less transparent kind of "indirection" than those Polonius was recommending to Reynaldo at lines 59-65.

Like Hieronimo in Kyd's *Spanish Tragedy*, in order to hide his real purposes, Hamlet wishes the court to believe that he is mad. Having had the "tenders of his affection" rejected by Ophelia under orders from her father (I.iii.132-34 and lines 106-107 here), Hamlet makes use of the opportunity provided by this circumstance to suggest to the court via Ophelia and Polonius that he is mad for love. He therefore puts on an act, dressing and behaving like the standard cliché image of the unrequited lover, including the perusal of her face and the great sigh, cf., *As You Like It* III.ii.373-81. Ophelia does not understand its import, but Polonius does and jumps immediately to the conclusion intended by Hamlet.

Thus the "wisdom and reach" Polonius boasted of earlier in the scene are ironically trumped by the greater subtlety of Hamlet while the Shakespearean audience, unlike too many modern ones, is let in on Hamlet's performance. The idea that Hamlet's true mental condition is inaccessible to us is nonsense.

POLONIUS
  Mad for thy love?

OPHELIA
          My lord, I do not know,
  But truly I do fear it.

POLONIUS
          What said he?

OPHELIA
  He took me by the wrist, and held me hard.
  Then goes he to the length of all his arm,   85
  And with his other hand thus o'er his brow
  He falls to such perusal of my face

  As a would draw it. Long stayed he so.
  At last, a little shaking of mine arm,

  And thrice his head thus waving up and down,   90

  He raised a sigh so piteous and profound

  As it did seem to shatter all his bulk
  And end his being. That done, he lets me go,
  And with his head over his shoulder turned
  He seemed to find his way without his eyes,   95
  For out a' doors he went without their helps,

  And to the last bended their light on me.

Shakespeare did not write plays in order to be obscure, and he believes what Hamlet tells Ophelia at III.ii.141–42, "The players cannot keep counsel; they'll tell all." That Hamlet is making rather unfeeling use of his beloved may strike us as unkind or even unjust. His justification lies in 1) his responsibility for all Denmark as prince and heir to the throne and (if the Ghost has spoken honestly) as rightful king, and 2) his illustration to Ophelia and to Polonius of the danger of assuming knowledge of another's soul. False presumption and breach of love can drive a true lover to madness, as he successfully has them think, erroneously, that theirs have driven him.

Mad … love?: Polonius leaps directly to the conclusion that Hamlet intended for him.

length of all his arm: holding her at arm's length.

thus: Ophelia illustrates Hamlet's gesture.

perusal: detailed examination, cf., IV.vii.136 and *Troilus and Cressida* IV.v.232.

As a would draw it: as if he wished to or intended to draw it. **a:** he. **As a would … stayed he so:** I read the stresses "Ás a would dráw it. Lóng stáyed he só," though Abbott finds only four stresses with a stress on "he" ("a"), one on the caesura, and no stress on "long" (§507), a reading that seems to contradict the intended emphasis.

thrice: three times. **his head thus waving:** We may easily read "waving" as a participle modifying "He" in the next line, though Abbott finds it a gerund (with the "of" [his head] omitted because the object comes before the verbal), parallel to "a … shaking of mine arm" in the previous line (§178).

so … As: so much … that, cf., lines 79–80 and Abbott §109. **piteous:** pitiful, as two syllables.

bulk: torso, trunk of the body.

their helps: i.e., the help of his eyes, staring back at her the whole time, for the plural see I.i.173 note.

bended their light: According to a medieval and Renaissance theory of optics, sight was made possible by the reflection from an object of an invisible beam of light proceeding from the eye (cf., Donne's "Ecstasy," lines 7–8).
  ● If the image of Hamlet looking back at his beloved as he leaves her is a reference to Orpheus and Eurydice in Ovid's *Metamorphoses* (X.57), as Jenkins suggests, it may be deliberate on Shakespeare's part but cannot be so on the

POLONIUS

Come, go with me. I will go seek the King.

This is the very ecstasy of love,

Whose violent property fordoes itself   100

And leads the will to desperate undertakings
As oft as any passion under heaven
That does afflict our natures. I am sorry—

What, have you given him any hard words of late?

OPHELIA

No, my good lord, but as you did command   105
I did repel his letters and denied
His access to me.

POLONIUS

                    That hath made him mad.

I am sorry that with better heed and judgment

I had not coted him. I feared he did but trifle

---

part of Hamlet, who cannot know that Ophelia
will be lost to him as Eurydice was to Orpheus.

go with me: "So at line 114. But at II.ii.39
Polonius arrives alone" (Jenkins, but cf., his LN).
• There is no difficulty. By II.ii some time has passed.
The ambassadors have returned, Hamlet is already
known at court to be mad, and Polonius has had time
to plan how to tell the King about Ophelia's rejection
of the Prince. The haste of Polonius here, no longer
relevant there, is easily explained by a change in his
plans, though such speculation is clearly not the
point, there being no time for it in the theater,
cf., II.ii.5 note.

This is ... our natures: The characteristic violence
of love-madness both destroys the love-madness
itself and tempts the free will to acts of despair, i.e.,
suicide, as often as any passion that afflicts human
nature. **ecstasy:** a standing outside of oneself (from
the Greek *ex-*, out, and *histanai*, to cause to stand),
whether because of joy, pain, physiological disease,
demonic possession, or any other cause, and often a
synonym for madness, as at III.i.160, III.iv.74, 138.

violent property: characteristic violence, "property"
means "that which is proper or natural to anything"
(Jenkins); the *o* in "violent" is elided. **fordoes:**
destroys, cf., V.i.221 ("did ... Fordo"). **itself:** i.e.,
the "ecstasy."

desperate undertakings: acts of despair.

I am sorry—: "Polonius breaks off what he was going
to say and resumes it at line 108" (Jenkins).

What: a sign of interrogation, as at I.i.19 and 21
(OED A. 21).

as you did command: at I.iii.121, 130–35.

That hath ... mad: • Polonius is sure, as the
monosyllables punctuate. He is so sure because a)
Hamlet is a good actor, and b) Polonius is proud of
his own "wisdom" and "reach" (line 61). In being
so, he becomes a foil for Hamlet, who in III.iii
will also a) be fooled by an appearance (Claudius
seemingly penitent in prayer), and b) trust too
much to his own "wisdom" and "reach" in the
judgment of Claudius's soul.

better heed: closer attention. **heed and judgment:**
possibly a hendiadys (Wright, page 186).

coted: observed, scrutinized (a variant form of
quoted, as in F, from the French *coter*, to put a number
on, from Latin *quotus*, how many, OED quote *v*.5.b.),
cf., *Romeo and Juliet* I.iv.31 and *Troilus and Cressida*
IV.v.233. According to Abbott (§472) the "-ed" is not
pronounced, hence the pentameter is preserved.
• The sentiment is both well justified and ironic, for
Polonius should have given Hamlet more credit (as

he should have given his own son more), and at the same time he is still lacking "heed and judgment" even now, for he continues to judge Hamlet falsely, assuming to be love-madness what we the audience know to be only the pretense of it.

And meant to wrack thee. But beshrew my jealousy!   110

wrack: ruin, wreck, cf., *All's Well* III.v.22 (Jenkins substantially). **beshrew:** F, beshrow Q2, curse. **jealousy:** suspicion (OED 5.), cf., IV.v.19, *Much Ado* II.ii.49, *Twelfth Night* III.iii.8, and as a parallel meaning throughout *Othello*.

By heaven, it is as proper to our age
To cast beyond ourselves in our opinions
As it is common for the younger sort

proper to: characteristic of. **our age:** i.e., old age.

to cast beyond ourselves: to reach too far (beyond the scent in hunting), "to suspect more than they actually know" (Jenkins). • The antithesis is between exaggerated presumption of understanding in the old and lack of judgment in the young. This formulation of Polonius too is ironic. At this moment he is guilty of precisely the flaw of presumption he recognizes as characteristic of the elderly, for he is trusting his interpretation of Hamlet's madness when we know he is as much in error now, about Hamlet's being mad because of thwarted love, as he was before about the likelihood of Hamlet's betrayal of Ophelia. The further irony is that Hamlet, in his pretended madness, is exhibiting more discretion than Polonius in his self-approving rationality (Power).

To lack discretion. Come, go we to the King.
This must be known; which, being kept close, might
                                        [move   115
More grief to hide than hate to utter love.
Come.
                            Exeunt.

Come ... to the King: see line 98 note.

This must ... utter love: The last five words of this couplet may be variously interpreted: This thwarted-love madness of Hamlet ought to be made known to the King because it might cause more harm (and therefore "grief") in being hidden from the King and the Queen than it would cause offense ("hate") in being revealed. Or Polonius may mean more "grief" than "love" for himself, rather than for the King and Queen. Abbott renders the last phrase "than our unwillingness to tell bad news would excite love" (§390), i.e, than our hate of uttering the news ("hate to utter") would move the King and Queen to love of us for doing so. Warburton finds that the clarity of this sentence is compromised by the poet's determination to end the scene with a rhyming couplet, clarifying thus: "the hiding of Hamlet's love might occasion more mischief to us from him and the Queen, than the uttering or revealing of it will occasion hate and resentment from Hamlet" (in Furness). **This:** his conclusion that Hamlet is mad because of thwarted love of Ophelia. **must:** ought to (Abbott §314, §390). **be known:** be made known (to the King). **close:** secret, hidden. **to hide ... to utter:** being concealed, being spoken of, cf., Abbott §356 on indefinite uses of the infinitive.

Act II, Scene ii

Flourish. Enter King and Queen, Rosencrantz
and Guildenstern, cum aliis.

KING

Welcome, dear Rosencrantz and Guildenstern.
Moreover that we much did long to see you,
The need we have to use you did provoke
Our hasty sending. Something have you heard
Of Hamlet's transformation; so call it,   5

Sith nor th' exterior nor the inward man

Resembles that it was. What it should be,

More than his father's death, that thus hath put him
So much from th' understanding of himself

I cannot dream of. I entreat you both   10

That, being of so young days brought up with him,

Act II, Scene ii—The main audience room
of the castle.
s.d. *Cum aliis*: Latin, with others, i.e., attendants.

Moreover: besides, in addition to the fact.

sending: sending for you.

Hamlet's transformation: ● Hamlet's apparent
madness has already become known to the King
and Queen. Later in the scene Polonius appears to
announce not the fact that Hamlet is mad, as in the
previous scene he has said he would do, but the cause
(as Polonius believes it to be) of Hamlet's already
known condition. At some point since the previous
scene Rosencrantz and Guildenstern have been sent
for and have now arrived. Hence we conclude that
some time has passed since the previous scene.
One could speculate that after Act II, Scene
i, Polonius changed plans, deciding it would be
wiser first to report Hamlet's madness and only
later to offer his opinion about its cause, but in the
theater there is no time for an audience to engage
in such speculation. If the poet had meant that
change of plans to be present to our minds, it would
somewhere be articulated in words, cf., II.i.98 note
and Introduction, page 6 note 13. **transformation:**
the "-ion," pronounced as two syllables (Abbott §479),
fills out the pentameter.

Sith: *conj.,* since, seeing that, because (OED C.2.),
as at IV.iv.45 and IV.vii.3. **nor ... nor:** = neither ... nor.
nor th' exterior ... man: neither Hamlet's outward
look and behavior nor his inner character and mood.

should be: would, could, or might be, not "ought to
be" (Abbott §325).

put him ... from: caused him to be separated from;
th' understanding of himself: his rational self-
awareness, i.e., his reason.

cannot dream of: cannot even dream of, imagine, the
of redundant according to Abbott (§179).

of: from (OED *prep.* 2.), cf., Mark 9:21 ("Then he
asked his father, How long time is it since he hath
been thus? And he said, Of a child"), whose context
is Jesus' ridding a son of a madness-causing demon,
Two Gentlemen IV.iv.3 ("that I brought up of a puppy"),
and Abbott §167. **so young days ... with him:** ● At
III.iv.202 Hamlet confirms this comradeship with
Rosencrantz and Guildenstern in grammar school, a
childhood friendship incidental to circumstances.
Note that they are not students at Wittenberg, like
Horatio, with whom Hamlet's adult friendship is by
contrast a "marriage of true minds," cf., III.ii.54–74
and Sonnet 116. The King and Queen presume that
the former kind of friend will uncover for them

And sith so neighbored to his youth and havior,

That you vouchsafe your rest here in our court

Some little time, so by your companies
To draw him on to pleasures and to gather   15

So much as from occasion you may glean,
Whether aught to us unknown afflicts him thus

That, opened, lies within our remedy.

QUEEN
Good gentlemen, he hath much talked of you,

And sure I am two men there is not living   20
To whom he more adheres. If it will please you

---

information that will be granted in fact only to the latter.

And sith: and since that time, if *sith* is *adv.* (= sithen, from OE *siððan*), assuming that "young days" refers to childhood and "youth" to young manhood, the probable meaning (Abbott §132 note). It is possible that if "young days" and "youth" are meant to be synonymous, *sith* could mean *because* as at line 6 above (being so brought up with him and because so neighbored). **neighbored to:** familiar with. **youth and havior:** his characteristic manner, expression, demeanor, behavior from youth, another hendiadys (Wright, page, 186), cf., I.ii.81.

That: a redundancy for "That" in line 11. **vouchsafe:** consent to. **your rest:** your remaining (from French *rester*).

so: combining two senses of the word, a) in this way and b) in order [to]. **companies:** for the plural see I.i.173 note.

occasion: opportunity, cf., I.iii.54. **glean:** gather.

aught: anything. **to us unknown:** unknown to me (the royal plural).

opened: being revealed. **lies ... remedy:** is able to be remedied by me (the royal plural). ● That the King sets Rosencrantz and Guildenstern to spy on Hamlet is not in itself a suspicious gesture. It was a king's responsibility to be aware of what was going on in his kingdom, particularly in relation to an heir to the throne. Nonetheless, the King's ignorance of what the audience knows about the reason for Hamlet's "transformation" suggests limitation in what even a king can know. His charge echoes that of Polonius to Reynaldo, providing another example of the attempt "by indirections [to] find directions out," cf., II.i.63. More importantly, the royal charge to Rosencrantz and Guildenstern to find out what is in Hamlet's mind is mirrored at the end of the scene when Hamlet determines, by the indirection of the play within the play, to discover what is in the mind of Claudius, thereby to avoid "tainting his mind" in case the Ghost should be a devil and Claudius not guilty.

he: Hamlet. **hath much talked of you:** ● Considering the difference between Hamlet's manner toward Rosencrantz and Guildenstern and toward Horatio, we may consider this a bit of court flattery.

sure I am ... adheres: ● If not merely court flattery, an example of self-confident overreaching, a central theme of the play (cf., Hamlet, Claudius, Polonius, Fortinbras, Clown, etc.) This claim will soon be seen to be false: we have seen Hamlet to be far more intimate with Horatio than he will be with Rosencrantz and Guildenstern. **is:** (are F) "The singular is common after 'there' even with a plural subject. Abbott [§] 335" (Jenkins). **If it will please you:** again court flattery or the show of magnanimity in the form of a polite request in place of a command.

To show us so much gentry and good will
As to expend your time with us a while

For the supply and profit of our hope,

Your visitation shall receive such thanks   25

As fits a king's remembrance.

ROSENCRANTZ
                    Both your Majesties

Might, by the sovereign power you have of us,
Put your dread pleasures more into command

Than to entreaty.
GUILDENSTERN
                    But we both obey,

And here give up ourselves in the full bent   30

To lay our service freely at your feet
To be commanded.
KING
Thanks, Rosencrantz and gentle Guildenstern.
QUEEN
Thanks, Guildenstern and gentle Rosencrantz.

---

gentry and good will: perhaps a hendiadys for gentle good will (Wright, page 186). **gentry:** gentility, courtesy, cf., V.ii.110.

supply and profit: "fulfilment and furtherance" (Kittredge), or, more likely, a hendiadys (Wright, page 186) for profitable (= advantageous) supply (= fulfillment). **of our hope:** i.e., to gain information about Hamlet, leading to a restoration of Hamlet's wits.

visitation: visit, length of stay. **thanks … fits:** *thanks* is often singular, cf., I.i.8, but cf., Abbott §247, who finds that the relative takes a singular verb even when the antecedent is plural.

As fits … remembrance: as is suitable for the appreciation of a king, a polite way of promising a substantial reward. **fits:** befits, is suitable or appropriate for. ● The Queen promises to reward Rosencrantz and Guildenstern for providing information about Hamlet.

Both your Majesties: i.e., the King and the Queen, for the plural, cf., I.i.173 note. **Majesties:** perhaps the *e* is elided, making the word two syllables (Abbott §468).

of: over (cf., OED 10 and 29.c., Abbott §174).

dread: "held in awe, deeply respected" (Jenkins), cf., I.ii.50, here modifying not the "pleasures" themselves but the King and Queen whose pleasures they are, cf., III.iv.108. **pleasures:** desires.

Than to … both obey: ● NOTE TO ACTORS: The sharing of line 29 between Rosencrantz and Guildenstern punctuates the impression that they are two of a kind, speaking as if in one voice, equally obedient and equally obsequious to the King and Queen, one acknowledging their appreciation of the Queen's civility in expressing her wish as a request rather than a command, the other committing them both to fulfilling that request.

give up: devote. **in the full bent:** entirely, "to the limit of our capacity" (Jenkins), from the image of bending a bow to its greatest possible tension in shooting an arrow, cf., III.ii.384 and *Much Ado* II.iii.223.

lay … at your feet: an ancient image of service, worship, sacrificial offering.

Thanks … gentle Rosencrantz: ● Because the names of the two courtiers are metrically identical, each an amphimacer fitting easily into an iambic line, the King and Queen can change the order in which they thank them. This reversal of the names, like the identity of their metrical structure, is another sign of the interchangeability of Hamlet's two schoolfellows. Directors often make of this line a visual joke, having the King address each by the other's name and having the Queen subtly correct him by addressing them accurately. The King's imaginary blunder, though in production it comically reinforces the notion that the two courtiers are rather indistinguishable, does not seem in character for the apparently competent Claudius. Lacking a stage direction indicating otherwise, we may presume that the King addresses them correctly and that the Queen wishes to forestall the suggestion that one is favored over the other, a subtler but similarly effective and verbally comical way of equating the two in our minds.

And I beseech you instantly to visit 35
My too much changèd son. Go some of you

instantly: immediately.

too much changèd: for the phrase compounded into an epithet modifying the noun see Abbott §434.
some: some one of you (indefinite singular). Most editors take it for plural and add '*attendants*' to the stage direction at line 39, but cf., *Pericles* V.i.9–10, "there is some of worth would come aboard; / I pray greet him fairly" and *Richard II* IV.i.268 (Jenkins substantially).

And bring these gentlemen where Hamlet is.

bring … where: bring to where.

GUILDENSTERN
Heavens make our presence and our practices

practices: activities, with an ironic play on the sense "deceptive plots" that Guildenstern does not intend.

Pleasant and helpful to him.

Pleasant: pleasing.

QUEEN
                    Ay, amen.

Exeunt Rosencrantz, Guildenstern, and an Attendant.

s.d. *an Attendant*: see line 36 note

Enter Polonius.

s.d. *Enter Polonius*: without Ophelia, despite II.i.98 and 114 and her entrance here in Q1 and in many modern productions. Polonius has presumably completed his initial plan earlier, or changed it. It is some time since Hamlet's madness has become known, though only now does Polonius try to report his opinion of its cause—see II.i.98 note.

POLONIUS
Th'ambassadors from Norway, my good lord, 40
Are joyfully returned.

ambassadors from Norway … returned: not ambassadors from Norway but our ambassadors are returned from Norway.

KING
Thou still hast been the father of good news.

still: always, as is usual in Shakespeare (Abbott §69).

POLONIUS
Have I, my lord? I assure my good liege
I hold my duty as I hold my soul,

liege: sovereign, lord to whom fealty is owed.
I hold … soul: I value my duty as I value my soul, i.e., it is a sacred trust.

Both to my God and to my gracious king; 45
And I do think—or else this brain of mine

Both … king: In the hierarchical universe that Shakespeare and his audience inherited, a king's realm is a microcosm of God's, and duty to the king is therefore a subset of duty to God.
to … and to: i.e., duty to.

Hunts not the trail of policy so sure

Hunts not … policy: "does not pursue the path of statecraft," with an ironic play on the sense of "policy" as secret plotting, a synonym for "practice," unintended by the speaker, as at line 38. **sure:** surely.

As it hath used to do—that I have found

hath used to do: has been used to doing (OED use *v.* 20.b.), an older active form of the still common passive form.

The very cause of Hamlet's lunacy.

KING

O speak of that; that do I long to hear.   50

POLONIUS

Give first admittance to th'ambassadors;

My news shall be the fruit to that great feast.

KING

Thyself do grace to them, and bring them in.

Exit Polonius.

He tells me, my dear Gertrude, he hath found

The head and source of all your son's distemper.   55

QUEEN

I doubt it is no other but the main,

His father's death and our o'erhasty marriage.

KING

Well, we shall sift him.

Re-enter Polonius, with Voltemand and Cornelius.

Welcome, my good friends.

Say, Voltemand, what from our brother Norway?

VOLTEMAND

Most fair return of greetings and desires.   60

Upon our first, he sent out to suppress

---

lunacy: madness, from an insanity, interrupted by lucid intervals, once thought to be influenced by the phases of the moon (from *lunatic*, from Latin *luna*, the moon).

Give first: i.e., first give. **admittance:** to the King's audience chamber.

fruit: dessert.

do grace: show honor. ● "With a play on grace before meat the King takes up Polonius's [feast] metaphor" (Jenkins).

head: "synonymous with *source*" (Riverside), cf., *fountainhead*. **distemper:** disease, in this case mental, from the idea that man's normal nature in health is a harmony or tempering of the four humors, cf., SPEECH NOTE after I.iv.38. We associate losing one's temper[ament] with the choleric complexion, but originally *distempered* meant suffering from a temporary or ongoing and characteristic excess or imbalance in any of the four humors or in their interrelations, which led to a *complexion* or *temperament* tending to a corresponding excess of the related emotion. Excess blood produced the *sanguine* or cheerful complexion, excess phlegm the *phlegmatic* or dull, excess black bile the *melancholic* or morose and depressed, and excess yellow bile the *choleric* or excitable and easily angered. Here Claudius is not diagnosing the particular form of distemper but merely using the word as a general term, as we might say "sickness" without specifying a disease.

doubt: suspect. **main:** main cause or source.

o'erhasty: over-hasty, precipitous. ● The Queen here acknowledges the speed of their marriage, which so upset Hamlet as shown in his soliloquy at I.ii.129–59. She is confirming that neither she nor the King has any notion of the Ghost or Hamlet's suspicions. Hamlet's friends have maintained their secrecy and their loyalty to him, in contrast to Rosencrantz and Guildenstern, who, in understandable obedience to their sovereigns, have agreed to spy on him for them.

sift him: closely question Polonius, from the image of passing something through a sieve to separate the coarse grains from the fine or the grain from the chaff. The audience may also hear a hint that the King's intention to investigate may apply to Hamlet.

what from: what message from. **our:** the royal plural. **brother Norway:** fellow-king, the King of Norway.

Most fair ... desires: The king of Norway returns the same greetings and good wishes to Claudius that Claudius has sent to him via the ambassadors. **desires:** for health, well-being, etc.

our first: as soon as we had informed him of what was happening. **sent out:** i.e., officers with orders. **to suppress ... levies:** to stop the enlisting of soldiers,

His nephew's levies, which to him appeared
To be a preparation 'gainst the Polack;
But better looked into, he truly found
It was against your highness; whereat grieved   65

That so his sickness, age, and impotence

Was falsely borne in hand, sends out arrests

On Fortinbras; which he, in brief, obeys,

Receives rebuke from Norway, and, in fine,
Makes vow before his uncle never more   70

To give the assay of arms against your Majesty.

Whereon old Norway, overcome with joy,

Gives him three thousand crowns in annual fee

And his commission to employ those soldiers,
So levied as before, against the Polack,   75
With an entreaty, herein further shown,

[Giving a paper.]

That it might please you to give quiet pass
Through your dominions for this enterprise

On such regards of safety and allowance

---

fulfilling the request that Claudius had sent to King of Norway, cf., I.ii.27–31.

to him: i.e., to the King of Norway.

a preparation 'gainst: a preparation of war to be fought against. **the Polack:** i.e., the King of Poland.

whereat: at which. **grieved:** aggrieved, offended (Riverside).

so: in this way, and also to this great degree. **impotence:** lack of strength.

Was: for the singular verb with plural subject see Abbott §336. **falsely borne in hand:** deceived, kept in a false belief, from French *maintenir* (OED bear *v.*[1] 3.e.), cf., *Much Ado* IV.i.303–304, *Macbeth* III.i.80, *Cymbeline* V.v.43 (Jenkins substantially). **sends:** for the missing "he" (elliptical nominative) see Abbott §399 and cf., III.i.8 and IV.i.10–12. **arrests:** orders to halt (French *arrêter*) his activities.

he: Fortinbras. **in brief:** to speak concisely (OED brief *a.*B.a.).

Receives rebuke from Norway: accepts chastisement from the King of Norway. **in fine:** at last, in the end (Latin *finis*).

assay: trial, attempt, challenge. **majesty:** probably two syllables with the *e* elided (Abbott §468).

Whereon: whereupon, at which (i.e., Fortinbras's vow).

three thousand: F, where Q2 has "threescore thousand," which, as Jenkins points out, is not only a colossal sum for an annual income but is unmetrical. Probably *thousand* was meant to substitute for *score*, which remained undeleted in the ms.. **annual fee:** yearly payment.

employ ... the Polack: use those previously enlisted soldiers to wage war against the King of Poland.

herein further shown: i.e., in this document, which Voltemand now hands to the King.

quiet pass: free and unmolested passage (through Denmark to Poland). "In the geography of the play Denmark seems to be thought of as lying between Norway and Poland," but "it is not profitable to seek geographical precision for what Shakespeare is content to leave vague. The play is consistent with itself in making Fortinbras plan an invasion of Denmark ... , switch his troops against Poland ... , proceed there by way of Denmark, and return by the same route" (Jenkins LN).

On such regards: according to such specific terms. **safety and allowance:** presumably Norway's guarantee of Denmark's safety from its forces and Denmark's allowance of safe passage for Norway's forces, or possibly a hendiadys (Wright, page 186). Kittredge's gloss is "on such conditions with regard to the public safety (or your own safe-conduct) as are (in this document) submitted for your approval [= 'allowance']."

As therein are set down.

therein: in that document. **set down:** explicitly written.

●SPEECH NOTE: The previous passage describing the relation of Fortinbras to his uncle, the King of Norway, is a crucial foil by which the main plot of Hamlet is illuminated. Fortinbras, to win honor, has gone off on his own, hiring mercenary soldiers to fight an illegitimate war against the King of Denmark by his own will and without the permission of his own rightful king. He is thus guilty of a major act of pride and insubordination. When the King of Norway stops him, he obeys, and when the King rebukes him, he is penitent and vows never again to pursue the illegal and impolitic vengeful war with Denmark. The King of Norway is overjoyed at the submission and obedience of his nephew and rewards him by giving him a substantial annual income and an honorable enterprise to pursue under legitimate orders. As we will see, Fortinbras's false initial step of self-willed revenge against Denmark, followed by true repentance and honorable obedience, prepares us to understand what is going on in the deeper plot of Hamlet's relation to his father, his uncle, and God. Hamlet too will take a false moral step in III.iii and will, by Providence, be obstructed, corrected, and chastened. The foil formed by Fortinbras's march to fight in Poland, from which he returns to an inheritance unlooked for, will find its parallel in Hamlet's sea voyage. What Denmark is to Fortinbras, namely a kingdom he wrongly tries to despoil and unimaginably inherits in the end, Heaven is to Hamlet.

KING

           It likes us well,   80

It likes us: We (the royal plural) are pleased, an impersonal use of the verb (OED like $v.^1$ I. and Abbott §297), cf., V.ii.265.

And at our more considered time we'll read,
Answer, and think upon this business.

more considered time: time more suitable for consideration, for the indefinite use of the passive participle, see Abbott §374. **read, /Answer, and think upon:** either metrical considerations outweigh chronological ones in the proposed order of these activities or "answer" refers to an immediate acknowledgement of receipt of Norway's proposal with the response to the proposal itself to follow after deliberation. ●Claudius will approve of the King of Norway's plan, perhaps to encourage Fortinbras to do something with his army besides attacking Denmark, and will give permission for him to cross Denmark on his way to fight the Poles (cf., IV.iv.2–4), who have in the past been enemies to Denmark as well, cf., I.i.63.

Meantime we thank you for your well-took labor.

well-took: fruitful, "usefully expended" (Raffel), on *took* for *taken* see Abbott §343.

Go to your rest; at night we'll feast together.

feast: a reasonable form of celebration for such a diplomatic victory, offering little support in this case for Johnson's accusation of intemperance in the King, cf., I.ii.125–28 note.

Most welcome home.

Most welcome home: "You are" is understood.

Exeunt Voltemand and Cornelius.

POLONIUS

This business is well ended.   85

My Liege and Madam, to expostulate

What majesty should be, what duty is,
Why day is day, night night, and time is time,
Were nothing but to waste night, day, and time.

Therefore, since brevity is the soul of wit,   90
And tediousness the limbs and outward flourishes,

I will be brief. Your noble son is mad.
Mad call I it, for to define true madness,

---

well ended: concluded successfully.

● **SPEECH NOTE:** Polonius's following speech is a satirical version of a formal rhetorical oration, whose structure—*exordium* (introduction), *narratio* (statement of the facts), *divisio* (division of the agreed on from the contested), *definitio, confirmatio* (proof), *confutatio* (refutation), *conclusio* (conclusion)—Shakespeare would have learned in his grammar school curriculum, which, after William Lily's Latin Grammar, would have included Cicero (*Ad Herennium* and *Topica*), Susenbrotus (*Epitome Troporum*), Aphthonius (*Progymnasmata*), Quintilian (*Institutio Oratoria*), and Erasmus (*De Copia*). "The particular form of [the speech] points ... unmistakably to *Ad Herennium* for its main outline ... [and] is a sufficient guarantee that Shakspere had the conventional rhetorical tricks at complete command" (Baldwin II.377). Jenkins points out (LN) that Shakespeare is satirizing a "stylistic controversy" of the time between imitators of the elaborated style of the ancient orator Cicero and opposers of that style (e.g., Thomas Campion and later Joseph Hall), who favored conciseness. Polonius claims to be on the side of brevity while in practice engaging in unnecessary rhetorical elaboration. "This misapplication of correct technical doctrine is ... one of Shakspere's favorite comic devices" (Baldwin II.375).

My Liege: the King, see line 43 note. **Madam:** the Queen. **expostulate:** any or all of three senses may be meant in Polonius's word: to demand to know, to debate about, to discourse upon (OED 1b., 2b., 3b.).

What majesty ... and time: ● An elaborate rhetorical introduction, wasting time in saying that to inquire into his list of abstractions is to waste time and then concluding with the ironic self-contradiction "I will be brief." According to Johnson (quoted in Furness and Jenkins), Shakespeare is satirizing the irrelevant prefaces in the speeches of the time, and Baldwin (II.373–77) shows how Polonius is announcing the traditional sections of a formal oration, pretending to dispense with them for the sake of brevity, and doing so with elaborate and unnecessary rhetorical art, which evokes the Queen's response at line 95.

wit: intelligence, understanding.

tediousness ... flourishes: in both words the *i* may be elided, making the former three syllables, the latter two (Abbott §467), but perhaps Polonius in vanity forgoes the elisions, in effect making the line itself tedious. **tediousness:** tiresome length, prolixity causing weariness (OED 1.). **limbs:** brevity being the soul or essence of wit, decorative elaboration is the outwardly visible physical body. **flourishes:** decorations.

I will be brief: ● The joke is that Polonius is wordy in recommending brevity. His introduction thus embodies his character in that he regularly misses the immediate application to himself of the point he

What is't but to be nothing else but mad?

But let that go.
QUEEN
                    More matter with less art.   95

POLONIUS
Madam, I swear I use no art at all.
That he is mad, 'tis true; 'tis true 'tis pity;
And pity 'tis 'tis true—a foolish figure,

is making, thus generally revealing his failure to know himself, cf., II.i.99, 107,111–14, this scene lines 189, 210–11, 498, III.i.45–48, etc. The more general implication is that words, like men and like ghosts, can say or look like one thing but mean or be another. **Your noble son is mad:** This is indeed brief, but it is followed by more self-indulgent, because unnecessary, elaboration.

nothing else but mad: If Polonius is here referring to Horace, *Satires* II.iii.41, where "The theme of the satire is that the accepted madman is no madder than anyone else. Hence the *true madness* is that of the world in general" (Jenkins), then the point here is that Polonius is failing to see that the observation he applies to others applies pointedly to himself, a self-deception analogous to Hamlet's accusation of his mother later, cf., III.iv.88 note. Polonius also lands in a simple tautology, which not only extends the discourse with unnecessary rhetorical devices but does so without adding any content to his speech to the King and Queen. It is an example of the disjunction between form and content that will become most crucial in III.iii, when Hamlet's actions and intentions become diametrically opposed.

that: i.e., that figure of speech and line of reasoning.

matter: content or substance, as opposed to form. **art:** the art of rhetoric—for a discussion of Shakespeare's persistent theme of the relation between matter and words (or phrase), essential meaning and manner of delivery, content and form, see Baldwin (II.183–84) and cf., lines 442–43 ("matter in the phrase"), II.ii.442–43, III.iv.143, and *Love's Labor's Lost* I.i.192–93, V.i.16–17, *Merchant of Venice* III.v.69–70, *Twelfth Night* I.v.210–11, *Measure for Measure* V.i.90, *1 Henry IV* II.iv.436, *King Lear* I.i.55, III.ii.81, IV.vi.8, *Troilus and Cressida* V.iii.108, *Antony and Cleopatra* II.ii.24–25, 111–112, and *Cymbeline* I.iv.16–17.

art: here artifice, as opposed to truth or nature.

'tis true 'tis pity … 'tis true: It's true that it's a pity, and it's a pity that it's true. **figure:** of speech. ● Polonius is again claiming to say the simple truth but saying it in a fused-together heap of many of the rhetorical devices of repetition that Shakespeare would have mastered in grammar school (including anadiplosis, antimetabole, antistasis, chiasmus or commutatio, diacope, epanalepsis, epizeuxis, exergasia, homiologia, pleonasmus, polyptoton, tautologia), with the alliteration, consonance, and assonance attendant on such repetitions. ● NOTE TO ACTORS: Notice especially the chiasmus of grammatical structures (a: "that he is mad," b: "'tis true," b: "'tis true," a: "[that] 'tis pity," etc.), of diction, called antimetabole ("true/pity/pity/true," lines 97–98; "cause/defect/defective/cause," lines 102–103; "thus/remains/remainder/thus," line 104), and consequently of sounds.

But farewell it, for I will use no art.

farewell it: farewell to that figure of speech. **use:** employ, practice, or speak in the form of. **art:** artifice, as Polonius intends, but with an ironic play on the art of rhetoric.

Mad let us grant him then, and now remains   100

and now remains: for the ellipsis of *it* see Abbott §404.

That we find out the cause of this effect,
Or rather say the cause of this defect,
For this effect defective comes by cause.

this effect defective: this effect that amounts to a defect in Hamlet, another instance of the figure of speech polyptoton, repetition of a root word in various forms. **comes by cause:** must come as the result of some cause, another instance of tautology.

Thus it remains, and the remainder thus:

Thus it remains … remainder thus: another instance of chiasmus and a pleonasm dressing up a tautology. **it:** may refer to the madness of Hamlet, to the "that" clause beginning at line 101, to the rhetorical (but not logical) argument's conclusion that is to follow, or to all three of them in Polonius's maze of rhetoric. **the remainder thus:** what remains to be said is as follows.

Perpend—   105

Perpend: a pretentious way of saying "consider," from the Latin "to weigh thoroughly," and, as Jenkins notes, used elsewhere in Shakespeare only by clowns, cf., *As You Like It* III.ii.67, *Twelfth Night* V.i.299, and *Henry V* IV.4.8, and, like "mark" at line 107 and "gather, and surmise" at line 108, another example of Polonius's characteristic attention-getting device, cf., II.i.6 note For the "interjectional line" see Abbott §512.

I have a daughter—have while she is mine—
Who in her duty and obedience, mark,
Hath given me this. Now gather, and surmise.

have … mine: more unnecessary rhetorical elaboration.
mark: see line 105 note.

this: a paper in his hand. **gather:** infer, deduce, conclude, from the idea of gathering knowledge from observation or reasoning (OED 10). **surmise:** conceive, imagine (OED 3.b.), and see line 105 note.

[*Reads.*] "To the celestial and my soul's idol, the

● SPEECH NOTE: **To the celestial … machine is to him, Hamlet:** Some editors doubt whether Hamlet's letter is in earnest, but there is no reason to think it is not. As Jenkins says, "It is unquestionably an affirmation of Hamlet's love…. The letter is offered (and accepted [by the King at lines 128–29]) as evidence not of Hamlet's present madness but of the love which, frustrated, led to it [according to Polonius]" (Jenkins LN). Some editors worry about whether it was sent before or after Polonius's command to Ophelia to "repel his letters," which was not made in I.iii, where only "words or talk" are forbidden to Ophelia, but is reported by Ophelia at II.i.105–106. Given the letter's invitation to Ophelia to "doubt" anything but Hamlet's love, we may assume that the letter was sent after Polonius's initial prohibition and before the instruction to "repel his letters," which may have been inspired by this one. However, none of this speculation is necessary since in the context of the reading of the letter here, no such calculations of timing can be in the audience's mind and must therefore be irrelevant. The point of the letter

here, apart from the use Polonius is making of it, is to
provide us evidence that Hamlet's assertions of true
love, reported by Ophelia at I.iii.99–114, were genuine,
as is confirmed later in his passionate outburst
at V.i.269. It is the information of the Ghost, not
Ophelia's rejection, that has driven Hamlet to make
the use of his beloved and of her apparent rejection
of him in the playacted performance that Ophelia
reports at II.i.72ff.

most beautified Ophelia"— That's an   110
ill phrase, a vile phrase; "beautified" is a

beautified: beautiful. ● The Elizabethan Homily on
the State of Matrimony asserts that in marriage a
woman "shall be most excellently beautified before
God and all his angels and saints" (II:18.1–188);
"The use of the word in religious contexts (cf. here
celestial, soul's idol) seems to have been encouraged
by confusion with 'beatified,'" and "dedications
to 'the most beautified lady' and 'the most worthily
honoured and most virtuous beautified lady' occur
respectively in Nashe's *Christ's Tears* (1594) and the
Diella of R.L. (1596). They forbid us to regard Hamlet's
superscription as wildly extravagant" (Jenkins LN).
But the word was not limited to religious contexts, for
"In his criticism of 'beautified' as an ill and vile phrase,
Polonius disagrees with the standard grammar-
school authority of his time upon phrases. The index
to the *Phrases* of Aldus Manutius under 'Beautified
bothe with riches and wit' refers one to ... 'Beautified
with the gifts of minde and of fortune'" (Baldwin
II.364). Polonius's opinion of the phrase is not shared
by the audience, and even if the word indicates a high
rhetorical style, the point of Polonius's disapproval
is that while objecting to Hamlet's rhetorical flourish
he cannot see the self-indulgence in his own.

vile phrase. But you shall hear—Thus:
[*Reads.*] "In her excellent white bosom, these"—[& c.]

But you shall hear — Thus: "In: This edition, but
you shall heare: thus in Q2, but you shall heare these
in F, and many alternative emendations. Jenkins
argues for "these" (LN), see next note. **In her ... these:**
part of the formal heading of Hamlet's letter, probably
continuing with something like "these poor lines
(or perhaps letters) shall come," cf., *Two Gentlemen*
III.i.250–52 ("Thy letters ... shall be delivered / Even in
[= into] the milk-white bosom of thy love"), for "The
plural (from Latin *litterae*) with singular sense was
very common. (cf. IV.vi.2 note)" (Jenkins).
In: into (Abbott §159). **[& c.]:** only in Q2, *et cetera*.
● The abbreviation probably indicates that the actor
playing Polonius, rather than pronouncing the
words *et cetera*, is to go on with the standard language
of letter headings until the Queen interrupts him,
though some take it as being spoken by Polonius and
meaning that he is skipping over phrases he finds
irrelevant to his purpose.
this: the letter.

QUEEN
  Came this from Hamlet to her?
POLONIUS
  Good madam, stay awhile; I will be faithful.   115

stay: wait.

[*Reads.*]
   "Doubt thou the stars are fire,
   Doubt that the sun doth move,
   Doubt truth to be a liar,
   But never doubt I love.

O dear Ophelia, I am ill at these numbers. I have   120

not art to reckon my groans. But that I love thee
best, O most best, believe it. Adieu.

●**SPEECH NOTE: Doubt thou ... never doubt I love:** Whatever sense is given to "doubt" in line 118, I cannot agree with Jenkins that Hamlet's poem "leaves the status of truth and hence of Hamlet's love in some ambiguity." Nothing in the context of the letter puts the genuineness of Hamlet's love for Ophelia into doubt, and ambiguity about it can only be externally imposed by the critic. Some commentators wish to complicate Hamlet's verse by suggesting that, being aware of the new Copernican astronomical paradigm, Shakespeare meant Hamlet's lines to cast doubt on the undoubted certainties themselves (that the stars are fire, that the sun moves). Again, such an argument injects a modern ambiguity irrelevant to the play. Hamlet is calling upon the surest things he can think of, capped by the truth of truth itself, to exhort his beloved to believe what both her brother and her father have labored to persuade her *not* to believe, namely that he genuinely loves her. Jenkins asserts that Shakespeare, though not Hamlet, "must have been aware" of the irony in the lines' assertion of "what had now begun to be doubted," i.e., the astronomical verities. Perhaps, but the point is irrelevant to the play and its audience. The dramatic sense of the letter depends on Hamlet's meaning the listed phenomena to be self-evidently true.
Doubt: The senses are "disbelieve" in lines 116 and 117 (OED 2.), "fear" (OED 5.b.) or "suspect" (OED 6.b.) in line 118 (that truth is a liar), and "disbelieve" again in line 119, though it is possible that in line 118 the sense is also "disbelieve" with an elliptical implication = disbelieve in truth itself in that it may be being a liar (cf., Abbott §356).

ill: not good at, bad at. **numbers:** metrical lines of verse.

art: of verse-writing and of counting. **reckon:** express (by the art of poetry), count (by the art of arithmetic). ●Hamlet says he has not the art either to make metrical verse lines or to count up his groans of unhappiness at her doubting and rejecting him. The simplicity of Hamlet's verse is evidence not of its falsity but of the opposite. He himself confesses to be unable to express in verse how much he loves her. By contrast, Polonius has shown that his own rhetorical abilities are perfectly equal to the task of saying nothing much in a lot of words. Baldwin finds the influence of Erasmus (*Modus Conscribendi Epistolas*), who recommends that "if we shall solicit the mind of a girl to mutual love, we use especially two battering rams, praise, and pity. For all people but especially girls delight in praise, especially of beauty.... Then because that ilk is tender hearted and easily moved to pity, we will study to be as suppliant as possible." "Hamlet has used the two battering rams, praise of the lady's beauty [lines 109–110], and pity for the lover's groans [line 121]" (Baldwin II.284–85).

Thine evermore, most dear lady, whilst this machine
is to him,
            Hamlet."
This in obedience hath my daughter shown me   125

And, more above, hath his solicitings,
As they fell out by time, by means, and place,
All given to mine ear.

KING
                    But how hath she
Received his love?

POLONIUS
                    What do you think of me?

KING
As of a man faithful and honorable.   130

POLONIUS
I would fain prove so. But what might you think,
When I had seen this hot love on the wing—
As I perceived it, I must tell you that,
Before my daughter told me—what might you
Or my dear Majesty your queen here think   135

If I had played the desk or table-book,

Or given my heart a winking, mute and dumb,

Or looked upon this love with idle sight—

What might you think? No, I went round to work,

And my young mistress thus I did bespeak: 140

---

this machine: his body, in the sense of a complex and natural physical entity with interrelating parts and motion, rather than in the sense of the artificial mechanical tool with which we associate the word after the Industrial Revolution. **is to:** belongs to, "cf. our idiom, There is a great deal *to* him" (Jenkins). **more above:** F, in addition, furthermore (Q2 has "more about"). **hath ... given:** the subject of the verb is still "my daughter," i.e., Ophelia has told me ("given to mine ear") his wooing ("solicitings") in all particulars. **fell out:** happened. **by:** according to, along with (cf., Abbott §145). **time ... means, and place:** three of the "circumstances" (systematized from Aphthonius and Quintilian by Johannes Veltkirchius in his edition of Erasmus' *De Copia*, 1534) with which students in Shakespeare's grammar school would have been taught to "amplify" and "dilate" a narrative. The nine circumstances were person, time, place, mode (means), cause, occasion, instrument, number, and accident, with some authors listing opportunity, thing, and act (Baldwin II.316–319), cf., line 157.

fain: as verb = desire to, as an adverb = gladly, willingly.

As I perceived it: The evidence of I.iii.91–99 suggests that Polonius did not actually know it was "hot love" before Ophelia told him, though he seems to have heard something of court gossip (I.iii.91). His claim that he did perceive it continues Polonius's willingness to exaggerate his own perceptiveness and to adjust the truth for his own purposes, as he taught Reynaldo to do in II.i.

desk: on which letters are written. **table-book:** writing-tablet, cf., Hamlet's metaphorical "tables" at I.v.107 and note ● The desk and table-book are themselves speechless, passive observers (not, as Jenkins has it, givers of active assistance). To have "played the desk" must mean to have behaved like an inanimate piece of furniture, ignoring what was taking place on it.

winking: shutting the eyes, being willfully blind, connivance (Clarendon in Furness), cf., *Henry V* II.ii.55, V.ii.300ff., *Macbeth* I.iv.52, *Cymbeline* V.iv.186–87, etc.. **dumb:** silent. ● The contrast with the previous line is that here an animate being is actively choosing to be silent.

idle: detached, uncaring, "as distinct from the deliberate connivance of the previous line" (Jenkins).

round: roundly, i.e., thoroughly (OED 2.), plainly (OED 3. and 4.), sharply, or severely (OED 5.), cf., III.i.183, III.iv.5, and Abbott §60.

my young mistress: "a condescending" phrase (Jenkins), self-protectively implying to the King and Queen a chastising tone toward Ophelia. **bespeak:** address formally, cf., Abbott §438.

"Lord Hamlet is a prince out of thy star;

out of thy star: beyond your degree of fortune, thought of as determined by astrological influence, cf., I.iv.32 and *Twelfth Night* II.v.143–44. ● As we know, this is not what Polonius actually said in I.iii, where he was concerned with Hamlet's potential compromising of Ophelia's virtue, not with her trying to rise in station. Here again he adjusts the truth to paint himself in colors calculated to win royal approval. That attempt is ironic in light of the Queen's implying at V.i.244 that she has intended Ophelia for Hamlet all along.

This must not be." And then I prescripts gave her,
That she should lock herself from his resort,

prescripts: instructions, orders (cf., *prescriptions*).
lock herself from: close herself off to. **resort:** visiting (OED 4.).

Admit no messengers, receive no tokens.
Which done, she took the fruits of my advice,   145

tokens: love-tokens, gifts.
took the fruits of: obeyed, followed, making the advice fruitful.

And he, repelled—a short tale to make—
Fell into a sadness, then into a fast,

repelled: cf., "repel" at II.i.106.
sadness: heavy seriousness of mood (not merely, as in the modern sense, unhappiness). **fast:** refusal to eat.

Thence to a watch, thence into a weakness,

Thence to … into a weakness: "The repeated 'thence' seems to require a pause" which "may excuse the absence of an unaccented syllable, additional stress being laid on the [following] monosyllable" (Abbott §483), here with minor stress on the *to* of "into" (Abbott §457a). **watch:** wakefulness, insomnia. **weakness:** physical and mental debility.

Thence to a lightness, and, by this declension,
Into the madness wherein now he raves   150

lightness: of brains, disorientation, a result of wakefulness, as in *Comedy of Errors* V.i.71–72. **declension:** decline. ● The order of debilities is standard for disappointed lovers, cf., Ophelia's description at II.i.75–97 and II.i.81 note, *Two Gentlemen* II.i.18–26, *Romeo and Juliet* I.i.131–224, and Burton III.2.3. But Polonius is only pretending to have observed the cliché symptoms. Shakespeare's early editor Warburton points out the irony: Polonius "would not only be thought to have discovered this intrigue by his own sagacity, but to have remarked all the stages of Hamlet's disorder … when all the while the madness was only feigned."

And all we mourn for.
KING
              Do you think 'tis this?
QUEEN
    It may be, very like.
POLONIUS
    Hath there been such a time—I would fain know that—

And all we: the pronoun "we" is stressed in parallel to "he" in the previous line, cf., Abbott §240.

like: likely.

fain: see line 131 note above.

That I have positively said "'Tis so"
When it proved otherwise?
KING
              Not that I know.   155

That: when, at which (Abbott §284).

Polonius [*Pointing to his head, then his shoulder,
then the paper.*]

Take this from this if this be otherwise.

If circumstances lead me, I will find
Where truth is hid, though it were hid indeed
Within the center.

KING

How may we try it further?

POLONIUS

You know sometimes he walks four hours together   160

Here in the lobby.

QUEEN

So he does indeed.

POLONIUS

At such a time I'll loose my daughter to him.

Be you and I behind an arras then,

Take this …: ● Polonius's rhetorical willingness to lose his head if he is wrong about this matter is comical (and Jenkins points out the parallel to the heroic Odysseus at *Iliad* II.259), but it also foreshadows the fatally ironic consequence in III.iv of Polonius's unqualified trust in his own interpretation of things.

If circumstances … center: "This was the ambition of every searcher for truth. By drawing his subject through the circumstances he hoped to *invent* or find out truth" (Baldwin II.320), referring to the nine "circumstances" of narration listed at line 127 note above. **though it were:** implying "I *would* find it though it were hid" because in conditional sentences "The consequent does not always answer to the antecedent in mood or tense" often because of "a change of thought" (Abbott §371). **center:** "the centre of the earth, traditionally thought of as its most inaccessible point and the most remote from the light of day. Cf. *Volpone,* I.i.9–10, 'the day Struck out of chaos, when all darkness fled Unto the centre'; Tourneur, *Atheist's Trag.,* IV.iii.282, 'I will search the centre'" (Jenkins). ● The center of the earth is also the point around which, in the Ptolemaic astronomy, all the concentric spheres of the created universe and its stars turn. Polonius's over-confidence in his ability to find truth we already know to be misplaced. But the passage also makes Polonius's pride a foil for Hamlet's excessive trust in his own judgment at III.iii and the fatal consequences of that trust.

try: test (cf., *trial*).

four: "Commonly used for 'several' and hence not to be taken precisely. Cf. *Duchess of Malfi,* IV.i.9, 'She will muse four hours together'. Elze collected many examples in *Sh*[*akespeare*] *Jahr*[*buch*], XI, 288–94" (Jenkins, cf., Furness).

lobby: passage, corridor, antechamber (OED 2., citing this passage and 2 *Henry VI* IV.i.61).

loose: release from restraint. ● Jenkins points out the contrast with line 143 above ("lock herself from his resort"), and suggests that "the mating sense of *loose … to him* can hardly be missed. Cf. [*Merry Wives*] II.i.[182–83]." Even if so, any sexual implication of loosening from restraint must be unintentional on the part of Polonius.

arras: a rich hanging tapestry woven with figures and scenes, named for the town (Arras in Artois) in which it was made, and used as a screen hung in front of the walls of great houses, sometimes distant enough from the wall to conceal a person (OED and Nares in Furness).

Mark the encounter. If he love her not
And be not from his reason fall'n thereon,   165
Let me be no assistant for a state,
But keep a farm and carters.

KING

                                        We will try it.

Enter Hamlet, reading on a book.

QUEEN
But look where sadly the poor wretch comes reading.

POLONIUS
Away, I do beseech you both, away.

I'll board him presently. O give me leave.   170
                    Exeunt King, Queen, and Attendants.
How does my good Lord Hamlet?

HAMLET
Well, God-a-mercy.

POLONIUS
Do you know me, my lord?

HAMLET
Excellent well; you are a fishmonger.

POLONIUS
Not I, my lord.   175

HAMLET
Then I would you were so honest a man.

POLONIUS
Honest, my lord?

HAMLET
Ay, sir. To be honest, as this world goes, is to be
one man picked out of ten thousand.

Mark: watch, pay attention to.

thereon: because of that, i.e., if Hamlet is mad for any reason other than obstructed love of Ophelia.

carters: horse-and-cart drivers, i.e., farm workers, who are of low status compared to the present position of Polonius.

try: test, attempt (cf., *trial* and line 159 above).

s.d. *a book:* not convincingly identified with any particular book known.

sadly: soberly, gravely (Raffel). **wretch:** miserable, unfortunate person, affectionately meant, cf., IV.vii.182 and V.ii.333.

Away: i.e., go away. **you both, away:** Jenkins, you both away Q2, you, both away F. ●NOTE TO ACTORS: Since Q2 and F differ, one may choose among the three alternatives depending on whether one wants greater stress on "away" (Jenkins and Q2) or on "both" (F).

board: approach, address, accost (OED 4.), from the idea of boarding a ship. **presently:** immediately, cf., line 591. **O give me leave:** i.e., leave me (Raffel), give me the benefit of your departure, explained by Jenkins as follows: "A formula not of accosting, as often supposed, but of farewell. From being a request for permission (to depart), it came to be a courteous form of dismissal. Probably [here] addressed to attendants who do not vanish with sufficient alacrity." F places the exit of the King and Queen after "I'll board him presently," leading some editors to take this phrase as the opening of the speech to Hamlet. But Polonius would not begin speaking to the Prince without some form of direct address, which is present in the next line. Hence either this phrase must be directed at attendants and mean what Jenkins and Raffel say, or else it is a reiteration (typical of Polonius) of what he has already said to the King and Queen: go away, I'll speak to Hamlet immediately, please allow me (to do so).

God-a-mercy: God have mercy (on you), meaning "thank you" as in *King John* I.i.185 (Jenkins substantially).

know: recognize.

fishmonger: seller of fish, probably also one whose wife or daughter is particularly lusty and fertile (Jenkins LN), and possibly also a bawd, though the evidence is scanty for the word's use in that sense.

so: as (honest as a fishmonger), cf., Abbott §275. **honest:** respectable, honorable, but also sexually upright.

picked: chosen for particular excellence, "the more usual formula, as cited by Tilley (M 217), [being] 'a man among a thousand'" (Jenkins).

POLONIUS

That's very true, my lord.   180

HAMLET

For if the sun breed maggots in a dead dog, being
a good kissing carrion—Have you a daughter?

POLONIUS

I have, my lord.

HAMLET

Let her not walk i' th' sun. Conception is a blessing,
but as your daughter may conceive—friend, look   185
to't.

For if the sun ... dead dog: As Jenkins explains (LN),
the sun, in ancient times thought of as a god, was
believed to be the source of life (cf., Spenser, *Faerie
Queene* III.vi.9) and into Elizabethan times was
imagined to breed life in earthly bodies, e.g., spirits
(alcohol) in grapes, serpents and crocodiles out of
Nile mud (cf., *Antony and Cleopatra* II.vii.26–27), and
flies out of rotting flesh, though any corruption bred
by the sun was a function of the corruption of the
body in which it was bred, heir of Adam's fall, and not
of the sun itself. **being:** modifying the dead dog, not
the sun. **good kissing carrion:** *carrion* is the dead
and rotting flesh of a carcass, and *good kissing* may be
either good to kiss, hence "flesh good enough for the
sun to kiss" (Riverside), for which Jenkins (following
Caldecott and Corson, quoted in Furness, I.148–50)
offers the analogies "good eating apple" and "too
hard-a-keeping oath" (from *Love's Labor's Lost* I.i.65),
or kissed by the good, hence "carrion that the good
(sun) kisses."

Conception: conceiving an idea (= rational thought)
and conceiving a child, cf., the same pun in *King Lear*,
I.i.12–13. **may conceive:** may understand the subject,
may get pregnant. **look to't:** take care, be wary.
● SPEECH NOTE: **you are a fishmonger ... look to't:**
The whole previous passage is playacted madness,
primarily intended to confirm Polonius's
interpretation of Hamlet's "transformation" (line 5
above) as caused by thwarted love for Ophelia, yet
also implying some "method" (line 206), cf., the
Gentleman's description at IV.v.7–13 of the court's
seeking meaning in Ophelia's mad words. Hamlet's
giving Polonius the occupation of *fishmonger* (line
174) suggests that Hamlet is a) insultingly demoting
Polonius, b) implying, to us, though Hamlet has not
heard it (line 162), that Polonius will use his daughter
as bait in fishing for the cause of Hamlet's madness,
c) ironically taunting him with having a lusty
daughter when he has in fact forbidden her to speak
with Hamlet for fear of injury to her chastity, and d)
accusing Polonius of thinking of his daughter as so
much marketable, and spoilable, flesh.

From these insults Hamlet moves to the theme
of honesty, implying a) that Polonius is less honest
than a simple tradesman, b) that an honest man is a
rarity, one among many, as a fish sold at market is one
picked out of a sea of multitudes, and c) that Polonius
is dishonest, meaning both dishonorable and not
himself chaste, in not trusting to the chastity of his
daughter and to the honor of Hamlet and perhaps in
approving the "o'erhasty" royal marriage.

In the next image Hamlet employs an extreme
oxymoron, bringing together the "god of day" of
I.i.152 and maggots in a dead dog, spanning almost
the whole range of creation, a) to punctuate the great

distance between the source of good (honesty) and corruption (dishonesty), b) to imply that if the sun can breed maggots in a dead dog, then perhaps honesty *may* be found in fallen man, though in not more than one in ten thousand, continuing the implication of the dishonesty of Polonius, and c) to warn Polonius not to walk in the sun, with a play on *son*, implying the danger of presuming to fathom Hamlet's mind, lest Polonius's own corrupt nature, like that of a dead dog, breed further corruption. Coleridge's gloss ("if the sun ... can raise life out of a dead dog, why may not good fortune, that favors fools, have raised a lovely girl out of this dead-alive old fool?"), though attractive, misses both the insult intended to Polonius and the thwarted lover's mad sex-aversion from which Hamlet is pretending to suffer.

Finally, moving from "breed" to "conceive" and from Polonius to Ophelia, Hamlet moves from the *sun/son* pun of line 181 to *daughter* in line 182, implying that in denying Hamlet access to Ophelia, Polonius is treating her as if she were sure to be corrupted by walking in the presence of Hamlet. The *sun/son* of Denmark (cf., *Richard III* I.i.2) is chiding Polonius for keeping Ophelia ("good kissing" flesh) from his presence for fear she will breed corruption by him and implying that the real corruption lies in Polonius himself, who thinks of Ophelia as merely carrion, i.e., flesh in which breeding may happen, rather than as a person with virtue of her own.

In all of this it is crucial to remember that Hamlet has in mind the Ghost's accusation of Gertrude (I.v.45–46), her "o'erhasty" marriage, and Ophelia's rejection of his attentions. That his mother has become tainted (cf., III.iv.34–196) causes Hamlet to fear the same threat to the virtue of his beloved. None of this imagery signifies that Hamlet is in fact obsessed by sex and reproduction, or (*pace* Jenkins) that Hamlet suffers from some characteristic "malaise." In response to the call of his particular situation, Hamlet is performing the role of the melancholy lover and using that disguise to express his exasperation with the "tedious old fool" Polonius. He is disgusted by his mother's having been won to Claudius's lust (I.v.45) and by the presumption of Polonius that Hamlet's intentions about Ophelia were illicit. Fueled by that disgust, he is playacting one of the familiar forms of madness known to the Renaissance, namely abhorrence of sex arising from thwarted love in the form of *melancholia adust*, the excess and then corruption of the humor of melancholy (= black bile) (see Introduction, pages 12–13 and Burton III.2.3, page 721 and passim). Just as Ophelia's description of Hamlet's behavior in II.i revealed that Hamlet was performing the role of cliché thwarted lover, so here he performs the next stage of that role, which is an exaggerated preoccupation with sex, chastity, and purity that ends in irrational abhorrence of sex and even

POLONIUS [*aside.*]
> How say you by that? Still harping on my

daughter. Yet he knew me not at first; a said I was a
fishmonger. A is far gone. And truly in my youth I
suffered much extremity for love, very near this. I'll   190
speak to him again.—What do you read, my lord?

HAMLET
> Words, words, words.

POLONIUS
> What is the matter, my lord?

HAMLET
> Between who?

POLONIUS
> I mean the matter that you read, my lord.   195

HAMLET
> Slanders, sir; for the satirical rogue says here that old
men have grey beards, that their faces are

wrinkled, their eyes purging thick amber and
plum-tree gum, and that they have a plentiful lack of
wit, together with most weak hams—all which, sir,   200
though I most powerfully and potently believe, yet I

hold it not honesty to have it thus set down, for

yourself, sir, shall grow old as I am, if like a crab you
could go backward.

of marriage. The performance reaches its peak at
III.i.102–149. In short, throughout this passage Hamlet
is continuing the ruse that he is mad for love of Ophelia.
In addition, in ironically advising Polonius to do what
we know he has already done, i.e., forbidden Ophelia
to see Hamlet, he is ridiculing Polonius for lack of faith
in Ophelia's virtue and in Hamlet's, thereby accusing
Polonius of not knowing with whom he is dealing.

How say you by that: "A triumphant exclamation"
(Kittredge), "What do you say about that!" (Jenkins),
for *by* meaning *about*, cf., Abbott §145, *Merchant of Venice*
I.ii.54, and *All's Well* V.iii.237. **Still:** always.**harping:** to
dwell on repeatedly, from "harping on one string"
(OED *v.* 3.).

a: he.
A: he.

matter: Polonius means the subject matter.

Between who?: Hamlet "deliberately misunderstands"
(Jenkins), taking *matter* in the sense of an issue of
contention. **who:** for *whom*, cf., Abbott §274 for the
often neglected inflection.

satirical rogue: The passage Hamlet reads, or pretends
to read, is by an imaginary author, or by Hamlet himself.
Its satire of the debilities of old age possibly alludes to
Juvenal, *Satires* 10.188ff. (Warburton), in a passage that
would have been known to Shakespeare and members
of the audience from grammar school (Baldwin
II.526–28), though Jenkins rejects the identification of
the book Hamlet is reading with any known work put
forward by others as candidates (e.g., Juvenal, Erasmus'
Praise of Folly, and Guazzo's *Civil Conversation*).

purging: dripping, exuding. **amber:** ambergris.

plum-tree gum: sap, referred to in Gerard's *Herbal*
but possibly proverbial (Jenkins). **hams:** thighs and
buttocks (OED *sb.*[1] 1.b.; Crystal), possibly knee-joints
(OED *sb.*[1] 1.a.; Schmidt).

honesty: appropriateness, decorum, cf., *Othello*
IV.i.277–78, with added implications there.

old as: as old as, the first *as* is sometimes omitted
(Abbott §276). **old as I am if ... backward:**
● Hamlet's point is that though the supposed author's
statements are true, it is not proper ("honest") to write
them because no one can help growing older. One
cannot go back in time as a crab can go backward in
space. Thus facts used to satirize what can't be helped
are roguish. Whether Hamlet is reading or making up
the satire, he is reminding Polonius that the latter is old
and ought to realize that he has less wit than he thinks.

POLONIUS [*aside.*]
  Though this be madness, yet there is method in't.   205

  —Will you walk out of the air, my lord?

HAMLET
  Into my grave?

POLONIUS
  Indeed, that's out o' the air. [*Aside.*] How pregnant

  sometimes his replies are—a happiness that often
  madness hits on, which reason and sanity could not   210

  so prosperously be delivered of. I will leave him and

  suddenly contrive the means of meeting between
  him and my daughter.—My lord, I will take my leave
  of you.

HAMLET
  You cannot take from me anything that I will more   215
  willingly part withal—except my life, except my life,
  except my life.

POLONIUS
  Fare you well, my lord.

HAMLET
  These tedious old fools!

              Enter Rosencrantz and Guildenstern.

POLONIUS
  You go to seek the Lord Hamlet; there he is.   220

ROSENCRANTZ [*To Polonius.*]
  God save you, sir.

                                        Exit Polonius.

GUILDENSTERN
  My honored lord.

ROSENCRANTZ
  My most dear lord.

HAMLET
  My excellent good friends. How dost thou,
  Guildenstern? Ah, Rosencrantz. Good lads, how   225
  do you both?

madness … method: Possibly an allusion to Horace (*Satires* II.3.265–71), but "it was inevitable in a rhetorical age that madness and method should mount the opposite ends of a see-saw" (Baldwin II.516). ● Polonius, as usual, misses the point: Hamlet succeeds in keeping up the illusion of his madness while Polonius, recognizing "method," i.e., rational order of ideas, in Hamlet's words, yet misses, as he is meant to do, that the madness itself is Hamlet's method to achieve something of which Polonius knows nothing. The audience recognizes that given Polonius's ignorance of the hidden facts, a degree of humility is called for that he does not have.

out of the air: in from the outdoors, which was thought to be bad for the ill. Like lines 299–301 and III.ii.376, the line gives an instance of the "unlocalized stage" (Jenkins LN). ● Hamlet again deliberately takes the phrase literally.

pregnant: imaginative, inventive, resourceful, particularly in one's wit (OED *a*².3a. and b.), full of potential meaning, which may or may not be born, cf., "delivered of" at line 211 and "conceive" at line 185.

happiness: good fortune.

hits on: comes upon, finds, meets with (OED *v.* 12). **sanity:** F, sanctity Q2.

be delivered of: give birth to, cf., "pregnant" at line 209.

suddenly: immediately, right away.
take my leave: This form both announces one's departure and asks permission for it, cf., *1 Henry IV*, I.iii.20 ("You have good leave to leave us").

cannot take: Q2, cannot Sir take F. **will more willingly:** F, will not more willingly Q2. The double negative was common as an expression of emphasis (Abbott §406), but F corrects it. Hamlet is saying "good riddance". **except my life:** intended to reinforce the impression of the melancholy madness of thwarted love (cf., Burton III.2.4).

These tedious old fools!: ● An obvious aside to the audience and a reminder that Hamlet is not mad in any sense, and that Polonius is foolish, not merely because Hamlet has succeeded in fooling him but because in general he casts beyond himself in his opinions, cf., II.i.112.

ROSENCRANTZ
  As the indifferent children of the earth.

GUILDENSTERN
  Happy in that we are not over-happy;

  On Fortune's cap we are not the very button.

indifferent: middling, average, neither at one extreme nor at another (OED 6. and 7.).

Happy: fortunate. **not over-happy:** cf., Polonius's recommendation of the golden mean to Laertes at I.iii.59–80.

Fortune's cap: • From ancient times, Fortuna was thought of as a goddess, blindfolded, enthroned above the world and turning a great wagon or spinning wheel, by which motion she continually redistributes all worldly goods and fortunes. The wheel was often pictured with a king enthroned at the top and a beggar at the bottom, which, as Fortuna turned her wheel, changed places, the king falling to ruin on one side as the beggar climbed to great fortune on the other. In Christian art and literature (e.g., Dante's *Divine Comedy*), Fortuna was sometimes thought of as serving God, by her often unmerited redistributions reminding men to attach themselves not to worldly goods and mutability but to God and virtue. Many medieval cathedrals depict Fortune's wheel above their west entrances with the spaces between the spokes being stained-glass windows. The same architectural structure that from the outside appeared to be the wheel of fortune, its material spokes bright in the sunlight and spaces dark, representing worldly things, is revealed when seen from inside the church to be a great window in the form of a rose, the material frame dark and the glass petals light. The rose symbolized both the Virgin Mary, to whom the medieval cathedrals were dedicated, and the heavenly host of saved souls. Cf., the White Rose in Dante's *Paradiso*, Cantos XXX–XXXI. **button:** at the top of the cap, the peak of good fortune.

HAMLET
  Nor the soles of her shoe?   230

ROSENCRANTZ
  Neither, my lord.

HAMLET
  Then you live about her waist, or in the middle of
  her favors?

soles of her shoe: the lowest point, the nadir of bad fortune.

Neither: not that either.

favors: Q2 ("favour" in F), regard, attention, disposition toward (OED 1.c.), with a pun on clothing decoration (ribbons, cockades, rosettes, etc.) parallel to "cap" and "shoe" (OED 7.b.), and on physical features (OED 9.c.), or, if F has the correct reading, her beauty, attractiveness, or her aspect, look, and hence her person, body (OED 8. and 9.)

GUILDENSTERN
  Faith, her privates we.

HAMLET
  In the secret parts of Fortune? O most true; she is a   235
  strumpet. What news?

privates: ordinary subjects, neither slaves nor office-holders, with a pun on genitalia, picked up by Hamlet in the next line as "secret parts."

strumpet: whore, another common image of Fortuna in the Renaissance because she is faithful to no man, cf., line 493.

ROSENCRANTZ
None, my lord, but the world's grown honest.

HAMLET
Then is doomsday near. But your news is not true.

Let me question more in particular. What have you,
my good friends, deserved at the hands of Fortune,   240
that she sends you to prison hither?

GUILDENSTERN
Prison, my lord?

HAMLET
Denmark's a prison.

ROSENCRANTZ
Then is the world one.

HAMLET
A goodly one, in which there are many confines,   245
wards, and dungeons, Denmark being one o' th'
worst.

ROSENCRANTZ
We think not so, my lord.

HAMLET
Why then 'tis none to you; for there is nothing
either good or bad but thinking makes it so.   250
To me it is a prison.

but the: Q2, but that the F. **honest:** upright, virtuous, truthful, cf., lines 176–79 and 202, an obviously ironic throwaway line, from their point of view intended to evoke verbal wit but to the audience hinting at the moral obtuseness of these two spies for the King.

doomsday: The day of the Last or Final Judgment, on which the dead will be raised and both the living and the dead judged by God for heaven or hell. **near:** because dishonesty is so universally a characteristic of fallen mankind (cf., lines 178–79), the world "grown honest" would signify the end of time.

Let me question ... dreadfully attended: This passage is not in Q2, only in F, more likely a cut in the printing of Q2 than added in the printing of F, which we deduce because the omitted passage leaves us with two "but" clauses and a capital after a semicolon ("but your news is not true; But in the beaten way of friendship, what make you at Elsinore?") and with a "discontinuity of thought," which the passage in F supplies, the "link between the discussion of Fortune's treatment of the new arrivals and the reason for their coming." Why the passage was omitted is not certainly known, though some suspect suppression of "derogatory references to Denmark, out of deference to Anne of Denmark, James I's queen" (Jenkins substantially).

prison: "The feeling of being in prison was a recognized symptom of melancholy. Cf. Bright, page 263" (Jenkins), and cf., Burton, I.3.1.2, page 337.

goodly: good-looking, sizeable, excellent, all also possibly ironically meant (OED 1., 2., 3., and 3b.). **confines:** enclosures, places of confinement (OED sb.² 5.), probably stressed here on the first syllable. **wards:** prison cells.

none to you: not one (i.e., a prison) to you. **there is nothing ... thinking makes it so:** ● Perhaps the most dangerous line in the play to be misunderstood, as it often is. Hamlet cannot possibly mean, like a modern-day Existentialist, that there are no moral absolutes, that everything is relative. Such a meaning is only possible in an age that has ceased to believe in God. For all the doubts and questioning that characterize the philosophical, moral, and religious investigations of the Renaissance, such a meaning is still foreign to it, and not only Hamlet's character as portrayed but the entire play would fall into ruin if such an intent were taken to be a general principle. The real point of the statement is that it is only in thought that anything is experienced as positive or negative. If you *think* Denmark is a prison, then for you it is, and if you do not think so, then for you it isn't. In addition, Denmark (and the world) are always from one viewpoint prisons and always from another viewpoint not prisons, and whether or not they are so to a given man at a given time will depend upon his own thinking, that is, on the state of his soul. A smile is good if it is a smile revealing goodness, but "one may smile, and smile, and be a villain" (I.v.108). Good and evil are perceived and experienced in relation to the state of the soul of the perceiver. As Hamlet and the audience will learn, if you think the actually bad is good, then to you it appears to be good, but in thinking so you have become bad. (An earlier statement of this idea appears in Rappaport "R&R"). See Jenkins LN, which provides comparable passages: Montaigne, *Essays* I.40: "That the Relish for Good and Evil Depends in Great Measure upon the Opinion We Have of Them"; Lyly: "It is the disposition of the thought that altereth the nature of the thing"; Nashe: "So that our opinion (as Sextus Empiricus affirmeth) gives the name of good or ill to every thing"; Spenser, *F.Q.* VI.ix.30: "It is the mynd that maketh good or ill, / That maketh wretch or happie, rich or poore"; Donne, "Metempsychosis: The Progresse of the Soule," 518–20: "Ther's nothing simply good, nor ill alone, / Of every quality comparison, / The onely measure is, and judge, opinion"; and other examples in Tilley M254. "[T]he inference that Hamlet maintains that there are no ethical absolutes (Levin, *The Question of Hamlet*, page 75) is false" (Jenkins LN).

ambition: • As Polonius assumes Hamlet's madness arose from frustrated love, so Rosencrantz and Guildenstern assume that Hamlet is suffering from "frustrated ambition (for the throne)" (Jenkins), thwarted ambition being another well-established cause of melancholy, cf., Burton, I.2.3.11: "*Ambition*, a proud covetousness, or a dry thirst of honour, a great torture of the mind.... If they do obtain their suit, ... their anxiety is anew to begin, for they are never satisfied ... If he chance to miss, ... he is in a hell on the other side ... if he cannot satisfy his desire ... he runs mad. So that both ways, hit or miss, he is distracted so long as his ambition lasts, he can look for no other but anxiety and care, discontent and grief, in the mean time; madness itself, or violent death, in the end," pages 243–44, and cf., Francis Bacon, Essay XXXVI: "Of Ambition." As with Polonius's assumption that love is the cause of Hamlet's supposed madness, to serve his purposes Hamlet will also cultivate the misconception of Rosencrantz and Guildenstern that ambition is the cause. These two forms of madness ironically reflect the two motives for the King's crimes, love and ambition, cf., III.iii.55.

I could be bounded ... infinite space: • Hamlet is both expressing his anguish at his actual situation and revealing that he in fact has no particular ambition to be king on his own account.

bad dreams: • Here Hamlet intentionally misleads

ROSENCRANTZ
Why then your ambition makes it one: 'tis too narrow for your mind.

HAMLET
O God, I could be bounded in a nutshell and count myself a king of infinite space—were it not that I   255

have bad dreams.

GUILDENSTERN

Which dreams indeed are ambition, for the very
substance of the ambitious is merely the shadow
of a dream.

HAMLET

A dream itself is but a shadow.   260

ROSENCRANTZ

Truly, and I hold ambition of so airy and light a
quality that it is but a shadow's shadow.

HAMLET

Then are our beggars bodies, and our monarchs and
outstretched heroes the beggars' shadows.

Rosencrantz and Guildenstern, bad dreams being
another symptom of melancholy, cf., Bright, page 124,
Burton I.1.3.3, I.3.1.1, III.2.3.

Which dreams ... shadow of a dream: ● An instance
of "reasoning," in the sense of clever rhetorical
exchanges of argument and counter-argument,
whether actually logical or not, cf., line 265. Here
Guildenstern engages in a kind of chop-logic that
plays on two senses of the words "dream" (goal
and illusion) and "shadow" (an image without
actuality, like that produced by an object blocking
the sun, and illusion). *Substance* (from Latin *sub*,
under + *stare*, to stand), an important term inherited
from medieval scholastic philosophy, means the
underlying essence of something, not its physical
material. Here the essence of the ambitious man is
his mental image ("shadow") of the goal of actual
attainment of high place in the world, which actual
attainment is both a reflection ("shadow") of the
goal ("dream") and an illusion ("dream") because
of the mutability of fortune. The image of ambition
or fame as shadow was available to Shakespeare in
Florio's translation of Montaigne (II.352 "Of Glory")
but also in Cicero (*Tusculanae Disputationes* I.110
and III.3), Seneca (*Epistulae Morales* LXXIX.13), and
quotations from Plutarch in commonplace books by
Mirabelli (*Polyanthea* under "Gloria"), Meres (*Wit's
Commonwealth* under "Glory"), and Cawdrey (*A
Treasury or Storehouse of Similies* under "Ambition")
(Harmon, pages 993–94).

dream itself is but a shadow: a dream is itself not an
actual thing but only an image, hence a shadow. Like
the previous image, this of ambition or fame as dream
was available to Shakespeare in Florio's translation
of Montaigne (II.352 "Of Glory" and I.296, quoting
Tasso) but also in Pindar (*Pythian Hymns* VIII),
and in Erasmus quoting Pindar (*Adagia* II.iii.48
under "Homo bulla") (Harmon, page 993).

hold: consider. **so airy and light a quality:** so
insubstantial in the medieval sense, lacking in
underlying substance or real essence, because of
mutability and, possibly, for one of his rank, a pure
fantasy, cf., Seneca *Epistles* CXXIII.16 (ref. in Harmon,
page 993).

Then are our beggars bodies ... shadows: Then
beggars are material bodies, and kings and heroes
are the mere shadows of them, "outstretched" like
elongated shadows "looking bigger than they are"
(Jenkins, Riverside). ● Hamlet, playing on the literal
meaning of "shadow," points out the absurdity of
the argument by saying that if Rosencrantz is correct
at lines 261–62, then we would have to conclude that
monarchs and heroes, the highest beings ambition
might seek to become, are merely shadows, cast by
the dreams of the lowest of men, beggars, who are
the only beings with actual substance, a manifest
absurdity. There may also be an implication that
Claudius is merely the shadow of a king, not a
king of substance but a beggar made what he is by

Shall we to th' court? For, by my fay, I cannot reason.   265
BOTH [*Rosencrantz and Guildenstern*]
　We'll wait upon you.
HAMLET
　No such matter. I will not sort you with the rest of
　my servants, for, to speak to you like an honest

　man, I am most dreadfully attended. But in the

　beaten way of friendship, what make you at Elsinore?   270

ROSENCRANTZ
　To visit you, my lord, no other occasion.
HAMLET
　Beggar that I am, I am even poor in thanks, but I thank
　you. And sure, dear friends, my thanks are too dear
　a halfpenny. Were you not sent for? Is it your own
　inclining? Is it a free visitation? Come, come, deal   275
　justly with me. Come, come. Nay, speak.
GUILDENSTERN
　What should we say, my lord?

HAMLET
　Anything but to th' purpose. You were sent for,
　and there is a kind of confession in your looks, which

his own ambition. Cf., the Ghost's "wretch whose natural gifts were poor / To those of mine" at I.v.51–52 and Hamlet's "The King is a thing ... Of nothing" at IV.ii.27–30.

to: go to. **by my fay:** by my faith. **reason:** play at the game of witty pseudo-logical repartee.

wait upon: escort, attend (Jenkins).

No such matter ... my servants: ● Hamlet plays on the phrase "wait upon" in the sense of serve. **sort:** categorize, catalogue, class.

dreadfully attended: ● Hamlet is taking the opportunity of the two senses of "wait upon" to reinforce the impression that he is ambitious by complaining about the incompetence of his servants, implying that he deserves better. Compare this pretense with his genuine magnanimity toward Horatio at I.ii.163 and toward Horatio, Marcellus, and Barnardo at I.ii.253.

beaten way of friendship: the well-worn path of honesty between friends, i.e., tell me honestly and not in the roundabout rhetoric we've been using. Cf., the Queen's "More matter with less art" at line 95. **what make you:** what are you doing here, what are you up to? ● Hamlet is about to extract the motives of those who have failed to extract his.

occasion: grounds, cause, purpose. ● Rosencrantz is lying: they were sent for by the King, cf., lines 3–4.

Beggar that I am: ● Another expression of Hamlet's supposed ambition, picking up the image of beggars from lines 263–64. **too dear a halfpenny:** too expensive, *dear* playing on "dear friends," even at the smallest fraction of money, costing them more than the thanks are worth. ● For the understanding of Rosencrantz and Guildenstern Hamlet implies that he "lack[s] advancement" (III. ii.340) and so has not much to offer them. For the audience's understanding, Hamlet suggests that Rosencrantz and Guildenstern are not going to be rewarded for their trouble with his telling them the truth. Jenkins, following Dover Wilson, suggests that Hamlet may mean his thanks are too dear *by* a halfpenny because "even his poor thanks are (a halfpennyworth) more than the visitors deserve (if they have not come of their own free will)," as the next line suggests. ● NOTE TO ACTORS: *halfpenny* is pronounced *hā-p'ny*, with the stress on the first syllable.

but: Abbott (§128) sees a possible "studied ambiguity" here: *but* can mean *only*, suggesting that Rosencrantz and Guildenstern may say anything so long as it is relevant, an inferior reading according to Jenkins, and can also mean "except," suggesting sarcastically that Hamlet knows Rosencrantz and Guildenstern will say anything except what is actually true or relevant.

your modesties have not craft enough to color. I   280
know the good King and Queen have sent for you.

ROSENCRANTZ

To what end, my lord?

HAMLET

That you must teach me. But let me conjure you, by

the rights of our fellowship, by the consonancy of our
youth, by the obligation of our ever-preserved love,   285

and by what more dear a better proposer could charge

you withal, be even and direct with me whether you
were sent for or no.

ROSENCRANTZ [aside to Guildenstern.]

What say you?

HAMLET [aside.]

Nay then I have an eye of you.—If you love me,   290

hold not off.

GUILDENSTERN

My lord, we were sent for.

HAMLET

I will tell you why; so shall my anticipation prevent
your discovery, and your secrecy to the King and

---

modesties: for the plural of abstract qualities possessed by more than one person, cf., I.i.173 note. **color:** paint over, i.e., disguise, as at III.i.44.

To what end: for what purpose, aim.

teach me: with emphasis on "me," turning their question back on them. **conjure you, by:** implore or entreat in the name of, followed by the grounds of appeal, cf., lines 11–12.

rights of our fellowship: what is due to friendship. **consonancy of our youth:** harmony of our ages, with perhaps the idea of shared interests and qualities in the past. **obligation of our ever-preserved love:** duties based on our long friendship. ● All of these grounds are expressed in a satirically exaggerated formal style and undercut by "what more dear a better proposer could charge you withal," i.e., grounds even more precious by which someone more capable of coming up with grounds could appeal to you.

dear: valuable, precious. **proposer:** person proposing grounds (for your being honest). **charge:** load, burden, with the added sense of imposing one as a duty. See Introduction, pages 13–14, for discussion of the theme of imperatives.

even: frank, honest, direct (Riverside suggests the modern parallel "level with me"). **whether ... or no:** whether or not you were sent for, as Hamlet suspects and we know they were.

have an eye of: have an eye on (Abbott §174), am onto, am watching. **hold not off:** don't hold back.

● **SPEECH NOTE: I will tell you why ...:** In the following speech Hamlet expresses the conventional mood and attitude of the melancholic character. His sincerity in the feeling is supported by his explicit confession later that he suffers from melancholy (line 601). At the same time, however, he does not reveal to Rosencrantz and Guildenstern the actual cause of this "distemperature," which is neither thwarted love, as he would have Polonius believe, nor thwarted ambition, as he would have Rosencrantz and Guildenstern believe, but rather, as we know, his father's death, his mother's "o'erhasty marriage," the appearance and charge of the Ghost, his mission of revenge, and the fear of damnation he will reveal to us at the scene's end. **prevent your discovery:** come before and therefore forestall your uncovering (Abbott §439), i.e., of what the King and Queen have asked of you.

Queen moult no feather. I have of late, but wherefore   295

I know not, lost all my mirth, forgone all custom
of exercises; and indeed it goes so heavily with my
disposition that this goodly frame the earth seems to

me a sterile promontory; this most excellent canopy
the air, look you, this brave o'erhanging firmament,   300
this majestical roof fretted with golden fire, why, it

appeareth nothing to me but a foul and pestilent

congregation of vapors. What piece of work is a
man, how noble in reason, how infinite in faculties,

moult no feather: remain intact, like a bird not losing even one of its colorful feathers, cf., "color" at line 280. **wherefore:** why.

forgone all custom of exercises: given up all customary activities, including but not limited to athletic ones, though Hamlet later says to Horatio, to whom he speaks only honestly when they are together in private, that he has been "in continual practice" at fencing (V.ii.211). **it goes so heavily ... that:** "this is the impersonal construction, as in 'How goes it with ... Antony?' (*Ant*[*ony and Cleopatra*] I.v.38)" (Jenkins), cf., *Measure for Measure* I.i.57, *King John* V.iii.1, *Richard III* III.ii.96, the point being "it goes so heavily with me that ...". **disposition:** mental constitution or temperament (OED 6.), probably from the notion of the ordering or arrangement of the elements or humors within the human body and mind under divine or astrological influence, cf., SPEECH NOTE after I.iv.38. **goodly:** excellent or splendid, cf., line 245 above. **frame:** structure (OED 8.).

promontory: • "The metaphor suggests that man's earthly existence is surrounded by some different element vastly greater than itself" (Jenkins). **canopy ... golden fire:** • In the Ptolemaic cosmology, surrounding the earth beneath the sphere of the moon was a sphere of fire, and beneath that was the sphere of the air. This hierarchy corresponded to the hierarchy of the elements, earth being the lowest, then water, then air, then fire being the highest and closest to heavens and spirit. Here Hamlet takes the sphere of the air to be a firmament or vault with a canopy or roof decorated with the heavenly bodies moving in the crystalline spheres beyond it, on the analogy of a building with a decorated vaulted ceiling or the embossed and painted canopy roof overhanging the stage of the Globe theater, which was decorated with blue sky and golden sun, moon, and stars and called "the heavens," cf., I.v.151 note. Many locate the source of this passage in Florio's translation of Montaigne's *Essays* (II.141), but "descriptions of the beauty and order of the universe as contemplated by the mind of man ... are a set piece in classical works popular in the Renaissance," including Cicero's *De Natura Deorum* (II.4, 15, 90, 98, etc., II.95 quoting Aristotle's lost *De Philosophia*) and *Tusculanae Disputationes* (V.69), Seneca's *De Otio* (V.3ff.) and *De Providentia* (I.2), Plutarch's *De Tranquillitate Animi* and elsewhere, and Twyne's translation of Petrarch's *De Remediis Utriusque Fortunae* in *A Phisicke against Fortune* (1579, folios 281–82) (Harmon, pages 994–97). **brave:** decorated, splendid. **fretted:** decorated with carving or embossing (OED *v.*² 2.).

foul: offensive, corrupt, putrid, filthy. **pestilent:** pernicious, infectious, destructive, from Latin *pestis*, pest, plague, infectious disease. **congregation:** gathering together. **vapors:** steamy or imperceptible exhalation, figuratively denoting something unsubstantial or worthless (OED 1, 2.c.).

• SPEECH NOTE: **What piece of work is a man ... paragon of animals:** The speech that follows forms a peak in the expression of the commonplace conception of ancient, medieval, and Renaissance thought: the magnificence of the created world with man as at once its finest and its most problematic creation, finest in being the summation of all qualities in the created universe and problematic in being corrupted in those qualities as a consequence of having fallen from grace by his own free will, and in having to suffer the consequences of that fall. "Man is called a little world ... because he possesses all the faculties of the universe.... [of] gods, the four elements [see line 306 note], the dumb beasts, and the plants. Of all these man possesses the faculties: for he possesses the godlike faculty of reason; and the nature of the elements, which consists in nourishment growth and reproduction. In each of these faculties he is deficient ... For we possess the faculty of reason less eminently than the gods; ... our energies and desires are weaker than the beasts'; our powers of nurture and of growth are less than the plants'. Whence, being an amalgam of many and varied elements, we find our life difficult to order. For every other creature is guided by one principle; but we are pulled in different directions by our different faculties. For instance at one time we are drawn towards the better by the god-like element, at another time towards the worse by the domination of the bestial element, within us" (Photius, *Life of Pythagoras*, quoted in Tillyard, page 66).

It is often asserted that Hamlet's contrasting the glory of the heavens and the paltriness of man comes from a passage in Montaigne: "Let us then, for once, consider a man alone ... how he stands in this fine equipage.... Who has made him believe that this admirable motion of the celestial arch, the eternal light of those luminaries that roll so high over his head, the wondrous and fearful motions of that infinite ocean, should be established and continue so many ages for his service and convenience? Can any thing be imagined so ridiculous, that this miserable and wretched creature, who is not so much as master of himself, but subject to the injuries of all things, should call himself master and emperor of the world, of which he has not power to know the least part, much less to command the whole?" (*Apology for Raimond Sebond*). But though we know that Shakespeare read Montaigne, possibly in the original French but certainly also in Florio's translation (1603), as a passage in *The Tempest* (II.i.148–65) that closely follows one in Montaigne's essay "Of the Cannibals" demonstrates, both Shakespeare and Montaigne would independently have seen such "descriptions of the beauty and order of the universe as contemplated by the mind of man ... [which] are a set piece in classical works popular in the Renaissance [e.g., Cicero, Seneca, Plutarch]. These conventional pieces were no doubt models for the many descriptions of the heavens which occur in the literature of the sixteenth century [e.g., Petrarch's *De Remediis Utriusque Fortunae*, translated by Thomas Twyne in

Phisicke against Fortune, 1579]" (Harmon, page 995), cf., lines 299–301 note.

   The punctuation of the passage is the subject of much debate, Q2 and F differing in where the pauses come. Where F has "in form and moving how express and admirable? in action, how like an angel? in apprehension, how like a God?" (the question marks intended to indicate exclamation), Q2 has "in form and moving, how expresse and admirable in action, how like an angel in apprehension, how like a God." The logic, philosophical background, and rhythm of the passage all argue for the F punctuation. As the following notes indicate, in the tradition "action" is characteristic of angels and "apprehension" of gods. In addition, as Jenkins argues, "the pattern of the present speech—'how like ... in'—seems to require continuation with 'how like a god' *in* some particular respect.... After an unlimited comparison of man as 'like a god', to celebrate him as 'the paragon of animals' would be bathos, whereas to pass from '*in apprehension ...* like a god' to man as 'the paragon of animals' shows a natural progression of thought. For man *is* an animal [in the sense of having a soul], as the play elsewhere will tell us (IV.iv.33–39), yet is raised above other animals by his 'godlike reason', through which he is 'the paragon' of them (cf. Pico [della Mirandola], *On the Dignity of Man*, 'Man is rightly ... thought to be ... the animal really worthy of wonder,')" (Jenkins LN).
What piece: Jenkins gives examples of the idiomatic construction without the article, calling "a piece" in F a modernization, cf., Abbott §86, and examples: *Julius Caesar* I.iii.42, *Twelfth Night* II.v.112, *Two Gentlemen* I.ii.53, *Measure for Measure* II.iv.154, *Cymbeline* IV.ii.207, *Winter's Tale* I.ii.352, etc.. **piece of work:** instance of artistic making, craftsmanship, especially an excellent, exemplary, superior one, as we would say "masterpiece," cf., "piece of work" at III.ii.46 and *Midsummer Night's Dream* I.ii.13, *Taming of the Shrew* I.i.253, *Timon of Athens* I.i.199, *Julius Caesar* II.i.327, *Macbeth* II.iii.128, *Othello* IV.i.151, *Antony and Cleopatra* I.ii.154, and *Cymbeline* II.iv.72. For *piece* as in itself implying excellence see *King Lear* IV.vi.134, *Winter's Tale* IV.iv.32, 422, V.i.94, etc.

in form and moving how express and admirable, in   305

in form and moving ... admirable: "*express* is appropriate for 'form' (as in 'the express image' of Hebrews i.3 [in the KJV, where the Geneva Bible has 'engraved form,' glossed there as 'the lively image and pattern,']) and shows indeed a turn of thought characteristic of Shakespeare, who joins 'form' and 'pressure' at I.v.100 and III.ii.24. From Latin *exprimo*, *expressus*, to press out, the word refers to the clear impression made by a die or seal and so to the faithful reproduction of an original. Hence it describes a man as not only well designed but well executed, and so sustains the idea of a 'piece of work', which can inspire the wonder that leads on to 'admirable' [= to be wondered at]" (Jenkins LN). On the above grounds, I doubt Wright's claim (page 186) that "form and

action how like an angel, in apprehension how like a
god, the beauty of the world, the paragon of
animals—and yet to me what is this quintessence
of dust? Man delights not me—nor woman neither,
though by your smiling you seem to say so.   310

moving" is a hendiadys, but "express and admirable"
may be a hendiadys for "admirably express" in the
above sense.

action ... like a god: ● Action is the characteristic quality
of angels in relation to man: "... the action performed by
the angel who is sent, proceeds from God as from its first
principle, at Whose nod and by Whose authority the
angels work" (St. Thomas Aquinas, *Summa Theologica*,
III.cxii.I). Apprehension, in the sense of understanding,
intellectual grasp, is the characteristic of the mind of
a god. Man is of course only "like" an angel and a god,
gifted with discursive rather than the intuitive reason
of those higher beings called pure intelligences or
angels, cf., I.ii.150 note, though the two are "Differing
but in degree, of kind the same" (Milton *Paradise Lost*,
V.490), cf., Jenkins I.ii.150 LN and II.ii.304–6 LN. Hamlet
speaks here with the authority of a long scholastic
tradition, whose contents he would have been learning
at Wittenberg. **paragon of animals:** the model or pattern
of excellence or perfection in an animated being, i.e.,
one with a soul (Latin *anima*). **quintessence of dust:**
● To the four elements or essences (earth, water, air,
and fire), of which according to the ancients all natural
things are made, Aristotle and the Pythagoreans joined
a fifth (*quint-*) essence, which composed the heavenly
bodies. In the medieval and Renaissance world view
that Shakespeare and his audience inherited, the four
elements were characterized by four qualities in pairs
and corresponded to the four humors mixed in man
(ideally, mixed in right proportion): earth (cold and
dry) to melancholy, water (cold and moist) to phlegm,
air (hot and moist) to blood, and fire (hot and dry)
to choler (see Tillyard, page 69, and SPEECH NOTE
after I.iv.38). Man's quintessence was the intellectual
soul, characterized by the capacity for discursive
reason. Angels, having no physical body, consisted of
the intellectual soul only, in their case characterized
by intuitive reason. In the phrase "quintessence of
dust," Shakespeare compresses man's complex relation
to the cosmos into an oxymoron expressing man's
double nature. From one viewpoint man is the crown
of physical creation, dust (earth, the lowest element)
raised up to spirit. From another, man is essentially
dust however spiritual in aspiration. This speech,
made particular to himself by Hamlet, thus gives to a
commonplace ancient, medieval, and Renaissance idea
a "local habitation and a name" (*Midsummer Night's
Dream* V.i.17), seamlessly uniting the universal and
the particular into a profound experience of our own
complex nature. His description having reached this
pinnacle of creation—man, the image of God and a
microcosm of the universe—Hamlet now plunges
himself and us back into his particular melancholy
"distemperature" with the word "dust" and the phrase
"Man delights not me." Of that "distemperature," to the
extent that it is real, only the audience so far knows
the cause. To the extent that it is acted, it continues the
pretense of the madness of thwarted ambition enacted
for the sake of the King's spies.

ROSENCRANTZ

My lord, there was no such stuff in my thoughts.

HAMLET

Why did ye laugh then, when I said man delights
not me?

ROSENCRANTZ

To think, my lord, if you delight not in man, what   315
Lenten entertainment the players shall receive from

you. We coted them on the way, and hither are they
coming to offer you service.

HAMLET

He that plays the king shall be welcome—his Majesty
shall have tribute on me, the adventurous knight   320
shall use his foil and target, the lover shall not sigh
gratis, the humorous man shall end his part in peace,
the clown shall make those laugh whose lungs are
tickle o' th' sere, and the lady shall say her mind
freely, or the blank verse shall halt for't. What players   325
are they?

stuff: matter of thought (OED 7.b., citing this passage
alone), possibly with a disparaging sense (OED 7.a.
and 8.b.)

Lenten: meager, minimal, from Lent, the period
between Ash Wednesday and Easter, when Christians
were expected to give up self-indulgences and
pleasures, including certain foods and also theatrical
performances, "confirmed by the Privy Council on
22 June 1600" (Jenkins). **entertainment:** reception.
players: troupe of actors, cf., I.ii.174 note.
coted: overtook and passed, cf., "o'erraught"
at III.i.17, said of one hunting dog in relation to another
in the chase.

● SPEECH NOTE: **He that plays ... halt for't:**
Hamlet lists some of the stock roles that particular
members of an acting company would typically play:
king, knight, lover, humorous man, clown, and lady
(played by a boy).
his Majesty: the actor who plays the king. **tribute:**
honor and money, implying that Hamlet will be a
patron to the company. **on:** of, from (OED 23.), cf.,
King Lear V.iii.166. **adventurous:** daring, possibly
also rash, likely to have adventures (OED 3. and 4.).
foil and target: fencing sword and shield. **sigh:** in
longing for his lady. **gratis:** without being paid by me,
whether he is rewarded with love of the lady or not.
humorous man: the sort of character who exhibits a
disproportion in the mix (complexion, temperament)
of humors, whether tending to the melancholic (e.g.,
Jaques in *As You Like It*, Don John in *Much Ado*), the
choleric (e.g., Katherine in *Shrew*, Mercutio in *Romeo
and Juliet*, Hotspur in *I Henry IV*), the sanguine (e.g.,
Falstaff in *1* and *2 Henry IV*), or the phlegmatic (cf., line
567 and I.v.32–34), tendencies that might be brought
into better temperament by correction of the will. **in
peace:** both peaceful resolution of his conflict in the
play and permission to achieve it without heckling
from the audience, cf., the invitations to the humorous
men Jaques and Malvolio to join in the concluding
celebrations in *As You Like It* (V.iv.194) and *Twelfth
Night* (V.i.380). **clown:** originally an uneducated
country fellow, hence a rude and boorish person,
hence one likely to be laughed at, and eventually,
as here, a professional jester. At different times
Shakespeare uses the term in all these senses. **tickle
o' th' sere:** easily caused to laugh, from *tickle*, easily
susceptible to influence. **sere:** the part of a gun that
holds the hammer in place till the trigger is pulled.
freely ... halt for't: to avoid making the blank verse
(unrhymed iambic pentameter) halt (= limp, walk
lamely), the boy playing the lady should feel free not
to omit any indelicate words that a lady would not say
when speaking before royalty instead of before the

ROSENCRANTZ
    Even those you were wont to take such delight in,
    the tragedians of the city.

HAMLET
    How chances it they travel? Their residence,
    both in reputation and profit, was better both   330
    ways.

ROSENCRANTZ
    I think their inhibition comes by the means of the late
    innovation.

HAMLET
    Do they hold the same estimation they did when I was
    in the city? Are they so followed?   335

ROSENCRANTZ
    No indeed are they not.

HAMLET
    How comes it? Do they grow rusty?

general public. ● The prince is both magnanimously inviting ease in the actors and countenancing their fidelity to the intentions of their plays' authors.

wont: accustomed. **the city:** no particular city of Denmark is intended within the story but rather the idea that the troupe has left the world of sophistication and profit to travel. But of course to Shakespeare's audience the image of London is implied.

how chances it they travel: *chance* used as an indefinite verb (Abbott §37). **residence:** remaining residing in the city as opposed to going on tour. **was better both ways:** they would have been better off, both in reputation and in profit.

inhibition … innovation: Some editors take "inhibition" to refer to a prohibition against theater companies in London and "innovation" (which can mean insurrection) to refer to the Essex rebellion of 1601 against Queen Elizabeth. While the audience may well have made the latter association, I think "inhibition" need not be taken to refer to a particular historical action but refers to the company's resistance to playing in the city because of the conflict arising from the growth of the boy-actor companies in the private theaters referred to several lines below. "Innovation" then opens up a topic which Hamlet guesses at in his next question and which Rosencrantz develops.

estimation: value (in the eyes of the public).

● SPEECH NOTE: **How comes it? … and his load too:** The following passage appears only in F. It alludes to the so-called "War of the Theaters" of 1599–1602, called *"Poetomachia"* by playwright Thomas Dekker, in which Dekker and playwright John Marston on one side and playwright Ben Jonson on the other, satirized one another in plays written for different acting companies. Dekker and Marston wrote for the Lord Chamberlain's Men, an adult-actor and public theater company, and also for the Children of Paul's, who performed at the royal court and at the grammar school attached to St. Paul's Cathedral. Jonson wrote for the Children of the Chapel, a boy-actor company, who performed at court and at the Blackfriars buildings, converted in 1596 into a private theater by James Burbage. Here, according to Halliday (page 379), "the adult actors are described as being forced to travel in the provinces owing to the popularity of the boys' companies, who presented most of the plays in the controversy." But the controversy seems to have been not merely between two sets of boys'-company writers but between the writers for the private (boys'-company) theaters and those writing for the public (men's-company) theaters. Hence "the boys carry it away" at line 360. There is one

ROSENCRANTZ

Nay, their endeavor keeps in the wonted pace; but

there is, sir, an eyrie of children, little eyases,

that cry out on the top of question, and are most   340

tyrannically clapped for't. These are now the fashion,

and so berattle the common stages— so they call

them—that many wearing rapiers are afraid of
goose-quills and dare scarce come thither.

HAMLET

What, are they children? Who maintains 'em? How   345

---

reference to Shakespeare's making a jibe at Jonson. It appears in *The Return from Parnassus, Part 2* (1601), an anonymous play performed by the students of St. Johns College, Cambridge. The author seems to have assumed erroneously that Shakespeare had a hand in Dekker and probably Marston's *Satiromastix* (1601), where Jonson is satirized. Except for this reference, "there is no other obvious indication of Shakespeare's being involved in the quarrel, which was made up by 1604, when Marston dedicated *The Malcontent* to Jonson" (Halliday, pages 99–100, 354, 379, 431).

keeps: continues. **wonted:** usual—their quality remains consistent.

eyrie: ayrie F, nest of an eagle or other bird of prey. **of children:** "A clear topical reference to the Children of the Chapel, who began to act at the Blackfriars theatre towards the end of 1600" (Jenkins), and possibly to the Children of Pauls, who had begun acting again after a hiatus of nine years (Halliday, page 100). **eyases:** clamorous unfledged hawks who (according to Capell) fly "at game above them," with a possible pun on the Greek pronunciation of Ajax (Aias, from the Greek word for eagle), ironically implying small would-be versions of the large and strong but "blockish" Homeric hero (cf., *Troilus and Cressida* I.iii.374, etc.).

cry out on the top of question: A disputed phrase: shout louder than the subject of the play warrants, or than argumentation itself, or than can be answered by counter-argument. •The satire performed by the boys' companies is so extreme, extending the idea of the noisiness of "eyases" and reading the phrase as analogous to "top of my bent" (III.ii.384) and "at the top of one's voice" (Jenkins substantially), that they are more forceful than the subject of the plays warrant, or than argument can answer. The result, seen in the following lines, is that the boys' companies have become so popular as to steal audiences away from the public theaters, a consequence possibly implied here if "on the top of question" is read as analogous to "cried in the top of mine" (lines 438–39). **question:** argument, discussion, subject of a debate or of a play.

tyrannically: frantically, wildly (cf., "out-Herods Herod, III.ii.14 and note).

berattle: noisily satirize, berate. **common stages:** public theaters. **so they call them:** "The term 'common stages' was contemptuously used in *Cynthia's Revels* (Ind. 182; IV.iii.118). Cf. the Privy Council's use of 'common playhouses' (Chambers, *El. St.* iv.322)" (Jenkins).

rapiers ... thither: armed gallants trained in fencing are afraid to attend the theaters for fear of being satirized, hence the boys' companies are driving audiences away from the public theaters toward the private ones and thereby "carry it away" (cf., lines 360–61), i.e., triumph in the controversy. **goose-quills:** pens (of the satirizing

are they escotted? Will they pursue the quality no

longer than they can sing? Will they not say afterwards,

if they should grow themselves to common players—

as it is most like, if their means are no better

—their writers do them wrong to make them exclaim   350
against their own succession?

ROSENCRANTZ
Faith, there has been much to do on both sides, and

the nation holds it no sin to tar them to controversy.

There was for a while no money bid for argument
unless the poet and the player went to cuffs in the   355
question.
HAMLET
Is't possible?
GUILDENSTERN
O, there has been much throwing about of
brains.
HAMLET
Do the boys carry it away?   360
ROSENCRANTZ
Ay, that they do, my lord—Hercules and his load too.

playwrights), "an instance of the pen's proving mightier than the sword" (Jenkins wittily).

escotted: supported, escoted F, but "if the infinitive is rightly *escot* (OED), the preterite should retain the short vowel. Cf. Cotgrave, *escotier*" (Jenkins), hence the double *t*. **quality:** profession (here, of acting).

sing: boy actors began and perhaps continued as choirboys—the question is whether they will give up acting when their voices change with puberty.

grow themselves to common players: later become professional adult actors in public theaters.

like: likely. **means:** funds, money, method of earning a living.

their writers … their own succession: the authors of the plays in which the boys act do the boys wrong by making them criticize the profession which the boys will themselves practice when later they continue working as adult actors in the public theaters. ●Hamlet's comment is not merely a way for Shakespeare to score a point in the topical controversy of the "War of the Theaters." The absurdity of the playwrights' having boy actors satirize the profession of public acting from which many of them will later have to make a living ("their own succession" = the profession to which they will succeed as heirs) is a metaphor for Claudius's having murdered his brother to become king, by which action he is "exclaiming against his own succession," for by his example he is teaching someone else how to succeed him, namely by killing him. Cf., *Macbeth* I.vii.7–12.

Faith: a mild oath. **to do:** ado, fuss, agitation. **both sides:** Ben Jonson on the side of the private theaters in *Cynthia's Revels* (1600) and *Poetaster* (1601) and Dekker and Marson on the side of the public theaters in *Satiromastix* (1601), see SPEECH NOTE at line 337.

tar: (F "tarre"), incite, as a master (cf., *King John* IV.i.117) or a bone (cf., *Troilus and Cressida* I.iii.390) drives dogs into a dogfight. ●NOTE TO ACTORS: rhymes with *mar*. **them:** the boy actors.

no money bid for argument: No one made a bid to buy an "argument" (= plot idea) for development into a full play, or possibly no one paid to hear even the argument (= summary) of a play, let alone attend it, unless the question (= issue) it addressed would lead to a fistfight ("cuffs" = fisticuffs, buffets) between the poets and actors of the competing boys' and men's companies.

carry it away: win the competition, cf., *Romeo and Juliet* III.i.74.

Hercules and his load too: "Hercules in the course of one of his twelve labors supported the world for Atlas; the children do better, for they carry away the world and Hercules as well. There is an allusion to

HAMLET

It is not very strange; for my uncle is King of Denmark,
and those that would make mouths at him while my
father lived give twenty, forty, fifty, a hundred ducats   365

apiece for his picture in little. 'Sblood, there is

something in this more than natural, if philosophy
could find it out.

A flourish.

GUILDENSTERN

There are the players.

HAMLET

Gentlemen, you are welcome to Elsinore. Your hands,   370

come then. Th'appurtenance of welcome is fashion
and ceremony. Let me comply with you in this garb,

lest my extent to the players, which I tell you must
show fairly outwards, should more appear like
entertainment than yours. You are welcome. But my   375
uncle-father and aunt-mother are deceived.

GUILDENSTERN

In what, my dear lord?

HAMLET

I am but mad north-north-west. When the wind is
southerly, I know a hawk from a handsaw.

Enter Polonius.

the Globe playhouse, which reportedly had for its
sign the figure of Hercules upholding the world"
(Riverside).

strange: unusual, extraordinary.

mouths: mocking faces, cf., IV.iv.50.

ducats: gold coins. The name was first used for a
coin struck by Roger II of Sicily as Duke of Apulia
in 1192 but spread because of the Venetian gold coin
first struck in 1284 depicting St. Mark and the Doge
(Duke) of Venice on one side and Christ on the
other. The word was later used for coins of various
European countries, including Denmark.

picture in little: miniature portrait.

'Sblood: shortened form of the oath "by his
(i.e., Christ's) blood."

more than natural, if philosophy ... find it out:
cf., I.v.167. ● Hamlet compares the supplanting of
the professional actors' popularity by that of the
boys' companies with the supplanting of Hamlet
Senior by Claudius in the estimation of the people of
Denmark. With "more than natural" Hamlet implies
both the unnaturalness of Claudius's succeeding
to the throne through murder (and cf., I.ii.65) and
the supernaturalness of the Ghost's appearance,
knowledge of either being beyond discernment by
rational thought or study ("philosophy").

S.D. *flourish:* trumpets announcing an arrival.

Your hands: ● Hamlet offers his hand to shake theirs,
another example of magnanimous condescension.

appurtenance of welcome: what appertains to
the welcoming of visitors. **fashion and ceremony:**
perhaps a hendiadys for "fashionable ceremony" =
appropriate and customary formality (Wright, page
186). **comply:** to observe the formalities of courtesy
and politeness (OED *v.*¹ 2. citing this passage), cf.,
V.ii.187. **garb:** style, form of behavior (OED *sb.*² 3.),
i.e., shaking of the hands.

extent: extending of welcome.

more appear like entertainment: seem more
favorably welcoming. ● Suspicious of Rosencrantz
and Guildenstern (cf., line 290), Hamlet makes a
show of warm welcome to them lest his warmer
welcome to the players arouse in them suspicion of
his mistrust. His intimation that his welcome to the
players must "show fairly outwards" disguises from
the suspected and undiscerning school friends that
this gesture of hand shaking is more outward show
than genuine inward welcome.

north-north-west ... southerly: Perhaps
Shakespeare had in mind winds commonly thought
to be harmful (north) and healing (south) to the
melancholic. **When ... southerly:** "in my more lucid

POLONIUS
Well be with you, gentlemen.   380

HAMLET [*aside to Guildenstern, then Rosencrantz.*]
Hark you, Guildenstern, and you too—at each ear a
hearer. That great baby you see there is not yet out of
his swaddling-clouts.

ROSENCRANTZ [*aside to Hamlet.*]
Happily he is the second time come to them, for they
say an old man is twice a child.   385

HAMLET [*aside to Rosencrantz and Guildenstern.*]
I will prophesy he comes to tell me of the players.
Mark it.—You say right, sir, a Monday morning; 'twas
then indeed.

POLONIUS
My lord, I have news to tell you.

HAMLET
My lord, I have news to tell you. When Roscius was   390
an actor in Rome—

POLONIUS
The actors are come hither, my lord.

HAMLET
Buzz, buzz.

POLONIUS
Upon my honor—

HAMLET
Then came each actor on his ass—   395

moments" (Jenkins). **hawk ... handsaw:** perhaps two kinds of tool, pickax and saw, or two kinds of bird, hawk and heron (hernshaw or heronshaw), or one of each. Jenkins suggests that Hamlet is intimating that he can tell a bird of prey (the King) from a mere tool (Rosencrantz and Guildenstern) or perhaps from the raptor's victim. In any case, Hamlet pretends to be intimating to Rosencrantz and Guildenstern that at times he knows what's what, but he does so in a way that only confirms his madness to them. Only the audience and not Rosencrantz and Guildenstern recognize that Hamlet's madness is not genuine but an act.

Well be with you: may it be well with you, addressed to Rosencrantz and Guildenstern. For the impersonal verb see Abbott §297.

Hark: listen. **at each ear:** i.e., one of you on each side of me. **That great baby:** referring to Polonius and still playing at madness. **swaddling-clouts:** infant's swaddling clothes.

Happily: haply, by hap, perhaps, cf., Abbott §42.
old man is twice a child: proverbial ● cf., *As You Like It*, II.vii.165, and "instances are given in Tilley, M 570" (Jenkins).

Mark it: watch, pay attention. **— You say right, sir:** Hamlet comes out of his aside and, aloud, pretends to be discussing something else as Polonius approaches. **a Monday:** for "a" see I.v.19 note and cf., IV.v.183 and *Romeo and Juliet* III.iv.20.

When Roscius ... Rome: Hamlet makes fun of Polonius for bearing news already known by pretending to give even older news, i.e., about the most famous comic actor of ancient Rome (d. 62 B.C.).

Buzz, buzz: mocking response to "idle talk" (Johnson in Furness) or old news (Blackstone substantially in Furness), or "to command silence" (Schmidt).

Upon my honor: an oath confirming the truth of the news.

Then came ... his ass: Perhaps a quotation from an older ballad, as at lines 407–408, 416, and 418. **on his ass:** on his donkey. ● Hamlet pretends that Polonius means the actors have literally ridden in upon him ("upon my honor" = on me, cf., "your honor" or "your majesty") and implies thereby that they have ridden each on an ass (= fool), thus calling Polonius an ass. Polonius misses or ignores the point, perhaps taking it, as Hamlet intends, to be more evidence of nonsensical madness.

POLONIUS

The best actors in the world, either for tragedy,
comedy, history, pastoral, pastoral-comical,

historical-pastoral, tragical-historical,
tragical-comical-historical-pastoral, scene individable,
or poem unlimited. Seneca cannot be too heavy,   400
nor Plautus too light. For the law of writ, and the
liberty, these are the only men.

HAMLET

O Jephthah, judge of Israel, what a treasure hadst
thou!

POLONIUS

What a treasure had he, my lord?   405

HAMLET

Why,

        "One fair daughter and no more,

        The which he lovèd passing well."

POLONIUS [*aside.*]

Still on my daughter.

HAMLET

Am I not i' th' right, old Jephthah?   410

POLONIUS

If you call me Jephthah, my lord, I have a daughter that
I love passing well.

● **SPEECH NOTE: best actors ... only men:** Trying to impress, Polonius attempts an exhaustive list of dramatic categories. This recitation suggests that, like Osric (V.ii.190–94), he has only "got the tune of the time," here as relates to the theater, and when it comes to his trial later in the scene, namely the First Player's recitation, the "bubble" is "out," i.e., his knowledge is a mere bubble that pops when put to the test.

tragical-historical: "The first play to be so designated on its title-page was 'The Tragicall Historie of Hamlet' (Q1, Q2)" (Jenkins). **scene individible ... poem unlimited:** "play observing the unity of place" and "play ignoring rules such as the three unities [of time, place, and action]" (Riverside), though Jenkins suggests that "these meanings are not obvious, and both terms [may bring] the already ridiculous categories to a climax in an all-inclusive (*unlimited*) and unclassifiable (*individible*) drama." **Seneca ... Plautus:** Roman playwrights of tragedy (heavy, serious, sober, Latin *gravis*) and comedy (light) respectively, cf., Meres, *Palladis Tamia* (1598) (Jenkins substantially). **law of writ, and the liberty:** both for plays written ("writ") in adherence to formal rules ("law") and plays taking liberties with them ("liberty"), "law" and "liberty" being the significant antithesis, with possible quibbles on plays performed at court and plays performed in public. In London the "liberties" were areas outside official city jurisdiction (Jenkins substantially). **only men:** by far the best—these actors are the best at performing both formally and informally written plays.

Jephthah: The biblical story of Jephthah (Judges XI.30–40), who sacrificed his daughter in order to keep a careless vow, was a common subject for homilies, and though Shakespeare may have known the story from the Bible and from a popular Latin drama called *Jephthes* (1554) by George Buchanan (Baldwin I.683), Hamlet at lines 407–408 is actually quoting lines 2–6 of the first eight-line stanza of a popular ballad version (given in full in Jenkins LN). ● Hamlet is adding to his earlier characterization of Polonius as a "fishmonger" (line 174) the accusation that he would sacrifice his own daughter to his self-importance, cf., line 185 note. **passing:** surpassingly.

Still: always.

HAMLET
  Nay, that follows not.
POLONIUS
  What follows then, my lord?
HAMLET
  Why,   415
    "As by lot, God wot,"
  and then, you know,
    "It came to pass, as most like it was"—
  The first row of the pious chanson will show you

  more, for look where my abridgement comes.   420

                    Enter the Players.

  You are welcome, masters, welcome all.—I am glad to
  see thee well.—Welcome, good friends.—O, old

  friend, why thy face is valanced since I saw thee last.

  Com'st thou to beard me in Denmark?—What, my

  young lady and mistress! By'r lady, your ladyship is   425
  nearer to heaven than when I saw you last by the

  altitude of a chopine. Pray God your voice, like a

---

that follows not: that is not how the ballad goes, and also it does not follow that you love your daughter so very well.

As by lot ... most like it was: quoting lines 5–6 of the ballad, see line 403 note

row: stanza. **pious chanson:** song (French *chanson*) based on holy scripture, i.e., the familiar ballad.
abridgement: interruption, the cutting short of his conversation, with a pun on entertainment, the making of time seem shorter with their performances, cf., *Midsummer Night's Dream* V.i.39 (Jenkins substantially).
s.d. the Players: the number is unstated in Q2, where F, which "estimates the practical requirement," has "*four or five.*" "The play of III.ii will have four speaking parts, of which two may be doubled, plus at least '*two or three Mutes*' ... , so that at least five will be needed then. It does not follow that all must appear now" (Jenkins). However it seems likely that all the players who are to appear later would enter here as a group because a) "*the Players*" seems to imply the whole troupe, b) Hamlet uses and repeats the word "all" (lines 421 and 429), and c) at III.ii the s.d. has "three of the Players."
masters: because they are masters of their art.
thee: the informal and personal manner of address to an inferior or an intimate, here a fulfillment of Hamlet's intimation (line 373) that he would be extending an outwardly warmer welcome to the Players than to Rosencrantz and Guildenstern, whom he has addressed with the more formal and respectful "you."
valanced: fringed (Riverside), draped (Jenkins), i.e., with a beard.
beard me: Hamlet intends two senses of *to beard*: a) to wear a beard, with "me" as an ethical dative, and b) to challenge or defy, with "me" as a direct object.
lady and mistress: directed to the boy who plays the female roles and ironically returning to the formal "you" as if speaking to the upper class character the boy plays. **By'r lady:** By Our Lady (i.e., the Virgin Mary), a mild oath, F "Byrlady," Q2 "by lady." At III.ii.133 Q2 has "ber Lady." Cf., *Titus Andronicus* IV.iv.48 Q1–3 "be lady," F "ber lady." The variety suggests the possibility that any of these forms may have been in use.
chopine: an elevator shoe worn by short women (in Cotgrave), the point being that the boy has grown in height (Jenkins LN).

piece of uncurrent gold, be not cracked within the
ring.—Masters, you are all welcome. We'll e'en to't

uncurrent ... ring: An illegal way of amassing
gold without detection was to shave or clip a thin
wedge ("crack") from the edge of a gold coin of the
realm which remained legal tender ("current") so
long as the crack did not cross through the raised
"ring" around the image of the sovereign. Hamlet
hopes the sound ("ring") of the boy's voice has not
changed with puberty so much that it has become
unfit for the female roles, with an additional pun
on the cracking of the lady's virginity (the hymen
protecting her "ring") and consequent loss of the
value of her virtue. ● With the last pun, Hamlet
may be seen by Polonius and Rosencrantz and
Guildenstern as madly taking the boy actor for
an actual lady, and by the Players as engaging in
witty repartee. The image of the boy's eventually
outgrowing the lady's part may hint at the theme of
lines 347–51. **e'en to't:** even to it—we'll get right to it.

like French falconers, fly at any thing we see. We'll   430

like French falconers ... any thing we see: An insult
to French hunters, who send their falcons after
all kinds of quarry rather than after the particular
kinds of quarry English falcons were trained to
hunt, implying that Hamlet wishes to hear a speech
immediately without caring what its subject or style
might be.

have a speech straight. Come, give us a taste of your
quality. Come, a passionate speech.

straight: immediately.

quality: "professional skill," cf., line 347 (Jenkins).
passionate: emotional, impassioned (OED 2.b.),
with the possible overtone of evoking compassion
and pity (OED 5.c.).

FIRST PLAYER
What speech, my good lord?
HAMLET
I heard thee speak me a speech once, but it was never
acted, or if it was, not above once, for the play,   435

me: the ethical dative (Abbott §220).

above: more than. **the play:** "There is no justification
for identifying this with Marlowe and Nashe's
Tragedy of Dido, which also gives 'Aeneas' tale to Dido'
(see lines [446–47]), but from which Shakespeare's
version is not taken ... though Shakespeare may have
been influenced by the prominence *Dido* gives to the
slaying of Priam and by one or two particular details"
(Jenkins).

I remember, pleased not the million; 'twas caviary
to the general. But it was—as I received it, and

million: multitudes. **caviary to the general:** caviar to
the general public, i.e., too refined a delicacy for the
taste of the multitude. ● Jenkins quotes Harbage's
comment (in *Shakespeare and the Rival Traditions*,
page 292) that "caviar to the general" "has passed
into general currency in a sense quite contrary to
the speaker's apparent intention ... with purveyors
of 'caviar' receiving the cuff rather than 'the general'
who fail to relish it." The alteration of original intent
of the phrase (as with I.iii.78 and line 250 above) is
a measure of the change in underlying cultural and
philosophical assumptions from Shakespeare's
time to ours. In a hierarchical society, greater
rank was assumed to be accompanied by more
refined taste, royalty setting the standard for the
rest of the population ("the general"), whereas in
an egalitarian society, the common taste sets the
standard and refinement is a sign of effeteness if not

others, whose judgments in such matters cried in the
top of mine—an excellent play, well digested in the

scenes, set down with as much modesty as cunning.   440

I remember one said there were no sallets in the lines to

make the matter savoury, nor no matter in the phrase
that might indict the author of affection, but called it
an honest method, as wholesome as sweet, and by very

much more handsome than fine. One speech in't   445

I chiefly loved; 'twas Aeneas' tale to Dido, and

thereabout of it especially when he speaks of

---

of snobbery. About plays here and at III.ii.25–27 and 41, like Polonius about clothing at I.ii.73–74, Hamlet, following the tradition begun by Socrates in Plato's *Crito* and elsewhere, asserts the higher value of the opinions of the judicious few than of the many.

cried in the top of: had superior authority to, cf., line 340 and note. **digested:** arranged, ordered, cf., *Richard III* III.i.200.

scenes: stage representation with the secondary sense of division of an act (OED 3., 5.). **modesty:** decorum, propriety, cf., III.ii.19 and V.i.208. **cunning:** artistry, skill, cf., line 590.

sallets: salads (from the Latin *sal*, salt), whose use in the first-century Roman rhetorician Quintilian's *Institutio Oratoria*, a fundamental text in Shakespeare's grammar school, is defined in Thomas Cooper's *Thesaurus* (1565) as "pleasant wittinesse … mery conceites in woordes or otherwyse" (quoted in Baldwin II.202), hence sharp-tasting or spicy bits, as distinct from "sweet" at line 444, and "hence ribaldries" (Jenkins).

savoury: here inappropriately sharp tasting. **matter … phrase:** subject matter … words, expression. Based on Quintilian, "phrase and matter are separate entities, but must be suited to each other" (Baldwin II.183), cf., line 95 note. **matter in the phrase … affection:** the author added no subject matter of his own, outside that of the received story, by which he could be accused ("indict") of affectation, the worst of all rhetorical vices according to Quintilian (Baldwin II.216).

handsome: serviceable in style, "natural grace" (Jenkins). **fine:** elaborated or showy, "artful workmanship" (Jenkins).

I chiefly loved: ● With this assertion Hamlet wants to justify his desire to hear the passage, his real motive remaining a secret, see SPEECH NOTE following line 449. The excellence of the play is emphasized so as to cause us in the audience to take it seriously and to believe in its moving power. The whole passage, as Baldwin shows (II.202–203), derives from the standards of Quintilian, though Baldwin misreads the intent of the "one" mentioned in line 441 as critical rather than laudatory. Like Hamlet, the "one" wanted no excess of "sallets" and no affectation, cf., line 436 note. **Aeneas' tale:** For the source of the passage see Book II of Virgil's *Aeneid*, which Shakespeare would have studied in grammar school (Baldwin II.420). Guided by the gods, Aeneas left the falling Troy, carrying with him his father and son (past and future), and, on his way to Italy to found Rome, paused at Carthage, where he told his story to the widowed queen, Dido, who fell in love with him and killed herself when Aeneas followed the gods' orders to leave her and sail onward.

thereabout of it: thereabouts in the speech.

Priam's slaughter. If it live in your memory,

begin at this line—let me see, let me see—

Priam's slaughter: Priam, King of Troy, father of fifty sons, including Paris and Hector, was slain by Achilles' son Pyrrhus following the successful ruse of the Trojan Horse conceived by Ulysses (Odysseus), cf., *Aeneid* II.506–559.

let me see: Hamlet is trying to remember the speech. ●**SPEECH NOTE:** The lines of Hamlet and the Player that follow, like those from "The Murder of Gonzago," which Hamlet will soon commission the players to perform with a few lines added by himself (see lines 540–43) to "catch the conscience of the king" (see line 605), come from imaginary plays written by Shakespeare in older styles, florid blank verse and heroic couplets, respectively, not to satirize those styles but to distinguish them from the contemporary style of his own play. Both "plays" are constructed to be thematically relevant in many respects, the central one being the subject of the killing of kings.

From this first play Hamlet wants to hear about Pyrrhus' killing of Priam. His motive is not necessarily to be moved to follow Pyrrhus' example. It is to envision the fall of a great king at the hands of a villain and the grief of that king's wife. Pyrrhus appears here not as the heroic avenger of his father Achilles but rather as a treacherous villain. And Priam appears as an ancient, noble, and tragic archetype, partly because in the matter of the Trojan War Shakespeare and his audience identified with the Trojans rather than the Greeks, and more specifically because Hamlet wants to experience, through the mirror of nature that is theater (cf., III.ii.22), the horror of the death of his father in that of Priam and the significant lack of grief of his mother in the contrasting envisioned grief of Hecuba. Thus will history provide him inspiration and justification for his revenge.

In addition to "lead[ing] on to Hamlet's plot against the King and [giving] prominence to the players in preparation for their crucial role in it, [and to providing] occasion for the contrast, elaborated in the soliloquy of lines [549]ff., between the Player's reaction to a fictional calamity and Hamlet's reaction to a real one," the speech, which (*pace* Jenkins) belongs *both* to the hero's design *and* to the dramatist's, reproduces "the play's basic motifs in exaggerated form" (Jenkins LN). The themes and motifs of the speech that are relevant to the play as a whole include vengeance, hellishness and hell, secret plotting, the fall of kings, the fickleness of fortune, the pause before the death blow, the grief of Hecuba contrasted with the lack of it in Gertrude, the power of theatrical drama to move, the fall of a great city, and in Pyrrhus a combined foil for Claudius, Hamlet, Lucianus (in the "Murder of Gonzago" play), Laertes, Fortinbras, and even Horatio. Finally, using the speech to lend heroic weight and meaning to Hamlet's own situation, which is closer than the fall of Priam to one that might be our own, Shakespeare deftly joins heroic universality and personal immediacy into a single experience for his audience, as well as for Hamlet himself.

"The rugged Pyrrhus, like th' Hyrcanian beast"—   450

rugged: "An apt epithet for both the landscape and the beasts of Hyrcania (see next note), corresponding to Virgil's *horrens* [whence *horrendous*]. Hence terrifyingly wild in appearance. Cf. *Mac[beth]* III.iv.[99–100]" (Jenkins).

Hyrcanian: "Hyrcania, a region on the southern shores of the Caspian, in literature famous for tigers…. Virgil's Dido (and Marlowe's) denounces Aeneas, when he deserts her, as having been suckled by them (*Aeneid*, IV.367). Shakespeare refers to them [in *3 Henry VI* I.iv.155 and in *Macbeth* III.iv.100]. Hamlet's slip of memory thus stresses the savagery of Pyrrhus from the start" (Jenkins).

'Tis not so. It begins with Pyrrhus—

'Tis not so … with Pyrrhus: That is not the way the lines go. The speech begins with a fuller description of Pyrrhus.

"The rugged Pyrrhus, he whose sable arms,
Black as his purpose, did the night resemble
When he lay couchèd in the ominous horse,

sable arms: black armor, another image of villainy, as the next lines reinforce.

ominous: fateful, full of bad omen. **horse:** The wooden horse was offered to Troy in a stratagem. Apparently a gift from the defeated and departing Greeks, it actually hid within it a company of Greek heroes who, once inside Troy, came out of the horse to open the Trojan gates to the Greek forces, who then proceeded to destroy the city.

Hath now this dread and black complexion smeared   455

black: fourth use of the idea in as many lines.
complexion: complex of qualities: color, general appearance, and character of Pyrrhus' whole form (cf., line 306 note and SPEECH NOTE after I.iv.38).

With heraldry more dismal. Head to foot

heraldry: the art of symbolism in armor and crests, here referring to the significant decoration of Pyrrhus himself in armor, as if he were an image of his own coat of arms, and in particular to its color, which is now more fatally ominous ("dismal") than merely black because he is smeared all over in "gules," the heraldic name for the color red, here with blood.

Now is he total gules, horridly tricked
With blood of fathers, mothers, daughters, sons,

tricked: delineated, decorated, another heraldic term.
blood of fathers … sons: the blood of the people of Troy being slaughtered.

Baked and impasted with the parching streets,

Baked and impasted: the blood upon Pyrrhus is baked into paste. **parching streets:** the burning city is giving off heat that parches the wet blood covering Pyrrhus.

That lend a tyrannous and damnèd light   460

tyrannous and damnèd light: possibly a hendiadys for "damnably pitiless, or the kind of pitiless light that shines on the damned" (Wright, page 186).
● The light from the fires of the burning city is like the fires of hell in illuminating in its blood-red glow the violent, bloody, and harsh ("tyrannous") act of the killing of Priam.

To their lord's murder. Roasted in wrath and fire,

Roasted in wrath and fire: wrath being one of the seven capital sins, the image has Pyrrhus both

And thus o'ersizèd with coagulate gore,

With eyes like carbuncles, the hellish Pyrrhus

Old grandsire Priam seeks."
So proceed you.   465
POLONIUS
'Fore God, my lord, well spoken, with good accent

and good discretion.

FIRST PLAYER
            "Anon he finds him

Striking too short at Greeks. His ántique sword,

burning in the sin of wrath itself and imaging the punishment of that sin in hell, cf., "hellish" in line 463.

o'ersizèd: smeared, glazed, and stiffened with blood as with "size," the glutinous substance made from glue, flour, varnish, resin, etc., used to fill pores in paper, textiles, plaster, or leather to prepare them to be painted, decorated, etc. **coagulate:** clotted. **gore:** blood.

carbuncles: red gemstone, implying bloody purpose, "[F]iery red in colour, [they] were thought to have a light of their own by means of which they shone in the dark. Cf. line [461], where the heat comes from within as well as without. For Shakespeare an eye glowing red carries particular menace. Cf. *Cor*[*iolanus*] V.i.63[–64] … [*King*] *John*, IV.ii.163, [and] *2 H*[*enry*] *VI* III.i.154" (Jenkins). **hellish:** • Summing up all the previous images. **Pyrrhus … Priam seeks:** that is, Pyrrhus (subject) seeks Priam (direct object). **grandsire:** grandfather.

So proceed you: instructing the Player to proceed in the speech from there.

'Fore God: Before God, an oath used for emphasis. **accent:** emphasis, stress (Raffel).

discretion: the same good judgment in delivering the speech that earlier Hamlet had claimed in judging the play (lines 437–40). • According to Polonius, Hamlet's delivery of the lines is excellent, and though Polonius's praise is no doubt spoken in flattery, there is no reason not to believe his description to be essentially true. More importantly, Hamlet's accuracy is like that of a professional actor, and this contributes to the characterization of the Prince: Hamlet is, as Ophelia later describes him, the ideal courtier, soldier, and scholar, and is "unmatched" in bearing man's "most noble and sovereign reason." Memory is an essential characteristic for an ideal prince and an ideal scholar, as it is for an actor and a playwright, and Mnemosyne (Memory) was the mother of the muses. Shakespeare is giving us one more example of Hamlet's excellence while at the same time suggesting that he has recalled and begun the speech so vividly because the horror of the fall of the great king Priam has been called to his mind by the Ghost's description of the fall of his own father.

Anon he finds him: • This half line completes the pentameter line that began with the last half line in Hamlet's recitation of the speech (line 464), suggesting not only the Player's continuation of the same line without break, keeping to the meter and being quick in obedience to Hamlet's request at line 465, but his ignoring of Polonius's flattering interruption in prose.

Striking too short: his sword thrusts are not able to reach their targets. **ántique:** his sword is ancient, like

Priam himself, and was used long ago when Priam was young. ●NOTE TO ACTORS: The word is stressed on the first syllable.

Rebellious to his arm, lies where it falls, 470

Rebellious to his arm: the sword does not obey Priam's attempt to wield it (because Priam is so old).

Repugnant to command. Unequal matched,

Repugnant: literally "fighting against" Priam's commands. ● The three lines, metaphors for Priam's hopeless weakness in combat because of his old age, also suggest the theme of failing to fulfill a charge. **Unequal matched:** Pyrrhus is matched against an opponent who, because of his age, is not equal to him as a fighter.

Pyrrhus at Priam drives, in rage strikes wide,

drives: lunges at. **strikes wide:** swings and misses, wide of the mark.

But with the whiff and wind of his fell sword

But: though the sense "however" is implied, the primary sense is only or merely (cf., "even" at *Troilus and Cressida* V.iii.41). **whiff and wind:** a hendiadys (Wright, page 186), the gust of wind generated by the missed stroke.

Th'unnervèd father falls. Then senseless Ilium,

unnervèd: abandoned by his strength, "enfeebled … the first recorded use of the word" (Jenkins). **father:** Priam, who is so weakened with age that he falls from the mere puff of wind from the sword of Pyrrhus. **Then senseless Ilium:** Ilium is the citadel of Troy, insensible ("senseless") because made of stone (these three words, in F, are missing in Q2).

Seeming to feel this blow, with flaming top 475

Seeming to feel: Jenkins notes that despite its natural insensibility, the citadel nonetheless seems to feel *this* blow, so horrible is the act of murder of the great but ancient and weakened king by the young, strong warrior, cf., III.iv.126–27. **flaming top:** burning towers, cf., Marlowe's *Doctor Faustus* V.i.96 ("And burnt the topless towers of Ilium").

Stoops to his base, and with a hideous crash

Stoops to his base: collapses to the ground, "his" being a normal genitive form of "its" (Abbott §228). **hideous:** terrifying, cf., I.iv.54.

Takes prisoner Pyrrhus' ear. For lo, his sword,

Takes prisoner Pyrrhus' ear: the sound of the great crash, in a metaphor appropriate to a battle, grabs and holds Pyrrhus' attention ("ear"). **lo:** behold.

Which was declining on the milky head
Of reverend Priam, seemed i' th' air to stick,

declining: coming down upon, "A rare use, though again said of a sword in *Troilus and Cressida* IV.v.189" (Jenkins). **milky:** white-haired with age.

So as a painted tyrant Pyrrhus stood 480

painted tyrant: Pyrrhus, a tyrant in his own right because of what he is trying to do, cf., line 460, stands stock still as if he were an image in a painting or on a painted cloth. ●NOTE TO ACTORS: Stress the word "painted" here to make the point of his temporary stillness.

And, like a neutral to his will and matter,

neutral … matter: Pyrrhus stands immobilized between his "will" to kill Priam on one hand and the actual killing of Priam (the "matter") on the other, as if in a state of neutrality between them.

Did nothing.

Did nothing: ● This arrested motion of Pyrrhus is a crucial image in the play. Shakespeare makes this line one and a half feet (an iamb plus an unstressed syllable), the soundless empty three and a half feet of the rest of the pentameter line causing us to feel the motionlessness. The same metrical device will recur at the very point of the climax of the play (III.iii.87), when Hamlet too pauses between the "will" and the "matter" of killing Claudius. In externals that pause will end differently. Internally it is the moment that Hamlet becomes more like the "tyrant" Pyrrhus than even Claudius has been.

But as we often see against some storm

see: "Loosely used to include perceiving by other senses" (Jenkins). **against:** immediately before.

A silence in the heavens, the rack stand still,

rack: "Clouds, or a mass of cloud, driven before the wind in the upper air" (OED *sb.*¹ 3.).

The bold winds speechless, and the orb below   485
As hush as death, anon the dreadful thunder

orb below: the earth.

hush: quiet, silent, "regarded by Abbot ([§]22) as an adjectival use of the noun, but explained by OED as a modification of the adjective *husht*, which derived from the interjection and was then mistaken for a past [participle]" (Jenkins). **anon:** soon.

Doth rend the region; so after Pyrrhus' pause

rend: "Used to denote the effect of sounds, esp. loud noises, on the air" (OED *v.*¹ 4.b., which cites this as the first use in this sense). **region:** heavens, sky, the sphere of the air, that region of the Ptolemaic universe of concentric spheres that was conceived to surround the globe of the earth and be surrounded itself by the sphere of fire, cf., lines 299–301 note.

Arousèd vengeance sets him new awork,

Arousèd vengeance: "Though the element of revenge is inherent in the story of Pyrrhus (his father Achilles had been slain by Priam's son Paris), it receives little stress in Virgil or the medieval writers. It becomes conspicuous, however, in some of Shakespeare's predecessors": Marlowe and Nashe in *Dido* (II.i.259–60) and Peele in *Tale of Troy* (lines 440–44) (Jenkins). • This newly aroused rage of Pyrrhus will be contrasted with Hamlet's form of vengeance in III.iii, which will seem externally to be far less fierce but internally to be far more so. Where the horror of this scene lies in the action, in III.iii it will lie in the will. **him:** Pyrrhus. **new:** newly. **awork:** to work, contraction of an older prepositional phrase "on work" (see Abbott §24, and cf., *King Lear* III.v.8).

And never did the Cyclops' hammers fall
On Mars's armor, forged for proof eterne,   490

never … / With less: the double negative emphasizes the ferocity. **Cyclops' hammers … Mars's armor:** Vulcan, the blacksmith and armorer of the gods, used the Cyclopes as workers, here seen forging and shaping the armor of Mars, the god of War. **proof eterne:** eternal defense or protection, "proof" being both a general term (being proven, standing up to testing) and a particular term in relation to armor, "the quality of armour which has been specially 'proved' or tested for its power of resistance. Cf. *Ant[ony and Cleopatra]* IV.viii.15 [and] *R[ichard]* 2 I.iii.73" (Jenkins).

With less remorse than Pyrrhus' bleeding sword
Now falls on Priam.

remorse: pity, compassion. **bleeding:** i.e., bloody.
Now falls on Priam: The empty feet again make a pause of silence for effect.

Out, out, thou strumpet Fortune! All you gods,

Out: a condemnation, as we might say "get out!" **strumpet:** whore, cf., line 229 note and line 236.

In general synod take away her power,
Break all the spokes and fellies from her wheel,   495

And bowl the round nave down the hill of heaven
As low as to the fiends."

POLONIUS
This is too long.

HAMLET
It shall to the barber's with your beard.—Prithee say
on. He's for a jig or a tale of bawdry, or he sleeps.   500

Say on; come to Hecuba.

FIRST PLAYER
"But who—ah woe—had seen the mobled queen—"
HAMLET
"The mobled queen."

POLONIUS
That's good.
FIRST Player
"—Run barefoot up and down, threatening the flames   505

With bisson rheum, a clout upon that head

Where late the diadem stood, and for a robe,
About her lank and all o'erteemèd loins
A blanket, in the alarm of fear caught up—

Who this had seen, with tongue in venom steeped,   510

---

general synod: council of all.

fellies: "curved pieces composing the outer rim of the wheel" (Raffel).

bowl: to send rolling, derived from the game of bowls (OED v.¹ 2.). **nave:** the wheel's hub, "all of the wheel that is left when the spokes and fellies are gone" (Jenkins) ● In horror at the destruction of the great Priam, the speaker (Aeneas) calls upon the gods to act as one in overturning Fortune's own greatness and power by breaking up her instrument of alteration, to reverse the fortune of Fortune as she has reversed the fortunes of men, see line 229 note.

This is too long: ● Polonius is unmoved by the fall of Priam because he sees the world in terms of policy rather than tragedy and has little patience for words when they are not his own. He objects to the Player's or playwright's overdoing the length of the speech in the matter of Troy. Ironically, he will fail to recognize and limit his own overdoing in the matter of Denmark, a failure that leads to his own reversal of fortune and tragic fall.

beard: "The conspicuous feature of an inveterate chin-wagger" (Jenkins). **jig:** comical farce involving singing and dancing performed after serious plays in the public theaters. **tale of bawdry:** ribald or licentious story.

come to Hecuba: Though Hecuba is a classical heroine particularly famous for her many sufferings, Shakespeare here focuses attention specifically on her response to the violent death of her husband to emphasize Hamlet's interest in the contrast to his mother's response to her own husband's death (Jenkins substantially).

mobled: muffled, head and face covered up, here in her grief. It is uncertain whether the pronunciation should be as spelled or as "mobbled" or why it attracts Hamlet's musing, unless, as Jenkins suggests, the usage was rare.

That's good: ● With flattery Polonius is trying to make up for his earlier faux pas (line 498), which seems to have offended the Prince (lines 499–500). "F's addition ["mobled queen is good."] is a characteristic piece of ad-libbing [that made its way into the copy for F]" (Jenkins).

bisson: blinding, from an old word (*bisene, bisne*) whose etymology the OED finds uncertain.
rheum: watery discharge, here tears. Hecuba's tears are so profuse that they threaten to douse the "flames" of the burning city, cf., *Rape of Lucrece* line 1468. **clout:** cloth, rag.

late: recently. **diadem:** crown.

lank: thin. **o'erteemèd:** from at least three meanings of *to teem*: to bring forth or give birth, to become pregnant, and to abound. Hecuba's loins are "over-teemèd," worn to thinness from much childbearing.

venom steeped: drenched in venom, i.e., with venomous words.

'Gainst Fortune's state would treason have
                            [pronounced.
But if the gods themselves did see her then,
When she saw Pyrrhus make malicious sport
In mincing with his sword her husband's limbs,
The instant burst of clamor that she made,   515
Unless things mortal move them not at all,
Would have made milch the burning eyes of heaven

And passion in the gods."

state: both government or rule and position of authority in the universe.

if the gods ... did see ... Would have made: In conditional sentences, "the consequent does not always answer to the antecedent in mood or tense" (Abbott §371). **in mincing:** in the act of mincing (Abbott §164). **Unless things mortal move them not at all:** The ancient doctrine of Epicurus (followed by Lucretius in *De Rerum Natura*), who taught that, "Fashioned of finer stuff than we, [the gods] dwell afar in the intermundial spaces ... , neither troubling nor troubled by the affairs of humanity, neither rewarding virtue nor punishing sin in this life. And ... there is no life to come" (*Enc. Brit.* 8.649), a doctrine that could be considered seriously by Aeneas, the speaker of the quoted speech, before his descent to the underworld, but only as an ancient error or heresy by Hamlet, Shakespeare, and all but a rare few skeptics in Shakespeare's audience. **milch:** milk-giving, here tear-producing. **burning eyes of heaven:** the stars, with the added sense of eyes burning from weeping in sorrow. I.e., the extremity of Hecuba's grief would have made the element of fire (stars) yield the opposite element of water (tears), a miraculous transformation, like that of the next line.

passion in the gods: an oxymoron, the second object of "made" in the previous line. *Passion* (from the Latin deponent verb *patior*, to bear or suffer) means intense anguished emotion, whether evoked by love, hate, revenge, misfortune, or any other cause.
● This image forms another extreme reaction to the grief of Hecuba like that in the previous line. Though "passion in the gods" was not uncommon in classical myth, cf., Ovid *Metamorphoses* XIII.573, in this image the immortal gods are implied to be blissfully above such weakness. And in the philosophical and theological tradition that Shakespeare inherits, it was as much an impossibility as the water from fire of the previous line was an impossibility in nature. Considering how upset Hamlet has been about Gertrude's lack of response to the death of Hamlet's father (cf., I.ii.129–59 and 180–83), it makes sense that Hamlet has wished to hear retold this passionate grief of Hecuba. The telling also furthers the author's purposes, for the emotion of the Player, who is himself moved to tears (lines 519–20, 554–57), occasions Hamlet's questioning of his own motives and purposes. In addition, passion's overruling the government of reason will become one of the main subjects of the play. Hamlet is a man whose passion occasionally, for good cause, overcomes him but whose reason normally reasserts itself appropriately. This characteristic restoration will fail at the crucial moment (III.iii) that forms the climax of the play. Cf., SPEECH NOTE after line 600.

POLONIUS

Look, whe'er he has not turned his color and has tears
in's eyes. Prithee no more.   520

HAMLET

'Tis well. I'll have thee speak out the rest of this
soon.—Good my lord, will you see the players well

bestowed? Do you hear, let them be well used, for they
are the abstract and brief chronicles of the time. After
your death you were better have a bad epitaph than   525
their ill report while you live.

POLONIUS

My lord, I will use them according to their desért.

HAMLET

God's bodkin, man, much better. Use every man

after his desert, and who shall scape whipping?   530
Use them after your own honor and dignity;

Look, whe'er he has not: "whe'er" = whether, i.e.,
"note how he has" (Riverside). **turned his color:**
gone pale, cf., line 554. **turned ... in's eyes:** ● Polonius
informs us that the Player has been moved to tears
by his own speech, a motif that derives from Plato
(*Ion*, 535 b–d), Cicero (*De Oratore*, II.xlv.189), and most
influentially Quintilian, who writes, "I have often
seen actors, both in tragedy and comedy, leave the
theatre still drowned in tears after concluding the
performance of some moving role. But if the mere
delivery of words written by another has the power
to set our souls on fire with fictitious emotions,
what will the orator do whose duty it is to picture to
himself the facts and who has it in his power to feel
the same emotion as his client whose interests are
at stake? ... I have frequently been so much moved
while speaking, that I have not merely been wrought
upon to tears, but have turned pale and shown all the
symptoms of genuine grief" (Quint., VI.ii.35–36, Vol.
II, page 437), a passage to which Montaigne refers
(*Essays* III.4, "Of Diversion") and which Shakespeare
would have read in Florio's translation (1603), cf.,
Baldwin II.204–205. "Among those whose woes it
affected Ion to recite were Hecuba and Priam; and ... it
was 'the miseries of Hecuba', seen in a performance
of the *Troades* of Euripides, that drew tears from the
tyrant Alexander of Pherae.... Plutarch's account
of this (in the Life of Pelopidas, *Lives*, Tudor Trans.,
ii.323) is remembered by Montaigne (II.27) and cited
by [Sir Philip] Sidney as an instance of the power of
tragedy" (Jenkins LN). The Player's being moved sets
up Hamlet's own response in the following soliloquy
(lines 550ff.). **Prithee:** I pray thee, please.

bestowed: lodged, taken care of. **used:** treated.

the abstract and brief chronicles: perhaps a
hendiadys (Wright, page 187), but "the abstract"
is "A noun, as always in Shakespeare, and apparently
synonymous with *brief chronicles*" (Jenkins),
signifying the précis, summary, or epitome (OED
sb. B. 1. and 2.), cf., *Richard III* IV.iv.28 and *King John*
II.i.101. **brief chronicles:** historical summaries.
of the time: of the age, the historical period.
After your death ... while you live: cf., Horace *Satires*,
II.i.45–46 (Baldwin II.513). **you were better have:**
you would be better off having, replacing the older
form "to you it were better" with *you* as a nominative,
cf., Abbott §230.

desért: deserving, stress on the second syllable.
(In Riverside this word forms line 528 .)

God's bodkin: an oath, "By God's (meaning Christ's)
little body."

after: according to. **scape:** escape. **whipping:**
Jenkins notes that whipping was "the statutory
punishment for unlicensed players, who were held
to be vagabonds." ● But the point is not merely

the less they deserve, the more merit is in your bounty.
Take them in.

POLONIUS
Come, sirs.

HAMLET
Follow him, friends. We'll hear a play   535
tomorrow.

[*Aside to First Player.*] Dost thou hear me, old

friend? Can you play *The Murder of Gonzago*?

FIRST PLAYER
Ay, my lord.

HAMLET
We'll ha't tomorrow night. You could for a need   540
study a speech of some dozen or sixteen lines,
which I would set down and insert in't, could
you not?

FIRST PLAYER
Ay, my lord.

---

that Hamlet threatens Polonius and himself with
the specific punishment for vagabonds. It is more
importantly that no man, in this world or the next,
is safe from punishment if he is held strictly to the
account of justice and not shown mercy.

bounty: generosity, kindness. • Hamlet is
expressing a commonplace of Christian thought:
All men, being fallen, are sinners and deserve
punishment, from which they are redeemed only
by Christ's sacrifice and their faith in it, in other
words, by God's "bounty" (= mercy, kindness). In his
exhortation to Polonius to treat the players better
than they deserve Hamlet is recommending the
Christian attitude of the Paternoster's "forgive us
our debts, as we also forgive our debtors" (Matthew
6:12), which makes mercy a higher value than justice
and suggests that it is also a universal necessity for
all men (cf., *Merchant of Venice* IV.i.199–200). Hamlet
also emphasizes the good ("merit") that kind actions
accrue to one's own soul. Similarly, the threat to one's
own soul from unkind (vengeful) actions will be
illustrated by Hamlet's own situation when he makes
his fateful decision in III.iii.

hear a play: • Shakespeare's audience, as this
phrase confirms, generally spoke of "hearing" a play
rather than "seeing" one as we would say. Hence we
gather that language was more crucial than gestures,
costumes, and sets in the Renaissance audience's
experience of the theater. Though the theater
companies did what they could to make the visuals,
and particularly costumes, as elaborate as they could,
the convention of Shakespearean drama put primary
focus on poetic speech as the medium for conveying
story, character, and meaning.

Dost thou hear me: Hamlet is calling the First Player
aside to speak to him privately.

***The Murder of Gonzago*:** • Though there may be some
connection between the idea of the play within the
play (and of the play *Hamlet* itself) and the actual
murder of the Duke of Urbino by his wife's relative,
Luigi Gonzaga, in 1538, the play within the play that
Hamlet commissions is Shakespeare's own invention.
See SPEECH NOTE following line 449.

Ha't: have it (performed). **for a need:** if necessary,
F, for need Q2.

I would: I wish to, I would like to (Abbott §331).
set down: write down. • It is useless to seek for these
foretold lines in the lines actually delivered in III.ii.
We are given no specific information about which of
the lines that we will actually hear were written by
Hamlet. The point is that we are being prepared here
for "hearing" the play within the play as particularly
relevant to what the Ghost has reported about
Hamlet Senior's death.

HAMLET

Very well. Follow that lord, and look you mock him   545
                    [*Exeunt Polonius and Players.*]
not [*To Rosencrantz and Guildenstern.*] My good friends,
I'll leave you till night. You are welcome to Elsinore.

ROSENCRANTZ

Good my lord.
                    Exeunt [*Rosencrantz and Guildenstern*].

HAMLET

Ay, so, God buy you. Now I am alone.

O what a rogue and peasant slave am I!   550

Is it not monstrous that this player here,
But in a fiction, in a dream of passion,

Could force his soul so to his own conceit

Follow that lord: i.e., Polonius. ● Polonius and the other Players have waited apart for Hamlet to finish his words with the First Player, and now Hamlet instructs the latter to join them in following Polonius to their place of lodging (Jenkins substantially).
mock him not: ● Hamlet has a prerogative, both as the prince and as a presumed madman, that the players do not, and he does not want the players to take up the mocking of Polonius because a) Polonius is the King's chief counselor and authority is not to be insulted, b) Hamlet does not want the players to get into trouble with Polonius or the King, and c) Hamlet wishes to reserve for himself the role of abnormal behavior at court.
Good my lord: Rosencrantz's parting salutation as he and Guildenstern too leave the Prince.

God buy you: This phrase is said as Rosencrantz and Guildenstern are leaving the stage. Q2 has "God buy to you," F "God buy 'ye." Both are versions of the contraction, already common in Shakespeare's time, of "God be with you" (which later became "Good-bye"), upon which usage had also superimposed the meaning "God (i.e., Christ) buy (= redeem) you (from sin)." I have eliminated the "to" from the Q2 version on the grounds that a) it is redundant in both the contractions' senses, and b) it adds an excess unstressed syllable, making the line, which ends with "Now I am alone," less metrical, though with the "to" the meter would be retained if "I am" were elided to "I'm."

● SPEECH NOTE: **O what a rogue ... of the King:** The following speech, Hamlet's second great soliloquy, repeats the pattern, established by the first (I.ii.129ff.), according to which Hamlet pursues a line of thinking that drives him into a passion, whereupon his reason reasserts itself and he comes to a rational conclusion. The turn comes at line 582.
rogue ... peasant slave: terms of abuse. **rogue:** a lawless and immoral person, a villain. **peasant:** one who is low and subservient. **slave:** the lowest human level in the hierarchy of creation and of rank, one step above a brute beast.

monstrous: strange and unnatural.

But: only, merely (Abbott §129), i.e., in a mere fiction, a mere dream, as opposed to having a real external occasion of passion. "Elizabethans saw it as a characteristic of the player's art, which was thus distinguished from the orator's, that he feigned a passion he did not really feel (e.g. Thos. Wright, *The Passions of the Mind*, rev. 1604, page 179). Cf. the 'actions that a man might play', I.ii.84. Hence *monstrous*" (Jenkins), cf., lines 519–20 note.

force ... to: force his soul, his inner self, to fit or be in accord with. **conceit:** conception, idea in his mind.

That from her working all his visage wanned,

her: the soul's (Abbott §229). **working:** operation (in response to the conception). **visage:** face. **wanned:** turned pale.

Tears in his eyes, distraction in his aspéct,   555

distraction: madness. **aspéct:** his look, his face, accented on the second syllable (Abbott §490), the second "in his" being contracted to "in's" for the meter, as in F.

A broken voice, and his whole function suiting

function: operation of his physical powers, cf., *Macbeth* I.iii.140. **suiting:** making itself fit or appropriate.

With forms to his conceit? And all for nothing!

forms: outward gestures and expressions. **conceit:** his mind's conception or idea. **nothing:** i.e., not a real person but the mere idea of Hecuba, created out of words. • There is brilliant and daring irony in Shakespeare's dramatic trick here. First, the lines acknowledge that theatrical characters and their emotions are illusions created out of words from a concept in the mind, though the Renaissance audience still largely believed in the authenticity of the ancient stories (as compared with the distrust of historical authenticity that modern audiences experience, the legacy of nineteenth century historicism). Second, partly by acknowledging this illusion, the lines create at the same time the illusion that Hamlet, also made of words, is more real to us than Hecuba. Third, to the extent that the audience is moved by the First Player's being moved, the lines confirm the power of words to move both actor and audience, cf., lines 519–20 note. All three previous points come into the service of the fourth and main point: Hamlet's observation that the Player is moved evokes Hamlet's self-loathing and frustration, which the Player's emotion at first seems to him to justify.

For Hecuba!
What's Hecuba to him, or he to her,

For Hecuba!: for interjectional lines see Abbott §512.

he to her: Q2, F's "he to Hecuba" being an actor's unmetrical over-emphasis (Jenkins substantially).

That he should weep for her? What would he do   560

weep for her: • NOTE TO ACTORS: The stress of the line should come on "weep" rather than on either of the pronouns, where stress would obscure the point. **What would he do?:** Baldwin observes, "It was clearly Quintilian [who "had seen actors … come out weeping"] who shaped Hamlet's thought here" (II.205), cf., lines 519–20 note.

Had he the motive and the cue for passion

motive … / That I have: the real (as opposed to the Player's theatrical) reason for Hamlet himself to be in a passion of anguish and grief, namely the Ghost's description of Hamlet Senior's death and the charge to revenge his murder. • Hamlet's use of the theatrical word "cue," the line of one actor coming just before the start of another actor's speech and in a sense evoking it, turns our attention from the Player's "conceit"-inspired passion to Hamlet's reality-inspired passion.

That I have? He would drown the stage with tears,

drown the stage: a hyperbole, the antithesis of having tears only in his eyes.

And cleave the general ear with horrid speech,

cleave the general ear: tear through the ears of the public, the whole crowd, cf., III.ii.10–11 ("split the ears of the groundlings"). **horrid:** frightful.

Make mad the guilty and appall the free,

mad: out of one's mind, here because of the weight of guilt. ● "Note that what the Player 'would' do is what Hamlet presently does (lines 588ff.): it is the example of the Player that leads to [Hamlet's] device of the play [within the play]" (Jenkins). **appall:** make pale with fear or dismay. **the free:** i.e., free of sin, the guiltless, cf., III.ii.241–42 and *As You Like It* II.vii.85.

Confound the ignorant, and amaze indeed   565

Confound: baffle. **amaze:** perplex, stun, confuse, cf., I.ii.235, III.iv.112.

The very faculties of eyes and ears.

very faculties: inherent power or capacity, essential function (OED faculty 3.), cf., *Julius Caesar* I.iii.67.

Yet I,

Yet I: Following Q2 and F, Riverside includes the phrase on the previous line (which accounts for the anomaly in line numbering here), making a supposed hexameter, but see Abbott §511 on single short lines in speeches of passion.

A dull and muddy-mettled rascal, peak   567

dull: unmoved, inert, lethargic. **muddy-mettled:** dull-spirited, phlegmatic. *Mettle*, from the same root as *metal*, means the substance of which something is made, hence, for a human being, his essential spirit, the stuff of his soul, here muddied like a stirred-up pond or creek, with perhaps the associated meaning of bright metal muddy with rust or dirt. **rascal:** from the French for "worthless foot-soldier," a base and therefore insufficient person, with the associated meaning of an immature deer not worth the hunting, cf., "muddy rascal" and Falstaff's punning rejoinder at 2 *Henry IV* II.iv.39–41. **peak:** grow weak, dwindle, languish, cf., *Macbeth* I.iii.23.

Like John-a-dreams, unpregnant of my cause,
And can say nothing—no, not for a king,

John-a-dreams: "a nickname (like *John-a-nods*) for a listless, dreamy fellow (a = of)" (Jenkins). **unpregnant:** barren, not bringing to birth, cf., *Measure for Measure* IV.iv.20. **cause:** mission, purpose, intention, goal, with the associated meaning of subject of a law case or suit.

Upon whose property and most dear life   570

property: from the Latin for "own," "belonging to oneself," "his proper person (including all that belonged to the essential quality of the man)" (Jenkins), to which we may add, including his kingship, cf., *Antony and Cleopatra* I.i.58. Though the word does not refer specifically to material possessions, through the Middle Ages and Renaissance possessions were thought of as extensions of a man's person, so that in Dante's *Inferno* theft of a man's possessions is punished as severely as crimes against his person. **dear:** precious.

A damned defeat was made. Am I a coward?

defeat: undoing, destruction, from French *defaire* from Latin *disfacere*, cf., I.ii.10, V.ii.58. **Am I a coward?:** In this passage (lines 571–77) Jenkins sees an echo of Thomas Nashe's pamphlet *Pierce Penniless His Supplication to the Devil* (1592) i.210–11 and notes that Emrys Jones (*Origins of Shakespeare*, pages 22–24) relates it to the self-reproaches of Atreus in Seneca's *Thyestes*, lines 176–80.

Who calls me villain, breaks my pate across,
Plucks off my beard and blows it in my face,

Tweaks me by the nose, gives me the lie i' th' throat

As deep as to the lungs—who does me this?   575
Hah! 'swounds, I should take it; for it cannot be

But I am pigeon-livered and lack gall

To make oppression bitter, or ere this

I should ha' fatted all the region kites

With this slave's offal. Bloody, bawdy villain!   580

Remorseless, treacherous, lecherous, kindless villain!

Why, what an ass am I! This is most brave,

Who calls me villain ... to the lungs: These five imaginary actions are all severe insults that would evoke a challenge to a duel from any aristocrat or gentleman in defense of his honor. **pate:** head.

gives me the lie i' th' throat: accuses me of lying with full intention, "the deeper its origin the worse. Kittredge quotes Webster, *Devil's Law-Case*, IV.ii.643–4, 'I'll give the lie in the stomach—That's somewhat deeper than the throat.'" (Jenkins).

me: an ethical dative (Abbott §220).

'swounds: an oath, by his (i.e., Christ's) wounds (yielding also the form *zounds*).
should: = probably would.

But: that not, except, i.e., "it cannot be that I am not pigeon-livered," "it cannot be any other way except that I am a coward" (Abbott §122). **pigeon-livered and lack gall:** "The pigeon was a symbol of meekness, being popularly believed to have no gall [= choler, yellow bile], which was notoriously the source within the liver of bitter and rancorous feelings" (Jenkins, who compares Dekker, *Honest Whore, Part I*, I.v.109 and *Othello* IV.iii.92–92), cf., SPEECH NOTE following I.iv.38. ● Hamlet accuses himself of feeling insufficient bitterness at the deeds ("oppression") of his uncle to rouse him to action.

oppression: pressure of outward circumstances, grief, or trouble (OED 2.a.). **ere this:** before now.

ha' fatted: have made fat by feeding. **region:** of the air, cf., line 487 note. For its use as an adjective cf., Sonnet 33.12 and Abbott §22 and §430. **kites:** small hawk-like scavenging birds of prey.

slave: cf., line 550 note above. ● Hamlet has turned the rage expressed in this epithet from himself (line 550) to Claudius. **offal:** guts, the unusable viscera of dead animals. From ancient times the bodies of slain men meant to be utterly dishonored were thrown upon the trash heaps to be food for carrion-eating birds, cf., *2 Henry VI* V.ii.11 and *Macbeth* III.iv.71–72. **Bloody:** murderous. **bawdy:** sexually immoral.

Remorseless: without pity or regret, cf., line 491. **kindless:** unnatural, hating his own kind, cf., I.ii.65 note. **villain!:** following this word F adds "Oh vengeance!" which, though many actors and directors keep it, "has all the marks of an actor's addition [since] Hamlet accuses himself of cursing (line [586]) but not of threats, and his change from self-reproach ... occurs only at line [588]" (Jenkins), when he "abandons his self-reproaches and plans action" (Jenkins *Stud. Bib.*, page 37, quoted in Hoy). Neither does the phrase fit with the meter of either the previous or the following line, though Abbott calls it an interjectional line (§512).

brave: splendid, admirable, as we might say, "a fine show," here meant sarcastically, with a possible secondary sense of courageous, i.e., in words but not in deeds, also sarcastically.

That I, the son of a dear father murdered,

Prompted to my revenge by heaven and hell,
Must like a whore unpack my heart with words   585

And fall a-cursing like a very drab,
A scullion! Fie upon't! Foh! About, my brains.

Hum—I have heard
That guilty creatures sitting at a play

Have, by the very cunning of the scene,   590

Been struck so to the soul that presently
They have proclaimed their malefactions;

For murder, though it have no tongue, will speak

With most miraculous organ. I'll have these players
Play something like the murder of my father   595
Before mine uncle. I'll observe his looks;

father: not in Q2 or F, but in Q3 and also in Q1, which "authenticates the addition" (Jenkins).

heaven and hell: perhaps because "both ... are reflected in that 'nature' to which the Ghost has appealed (I.v.81)" (Jenkins), but more pointedly because heaven calls for justice and hell for the soul of Claudius.

drab: whore.

scullion: F, "A kitchen menial of either sex, 'proverbially foul-mouthed' (Sisson, *NR*). The word was in common use as a term of contempt" (Jenkins), cf., OED *scullion* and *scullery*. Q2 reads "stallyon," which many editors accept as meaning male whore, but Q1 reads "scalion," which, according to Jenkins, points to pronunciation and may represent the original ms. spelling "scallion." ● In either case, Hamlet is repudiating his previous outburst as beneath him and turns his attention to dispassionate reasoning. **About:** both "get busy" as in "get about it," cf., *Julius Caesar* III.ii.204 and *Merry Wives* V.v.55, and turn in a different direction, as in the nautical "come about" (OED 6.).

Hum—: ● NOTE TO ACTORS: This is not a word but indicates the musing sound we would spell "hmm ...". **I have heard ... malefactions:** Instances of "the self-betrayal of those who witness an actual image of their own crimes ... which playwrights like to cite as evidence of the drama's power" include *A Warning for Fair Women* (1599, sig. H2. Bullough, page 181), "'lately' acted by Shakespeare's company," and *Friar Francis* (1593, as reported, with other examples, in Heywood's *Apology for Actors*, 1612), both of which plays tell that "at Lynn in Norfolk a woman was so moved by watching a guilty wife in a tragedy that she confessed to having murdered her own husband" (Jenkins), and cf., lines 519–20 note above.

cunning: artfulness, skill, cf., line 440. **scene:** staging, representation.

presently: immediately, instantly, cf., line 170.

proclaimed: confessed publicly. **malefactions:** evil deeds, *-ion(s)* pronounced as two syllables as is common at the ends of lines (Abbott §479).

though it have: though it may have, "used to express a concession for the sake of argument, not a fact" (Abbott §366).

organ: instrument of speech (combining senses OED 5b. and 7.), cf., III.ii.367. **I'll have ... before mine uncle:** ● Hamlet has already put this plan into action. Here Shakespeare is having him speak his mind so that we may understand his motivation in having done so. Though we may feel that logically either this speech ought to have come earlier or the instruction to the First Play later, in the theater the matter of timing is irrelevant compared with the significance of the thought. As important as Hamlet's device is to the plot of the play, far more crucial to the play's meaning is Hamlet's motive for planning

I'll tent him to the quick. If a do blench,

I know my course. The spirit that I have seen
May be a devil, and the devil hath power
T'assume a pleasing shape, yea, and perhaps   600

it. Having planted the idea in our minds, Shakespeare now reveals the point of it. If we must have logical justification for this order of action before expression of the thought, cf., V.ii.6–9 and 30–31.

tent: here a verb, from the noun for the instrument used to probe and cleanse a wound covered over with tissue or scab, cf., Sidney, "the high and excellent tragedy, that openeth the greatest wounds, and showeth forth the ulcers that are covered with tissue; that maketh kings fear to be tyrants, and tyrants manifest their tyrannical humors" (¶48). **to the quick:** down to the living flesh. **a:** he. **blench:** turn aside, shy, flinch, as with pain when a wound is probed (OED *v.*¹2, unrelated to *blanch*, with which it is later [19ᵗʰ C.] confused).

● SPEECH NOTE: **The spirit ... damn me:** This sentence is central to the drama of *Hamlet*. Many critics and directors, reading this speech in light of the soliloquy at IV.iv.32ff., especially lines 43–46, and taking those lines to be self-evidently accurate, have read this speech as rationalization. According to that view, Hamlet is here inventing an excuse for not acting that hides his true motives, which then the critics are free to invent for themselves and argue about *ad infinitum*, an example of J. V. Cunningham's dictum that "there is less to be said about *Hamlet* than has been said" (Cunningham Sem.). But given the context of the time, the beliefs of Shakespeare's audience, the language and imagery of this play as well as others, and the style of Shakespearean drama, according to which we are to believe what a character says, especially in soliloquy, unless we are given explicit reason to doubt it (e.g., Macbeth's or Iago's hypocrisy)—as Hamlet himself later says at III.ii.141–42, "The players cannot keep counsel; they'll tell all"—it is certain that we are to take it that Hamlet means this sentence in utter seriousness and that it accurately expresses his real motive. Any unconscious motives we might wish to ascribe to Hamlet here are products of the modern critic's imagination, not of Hamlet's or indeed of Shakespeare's.

  Earlier in this soliloquy we have seen that Hamlet is upset with himself for not having taken vengeance already. *Why* he has not is here made clear to us. The reason is that he recognizes that the Ghost may actually have been a devil who means to tempt Hamlet into action that would damn him, and Hamlet is applying his reason, despite his passionate desire for revenge, to prevent such an outcome. As in his first soliloquy (I.ii.129ff.) the anguish at his father's death and mother's marriage surrendered to the reasonableness of "But break my heart for I must hold my tongue," so here the passionate desire for revenge gives way to the reasonable development of a plan of action that may prevent Hamlet's damnation. That Hamlet's reasoning is sound here we know because earlier both he and Horatio, the rational

man, expressed fear that the ghost might be demonic
(I.iv.40, 69–74, and I.v.93, and see II.ii.599–600 note
below). Hamlet here is not delaying out of any flaw in
character, neither the cowardice of which he accuses
himself hypothetically both earlier (line 571 above)
and later (IV.iv.43), nor the excessive thinking or
melancholy self-regard of which modern critics love
to accuse him. He is delaying, quite rightly, exactly
as he did at I.v.1 ("Speak, I'll go no further"), out
of clear and virtuous reason. Hamlet is no coward
afraid of physical danger. We will later hear that he
has leapt aboard a pirate ship with selfless courage
regarding his physical person (IV.vi.18–19). Before
he undertakes an action not merely so physically
dangerous but so potentially damnable as the killing
of a king, he wisely seeks more reasonable grounds
than his mere desire for vengeance. He chooses to
learn for sure the truth of the King's guilt before
acting against him. The play within the play will
make available to Hamlet the kind of knowledge
that no direct discourse would reveal, because "one
may smile, and smile, and be a villain" (I.v.108).
Finally, here again we find that the significance of
drama is confirmed by the drama itself, and we are
reminded that the play *Hamlet*, if we allow it, may
tent *us* to the quick.

my course: what to do. **May be a devil:** a possibility
that both Hamlet and Horatio have entertained from
the first, cf., I.i.48, I.ii.244–45 and note, I.iv.40–42,
69–74, I.v.93. **power / T'assume a pleasing shape:**
Jenkins (LN) cites many examples of the belief that
"when an apparition claims to be the spirit of a
particular person, one should suspect a deception of
the devil," including St. Chrysostom (quoted in
Pierre Le Loyer, *IIII Livres des Spectres out Apparitions
et Visions d'Esprits, Anges et Demons*, 1586, III.7), Lewes
Lavater (*Of Ghosts and Spirits Walking by Night*, 1570
[in Latin], 1572 [translated by Robert Harrison], II.
ix), James I (*Demonology*, III. Ch. 1), Thomas Browne
(*Religio Medici*, I. 37), and Nashe (*Terrors of the Night*,
i.348), to which Stoll (pages 47–48) adds the
Elizabethan preacher Henry Smith (d. 1591) in
Pilgrim's Wish, Andrew Willet in *Hexapla in Exodium*
(1608), and others. ● Nonetheless, if the dilemma of
Hamlet is to be taken seriously, we must also
entertain the idea that the spirit Hamlet has seen
may *not* be a devil trying to damn him. It is precisely
because Hamlet does not know whether the Ghost is
a legitimate messenger from God or a demonic
tempter that he proposes to test for Claudius's guilt
with the play-within-the-play.

Out of my weakness and my melancholy,

my weakness and my melancholy: ● These are a
function of Hamlet's particular grief at the death of
his father and the "o'erhasty" marriage of his mother,
that "woe" within "which passes show" (I.ii.85–86).
Though some understand Hamlet's general
disposition (i.e., his "complexion," cf., SPEECH NOTE
after I.iv.38) to tend to the melancholic, nothing in

the play indicates that Hamlet has had any predisposition to melancholy independently of the death of his estimable father and the hasty marriage of his mother. Ophelia's description of what he has been (III.i.150–54) suggests him to have been a man of exemplary qualities and reinforces that Hamlet's melancholy is an uncharacteristic but natural response to the unfortunate and unhappy circumstances of his father's death. And, as Jenkins reminds us, the word appears only twice in the play, here and at III.i.165. There the King rightly recognizes that there is "something in [Hamlet's] soul / O'er which his melancholy sits on brood," not knowing, as we do, that that "something" is in fact the appearance and the imperative of the Ghost. As we have seen (SPEECH NOTE after II.i.81 and line 252 note above), Hamlet himself can pretend to two distinct hypothetical causes of his melancholy to mislead the court, but he has no reason to mislead the audience. His "but wherefore I know not" (lines 295–96) is meant to mislead Rosencrantz and Guildenstern, not us. In any case, Shakespeare emphasizes not Hamlet's melancholy itself but the occasion for it and the danger that occasion presents to his soul. Not melancholy but temptation to sin is what threatens Hamlet, temptation that might come to anyone whatever humor may predispose him or her. *Hamlet* is a tragedy about the moral life, not about melancholy.

As he is very potent with such spirits,

potent: powerful in using a man's own weaknesses to deceive him and cause him to deceive himself (Jenkins substantially). **such spirits:** as the "weakness and melancholy" in the previous line.

Abuses me to damn me. I'll have grounds

Abuses: deludes, tricks, lies to, cf., *King Lear*, IV.vii.52, 76, *Pericles* I.ii.38. **to:** i.e., in order to.

More relative than this. The play's the thing

relative: related to his situation, relevant, persuasive, perhaps also sufficient to serve as evidence if told (related) to others.

Wherein I'll catch the conscience of the King.   605

Exit.

conscience: Of the eight uses of this word in the play, four—this one, III.i.49, 82, and V.ii.58—imply not the inner lawgiver about right and wrong, nor the faculty of knowing that distinction, but the secret inner awareness of having done wrong (cf., Lewis *Studies*, Ch. 8). The lawgiver sense (which Lewis calls *synteresis*) will appear at IV.vii.1 and V.ii.67. At IV.v.133 and V.ii.296, as we will see, the uses of the word conflate several senses. Here Hamlet means that the play-within-the-play is the means by which Claudius will be driven to express by outward signs his own awareness of guilt for his crimes should he in fact be guilty.

Act III, Scene i

*Enter King, Queen, Polonius, Ophelia,
Rosencrantz, Guildenstern.*

KING
And can you by no drift of conference

drift: the noun for the act of driving (OED *sb.*1.), hence not merely the movement or course of the conversation but their active directing of it, cf., line 9. **conference:** conversation (Riverside), talk, as at line 185 (Jenkins).

Get from him why he puts on this confusion,
Grating so harshly all his days of quiet
With turbulent and dangerous lunacy?

puts on: adopts, assumes, takes upon himself (OED put *v.*¹ 46.d.), not necessarily falsely, though because Hamlet uses it so at I.v.172, it may hint at "the King's suspicion that Hamlet's *confusion* (mental disturbance) is not altogether involuntary" (Jenkins), but cf., the sense of genuine transformation at I Corinthians 15:53 (Geneva, King James).

ROSENCRANTZ
He does confess he feels himself distracted,   5
But from what cause he will by no means speak.

distracted: mad, mentally confused, cf., I.v.97, IV.v.ii, V.ii.230.

GUILDENSTERN
Nor do we find him forward to be sounded,

forward: eager, inclined (OED 6.). **sounded:** probed, investigated, measured, as the depth of a body of water (OED *v.*² 6.).

But with a crafty madness keeps aloof
When we would bring him on to some confession

crafty: artful, cunning, guileful ● Guildenstern means that the madness itself is clever at avoiding being discovered, or perhaps "the shrewdness that mad people sometimes exhibit" (Riverside), but in any case the audience perceives dramatic irony in knowing that it is Hamlet himself, not his madness, who is being crafty. **keeps:** for the missing "he" (elliptical nominative) see Abbott §399 and cf., II.ii.67 and IV.i.10–12.

Of his true state.

state: mental condition.

QUEEN
        Did he receive you well?   10
ROSENCRANTZ
Most like a gentleman.
GUILDENSTERN
But with much forcing of his disposition.

disposition: inclination, mood, state of mind, cf., II.ii.298.

ROSENCRANTZ
Niggard of question, but of our demands

Niggard: grudging, stingy (from the ME for "miser," not the Latin for "black"). **question:** intellectual discussion, argument, debate. **of:** in respect to, as regards (Abbott §173). **demands:** questions, inquiries.

Most free in his reply.

free: generous, opposite of "Niggard." ● To Rosencrantz and Guildenstern, Hamlet has resisted engaging in discussion and philosophical argument but has generously and openly responded to their inquiries. The audience knows that his responses are intended to direct the thoughts of Rosencrantz and Guildenstern to the conclusion that he is suffering from the madness of thwarted ambition.

Act III, Scene i—An audience room of the castle.

QUEEN

             Did you assay him
To any pastime?   15

ROSENCRANTZ

Madam, it so fell out that certain players
We o'erraught on the way. Of these we told him,
And there did seem in him a kind of joy
To hear of it. They are here about the court,
And, as I think, they have already order   20
This night to play before him.

POLONIUS

                   'Tis most true,
And he beseeched me to entreat your Majesties
To hear and see the matter.

KING

With all my heart, and it doth much content me
To hear him so inclined.   25

Good gentlemen, give him a further edge,
And drive his purpose on to these delights.

ROSENCRANTZ

We shall, my lord.

          Exeunt Rosencrantz and Guildenstern.

KING

          Sweet Gertrude, leave us too;
For we have closely sent for Hamlet hither

That he, as 'twere by accident, may here   30

Affront Ophelia.
Her father and myself, lawful espials,

---

assay him to: test his inclination about, tempt him in regard to.

fell out: happened. **players:** actors.
o'erraught: overtook (OED overreach *v.* 2.).

This night: "A day has intervened since II.ii.[535–40]" (Jenkins).

beseeched: strongly requested, begged.

hear and see: • Shakespeare's audiences normally went to *hear* a play rather than, as we say, to *see* one, and their phrase reminds us how much more important was language than spectacle as the medium of experience in the theater, though the players did their best to make the latter too as dramatic as possible. **matter:** the performance (OED 19.).

With all my heart: "amphibious" in forming both the last part of the previous line and the first part of its own (Abbott §513).

give him a further edge: sharpen his appetite. **drive:** cf., "drift" at line 1.

shall: are certain to (Abbott §315).

us: the royal plural. **too:** F, two Q2.
For we ... suffers for: cf., II.ii.160–64. **closely:** secretly, privately. **hither:** to us here.
That: in order that. **as 'twere:** as it were, as if it were (a common use of the subjunctive mood in Shakespeare).
Affront Ophelia ... lawful espials: Q2 Affront Ophelia; her father and my selfe, F Affront Ophelia. Her father and my selfe (lawful espials). "The absence of ['lawful espials'] from Q2, together with the metrical redundancy, has brought them under suspicion. But it may well have been the metrical irregularity that led to their omission. They are most unlike an actor's elaboration and they fit the line [both metrically and logically] as 'Affront Ophelia' does not" (Jenkins). Retaining the phrase, we may understand a pause of two and a half empty feet after "Affront Ophelia." These two lines make up line 31 in the Riverside lineation, which follows Q2 here. **Affront:** intentionally meet (OED 4.). **lawful espials:** legal or legitimate spies, stress on the second syllable (es-PIE-əls). • Here, as so often in Shakespeare, as J. V. Cunningham puts it, "foreground is background" (Sem.). Claudius is telling us what Shakespeare's audience knew to be the accepted justification for royal spying. As the King sends Rosencrantz and Guildenstern to investigate Hamlet (II.ii), and as

Hamlet tests the validity of the Ghost's words, so here the ruler appears justified in using deceptive means for the good of the commonwealth. It is lawful to deceive when the sanity of the heir to the throne is at stake (cf., the Duke in *Measure for Measure*, Prince Hal in 1 *Henry IV*, Kent and Edgar in *King Lear*, Prospero in *The Tempest*, etc.). However, this justification dissolves if the deceiver is revealed to be serving his own evil ends rather than the common good, a point hinted at by Polonius below (lines 45–48).

We'll so bestow ourselves that, seeing unseen,

We may of their encounter frankly judge,

And gather by him, as he is behaved,

If 't be th' affliction of his love or no   35

bestow: place, stow away (Raffel). **seeing:** elided to one syllable (Abbott §470).

frankly: without constraint, freely, unrestrictedly (OED 1.).

gather by: infer or deduce from (OED 10.). **is behaved:** is behaving.

affliction of his love: the trouble or misery caused *by* his (thwarted) love of Ophelia, with a secondary sense of the distress *to* his love of Ophelia caused by her distancing herself from him. **or no:** or not.

That thus he suffers for.
QUEEN   I shall obey you.
And for your part, Ophelia, I do wish
That your good beauties be the happy cause
Of Hamlet's wildness. So shall I hope your virtues
Will bring him to his wonted way again,   40
To both your honors.
OPHELIA   Madam, I wish it may.
                                    Exit Queen.

thus: in this way, i.e., his apparent madness. **for:** because of.

shall: "perhaps there is a mixture of 'I am bound to' and 'I am sure to.' Hence [*shall*] is often used in the replies of inferiors to superiors" (Abbott §315). **be:** may indeed be, cf., Abbott §368 on the subjunctive.

wonted: normal, usual.

To both your honors: to the credit of both of you, and for both your sakes. It will honor Hamlet to be brought to reason again and honor Ophelia to be the means of that healing.

POLONIUS
Ophelia, walk you here.—Gracious, so please you,

Gracious: addressed to the King—since "its use without a noun is unparalleled" (Jenkins), we may infer that Polonius is eager to get the King and himself into position. **so please you:** both may it please you and if it please you.

We will bestow ourselves. [*To Ophelia.*] Read on this book;

That show of such an exercise may color

Your loneliness. We are oft to blame in this—   45

bestow: place (in hiding). **on:** in (Abbott §180). **this book:** a prayer book.

show: appearance, outward seeming. **exercise:** religious or devotional practice. ● "In iconographic convention a solitary woman with a book represented devoutness.... The book is ... traditional in pictures of the Annunciation" (Jenkins). **color:** disguise, cover, cf., II.ii.280.

loneliness: being alone. ● Ophelia would not normally be alone in the court without a family member or servant as chaperone, but being at prayer would make her solitude seem less surprising. **We are:** probably elided to *we're* to preserve the meter.

'Tis too much proved—that with devotion's visage

too much proved: too often shown by experience; **devotion's visage:** the mere face, appearance, or outward show of religious devotion.

And pious action we do sugar o'er
The devil himself.

sugar o'er: hide under superficial sweetness.

KING [*Aside.*]
              O, 'tis too true.
How smart a lash that speech doth give my conscience!

The harlot's cheek, beautied with plast'ring art,   50

Is not more ugly to the thing that helps it

Than is my deed to my most painted word.
O heavy burden!

POLONIUS
I hear him coming. Let's withdraw, my lord.
               Exeunt King and Polonius.

        Enter Hamlet.

conscience: the awareness of having done wrong, see II.ii.605 note and cf., line 82 and V.ii.58. ● Here, for the first time, Claudius, who until now has appeared competent and rightful despite his "o'erhasty marriage" to the Queen, reveals to us that he feels guilt, though he has not yet confirmed why. Despite Hamlet's doubt, the authority of the Ghost begins to be restored in the minds of the audience. In addition, "it forewarns [the audience], by revealing the *conscience* that is to be caught, what the effect of Hamlet's play-acting device (II.ii.[588–605]) will be. Thus, even while the King is enacting the plot to spy on Hamlet, expectation of Hamlet's plot to spy on the King gains force" (Jenkins). The truth is unfolding slowly and suspensefully, to us as to Hamlet. Its final confirmation will be part of the climax at III.iii.

harlot's: prostitute's. **plast'ring art:** makeup, much deplored as ungodly vanity by homiletic writers, see line 142 note and V.i.193–95.

to: compared to, in comparison with, here and in the next line (Abbott §187). **the thing that helps it:** the makeup that covers it.

painted: covered with makeup, hidden by coloring, cf., line 44. ● Claudius reveals not only that he is guilty but that he is disguising his guilt with falsehood, comparing himself to a prostitute who under makeup attempts to hide a complexion marred by the effects of venereal disease.

Let's: F, not in Q2.

● **SPEECH NOTE:** The following speech, because it is philosophical, universal, and eloquent, has had the misfortune of becoming the most famous speech in the play. As a result it has been mistaken for being also the most important and the most thematically central speech. It is a profound speech with universal import, and it is integral to the understanding of Hamlet's spiritual condition at this moment. But it would be a deformation of the play to take it as the expression of the play's essence. The speech is meditative but not passionate and must be performed as the careful reasoning of a "Renaissance graduate student" (see Introduction, page 11) about the pressing spiritual and philosophical matter raised in the passionate soliloquy of II.ii.550–605, as will be seen in the notes. In keeping with the soliloquy convention, we are to understand that the speech depicts Hamlet's thought to the audience only and is not overheard either by the King and Polonius, who are behind the arras, or by Ophelia, who is elsewhere on the stage pretending to be reading in a devotional book. Hamlet's conversation with Ophelia begins only with her words at line 89.

HAMLET

To be, or not to be—that is the question: 55

question: the medieval literary form called in Latin
quaestio (Cunningham Sem.), which Hamlet would
have known well from school at Wittenberg (as a
quaestio disputata, set by the rector, or *quaestio de
quodlibet*, raised by anyone). It involved responding
to a general hypothetical question of moral,
philosophical, or theological import with *pro* and
contra answers, for each of which supporting and
contrary arguments were presented. The question
could be as fundamental as "Does God exist?" or
"Does man have free will?" or, as in Hamlet's question
here, "Is it better to be alive or not?" • In this
soliloquy Hamlet closely follows the format, raising
the question, giving the reasons it is better "not to
be," then the reasons why people do not choose "not
to be." The context for Hamlet's meditation is his
postponing the killing of Claudius until he verifies
the Ghost's tale lest Hamlet risk damnation, his
intermediate conclusion at the end of the previous
scene. Though he raises the question here as an
academic philosophical exercise in order to illuminate
the question particular to himself (whether or not
to take action against the King and thereby probably
to die), the speech (as Kittredge [quoted in Jenkins
LN] rightly holds) is not personal or passionate but a
general and coolly rational inquiry into the universal
conditions of man within which any individual's
choices must be made. There is no suicidal tendency
here. Well knowing that suicide is forbidden in the
Christian dispensation (cf., I.ii.131–32) and would
lead inescapably to damnation, Hamlet is expressing
no personal desire to kill himself. He considers the
abstract knowledge that men *could* kill themselves, or
do something that would get them killed by others, to
escape life's miseries and then considers the reason
why they tend not to do so, namely the possibility or
likelihood of even greater suffering after death, i.e.,
in hell. Baldwin (II.603–608) sees in the rhetorical
framework of the speech the influence of Cicero's
translation and treatment (in *Tusculan Disputations*
I.97–99) of Socrates' discussion of death in Plato's
Apology (40d), and indeed argues that the learned
in Shakespeare's audience would have recognized
Hamlet's *quaestio* as "the fundamental 'question' of the
first ... of those 'five questions' which Tully [= Cicero]
held at Tusculum (II.607)." However, whereas Cicero
was defending a stoical fearlessness of death based
on the Socratic presumption of innocence before the
just gods, "Christian Hamlet in England at the turning
of the centuries could not brush Hell aside" (II.605).
Just the contrary: the possibility of hell is precisely
Hamlet's central concern in the speech. In a "typical
grammar school exercise upon the speech of Socrates"
(II.607), Shakespeare has transposed the classical
motif into the Christian context (see Introduction,
pages 2–3) with the effect of justifying a postponement
of the taking of revenge until such time as the King's

Whether 'tis nobler in the mind to suffer

The slings and arrows of outrageous fortune,

Or to take arms against a sea of troubles

response to the play-within-the-play confirms his guilt so that Hamlet may execute him, if he is guilty, with justice and thus avoid his own damnation.

Whether ... end them: The sentence is a parallel and more particular restatement of the initial general question (whether to be or not to be is better). Is it better to suffer life's pains patiently and live, or to fight against them and, dying in the fight, to end them? **nobler:** more virtuous, more appropriate to a nobleman. **in the mind:** a squinting modifier, which Jenkins humorously glosses by quoting Kittredge as saying it modifies "nobler" and Dowden as saying it modifies "to suffer." Shakespeare intends it to work both ways. The primary meaning is nobler as judged by rational thought as opposed to public opinion or external effects, and the secondary meaning is an underscoring of Hamlet's particular mode of suffering, which is mental as opposed to physical, cf., I.ii.85 ("that within which passes show") and is in keeping with the play's emphasis on the free will rather than the external action as the locus of virtue and sin. **to suffer:** to bear patiently, to put up with.

slings: projectiles from slingshots, cf., "wyth slyngs, shot of arrows, and other artillery" from Golding's translation of Caesar's *Gallic War* (cited in Jenkins). **outrageous:** excessive, unbounded by rule or law, "because capricious, obeying no principle" (Jenkins), from French *outré*, Latin *ultra*, meaning beyond (bounds), plus *-age*, indicating an abstract noun, but the word was influenced in English by the imaginary derivation from "out" and "rage." **fortune:** see II.ii.229 note.

sea: either the sea itself or the nautical sense of a huge wave that washes over a ship. **sea of troubles:** The phrase is not merely a mixed metaphor but stresses "the futility of fighting against an uncontainable and overwhelming force" (Jenkins), and with "arms" like swords and guns that can do nothing against a sea. Shakespeare probably had read (in Abraham Fleming's translation of Aelian, *A Registre of Hystories*, 1576, in Aristotle's *Eudemian Ethics*, III.i, or in other ancients) that "the Celts ... rather than show fear by flight, would draw their swords and throw themselves into the tides as though to terrify them," and, according to some versions, "perished in the waves.... It is precisely because the heroic gesture is necessarily disastrous that argument becomes possible about whether it is noble" (Jenkins LN). Shakespeare has in mind Aristotle's discussion of courage as a mean between rashness and cowardice in the Nicomachean Ethics (III.vii), and cf., Polonius's advocacy of the golden mean to Laertes at I.iii.58ff. The point here is that to take arms against Hamlet's troubles (i.e., by killing the King) is almost certainly to die as a consequence, and so to end the troubles. However, the speech

And by opposing end them. To die—to sleep,
No more; and by a sleep to say we end   60
The heart-ache and the thousand natural shocks

That flesh is heir to. 'Tis a consummation
Devoutly to be wish'd—to die, to sleep—

To sleep, perchance to dream—ay, there's the rub,

For in that sleep of death what dreams may come,   65

When we have shuffled off this mortal coil,

Must give us pause. There's the respect

That makes calamity of so long life.

moves beyond the classical question of virtue and the aristocratic question of nobility. Shakespeare has set this play in the context of the universe as Christian scripture revealed it and his audience believed it to be, the context of heaven, hell, and divine judgment (see Introduction, pages 2–3). Hence, Hamlet's speech moves from the Aristotelian question of whether an action leading to death would be noble in the rational judgment of men to the more pressing question to Hamlet of whether it would be damnable in the judgment of God.

To die—to sleep, / No more: to die is merely to sleep, no more than that.

natural shocks: "The primary sense [of the word *shocks*,] 'clashes of arms'[,] is usual in Shakespeare (cf. *R[ichard] II* I.iii.136, *R[ichard] III* V.iii.93, etc.) and here resumes the battle metaphor of lines [57–58]" (Jenkins), but the addition of "natural" implies all the conflicts that man's nature, being fallen, incurs.

flesh is heir to: inherent in mortal bodies as a legacy of the original sin of Adam and Eve. **consummation:** F, (Q2 consumation), ending, completion, with a conjoined sense of being consumed and destroyed, cf., OED *consummation* 2. and 4., citing this passage, and *consumation*, and also *Cymbeline* IV.ii.280, *King Lear* IV.vi.129 (Q "consumation'), and *Edward III* IV.ix.43.

perchance: possibly, perhaps. **rub:** obstruction, impediment, as in *Henry V* V.ii.33, from the term for anything hindering the course of the bowl in the game of bowls (lawn bowling).

in that sleep … must give us pause: ● The analogy is that as sleep is to death so dreams are to what? It is death's unknown experiences analogous to the known dreams of sleep that give us pause in contemplating actions that may lead to death. Those unknown "dreams" in death are known to Christians to be hell, purgatory, and heaven, the uncertainty being to which of those spiritual conditions of the afterlife one may be assigned.

shuffled off: cast off or got rid of in a perfunctory way (OED 5.d.), cf., *Twelfth Night* III.iii.16. **mortal coil:** the tumult, fuss, bother, turmoil of mortal human life (OED *coil sb.²*).

give us pause: cause us to pause (in taking action that might lead to death), with a full foot caesura to punctuate it, an example of Shakespeare's uniting of form and content in a single experience, cf., Abbott §484, §508. **respect:** consideration, regard.

makes calamity of so long life: makes calamity live so long, i.e., that is the observation that keeps one living on in spite of troubles. ● The sense of long life being itself a calamity cannot be intended, despite our temptation to detect a double meaning, because consideration of what might come after death would make no more calamity of a long life than of a short one, and because there is nothing to which "so long" read this way could be referring.

For who would bear the whips and scorns of time,

of time: temporal life, living in time as opposed to eternity.

Th' oppressor's wrong, the proud man's cóntumely, 70

cóntumely: instance or words of contempt. • NOTE TO ACTORS: the stress is on the first syllable.

The pangs of déspisèd love, the law's delay,

déspisèd: Q2 "despiz'd" F "dispriz'd". • In either reading what is implied is whatever Hamlet actually suffered because of the repelling of his letters and the denial of access to Ophelia (II.i.106–107) and, more importantly, the kind of unrequited love that Hamlet pretends to be suffering from in his appearance to Ophelia reported in II.i.72ff. That his behavior there was a performance rather than a true passion is further reinforced by his ability to think dispassionately here of "despised/disprized love" as an abstraction. • NOTE TO ACTORS: in either reading, the stress is on the first syllable. **law's:** law courts', justice system's.

The insolence of office, and the spurns
That patient merit of th' unworthy takes,

of office: of those in official positions of authority.
spurns … takes: the kicks or rejections that those who are worthy patiently bear from those who are not.

When he himself might his quietus make

quietus: literally release or quittance from a debt (cf., "quit" and "requite") with a play on "quiet." • It was a Renaissance commonplace that death paid all debts, cf., *1 Henry IV* III.ii.157 ("the end of life cancels all bands [= bonds]") and *Tempest* III.ii.131 ("He that dies pays all debts"), and "*Quietus est*, he is quit, were the words written against an account to indicate that payment had been made" (Jenkins). • NOTE TO ACTORS: The stress is on the second syllable (kwī-Ē-təs).

With a bare bodkin? Who would fardels bear, 75
To grunt and sweat under a weary life,

bare: mere, unsheathed being an unlikely though possible secondary sense. • The internal rhyme "bare/bear" suggests the underlying antithesis. **bodkin:** small dagger. • "Ernst Honigmann has drawn my attention to the anticipation of this in Seneca, *Epist.*, 70, 'scalpello aperitur ad illam magnam libertatem via et puncto securitas constat'" (Jenkins) ["a lancet will open the way to that great freedom, and tranquillity can be purchased at the cost of a pin-prick," Seneca *Epist.*, 70.16]. **fardels:** bundles, burdens, packs carried on the back, *farthel* being a variant, cf., *Winter's Tale* IV.iv.708ff. and V.ii.3, 116.

But that the dread of something after death,
The undiscovered country from whose bourn

But that: except that, if it were not that.

undiscovered: not known to men, unrevealed.
bourn: boundary, implying the line between life and death which no one recrosses, taken by many editors as a metaphor for "region" under the influence of the following image.

No traveler returns, puzzles the will,
And makes us rather bear those ills we have 80
Than fly to others that we know not of?

No traveler returns: cf., Job 10:21 and the apocryphal Wisdom of Solomon 2:1. • There is no contradiction between this observation and the appearance of the Ghost. First of all, Hamlet is not yet sure that the Ghost was indeed the returned spirit of his father rather than a devil in disguise. Second, "We must not, and we do not (as Hamlet himself does not), connect the Ghost at all with this general reflection. Shakespeare allows Hamlet to utter it because it is what would occur to any well-read Renaissance man meditating upon death" (Jenkins, who lists additional sources for the commonplace metaphor, including Catullus, Seneca, Aelian, Cardan, La Primaudaye, and Marlowe's *Edward II* [V.vi.65–66]). **puzzles:** stymies, confounds, cf., *Twelfth Night* IV.ii.43–44 (a reference to Exodus 10.21–23) and *Antony and Cleopatra* III.vii.10. **will:** in this context, the intention to accomplish some act that risks or may hasten death and thereby to achieve that "consummation" spoken of in lines 62–63.

Thus conscience does make cowards of us all,

conscience: the awareness of having done wrong, hence the awareness of the possibility or likelihood of being damned, see II.ii.605 note, and cf., line 49, IV.v.133, and V.ii.58, and "nothing more or less than 'fear of Hell'" (C. S. Lewis, *Studies in Words*, page 207). **does make:** turns us into, causes us to be. **cowards:** not in general but in this specific case of being afraid to rush to death and possibly damnation. **conscience ... us all:** • Whether or not we are cowardly by nature, as Hamlet is not (as we will see from his letter to Horatio, IV.vi.18–19), the awareness of being sinners, subject to the judgment of God and consequent punishment, makes all men fear death. Jenkins holds that "conscience" here means either "inner voice of moral judgment" or "consciousness," and therefore that Hamlet is concerned about the evil potential of what he contemplates doing. In fact the abstractness and universality of this soliloquy suggest that Hamlet means by "conscience" that awareness of being a sinner which makes all men "cowards" in not choosing to rush to a death that might send them to hell. Later in the speech "this regard" refers not to thinking too much, the common modern reading of "conscience," but the recognition of the possibility of damnation.

And thus the native hue of resolution

native hue: natural color or complexion. **resolution:** a quality of the sanguine (cheerful, positive, jolly, hopeful) temperament, a result of the predominance of the humor of blood in the complexion, its hue consequently red, cf., SPEECH NOTE after I.iv.38. • Here "resolution" is an abstract term for a hypothetical resolute person whose native hue, red, pales in the face of the contemplation of the risk not of death but of damnation.

Is sicklied o'er with the pale cast of thought,

sicklied: Shakespeare coins the word here. **cast:** shade or coloring, tinge. **thought:** in the context, not thought itself in general, which may bestow any kind of "cast" depending on its content, nor melancholy brooding, which editors read into this passage from the generalization about Hamlet's character they abstract from the play as a whole and then apply when convenient, but the specific thought with which this soliloquy is concerned, namely the awareness that rushing to death may mean rushing to damnation. It is this thought (parallel to "this regard," line 86) which turns the reddish hue natural to health and resolution into the sickly pallor natural to fear.

And enterprises of great pitch and moment   85

pitch: "the height to which a falcon soared before she stooped upon her prey" (from Robert Nares, *A Glossary*, quoted in Jenkins). ● The metaphor's allusion to the enterprise Hamlet has in mind, the killing of Claudius, along with "the association of *pitch* with *resolution*" in *Richard II* I.i.109 ("How high a pitch his resolution soars!"), as Jenkins points out, argues for this Q2 reading as against F's "pith." **moment:** importance, significance.

With this regard their currents turn awry

this regard: again, the idea of what might come after death, the possibility of damnation, see line 84 note. **their currents:** the course, as of tides of the sea or currents of rivers, of the "enterprises" of the previous line, cf., *Julius Caesar* IV.iii.218–24, "where the imagery of sea and tide is explicit" (Jenkins).

And lose the name of action. Soft you now,

lose the name: The "enterprises," prevented from being enacted by the fear of death that might lead to damnation, remain as thoughts and so cannot be called "actions." ● The speech concludes with no alteration in Hamlet's plan (II.ii.594–96, 604–605) to test whether the Ghost was honest and the King is guilty before he takes any action that might lead him to death and perhaps to hell. This soliloquy, unlike the two previous ones in which passion is supplanted by reason, is a speech of clear reason throughout. It puts into a calm, rational context and universal terms Hamlet's particular concern about acting against the King before he is morally certain that the King is guilty of the Ghost's accusations. That Hamlet is not the less passionate when provoked we will see several lines below when his passion, as always evoked by external circumstances, bursts out. **Soft you now:** Hush, stop talking, spoken to himself (OED soft *adv.* 8.).

The fair Ophelia. Nymph, in thy orisons
Be all my sins remembered.

fair: beautiful, possibly also implying fair-skinned and blonde, ideal qualities of feminine beauty in Shakespeare's time. **Ophelia:** three syllables, not four (Abbott §469). **Nymph:** beautiful girl; cf., *Midsummer Night's Dream* III.ii.137 and 226–27. ● Though not the mad unrequited lover he intentionally appeared to Ophelia to be, Hamlet does love her. **orisons:** prayers, with the stress on the first syllable. ● Hamlet takes Ophelia to be praying, which explains her being alone, as was intended by Polonius at lines 43ff. We know lines 88–89 are not spoken aloud to her for she makes no direct response to them. Hamlet speaks them from the heart to himself. Her greeting then opens their conversation.

OPHELIA
                              Good my lord,
How does your honor for this many a day?   90

How does … many a day?: for the present tense with the prepositional phrase signifying past action up through the present, see Abbott §346.

HAMLET
I humbly thank you, well.

I humbly … well: Jenkins points out, quoting Dowden, that Hamlet's response is as if to a stranger, made in the same form as that he uses with the Norwegian Captain (IV.iv.29) and Osric (V.ii.82). The repetition of "well" in F "appears to be no more than an actor's elaboration" (Jenkins). ● Hamlet is again playacting at the madness of thwarted love but now exhibiting a mood opposite to the mood in which Ophelia last saw him. Then it was the wild desperation of the unrequited lover. Now it is the same rejected lover in a calm distraction, pretending to an imaginary distance in their acquaintanceship. Hamlet's line is only three metric feet, as is line 95. In both cases, the two empty feet, presuming they come after Hamlet's lines, suggest a pause in which Ophelia a) tries to absorb Hamlet's strangeness and to find the best way to reply to his inappropriate statements, and b) hesitates because she knows the King and her father are eavesdropping.

remembrances: keepsakes, love tokens.

OPHELIA

My lord, I have remembrances of yours
That I have longèd long to redeliver.
I pray you now receive them.

HAMLET

                    No, not I.
I never gave you aught.   95

aught: anything. • Hamlet continues to playact the calm detachment of a despairing spurned lover to keep up the pretense of madness to an Ophelia who, as Hamlet thinks, will surely report his behavior and speech to her father and thereby to the King. He is perhaps sad that he must do so under the pressure of a duty that pre-empts the expression of his earnest love just revealed in the last lines of the previous soliloquy. His denial of the gifts is neither petulance nor provocation in Hamlet's attitude but rather the playacted confirmation of his being mad.

OPHELIA

My honored lord, you know right well you did,

right well: very well. **you did:** give me the "remembrances" of line 92.

And with them words of so sweet breath composed

words ... composed: the words, made of sweet breath, like flowers, gave off sweet airs, i.e., were spoken so lovingly as to make the physical remembrances the more valuable.

As made these things more rich. Their perfume lost,

these things: Q2, the things F. **perfume lost:** "ironically recalling [Laertes' warning at] I.iii.7–9" (Jenkins).

Take these again, for to the noble mind
Rich gifts wax poor when givers prove unkind.   100

these: the "remembrances" of line 92.
noble mind ... unkind: • The rhymed couplet serves both to punctuate Ophelia's genuinely intended maxim and to contrast with the wild and seemingly chaotic prose that follows. **wax:** become, turn (OED wax $v.^1$ 9.a. (*b*)). **unkind:** ungentle, harsh (OED 6.), with the secondary sense unnatural.

There, my lord.

There: Ophelia hands Hamlet the "remembrances" of line 92.

HAMLET

Ha, ha! Are you honest?

OPHELIA

My lord?

HAMLET

Are you fair?

OPHELIA

What means your lordship?   105

Ha, ha! Are you honest? ... Are you fair?: • With this line Hamlet suddenly flies into a passion and begins one of Shakespeare's most amazing verbal accomplishments, the depiction of a sane man expressing his genuinely passionate anger in the form of a pretended madness. None of the following speeches is to be seen as conveying intentional cruelty toward Ophelia for revenge or any other reason. Since nowhere else in the play does Hamlet

fly into a passion without some occasioning spur
(the "o'erhasty marriage" before I.ii.29ff., the Ghost's
words before I.v.92ff. and II.i.72ff., the Player's speech
and tears before II.ii.550ff., the King's reaction to the
play in III.ii.265, 269, Polonius's cry at III.iv.22ff., and
Laertes' attack before V.i.266, foil thrust at V.ii.302,
and confession before V.ii.321), and since there is
nothing in Hamlet's thoughts or Ophelia's words to
alter Hamlet's calm demeanor here, we must assume,
despite the absence of a stage direction, that Hamlet
has suddenly seen through the hypocritical "color"
(line 44) of Ophelia's supposed prayers because of a
movement of the arras or some such stage business
revealing the presence of at least one eavesdropper.
Knowing his busybody nature, Hamlet rightly
assumes the spy to be Polonius and immediately puts
on an extreme version of the thwarted-love madness
meant for Polonius (as opposed to the thwarted-
ambition madness he would enact if he thought
the spies were Rosencrantz and Guildenstern).
The form of melancholy madness Hamlet here
plays at is the sexual preoccupation mania that he
has earlier put on for Polonius ("Conception is a
blessing" etc. at II.ii.184ff.) and that Ophelia will
later exhibit in reality (IV.v.23ff.), now carried to its
extreme form, a puritanical sex-revulsion to which
it was thought that thwarted love could lead (cf.,
Twelfth Night IV.ii.25–26, *King Lear* III.iv.86–100 and
IV.vi.122–29, *Winter's Tale* I.ii.108–146, and Burton,
where Religious Melancholy is classified as a subset
of Love-Melancholy, see III.4.1–2, especially pages
919 and 921). Hamlet's ensuing taxing of marriage
and of breeding is no more a true picture of his
actual thought than his claims to Rosencrantz and
Guildenstern to be "dreadfully attended" (II.ii.269)
or to "lack advancement" (III.ii.340). We know from
all the evidence of the play, including speeches and
asides (cf., I.v.171–72, II.ii.205–206, 219, and 378, III.
ii.384–85, and III.iv.187–88), that Hamlet is never
really mad, that he has no objection to marriage in
principle or to his marrying Ophelia. Thus (*pace*
Jenkins) any attempt to find justification in Hamlet's
actual psychology for this outburst of passion
requires a mangling of his character and a denial of
the essential through-line and themes of the play.
However, Hamlet *is* in a passion. He sees woman's
"frailty" being abused in Ophelia just as Gertrude's
has been abused previously (cf., I.ii.146). All the
energy of his anguish at the king's corrupting of his
mother now pours out in rage at the corrupting of his
beloved, occasioned by the discovery that Polonius,
in service to the hated King, has driven Ophelia into
hypocrisy (putting on the "devotion's visage" of line
46) to entrap him. The corruption by corrupt men of
the two women Hamlet cares for fuels this passion
disguised as madness. It is true that he has himself,
in a sense, "used" Ophelia to convey to the court
that he was mad (II.i.72ff.). But his motives, unlike
those of Claudius according to the Ghost, were not

HAMLET

That if you be honest and fair, your honesty should
admit no discourse to your beauty.

selfish, and he was driven to that deception, as to this,
by the need to respond to the Ghost's charge, which
takes precedence over matters more personal. It is
one of the many examples of how the corruption
of the monarch poisons the entire body politic and
of Hamlet's treating personal matters as secondary
to his obligations as son, heir to the throne, and
(if Claudius proves guilty) rightful king, just as
Claudius in public had quite properly subordinated
personal matters to matters of state in I.ii (see
I.ii.42 note). **honest:** truthful, literally meant, with
the secondary sense of chaste, meant to introduce
the anti-marriage madness that will "color" (i.e.,
disguise) his own rage. **fair** beautiful. ● Hamlet's
real though rhetorical questions to Ophelia are the
introduction to a diatribe against the corruption of
women by men (see line 102 note).

That if you be ... To a nunnery, go. (lines 106–149):
Prose, often chosen to express "frenzy," "madness,"
or "the higher flights of the imagination" (Abbott
§515a), here expresses Hamlet's genuine passion
conveyed through pretended madness. **honest
and fair:** chaste and beautiful. **if you be honest ...
to your beauty:** "(1) Your chastity should permit
no one to have converse with your beauty.... (2)
Your chastity should permit itself no converse with
your beauty" (Jenkins). ● The first sense is an echo
of Laertes' warning (I.iii.29–42) and Polonius's
command that Ophelia have no discourse with
Hamlet (I.iii.132–34). Ophelia, in her next speech,
answers Hamlet in the second sense. But "[i]t does
not follow ... that she misunderstands Hamlet's
meaning. And she may understand, though
she does not accept, the implication that in the
association of chastity and beauty chastity will
suffer. Where the speakers agree is in assuming that
a woman is vulnerable through her *beauty*, which it
is the office of her *honesty* to protect" (Jenkins). On
the subject of the Elizabethan commonplace, the
"proverbial incompatibility of beauty and chastity,"
Jenkins cites Tilley (B 163), Pettie's translation of
Guazzo's *Civil Conversation*, *As You Like It* I.ii.37–38
and III.iii.28–39, John Donne's *Paradoxes and
Problems* (7) and "Of the Progress of the Soul: The
Second Anniversary" (line 364, which may owe
something to Psalm 85:10). Donne's "Song" ("Go
and catch a falling star") analogously finds beauty
and fidelity mutually exclusive. However, the
pairing of beauty and honesty here also refers to
a contrary commonplace, the neo-Platonic ideal
of the correspondence between moral virtue and
physical beauty, cf., *Tempest* I.ii.458–60 ("There's
nothing ill can dwell in such a temple. / If the ill
spirit have so fair a house, / Good things will strive
to dwell with't"). Miranda's words there rightly
apply to Ferdinand, though Prospero knows that
Miranda's belief does not apply universally. Here,
Hamlet has the evidence of his mother's behavior

OPHELIA

Could beauty, my lord, have better commerce than
with honesty?

HAMLET

Ay, truly, for the power of beauty will sooner   110
transform honesty from what it is to a bawd than
the force of honesty can translate beauty into his
likeness. This was sometime a paradox, but now

the time gives it proof. I did love you once.

OPHELIA

Indeed, my lord, you made me believe so.   115

HAMLET

You should not have believed me, for virtue cannot so
inoculate our old stock but we shall relish of it.

I loved you not.

and now Ophelia's to show the frailty of "honesty" in
a woman who is "fair." **commerce:** business dealings,
but here general "intercourse in the affairs of life,
dealings" (OED 1., 2.). ● Ophelia does not intend the
third sense, sexual dealings (OED 3.), but Hamlet
takes up her words in that sense.

beauty … likeness: it is likelier for a woman's beauty
to procure her loss of chastity than for chastity
to persuade her beauty to be chaste. **bawd:** pimp,
procuress (Raffel). **his:** its (Abbott §228), meaning
honesty's. ● Theobald saw parallels in this passage to
Juvenal (*Satires* 10.297–98) and Ovid (*Heroides*, 16.289–
90) (Baldwin II.529).

was sometime: was once thought to be. **paradox:**
"a thing contrary to received opinion or rational
explanation (the usual Elizabethan sense)" (Jenkins),
i.e., not the sense of "the figure defined by Susenbrotus
from Quintilian" (self-contradiction) but "the sense
… derived from Cicero's *Paradoxes*" and defined in
T. Cooper's *Thesaurus* as "Sentences straunge and
contrarie to the opinion of the most parte" (Baldwin
II.599).

the time gives it proof: the present time provides
evidence for its truth, i.e., in the form of his mother's
"o'erhasty marriage," the Ghost's accusations against
her, and now Ophelia's being used. **I did love you
once:** ● A sign not that he does not in fact still love
her now but that his pretended madness continues
to speak. Under the playacted mania, Hamlet reveals
his actual frustration at the compromise of Ophelia's
virtue toward him in her serving as her father's "bait of
falsehood" to take Hamlet's "carp of truth," cf., II.i.60,
and suggests that his love for her was always tied to
her virtue, not just to her beauty, refuting Laertes' and
Polonius's suspicions at I.iii.5, 10, 107–131.

You should not have believed me: ● Another echo of
Laertes' advice at I.iii.10 and Polonius's at I.iii.127, now
in the voice of Hamlet's outrage (at Gertrude's and
Ophelia's abused frailty) disguising itself in playacted
anti-sex mania. **virtue … relish of it:** the image is from
grafting in horticulture. Virtue, like the slip of a plant,
cannot be so grafted (for the sake of its more refined
or superior qualities) onto our old fallen nature, the
hardier but coarser root stock, without our retaining a
hint (flavor, "relish") of our old sinfulness, the quality
of the root stock. **but … relish:** without our continuing
to relish (Abbott §121).

I loved you not: ● i.e., "All men being sinners, and love
therefore being tainted with lust, I cannot be said truly
to have loved you." Hamlet is continuing the pretense
of a moral revulsion against erotic love in the language
of puritanical anti-sex mania as a way to keep in his
disguise while at the same time giving vent to his actual
anger at the King's playing upon the moral weakness
("frailty") of his mother and now at Polonius's playing
upon that of Ophelia, see line 102 note. If the stage
business includes Hamlet's seeing not only Polonius
but the King too behind the arras, his rage is doubly
justified.

OPHELIA

I was the more deceived.

HAMLET

Get thee to a nunnery. Why wouldst thou be a   120

breeder of sinners? I am myself indifferent honest,

but yet I could accuse me of such things that it were
better my mother had not borne me. I am very proud,
revengeful, ambitious, with more offences at my beck
than I have thoughts to put them in, imagination to   125
give them shape, or time to act them in. What should
such fellows as I do crawling between earth and
heaven? We are arrant knaves all; believe none of us.
Go thy ways to a nunnery.

I was ... deceived: ● In believing that he loved her and
that his virtue had prevailed over his fallen nature
("our old stock").

nunnery: ● In the context, the word means
a convent and not, as some have liked to believe, a
brothel. As Jenkins shows, the only two references to
the brothel sense of the word in Shakespeare's time
(*Gesta Grayorum*, MSR, page 12, and Nashe's *Christ's
Tears*, 79 b.) had to announce themselves explicitly
and were intended as ironic jokes, whereas here the
passage requires the primary sense of "sanctuary
from marriage and from the world's contamination"
"where [Ophelia] will preserve her chastity and
be safe from love, marriage, and the breeding of
sinners.... [T]o insist on [the occasional sarcastic
sense here] at the expense of the literal meaning ...
is perverse" (Jenkins line 120 note and LN).

Why: Jenkins argues (without textual authority) for
a comma after the word, making it an interjection
(OED IV.7.b.), the question being "wouldst thou?"
rather than "why wouldst thou?" "Why do you want
to breed sinners?" and "Do you want to breed
sinners?" are both rhetorical questions with similar
emotional implication, but to my ear the former
sounds more Hamlet-like, cf., V.i.98 and 203.

breeder of sinners: ● Because it was a universal
belief that all men were born in sin, a melancholy or
religious mania would be haunted by the fact that to
give birth to children is to give birth to sinners.
indifferent: moderately, more or less. **honest:**
virtuous, decent, with the secondary sense of chaste,
as at lines 102–112.

accuse me: accuse myself (Abbott §223). **I am ... act
them in:** ● Continuing the enacting of the religious
mania form of melancholy. **at my beck:** at my
command, on call (from *beckon*), hence "waiting
to be committed" (Jenkins).

such fellows as I ... We: ● The shift from first-
person singular to first-person plural is a function
of the generalized sermonizing Hamlet is enacting
in his guise of religious mania. He does of course
recognize that, like all men, he is a sinner, but the
confession in the singular here is no more meant to
be accurate about himself than his earlier complaints
about being dreadfully attended (II.ii.269), and his
move to the plural is sermonizer's rhetoric. **arrant
knaves:** extreme villains. **all:** F, not in Q2. **believe
none of us:** ● That is, do not believe me (as your
father commanded you), your father (who is using
your beauty and pretense of praying to entrap
me, and who by the way was wrong about me), or
any man. The thrust of Hamlet's speech here is to
play at a puritanical preoccupation with sexual
crimes and purity, a preoccupation recognized to
be characteristic of certain kinds of melancholy
madness and a cliché on the stage. He is energized by,
even as he is disguising, his actual rage at the abuse

Where's your father?

of the two women in his life by Claudius and Polonius. Pretending madness, he asserts that only in a nunnery is a woman safe from sexual depredations. In reality, he is feeling that only in a metaphorical nunnery is Ophelia safe from the machinations of the court. In his passionate focus on universal sin, from which the only safety lies in spiritual retreat, Hamlet is intentionally and half-satirically exhibiting, in the language of homiletic preaching, an exaggerated display of the qualities precisely opposite to those he was accused of by Laertes and Polonius in I.iii, which served as the justification for Ophelia's rejection of Hamlet's overtures. Cf., the form of madness Edgar plays at as Tom o' Bedlam in *King Lear*, especially at III.iv.80–98 and IV.i.58–63. **Go thy ways:** see I.iii.135 note.

Where's your father?: • Because of the lack of a stage direction to indicate that Hamlet has discovered that at least Polonius is hiding behind the arras, Jenkins asserts that Hamlet does not know he is being secretly observed. Jenkins' argument depends not only on his understanding of the stage convention that "a character's awareness of being overheard is normally made explicit in the dialogue," but also on a convoluted understanding of Hamlet's psychology, dubbed his "'antic' vein," according to which "Hamlet's love for Ophelia has all along been entangled with her father" and seeing Ophelia herself, Hamlet "suddenly thinks of her father." On this fanciful basis Jenkins dismisses as fanciful all earlier arguments that Hamlet suddenly realizes there is a spy. The implication is the erroneous notion that the madness—or at least the intellectual and emotional vagaries—that Hamlet exhibited earlier and now exhibits here is real, and that it alone explains the outbursts. In fact, however, 1) we have been explicitly told before (I.v.171–72) and will be told again (III.iv.187–88) that Hamlet is "mad in craft," thus imitating the example set for stage avengers by Kyd's *Spanish Tragedy*; 2) this being so, we have no reason to think that Hamlet's mad-appearing outburst and rage at Ophelia are functions of his own actual psychology, as if he indeed suffered from puritanical sex-revulsion mania; and 3) Hamlet's awareness of the eavesdropper(s) *is* made obvious in the dialogue, in keeping with the stage convention (though more subtly here than elsewhere, as suits Shakespeare's purposes), by the suddenness of his shift in tone and by the aptness of his question here and pointed intentions later (lines 132 and 148). Hamlet has determined to play at various forms of madness depending on his various audiences, and here as before we see his shift of performance tactics as a consequence of a shift in external circumstances. Not only is there no other reasonable explanation for Hamlet's sudden rage at Ophelia (unless we adopt the thoroughly un-Shakespearean principle that Hamlet's inner life is intended by the author to be and remain an impenetrable mystery), but this explanation is entirely in keeping with the overall structure of the play, for it is precisely the parallel between his mother and his intended wife that drives Hamlet into the present passionate rage, expressed through pretended but not actual madness. As Gertrude's will was turned against Hamlet Senior under Claudius's influence, so Ophelia's will has now, for the second time, been turned against Hamlet under Polonius's and possibly also Claudius's influence. Hamlet's angry rhetorical question, which challenges her "honesty," now not in the sense of chastity but in that of truthfulness, drives Ophelia again to have to choose between obedience to her father and loyalty to her lover.

OPHELIA

At home, my lord.   130

At home, my lord: ● Ophelia's response we know to be false, and there is no reason for Hamlet to have asked the question unless he knows so too and asks it as a rhetorical test of Ophelia's "honesty." And though it is forgivable, because she believes Hamlet to be mad, her answer is dishonest, so that the truthful answer to the question of line 102 ("Are you honest?") would (ironically) be "No." Tragically caught between her duty to father and king and her duty to her lover and prince (who, if the Ghost is honest, is also her rightful king), and frail like all women, as the commonplace had it, or at least like a certain type of woman, she fails Hamlet's test here, as Hamlet will fail his test in III.iii, as Gertrude has failed hers, and as Fortinbras, Laertes, Osric, and even Horatio will each fail his. However, only Claudius, resolute in sin despite his opportunities for repentance, will fail irredeemably.

HAMLET

Let the doors be shut upon him, that he may play the fool nowhere but in's own house. Farewell.

Let the doors ... own house: ● Strong evidence that Hamlet knows the truth of Polonius's whereabouts but is keeping up the fiction, to protect both Ophelia's cover and his own. Polonius is "playing the fool" in secretly spying on one who now knows he is doing so. **in's:** in his.

OPHELIA

O help him, you sweet heavens!

help him: ● Ophelia believes that Hamlet's speech exhibits madness, as Hamlet intended. Only we, the audience, recognize the madness as a performance fueled by real and legitimately evoked passion.

HAMLET

If thou dost marry, I'll give thee this plague for thy dowry: be thou as chaste as ice, as pure as snow,   135

If thou dost marry ...: ● It is not Ophelia's marrying in itself that enrages Hamlet, as Jenkins argues (though he is right to defend the literal meaning of "nunnery" above, line 120), but the likelihood of her betrayal of her husband, as Hamlet's mother has betrayed his father and as Ophelia is now betraying Hamlet, Claudius being the instigator of the first betrayal directly and of the second at one remove.

thou shalt not escape calumny. Get thee to a nunnery, farewell. Or if thou wilt needs marry, marry a fool, for

calumny: slander, false accusation that threatens the ruin of one's reputation. ● Even if one is chaste, people will think one is not, a commonplace complaint that echoes Laertes at I.iii.38, cf., *Measure for Measure* III.ii.186–87, *Winter's Tale* II.i.73–74, and Tilley E175.

wise men know well enough what monsters you make of them. To a nunnery, go, and quickly too. Farewell.   140

monsters: ● An allusion to the horns that supposedly grew on the forehead of a cuckold, making him half man, half beast, hence a monster, cf., *Othello* IV.i.62. The husband was the last to see

OPHELIA

Heavenly powers, restore him!

HAMLET

I have heard of your paintings well enough. God
hath given you one face, and you make yourselves

another. You jig and amble, and you lisp; you

nickname God's creatures and make your wantonness   145
your ignorance. Go to, I'll no more on't; it hath made

me mad. I say we will have no more marriage. Those

that are married already—all but one—shall live. The
rest shall keep as they are. To a nunnery, go.

Exit.

the horns on his own forehead, meaning the last to know his wife was unfaithful. This notion underlies the still common prank of holding up two fingers behind the head of one's neighbor (as in a group photograph). **you:** you women. ● Jenkins, still taken in by Hamlet's performance, again misses the point in saying that Hamlet "has ceased to think of Ophelia as an individual." In fact, Hamlet is angry at her as an individual, as at his mother, and in his preacher-like denunciation of all women is expressing that anger dressed in the sex-revulsion mania that is a form of love melancholy.

Heavenly powers restore him!: ● Ophelia's prayer for the healing of Hamlet's madness recalls to him her false praying earlier in the scene and evokes his further outburst.

paintings: use of makeup, cf., V.i.193–94, a common reproach of preachers against unchaste women (Jenkins cites examples in Guazzo's *Civil Conversation*, Tilley, the Book of Homilies, and Philip Stubbes, *Anatomy of Abuses*, and says "Donne's argument 'That women ought to paint' [in *Paradoxes* No. 2] is correspondingly outrageous" (Jenkins).

jig: dance a jig, which involves moving up and down or to and fro with a rapid jerky motion (OED 2.), implying affectation, and possibly inconstancy. **amble:** dance in a way that imitates the easy pace of a walking horse, gliding or walking affectedly (OED amble *v.* 3. and ambling *vbl. sb.* 2.), implying affectation or coquetry, cf., *Romeo and Juliet* I.iv.11, 1 *Henry IV* III.ii.60, *Richard III* I.i.17, *I Return from Parnassus* line 1310, and Shirley, *Lady of Pleasure* V.i.395 (all cited in Jenkins). **lisp:** seductive affectation of speech, cf., Chaucer, *Canterbury Tales,* General Prologue, line 264.

nickname: name incorrectly or improperly as an affectation (OED 1.). **make your wantonness your ignorance:** pretend that your (intentional) affectation or looseness of behavior (including sexual behavior) comes from not knowing any better.

no more marriage: For F "more" Q2 has "mo" " = *more* but not a corruption of it. O.E. *má*" (Jenkins, OED mo). ● We know from the soliloquy (lines 55ff.) that Hamlet is perfectly sane. His playing at this mania of moralistic asceticism allows him to get away with expressing his intense feelings about the King while continuing the fiction of his being mad, see line 102 note.

all but one: ● Clearly the audience realizes that the line refers to the King, but in the midst of such a diatribe against marriage in general, Hamlet is safe within his assumed madness from any accusations of treason. He might have meant himself, or anyone. It may be as Jenkins asserts, that "the effect depends on our knowing, but not on Hamlet's knowing, of the King's presence," but the effect intended also depends on Hamlet's knowing quite well that at least Polonius is behind the arras. Additional symbolic evidence lies

OPHELIA

O, what a noble mind is here o'erthrown!   150

The courtier's, soldier's, scholar's, eye, tongue, sword;

Th'expectancy and rose of the fair state,

The glass of fashion and the mold of form,

Th' observed of all observers, quite, quite down!

And I, of ladies most deject and wretched,   155
That sucked the honey of his music vows,

Now see that noble and most sovereign reason

Like sweet bells jangled out of tune and harsh;

---

in the fact that here, before Hamlet's fall (in III.iii), he can tell who is hiding behind an arras whereas later (III.iv) he cannot.

noble mind … o'erthrown: ● Ophelia laments the destruction of Hamlet's exemplary intellect. **noble:** admirable, aristocratic, and honorable, cf., line 56.

courtier's … sword: that is, the courtier's eye, implying refined attention, judgment, and discretion (cf., OED 6. and 8.), the soldier's sword, implying adeptness in military art and courage, and the scholar's tongue, implying exemplary knowledge and speech, cf., I.i.42. ● i.e., the ideal prince, cf., *Measure for Measure* III.ii.146. The different order of the modifiers and the nouns modified is not uncommon, cf., *Rape of Lucrece* lines 615–616, *Antony and Cleopatra* III.ii.16–17, IV.xv.25–26, and Quintilian (quoted in Baldwin II.201).

expectancy and rose: possibly a hendiadys (Wright, page 187). **expectancy:** F, expectation Q2, hope for the future, promising heir to the throne. **rose:** symbolizing the blossom of perfection, cf., IV.v.158 and *1 Henry IV* I.iii.175. **fair state:** the rose (Hamlet) that makes the state (Denmark, its court) fair (= beautiful).

glass … form: "cf. … North's Plutarch 'as if I looked into a glass, to frame and fashion my life, to the mould and pattern of these virtuous noble men' (Life of Paulus Aemilius, Tudor Trans., ii.196)" (Jenkins). **glass:** mirror in which fashion, as well as the person who would be fashionable, sees the ideal to be emulated, cf., *2 Henry IV* II.iii.31–32. **mold of form:** (mould Q2 and F), pattern of perfection in courtly behavior.

observed: paid respectful attention, honored, revered, perhaps also emulated (OED observe 4.b.).

deject: dejected (for the omitted -ed, see Abbott §342).

sucked … vows: ● Hearing Hamlet's vows of fidelity was like tasting honey or hearing harmonious music, the F variant "music" chosen over Q2 "musickt" (= musicked) because "it is not so much that he spoke the vows musically as that they were like music to her. Abbott ([§] 22, 430) treats *music vows* as a noun compound" (Jenkins).

most sovereign: reason, as the highest of man's faculties, properly ruled the lesser faculties of emotion and sensation, cf., I.iv.73 and note. **most:** the intensifier may add the sense that Hamlet's reason was most like that of a sovereign, or of what a sovereign ought to be.

jangled: rung noisily, with inharmonious clanging. **out of tune and harsh:** Though Jenkins quotes Corson's assertion that "out of tune" is "an adverbial element to *jangled*, and not an adjective element to *sweet bells*," the phrase works both ways at the same time. The F reading "tune," where Q2 has "time," is chosen only because "Shakespeare elsewhere combines *out of tune* with *harsh*: see

That unmatched form and feature of blown youth

Blasted with ecstasy. O woe is me,   160

T' have seen what I have seen, see what I see.

Re-enter King and Polonius.

KING

Love? His affections do not that way tend,
Nor what he spake, though it lacked form a little,
Was not like madness. There's something in his soul

O'er which his melancholy sits on brood,   165

And I do doubt the hatch and the disclose

Will be some danger, which for to prevent
I have in quick determination

Thus set it down: he shall with speed to England

Rom[eo and Juliet] III.v.27–28 and *Othello* V.ii. [115–16]" (Jenkins). The two words could be almost interchangeable, as exemplified by *As You Like It* V.iii.35–38, and cf., *Richard II* V.v.42–46. "Either *time* or *tune* must be a mimin error [of the typesetter], but as both make excellent sense we cannot be certain which" (Jenkins LN).

unmatched: matchless, unequaled. **form and feature:** shape and fashioning, "(of the whole body, not specially of the face). (Fr. *faiture*.) Cf. *R[ichard III]* I.i.19[–20]" (Jenkins). F feature, Q2 stature. **blown:** fully blossomed, in full bloom, cf., III.iii.81, *Much Ado* IV.i.58, and *Antony and Cleopatra* III.xii.39.

Blasted: blighted (Raffel), withered (Riverside). **ecstasy:** madness, cf., II.i.99 and note and III.iv.74, 138.

T' have: To have. **seen ... see:** i.e., to have seen Hamlet in the past as so fine an example of noble young manhood and to be seeing him in the present in the apparent ruin of madness.

● **SPEECH NOTE:** Lines 150–161 sum up the ideal youth that Hamlet is seen to be by Denmark in general and by Ophelia in particular, and the disastrous loss that his (to us, only apparent) madness is seen to be to the state. In addition to revealing the success of Hamlet's performance, it also sets up the terrible irony of Ophelia's own later fate. What is here a brilliant show of madness will become, because of a combination of events, including Hamlet's error in III.iii and action in III.iv, a tragic reality in Ophelia herself.

affections: mental state, emotions, inner feelings, the way in which one is affected by things (OED 2.).

Was not like madness: ● The King, more astute than Polonius, realizes a) that what is disturbing Hamlet is not a mad reaction to unrequited love, which is Polonius's theory expressed earlier, b) that Hamlet is brooding on something, and c) that danger is threatened. His observation here is yet more evidence that Hamlet is not mad, as he means Polonius and the others to think he is.

sits on brood: like a hen (for "on brood" see Abbott §24), leading to "hatch" and its synonym "disclose" in the next line.

doubt: fear (OED 5), suspect (OED 6.b.) as at I.ii.255. **hatch and disclose:** possibly a hendiadys (Wright, page 187). **disclose:** synonym for "hatch," the setting free of the young bird from the shell of an egg, cf., V.i.287 (OED *sb.* and *v.* 3.b.), another example of a verb used as a noun, cf., *avouch* I.i.57, *inquire* II.i.4, *supervise* V.ii.23 (Abbott §451) (Jenkins substantially).

for to: in order to (Abbott §152).

determination: ● NOTE TO ACTORS: The word may be pronounced with six syllables (*-tion* as *shi-un*), implying irony after the word "quick," or elided to five (*shun*) to embody the claimed quickness.

set it down: decided, determined, resolved. **he shall with speed to England:** ● "The dramatist, if not the King, is already preparing the plot against Hamlet's life.

For the demand of our neglected tribute.   170

As an instance of Shakespeare's construction see this developing at III.iii.3–7 and III.iv.[200–205] before becoming explicit at IV.iii.[55–68]" (Jenkins). **shall ... to:** shall go to.

neglected tribute: ● Paid by the English to forestall Danish (Viking) attacks. The money was collected as a tax called Danegeld levied from 991 until 1163. According to Jenkins (referring to Horsey's *Travels* [Hakluyt Soc.], pages 240–44, and the British Calendar of State Papers, Domestic, 1598–1600, page 59), the reference was topical in Shakespeare's time because "the Danish kings had recently sought to reimpose an annual payment."

Haply the seas and countries different

Haply: perhaps, maybe. **seas:** "A recognized cure. Cf. *Wint[er's Tale]* IV.iv.[762–63]" (Jenkins).
different: ● NOTE TO ACTORS: pronounced as three syllables but cf., line 168 note.

With variable objects shall expel
This something-settled matter in his heart,

objects: "notable sights" (Jenkins), cf., I.i.156 note.
something-settled matter: a compressed metaphor. This unidentified matter ("something," as in line 164) settled in his heart, i.e., an unidentified thing settled (Jenkins substantially) rather than a known thing somewhat settled (as in Abbott §68). ● "Schmidt compares *R[ichard II]* II.ii.36, 'my something grief' ('i.e. existing, but of uncertain nature')" (Jenkins).

Whereon his brains still beating puts him thus
From fashion of himself. What think you on't?   175

Whereon ... himself: the continuous harping of his mind on which (i.e., the "matter" of the previous line) separates him from his normal behavior. **still:** always.
puts: "the subject is ... the whole preceding phrase" (Jenkins), i.e., the participial phrase "Whereon his brains still beating" is understood as a substantive (Abbott §413) with a singular verb (Abbott §337).
fashion of himself: normal behavior (Jenkins, Raffel). **on't:** of it.

POLONIUS
It shall do well. But yet do I believe
The origin and commencement of his grief

But yet ... love: ● Polonius continues to trust his own impressions despite the King's more astute observation, trying to shore up his own and his daughter's importance and confirming Hamlet's accusation that he is a fool (line 132).

Sprung from neglected love.—How now, Ophelia?
You need not tell us what Lord Hamlet said;
We heard it all.—My lord, do as you please,   180
But if you hold it fit, after the play
Let his queen-mother all alone entreat him
To show his grief. Let her be round with him,

And I'll be placed, so please you, in the ear

neglected: unrequited. **How now:** how is it (are you) now?

hold it fit: find it appropriate.

round: outspoken, direct, cf., II.ii.139, III.iv.5, and *Henry V* IV.i.203.

so please you: if (or may) it please you. **in the ear:** within hearing. ● Polonius has tried twice to discern Hamlet's mind, once with direct address, once with eavesdropping. The third attempt will be fatal.

Of all their conference. If she find him not,   185
To England send him, or confine him where
Your wisdom best shall think.

find him: smoke him out, get to the bottom of his thinking, learn the truth.

KING

It shall be so.
Madness in great ones must not unwatched go.

Exeunt.

Act III, Scene ii

Enter Hamlet and three of the Players.

HAMLET

Speak the speech, I pray you, as I pronounced it to you,

so / go: Kennedy notes that III.iii too ends with a couplet rhyming on the word "go."

Act III, Scene ii: A hall in the castle.

S.D. *three*: Q2, where F has "*two or three*," "is unexpectedly precise but corresponds (if we discount the Prologue) to the number of speaking parts in their play" (Jenkins). Cf., II.ii. 420 S.D. and note.

● SPEECH NOTE: **Speak the speech … fool that uses it:** In his instructions to the players, Hamlet articulates his high standards for theatrical art, revealing his "noble mind" (III.i.150) and good judgment in general and his "scholar's tongue" (III.i.151) in particular. The speeches also advertise the quality of Shakespeare's own plays and provide scholars a valuable illumination of Elizabethan theatrical customs and expectations. "The standards are … those sanctioned by the critical tradition. (See [B. L.] Joseph, *Elizabethan Acting*, pages 146–9). The principle of ease and naturalness of gesture corresponds with what is advocated in Heywood's *Apology for Actors*, 1612 [C4]" (Jenkins LN). The primary function of these speeches, however, is thematic. The charge that Hamlet gives the players, whose art is meant to reflect the reality of the human world ("hold … the mirror up to nature," line 22), is the central metaphorical paradigm of every charge given in the play (see Introduction, pages 13–14, 17–18). Like the Ghost's charge to Hamlet, Hamlet's own instructions to the players require them to do an action in a certain way without overdoing it. As in Polonius's speech to Laertes at I.iii.58ff., so in these speeches the golden mean is urged, here in language pregnant with universal implications. Acting on the stage was a common metaphor for life that Shakespeare had learned in grammar school, and the theater in which this play was performed was called the Globe, whose sign depicted Hercules holding the world on his shoulders and whose motto was *totus mundus agit histrionem* ("the whole world plays [the role of] actor")—cf., Sonnet 15.3, *As You Like It* II.vii.139–40, *Merchant of Venice* I.i.78, *2 Henry IV* I.i.155, *King Lear* IV.vi.183, *Macbeth* V.v.24–25, and *Winter's Tale* V.i.58. Hence, every phrase in these speeches applies not only to the way the actors are to perform the play before the King, upon which more depends than the actors can know, but also to the way any man must live his life in the world, on which also more depends than he can comprehend. The resonances of Hamlet's words here affect our understanding of all else that happens in the play, in particular the significance of the enlightenment Hamlet exhibits in Act V.

trippingly on the tongue; but if you mouth it as many
of your players do, I had as lief the town-crier spoke

my lines. Nor do not saw the air too much with your

hand, thus, but use all gently; for in the very torrent,   5

tempest, and, as I may say, whirlwind of your passion,

you must acquire and beget a temperance that may
give it smoothness. O, it offends me to the soul to hear

a robustious periwig-pated fellow tear a passion to

tatters, to very rags, to split the ears of the groundlings,   10

who for the most part are capable of nothing but
inexplicable dumb shows and noise. I would have such

a fellow whipped for o'erdoing Termagant. It out-

Herods Herod. Pray you avoid it.

the speech: the one Hamlet has written for them to insert in "The Murder of Gonzago," II.ii.540–43 and line 4 ("my lines") ● Shakespeare does not provide any clear indication of which speech that is, nor does seeking for it serve any dramatic purpose. The play has the effect Hamlet intends, and that is what matters.

trippingly: lightly and lively. **mouth:** over-articulate, declaim exaggeratedly. **your:** F, our Q2, the colloquial indefinite use, cf., I.i.138 note and Abbott §221. **I had as lief:** I had just as soon, I would just as willingly, Q2 and F "live" is a variant spelling (OED Lief 1.d.). **town-crier:** an official of the town, sometimes called a bellman, charged with making public pronouncements of royal edicts, local laws, and other significant news.

saw the air: "Cf. Quintilian's objection to this kind of hand movement in oratory ... (*Inst. Orat.*, XI.iii.119). Bulwer, *Chironomia*, 1644, echoing Quintilian, refers to 'the action of one that saws or cuts' (pp. 102–3)" (Jenkins).

gently: in two senses, "with moderation" and "in the well-bred manner of a gentleman" (Jenkins).

tempest ... whirlwind: cf., Jeremiah 23:19 and Amos 1:14.

acquire and beget: "acquire, through training and practice; beget, through a native artistic impulse" (Dowden, quoted in Jenkins).

robustious: boisterous, noisily assertive, cf., *Henry V* III.vii.148. **periwig-pated:** i.e., wig-headed, wearing a wig (from French *perruque*), implying dressed for the stage, artificial.

split: F, Q2 "spleet," a synonym which OED finds etymologically "Obscurely related to Split," cf., *Antony and Cleopatra* II.vii.124. **groundlings:** audience members who paid the lowest entrance fee and stood on the ground in the "pit" rather than sitting on seats in the galleries.

capable of: able to appreciate, receptive to.

inexplicable: too shallow or obvious for explication or for expression in words (rather than, as OED 3. has it, citing this line, "inscrutable, unintelligible"), perhaps simply "nonverbal (and therefore unable to be explained in words)" (Raffel). **dumb shows:** pantomimes, scenes acted in gestures without words, as at line 135 S.D.

o'erdoing Termagant: overacting the loud and violent stock character of the medieval mystery plays, the supposed false god of the Saracens.

Herod: another stock character of the medieval mystery plays, the king of Judea in Matthew 2:16, who was depicted as a ranting and raving tyrant. ● Hamlet's instruction that the Players not overdo their parts expresses in the terms of art the major theme of fulfilling a charge without overdoing it, a theme we have seen conveyed in the King's caution to Cornelius and Voltemand at I.ii.36–38, Polonius's

FIRST PLAYER

   I warrant your honor.   15

HAMLET

   Be not too tame neither, but let your own discretion

be your tutor. Suit the action to the word, the word

to the action, with this special observance,
that you o'erstep not the modesty of nature.

For anything so o'erdone is from the purpose of   20
playing, whose end, both at the first and now, was

and is to hold as 'twere the mirror up to nature; to

show virtue her own feature, scorn her

own image, and the very age and
body of the time his form and pressure. Now this

---

advice to Laertes at I.iii.59ff., Hamlet's ultimatum at I.v.1, most centrally, the Ghost's warning to Hamlet at I.v.84–86, and elsewhere through the play. **warrant:** assure, promise (that we will avoid it).

Be not too tame neither: ● The golden mean is the ideal in acting, as Polonius suggested it was in the practical affairs of a young man's life (I.ii.59ff.), underdoing potentially as great a breach as overdoing, as we will see at the moment of Hamlet's climactic crisis in III.iii. **discretion:** discernment, wisdom, ability to distinguish right from wrong, better from worse, etc.

Suit the action to the word: ● By the end of the play, the latent implication of this phrase will become visible, notably at V.ii.10–11. Every man must suit his action to the Word, that is, to the reason or logic of God as revealed through the incarnated *logos* of John 1:1. **observance:** care, heed (OED 4.).

modesty: moderation (Riverside), absence of excess, cf., II.ii.440, V.i.208. **of nature:** ● Again the theme of the golden mean, which is exhibited by nature itself (including human nature), whose creation is ordered to avoid extremes when its elements are not misdirected by perverse will, as by the original sin of Adam and Eve and all excesses arising from it.

anything: Q2, F any thing, always as two words originally (OED). **from:** apart from, away from, contrary to (Riverside), i.e., overdoing departs from the purpose of acting (Abbott §158). **playing:** playacting, theatrical drama. **end:** goal, purpose, foreshadowing the double meaning of "ends" at V.ii.10.

as 'twere: as it were, so to speak. **mirror up to nature:** "The widespread Renaissance theory of drama as an image of actual life derives from [the 4th c. Roman grammarian] Donatus on comedy, where it is attributed to Cicero (*Commentum Terenti*, ed. Wessner, i.22)" (Jenkins). Baldwin stresses the importance of invention added to imitation (II.406) and notes elsewhere that "Hamlet is conscious of the historical perspective of his statement, 'both at the first and now, was and is' [line 21]. [N]o sixteenth century critic on Terence … omits it. The statement … was and is a threadbare platitude; that is why we shall cherish it always" (Baldwin *Five-Act*, page 567), cf., the characteristics of success in this endeavor at II.ii.439–45 and the contrast with the work of "Nature's journeymen" at lines 28–35.

feature: shape, form, appearance (Jenkins, Raffel), cf., III.i.159. **scorn:** that which merits scorn, object of scorn (OED *sb.* 3. and 4.), cf., *Comedy of Errors* IV.iv.103, *Love's Labor's Lost* I.i.309, *2 Henry VI* IV.ii.12, *Titus Andronicus* I.i.265, etc.

age and body of the time: "*age* does not correspond with *body* as an attribute of 'the time' but with the whole phrase *body of the time*. *body*, 'the essential and

overdone or come tardy off, though it makes the   25

unskillful laugh, cannot but make the judicious grieve,

the censure of which one must in your allowance
o'erweigh a whole theatre of others. O, there be players
that I have seen play—and heard others praise, and

that highly—not to speak it profanely, that   30

vital part' (Schmidt), but also with a suggestion of
the 'substance' of which the players give the image
(*OED* body 24)" (Jenkins). Wright (page 187) less
convincingly finds the phrase a hendiadys, the era
and what's happening in it. **his:** its, cf., I.i.37 note.
form and pressure: likeness as in an impression
of a seal in wax, cf., I.v.100 note and II.ii.305 note, a
hendiadys (Wright, page 187), cf., I.1.57 note.

come tardy off: Though Jenkins' gloss, "executed
inadequately" (based on OED 3. on the analogy
of *Romeo and Juliet* II.vi.15), may be present as a
secondary sense, implying "underdone" as an
opposite extreme to "overdone," nonetheless the
primary meaning remains delayed beyond the
appropriate time, late, even in the phrase "to come
off" meaning to turn out, to end up (cf., OED come
v. 61. i., and cf., Abbott §165 for the possibility that
off may be *of*). ● Hamlet's choice in the next scene
shows him overdoing his performance as avenger
and thereby literally retarding it (from III.iii to V.ii)
as well as performing it inadequately. It is precisely
the delay for reasons of overdoing, which we will be
shown in III.iii, that leads to the tragic outcome for all
the main characters except Fortinbras.

unskillful: in appreciating the art of drama. **cannot
but:** i.e., cannot not, cannot other than. **judicious:**
discerning, antithesis to "unskillful."

censure: judgment, criticism, cf., I.iii.69. **of which
one:** Q2, where F has "of the which One." The
apparently problematic syntax (in both Q2 and F) is
resolved if (in light of Abbott §269 & §270) we take
"which" to be an adjective modifying "one," "one" to
be the object of the preposition "of" referring back
to a singular judicious person, and "censure" (not
"one") to be the subject of "must o'erweigh." The
phrase thus means "the censure of which judicious
(person) must o'erweigh." The addition of "in" before
"the censure" would justify Riverside's gloss "(even)
one of whom," which makes "one" the subject of
"o'erweighs," but there is no textual authority for
it. In any case, the general import of the phrase is
clear: the judgment of one who is judicious ought
to outweigh the judgment of a whole theater-full of
others. ● NOTE TO ACTORS: The antithesis to bring
out is between "the censure of the (judicious)" and "a
whole theatre of others." That is, the weight is rather
on judicious vs. others than on one vs. many. The
following quotation from Ben Jonson's *Poetaster* (To
the Reader) will help clarify: "Auth…. if I prove the
pleasure but of one, / So he judicious be, he shall b[e]
alone / A theatre unto me". **allowance:** acceptance,
acknowledgment, admission. **be:** usually with plural,
here referring to a kind or class (Abbott §300).

not to speak it profanely: not intending to take the
word "Christian" (which contains the name Christ)
in vain in what follows and thereby to break the
third of the Ten Commandments. ● The potential
profanity Hamlet is disclaiming is "that there

neither having th' accent of Christians nor the gait of
Christian, pagan, nor man, have so strutted and
bellowed that I have thought some of Nature's

journeymen had made men, and not made them well,

they imitated humanity so abominably.   35

FIRST PLAYER

I hope we have reformed that indifferently
with us.

HAMLET

O reform it altogether. And let those that play
your clowns speak no more than is set down for

them, for there be of them that will themselves laugh,   40

to set on some quantity of barren spectators to laugh
too, though in the mean time some necessary question
of the play be then to be considered. That's villainous,

and shows a most pitiful ambition in the fool that uses

it. Go make you ready.   45

Exeunt Players.

Enter Polonius, Rosencrantz, and Guildenstern.

How now, my lord? Will the King hear this piece
of work?

POLONIUS

And the Queen too, and that presently.

---

can be men not of God's making" (Jenkins), i.e., that
the making of men, whether by Nature herself or by
"Nature's journeymen," is not by God's will, or that God's
making of men via Nature may be flawed.

Christians: "ordinary decent beings" (Jenkins).

Christian: redeemed man. **pagan:** unredeemed man.

nor man: nor any man whatsoever, cf., Jonson, [*Epicoene,
or the*] *Silent Woman*, IV.i.1–2 ["Was there ever poor
bridegroom so tormented? Or man, indeed?"] (Jenkins
substantially).

journeymen: hireling, day-worker, drudge, as opposed
to the master artisan that is Nature herself.

abominably: from the Latin *abominari* (to deprecate as
a bad omen—from *ab* + *omen, ominis*) but playing on the
common Elizabethan spelling ("abhominable") based on
the false derivation from *ab* (away from)
+ *homo, hominis* (man).

indifferently: moderately, pretty well, cf., III.i.121.

● SPEECH NOTE: **O reform … ready:** The following
speech is a metaphor for Hamlet's own error to come: In
the next scene, "(literally) damnably unready" as Philip
Thompson writes (see Introduction, page 5), Hamlet
will be the overweening clown attempting in villainous
spiritual ambition to do more than is "set down" for
him by God, even as the most "necessary question of
the play," executing the murderous usurper, is then to
be accomplished, an ambition that, seen at the end of
the play in the light of ultimate divine reality, is both
contemptible and pitiable. Playing on the stage being a
metaphor for life, in this speech Shakespeare has Hamlet
articulate parabolically the central theme of Hamlet's
own life, of the play, and of all human life.

altogether: entirely, completely.

clowns: the actors playing the role of country bumpkin,
fool, or court jester. **no more than is set down:** only
what is written, no ad-libbing, as was a common practice,
cf., Brome, *The Antipodes* II.ii.40–49 (cited in Jenkins).

there be of them that: there are some among them who,
cf., line 28 note, Abbott §300.

quantity: small fragment (OED II.8.b.). **barren:** i.e., of
mental fruits, witless.

villainous: echoing Hamlet's own word for Claudius, the
villainous usurper, at II.ii.580–81.

pitiful: pitiable for its insignificance, contemptible.

fool: both a foolish person and an actor playing the role
of the fool.

ready: to perform the play, and foreshadowing the
"readiness" of Hamlet's enlightenment (V.ii.222).

Will: both future, "will he hear it," and optative, "does
he wish to hear it." **piece of work:** instance of artistry, in
this case a play, cf., II.ii.303 and note.

And: yes, and (Abbott §97). **that:** i.e., hearing the play.
presently: right away, immediately.

HAMLET

Bid the players make haste. [*Exit Polonius.*] Will you
two help to hasten them?   50

ROSENCRANTZ

Ay, my lord.

[*Exeunt Rosencrantz and Guildenstern.*]

HAMLET

What ho, Horatio!

Enter Horatio.

HORATIO

Here, sweet lord, at your service.

HAMLET

Horatio, thou art e'en as just a man

As e'er my conversation coped withal.   55

HORATIO

O, my dear lord—

HAMLET

Nay, do not think I flatter,
For what advancement may I hope from thee
That no revénue hast but thy good spirits
To feed and clothe thee? Why should the poor be
                                              [flattered?

No, let the candied tongue lick ábsurd pomp   60

S.D. *Exeunt Rosencrantz and Guildenstern:*
● "The dismissal of the King's agents (who seem
to have been brought on for no other purpose) just
when Hamlet summons his own confidant effects a
contrast between them which the ensuing discourse
on flattery reinforces" (Jenkins).

sweet: dear (Raffel), "a frequent epithet in
complimentary or affectionate [courtly] address"
(Jenkins), cf., III.i.28, III.iv.96, IV.v.27, V.i.83,
V.ii.89, 359, etc.

e'en: even, steadily, regularly, uniformly (OED 1.)
with a possible sense of quite, fully (OED 7.). **just:**
rightly harmonized in qualities, i.e., balanced in the
elements or humors that make up the "temperament"
or "complexion" of a man (cf., I.iv.38 SPEECH NOTE)
and therefore even-tempered, with the additional
sense, derived from Plato's *Republic*, that the just man
is the one in whom right reason (mind) governs the
other two divisions of the self, the will or passions
(heart) and the desires (body), and is not governed
by them.

e'er: ever. **conversation:** social intercourse,
association, not just in speech (OED 2.). **coped
withal:** had to do with, encountered (OED *v.*² 5.).

advancement: practical advantage, upward mobility.

revénue: income, assets, with the stress on the
second syllable. **good spirits:** positive disposition,
good character (OED 18.b.) with underlying reference
again to those elements or humors that mediate
between body and soul, cf., Donne's "Exstasie," line
62 ("spirits, as like souls as it can").

let the candied ... fawning: ● "The basic idea is that
flattery (here figured as fawning and genuflecting)
should direct its attentions where it may expect
profit (*thrift*) to ensue. The *candied tongue* suggests
an obsequious dog whose physical licking affords
an image of the flatterer's sugary words. The
association of dog and candy belongs to a famous
Shakespearean 'image cluster' (see Spurgeon,
Sh[akespeare]'s Imagery, pages 194–[97]; Armstrong,
S[hakespeare]'s Imagination, pages 154–[56]). The
candy is of course what the tongue bestows, not (as
Spurgeon) sweetmeats the dog has eaten. Cf. *1 Henry
IV* I.iii.251–[52]" (Jenkins). Hamlet is denying that he,
the rich prince, is flattering the poor Horatio, for it
makes no sense for any but the rich, from whom one
may gain advantage, to be flattered. (Shakespeare's
deprecation of dogs as mere flattering fawners

And crook the pregnant hinges of the knee

Where thrift may follow fawning. Dost thou hear?

Since my dear soul was mistress of her choice
And could of men distinguish her election,

Sh' hath sealed thee for herself, for thou hast been   65

As one in suff'ring all that suffers nothing,
A man that Fortune's buffets and rewards
Hast ta'en with equal thanks; and blest are those

Whose blood and judgment are so well comeddled

That they are not a pipe for Fortune's finger   70

To sound what stop she please. Give me that man

That is not passion's slave, and I will wear him
In my heart's core, ay, in my heart of heart,

---

suggests that he cannot ever have owned and loved a good dog himself, the only flaw in the poet's character that I have ever detected. That Launce's love for the disreputable Crab in *Two Gentlemen of Verona* is satirized only reinforces the point.). **candied:** sugar-bearing, i.e., flattering. **ábsurd:** senseless, ridiculous, possibly insipid, tasteless (Jenkins, citing Hulme, pages 160–62, and Cotgrave), stressed on the first syllable, cf., I.iv.52 note, from Latin *absurdus*, inharmonious, jarring to the ear. **pomp:** ceremonial splendor, here a metaphor for higher rank, royalty itself.

pregnant: ready, receptive to influence, disposed (OED *a.*² 3.d.), cf., *King Lear* IV.vi.223.

thrift: the noun from the verb *to thrive*, thriving, profit, parallel to "advancement" and "revenue." **fawning:** servility. **Dost thou?:** the intimate and personal form of address.

was mistress ... election: reached the age of rational free will and thereby gained the power to discriminate and to make choice among men, cf., *Measure for Measure* I.i.17–18. **her ... her:** "Her is very often applied by Shakespeare to the mind and soul" (Abbott §229). **of:** about, concerning (Abbott §174).

Sh' hath: she hath, i.e., my soul has, elided to one syllable, Q2 S'hath, F Hath, Q3 S hath, Q4 Shath, Q5 Sh'ath. **sealed:** not only written but finalized by stamping with a seal, the soul being the sovereign of the self, as the king (who seals state documents) is of the state, cf., V.ii.47–52.

As one ... equal thanks: ● The following description is theoretical, implying no particular agonies of Horatio but a Stoical ideal, cf., "more an antique Roman" (V.ii.341). **in:** while, in the act of (Abbott §164). **suff'ring all:** in two senses, undergoing or experiencing all that he has experienced, and bearing up under any afflictions that have come to him. **suffers nothing:** has no anguish, bears without mental pain. ● Hamlet observes that Horatio bears whatever happens to him with equanimity. **equal thanks** for both bad ("buffets" = blows, punches) and good ("rewards").

blood and judgment: passion and reason, cf., I.iii.6, 116, II.i.34, III.iv.69, and IV.iv.58. **comeddled:** comedled Q2, co-mingled F, blended or mingled together (cf., "comutual," line 160).

pipe ... stop: "The metaphor will recur in lines [364–72]" (Jenkins). **Fortune's:** see II.ii.229 note.

stop: the hole in a musical wind instrument that determines the pitch of the sound, cf., line 365.

passion's slave: see line 54 note.

heart's core ... heart of heart: "Both phrases mean the same, on the supposed etymology of *core*, from Latin *cor*: in the very centre of my heart" (Jenkins), a derivation that Shakespeare may have assumed though the OED finds it dubious. ● Hamlet declares his admiration and love for the man whose passions and reason are in harmony, in whom Hamlet sees the ideal embodiment of the golden mean that Polonius has advised in his "precepts" to Laertes (I.iii.58ff.). In this admiration for Horatio Hamlet reveals that his earlier conclusion that "Man delights not me" (II.ii.309) was not absolute but an instance of his playacted madness for the ears of Rosencrantz and Guildenstern. Jenkins notes, "It is regularly observed that Hamlet values in Horatio what he knows to be lacking in himself." However, though his passions may be more powerful than Horatio's and his reason perhaps superior, it is not that Hamlet is lacking the capacity to balance reason and passion, cf., Ophelia's description of him at III.i.150ff. It is that Hamlet is driven painfully from one to the other by the extremity of his situation, even as he observes and admires the seemingly unalterable equanimity of his friend. By the end of the play, we will see that Hamlet achieves a harmony between passion and reason through readiness to respond rightly, with either of them, to the call of the moment. We will also find that even the apparently balanced Horatio departs from his equanimity in a passion when driven by the agonizing external circumstances of the denouement, when it will be Hamlet's reason and passion combined that restore Horatio to balance: there Hamlet's reason will oppose Horatio's suicide and give him cause to live, and Hamlet's passion will force the poisoned cup from Horatio's hands (V.ii.342–49).

As I do thee. Something too much of this.
There is a play tonight before the King;   75

Something too much of this: ● "The genuine manliness of this little sentence ... is precisely one of Shakespeare's exquisite touches of innate propriety in questions of feeling. Let any one, who doubts for a moment whether Sh[akespeare] intended that Ham[let] should merely *feign* madness, read carefully over the present speech, marking its sobriety of expression even amid all its ardor, its singleness and purity of sentiment amid its most forcible utterance, and then decide whether it could be possible that he should mean Hamlet's wits to be touched. That his heart is shaken to its core ... we admit; but that his intellects are in the very slightest degree disordered, we cannot for one instant believe" (Clarke).

One scene of it comes near the circumstance
Which I have told thee of my father's death.

circumstance ... father's death: Q2, where F has "Circumstance / Which I have told thee, of my Fathers death." Corson (cited in Furness) correctly notes that "of my father's death" modifies "circumstance," which invites two commas (of which F supplies only one) to set off the subordinate clause, but the absence of commas in Q2 preserves the forward motion of the verse. ● At some point after I.v and before this scene Hamlet has shared with the trusted Horatio what he has heard from the Ghost, thereby making Horatio a witness to the motives for Hamlet's pretended madness and for any act against the king that may be to come.

I prithee when thou seest that act afoot,

I prithee: I pray thee. **that act:** the action to be depicted in the "one scene" mentioned in line 76, not a division of the play. **afoot:** in progress.

Even with the very comment of thy soul

with the very comment: (observe him) with true and deliberate interpretation (of his response to the play) (OED comment *sb.* 2.). **thy soul:** "The 'just' Horatio will be the perfect witness" (Jenkins), cf., line 54 note.

Observe my uncle. If his occulted guilt   80

occulted: covered up.

Do not itself unkennel in one speech,

unkennel: come out, escape from its enclosure (in feigning or hypocrisy). **one speech:** presumably the one mentioned at lines 1–4 and II.ii.541.

It is a damnèd ghost that we have seen,
And my imaginations are as foul

damnèd ghost: ● Hamlet repeats here to Horatio his central concern about taking revenge before being certain that the Ghost is not a demon in disguise trying to tempt him to damnable action, cf., I.iv.40, 69, 72, II.ii.598ff., below at lines 286–87, and the import of III.i.55ff. and note.

As Vulcan's stithy. Give him heedful note;
For I mine eyes will rivet to his face,   85

Vulcan's: Vulcan was the blacksmith of the gods of ancient Rome. **stithy:** forge, hence foul in being filthy and black, the more so for being that of a god ● If the Ghost is lying, then Hamlet's imagination of Claudius's crimes is itself damnably foul.
note: attention.

And after we will both our judgments join
In censure of his seeming.

after: afterwards.

censure: judgment, cf., line 27 and I.iii.69. **seeming:** what the King's behavior appears to be, with the implication that his "seeming" may be a pretense or false show hiding a foul reality, cf., I.ii.83–86 and *Measure for Measure* II.iv.150.

HORATIO

                    Well, my lord.

If a steal aught the whilst this play is playing

a: he, as often in the play. **aught:** anything. **whilst:** while, during the time that, cf., Abbott §137.

And 'scape detecting, I will pay the theft.

'scape detecting: avoid being found out, "'scape" for *escape*. **pay the theft:** reimburse for what he has stolen. ● Horatio's fanciful metaphor confirms his intention to fulfill Hamlet's request by closely watching the King during the performance.

Enter Trumpets and Kettle-drums.

S.D.: see I.iv.11 note.

HAMLET
They are coming to the play. I must be idle.   90

be idle: be seen to be a) "unoccupied. They must not be seen conspiring. (So Greg, *MLR*, XIV, 362–3)" and b) mad, "as in his next speech Hamlet does [pretend to be]" (Jenkins).

Get you a place.

Get you: find for yourself.

*A flourish. Enter King, Queen, Polonius, Ophelia,
Rosencrantz, Guildenstern, and other Lords attendant,
with [the King's] Guard carrying torches.*

S.D. *flourish:* fanfare of horns, trumpets, drums, etc.

KING
How fares our cousin Hamlet?

How fares: How is he doing, use of the third person suggesting that the question is meant for any or all to hear. Hamlet, pretending the madness of thwarted ambition, will take the word in the sense of eating. **our:** the royal plural. **cousin:** relative, here nephew and stepson, cf., I.ii.64.

HAMLET
Excellent i' faith, of the chameleon's dish. I eat
the air, promise-crammed. You cannot feed
capons so.   95

i' faith: in faith, truly. **of:** "used to separate an object from the direct action of a verb … when the verb is used partitively, as 'eat of'" (Abbott §177). **chameleon's dish … promise-crammed:** Hamlet likens himself to the chameleon, which, in addition to being thought to change color to simulate what it touched, was believed to feed on the air, cf., Ovid *Metamorphoses*, XV.11–12, Browne *Vulgar Errors*, III.21, Tilley M 226, and *Two Gentlemen* II.i.172–74 (all cited in Jenkins). ● Hamlet implies that he is being fed on nothing but promises, hence "air," with a pun on *heir* (cf., I.ii.109 and lines 341–42 below), continuing to play, for the King's ears, at the thwarted-ambition mania that he took up in response to the accusation of Rosencrantz and Guildenstern (see II.ii.252 and note) and that he presumes they will have reported to the King. **capons:** castrated roosters fattened for slaughter, but not (like the chameleon) on air or (like Hamlet) on the promise of being the heir, "A veiled hint that Hamlet suspects the King of designs against him" (Jenkins).

KING

I have nothing with this answer, Hamlet. These words are not mine.

have nothing with: do not understand (Riverside). **These words are not mine:** I am not master of them because I cannot make sense of them, or perhaps "They grow not out of mine; have no relation to anything said by me" (Caldecott), or they are not "an answer to my question" (Riverside), or they are not "for me, to do with me" (Jenkins).

HAMLET

No, nor mine now. [*To Polonius.*] My lord, you

nor mine now: "A man's words, says the proverb, are his own no longer than he keeps them unspoken" (Samuel Johnson, quoted in Furness), Tilley W 776 (cited in Jenkins). **S.D.** [*To Polonius*]: Q2 nor mine now my Lord. / You playd, F nor mine. Now my Lord, you plaid. Both seem corrupt. "Q1 [My lord, you playd] suggests [that the words 'My lord'] were said to Polonius in performance" (Jenkins). For Hamlet's addressing Polonius as "my Lord" cf., II.ii.522.

played once i' th' university, you say?

played: acted.

POLONIUS

That did I, my lord, and was accounted a good actor.   100

HAMLET

What did you enact?

POLONIUS

I did enact Julius Caesar. I was killed i' th' Capitol. Brutus killed me.

Julius Caesar: Shakespeare's own *Julius Caesar* appeared three years before Q1 and five before Q2 of *Hamlet*. **Brutus killed me:** In a metatheatrical point, Jenkins writes, "It is likely enough that the roles of Caesar and Brutus in [Shakespeare's *Julius*] *Caes*[*ar*] (first performed in 1599) were taken by the same actors as now played Polonius and Hamlet; so that 'Hamlet' would already have killed 'Polonius' in a previous play, and, ironically, is to do the same 'brute part' in this."

HAMLET

It was a brute part of him to kill so capital a calf there.   105

brute: brutish, with a pun on Brutus. **part:** role (in a play), undertaking (historically). **so capital a calf:** a complex layering of puns. The relevant senses of *capital* that the OED records in use at the time include (1.) relating to the head, (2.) involving loss of the head, mortal (as a capital crime), and (6.) "chief, principal" (Schmidt), head, used of persons, like a "capital burgess," or places, like "a capital manor" or "a capital town." The word was not yet in use in sense (7.) excellent, first-rate. Shakespeare treated the assassination of Julius Caesar, in *Hamlet* and elsewhere, as an archetypal historic political disaster, cf., I.i.113ff. and V.i.213–216. Hence, as in *Julius Caesar*, Brutus's killing of Caesar was terribly wrong however nobly intended. Shakespeare is here using the word in sense (6.) but pushing it beyond itself to mean "of the nature of a chief, leader-like," with additional puns on sense (2.) "a calf so mortally dangerous to be killed" and on "Capitol" in the previous line. Hence, it was brutish for Brutus to kill so world-leader-like, so dangerous-to-be-sacrificed, and so Roman-Capitol-worthy a victim. As applied to Caesar "calf" means "sacrificial animal," with the various senses of "capital" genuinely intended. As applied to Polonius it means "fool," with the various senses of "capital" meant ironically. E. K. Borthwick suggests that "calf" may also be a pun on Latin *calvus*, "bald." And "to kill a calf" seems to have been the name of a kind of skit or possibly a declamation performed in mummery plays. ● Hamlet's excitement over the potential outcome of the play-within-the-play has energized his wit to the "top of his bent."

Be: cf., line 28 note, Abbott §300. **ready:** cf., line 45 and note and V.ii.222. ● Hamlet's own "readiness" will be tragically absent in the next scene but become evident in his regeneration in V.ii.

stay upon your patience: wait for your permission (Raffel).

Be the players ready?

ROSENCRANTZ
Ay, my lord, they stay upon your patience.
QUEEN
Come hither, my dear Hamlet, sit by me.
HAMLET
No, good mother, here's metal more
attractive.   110

metal more attractive: a double pun: literally metal more magnetic and figuratively mettle (= spiritedness) with more personal and erotic drawing power for him. **metal:** Q5, mettle in Q2 and F. The two words were originally one, but their distinct senses had separated before the two spellings did in the 18th C. See morphology at OED Mettle, and cf., I.i.96.

[*Turns toward Ophelia and lies at her feet.*]

s.d.: not in Q2, F, or Q1. Light on such "customs of gallantry may be given by Fletcher, *Queen of Corinth*, I.ii.194–7, 'The fine courtier ... tells my lady stories, ... lies at her feet At solemn masques', and Gascoigne, 'The Green Knight's Farewell to Fancy' (line 16), which lists among court pleasures 'To lie along in ladies' laps'" (Jenkins).

POLONIUS
[*Aside to the King.*] O, ho! do you mark that?

O, ho! do you mark that?: ● Polonius remains fixed upon the idea that Hamlet's madness derives from thwarted love of Ophelia, and Hamlet intentionally reinforces that notion.

HAMLET
Lady, shall I lie in your lap?
OPHELIA
No, my lord.
HAMLET
I mean, my head upon your lap?
OPHELIA
Ay, my lord.   115

shall I lie in your lap: with a pun on the female genitalia (OED *sb.*¹ 5. and 2.b.). "Hamlet first implies, then [line 114] affects not to have meant, an indecent meaning .... But more significant [than lying at Ophelia's feet] is the situation in the Morality plays (as excellently shown by M. Collins, *N&Q*, CCXXVI, 130–2), where a youth, by lying in the lap of a temptress, puts himself in her power and is betrayed"

HAMLET
Do you think I meant country matters?

(Jenkins). Thus Hamlet is offering to let Ophelia betray him yet again as she did in the previous scene, and as his mother (if the Ghost is an honest one) betrayed his father.

country matters: sexual love, the first syllable of *country* being a common pun on the female pudendum (spelled "queynte" in Chaucer and apparently derived from the adjective now spelled "quaint"), cf., Donne, "The Good-morrow" line 3, *Birth of Merlin* II.i.18, and Dekker, *Westward Ho* V.i.170 (all three cited in Jenkins). • As at lines 93–95 Hamlet continued to play at thwarted-ambition mania, here he is continuing to play at the sex preoccupation mania that he took up in response to Polonius's unjust presumption about him and Ophelia's rejection, which invited him to choose the cliché madness of the unrequited lover with which to begin his pretense of madness, cf., II.ii.72ff. and III.i.102ff. and notes.

OPHELIA
I think nothing, my lord.

nothing: • Ophelia is trying to humor him.

HAMLET
That's a fair thought to lie between maids' legs.

fair: a) lovely (partly earnest, partly sarcastic), b) chaste, pure, setting up the following pun.
maids': virgins'.

OPHELIA
What is, my lord?   120

HAMLET
Nothing.

Nothing: not anything, implying virginity (Jenkins), with a complex pun on "no thing," *thing* implying either the male or the female genitalia (*nothing* = figure 0). Hence, it is a) a chaste thought to think of virginity, b) a pure thought to think of no male "thing" between virgins' legs, and c) a (sarcastically) lovely (= inappropriate, strange) thought to think of no female "thing" "between maids' legs," and cf., II.ii.428 and note.

OPHELIA
You are merry, my lord.

merry: full of jokes, happy.

HAMLET
Who, I?

OPHELIA
Ay, my lord.

HAMLET
O God, your only jig-maker. What should a man   125
do but be merry, for look you how cheerfully my
mother looks, and my father died within's two hours.

your only: the best. **your:** the colloquial indefinite sense, cf., I.i.138 note. **only:** in the sense "above all," "surpassing," Abbott §58, cf., IV.iii.21. **jig-maker:** merry-maker, maker of jigs, the comical music and dance routines performed after serious plays, cf., II.ii.500 and note. **but:** if not, except. **within's:** within these, i.e., within these last two hours, a sarcastic exaggeration that Ophelia takes as further evidence of madness to be humored.

OPHELIA
Nay, 'tis twice two months, my lord.

twice two months: • An example of Shakespeare's freedom in indicating the passage of time. At certain moments we are to feel that only hours or days have passed, at others, as here, months. Some time has passed as implied by comparing this line with I.ii.147–51, but the intention is not strictness of chronology but relevance to the development of plot, character, and theme.

HAMLET

So long? Nay then, let the devil wear black, for I'll have
a suit of sables. O heavens, die two months ago, and   130
not forgotten yet? Then there's hope a great man's
memory may outlive his life half a year.

But by'r lady a must build churches then, or else shall

a suffer not thinking on, with the hobby-horse, whose
epitaph is "For O, for O, the hobby-horse is forgot."   135

The trumpets sound. A dumb-show follows.

black: simple mourning clothes, and the color of the devil. **sables:** sober clothes edged in the fur of the sable, a species of weasel. • Most commentators imagine a contrast between mourning clothes (black) and fancy court wear (sables) and find Hamlet offering sarcastically to change out of mourning clothes since his father has been dead so very long. But "sable" was also a synonym for black and was associated with melancholy and mourning. Hamlet's sarcasm lies in his offer to bequeath his youth's simple black mourning clothes to the devil and to take up an old man's sober wear, the point being that the four months Ophelia makes seem like a long time, which it is in relation to Hamlet's earlier "two hours," is, in relation to the memory of the dead king, equivalent to the time it takes a young man to turn old (Jenkins LN substantially).

by'r lady: an oath, by the Virgin Mary. **a:** he, as often in the play, including the next line. **churches:** monuments to his reign to be remembered by.

not thinking on: not being thought of. **hobby-horse:** "a traditional character in the morris dance and the May Games" is "described by Nares as 'the figure of a horse fastened round the waist of a man, his own legs going through the body of the horse, and enabling him to walk, but concealed by a long foot-cloth; while false legs appeared where those of the man should be, at the sides of the horse.'" The figure appeared in the refrain of a popular song, "For O, for O, the hobby-horse is forgot" (cf., *Love's Labor's Lost* III.i.28–29). "From its frequent use we seem to have an instance of a catch-phrase continuing in popularity after the original point of it had been lost. What is certain is that the hobby-horse, while very much remembered, became a byword for being forgotten and as such the occasion for numerous jokes in Elizabethan plays" (Jenkins LN).

S.D.: • As Jenkins discusses in an excellent long note, though dumb-shows were common, the following one is unusual in being an exact pantomime of the plot of the play-within-the-play about to be performed. This literal 'prequel' Shakespeare invents for the sake of dramatic irony and tension. Because we in the audience have heard the Ghost's recounting of the facts surrounding his death, we are more awake to the import of the dumb show than the characters onstage. Ophelia represents the innocent bystander who cannot be expected to get the "point" of the dumb show without explication. As Professor Mary Holmes taught, calling the medieval cathedral "the Bible of the illiterate" is erroneous. One cannot learn a story from a visual image alone. One must know the story already for the image to convey significance. But even if Claudius, based on what we find out later, must see in the dumb show an unsettling parallel to his own actions, he does not react to it. It is the reenactment of the poisoning in the spoken play, whose words make the meaning of the gesture explicit, together with Hamlet's commentary about the winning of Gonzago's wife, that drives Claudius to burst out of self-control. Whether or not the dumb-show has initiated that movement, it has heightened the expectation of the King's outburst in us, the audience, which is its purpose. And it is important to remember that until Claudius rises, and in fact not for certain until the next scene, do even we know whether the report of the Ghost has been a true one. Thus both dumb show and the play-within-the-play, differently for the various characters and for the audience, are arranged to place all the focus of tension on the moment of Claudius's outburst and on his soliloquy in the next scene.

Raising the un-Shakespearean but common question "how is it that the King, whose conscience is so well caught when he sees his crime re-enacted in the play, remains unmoved by the dumb-show?" Jenkins quite effectively dispenses with various critical "explanations": 1) There is a "textual anomaly, whereby alternative versions are conflated"; 2) Claudius missed seeing the dumb-show, being busy whispering with Gertrude or placed where he could not see it; 3) Claudius saw it but didn't understand it; 4) Claudius saw it and understood it but "was strong enough to stand the sight of his crime once but not twice." All these theories depend on hypothetical additions to what Shakespeare has given us. But "It is surely not an oversight but Shakespeare's dramatic tact which leaves the King out of the dialogue at this stage: how *he* reacted to the dumb-show is a question the play not only does not answer but is careful not to ask. And though it reckons without the critic in the study, it counts on the spectator in the theatre not to ask the question either. He will see the King's suspicions rising first in the questions of lines [232–33]: the numerous critical accounts of a tense struggle going on before that between the King and Hamlet or within the King himself describe what is in the critics' minds and not in the play at all.

●NOTE TO ACTORS "The problem which is thus, strictly, no problem may nevertheless present itself ... to the producer and still more to him that plays the King. How should the actor behave during the dumb-show? If he wishes to be faithful to Shakespeare, as many do not, he will neither blench at seeing the dumb-show nor whisper so as not to see it. To the curious spectator's eye, giving no more clue than the text does, he must remain inscrutable" (Jenkins LN).

s.d. *She kneels ... him*: F, not in Q2, "*She kneels* must, in view of *he takes her up* [which *is* in Q2], represent an omission in Q2" (Jenkins). *protestation*: affirmation (of her love). *declines*: leans, lowers. *lies him*: he lies down, lays himself down, "*him*" being an ethical dative. *bank of flowers*: likely to be a stage property (Jenkins substantially). *Anon*: right away. *passionate action*: emotional gestures. *seem to condole*: pretend to express sorrow for her. *gifts*: cf., I.v.43. *harsh*: resistant to his seduction.

Enter a King and a Queen, the Queen embracing him, and he her. She kneels and makes show of protestation unto him. He takes her up and declines his head upon her neck. He lies him down upon a bank of flowers. She, seeing him asleep, leaves him. Anon comes in another man, takes off his crown, kisses it, pours poison in the sleeper's ears, and leaves him. The Queen returns, finds the King dead, makes passionate action. The Poisoner with some three or four come in again, seem to condole with her. The dead body is carried away. The Poisoner woos the Queen with gifts. She seems harsh awhile, but in the end accepts love.

[Exeunt.]

OPHELIA

What means this, my lord? 136

HAMLET

Marry, this is miching malicho. It means mischief.

OPHELIA

Belike this show imports the argument of the play. 140

Enter Prologue.

HAMLET

We shall know by this fellow. The players cannot keep counsel; they'll tell all.

What means this: Ophelia, not knowing of the Ghost's appearance to Hamlet, cannot get the point of the dumb show on her own, see S.D. note after line 135.

miching: Q2 *munching*, F *Miching*, Q1 *myching*, sneaking, lurking, being up to no good, pronounced with short *i*, the *ch* pronounced as in *chin*, and the stress on the first syllable, cf., Florio *WW*, page 4 ("*acciapinare*: to miche, to shrug or sneake in some corner") and John Minsheu, *Ductor in Linguas, the Guide into Tongues*, 1617 ("To Miche, or secretly to hide himself out of the way, as Truants doe from schoole") (both quoted in Jenkins LN), and cf., *1 Henry IV* II.iv.408. **malicho:** Q2 *Mallico*, F *Malicho*, Q1 *Mallico*, mischief (from Spanish *malhecho*, bad deed, evil action), pronounced with a short *i*, the *ch* pronounced as in *chin*, and the stress on the second syllable. ● Hamlet picks up Ophelia's two *m*'s and multiplies the alliteration (and consonance on ch and assonance on the short i), climaxing in the word *mischief*, which the play-within-the-play both depicts and embodies, for it is mischievously (if the Ghost is not honest) using the image of mischief to unmask the King's mischief (if the Ghost is honest).

Belike: perhaps. **argument:** plot, message, or point. ● Ophelia is correct that it does.

know by this fellow: "Dumb-shows, like the pageants from which they derived, often had a 'presenter' to explain their meaning to the spectators. Cf. the Act-Prologues in *Locrine*; *Spanish Trag[edy]* I.iv.138ff.; *M[idsummer] N[ight's] D[ream]* V.i.12[7]ff. But the 'fellow' in this case does not do as expected, so that the play begins with the stage-audience unwarned" (Jenkins), cf., S.D. note after line 135.
The players ... tell all: ● This is not only a joke based on the obvious fact that players come onto the stage to speak, not to keep secrets. It is also a fundamental principle of understanding Shakespeare's drama. Though too many critics have spent too much ink in inventing meanings Shakespeare does not give us based upon assumptions he did not make, Hamlet here reminds us that the purpose of a play is not to keep things hidden but to reveal them, and like the play-within-the-play, *Hamlet* itself will reveal all. The most salient example of misreading based on the ignoring of this principle is the belief that Hamlet's essence is too mysterious for us to comprehend, see line 366 note and Introduction, page 1. **keep counsel:** keep a secret (OED *counsel sb*. 5.d.), cf., IV.ii.11–12.

OPHELIA
Will a tell us what this show meant?

HAMLET
Ay, or any show that you will show him. Be not
you ashamed to show, he'll not shame to tell you   145
what it means.

OPHELIA
You are naught, you are naught. I'll mark the
play.

PROLOGUE
For us and for our tragedy,
Here stooping to your clemency,   150
We beg your hearing patiently.

                                            [*Exit.*]

HAMLET
Is this a prologue, or the posy of a ring?

OPHELIA
'Tis brief, my lord.

HAMLET
As woman's love.

            Enter [the player] King and Queen.

PLAYER KING
Full thirty times hath Phoebus' cart gone round   155

a: he. **show:** the dumb-show.

or any show: "The obvious indecency, acknowledged
by Ophelia's rebuke, may be heightened by a pun
on shoe, referring to the woman's sexual part
(Trivium, IV, 108-11)" (Jenkins). In that article G.I.
Williams contends that shoe as a "symbol for the
female genitals" was widespread among Elizabethan
dramatists, that *show* and *shoe* were homonymic, and
that the pun is "probable" here (Williams). If so, it
operates only in line 144, where the first "show" is a
noun, and suggests with the sense "show" Ophelia's
duplicity in III.i, and with the sense "shoe" more of
Hamlet's pretense of thwarted-love madness become
indecent sex mania. **Be not you:** if you be not, so long
as you be not (subjunctive).

naught: naughty, immoral, from the literal sense
"nothing" via the sense "of no worth."

For us ... patiently: ● These three tetrameter rhyme
lines announce the beginning of the onstage play to
both the play-acting audience and the real one. They
and the rhymed couplets, archaic diction, inversions
of word order, and aphorisms that follow distinguish
the style of the play-within-the-play as both serious
and artificial, so that we recognize it as a significant
work of art in the context without confusing it
with the "real" world of the play we are watching.
stooping: bowing. **clemency:** mercy (in judging our
performance). **patiently:** modifies "your hearing,"
not "We beg."

posy: "a syncopated [i.e., abbreviated] form of
poesy (which, even when written in full, was often
pronounced in two syllables) ... a short motto,
originally a line or verse of poetry, and usually in
patterned language, inscribed on a knife, within a
ring, as a heraldic motto, etc." (OED). Inscribed on
the inner surface of a ring, it was "necessarily short"
(Riverside). Cf., *As You Like It* III.ii.270–72, *Merchant of
Venice* V.i.147–50, Middleton *Chaste Maid in Cheapside*,
I.i.188–91 and other references (cited in Jenkins).

As woman's love: ● Hamlet is thinking of his mother
as well as playing again at the madness of the broken-
hearted lover.

Full thirty times ... sacred bands: The "artificial
elaboration of style characteristic of an older period
... is especially manifest in the opening periphrastic
time-formulae, with which compare Green's
Alphonsus, IV.i.9ff... . and *Selimus*, lines 37ff... . There
is no reason to suspect parody" (Jenkins LN). The
style was not necessarily limited to older works: "The
Player King is exercising his grammar school learning
in elegant variation," a style "admired and approved
by the pedants of the time, both in verse and in prose,"
and "So late as 1688, John Twells, Schoolmaster, [in

Neptune's salt wash and Tellus' orbed ground,

And thirty dozen moons with borrowed sheen
About the world have times twelve thirties been
Since love our hearts and Hymen did our hands
Unite comutual in most sacred bands.

PLAYER QUEEN
So many journeys may the sun and moon

Make us again count o'er ere love be done.
But woe is me, you are so sick of late,
So far from cheer and from your former state,

That I distrust you. Yet though I distrust,
Discomfort you, my lord, it nothing must.
For women's fear and love hold quantity,
In neither aught, or in extremity.

Now what my love is, proof hath made you know;
And as my love is sized, my fear is so.
Where love is great, the littlest doubts are fear;
Where little fears grow great, great love grows there.

PLAYER KING
Faith, I must leave thee, love, and shortly too.
My operant powers their functions leave to do,

And thou shalt live in this fair world behind,
Honored, beloved, and haply one as kind
For husband shalt thou—

PLAYER QUEEN
                            O confound the rest.

Cicero Redivivus, page 43] is to point out a similar elegancy" (Baldwin II.400–401). • This play-within-the-play, to be clear, is Shakespeare's invention and imitation, not a quotation from any actual play of the time. And we are never told specifically which if any of the lines we hear are penned by Hamlet, cf., line 180 note. **Phoebus' cart:** the chariot of Apollo, god of the sun. **gone round:** the yearly (not the daily) cycle, hence thirty years.

Neptune's salt wash: Neptune is god of the sea, hence the ocean. **Tellus' orbèd ground:** Tellus is the goddess of the earth, hence the globe of the earth.

moons: i.e., months. **borrowed sheen:** reflected shining.

Hymen: god of marriage.

160 **comutual:** mutually (cf., "comeddled," line 69). **bands:** bonds. • As in Kyd's *Spanish Tragedy* and its Senecan precursors, the implied metaphysical background of the play-within-the-play is classical rather than explicitly Christian, from which custom Shakespeare's own play is a radical departure, cf., line 258 and Introduction, pages 2–3.

o'er: over. **ere:** before.

cheer and ... former state: a hendiadys for former state of cheerfulness (Wright, page 187). **state:** condition.

165 **distrust:** fear for (Riverside); worry about (Raffel).
nothing: not at all, used adverbially (Abbott §55).
hold quantity: are proportional one to another, for F holds, cf., Abbott §336. **In neither ... extremity:** a compressed image: [either] in neither [love nor fear] anything, or excess [in both], i.e., when women love they also fear and they do both either not at all or extremely (Abbott §388a).
proof: experience (having proven).

170 **And as ... is so:** my fear is as great in size as my love.

Faith: a mild oath, in faith, by my faith.
operant powers: vital faculties, cf., Heywood, *Royal King and Loyal Subject* I.i.37–38, and Webster, *Appius and Virginia* V.ii.108 (cited in Jenkins). **leave to do:** cease to perform, leave off functioning, the infinitive used as a noun (Abbott §355).

175 **behind:** after me.
haply: perhaps.

confound the rest: • The Player Queen interrupts the Player King, wishing destruction on the uncompleted idea that she would remarry. Her phrase, intended by the imaginary author of "The Murder of Gonzago" (or by Hamlet, if he wrote

Such love must needs be treason in my breast.
In second husband let me be accurst;
None wed the second but who killed the first.   180

HAMLET
[*Aside.*] That's wormwood.

PLAYER QUEEN
The instances that second marriage move

Are base respects of thrift, but none of love.

A second time I kill my husband dead
When second husband kisses me in bed.   185

PLAYER KING
I do believe you think what now you speak,

---

these words) to heighten the irony, foreshadows the greater irony of the destruction that will literally fall upon Gertrude's remarriage.

must needs: must necessarily.

None wed … kisses me in bed: ● If these lines were written by Hamlet, neither in them nor at III.iv.29 is Hamlet accusing Gertrude of literally participating in the murder of his father. The intent, both here and there, is metaphorical. In refusing to see and distance herself from Claudius's guilt, Gertrude becomes morally culpable. **None wed … the first:**
● The sentence is hyperbole, whether the lines are by Hamlet or not, and its metaphor can be taken in two senses. Either the phrase uses the plural sense of "none" (OED 2.b.) and an indicative verb, i.e., generally no women wed a second husband except those who have killed their first (Jenkins substantially), or let no woman marry a second husband except she who (will admit to having) killed her first husband (Kittredge substantially). For the subjunctive used optatively or imperatively, see Abbott §364.

wormwood: a very bitter herb (*Artemisia absinthium*).

instances: causes, impelling motives (OED 2.), the subject, not the object, of "move," i.e., what causes people to remarry. **move:** cause, prompt, "second marriage" being the direct object.

base respects of thrift: merely low and unworthy considerations of success or thriving, i.e., practical advantage. **none of love:** i.e., are not at all considerations of love.

kill … dead: "The tautology is idiomatic. Cf. *Tit[us Antronicus]* III.i.92 … and see *OED* kill *v.* 2c. Hence it is unnecessary to explain, with Dowden and Kittredge, that the second killing is of a husband already dead" (Jenkins), i.e., "I kill my husband a second time when I kiss a second husband." But the poet of the Sonnets is perfectly capable of reinforcing the doubleness (of killing and of marriage) in the meaning of the couplet with doubleness in its form, possibly adding to the couplet form itself the ambiguity of the two senses of "kill my husband dead" (to "kill dead" and "dead husband"), knowing that either sense in which members of the audience hear the phrase will convey the meaning and perhaps that some of them will hear it in both senses, cf., "He hath" at I.ii.58 and note.

● SPEECH NOTE: **I do believe … first lord is dead:** The Player King's disquisition on the alteration of purpose with time ironically foreshadows the Player Queen's betrayal of her intention and prefigures the speech of Claudius to Laertes at IV.vii.110–23. Jenkins properly notes that "The echo here of sentiments expressed elsewhere by Hamlet reflects … not Hamlet's mind but that of the creative dramatist fashioning his design…. With *purpose … memory … forget* (ll. [188, 192] cf. Hamlet's vow to *remember* (I.v.92–112) … ; with the interdependence of friendship and fortune (ll. [200–209] cf. II.ii.[363–66], III.ii.60–71, and the whole career of Rosencrantz and Guildenstern; with the discrepancy between intention and achievement (ll. [211–13]) cf. V.ii.[382–85]" (Jenkins LN). However, the speech goes beyond the commonplaces about changes of mind arising from changes of fortune to hint at the deeper question of the moral and spiritual direction of such turnings. It thus serves as foreshadow and foil for all alterations of purpose in Hamlet and in his foils. Fortinbras goes wrong in revolting against the terms of his father's combat with Hamlet Senior (I.i.86–95 and I.ii.24) but goes right in heeding his uncle's chastisement (II.ii.68–70), for the latter turning reaping the reward of a kingdom. Laertes errs in allowing his purpose of revenge to be turned by Claudius to betrayal and murder but then is righted by the prospect of immediate death, which turns his purpose to repentance and forgiveness. Horatio errs in purposing desperate suicide but then submits to Hamlet's correction and the better purpose of telling Hamlet's story. Most centrally Hamlet will go wrong in turning his purpose from killing Claudius to damning him (III.iii) and will go right in heeding the correction of Providence, revealed on the sea voyage and in the graveyard, by which his will is turned toward "readiness" (V.ii.10–11 and 219–24).

> But what we do determine oft we break.
> Purpose is but the slave to memory,
> Of violent birth, but poor validity,
> Which now, the fruit unripe, sticks on the tree,   190
> But fall unshaken when they mellow be.

determine: intend.

Purpose ... mellow be: Purpose is at first held firmly in the mind by the one who conceives it, as unripe fruit is firmly attached to the tree that produces it, but in time, as ripened fruit falls from the tree by no external force ("unshaken"), so purpose is abandoned. **Purpose:** intention. **Of violent birth:** born in intense feeling. **validity:** health and strength, hence longevity. **Which:** i.e., the "Purpose" of line 188. **Which ... sticks ... fall ... they:** "The subject ['Which,' referring to 'Purpose'], which is singular, is here confused with, and lost in, that to which it is compared ['fruit'], which is plural" (Abbott §415). **mellow:** ripe. • "For a rewording of the thought, see lines [194–95]" (Jenkins).

> Most necessary 'tis that we forget
> To pay ourselves what to ourselves is debt.

necessary 'tis: it is inevitable. **that we forget ... debt:** that we neglect to fulfill promises we make only to ourselves.

> What to ourselves in passion we propose,
> The passion ending, doth the purpose lose.   195

What ... lose: Intentions or plans ("What ... we propose") that we make in moments of passion we neglect to fulfill when the passion ends. • This theme will be dramatically and to the Renaissance audience shockingly realized in the following scene, when Hamlet's own purpose alters at III.iii.87 (see SPEECH NOTE at line 186).

> The violence of either grief or joy
> Their own enactures with themselves destroy.

The violence ... destroy: Extreme grief and extreme joy destroy the actions they inspire along with themselves in the process. For the number shift cf., I.ii.38 and Abbott §412, and cf., lines 188–91 note and Abbott §415. **violence:** extremity, vehemence (OED

Where joy most revels, grief doth most lament,
Grief joys, joy grieves, on slender accident.

This world is not for aye, nor 'tis not strange   200

That even our loves should with our fortunes change,
For 'tis a question left us yet to prove,
Whether love lead fortune, or else fortune love.
The great man down, you mark his favorite flies;

The poor advanced makes friends of enemies.   205
And hitherto doth love on fortune tend,

For who not needs shall never lack a friend,
And who in want a hollow friend doth try

Directly seasons him his enemy.

But orderly to end where I begun,   210

Our wills and fates do so contráry run
That our devices still are overthrown;

Our thoughts are ours, their ends none of our own.

So think thou wilt no second husband wed,
But die thy thoughts when thy first lord is dead.   215

PLAYER QUEEN
Nor earth to me give food, nor heaven light,

Sport and repose lock from me day and night,

5.). **enactures:** acts, deeds, carryings out in action (OED's only instance). **with themselves:** together with themselves, i.e., extremes of both grief and joy destroy themselves along with the actions that proceed from them.

Where joy … joy grieves: Where joy and grief are greatest, they turn to their opposites. **on slender accident:** "with slight occasion" (Riverside).

This world … his enemy: "These sentiments on friendship and fortune go back ultimately to Cicero's *De Amicitia*. With line [203] cf. Cicero's 'Non igitur utilitatem amicitia, sed utilitas amicitiam secuta est'. For the tradition, see [James I. Wimsatt, 'The Player King on Friendship', in *Modern Language Review*, 65.1 (1970), 1–6]" (Jenkins). **aye:** always, ever.

loves: cf., I.i.173 and note.

question: a medieval *quaestio* as at III.i.55. **left us yet to prove:** yet remains to be resolved.

you mark: you will see that. **favorite:** Q2, "one chosen as an intimate by a superior" (OED 2.), F "favorites." Abbott argues for the F reading on the grounds that the intention is "to describe the *crowd of favourites scattering in flight* from the fallen patron" (§333, "Third person plural in –s"), but the departure from Q2 is unnecessary if one takes the singular "favorite" as representative of a type. **flies:** flees, runs away.

advanced: having risen in fortune.

hitherto: thus far. **tend:** wait, depend. • i.e., love depends on fortune (answering the question of lines 202–203) to the extent illustrated in the previous two lines and further illustrated in the following three.

who not needs: whoever does not need (a friend).

in want: in need. **hollow:** empty, not to be trusted. **try:** test.

seasons him: ripens him into, brings him to maturity as (OED *v.* 4.), cf., I.iii.81, III.iii.86.

begun: began, "past indicative forms in *u* are very common in Shakespeare" (Abbott §339).

contráry: stress on second syllable (Abbott §490).

devices: plans, intentions, purposes. • cf., "deep plots" at V.ii.9. **still:** always.

ends: outcomes, results, cf., V.ii.10. **none of our own:** not belonging to us, not in our control, cf., line 97.

think … / But die thy thoughts: Several combinations of indicative and subjunctive senses may be intended: if you think, or you may think, or go ahead and think, but your thoughts will die, or they must die, or go ahead and let them die.

Nor: neither. **give … lock … turn … be … meet … destroy … pursue:** optative subjunctive forms of the respective verbs, i.e., let neither earth give me food nor heaven give me light, etc. (Abbott §364).

Sport … night: let day shut me out from (OED lock *v.*¹ 4.) recreation and night from rest.

To desperation turn my trust and hope,
An anchor's cheer in prison be my scope,

anchor's cheer: the condition, including but not limited to food, of an anchorite or hermit. **scope:** goal, aim, range of mental or physical activity (cf., OED senses 2., 6., and 7.).

Each opposite that blanks the face of joy   220
Meet what I would have well and it destroy,

Each opposite ... destroy: Let whatever would ruin my joy destroy whatever I might wish to have succeed. **blanks:** "blanches, makes pale (a symptom of grief)" (Riverside) or "less probably, makes blank, nullifies" (Jenkins).

Both here and hence pursue me lasting strife,

here and hence: "in this world and the next" (Kittredge). • The effects in the afterlife of choices made in the life in this world are a central concern of the play, cf., Introduction and II.ii.603, III.i.78 ("The undiscovered country"), III.iii.61 ("There"), III.iii.86 ("passage"), IV.v.135 ("both the worlds"), etc.

If once a widow, ever I be wife.

If once ... wife: F, Q1, and Riverside, Q2 "If once I be a widow, ever I be a wife," Jenkins "If, once a widow, ever I be a wife." Both Q2 and Jenkins, given the style of the play-within-the-play and the position of this ending rhymed couplet, are less satisfactory metrically.

HAMLET
If she should break it now.

PLAYER KING
'Tis deeply sworn. Sweet, leave me here awhile.   225

If she ... now: • Opposing the practical wisdom of the Player King, the Player Queen has called seven lines of curses upon herself if she ever breaks her promise, and Hamlet here, the Player King in line 225, and Gertrude in line 230 recognize the hyperbole in her words.

My spirits grow dull, and fain I would beguile
The tedious day with sleep.
                                        [*He*] *sleeps.*

fain: gladly, willingly. **beguile:** while away.

PLAYER QUEEN
                    Sleep rock thy brain,
And never come mischance between us twain.
                                        [*Exit.*]

mischance: misfortune.

HAMLET
[*to Gertrude*] Madam, how like you this play?

QUEEN
The lady doth protest too much methinks.   230

protest: declare solemnly. **methinks:** it seems to me, from the obsolete verb *think* (OED *v.*¹), meaning to seem or appear, with the dative of the pronoun.

HAMLET
O but she'll keep her word.

KING
Have you heard the argument? Is there
no offence in't?

argument: theme or subject-matter or the summary of either (OED 6. and 7.). **offense:** "cause for objection" (Jenkins), "offensive matter" (Riverside). • "the pointed remarks on second marriage are ... provocation enough [to evoke the question]. The King appears to be alerted first on the Queen's behalf rather than his own" (Jenkins).

HAMLET
No, no, they do but jest, poison in jest. No offence
i' th' world.   235

KING
What do you call the play?

jest: pretending, "make believe" (Jenkins).
poison: • Though the dumb show implied the idea, Hamlet here verbally anticipates the play-within-the-play. **offence:** as at I.v.137, Hamlet quibbles on the word, now intending the sense "crime" (Riverside and Jenkins substantially).

HAMLET

The Mousetrap. Marry, how? Tropically. This
play is the image of a murder done in Vienna.

Gonzago is the duke's name, his wife, Baptista.

You shall see anon, 'tis a knavish piece of work, but   240

what of that? Your Majesty and we that have

free souls, it touches us not. Let the galled jade
wince; our withers are unwrung.

Enter Lucianus.

The Mousetrap: ● The irony of the phrase is
intensified by our knowledge that the actual title of
the play is "The Murder of Gonzago" (II.ii.537–38),
and of course by II.ii.604–605. There may also be a
reference to St. Augustine's "allusion to the cross of
Christ as the mousetrap of the devil, who is trapped
by his own corruption" (Jenkins, referring to J.
Doebler in *SQ*, xxiii, 161ff.). **Marry, how? Tropically:**
I am not persuaded by Jenkins' argument that Q2's
reading, "mary how tropically" (which he edits to
"marry, how tropically!"), as "Hamlet's delighted
exclamation at his own conceit" is better than the
F reading, adopted here and by most editors, which
indicates a directly wild and whirling intensification
of the conceit itself aimed at Claudius. **Tropically:**
by a trope or figure of speech. ● Baldwin argues that
here "Shakspere has referred specifically to tropes" as
defined in Chapter VI, *De tropis*, of Quintilian: "By
a *trope* is meant the artistic alteration of a word or
phrase from its proper meaning to another" (Baldwin
II.229 and note 123, quoting Quint. Vol. III, page 301).
There may also be a pun on "trap" (perhaps the point
of the Q1 spelling "trapically") and possibly an allusion
to the cry "marry trap!" (reversed here in "Mousetrap.
Marry"), apparently used to indicate having paid
someone back for a trick or an insult, cf., *Merry Wives*
I.i.167 (Jenkins substantially).

duke's: a slip, hinting at the original story of the
actual poisoning of the Duke of Urbino at the
instigation of Luigi Gonzaga, on which Shakespeare
presumably based the plot for "The Murder of
Gonzago" and the manner of Hamlet Senior's death,
changing the names and the place to Vienna. "It was
obviously the intention to translate the Duke and
Duchess of the original into a King and Queen the
better to image events in Denmark.... All three texts
read 'King' at line [244]" (Jenkins LN).

You shall see anon: The punctuation (after "Baptista"
in line 239, after "anon," and after "work") of neither
Q2 (commas) nor F1 (colons) resolves the question of
what the King shall see anon: the "murder" of line 238,
that it is "a knavish piece of work," or both. **anon:**
right away. **knavish:** meaning (to the King) vulgar
and (to the audience) also mischievous, deceitful, cf.,
line 137. **piece of work:** instance of artistry, in this
case a play.

we: nominative pronouns are used for objective
"when they stand quasi-independently at some
distance from the governing verb or preposition"
(Abbott §216).

free: i.e., of sin, not merely without the awareness
of guilt, but without guilt itself, cf., II.ii.564, V.ii.332.
Let the galled ... unwrung: Jenkins notes that "The
proverbial expression [linking the wincing horse to
the guilty conscience] is very common," citing Tilley
H 700 and quoting John Lyly's *Euphues* [page 107]:
"for well I knowe none will winch except she bee

This is one Lucianus, nephew to the king.
OPHELIA
You are as good as a chorus, my lord.   245

HAMLET
I could interpret between you and your love
if I could see the puppets dallying.

gawlded, neither any bee offended vnlesse shee be guiltie". **galled ... wince:** a jade is an old or worn-out horse, and to be "galled" is to be "rubbed sore, esp. on the withers through an ill-fitting saddle. For a literal instance, see *I H[enry] IV* II.i.[6]" (Jenkins). **wince:** Q1, winch Q2, F, the two words are "different forms of the same word" (Jenkins), which, when applied to a horse, meant not only to recoil or flinch but to "kick restlessly from impatience or pain" OED wince $v.^1$ 1. and winch $v.^1$ 2. **withers:** the ridge between a horse's shoulders. **unwrung:** not chafed, not rubbed raw.

nephew: ● Here, as with Pyrrhus in II.ii, Shakespeare achieves a double application in making the murderer the Player King's nephew, thereby drawing a parallel not only between Lucianus and Claudius as being near kin to their victims, but between Claudius and his own nephew, Hamlet, who in the next scene will seek not merely to kill him (as Claudius killed Hamlet Senior) but to damn him. Jenkins in his long note makes a strong point of the parallel, but there and in his introduction he finds in Hamlet's character both goodness and evil (Hyperion and satyr) as equal and necessary though opposite qualities (page 146): "the evil being ineradicable, the mission requires Hamlet to submit to its corruption. A man who embraces his human lot must consent to be a sinner" (page 157 note). This un-Shakespearean assertion would condemn Hamlet and all men to a living hell in which no choices of the human free will can be good. It is at once the fate-bound pagan world of *Oedipus Rex* and the nature-bound modern world in which Jenkins finds that Hamlet lives. In either of those worlds to do one's duty is inescapably to choose evil. This cannot have been a belief of Shakespeare, and it is not in reality the thrust of the play. Hamlet does go wrong, but not perforce. He need not, in order to fulfill the duty to revenge, seek to damn Claudius (with which intention he stabs Polonius through the arras) in addition to killing him. He chooses to do so. He might have chosen not to do so, and that is precisely the point of the play, to raise the question how a man may fulfill that duty without tainting his mind. And the play resolves the question by the end. A man who embraces his human lot may go wrong, but, providential opportunity provided, he may again go right before he dies. Shakespeare's vision is neither pagan nor Existentialist but essentially Christian.

interpret: "In a puppet-show the man who 'interprets' is he who supplies the verbal accompaniment of the puppet action and so makes clear to the audience what is going on. Cf. [*Two Gentlemen* II.i.95]" (Jenkins), *Timon of Athens* I.i.34, Greene *GW*, 1592, page 14. **between you and your love:** between her behavior (rejecting his advances, II.i.106–107 and serving as a decoy, III.i.42–45, 130) and her love for Hamlet, also between her and some imaginary lover with whom she is being unchaste, and also between her and her father and

OPHELIA
You are keen, my lord, you are keen.

HAMLET
It would cost you a groaning to take off mine
edge.   250

OPHELIA
Still better and worse.

HAMLET
So you mistake your husbands. Begin, murderer;

leave thy damnable faces and begin. Come, the

croaking raven doth bellow for revenge.

LUCIANUS
Thoughts black, hands apt, drugs fit, and time
                                                          [agreeing,   255

the King, with whom she is being morally unchaste
in betraying her true lover. **puppets:** cf., line 246
note. **dallying:** idly amusing themselves, especially
amorously. ● Hamlet says that if he could see what
the puppets (Ophelia and her "love") were doing,
he could supply the dialogue or the explanation.
He thereby implies that Ophelia has been a mere
puppet, worked by others, namely her father, who
has set her first to reject Hamlet's love (I.iii.131ff.)
and then to serve as decoy for his and the King's
eavesdropping (III.i.43ff.). He is also playing once
again ironically on the sex theme by implying that
Ophelia might be unchaste when the reality is that
she has been forbidden to associate with Hamlet in
order to preserve her chastity from his supposed
dishonorable lust, a focus that continues in the
following lines.

keen: bitterly sharp in wit, but Hamlet takes it in the
sense of sexually hungry, aroused.

groaning: the sound made at the labor (digging,
carving, killing) that dulls the edge of a sharp
instrument, the sound made during sexual
intercourse, and the sound made in childbirth.

Still: always. **better and worse:** more witty and more
indecent. ● "The better, the worse" was a common
catch phrase, from the Latin *"Quo melius, eo pejus,"*
reputedly what Diogenes said of dancers (Tilley B 333,
ref. in Jenkins), cf., *Twelfth Night* I.v.73–77.

you: i.e., women generally. **mistake:** i.e., mis-take,
"cf. *R[ichard]* II III.iii.16–17 … . *Bartholomew Fair*
II.ii.101–102 … . and other examples in Furness"
(Jenkins), and cf., "take" in the wedding vow "I *N.*
take thee *N.* to my wedded husbande, to have and to
hold from this day forewarde, for better, for worse"
in the Book of Common Prayer of 1552 (http://justus.
anglican.org/ resources/bcp/1552/Marriage_1552.
htm), implying, with Gertrude's and Ophelia's
betrayals in mind, that women take their husbands
falsely (not intending to do so for better *and* for
worse), with a pun on "must take," the Q1 reading,
which is how the audience might easily hear the
phrase.

leave: stop, leave off making. **damnable faces:**
perhaps an example of the overacting Hamlet
cautioned against at lines 17ff.. **begin:** i.e., speaking.

croaking … revenge: "Recognized by Simpson
(*Academy*, 19 Dec. 1874) as a telescoping of two lines
from the anonymous *True Tragedy of Richard III*"
(Jenkins), the main evidence that the play may have
been a source for Shakespeare's own *Richard III*. ● No
doubt "The Murder of Gonzago" was to end with an
avenger killing Lucianus, but Hamlet here, playing
at madness still, jumps the gun, calling for revenge
before the murderer has murdered. The line is evoked
perhaps by impatience, or by the same calculation
that a few lines later (lines 263–64) impels Hamlet,
possibly seeing the King already reacting to the
poisoning, to drive the point home by disclosing the

next part of the plot. But the line also suggests that even as the action of Lucianus sharpens the edge of Hamlet's own desire for revenge, as the violence of Pyrrhus was meant to sharpen it (II.ii.448ff.), Hamlet intends for both himself and the King to feel that murder and revenge are inextricable.

Confederate season, else no creature seeing,

Confederate: F, Q2 Considerat. **Confederate season:** "the time being my ally" (Riverside), an epithet for "time" in the previous phrase explicated by the following phrase. The time ("season") confederates with the murderer because no one is there to observe him committing the murder, cf., "the time / Which now suits with it" (*Macbeth* II.i.59–60). **else no creature:** no creature else.

Thou mixture rank of midnight weeds collected,

rank: foul-smelling, festering, loathsome, offensive (OED 12. and 14.), the several senses uniting to imply that the mixture both is foul in itself and causes corruption. **of:** from (Abbott §165), cf., IV.vii.141.

With Hecate's ban thrice blasted, thrice infected,

Hecate's ban: the curse of the goddess of witchcraft. ● An internal example of the observation that the metaphysical background of revenge plays before *Hamlet* was classical as opposed to Christian (see Introduction, pages 2–3). **thrice … infected:** Hecate was thought of as three-natured in various senses, usually as goddess of night, of the underworld, and of the moon, hence of dark magical arts, cf., *Midsummer Night's Dream* V.i.384, *King Lear* I.i.110, and *Macbeth*, II.i.52, III.ii.41, and the non-Shakespearean passages in *Macbeth* at III.v and IV.i.39–43. **blasted:** blighted.

Thy natural magic and dire property

Thy natural … property: the power nature gives and its capacity to produce horrible effects.

On wholesome life usurp immediately.   260

Pours the poison in his ears.

On wholesome life usurp: take over or steal the healthy life (of the victim), cf., OED usurp *v*. 2. and 9. (*To usurp on*). **usurp:** F, Q2 usurps. ● The F reading sorts far better with the direct address to the drug at line 257 ("Thou mixture"). Lucianus is not merely observing what the drug does but exhorting it to do its vile work, cf., V.ii.322. S.D. *Pours … ears*: F, not in Q2.

HAMLET

A poisons him i' th' garden for his estate. His

A: he. **for his estate:** "Apparently echoing a folklore motif. Cf. *The Revesby Play*, 'for your estate we do your body kill'" (Jenkins), as Claudius has killed Hamlet Senior for *his* "estate," i.e., the kingdom and the Queen. **him … His:** the sleeping king, cf., line 239 and II.ii.537–38.

name's Gonzago. The story is extant, and written

The story … Italian: "This was probably true … , though Shakespeare's actual source has not been traced" (Jenkins), cf., line 239 note. **extant:** existing, published.

in very choice Italian. You shall see anon how the murderer gets the love of Gonzago's wife.

choice: "fine, excellent" (Raffel). **You shall see … wife:** see line 254 note. **anon:** right away.

OPHELIA

The King rises.   265

The King rises: "Cf. an actual incident when, as a result of a 'scandalous representation' before Elizabeth [I], 'the Queen was so angry that she at once entered her chamber using strong language, and the men who held the torches … left [the actors] in the dark' (Cal[endar of] S[tate] P[apers], Spanish, 1558–67, page 375)" (Jenkins).

HAMLET

What, frighted with false fire?

QUEEN

How fares my lord?

POLONIUS

Give o'er the play.

KING

Give me some light, away!

POLONIUS

Lights, lights, lights!   270

Exeunt all but Hamlet and Horatio.

HAMLET

Why, let the strooken deer go weep,
    The hart ungallèd play;
For some must watch while some must sleep,
    Thus runs the world away.

Would not this, sir, and a forest of feathers, if the rest   275
of my fortunes turn Turk with me, with Provincial
roses on my razed shoes, get me a fellowship in a cry
of players?

HORATIO

Half a share.

HAMLET

A whole one, I.   280

---

frighted with false fire: frightened by the firing of a weapon with no bullet, i.e., a mere stage representation. ● Notice the alliteration expressing Hamlet's excitement, cf., lines 137–38 and note.

Give o'er: stop.

Give me some light: a call for torches to light his way out. ● With the inescapable implication that the King is suddenly feeling himself in the darkness of sin as well, which he has hinted at (III.i.49–53) and will confirm in the next scene (III.iii.36ff.).

s.h. Polonius: Q2, F "All," which "obviously means to increase the commotion" (Jenkins).

Why, let … world away: ● Whether Hamlet is quoting from or imitating a ballad unknown to scholarship (Jenkins LN substantially) or composing his own on the spot, the point of the distinction between wounded (female) deer and unwounded (male) hart and between watchers and sleepers is that the play has succeeded in dividing the guilty, wounded by the arrow that was the play-within-the-play, from the innocent, cf., *As You Like It* II.i.33–40ff., and "In one of Peacham's emblems a wounded deer running about with the arrow in its side represents a man of guilty conscience, whose characteristic is to 'seek his ease, by shifting of his ground' while neglecting the means which 'might heal the sin' rankling within (*Minerva Britanna*, 1612, page 4)" (Jenkins LN). **strooken:** struck, stricken, for *strucken*, an irregular form of the past participle (Abbott §344), cf., *Comedy of Errors* I.ii.45, *Love's Labor's Lost* IV.iii.220, *Julius Caesar* III.i.209. **ungallèd:** unwounded. **watch:** stay awake.

this: the success of the theatrical stratagem.
sir: Horatio. **feathers … roses:** "The flamboyance of feathers on the hat and rosettes on the shoes characterizes the costumes of actors" (Jenkins), particularly of "tragic actors" (Riverside). **turn Turk:** "lit. become an infidel; hence play false, be treacherous" (Jenkins). **Provincial roses:** thick multi-petaled decorative rosettes on costume shoes, originally growing out of and later hiding the shoe ties, that imitated an actual variety of French rose variously claimed to be Province (*Rosa centifolia*), Provins (*Rosa gallica*), or Damask (*Rosa damascene*) (Jenkins LN substantially). **razed:** decorated with slashes in the leather. **fellowship:** membership, part ownership. **cry of players:** pack (as of hounds) of actors, implying an analogy between the cry of hunting dogs and the speech of actors. ● As Hamlet has set the actors on to hunt the guilt of Claudius.

Half a share … whole one: "A sharer in a company of players, as distinct from a hired man, was joint owner of its property and participated in its profits (see Chambers, *El[izabethan] St[age]*, i.352–5).

For thou dost know, O Damon dear,
   This realm dismantled was
Of Jove himself, and now reigns here
   A very, very—pajock.

HORATIO
You might have rhymed.   285

HAMLET
O good Horatio, I'll take the ghost's word for a
thousand pound. Didst perceive?

HORATIO
Very well, my lord.

HAMLET
Upon the talk of the poisoning?

HORATO
I did very well note him.   290

HAMLET
Ah, ha! Come, some music; come, the
recorders.
For if the King like not the comedy,
Why then belike he likes it not, perdie.
Come, some music.   295

Enter Rosencrantz and Guildenstern.

GUILDENSTERN
Good my lord, vouchsafe me a word with
you.

HAMLET
Sir, a whole history.

GUILDENSTERN
The King, sir—

HAMLET
Ay, sir, what of him?   300

GUILDENSTERN
Is in his retirement marvelous distempered.

The system also permitted of half-shares"
(Jenkins), Halliday, page 19.

For thou ... pajock: probably not a quotation (Jenkins,
following Verity), as line 285 seems to confirm;
Damon: 4th century B.C. Pythagorean famous for
his mutually loyal friendship with Pythias (properly,
Phintias), possibly also "A traditional shepherd name
from pastoral poetry, appropriately addressed to one
who has the ancient virtues of the golden age before
the realm was 'dismantled'" (Jenkins). **dismantled:**
divested, robbed. **Of:** from, away from (Abbott §165,
§166), cf., *Antony and Cleopatra* III.vi.28–29 ("of the
triumpherate / Should be depos'd"). **Jove:** a reference
to Hamlet's father, cf., III.iv.56. **pajock:** Q2 paiock,
F Paiocke, F2 Pajocke. • The expected rhyme word
was *ass*, and Hamlet both implies that rhyme and
substitutes a word referring either to the pride of
Claudius (if it is a variant or misprint of "peacock,"
cf., Dyce quoted in Furness) or to his being a base,
degenerate fellow (assuming the word is a variant
of *patchock*, "a contemptuous diminutive of *patch*,"
i.e., fool, clown, dolt) and pronounced "*padge-ock*"
(Jenkins LN substantially).

talk: "The dialogue [of Lucianus at lines 255–60
and of Hamlet at line 261] and not merely the s.D.
[after line 260] (added in F) shows there to have been
more than talk" (Jenkins).

note: observe, notice. • Horatio, the rational
and balanced man, confirms the evidence of the
King's guilt.

recorders: small wooden wind instruments.

For ... comedy: referring to and playing on the
lines "And if the world like not this tragedy, / Hard
is the hap of old Hieronimo" from Kyd's popular
Spanish Tragedy (IV.i.191–92), referring also to a
play-within-the-play that was to be the instrument
of Hieronimo's revenge for the murder of his son, see
Introduction, page 2. **belike:** likely, probably. **perdie:**
the oath "by God," from the French *pardieu*, here
pronounced pur-DEE.

vouchsafe: grant.

retirement: withdrawal to his rooms. **marvelous:**
wondrously, extremely, here three syllables, Q2
meruilous, F maruellous, used adverbially, cf., II.i.3
and Abbott §1. **distempered:** angry, from the root
meaning out of temperament or unbalanced in the

HAMLET
With drink, sir?

GUILDENSTERN
No, my lord, with choler.

HAMLET
Your wisdom should show itself more richer
to signify this to his doctor, for for me to put   305
him to his purgation would perhaps plunge him
into more choler.

GUILDENSTERN
Good my lord, put your discourse into some frame
and start not so wildly from my affair.

HAMLET
I am tame, sir. Pronounce.   310

GUILDENSTERN
The Queen your mother, in most great affliction of
spirit, hath sent me to you.

HAMLET
You are welcome.

four humors, which were blood (Latin *sanguis*, excess of which caused a sanguine or jolly temperament), phlegm (Greek *phlegma*, excess of which caused a phlegmatic and dull temperament), black bile (Greek *melan*, black, + *chole*, bile, excess of which caused melancholy), and yellow bile (Greek *cholera*, a disease causing vomiting and excretion of bile, from *chole*, bile, excess of which caused a choleric or bilious temperament, quickness to anger), cf., SPEECH NOTE after I.iv.38, for *dis-* cf., Abbott §439.

drink: Hamlet pretends to take distemper in the sense of indigestion (a result of excess yellow bile) or drunkenness, a common meaning of the word, cf., the "heavy-headed revel" he criticizes at I.iv.17, *Henry V* II.ii.42, 54, and *Othello* I.i.99.

choler: anger, but Hamlet takes it in the root sense of yellow bile, cf., line 301 note.

more richer: a common doubling of the comparative, cf., II.i.11 and Abbott §11. **doctor:** ● Hamlet pretends to take the report of the King's anger to mean that the King has a medical problem that requires a physician to reduce the excess bile in his body. **for me to put ... would:** for pronoun and infinitive as subject see Abbott §354. **purgation:** both removing an excess humor from the body and, in Catholic doctrine, removing sin from the soul through repentance, specifically penance (= satisfaction, the third of the four parts of repentance, the others being confession, contrition, and absolution). Incomplete penance in this life requires the soul to complete it in Purgatory, whence the Ghost implies he has come, cf., I.v.10–13. **would perhaps... more choler:** because if the purgation of either the King's humor or his sin were up to Hamlet, the King might end up in still greater anger because a) being no doctor I might worsen his medical condition, and b) I might kill him and send his soul to Purgatory, or possibly to hell, where he would suffer the greater anger of God.

frame: order, "logical structure" (Riverside), "systematic form" (Jenkins), as recommended by Thomas Wilson in *The Art of Rhetorique* (1553) (quoted in Baldwin II.135–36), cf., I.ii.20, *Two Gentlemen of Verona* III.ii.75, *Love's Labor's Lost* III.i.191, IV.ii.138, *1 Henry IV* III.i.121–22, *Measure for Measure* V.i.61, and OED 5., which quotes this line. **start:** leap, rush (OED 2. and 4.). **from my affair:** away from the subject of my message to you.

The Queen ... to you: ● Trying to get a straight answer from Hamlet, Guildenstern postpones delivering his message with mere formalities of courtesy.

You are welcome: ● Willfully misunderstanding Guildenstern to mean that "sent me to you" is the point, Hamlet offers the intentionally misplaced courtesy of bidding him welcome, as if to a visitor from his mother, cf., V.ii.170 note.

GUILDENSTERN

Nay, good my lord, this courtesy is not of the right
breed. If it shall please you to make me a wholesome   315
answer, I will do your mother's commandment. If not,
your pardon and my return shall be the end of
my business.

HAMLET

Sir, I cannot.

GUILDENSTERN

What, my lord?   320

HAMLET

Make you a wholesome answer. My wit's
diseased. But sir, such answer as I can make,
you shall command, or rather, as you say, my
mother. Therefore no more but to the matter.
My mother, you say—   325

ROSENCRANTZ

Then thus she says: Your behavior hath struck her
into amazement and admiration.

HAMLET

O wonderful son that can so stonish a mother!

But is there no sequel at the heels of this mother's
admiration? Impart.   330

ROSENCRANTZ

She desires to speak with you in her closet ere you
go to bed.

HAMLET

We shall obey, were she ten times our mother.

---

right breed: appropriate kind, but also appropriate manners, proper form of politeness, breeding. **wholesome answer:** rational reply. **do your mother's commandment:** i.e., to deliver her message. **pardon:** indulgence, leave, cf., I.ii.56, IV.vii.46. **return:** to the Queen.

behavior: conduct, manners. **struck:** Q2's stroke is an early form of the same word. **amazement:** confusion, bewilderment. **admiration:** wonder (from Latin *ad* + *mirari*, to wonder, be astonished).

wonderful: full of wonders (playing on the root sense of "admiration" in the previous line), extraordinary. **stonish:** astonish.

sequel: follow-up, completion of the thought. **at the heels:** following. **Impart:** tell, relate. ● Hamlet's elevated diction ("Pronounce" at line 310, "sequel," "Impart") pokes fun at that of the courtiers, cf., V.ii.112–20.

She desires ... to bed: ● Hamlet's "behavior" and Gertrude's supposed "amazement and admiration" serve as convenient pretexts to summon Hamlet to a meeting already planned before the play (III.i.181–89) (Jenkins substantially). **closet:** private room, inner chamber, see II.i.74 note. **ere:** before.

We shall obey ... with us: ● Hamlet uses the royal plural ("We" and "us") in this speech "for the only time in the play" (Jenkins), perhaps because he now feels justified in thinking of himself as the rightful king of Denmark, cf., IV.iv.5 note. **were she ten times our mother:** Hamlet will go to chastise Gertrude even if she were his mother ten times over, and therefore to be honored tenfold, referring to the fifth of the Ten Commandments, "Honor thy father and thy mother" (Exodus 20:12, Deuteronomy 5:16) and possibly to those of the other nine commandments he believes Gertrude has broken, cf., *Richard II*, V.ii.101 ("twenty times our son"). The phrase may also imply the opposite of honoring her. He will obey his mother by going to her room even if she were ten times over the betrayer and morally the murderer of his father, as, after the reaction of the King to the play-within-the-play, he now knows she may be, cf., III.iv.29.

Have you any further trade with us?

ROSENCRANTZ

My lord, you once did love me.   335

HAMLET

And do still, by these pickers and stealers.

ROSENCRANTZ

Good my lord, what is your cause of distemper?

You do surely bar the door upon your own liberty if you
deny your griefs to your friend.

HAMLET

Sir, I lack advancement.   340

ROSENCRANTZ

How can that be, when you have the voice of the
King himself for your succession in Denmark?

HAMLET

Ay, sir, but while the grass grows—the proverb
is something musty.

Enter the Players with recorders.

O, the recorders. Let me see one.— [*to*   345
Rosencrantz and Guildenstern.] To withdraw
with you, why do you go about to recover the
wind of me, as if you would drive me into a toil?

GUILDENSTERN

O my lord, if my duty be too bold, my love is too
unmannerly.

HAMLET

I do not well understand that. Will you play upon   350
this pipe?

GUILDENSTERN

My lord, I cannot.

HAMLET

I pray you.

GUILDENSTERN

Believe me, I cannot.

HAMLET

I do beseech you.   355

GUILDENSTERN

I know no touch of it, my lord.

trade: business, commerce.

pickers and stealers: hands, from the Church of
England catechism, in which, just after the Ten
Commandments, the list of duties to one's neighbor
includes "to keep my hands from picking and stealing,"
with a play on the common oath "by this hand," and
possibly a reference to the falseness of the "trade" (line
334) of Rosencrantz and Guildenstern.

your cause of distemper: the cause of your distemper,
for the transposition see Abbott §423. **distemper:**
madness, cf., line 301 note.

bar the door ... liberty: cf., the talk of prisons at
II.ii.241–251. **deny ... to:** withhold from. **friend:**
● "It was a recognized function of a friend that you
could unburden your heart to him" (Jenkins).

advancement: promotion. ● Hamlet, to Rosencrantz
and Guildenstern, fosters the notion that his madness
arises from thwarted ambition, as to Polonius through
Ophelia he has fostered the notion that it arises from
unrequited love, see Introduction, page 13.

voice: expression of opinion, vote, approval.
cf., I.ii.108–109, V.ii.356. **succession:** to the throne.

proverb: i.e., "While the grass grows, the steed
starves," another attempt to keep Rosencrantz and
Guildenstern focused on ambition as the cause of
Hamlet's "distemper." **something musty:** a little stale,
therefore not worth quoting in full.

withdraw: draw apart, to speak privately.

recover the wind ... toil: an image from hunting: the
hunter goes upwind of the quarry, which gets his scent
and runs the opposite way into the "toil," the snare or
net set to catch it (Jenkins substantially).

if my duty ... unmannerly: the emphasis is on the
word "love": if my service (to King, Queen, and Prince)
offends by being too bold, it is my love (rather than any
bad motive) that is to be blamed for my discourtesy.

I do not ... that: Hamlet pretends not to follow the
logic, implying to us that actual love could not lead to
discourtesy, cf., Polonius's conclusion at I.iii.78–80.
pipe: recorder.

pray: request.

beseech: entreat, request more intensely.

HAMLET

It is as easy as lying. Govern these ventages with your fingers and thumb, give it breath with your mouth, and it will discourse most eloquent music. Look you, these are the stops.   360

GUILDENSTERN

But these cannot I command to any utterance of harmony. I have not the skill.

HAMLET

Why look you now how unworthy a thing you make of me. You would play upon me, you would seem to know my stops, you would pluck   365 out the heart of my mystery, you would

---

easy as lying: possibly proverbial. **ventages:** (from Latin *ventus*, wind) the holes in a wind instrument, seven for the fingers and one for the thumb, that determine the pitch of its notes, also called "stops," as in line 360.

But these cannot I command: "these" made emphatic by repetition from the previous line, whence the transposition (Abbott §425).

stops: cf., line 360.

mystery: ● J. V. Cunningham (Sem.) pointed out that the primary sense is derived from Latin *ministerium* (service, occupation, from Latin *minister*, servant) rather than from Latin *mysterium* (Greek *mysterion*, secret rites, from Greek *mystes*, priest of the secret rites of divine worship). Hamlet means that Rosencrantz and Guildenstern are trying to discover his ministry, his business, what he is up to. He does not mean they are trying to perceive the essence of his mystery in the other sense, as if Shakespeare were trying to convey that his character would never be understood, even by the audience. Of course Shakespeare could pun on the homonym, and whoever is responsible for Q1 seems to have taken it in the latter sense ("You would search the very inward part of my hart, / And dive into the secret of my soule.") But Shakespeare cannot have meant that Hamlet's inner life must be forever hidden not only from Rosencrantz and Guildenstern but from everyone, including his bosom friend Horatio and the audience, as if Hamlet were a living person, whose inner life no one could know, rather than a fictional character. The play is written precisely to reveal the trajectory of Hamlet's inner life to the audience, not to obscure it or to claim it to be unfathomable. The full implication of the pun comes in the next scene when Hamlet himself tries to pluck out the heart of God's mystery in both senses, what God is up to in the judgment of souls (*ministerium*) and the secrets of the divine will (*mysterium*). For God alone, not for Hamlet, *ministerium* and *mysterium* are one, not to be fathomed by mortal men. Rosencrantz and Guildenstern's attempt to fathom Hamlet's cause and Hamlet's attempt to play God arise out of ignorance and pride. All fail before knowledge and depth greater than their own. But the play is not about the eternal mystery of its main character. It is about the eternal necessity to perform each our *ministerium* by being ready to bow before the divine *mysterium*. The overweening of Rosencrantz and Guildenstern is a foil for Hamlet's own in a different realm. As with Hamlet's advice to the players, Hamlet's warning here ought to serve, *mutatis mutandis*, as a warning to himself.

sound me from my lowest note to the top of my compass; and there is much music, excellent voice, in this little organ, yet cannot you make it speak.

'Sblood, do you think I am easier to be played on than a pipe? Call me what instrument you will, though you fret me, you cannot play upon me. 370

Enter Polonius.

God bless you, sir!

POLONIUS
My lord, the Queen would speak with you, and presently. 375

HAMLET
Do you see yonder cloud that's almost in shape of a camel?

POLONIUS
By th' mass and 'tis, like a camel indeed.
HAMLET
Methinks it is like a weasel.
POLONIUS
It is backed like a weasel. 380
HAMLET
Or like a whale.
POLONIUS
Very like a whale.

sound: measure the depth of.

compass: musical range of an instrument.

this little organ: Hamlet is referring literally to the recorder (OED 1.), which he is holding, but there may be some reference to his own organ of speech if he points to his mouth or throat (OED 5.b., cf., *Twelfth Night* I.iv.33), and, by implication, to himself as an instrument of the intended revenge (OED 7.).

'Sblood: the oath "by his blood," referring to the blood of Christ.

fret: punning on a) annoy, irritate, vex, and b) furnish a musical instrument with frets, the cross bars on the neck of a lute or guitar to regulate the fingering. • "Hamlet switches from wind to stringed instrument for the sake of the pun on *fret*" (Jenkins).
fret me: This edition, following Jenkins, Q2 fret me not, F1 can fret me, Q1 can fret me, yet. • "Ed[itor]s almost invariably retain *can* [before "fret"], though this is surely an intrusion in F (and Q1) rather than an omission from Q2. Hamlet not merely can be but is being fretted, and the musical paradox is the greater if you actually fret the instrument and still cannot play it. Modern ed[itor]s who read *yet* with Q1 assume that the nonsensical *not* of Q2 is a misreading of it. This is also to assume, however, that the two good texts are each in error independently" (Jenkins).

presently: right away. • This report, concise and direct compared to that of Guildenstern at lines 311–27, reminds us that Polonius has the spy's reason for hastening Hamlet into Gertrude's rooms to "find him" (III.i.185), yet Polonius too, attempting to humor the apparently mad prince, will nonetheless be more manipulated than manipulating.

Do you see ... by and by: "Polonius, humouring the madman, would seem to know his stops; but it is Hamlet who calls the tune, and it is only when Polonius has piped to it that he consents to answer him" (Jenkins LN), cf., V.ii.101 note. **cloud:** not necessarily indicating a change of location: "the cloud may be as imaginary as the shapes Polonius is persuaded to see in it" (Jenkins LN). **in shape:** *the* is often omitted before a noun modified by prepositional phrase (Abbott §89).

By th' mass: an oath, "by the Eucharistic liturgy."

HAMLET

Then I will come to my mother by and by.—
[*Aside.*] They fool me to the top of my bent.—I will
come by and by.   385

POLONIUS

I will say so.

Exit.

HAMLET

By and by is easily said.— Leave me, friends.
Exeunt all but Hamlet.

'Tis now the very witching time of night,

When churchyards yawn and hell itself breathes out

Contagion to this world. Now could I drink hot blood   390

And do such bitter business as the day
Would quake to look on. Soft, now to my mother.

O heart, lose not thy nature. Let not ever

---

by and by: soon, cf., V.ii.293.

They fool me ... bent: • In his aside Hamlet is again reminding us that he is not in fact mad despite his mad-seeming speech. **top of my bent:** to the height of my capacity, cf., II.ii.30 note.

• **SPEECH NOTE:** In the following speech Hamlet is not exulting "in hate, vindictiveness, and blood lust," as Jenkins writes, but acknowledging that the time suits with the killing he knows he is now obligated to perform because the Ghost has been demonstrated to be honest. In relation to his mother the speech shows that chastening and not violence is on Hamlet's mind, indicating that his mind is not yet tainted. Hamlet *will* "come closest to the villain he would damn" (Jenkins LN), but not here. It is in the next scene that Hamlet wills not merely to kill but to damn Claudius and chooses to try to do so, and that will be his fall.

witching time: near midnight, the time of witchcraft, and just that time of night when the Ghost appeared on the battlements (I.i.7, I.iv.3–4).

churchyards yawn: graveyards open up to let out spirits of the dead.

Contagion to ... hot blood: a trimeter couplet according to Abbott §501, or possibly a regular pentameter line if "-gion to this" are elided into one unstressed syllable and "could I" similarly elided, "hot blood" being in any case a spondee. **Contagion:** poison, corrupting influence. **this world:** as distinct from the other world of heaven, hell, and purgatory. **drink hot blood:** • "It may not be irrelevant to recall that the rites of the witches' Sabbath included the drinking of human blood (cf. line [390])," writes Jenkins, who also sees in this passage, "in highly condensed form, the traditional night-piece apt to prelude a deed of blood" (Jenkins LN), cf., *2 Henry VI*, IV.i.1–7, *Macbeth*, II.i.49ff., *Rape of Lucrece* lines 162–68.

bitter business: "Revenge is 'bitter' in *Winter's Tale* I.ii.457, IV.iv.[773]" (Jenkins). **Soft:** hush, enough talking.

lose not thy nature: • It is characteristic of one's inherent feelings (and of the aristocratic ethos) to want revenge for the death of one's father (cf., I.v.81), and also not to want to hurt one's mother, an action the Ghost has forbidden (I.v.85–86), cf., the dilemma of Orestes in Aeschylus's *Libation Bearers*. Unlike Orestes, having expressed readiness to fulfill the first part of the Ghost's charge to avenge the murder of his father (I.v.25, 81–83), Hamlet now confirms his determination not to overstep the bounds by breaking the second part of the charge, which was not to harm his mother (I.v.84–86).

The soul of Nero enter this firm bosom.
Let me be cruel, not unnatural.   395

I will speak daggers to her, but use none.

My tongue and soul in this be hypocrites:

How in my words somever she be shent,

To give them seals never my soul consent.

Exit.

Act III, Scene iii

Enter King, Rosencrantz, and Guildenstern.

Nero: Roman emperor (54–68 C.E.), who killed his mother, Agrippina, who had killed the emperor Claudius, her husband and Nero's step-father, to make her son emperor.

speak daggers: cf., III.iv.95, "The image is anticipated in [*Much*] *Ado* II.i.[247–48] and *3 H[enry] VI* II.i.[98]" (Jenkins). **use none:** i.e., use no real dagger.
● NOTE TO ACTORS: The antithesis is between "speak" and "use."

hypocrites: pretenders to one another. ● What Hamlet thinks in his soul will not be represented in his words, i.e., he will threaten his mother in words without actually intending to harm her in action, as he makes clear in the next two lines.

How ... somever: Howsoever, however much, in whatever way or degree. **shent:** shamed, reproached (from the old verb *to shend*).

seals: a stamp in warm, soft wax that confirms a document, here a metaphor for an action confirming his words. **never my soul consent:** may my soul never consent to harming her however forcefully my words chastise her; the verb is "subjunctive (like line [397]) rather than imperative, with *my soul* nominative rather than (as often taken) vocative" (Jenkins).

Act III, Scene iii—A room in the Castle.
● SCENE NOTE: At the start of this scene, the climax and turning point of the play, we (the audience) have the following knowledge: a) that the King feels guilty for something, though we are not absolutely sure it is the murder of the former king, his brother; b) that Hamlet is now sure that the King is guilty of that murder; c) that Hamlet is now also sure of the Ghost's trustworthiness, and therefore of the justice of fulfilling the Ghost's imperative; d) that Horatio is in agreement with Hamlet; e) that Hamlet seems ready to act against the King; f) that Hamlet intends to chastise but not harm his mother, to whose room he is going first. As a result, we expect that when Hamlet next meets the King he will confront and kill him, either in a passionate rage or in cool reason. In either case we know that Hamlet has both the right and the duty to perform that act, as the receiver of the Ghost's explicit imperative, as the rightful king of Denmark, and as the chosen instrument of the divine vengeance. What actually happens in this scene is an utter surprise to the audience, partly because it takes place in a double-soliloquy rather than in dialogue and in non-action rather than in action, partly because it could not have been predicted from prevailing expectations based on Kyd's popular *Spanish Tragedy*, and most importantly because it signifies a terrible fall from grace in the soul of the protagonist of the play, whose wit, invention, and nobility have drawn us to identify with him and to approve of his mission.

KING

I like him not, nor stands it safe with us

> **like him not:** am not pleased with him, disapprove of him. **nor stands it safe with us:** nor is it safe for us (the royal plural).

To let his madness range. Therefore prepare you.

> **range:** move about freely, roam. ● In this speech the King shifts from the singular to the royal plural twice. The royal use of the plural arises from the Renaissance principle that a king is considered to have two bodies: He is both a particular individual and the embodiment of the state. Claudius first expresses a personal fear and then a public concern as the head of state, the alternation suggesting that after the play Claudius has just seen, the two bodies are not in harmony within him. Hamlet will play with this idea explicitly at IV.ii.27–28.

I your commission will forthwith dispatch,

> **I your commission will ... he to England shall:** transposition of verb and subject after emphatic words, here made emphatic by antithesis and "by natural importance" (Abbott §425). **commission:** instructions, charge. **forthwith:** immediately, speedily. **dispatch:** have executed, drawn up (Riverside).

And he to England shall along with you.

> **to England shall:** i.e., shall go, a common ellipsis (Abbott §405). ● the plan originated at III.i.169.

The terms of our estate may not endure   5

> **terms of our estate:** condition of my position or rank (as king).

Hazard so near's as doth hourly grow

> **Hazard:** risk, danger. **near's ... brows:** Q2, dangerous ... Lunacies F. Jenkins (LN) rejects the F readings here as not deriving from ms. copy, and there is no strong reason to mistrust Q2. **near's:** near us (again the royal plural).

Out of his brows.

> **brows:** his head, his mental condition, "the madness visible in his face (?)" (Riverside). Though Jenkins suggests "What grows out of the brows is generated in the head, i.e. plots, contrivances," Claudius is unlikely to be admitting to Rosencrantz and Guildenstern, lest he implicate himself, that the "Murder of Gonzago" performance constitutes a contrived plot against him, or even a form of defiance, as implied in the emendation of some editors to "braves" on the analogy of *Taming of the Shrew* III.i.15, *1 Henry VI* III.ii.123, and *Troilus and Cressida* IV.iv.137 (cited in Jenkins).

GUILDENSTERN

We will ourselves provide.
Most holy and religious fear it is
To keep those many many bodies safe
That live and feed upon your Majesty.   10

> **provide:** "equip, make ready. Cf. *A[s] Y[ou] L[ike It]* I.iii.[87]" (Jenkins).

> **many bodies ... Majesty:** i.e., the king's subjects, who depend on him for their welfare. **live and feed:** a hendiadys for "live by feeding" (Wright, page 187).

ROSENCRANTZ

The single and peculiar life is bound
With all the strength and armor of the mind

> **single:** individual. **peculiar:** personal, private, "of concern only to the individual possessor of it" (Jenkins).

To keep itself from noyance, but much more

> **noyance:** annoyance, harm.

That spirit upon whose weal depends and rests

> **weal:** welfare. **depends and rests:** the singular verb is often used with a following or deferred plural subject (Abbott §335).

The lives of many. The cess of majesty   15

Dies not alone, but like a gulf doth draw

What's near it with it. Or it is a massy wheel
Fixed on the summit of the highest mount,
To whose huge spokes ten thousand lesser things

Are mortised and adjoined, which when it falls,   20

Each small annexment, petty consequence,

Attends the boisterous ruin. Never alone

Did the king sigh, but with a general groan.

---

lives of many: cf., lines 9–10 note. **cess:** decease (OED *sb.*²), with a possible added sense of cessation, ending (OED *sb.*³). **majesty:** Q2 and F have Majesty, but Rosencrantz is speaking in general platitudes, not referring to Claudius specifically, cf., line 23 note.

gulf: maelstrom, whirlpool, with the possible additional sense of a yawning chasm.

it is: some editors emend "it is" to "'tis" to reduce the line from Q2's hexameter to pentameter, without textual authority (Jenkins substantially).
● NOTE TO ACTORS: If "Or" is given a heavy stress, even without elision to "'tis" "it is a" can easily be spoken as three quick unstressed syllables, making the line a regular pentameter. **massy:** huge and heavy, massive. **wheel:** Though this may recall it, this is not a reference to the wheel of Fortuna itself (cf., II.ii.229 note and 495 note), whose turning results in the fall of a king and to which the "summit of the highest mount" is irrelevant. Rather it is a metaphor for the king himself, whose fall drags his dependents down with him, though a confusion of the two images, suggested by the unusual image at II.ii.495–97, where it is Fortune's wheel that is to crash down a mountain, may be intended to signify a defect in Rosencrantz's understanding of Fortune's wheel (Jenkins substantially, citing Kittredge).

mortised and adjoined: joined, as the *tenon* or squared end of one timber is fitted into square hole or *mortise* of another. **which:** as to which, in relation to which (Abbott §272).

annexment: that which is annexed, attachment.
petty consequence: small result or effect, minor significance, and I think also "person of small consequence," deriving from the sense of OED consequence sb. 7.("Importance in rank and position"), though the OED does not record the use of the word to refer to a person.

Attends: waits upon, accompanies. **boisterous:** bulky, rough, noisy, violent. **ruin:** fall.

king: King in Q2 and F, but see line 15 note. **general:** universal, applying to all the people. Rosencrantz is not only flattering the King but also voicing a commonplace of the age. Since everyone in a state depends upon the health and wisdom of its king, his fall threatens ruin to all. Rosencrantz and Guildenstern, unaware of the guilt of Claudius, cannot know how immediate a threat their words will imply to Claudius, who responds to it by commanding speedy action. The audience hears in the speech the additional implication (unintended by Rosencrantz) of ruin attendant on the fall of Hamlet Senior. In the world of the play, the idea Rosencrantz expresses proves prophetically true, applying both to Claudius and to Hamlet, whose own moral fall in this scene will result in the ruin of the court.

KING

Arm you, I pray you, to this speedy voyage,

For we will fetters put about this fear   25
Which now goes too free-footed.

ROSENCRANTZ AND GUILDENSTERN

                    We will haste us.
          Exeunt Rosencrantz and Guildenstern.

          Enter Polonius.

POLONIUS

My lord, he's going to his mother's closet.

Behind the arras I'll convey myself

To hear the process. I'll warrant she'll tax him home,

And as you said, and wisely was it said,   30

'Tis meet that some more audience than a mother,
Since nature makes them partial, should o'erhear

The speech of vantage. Fare you well, my liege.
I'll call upon you ere you go to bed
And tell you what I know.

KING

                    Thanks, dear my lord.   35
                    Exit Polonius.

Arm you: make yourselves ready, a synonym for "prepare you" in line 2 above, cf., *Midsummer Night's Dream* I.i.117. **voyage:** F, viage Q2.

fetters: shackles, leg irons. **fear:** cause of fear.

free-footed: unshackled, unhampered.

he's going: as was suggested by Polonius himself at III.i.182–83 (Jenkins substantially) and pursued at III.ii.331–32, 374–75, and 392. **closet:** private room, see II.i.74 note.

arras: tapestry fabric, decorated with woven images, so called from the town of Arras in Artois, an area of Northern France just south of Flanders, where the cloth was made. The arras might screen an alcove or cover a wall at some distance from it, for adornment and presumably the retention of heat. **convey myself:** carry myself, steal. "This word often has the suggestion of furtiveness or stealth" (Jenkins), cf., *3 Henry VI* III.iii.160 and *Richard II* IV.i.317.

process: proceedings, conversation. **I'll warrant:** I assure you, probably pronounced as one syllable, as at I.ii.242. **tax:** accuse, reprove, blame, call to account. **home:** directly, thoroughly, to the heart of the matter. This speech is another of the many tension-building references to the coming meeting between Hamlet and his mother and to Polonius's third attempt (after II.ii.170ff and III.i.29ff.) to spy upon Hamlet in order to discern the true cause of his mad behavior, planned at III.i.181–85, set in motion at III.ii.331–33 and 374–75, continued at III.ii.392, and tragically completed in III.iv.

as you said, and wisely was it said: It was Polonius who first proposed (III.i.182–85) to eavesdrop on the conversation (Jenkins substantially), but neither he nor the King expressed the reason in these terms. This is flattery of the King characteristic of Polonius.

meet: appropriate, fitting. **audience:** hearer(s).

Since nature ... partial: Steevens notes a parallel to this platitude in Terence, *Heauton Timorumenos* (V.ii) (Baldwin *Five-Act*, 564). **them:** Gertrude and Hamlet, mother and son. **partial:** taking the side of one part, hence favoring, biased toward.

of vantage: the phrase modifies "o'erhear," not "speech," and implies any combination of three senses: a) in addition, cf., *Othello* IV.iii.84 and OED vantage 2b. and c., b) "from the vantage-ground of concealment" (Abbott §165), i.e., that position of observation or combat from which one gains an advantage, cf., *Macbeth* I.vi.7 and OED 3b., and c) taking the opportunity or chance, cf., *Cymbeline* I.iii.24 and OED

4b., to any of which senses may be added the possible overtone in Polonius's mind of a fourth more abstract sense d) from a superior position of knowledge (i.e., not being mad), cf., OED 4a. **Fare you well ... what I know:** The monosyllables here suggest a simplistic certainty in Polonius that will turn out to have been unwarranted.

● **SPEECH NOTE:** Only in the third line of the following speech do we the audience finally know for certain, thanks to the convention of the soliloquy as being the honest expression of the thought of the speaker, that Hamlet's suspicions were valid, that the Ghost told the truth, that the King is an incestuous fratricide and regicide, that Hamlet is the rightful king and therefore the rightful instrument of both human and divine justice in Denmark. Jenkins finds merely indecision in this speech, and ties it to a misreading of III.i.83–87, which he takes to imply a general "failure of resolution to translate itself into action." But the universe of this play is the Christian universe of Shakespeare and his audience. In the "To be" speech Hamlet was articulating not mere irresolution but fear of divine punishment for sin. Similarly here the King is not merely indecisive (cf., Epistle of James 1:8) but choosing to "retain the offense" when he is quite aware that to be saved he must surrender its fruits. As the inaction Hamlet contemplates at III.i.83ff. arises from the universal fear of eternal consequences of sin, here the King, similarly aware of the inevitability of divine judgment, is stuck in his sin for fear of giving up his this-worldly possessions and ambition.

Thus the King is an accurate analyst of his own spiritual condition. His will is not puzzled by lack of knowledge. Unlike the will of the repentant King David of 2 Samuel 12:1–13 and Psalm 51, whose sin in the matter of Uriah and Bathsheba that of Claudius resembles, the will of this king is frozen by attachment to the fruits of his sin. In a letter to James Hackett, Abraham Lincoln wrote "Unlike you gentlemen of the profession, I think the soliloquy in *Hamlet* commencing 'O, my offence is rank,' surpasses that commencing 'To be, or not to be.' But pardon this small attempt at criticism" (Lincolniana). Though he did not spell out what he meant by "surpasses," Lincoln is a profounder thinker than many a "gentleman of the profession." The King's soliloquy here dramatizes a man agonized in the throes of a profound moral crisis, aware of his situation and yet unable to resolve it. By contrast, Hamlet's "To be" soliloquy (III.i.55ff.) is a meditation on what all men generally do, and though it is applicable to the conditions of his own moral challenge there, it is calm and rational. The King's speech here conveys the moral agony of guilt. If we take Lincoln to mean surpasses in sheer emotional power, his opinion is entirely justified.

O, my offense is rank, it smells to heaven;

offense: the word appears four times in the speech, here and at lines 47, 56, 58, reflecting the repetitive, spiritually stuck condition of the King's thoughts. **rank:** gross, overgrown, foul, putrid. **to heaven:** cf., Genesis 4:10.

It hath the primal eldest curse upon't,

primal eldest curse: the reference is to Cain's murder of his brother Abel in Genesis 4, and specifically to the curse in verses 11–12, cf., I.ii.105 and V.i.77. ● Claudius has become not a physical but a spiritual fugitive.

A brother's murder. Pray can I not,

A brother's murder: ● In these words the honesty of the Ghost is finally confirmed for the audience. **A brother's murder. Pray can I not:** ● NOTE TO ACTORS: This is a pentameter line if both syllables of "murder" are stressed (Abbott §478) and "Pray can" is said as a trochee, or alternatively if "Pray" is given the length of a whole foot and "can" is stressed. **Pray can I not:** transposition after an emphatic word (Abbott §425). **Pray can I not, / Though ... will, / My stronger:** the commas of Q2, here retained, allow the subordinate "though" clause to modify either the previous or the following main clause. **inclination:** leaning, desire, impulse, natural tendency.

Though inclination be as sharp as will,

will: a layered term meaning literally that part of man's reason called "free will," the choice-making function that may choose to enact or to resist an "inclination," and having overtones of willfulness and also of sexual desire. ● He cannot pray for forgiveness even if his leaning toward doing so were as "sharp" (= intense, ardent, impetuous, cf., OED 4.) as will itself (the inner choice-maker and possibly also sexual desire), which, in reality, it is not, as he will explain. ● NOTE TO ACTORS: The subordinate clause "Though ... will" may be spoken as modifying either the previous or the following clause (or perhaps both as an intentional squinting modifier).

My stronger guilt defeats my strong intent,   40

guilt: sinfulness, attachment to the sin. **intent:** inclination or intention (here the intent to pray for forgiveness).

And, like a man to double business bound,

double business: namely continuing in his sin and turning in repentance. **bound:** sense a) tied to contrary purposes (OED bound *ppl. a.*² from *to bind*), and sense b) headed, directed in contrary directions (OED bound *ppl.a.*¹ from the ME verb *boun*).

I stand in pause where I shall first begin

stand in pause ... both neglect: ● the image echoes that of Pyrrhus standing as a "painted tyrant" doing nothing at II.ii.480–82 (Hogen substantially), as will Hamlet's own pause at line 75 below (cf., END NOTE below).

And both neglect. What if this cursèd hand
Were thicker than itself with brother's blood,
Is there not rain enough in the sweet heavens   45
To wash it white as snow? Whereto serves mercy
But to confront the visage of offense?

neglect: leave undone.

rain ... snow: cf., Deuteronomy 32:2, Psalms 51:7, Isaiah 1:18, Ecclesiasticus (Sirach) 35:20, and *Merchant of Venice* IV.i.184–85, also *Twelfth Night* V.i.392 and *King Lear* III.ii.77, where rain serves as a double image of both the trials of the material world and divine mercy working through them. **Whereto:** to what

And what's in prayer but this two-fold force,

To be forestallèd ere we come to fall,
Or pardoned being down? Then I'll look up.   50
My fault is past—but O, what form of prayer

Can serve my turn? "Forgive me my foul murder"?
That cannot be, since I am still possessed
Of those effects for which I did the murder:
My crown, mine own ambition, and my queen.   55
May one be pardoned and retain th'offense?

In the corrupted currents of this world

Offense's gilded hand may shove by justice,

And oft 'tis seen the wicked prize itself
Buys out the law. But 'tis not so above: 60

There is no shuffling; there the action lies

purpose, to what end. ●i.e., what is the purpose of mercy if not to address offense, since the unoffending do not require mercy.

what's in ... down: what else is prayer for but to plead either for help in avoiding sin or for pardon once one has sinned. **prayer:** probably two syllables for the meter, as in George Herbert (OED, cf., Herbert's "Prayer [II]").

forestallèd: prevented.

being down: i.e., already fallen into sin. **I'll look up. /My fault is past—:** Q2 and Jenkins, where F and some editors have "I'll look up, / My fault is past," linking these two sentences with a comma "as though Claudius's resolve to 'look up' were due to his fault's being past instead of to his confidence in the efficacy of prayer. [But] the 'twofold force' of prayer once recognized—to prevent or forgive sin—his admission that his own case requires the second begins the new train of thought: the fact that his fault is already committed determines the 'form' that his prayer must take" (Jenkins). **My fault is past—:** i.e., I have already sinned, am in the second of the two cases in which the force of prayer operates (past—Jenkins and this ed.; past, Q2 and Riverside; past. F).

serve my turn: avail me, answer the purpose.

am ... possessed / Of: possess, cf., Abbott §171.

effects: those things acquired by doing an action (OED *sb.* 4.).

and retain th'offense: and still keep possession of the benefits of the offense and therefore remain guilty of it. ●i.e., may one be both pardoned and yet impenitent? Cf., John 20:23, "Whosoever's sins ye remit, they are remitted unto them; and whosoever's sins ye retain, they are retained" (suggesting that one's sins cannot be both remitted and retained), and cf., the case of Guido, Count of Montefeltro, in Dante's *Inferno* 27.119 ("*nè pentère e volere insieme puossi / per la contradizion che nol consente*").

currents: course of events, streams of activity, "perhaps playing on the sense of 'currencies'" (Jenkins). **this world:** ●NOTE TO ACTORS: the emphasis is on "this," the antithesis being the world "above" (i.e., heaven) in line 60.

gilded hand: "gold-bearing, both as acquiring ill-gotten gains and as bestowing them in bribes; with a play on *gilt, guilt* (for which cf. *Mac*[*beth*] II.ii.[53–54]; *2 H*[*enry*] *IV* IV.v.[128], [and *Henry V* II.Chor.26])" (Jenkins). **shove by:** F, Q2 showe by, push aside, cf., "shuffling" at line 61 and note.

oft: often. **wicked prize:** ill-gotten gain.

Buys out: corrupts with bribery. **above:** i.e., in the heavenly court of justice.

There: ●NOTE TO ACTORS: The emphasis is on this word, referring to "above" (= heaven) in the previous line and being the antithesis of "this world" in line 57. **shuffling:** evasion, deception, trickery (OED *vbl. sb.*

4.), related to *shovel* (OED *v.*²) and thereby to *shove* (OED *v.*), hence "the word recalls *shove* (line 58), in order to enforce the contrast between 'this world' and 'above'" (Jenkins). **the action lies:** the deed remains revealed, with a pun on the legal terms "action" (= court case, suit) and "lies" (= is admitted for legal judgment), and "By a further quibble, that paradoxically *lies* which shows its *true* nature" (Jenkins).

In his true nature, and we ourselves compelled

his: its, cf., I.i.37 note. **and we … compelled:** even as we are compelled, we being compelled, cf., I.iii.62 note and Abbott §95.

Even to the teeth and forehead of our faults

Even: elided to one syllable, making a trochee with "to" and adding stress to the assonant "teeth." **to the teeth and forehead:** "in face-to-face confrontation" (Jenkins), nothing left out of view.

To give in evidence. What then? What rests?

give in: submit, provide, *in* being an "adv[erb] with *give* (not [a] prep[osition] with *evidence*)" (Jenkins). **rests:** is left, remains. • i.e., that being so, what remains for me to do?

Try what repentance can. What can it not?   65
Yet what can it when one cannot repent?

can … can … can: elliptical for "can do" (OED *v.*¹ 8.) with some influence of the old senses "to know" and "to be skilled at," on which meanings the word's fourth appearance in these two lines, in "cannot" in the sense "is (not) able to," forms a pun. • Anguished but as yet impenitent, the King correctly understands the theology of his spiritual condition. His sins cannot be forgiven unless he repents, but he has not repented. Repentance traditionally involves four elements (as elucidated in Sayers, pages 54–60): confession ("I did the crime and know it was wrong"), contrition ("I am sorry I did it, I renounce that in myself which impelled me to do it, and I wish never to do its like again"), satisfaction (= penance, reparation, restoring what one has taken or broken and amending one's own soul), and absolution (bestowed by priest in the Catholic sacrament or, in Shakespeare's more Protestant world at the time of *Hamlet*, by God in an act of grace). Note that once the first three elements of repentance are accomplished, absolution is *always* guaranteed by divine promise, and Hamlet knows this (hence "send / To heaven" in lines 77–78). The King may feel emotional anguish, guilt, and fear of judgment and of the damnation Hamlet contemplated at III.i.55ff., but so long as he will not give up "the effects for which I did the murder," refusing to do the penance essential to absolution, he is not in fact contrite. Hence absolution is unavailable and hell is his destiny, of which the fear drives him to the following outburst.

O wretched state! O bosom black as death!

state: condition, with an echo for the audience of the sense "nation and government of Denmark" that the King does not intend. **black:** also traditionally the color of the devil.

O limèd soul that struggling to be free

limèd: caught as in birdlime, a sticky substance (made from holly bark) that is smeared on twigs to catch birds, who proverbially were the more surely caught the more they struggled. • "a frequent metaphor in Shakespeare [and] proverbial. Cf. ... Tilley B 380. Battenhouse (*Shakesp[earea]n Trag[edy]*, pp. 377–8) shows its recurrence in [St.] Augustine's *Confessions* to describe the *death-like* state of the soul which entanglement in worldly pleasures keeps from God" (Jenkins), cf., Augustine, *Confessions*, III.6.10, VI.6.9 ("birdlime of death"), VI.12.22 ("stick so fast in the birdlime of that pleasure"), X.30.42 ("disentangled from the birdlime of concupiscence").

Art more engaged! Help, angels; make assay!

engaged: entangled, stuck. **assay:** test or trial, experiment, but also attempt, utmost effort, attack, all relevant senses (cf., OED Assay *sb.* 1., 3., 13–15), addressed to the angels, cf., II.ii.71, *Macbeth* IV.iii.143 (utmost effort), and *Henry V* I.ii.151 and Spenser's *Faerie Queene* V.iv.23.9 (attack) (Jenkins substantially).

Bow, stubborn knees; and heart with strings of steel,   70
Be soft as sinews of the new-born babe.
All may be well.

Bow ... knees: i.e., kneel.

[*Kneels.*]

Enter Hamlet.

HAMLET

Now might I do it pat, now a is a-praying;

pat: without missing the object or occasion, readily, aptly, opportunely, appropriately, promptly. **a:** he.

And now I'll do't; [*Drawing his sword.*] and so a goes
                                                [to heaven;

s.d. *Drawing his sword:* "That the sword, sheathed again at line 88, was drawn at this point appears from the wording of Q1: 'Ay so, come forth and work thy last'" (Jenkins).

And so am I revenged. That would be scanned: 75
A villain kills my father, and for that
I, his sole son, do this same villain send

would be: requires to be, needs to be, calls for being (Abbott §329). **scanned:** closely examined (OED 3.), from *scan* meaning examining a line of verse metrically (OED 1.). OED quotes this verse under 4., "to interpret," suggesting that the phrase means "that action would be interpreted by others as follows," a highly unlikely reading despite the lack of punctuation after "scanned" in Q2 (F has a comma). • This "scanning" is the heart of the play and of Hamlet's fall. He is not here worrying about how anyone (himself, God, the world) might interpret his action as a sending of the King to heaven. He is himself looking into what it means to do the deed to which the entire play has been leading him and which we expect him to accomplish at this moment. Hamlet's fate swings in the balance between "doing it pat" (i.e., immediately, say in a passion) and stopping to "scan" the deed he is about to do. But even the scanning itself would not be an error if the conclusion he came to after rational thought were to "do it" as an instrument of God's justice. But that is not his conclusion. Once again, as we shall see, there is no question here of thinking "too much" or of thought itself being the culprit in Hamlet's not killing the king. The soliloquy makes a point of giving us the *content* of Hamlet's thought, and it is that which forms the crisis of the play.

To heaven.

To heaven: "Single lines with two or three accents are ... often found in passages of soliloquy where passion is at its height" (Abbott §511). ● After these one and a half feet, the empty feet that complete the line indicate a pause, during which Hamlet's base motivation, the dram of evil glimpsed at I.ii.182–83 (where the word "heaven" was also central), comes into his mind, as evidenced in the next eight lines, which precede Hamlet's crucial decision, the act of will that will endanger his mission, his kingdom, and his soul.

Why, this is hire and salary, not revenge.

hire and salary: F; Q2 reads "base and silly," almost certainly a misreading of the manuscript. **hire:** payment for services or work, wages (OED *sb.* 2.). **salary:** reward or fee for services (OED *sb.* 2.). ● Hamlet indeed considers "hire and salary" to be base as against the satisfaction of his personal revenge, but what is called for is not his personal revenge but the accomplishment of that action for which he is metaphorically hired and salaried by the divine will as conveyed to him through the Ghost.

A took my father grossly, full of bread,   80

A: he. **grossly:** modifies the father's condition, not the manner of the taking, i.e., in a gross (material, worldly, not spiritually prepared) state, cf., I.v.76–79 and note. **full of bread:** an extension of "grossly," in the midst of the satisfaction of his physical needs, "hence unprepared for death. Cf. Ezekiel 16:49" (Jenkins).

With all his crimes broad blown, as flush as May;

crimes: sins, not any particular crimes, but in the sense that all men are sinners, being fallen. **broad blown:** in full bloom, cf., I.v.76. **flush:** vital, vigorous, full of life, lusty, cf., *Antony and Cleopatra* I.iv.52.

And how his audit stands who knows save heaven?

audit: accounting, here of good and bad deeds. ● Hamlet here utters the crucial and reasonable question that ought to deter him from the plan he is about to pursue. Who but God can know the account of a man's soul? The answer is no one, cf., Matthew 7:1, Luke 6:37, and especially John 7:24 ("Judge not according to the appearance"). But Hamlet will ignore the implication of his own question, "o'erstep the bounds of nature," as he warned the players not to do (III.ii.19), and do so far more egregiously than anyone else in the play filled with such overstepping, whether weighty or trivial, checked or not, as the King, Polonius, Gertrude, Fortinbras, Laertes, Horatio, Osric, and the Gravedigger all overstep the bounds of their respective places.

But in our circumstance and course of thought

in our circumstance and course of thought: given the limited human condition and manner of our thinking; a hendiadys, "as far as we mortals can judge" (Wright, page 187).

'Tis heavy with him. And am I then revenged

'Tis heavy with him: i.e., he is in bad shape, his soul is weighted down with sin, his "audit" or spiritual account is in a grave condition (from Latin *gravis*, heavy). ● As we know from the previous soliloquy, this conclusion is in fact correct, though Hamlet cannot know it for certain, but his next assumption (about "the purging of his soul"), as we will hear in the

To take him in the purging of his soul   85
When he is fit and seasoned for his passage?

No.

final couplet of the scene, turns out to be incorrect.
am I then revenged: ● The focus of this question on Hamlet's own personal desire to be revenged, rather than on his mission as avenger chosen by God via the Ghost, hints at the fatal decision to come.

purging: in a state of penitence.

fit and seasoned: spiritually prepared for death and judgment, as he appears to be by the fact that he is kneeling in prayer. **seasoned:** "matured (cf. I.iii.81), hence thoroughly prepared" (Jenkins). **passage:** i.e., to the next world, to judgment, and thence to heaven, purgatory, or hell. ● The assumption that the King is penitent can lead to Hamlet's answer only through Hamlet's substituting for his mission his own personal and private desire for revenge. He was told to revenge the murder of his father without tainting his mind, and were he to kill the King at this moment, he would have accomplished both tasks. But he asks not about the justice or mercy of this killing, but about whether his own personal desire for revenge will be satisfied if the King goes to heaven. This is a terrible substitution of his own desire for God's will, and of his pretending to know the state of another man's soul when he is in fact ignorant of the state even of his own. He has engaged not in violent rage but in a form of thinking that pretends to be reasonable but is in fact utterly benighted. He wills to be revenged by sending the King to hell, and his reason, pandering his will (cf., III.iv.88), seems to justify the one-word decision with which he risks the damnation of his own soul.

No: ● This one-syllable word is the climax of the play. It is the moment of choice in which Hamlet wills the damnation of the King and in doing so falls into sin greater even than the King's (see Introduction, pages 5–6). Followed (in Q2) by four empty feet, it forms the entire line as if to dramatize the centrality and significance of this moment of free will choice (cf., line 78 note). Hamlet is pretending to know about another man's soul what he cannot know, what only God can know. He feels that his personal desire for revenge can be satisfied only by the damnation of his uncle, not merely by his uncle's death. His mind has been tainted by that desire, and as a result he chooses to pretend to divine authority, his only form of false ambition (cf., Isaiah 10:15). Hence, his choosing *not* to kill Claudius here is a far worse crime in moral terms than that of Claudius, who only killed his brother without necessarily willing his brother's damnation. Everything has conspired providentially to bring Hamlet to kill the King here and now, either in a passionate rage or in rational service to his divinely ordained mission, and Hamlet says "No." In classical terms it is the moment of Hamlet's hubris. In Christian terms, it is his fall. And it is the turning point of the play, for directly from it comes all the "havoc" (V.ii.364) that Fortinbras finds in the final scene.

Up, sword, and know thou a more horrid hent:

When he is drunk asleep, or in his rage,

Or in the incestuous pleasure of his bed,   90
At game a-swearing, or about some act

That has no relish of salvation in't—
Then trip him, that his heels may kick at heaven,

And that his soul may be as damned and black
As hell, whereto it goes. My mother stays.   95

This physic but prolongs thy sickly days.

Exit.

KING [*Rising.*]
My words fly up, my thoughts remain below.
Words without thoughts never to heaven go.

Exit.

Up: away, into the scabbard, followed at some point between here and line 96 by the action of re-sheathing his sword. **know thou:** let you know, "have experience of" (Jenkins). **horrid:** rough, savage, dreadful, detestable. **hent:** grasping, act of being seized (if from the verb *hent*, related to *hend*, to lay hold of, seize) or opportunity, occasion (if from the verb *hint*)—in either case, the sword will be used on a nastier occasion, both in the sense that the King will be doing something evil, as opposed to the present action of praying, and in the sense that the result will be more dreadful, i.e., the sending of the King to hell rather than to heaven.

drunk asleep: asleep in drunkenness, cf., I.ii.127 note, Q2 drunk, a sleep, F drunk asleep.

incestuous: cf., I.ii.157 and note and I.v.42.

At game a-swearing: Q2 At game a swearing, implying swearing while gambling, F At gaming, swearing, implying either at gambling or at swearing, cf., Webster's *White Devil* V.i.70–72 for a parallel desire to cause a man to die swearing at tennis so that "He might have sworn himself to hell, and struck His soul into the hazard" (cited in Jenkins). Abbott's comment on the prefix *a-* (§24) would seem to apply to Q2's "a swearing" as well as to F's "At gaming."

relish: tinge, trace (OED *sb.*¹ I.c.).

Then: ● NOTE TO ACTORS: The stress is on this word, the antithesis of "now" in line 73, making a trochee that not only clarifies the antithesis but throws heavy stress on the last three feet of the line, which are further enhanced by the alliteration on *h* ("his heels ... heaven"). **kick at heaven:** "The metaphor suggests both that Claudius will be spurning heaven and that he will be plunging head first (into hell)" (Jenkins), like Lucifer.

that his soul ... it goes: "This speech, in which Ham[let], represented as a virtuous character, is not content with taking blood for blood, but contrives damnation for the man that he would punish, is too horrible to be read or to be uttered" (Samuel Johnson cited in Furness, page 283), "Yet some moral may be extracted from it, as all his subsequent calamities were owing to this savage refinement of revenge" (J. M. Mason, page 449, cited in Furness, page 283). Shakespeare's audience would have reacted with similar horror to Hamlet's malicious motive. **stays:** waits.

physic: medical remedy, here referring to the praying of the King as medicine for his soul, cf., "purging" at line 85 above (Jenkins substantially). **but:** only, merely. **prolongs ... days:** lengthens the period of your morally sick life.

My words ... heaven go: cf., Angelo in *Measure for Measure* II.iv.1–7 (Jenkins substantially). ● The terrible final irony of this final couplet is that the King has not in fact repented, so that had Hamlet killed him in this moment, the soul of the King might well have gone to hell, though not as a result of Hamlet's will. Waiting to kill the King when Hamlet can be sure the King's soul will go to hell, Hamlet puts himself into jeopardy of the same. (Kennedy notes that both at III.i.188 and here the King completes a scene-ending rhymed couplet on the word "go.")

• END NOTE: Let us look back over this scene and imagine seeing it without hearing the soliloquies. We would see the King in anguish fall to his knees in prayer, Hamlet enter, draw his sword, and hold it poised to kill the King, put the sword back into its sheath and exit. Would not this look to our eyes like mercy? But unlike Hamlet in relation to the King, we in relation to the characters are granted, through the medium of drama and the convention of the soliloquy, to participate in a quasi-divine perspective. We not only see the external gestures but hear the inner monologues and so know the conditions of the characters' souls. And hearing their words, we know the sin of each, Hamlet's being now the worse. Shakespeare has used the exquisite dramatic irony of this double-soliloquy climax to make visible for us the invisible moral drama of salvation. Hamlet's willful "No," despite his admitted ignorance of the true state of the soul of Claudius, his desire to place the satisfaction of his own desire for revenge above the imperative of the Ghost—this is his fall. He has tainted his mind, just as Fortinbras did when he challenged Denmark without his own uncle-king's permission, just as Polonius has done in jumping to his own conclusions, just as the King has done in killing his brother for the sake of ambition and lust. In this choice Hamlet has out-Heroded Herod (cf., III.ii.14), has not suited his action to the word of the Ghost, or to the Word (cf., III.ii.17), and has missed the perfect moment to fulfill his mission either in a rage or in reason. He has imitated reason to justify a will perverted by pride, his reason pandering his will (cf., III.iv.88 note), and the consequences will be immense.

Hamlet's pause, followed by the sheathing of his sword, recalls Pyrrhus' pause in holding his sword above the head of Priam in the Player's speech (II.ii.482). There too the First Player's "Did nothing" is followed by three and a half empty feet (cf., II.ii.482 note). Hamlet's pause here, like that one, is prelude to a horror, but here it lies in the motive for postponement rather than in the commencement of violence. Mulgrew would extend the parallel between this scene and the First Player's speech of Aeneas to Dido about the death of Priam at the hands of Pyrrhus by pointing out that both pauses, II.ii.482 and III.iii.87, reflect Aeneas' own pause before killing Turnus at the end of the *Aeneid*. He argues, based on Anchises' assertion that the arts of Rome will include "to spare the defeated" (*Aeneid* VI.984 tr. Fagles), that Aeneas commits a great error in killing Turnus (*Aeneid* XII.1109–1110 tr. Fagles). I am not persuaded that such is Virgil's intention, but if it were, the parallel could be understood thus: As in Aeneas the error was in killing, wrath overcoming mercy, so here the error is in not killing, vengeance overcoming justice. In any case, however Shakespeare thought of the killing of Turnus, he clearly intends Hamlet's spiritual and moral crime in *not* killing here to be seen as parallel to that of Pyrrhus in killing Priam in the First Player's speech in II.ii.

Many interpreters of this scene have claimed that Hamlet's expressed motive for delay, the desire to see Claudius not only dead but damned, is a pretense hiding a profounder and mysterious incapacity to act. They base this on a misreading of III.i.55ff. and take the soliloquy passage at IV.iv.39ff. to be words of self-knowledge and this speech to be words of self-delusion. In truth, both are speeches of self-delusion, as we see when Hamlet's right reason is restored at the end of the play. Jenkins makes a subtler error (LN to this speech). Rightly taking Hamlet at his word and crediting him with desiring the damnation of the King rather than rationalizing to disguise some different but unnamed motive, he ascribes Hamlet's attitude here to a persistent and universal aspect of his (and all men's) nature rather than to a particular fall from grace for which Hamlet must repent to be redeemed or else be damned. He sees the play as the presentation of a man with various sometimes contradictory qualities in various situations rather than as the unfolding of a spiritual journey. Ultimately, his view of the play is static rather than dramatic, and it leaves the play in the interpretive doldrums of having no moral direction but only descriptive significance: "this is how life is" instead of "this is how man falls and may be redeemed." The "dimming of belief in hell" has indeed softened the horror of Hamlet's choice for the modern critics Jenkins refutes. But in Jenkins we see the effects of a similar dimming of belief in Providence. Fortunately for whatever part of our moral and spiritual lives may be illuminated by drama, such a dimming effect was not the case with Shakespeare or the audience for which he wrote.

Act III, Scene iv

Enter Queen Gertrude and Polonius.

POLONIUS

A will come straight. Look you lay home to him.

Tell him his pranks have been too broad to bear with,

Act III, Scene iv—The Queen's closet (see III.iii.27): **closet:** private room, "the private apartment of a monarch or potentate" (OED 2. and see II.i.74 note), not her bedroom as John Dover Wilson maintained and the Olivier film (among others) depicts, under the influence of Freudian interpretations of Hamlet's relation to his mother.

A: he. **straight:** right away. **Look:** see that, be sure to. **lay home to him:** reprove him directly, cf., III.iii.29. **pranks:** tricks, which could be merely mischievous or malicious and wicked (OED *sb.²*, a.), hence the word is often modified (as here with "broad") to indicate the degree of seriousness or harmfulness, cf., *1 Henry VI* III.i.15, *Twelfth Night* IV.i.55, *Othello* II.i.142, III.iii.202, *King Lear* I.iv.238, *Winter's Tale* IV.iv.700. **broad:** unrestrained, out of all bounds (OED 8.). **bear with:** put up with, make allowance for (OED bear *v.*¹17.).

And that your Grace hath screened and stood between

Much heat and him. I'll silence me even here.

Pray you, be round.   5

QUEEN
        I'll war'nt you, fear me not.
Withdraw, I hear him coming.

[Polonius hides behind the arras.]

Enter Hamlet.

HAMLET
Now, mother, what's the matter?

QUEEN
Hamlet, thou hast thy father much offended.

HAMLET
Mother, you have my father much offended.   10

QUEEN
Come, come, you answer with an idle tongue.

HAMLET
Go, go, you question with a wicked tongue.

QUEEN
Why, how now, Hamlet?

HAMLET
        What's the matter now?

QUEEN
Have you forgot me?

HAMLET
        No, by the rood, not so.
You are the Queen, your husband's brother's wife,   15

---

that: for *that* omitted in the previous line and inserted here see Abbott §285. **your Grace:** you, an honorific title for the Queen, as for the King at V.ii.261.

heat: i.e., anger of the King. **silence me:** silence myself. ● "Ironically he does not (line 22) and so meets his death" (Jenkins), but also ironically he does indeed finally silence himself here, not intentionally but through his overreaching in this third attempt to fathom Hamlet's "mystery," see III.ii.366 note.

round: direct, forceful, severe (OED round *a.* 13 b. and c.), F "round with him," unmetrical, is probably "an addition in recollection of III.i.[183]" (Jenkins).

I'll war'nt … coming: Riverside treats as prose, hence the discrepancy in the numbering of lines 5-10. **war'nt:** warrant, assure, Q2 wait, F warrant, Wilson war'nt, Q2 "wait" "appears to be the misreading of an abbreviation in the copy" (Jenkins), cf., I.ii.242 and II.i.38 note. **fear me not:** do not fear (about) me (that I will not be "round"), the preposition is omitted with some verbs (see Abbott §200).

s.d. *arras*: cf., III.iii.28 and note, and IV.i.9.

what's the matter: what is the topic, subject of discussion, i.e., what have you called me to speak with you about, cf., III.ii.331-32.

thy father: implying the King. ● NOTE TO ACTORS: Note how in the four lines 9-12 the parallelism brings out the antitheses: "thou/you," "thy/my," "come/go," "answer/question," "idle/wicked."

my father: implying Hamlet Senior.

idle: foolish, trifling.

Why … Hamlet?: The question mark in Q2 and F may also imply exclamation, Gertrude's taking offense at Hamlet's accusation.

matter: topic, subject of discussion, as in line 8. **now:** the same "now" as in line 7. ● not "now as opposed to earlier" but "now what is the subject you called me here to discuss?" as if Hamlet, in bitterness, is pretending that the previous four lines were rather casual matters of fact than direct accusations and now pretends to return to his initial question, as if the four lines were no interruption.

Have you forgot me?: i.e., forgotten that I am your mother and the Queen, hence not to be insulted so.

by the rood: an oath by the cross (*rood* from OE *rod*).

husband's brother's wife: "A woman may not marry with her … husband's brother' ([from the Table of Kindred and Affinity in the] *Book of Common Prayer*)" (Jenkins), cf., I.ii.8 and I.ii.157 note.

And, would it were not so, you are my mother.

QUEEN

Nay, then I'll set those to you that can speak.

HAMLET

Come, come, and sit you down; you shall not budge.

You go not till I set you up a glass

Where you may see the inmost part of you.   20

QUEEN

What wilt thou do? Thou wilt not murder me?

Help, ho!

POLONIUS [behind the arras.]

     What ho, help!

HAMLET

          How now, a rat? [Drawing his rapier.]

Dead for a ducat, dead!   [Stabs through the arras.]

POLONIUS [behind the arras.]

        O, I am slain.

QUEEN

O me, what hast thou done?   25

HAMLET

        Nay, I know not.

Is it the King?

QUEEN

O what a rash and bloody deed is this!

HAMLET

A bloody deed. Almost as bad, good mother,

---

would: I wish, if only.

sit you down ... not budge: ● The Queen has presumably made a move to leave, and Hamlet forces her back to her seat.

glass: mirror. ● He means to set it up in words.

murder me: in fear that his madness might go so far, to the audience ironic in view of Hamlet's planned accusations of her and the King.

help!: ●NOTE TO ACTORS: This exclamatory word counts as a full foot in the shared verse line ("Help, ho! What ho, help! How now, a rat?").

How now ... dead!: Riverside treats as prose, hence the discrepancy in numbering lines 22–25. **a rat:** Taverner's *Proverbs*, notes that "rats proverbially cause their own deaths by drawing attention to themselves" (Jenkins). ● Taking the eavesdropper to be the King (lines 26 and 32), Hamlet is also commenting on his character. Later, when she knows that Hamlet is not in fact mad, Gertrude will pretend that Hamlet meant this metaphor literally in order to reinforce, in loyalty to him, the idea that Hamlet is indeed mad (IV.i.10).

for a ducat: I'll bet a ducat (that I kill him) (Riverside substantially), or possibly for the price of a ducat (a gold coin stamped with the head of the duke of Venice), i.e., I'll take as little as a ducat for killing him (Jenkins substantially). ● Hamlet clearly believes that it is the King he has stabbed (lines 26 and 32), and in precisely the sort of compromising situation in which he had hoped to find him (at III.iii.89ff.), intending to send his soul to hell.

S.D.: cf., IV.i.9–12.

O, I am slain: "amphibious" in filling up a pentameter as the last part of the previous line and as the first part of the following (Abbott §513).

Is it the King?: ● In the previous scene, his reason pandering his proud will, Hamlet fails to act to accomplish his mission. Now, in the passion of wrath, he acts in the belief that he is getting his way and sending the soul of the King to hell. But the wrong man is the victim. Having erred then in presuming to see into a man's soul through a gesture, now he cannot even see the external man through an arras. Moral blindness has become physical. Hamlet's act initiates the destruction that follows upon pride, cf., Proverbs 16:18, 29:22–23. Interpretations founded on the notion that Hamlet fails to act, whether out of melancholy or excessive thinking or cowardice or uncertainty about his role or some other psychological obstacle, fail to acknowledge that here Hamlet *does* act, thinking he is killing the King. The reason Hamlet's project goes wrong is not inaction in general, but inaction in the previous scene for the reason he there states explicitly. We need only take him at his word there to make sense of the entire play, and the convention of the soliloquy demands that we do so. Similarly, we are not to imagine that because we have just seen the King praying in another room, he could not have had time to arrive and hide here, implying that Hamlet ought to have known for sure that the King could not be behind the arras. Had we been meant to think so, someone would have had to say it. Hamlet's words show that he did indeed think he was killing the King.

kill a king: • Though the Ghost has not accused Gertrude of participation in the murder of Hamlet Senior, Hamlet sees her as complicit in that she ought to have known that the lust of Claudius and the death of Hamlet Senior were not unrelated. He thus employs the same hyperbole as the Player Queen at III.ii.180 and 184–85.
As kill a king? King. Q2, King? F.

As kill a king and marry with his brother.

QUEEN
As kill a king?
HAMLET
Ay, lady, it was my word.— 30
[*Lifts up the arras and discovers Polonius, dead.*]
Thou wretched, rash, intruding fool, farewell.

Thou wretched ... farewell: directed to the dead Polonius.
thy better: someone of higher rank, i.e., the King.
too busy: • Ironically Hamlet is pronouncing the same judgment upon himself without realizing it: Just as Polonius has been too busy in interfering in Hamlet's business, so in the previous scene Hamlet has been too busy in interfering in God's. The danger to him will come with the desire for revenge of the also too-busy Laertes.

I took thee for thy better. Take thy fortune;
Thou find'st to be too busy is some danger.—[*To Gertrude.*]
Leave wringing of your hands. Peace, sit you down,
And let me wring your heart, for so I shall 35

If it be made of penetrable stuff,

stuff: material or substance of which something is composed or made (OED 3.).
damnèd custom: the habit of doing evil, cf., III.iv.161–70. **brazed:** brasd Q2, braz'd F, "converted to, or covered with, brass" (Jenkins), hardened, cf., *King Lear* I.i.11 and the word *brazen*.

If damnèd custom have not brazed it so

That it be proof and bulwark against sense.

proof: strength-tested (proven) armor, cf., II.ii.490 note. **bulwark:** solid defensive plank or wall, fortification, protection. **sense:** feeling, emotion, with the additional implication of good sense, right feeling, cf., lines 71–74.

QUEEN
What have I done, that thou dar'st wag thy tongue
In noise so rude against me?
HAMLET
Such an act 40

Such ... that ... such ... as (lines 40–46): for "license in the use of these words" see Abbott §279.
act: • Despite the literal sense of the word here and at line 51, and of "deed" at line 45, neither the Ghost nor Hamlet accuses Gertrude of physical adultery while Hamlet Senior lived, though that possibility is never explicitly denied. In keeping with the central themes of the play, Hamlet's accusation focuses on the *will* of Gertrude in turning from Hamlet Senior to his brother, whatever her external behavior has been (cf.,

That blurs the grace and blush of modesty,

Calls virtue hypocrite, takes off the rose

From the fair forehead of an innocent love
And sets a blister there, makes marriage-vows

As false as dicers' oaths—O, such a deed   45
As from the body of contraction plucks

The very soul, and sweet religion makes
A rhapsody of words. Heaven's face does glow

O'er this solidity and compound mass

With heated visage, as against the doom,   50

Is thought-sick at the act.
QUEEN
                    Ay me, what act,

I.v.42 note), and reinforces the greater importance of human will than of physical gesture. In III.iii the King appears to pray but is unrepentant, and Hamlet appears to be merciful but is vengeful beyond measure. Similarly here Hamlet kills Polonius meaning to damn the King and accuses Gertrude of an adulterous act of will not necessarily exhibited in physical action.

blurs: stains, blemishes, blots, defiles. **grace and blush:** a hendiadys for the "innocent (blushing) grace of a modest young woman" (Wright, page 187).

rose: the flower, symbol of pure love, and the color both of the flower and of blushing, symbolic of youthful innocence and modesty, cf., "blush" in the previous line.

forehead ... blister: whether in fact whores were traditionally branded on the forehead, as many editors repeat, or not, as Henning argues, Shakespeare implies that chastity and unchastity may be seen revealed on the brow, cf., IV.v.119–21, *Comedy of Errors* II.ii.136, and *Measure for Measure* II.iii.12.

dicers: gamblers. **deed:** cf., line 40 note above.

from the body ... very soul: "Reduces to an empty form not merely the marriage-contract but *contraction*, the very principle of contracting solemn agreements of which the marriage-contract is the type" (Jenkins), i.e., Hamlet implies that Gertrude's presumed adultery removes the commitment of the spirit ("soul") from the form ("body") not only of marriage but of the principle of all contracts, which are the foundation of society.

religion ... words: makes of sacred vows merely a string, or perhaps a chaotic jumble, of words, cf., OED rhapsody 3. ● As in the previous image Gertrude's will has plucked the essence from the body of the social contract that is marriage, here it similarly reduces the spiritual contract, the sacrament of marriage, to its merely external form. **Heaven's face ... at the act:** cf., *Macbeth* II.iv.5–6. **glow:** with anger (Riverside).

this solidity and compound mass: a hendiadys, "solid compound mass" (Wright, page 187), i.e., the earth, which is a solid compounded of the four elements, earth, air, fire, water, and "threatened [with] disintegration at doomsday" (Jenkins).

heated visage: face burning with anger, cf., "glow" in line 48. **as against the doom:** as if in preparation for judgment day "(which is prophetically associated with signs in the heavens)" (Jenkins), for *against* in reference to time see Abbott §142.

thought-sick: sick at the awareness of, sick "as the result of thought" (Abbott §430). **act:** Gertrude's adultery of the will (cf., line 40 note), which "is here made to epitomize the guilt of the world" (Jenkins). ● Now that Claudius is confirmed to be a murderer by his reaction to "The Murder of Gonzago," Hamlet

That roars so loud and thunders in the index?

HAMLET
Look here upon this picture, and on this,

The counterfeit presentment of two brothers.

See what a grace was seated on this brow, 55

Hyperion's curls, the front of Jove himself,

An eye like Mars to threaten and command,

A station like the herald Mercury

New-lighted on a heaven-kissing hill,

A combination and a form indeed 60
Where every god did seem to set his seal

To give the world assurance of a man.
This was your husband. Look you now, what follows.
Here is your husband, like a mildewed ear

Blasting his wholesome brother. Have you eyes? 65

---

uses hyperbole to chastise effectively Gertrude's embrace of the King, as (at III.ii.396-99) he said he would do.

That roars ... index?: Q2 erroneously gives the line to Hamlet, F corrects, cf., IV.v.153 note. **index:** the indication of what is to come, as in a table of contents (OED 4. and 5.), cf., *Othello* II.i.257–58.

this picture ... this: • "Easily handled portraits were a favourite item in stage-business" (Jenkins LN), and whether they are miniatures (cf., II.ii.366) or somewhat larger, Hamlet shows Gertrude two portraits, one of Hamlet Senior probably in his own possession and one of the King probably in Gertrude's possession. By 19ᵗʰ-c. stage tradition, Hamlet wears one and Gertrude the other as pendants. Jenkins (LN) rather politely refutes the nonsensical argument that the audience would not be able to see for themselves in miniatures what Hamlet is describing. The point is that they see it in his words.

counterfeit presentment: painted representation, cf., *Merchant of Venice* III.ii.115.

seated: "firmly placed, fixed" (Crystal) in a place of eminence or dignity, enthroned. **brow:** forehead.

Hyperion: cf., I.ii.140 note. **front:** forehead. **Jove:** king of the Olympian gods in Roman mythology (in Latin Jupiter in the nominative case and Jov- when inflected), corresponding to the Greek god Zeus.

Mars: Roman god of war, corresponding to the Greek god Ares.

station: stance, bearing. **herald:** messenger, envoy. **Mercury:** winged Roman messenger god, corresponding to the Greek god Hermes, "whose bearing typified grace and beauty" (Jenkins).

New-lighted ... hill: just alighted, as upon Mount Atlas in Virgil's *Aeneid* IV.252–53, also alluded to in Milton's *Paradise Lost* V.285 (Jenkins substantially).

A combination ... form: a hendiadys (Wright, page 187), cf., I.i.57 note, a form made up of the combination of qualities, cf., I.v.100 note, II.ii.305 note, and III.ii.24 note. **A combination ... seal:** "The idea is that of an image formed on wax by the combined impression of many seals" (Jenkins). • Hamlet imagines that each of the gods had bestowed upon Hamlet Senior something of its own invisible characteristic quality and confirmed the gift with a visible sign ("seal"), "curls" (line 56), "front" (line 56), "eye" (line 57), and "station" (line 58).

a man: an ideal man, the product of the combined divine qualities, cf., *Julius Caesar* V.v.73–75.

mildewed ear: i.e., of grain, "of corn" in the Geneva Bible, a reference to Pharaoh's dream in Genesis 41:5–7, 22–24.

Blasting: blighting, Genesis 41:6, 23, 27 in the Geneva Bible, and cf., I.iii.42 and III.ii.258. **wholesome:** healthy, as at I.v.70 and III.ii.260. **brother:** i.e., its healthy fellow ear of grain.

Could you on this fair mountain leave to feed,

fair mountain: beautiful grazing land, referring to the picture of his father. **leave to feed:** leave off or cease feeding, cf., III.ii.174, for the infinitive used as a noun see Abbott §355.

And batten on this moor? Ha, have you eyes?

batten: glut oneself, or possibly thrive or grow fat at another's expense (OED batten *v.*¹ I. b. and c.). • The animal metaphors here and at lines 93–4, I.ii.150, and I.v.56–57 derive, "directly or indirectly, from Belleforest and ultimately from Saxo" (Jenkins). **moor:** infertile land, referring to the picture of Claudius. • "The contrast with a *fair* mountain suggests a play on blackamoor. This may be what prompts Q1 'With a face like *Vulcan*'" (Jenkins), though it could as likely be a play on "tawny moor," implying infidel.

You cannot call it love, for at your age

your age: • It does no good to guess at Gertrude's actual age, see Introduction, page 6, note 13, and cf., V.i.143 note.

The heyday in the blood is tame, it's humble,

heyday: excitement. **blood:** "As the source of sexual desire" (Jenkins), cf., I.iii.6 and note.

And waits upon the judgment, and what judgment   70

the judgment: • that judgment pronounced by God upon each person's soul after death, a central concern of the play. Shakespeare neatly avoids entering into doctrinal controversies among Catholics and Protestants. Catholics distinguish between the Particular Judgment, God's judgment of each person's individual soul at death, and the Final (Last, General) Judgment, God's judgment of all souls at the end of time. Protestants argued about the state of the soul between death and the Final Judgment. Except for his dramatic use in Act I of the imagery of Purgatory, about whose reality Catholics and Protestants disagreed, Shakespeare generally kept to terms on which all believers could agree. **what judgment:** here the human ability to distinguish, one of the five interior *wits* or *senses* that make up the human rational capacity, the other four being memory, fancy, imagination, and common sense.

Would step from this to this? Sense sure you have,
Else could you not have motion, but sure that sense

this to this: Hamlet Senior in one picture to Claudius in the other, cf., I.v.47–52. **Sense … motion:** "Sense" refers to the five outward senses or wits collectively, "what medieval psychologists called the sensitive (as distinct from the vegetable or rational) soul. [Hamlet] is making a clear and simple application of the maxim, originally Aristotelian [*De Sensu*, Ch. I, 436b (ref. in Jenkins)], that "the external senses are found in all creatures which have the power of locomotion" (Lewis *Studies*, pages 150–51).

Is apoplexed, for madness would not err

apoplexed: paralyzed, benumbed. **for madness … such a difference:** Even madness would not make such a mistake nor could the senses or the wits become so enslaved to illusion that they would not hold on to some modicum of the capacity to choose that would be useful in distinguishing between such extremely different men (as Hamlet Senior and his brother). **madness:** i.e., *even* madness.

Nor sense to ecstasy was ne'er so thralled
But it reserved some quantity of choice   75

To serve in such a difference. What devil was't

That thus hath cozened you at hoodman-blind?

Eyes without feeling, feeling without sight,
Ears without hands or eyes, smelling sans all,
Or but a sickly part of one true sense   80

Could not so mope. O shame, where is thy blush?
Rebellious hell,

If thou canst mutine in a matron's bones,
To flaming youth let virtue be as wax
And melt in her own fire. Proclaim no shame   85

---

ecstasy: frenzy, stupor, lunacy. **thralled:** enslaved.

But it reserved: without keeping or holding.
quantity: modicum, minimal amount, fragment
(OED quantity 8.b.), cf., *Taming of the Shrew* IV.iii.III,
King John V.iv.23, *2 Henry IV* V.i.62. **choice:** ability to
distinguish.

To serve: to be made use of. **in such a difference:**
in a case of such an obvious or extreme distinction.
What devil: which of the demons.

cozened: deceived. **hoodman-blind:** blindman's buff,
a group game in which a blindfolded player tries to
catch and identify by touch any of the other players.
● Hamlet implies that Gertrude, tricked by a demon
(as at II.ii.599–603 he was afraid he himself might
be) into losing her ability to distinguish identities,
or perhaps into the corruption of her modicum of
free will ("some quantity of choice" line 74 [Saven]),
has mistaken the worse husband (Claudius) for
the better (Hamlet Senior). Devils "in the general
belief not only deceived men but also undermined
their judgment so that they deceived themselves"
(Jenkins).

Eyes … smelling: individualizing four of the five
senses referred to collectively in lines 71–72, cf., *Venus
and Adonis* 433–46 (Jenkins substantially). **sans:**
without (from the French).

so mope: be so dazed, benumbed, cf., *Tempest* V.i.240.

Rebellious hell: An exclamation built on a quadruple
metonymy, referring to 1) the devils of hell, who,
having rebelled against God, now tempt human
beings to rebel in sin, 2) human sinfulness itself,
which tempts our feelings and bodily desires to rebel
against our reason, 3) those (particularly sexual)
desires themselves, and 4) the female sexual organs,
cf., Sonnets 129:14 and 144:12. ● In the Christian
tradition sin is figured as the rebellion of man's free
will against God. In *The Republic* Plato figures it as
the rebellion of the lower parts of the self against the
higher, i.e., the vegetable soul, implying the body
and its desires, and the sensible soul, implying the
heart and its passions, against the intelligible soul,
implying the mind and reason, cf., I.iii.44 note.

If thou canst mutine … own fire: ● Hamlet
hyperbolically and sarcastically suggests that if the
virtue of a mature matron can so succumb to sexual
desire as Gertrude's has done, then there is little
hope of preserving virtue from the greater sexual
heat in the young, cf., "mutines" at V.ii.6 note and
Hamlet's own moral mutiny in the previous scene.
mutine: to rebel or to mutiny (verb). **Proclaim no
shame … actively doth burn:** Still sarcastically, let
flaming youth, in whom irresistible sexual desire
("compulsive ardor") motivates sexual license, not
be reproved since older people like Gertrude ("frost,"
her passions cooled with age) burn with desire just
as hotly, and cf., I.iii.44, where Laertes also ties the
sexual heat of youth to the idea of rebellion of the
lower against the higher.

When the compulsive ardor gives the charge,
Since frost itself as actively doth burn

And reason panders will.

QUEEN

O Hamlet, speak no more.

ardor: Q2 ardure, F Ardure. **gives the charge:** gives the signal, as of a drum beat, to attack (i.e., against virtue), cf., *Rape of Lucrece* lines 433–39 and OED charge *sb*. 19., with *is in command* being a secondary sense in this play filled with imperatives, see, Introduction, page 13ff.

reason panders will: The power to reason serves as a procurer to what the will desires, cf., *Antony and Cleopatra* III.xiii.3–4. We would call it rationalization. *Will* here means in one sense pride or willfulness, in another passionate desire of any kind, and in a third sexual lust specifically, cf., *Rape of Lucrece* 243, 247, *Romeo and Juliet* II.iii.28, *Troilus and Cressida* I.iii.120, *Measure for Measure* II.iv.164 and 175, *All's Well* IV.iii.16, *Othello* III.iii.236, *King Lear* IV.vi.271, *Cymbeline* I.vi.47, etc., and Sonnets 134–36 and 143, which add a fourth sense, namely the sexual organs and play on the proverbial "A woman will have her will" (Riverside at Son. 135.1). *Panders* is a verb derived from the go-between Pandarus in Chaucer's poem *Troilus and Criseyde*, whom Shakespeare in his play *Troilus and Cressida* turns into an utterly disreputable, though not yet professional, procurer.
• This phrase is thematically central to the play. It is one thing for desire to rebel against reason. It is another for reason to justify desire in its rebellion. Hamlet here accuses his mother, rightly, of the very sin of which he himself has been guilty in the previous scene, and his failure to be aware of this error in himself will continue through Act IV, Scene iv. In accusing Gertrude of rationalizing her sin in succumbing to the seductions of Claudius, Hamlet also identifies why his own thought in the previous scene sounded so reasonable. His own reason was pandering his own will, rationalizing his desire to damn the King and his pride in imagining that such a judgment was up to him. Hamlet's soliloquy in III.iii is the play's central example, among many, of reason pandering will. The King in III.iii hopes "all will be well" without his giving up "my crown, mine own ambition, and my queen" and later justifies his two attempts to murder his nephew and heir. Polonius is guilty of it in ascribing Hamlet's madness to the Polonius-thwarted love of Ophelia, for it exalts Polonius's self-importance to have it so. Laertes reveals that his reason has pandered his will when he admits that his conscience objects to the King's plot of murder (V.ii.296). Horatio rationalizes suicide as Roman virtue (V.ii.341–42). Fortinbras may be said to rationalize his unapproved adventure against Denmark (I.i.95–104). Even Osric allows his reason to pander his will in his attempt to humor the mad prince without breaching courtly etiquette, cf., V.ii.92 note. Like Hamlet here, Polonius has seemed to be unaware of errors in himself that he sees in others, cf., II.i.111–14 and note, and II.ii.93–94 and note. And the King will claim to trust in a divine protection

Thou turn'st mine eyes into my very soul,
And there I see such black and grainèd spots   90

As will not leave their tinct.

HAMLET
                    Nay, but to live
In the rank sweat of an enseamèd bed,

Stewed in corruption, honeying and making love

Over the nasty sty!

QUEEN
                    O, speak to me no more.

These words like daggers enter in my ears.   95
No more, sweet Hamlet.

HAMLET
                    A murderer and a villain,
A slave that is not twentieth part the tithe

Of your precédent lord, a vice of kings,

A cutpurse of the empire and the rule

That from a shelf the precious diadem stole   100

---

for himself that he has denied to his brother, cf., IV.v.124–26 and note.

mine eyes … soul: F, my very eyes into my soul Q2.

grainèd: F (Q2 greeued), thoroughly dyed in, ingrained, indelible (Riverside). ● The word derives from a double origin: *to ingrain*, meaning to dye into the very texture or fiber of something, as wool before it is woven, and *in grain*, meaning in the deep scarlet dye made of the ground-up bodies of the insect kermes, which grows on oak trees in Europe and was originally thought to be a seed (hence "grain"), so that Gertrude implies that the spots she sees in her soul are deep scarlet dye (for sin), and are dyed into the fibers of her being, hence hard or impossible to remove.

not leave: F, leave there Q2. **leave their tinct:** lose their dark color, give up their stain, cf., *Macbeth* V.i.31–51 (Jenkins) and II.ii.57–60.

rank: excessive, gross, foul, rancid, lustful. **enseamèd:** larded, basted with fat, "saturated with seam (cf. *Troil[us and Cressida]* II.ii.[185]), i.e. animal fat, grease" (Jenkins).
Stewed: "bathed, steeped, with a play on *stew*, brothel" (Jenkins).

Over … no more: probably *Over* is shortened to *o'er* and unstressed to make a normal pentameter of the line (Abbott §498). **nasty:** disgustingly foul, filthy, or obscene. **sty:** pigsty, and by extension "an abode of bestial lust, or of moral pollution generally" (OED *sb.*³ 2.b., quoting this line among others), i.e., a brothel.

like daggers: cf., III.ii.396. **in:** into (Abbott §159).

slave: not merely a bound servant, but one who is slavish by nature and therefore the lowest possible rank of human being in the hierarchy of creation. **tithe:** tenth part.

precédent: previous, ●NOTE TO ACTORS: pronounced with a long second *e* and stress on the second syllable (pre-CEDE-ent). **vice of kings:** in one sense, a villain among kings, in another, an oxymoron, the comical trouble-making jester being opposite to the king in the hierarchic scale of the court. ● The image is based on the "vice" character of the old morality plays, a variously characterized combination of the personification of particular vices and the comical devil's assistant and mischief-maker, always damned in the end, or at least not redeemed, also called "Iniquity" as in *Richard III* III.i.82, *1 Henry IV* II.iv.453–54, *Measure for Measure* II.i.172.

cutpurse: pickpocket, not because he was not elected but because he murdered his brother to make that election necessary.

diadem: the royal crown.

And put it in his pocket—
QUEEN
                    No more.
HAMLET
                              A king
Of shreds and patches—

Enter Ghost.

Save me and hover o'er me with your wings,
You heavenly guards! What would your gracious
                                        [figure?
QUEEN
Alas, he's mad.   105
HAMLET
Do you not come your tardy son to chide,

That, lapsed in time and passion, lets go by

Th' important acting of your dread command?
O say.

---

shreds and patches: "In contrast to the complete man of lines 60–62" (Jenkins), with a possible allusion to the motley wear of the vice or jester or the rags of beggars.

S.D.: The stage directions in Q2 and F make no mention of the Ghost's dress, though Q1 adds "in his night gown," meaning in informal clothes as opposed to state dress or armor. If authentic, Q1's addition would indicate that the Ghost appears in a manner appropriate to the place and occasion, in armor on the battlements to soldiers, in informal dress in private rooms to his son. The only specification in the dialogue about the Ghost's dress in this scene is that he is said to appear "in his habit as he lived" (line 135).

Save me ... guards: Hamlet first prays for help, cf., I.iv.39, and then speaks in awe and terror, as Gertrude's later description of him confirms (lines 119–24). **What would ... figure:** What do you want, what is your desire or intention? • "your figure" is formal direct address in the third person, akin to "your majesty" or "your grace," the Ghost being a "figure" of a man but not a man. "'If, after the first appearance, the persons employed neglect, or are prevented from, performing the message or business committed to their management, the Ghost appears continually to them' (Grose, *Provincial Glossary* [Superstitions, page 14])" (Jenkins).

lapsed in time and passion: • Hamlet means that he has allowed time to pass and his passion either to distract him or to be weakened. But editors who take his reasoning here to be accurate ignore what they have just heard and seen. It is not time that has delayed Hamlet's killing of the King, nor has his passion been either too great (distracting him from action) or too little (weakening his resolve). In fact Hamlet has just engaged in the extreme passionate action of killing the King, which he thought he was doing when he killed Polonius, cf., line 32. Hamlet is indeed guilty of retarding (letting "go by") the fulfillment of his mission, but the reason is neither time nor passion but his evil intention, exhibited to us in III.iii, the error of *not* killing the King in that scene leading to the erroneous assumption that he was killing him in this. Nor has Hamlet yet grown enough in self-knowledge to be aware of the sinful cause of the lapse, though he has effectively made Gertrude aware of her own sin.

important: urgent, weighty. **dread:** i.e., causing dread, awe-inspiring.

GHOST

Do not forget. This visitation   110
Is but to whet thy almost blunted purpose.

Do not forget: cf., I.v.91.

but to whet: only, merely, to sharpen, i.e., not to chide Hamlet as Hamlet assumes at line 106.
● The Ghost's distinction between *chide* and *whet* is significant. It is Hamlet's excessive focus on the consequences, the rewards and punishments possibly in store for the King, that has tempted Hamlet into error. In compassion, the Ghost tries to redirect Hamlet's attention to his mission and away from fear of or desire for consequences so far beyond human knowledge and control as damnation. **almost blunted purpose:** From the Ghost's point of view Hamlet's purpose is to kill the King. What has blunted that purpose is not time or passion, as Hamlet thinks, but pride and self-will. Hamlet has substituted his own personal satisfaction for his divinely ordained mission, as we know from the previous scene (see Introduction, pages 5–7). The terms "whet" and "blunted" evoke an image of the sword that Hamlet almost used in III.iii but put up for later use, and then did use earlier in this scene. The very sharpness of his erroneous stabbing (of Polonius) ironically reveals and contrasts with the blunting of his actual (heaven-ordained) purpose.

But look, amazement on thy mother sits.

amazement: wonder, "Not merely 'astonishment' but 'bewilderment'. Cf. I.ii.235, II.ii.[565]" (Jenkins).

O step between her and her fighting soul.

step ... soul: get between her and her inner conflict, which the next line suggests may allude to her struggle with the "conceit" that Hamlet is mad indeed.

Conceit in weakest bodies strongest works.
Speak to her, Hamlet.

HAMLET
                      How is it with you, lady?   115

Conceit: the mental faculty of conceiving or forming images, imagination, here more particularly false images, fancy (OED 7.b). ● Jenkins quotes Florio's translation of Montaigne (I.20), the "weakest ... , whose conceit is so seized upon, that they imagine to see what they see not." The quotation is both apt and ironic, since Gertrude does not see all that is, namely the Ghost (cf., line 132), yet imagines that she does see Hamlet to be mad. Her misplaced certainty is parallel to Hamlet's in the previous scene, where he imagined he saw the King repenting, and in this scene, where he imagines it is the King behind the arras.

QUEEN
Alas, how is't with you,

That you do bend your eye on vacancy
And with th' incorporal air do hold discourse?
Forth at your eyes your spirits wildly peep,

bend ... on: turn ... to, look at. **vacancy:** emptiness.
incorporal: bodiless. ● Gertrude cannot see the Ghost.

Forth at your eyes ... peep: "A metaphor based on the theory that the physical signs of mental excitement were attributable to the agitation of the *spirits*. These were conceived of as fluids permeating the blood which ascended to the brain and determined its activity" (Jenkins), cf., I.iv.38 SPEECH NOTE.

And, as the sleeping soldiers in th' alarm,   120

as the sleeping soldiers ... stand an end: "The hairs are compared with soldiers who leap from their beds ... and stand stiff and erect for action" (Dover Wilson quoted in Jenkins). ● to imply Hamlet's terror at seeing the Ghost. **in th' alarm:** "when the call to arms is sounded" (Riverside).

Your bedded hair, like life in excrements,

excrements: outgrowths (from Latin *ex* + *cresco*, to spring forth, to grow). ● Hair and nails, because they

Start up and stand an end. O gentle son,

Upon the heat and flame of thy distemper

Sprinkle cool patience. Whereon do you look?

HAMLET
On him, on him! Look you how pale he glares.   125

His form and cause conjoined, preaching to stones,

Would make them capable.—[*to the Ghost.*] Do not
                                          [look upon me,
Lest with this piteous action you convert

My stern effects. Then what I have to do

Will want true color—tears perchance for blood.   130

QUEEN
To whom do you speak this?
HAMLET
                          Do you see nothing there?

QUEEN
Nothing at all, yet all that is I see.

---

had no sensation, were held to be not part of the living body, hence the unnaturalness of hairs standing up like suddenly awakened soldiers as if life were in them (Jenkins substantially).

Start up: are startled. **an end:** "an" is the prefix *a*- with the *n* retained for euphony, cf., I.v.19 note and see Abbott §24.

heat and flame: a hendiadys for "hot flame" (Wright, page 187). **distemper:** passion, imbalance in temperament, cf., I.iv.38. ● SPEECH NOTE: not a result of madness, as Gertrude thinks, but the body's natural reaction to an unnatural external situation that we who see the Ghost recognize.

Sprinkle cool patience: ● Gertrude not unreasonably wishes Hamlet to temper the heat of his passion with the coolness of the intellectual discipline and virtue of patience, meaning the practice of putting up with, enduring (from the Latin *patior*, to bear or suffer).

form: shape, appearance. **cause:** mission, purpose, intention, motive for appearing. **stones:** i.e., *even* to stones, cf., *Julius Caesar* I.i.35, III.ii.230, and Luke 19:40.

capable: i.e., of feeling and responding, cf., III.ii.11.

piteous action: pitying gesture. ● The Ghost pities Hamlet for his moral fall in the previous scene, which Hamlet does not yet see as a fall. **convert:** change, alter

stern effects: harsh intended actions (i.e., to kill the King).

want: lack. **color:** quality, character (OED *sb.* 16.), with the additional implications of justification (OED *sb.* 11), pretext for doing something (OED *sb.* 12), and the literal meaning, neutral color of tears for red color of blood (Jenkins substantially). ● Hamlet here fears that in the future he will be converted away from shedding the King's blood, not realizing that he has already been converted from doing so not by mercy but by a fiercer revenge than it was Hamlet's place to enact.

To whom ... nothing there: The apparent hexameters here and at line 133 may be seen as trimeter couplets (Abbott §500), or they may form a regular pentameter i "do you" is elided into one syllable and the stresses are placed on "whom," "speak," "Do," "noth-" and "there."

Nothing ... I see: ● Gertrude's certainty is not only an immediate dramatic irony but also the most directly articulated instance of the pride in one's own view of reality that is a central subject of the play. Polonius believes that he knows why Hamlet is mad, that he can pluck out the heart of Hamlet's "mystery," as Rosencrantz and Guildenstern believe they can. Hamle believes that the King is repenting when he is not (in III.iii) and that the King is behind the arras when he is not (line 32). Laertes will believe Hamlet to be entirely responsible for the death of Polonius and the madness of Ophelia. The Gravedigger will believe he is a master interpreter of "crowner's quest law." And so on. The question why Hamlet can see and hear the Ghost and Gertrude cannot is thus answered in two ways:

a) The visibility of a ghost to one person and not others is a commonplace of Elizabethan folklore and stage convention: "they may be seene of some, and of some other in that presence not seene at all" (Reginald Scot, *Discoverie of Witchcraft*, Appendix "Of Devils and Spirits," Ch. 28, page 449), and, referring to this scene, "the poet had ... an eye to a vulgar notion that spirits are only seen by those with whom their business is, let there be never so many persons in company" (Anon., *Remarks on the Tragedy of Hamlet*, 1736). See these and other examples, including James I, *Demonology*, III.1, in Stoll *SS*, page 212 note 47, and Jenkins LN, which cites these references.

b) The role the Ghost plays in general is essentially that of a messenger, appearing only to those to whom he must appear in order to get the message delivered. He needed to appear to the soldiers and Horatio so that they would be believed when conveying the message to Hamlet and so that Hamlet might have allies later. He needs to appear to Hamlet here to punctuate Hamlet's failure to do what he has been charged to do. The messenger function of the Ghost here has parallels in the play: Old Norway recalls Fortinbras from his false adventure, Laertes' conscience corrects Laertes in time for him to repent before he dies, and Hamlet will recall Horatio from his attempt at suicide. In the case of Gertrude, Hamlet himself is the only messenger she needs, and he has succeeded in delivering the message effectively. She being penitent already, no appearance of the Ghost is necessary to her situation. The distinction between seeing and not seeing the Ghost in this scene, while conventionally appropriate for reasons of plot, is at the same time a dramatization of heaven's ordination of events (cf., V.ii.48) and of the shaping of our ends (cf., V.ii.10). So thoroughly unified is Shakespeare's vision, that the conventional method and the thematic significance become seamlessly one, cf., the appearance of Banquo's ghost in *Macbeth* III.iv and Thomas Heywood, *2 Iron Age*, Part II, Act V (cited in Jenkins LN).

Nor did you ... ourselves: see previous note.

HAMLET
Nor did you nothing hear?

QUEEN
                    No, nothing but ourselves.

HAMLET
Why, look you there, look how it steals away—
My father, in his habit as he lived.   135

habit: clothing, "characteristic dress, as at I.iii.70" (Jenkins). **as he lived:** as he dressed when he was alive, cf., line 101 S.D. note.
portal: doorway, cf., *Rape of Lucrece* 309.

Look where he goes even now out at the portal.
                    Exit Ghost.

QUEEN
This is the very coinage of your brain.

coinage: invention, as of a newly "coined" word, from the act of coining money or the right to do so.

This bodiless creation ecstasy

Is very cunning in.

HAMLET

My pulse as yours doth temperately keep time   140
And makes as healthful music. It is not madness

That I have uttered. Bring me to the test,
And I the matter will re-word, which madness

Would gambol from. Mother, for love of grace,

Lay not that flattering unction to your soul   145
That not your trespass but my madness speaks.

It will but skin and film the ulcerous place

Whilst rank corruption, mining all within,
Infects unseen. Confess yourself to heaven,
Repent what's past, avoid what is to come,   150
And do not spread the compost on the weeds
To make them ranker. Forgive me this my virtue,

For in the fatness of these pursy times

---

bodiless creation: invention of an incorporeal being.
ecstasy: madness, "its synonym in line [141], cf., II.i.[99], III.i.[160], and line 74 above" (Jenkins).
cunning in: The ending preposition is a result of inverted word order. The sentence may be understood as "Ecstasy is very cunning in this creation of bodiless [beings]."

My: Q2, "Extasie? / My" F, probably an actor's addition for effect and to fill the empty feet.
temperately: evenly, ordinately, pronounced "temp'rately," elided to preserve the meter.
Bring me to the test: try me, test me.
matter will re-word: exactly restate all that we have just said, "matter" being the substance and "word" being the external form or ornament (Baldwin II.183–84).
gambol: wildly leap, spring away, like a horse, i.e., madness would shy away from restating, or from being able to restate, precisely what has just been said, cf., 2 Henry IV II.iv.251, where the word is associated with a "weak mind."

Lay not ... Infects unseen: Harmon (page 997) finds analogues if not sources for this passage not only in Florio's translation of Montaigne's *Essays* (III.67) but in Seneca's *De tranquillitate animi* (II.11–12) and *De ira* I.xvi.3), Nani Mirabelli's *Polyanthea* under "Voluptas," and Robert Cawdrey's *Treasurie or Storehouse of Similies* under "Continuance of Sinne." **Lay:** apply (OED lay $v.^1$ 15.). **that flattering unction:** that falsely soothing ointment, cf., IV.vii.141, identified in the next line, i.e., do not console yourself with the delusion that I am mad and that therefore you are not guilty.

skin ... unseen: "Kittredge cites Hughes, *Misfortunes of Arthur*, III.i.111–14, 'where the salve did soonest close the skin, The sore was oftener covered up than cured, which festering deep ... grew greater than at first'" (Jenkins). **skin:** cover over with skin, cf., *Measure for Measure* II.ii.136. **film:** cover with a film (OED film $v.1$.).
rank: cf., line 92 note. **corruption:** infection, here a metaphor for sin. **mining:** digging, eating away.

compost: manure, rotted organic matter.
ranker: more luxuriantly growing, with the additional implications of line 92 note. **my virtue:** his masculine strength in chiding her (*virtue* from Latin *vir*, man), with the possible added sense of authority, jurisdiction (Crystal 7).
pursy: swollen, puffed up, like a purse.
• "fatness" and "pursy" "suggest the physical (and metaphorically the moral) grossness that comes from undisciplined self-indulgence" (Jenkins), in particular that of the sin of pride. Cf., similar images of the corruption of the age and place at I.ii.135–37, II.ii.363–66, IV.iv.27–29, V.i.139–41, V.ii.189, and "bloat king" at line 182.

Virtue itself of vice must pardon beg,

Yea, curb and woo for leave to do him good.   155
QUEEN
O Hamlet, thou hast cleft my heart in twain.
HAMLET
O throw away the worser part of it

And live the purer with the other half.
Good night, but go not to my uncle's bed.
Assume a virtue if you have it not.   160

That monster, custom, who all sense doth eat
Of habits evil, is angel yet in this,
That to the use of actions fair and good
He likewise gives a frock or livery
That aptly is put on. Refrain tonight,   165

Virtue: ● Hamlet implies that he personifies virtue and his mother vice, but as we have seen, though he is in the role of virtue in relation to Gertrude, after the previous scene he is now also in the role of vice in relation to the imperative of the Ghost.

curb: bend, bow (from French *courber*, OED *v.*¹ 2.). **woo:** entreat, beg. **leave:** permission.

cleft: cloven, cut (past tense of *to cleave*). **twain:** two. ● Hamlet has succeeded in his plan of penetrating Gertrude's heart, cf., lines 20, 35–36, and the splitting of her heart is not "between regret for her conduct and loyalty to her present husband" (Jenkins) or between loyalty to her present husband and loyalty to her previous husband and her son. What Hamlet has broken apart is the illusory unity of her heart that, in her delusion, seemed to her to be loyal both to her first and to her second husband but now, in her contrition, is revealed to have been divided all along by the sinful desires and choices of her past. It is Hamlet who shifts her metaphor toward the distinction between loyalty to Claudius and the penance of renouncing his bed.

live: F, leave Q2.

Assume a virtue ... stamp of nature: Harmon (page 997) finds analogues if not sources for this passage not only in Florio's translation of Montaigne's *Essays* (III.29, 265, 347) but in Seneca (*Epistles* XXXIX.6), Nani Mirabelli's *Polyanthea* under "Consuetudo," Thomas Elyot's *Bankette of Sapience* under "Maners of men," William Baldwin's *Treatise of Moral Philosophy*, Robert Whittinton's *Mirror or Glass of Manners and Wisdom*, and Nicholas Ling's *Politeuphuia* or *Wit's Commonwealth* under "Of Labour." **Assume:** put on, as one puts on clothing, not in pretense but as reformed behavior.

That monster ... aptly is put on: Continuing the clothing metaphor of line 160, Hamlet asserts that custom, which is monstrous in devouring our sense of the evil in our bad habits, is also angelic in giving our practice of "fair and good" actions clothing (i.e., good habits) that we wear both readily and fittingly or appropriately ("aptly"). ● In other words, habit, which is a "monster" because through familiarity it devours what is otherwise normal, natural, and good in us, namely the perception of the evil in our bad habits, is nevertheless also the opposite of a monster ("angel") in that it makes the practice of good actions similarly habitual, that is, put on readily and appropriately. **custom:** habitual or usual practice (OED 1.). **eat / Of habits evil:** Theobald (Thirlby conjecture), eat / Of habits devil Q2, not in F. ● Thirlby's conjecture (adopted by Dover Wilson, Kittredge, Sisson, and Jenkins) makes excellent sense of the difficult passage, revealing that the essential antithesis is not the limited local contrast of devil vs. angel but rather the whole sentence's contrast of monster vs. angel. In this reading custom is monstrous in eating not all sense but all awareness ("sense") of the evil in evil habits. "[T]hat the emendation has been long and frequently resisted is due to the attractiveness of an antithesis (insisted on by Johnson) between *devil* and *angel*. Yet this seeming justification for the Q2 reading may well have been, as Theobald supposed, the source of its error" (Jenkins LN). **habits:** a) habitual behavior, b) clothing. **use:** practice, repeated action or behavior, performance. **frock:** dress, gown, cloak (Raffel). **livery:** distinctive garb, the characteristic clothing of a servant indicating whom he serves. **aptly:** fitly, suitably, appropriately (OED 2.) and readily (OED 3.). **put on:** a) worn, as clothing, b) adopted into practice, as a habit. The idea that virtue is achieved through habituation derives from Aristotle's *Nichomachean Ethics* (II.i–iv), and cf., *Two Gentlemen* V.iv.1.

And that shall lend a kind of easiness
To the next abstinence, the next more easy;
For use almost can change the stamp of nature

shall: is sure to (Abbott §315), "cannot but" (Jenkins).

use: habit, practice, cf., "Use is another nature" (Nashe, *Unfortunate Traveller* II.302, ref. in Jenkins), "Custom (Use) is another (a second) nature" (Tilley C 932). **almost:** because Aristotle asserts (*Ethics* II.i) that it cannot ("The moral virtues, then, are engendered in us neither *by* nor *contrary to* nature; we are constituted by nature to receive them, but their full development in us is due to habit"). **stamp:** "character bestowed or imprinted by. Cf. I.iv.31" (Jenkins).

And either [lodge] the devil or throw him out
With wondrous potency. Once more, good night,   170

And either … potency: since a word is missing in Q2, as we know from both sense and meter, and the passage is absent from F, we are left with either a blank or various editorial emendations, of which the best, perhaps, is "lodge" (= welcome, accommodate, give lodging to), Clarendon's conjecture, adopted by Jenkins and very tentatively here, though "the attempt to supply a word that is lost can only clutch at surmise" (Jenkins LN). The clear point is again that habituation ("use") makes it easy to engage in good as well as evil practices. **potency:** strength, "Stressing the less expected effect (that *use* can bring about good as well as evil)" (Jenkins), for the encouragement of Gertrude.

And when you are desirous to be blest,

desirous to be blest: repentant (Riverside), wishing to ask forgiveness.

I'll blessing beg of you. For this same lord

I'll blessing beg of you: ask for the traditional parental blessing of a child, cf., I.iii.57 and *King Lear* IV.vii.56–57 and V.iii.10–11. **this same lord:** i.e., Polonius.

I do repent; but heaven hath pleased it so
To punish me with this and this with me,

I do repent: ● a crucial phrase. Hamlet has not intended the death of Polonius, and his passion for revenge against the King has not entirely tainted his sense of justice. **heaven hath pleased … this with me:** ● This observation is truer than Hamlet can yet know, though he will know it more fully by the end of the play. He has not yet recognized the particular sin for which this disastrous error and its consequences are his punishment, but we have seen him commit it in III.iii. "'Even so doth God punish the wicked one by another' (P. de Mornay, *The Trewnesse of the Christian Religion*, ch. 12)" (Jenkins).

That I must be their scourge and minister.   175

their: of the heavens, pluralized from line 173, "The use of *heaven* in plural sense is common: see [William Sidney] Walker, [*A Critical Examination of the Text of Shakespeare*, 3 vols., 1860] II.110–13" (Jenkins), cf., *Richard II* I.ii.7. **scourge and minister:** possibly a hendiadys for "scourging minister" (Wright, page 187), but see the next two notes. **scourge:** literally "whip" (from late Latin *excoriare*, to strip off the hide [*corium*]) but in the phrase "scourge of God" (in Latin, *flagellum dei*, applied to Attila, 5th century leader of the Huns, and to Tamburlaine in Marlowe's play) implying the evil means of God's punishment of sinful mankind, cf., Isaiah 10:5–15. **minister:** instrument, servant, cf., III.ii.366 and note.
• As Hamlet is the scourge to punish the King and Polonius, the minister to effect the repentance of Gertrude, and both toward Laertes, so Laertes will become the scourge to punish Hamlet's sin. It may be that the role of scourge is not always "given only to the guilty" (Jenkins LN), but in III.iii Hamlet *is* guilty and Laertes is so in V.ii. Isaiah 10:15 ("Shall the axe boast itself against him that heweth therewith? ... as if ... the staff should exalt itself, as it were no wood") applies precisely to Hamlet in III.iii.

I will bestow him, and will answer well
The death I gave him. So, again, good night.

bestow him: stow away the body, "dispose of. Cf. IV.ii.1, IV.iii.12" (Jenkins). **answer well:** repent and do penance for.

I must be cruel only to be kind.

cruel ... kind: harsh with Gertrude in order to effect her genuine repentance.

This bad begins, and worse remains behind.

This: the killing of Polonius, cf., line 174. **worse:** the killing of Claudius, who is of higher rank, or perhaps the killing *and* damnation of Claudius, for Hamlet, despite his error in mistaking Polonius for the King, has given no sign of having renounced the latter intention. • Hamlet has already recognized that there must be some consequences for himself as a result of the death of Polonius (lines 174 and 177), and the audience is sure to hear the phrase as a reference to Hamlet's still unaccomplished mission. There is no language of prophecy here, as at I.v.40 or V.ii.212–19. Hence, if Hamlet's phrase is a "prophetic glimpse of the whole tragic outcome" (Jenkins), it is a foreshadowing given to the audience but not a foresight given to Hamlet. **behind:** still to come, yet to be accomplished. The metaphor is of events seen as marching toward us, the later ones coming behind the more recent ones.

One word more, good lady.
QUEEN
                              What shall I do?   180

One word ... lady: "F may be right to omit this. It seems intrusive after Hamlet's couplet, and the Queen's question in itself prompts him to resume" (Jenkins), but the point is not strong enough to adopt the F reading over Q2 here. **One word ... I do?:**
• NOTE TO ACTORS: The monosyllable "word" may be prolonged, by the vowel followed by *r*, to the value of two syllables, hence making "One word more" into

HAMLET

Not this, by no means, that I bid you do:

Let the bloat king tempt you again to bed,

Pinch wanton on your cheek, call you his mouse,

And let him, for a pair of reechy kisses,
Or paddling in your neck with his damned fingers,   185

Make you to ravel all this matter out

That I essentially am not in madness
But mad in craft. 'Twere good you let him know,
For who that's but a queen, fair, sober, wise,

Would from a paddock, from a bat, a gib,   190

Such dear concernings hide? Who would do so?

No, in despite of sense and secrecy,

Unpeg the basket on the house's top,
Let the birds fly, and like the famous ape,
To try conclusions, in the basket creep,   195
And break your own neck down.

QUEEN

Be thou assured, if words be made of breath,

And breath of life, I have no life to breathe
What thou hast said to me.

two iambs (Abbott §485), but it may be best to treat the line as four trochees and an iamb: "Óne wŏrd móre, gŏod ládў. Whát shăll Ĭ dó?"

Not this ... bid you do: By no means do what I am about to tell you (sarcastically) to do. ● NOTE TO ACTORS: This line restores the regular iambic meter from the trochaic feet of the previous line.

Let ... tempt: i.e., (with sarcasm) go ahead and let him tempt. **bloat:** flabby, puffy, swollen "as a result of self-indulgence" (Raffel), cf., line 153 note.

wanton: wantonly, self-indulgently (Abbott §1), or possibly "leave marks of his fondling which proclaim you a wanton" (Jenkins). **mouse:** "A term of endearment to a woman" (Jenkins), cf., *Twelfth Night* I.v.63, *Romeo and Juliet* IV.iv.11.

reechy: steamy, squalid, filthy.

paddling: fondling or tapping with the fingers, cf., *Othello* II.i.254, *Winter's Tale* I.ii.115, 125.

make: following "let him" in line 184. **ravel all this matter out:** disentangle the threads for him (by revealing what I've told you).

That I ... in craft: that I am not actually mad but only pretending. ● Once again, Hamlet confirms that all his supposed madness was playacting. **'Twere good ... own neck down:** The whole passage continues the sarcasm: why *wouldn't* a "fair, sober, wise" queen keep such important information concerning Hamlet from one so unsavory as the King?

paddock ... bat ... gib: toad, bat, gib-cat (castrated male cat), all three being animal forms that evil familiar spirits may take in their dealings with devil-worshiping human witches.

dear concernings: "matters of intense concern" (Riverside).

in despite of: in spite of, in defiance or contempt of. **sense and secrecy:** possibly a hendiadys, "good sense which calls for secrecy" (Wright, page 187). **sense:** good sense, wisdom. **secrecy:** confidentiality.

Unpeg ... neck down: Hamlet combines an old adage with an old fable now lost, urging Gertrude, sarcastically, to give away his secret and to destroy herself in the process. **Unpeg the basket:** release the peg that keeps the basket closed. Birds released on a roof from a basket in which they are confined fly away and cannot be recaptured, an image for giving away secrets, like "letting the cat out of the bag" (Jenkins substantially). **try conclusions:** make experiments. Apparently the "famous ape" tried to see whether he could fly if he crept into the basket and then leapt out of it like the birds, but he fell from the housetop to his death (Jenkins substantially). **in:** into (Abbott §159). **break ... down:** break by falling down from the roof (like the ape).

I have no life: I have no will, desire, ability. **to breathe:** to utter, even in a whisper.

● Having registered Hamlet's sarcasm, Gertrude

HAMLET
I must to England, you know that?
QUEEN
                              Alack,   200
I had forgot. 'Tis so concluded on.

HAMLET
There's letters sealed, and my two schoolfellows,

Whom I will trust as I will adders fanged,

They bear the mandate; they must sweep my way

And marshal me to knavery. Let it work,   205

For 'tis the sport to have the énginer

Hoist with his own petar, and 't shall go hard

But I will delve one yard below their mines

And blow them at the moon. O, 'tis most sweet

---

promises to keep from the King the idea that Hamlet is not in fact mad.

I must to England: ● How Hamlet knows that the King intends to send him to England before the King explicitly tells him so (IV.iii.40–46) is another question that arises in the study, not in the audience. The audience is aware of the plan, for the King has floated the idea as early as III.i.169. Shakespeare needs us to know here that Hamlet knows it but finds no need to tell us how he has found it out, and "if the matter were of any importance, we should not have been left in doubt" (Smith, see Introduction, page 6, note 13). If we must have a source for Hamlet's knowledge of it, we shall have to be content to locate it in the principle that "What great ones do, the less will prattle of" (*Twelfth Night* I.ii.33).
to: go to. **Alack:** an expression of sorrow or regret, from *a* + *lack* = lack, failure, fault, reproach (OED).

There's: for the singular verb with plural subject following see Abbott §335. **letters sealed:** ● No one in the theater during the play is concerned to know how Hamlet could know of these letters. This is not a Shakespearean blunder but an example of the theatrical conventions of the day, unfolding between the pure allegorical representations of the earlier drama and the slice-of-life verisimilitude of the later. A study-desk consistency of realistic detail is demanded only at later periods. For Shakespeare and his audience, of far greater importance is the immediate impression and a consistency of theme and meaning. **two schoolfellows:** Rosencrantz and Guildenstern, cf., II.ii.11.

trust … fanged: The phrase gives support to Hamlet's suspicion, when later he reads the King's letter requiring the English king to kill Hamlet, that Rosencrantz and Guildenstern are in on the plot, cf., V.ii.58 note.

mandate: formal authoritative order. **sweep my way:** clear my path, as escorting servants accompanying him on the journey.

marshal: conduct in an orderly way, usher. **to knavery:** i.e., to suffering from whatever villainous plot against him is brewing, cf., V.ii.19, *not* to committing any knavery himself.

'tis the sport: the game is. **énginer:** maker of military devices or "engines," accented on the first syllable, like "pioner" at I.v.163 (Abbott §492).

Hoist: blown up into the air, hence destroyed, past participle of the older verb *hoise* (OED hoise *v*. 2.b.), cf., Abbott §342. **petar:** petard, bomb, an explosive device for breaching walls or knocking out gates. **'t shall go hard / But I will:** things will go very badly if I don't (Abbott §120, §121).

delve: dig. **mines:** tunnels under a wall or fortification and also the explosive devices (gunpowder kegs) set there.

blow them at: explode them up to (Abbott §143).
● Hamlet's image is from siege warfare. Those laying siege to a walled town or castle would attempt to dig under the walls to "undermine" them or blow them up

When in one line two crafts directly meet.   210

This man shall set me packing.

I'll lug the guts into the neighbor room.
Mother, good night indeed. This counselor

Is now most still, most secret, and most grave,

Who was in life a foolish prating knave.   215

Come, sir, to draw toward an end with you.
Good night, mother.

Exit [dragging the body of Polonius].

---

from below in order to breach them and enter the city. Against such an attempt, the defense was to preempt the attack by digging from inside the walls below the besiegers' tunnels, undermining their mines, in order to blow them up outside and at some distance from the walls. The image is an apt one for the plots and counter-plots of Hamlet and the King, and later of Laertes, many of which, as Horatio reports, fall on the inventors' heads (V.ii.385), and all of which, under the divine shaping, come to their tragic completion in the play's final scene.

in one line ... meet: head for one another on a "collision course" (Jenkins). **crafts:** skilful activity, cunning plans (Crystal), plots (Raffel), and forms of artistry, here the arts of warfare.

This man: Polonius. **set me packing:** a) cause me to pack my bags in order to leave in a hurry for a journey, b) dismiss me summarily (from the court), and c) set me to contriving or plotting, which continues and puns on the previous images, cf., *Taming of the Shrew* V.i.118.

guts: the remains, the dead body.

indeed: in fact, actually, for he has said good night several times already (lines 159, 170, 177) but not left her.

grave: sober, serious. ● Hamlet's bitterness at Polonius's intrusion and at his own error in killing him is expressed in the sardonic pun.

prating: babbling, chattering. ● Once again, Polonius is a foil for Hamlet. The irony of the dead man's stillness, secrecy, and gravity in contrast to his busybody life is a foretaste of the *memento mori* of V.i and a reminder of Hamlet's own pretension to divinity in III.iii, which will, through the "indirection" (cf., II.i.63) of his killing of Polonius, lead to his own death. Just as Polonius thought he was smarter than Hamlet, so Hamlet has fallen into the belief that he can outflank that divinity that shapes our ends (V.ii.10). The question of the play is whether and how Hamlet, like his mother in this scene, will be chastened before it is too late. In this scene, Hamlet has acted as the chastener of his mother. In the next two acts the chastener of Hamlet will be Providence itself.

draw toward an end with you: finish up, conclude my business (Jenkins) or conversation (Riverside), with you, with a pun on the cognate *drag*.

S.D.: Q2 Exit, F Exit Hamlet tugging in Polonius, "in" meaning from the stage into the wings, tugging it offstage. "The F direction, which Greg thought 'one could swear ... was Shakespeare's' (*SFF* [*The Shakespeare First Folio*], page 319), appears in fact to be an editorial addition deriving, via a misprint, from the dialogue (*lug*, line [212])" (Jenkins).

● **End Note and Note to Directors:** Though the early editors marked this as the end of Act III, the scene is continuous with the next (IV.i). Gertrude does not leave the stage here, and Claudius, Rosencrantz, and Guildenstern enter to her private rooms immediately

after Hamlet's departure with the dead body. In Q2 the
Queen is listed among those entering, but her exit here
was not indicated. See next note.

Act IV, Scene i: Gertrude's closet.

Scene Note: Later editors follow a late quarto in
erroneously marking this scene as the beginning of
Act IV, though in Q2, F, and Q1 it is continuous from
the previous scene. Q2 has the Queen entering here
but indicates no previous exit for her. F omits her
superfluous entry. ● As soon as Hamlet leaves his
mother, his three enemies enter to her. **closet:** the
Queen's private chambers (not the modern sense of
a small room in which to hang clothes).

Act IV, Scene i

Enter King, Rosencrantz, and Guildenstern.

KING

There's matter in these sighs; these prófound heaves

There's matter … translate: F punctuation substantially,
Q2 punctuates with commas through line 3. **matter:**
meaning, import. **prófound:** ● NOTE TO ACTORS:
stress on the first syllable, cf., I.iv.52 note. **heaves:** deep
sighs. ● Gertrude does not speak but is sighing in grief,
"cf. 'penitential heaves' of *Revenger's Trag[edy]*, II.iii.12"
(Jenkins).

You must transláte. 'Tis fit we understand them.
Where is your son?

transláte: explain, construe, an allusion to the regular
grammar school procedure for addressing a passage in
Latin (Baldwin I.589). ● NOTE TO ACTORS: stressed on
the second syllable.
fit: fitting, appropriate, *that* is understood (fit that we
understand). **we:** the royal plural, used throughout the
scene.

GERTRUDE

Bestow this place on us a little while.
            Exeunt Rosencrantz and Guildenstern.
Ah, mine own lord, what have I seen tonight!   5

Bestow this place on us: leave us alone here.

KING

What, Gertrude, how does Hamlet?

What: not an interrogative as in F ("What Gertrude?")
but an exclamation (Abbott §73a), "Employed in calling
to persons, particularly when it is done with some
impatience" (Schmidt), or perhaps compassion (Jenkins)
given Gertrude's as yet unexplained heavy sighs.

GERTRUDE

Mad as the sea and wind when both contend

Mad … fit: ● Gertrude here proves faithful to her son in
keeping up the fiction of his madness.

Which is the mightier. In his lawless fit,
Behind the arras hearing something stir,
Whips out his rapier, cries, "A rat, a rat!"   10
And in this brainish apprehension kills
The unseen good old man.

mightier … old man: Both Q2 and F have a comma after
"mightier" and a lower case *i* for "in," and it is syntactically
possible that "Mad" serves as an introductory adjective
modifying the understood "he," the implied subject of
"Whips," "cries," and "kills," rather than an independent
answer to the King's question, especially if the length and
complexity of the sentence indicate that Gertrude has
been planning what to tell Claudius. On the other hand,
"mightier. In" is dramatically preferable if the shorter
answer is taken to fit with Gertrude's "sighs"
and "heaves," and most modern editors adopt it; for
the missing "he" (elliptical nominative) see Abbott
§399 and cf., II.ii.67 and III.i.8. **lawless:** mad,
ungoverned. **brainish:** "headstrong, passionate"
(OED), "deluded, frenzied" (Jenkins), "brainsick"
(Schmidt), "deluded, distracted, deranged" (Crystal),

KING

O heavy deed!
It had been so with us had we been there.
His liberty is full of threats to all—
To you yourself, to us, to everyone.   15
Alas, how shall this bloody deed be answered?

It will be laid to us, whose providence

Should have kept short, restrained, and out of haunt
This mad young man. But so much was our love,
We would not understand what was most fit,   20
But like the owner of a foul disease,
To keep it from divulging, let it feed

Even on the pith of life. Where is he gone?

GERTRUDE

To draw apart the body he hath killed,
O'er whom his very madness, like some ore   25
Among a mineral of metals base,
Shows itself pure: a weeps for what is done.

KING

O Gertrude, come away!
The sun no sooner shall the mountains touch,
But we will ship him hence: and this vile deed   30

"headstrong and entirely imagined" (Raffel).
apprehension: conception, imagination, notion.
heavy: grave, serious, severe, dire.
us ... we: the royal plural.
liberty: his freedom from the restraint usually applied to madmen.
answered: accounted for to the public and perhaps also paid for (avenged).
laid to us: blamed on me. **providence:** foresight, preparation in advance (from Latin *pro-vidēre* to see ahead).
short: on a short leash. **out of haunt:** away from places that people frequent.
fit: fitting, appropriate.

divulging: being revealed to others, intransitive "for refl[exive]" (OED 4.).
pith: vital essence, substance, core, cf., I.iv.22 note.

O'er whom ... what is done: It is tempting (as Jenkins does) to take the commas in Q2 to indicate that "O'er whom ... a weeps" is the single main clause of the speech and that "his very madness ... shows itself pure" is a parenthetical independent clause. Against this reading a) it is unlike Shakespeare to make parenthetical an entire independent clause containing its own parenthetical analogy, separating the subject and verb ("a weeps") so far from a prepositional phrase ("O'er whom"), and such a parenthetical would normally have called for "showing" instead of "shows," b) the distance separating the two prepositional phrases ("O'er whom" and "for what is done") is extreme, and c) the independence and brevity of the final clause ("a weeps for what is done") seems more dramatic than the long suspended sentence and more in keeping with Gertrude's "sighs" and "heaves," cf., line 8 note. ● Gertrude, while wanting to reinforce the idea that Hamlet is mad, also wants to suggest that there is good in Hamlet. Over the body of Polonius even Hamlet's madness, responsible for making that body dead, shows that it nonetheless has something pure in it, as gold may show itself amidst a mine or deposit of base metals. Faithful to Hamlet in lying to the King about Hamlet's being mad, Gertrude is also trying to assuage any anger the King may feel against Hamlet, whether she means Hamlet's weeping to be taken literally—we have not seen him weeping—which would be duplicitous to the King in loyalty to Hamlet, or as an honest metaphor for his genuine repentance. **some:** Q2 and F, Walker's conjecture (II.299) *fine*, adopted by Furness, Jenkins finds "very plausible." **ore:** "Often used by the Elizabethans for precious metal, and specifically for gold, perhaps through confusion with French and heraldic *or*" (Jenkins). **mineral:** mine (OED 3., Jenkins) or "mineral deposit" (Crystal). **base:** impure, non-valuable. **a:** he.

We must with all our majesty and skill
Both countenance and excuse. Ho, Guildenstern!

Re-enter Rosencrantz and Guildenstern.

majesty ... excuse: the parallelism is "with ... majesty... countenance [verb]" and "with ... skill ... excuse [verb]" (Braunmuller substantially). **countenance:** to grace, to put a good aspect on, to make a proper show of (OED 4.). **excuse:** to seek to clear the blame, from Hamlet (OED *v.* 1.a.) or from his offense (OED *v.* 1.b.). The King says that he must use the majesty of his office to put a good face on the deed and all his political skill to get Hamlet publicly off the hook. Wright (page 187) finds "majesty and skill" a hendiadys, but this is perhaps a case in which the line between "clearly parallel" (page 185) and hendiadys is not distinct.

Friends both, go join you with some further aid.
Hamlet in madness hath Polonius slain,

Friends both... aid: You two friends (to me) please go join with (= gather) some additional attendants. **join:** intransitive. **you:** nominative. **further aid:** additional attendants.

And from his mother's closet hath he dragged him.   35

closet: private room, see II.i.74 note and SCENE NOTE above.
fair: politely, nicely.

Go seek him out—speak fair—and bring the body
Into the chapel. I pray you haste in this.

Exeunt Rosencrantz and Guildenstern.

Come, Gertrude, we'll call up our wisest friends
And let them know both what we mean to do
And what's untimely done. [So envious slander]   40

[So envious slander]: Jenkins, Q2 has two empty feet, F reads "And what's untimely done. Oh come away," omitting lines 41–44 through "air" entirely. Riverside indicates that words supplying the two empty feet are missing ("[...]"). Jenkins, following conjectures of Theobald ("For, haply, Slander"), Capell ("So, haply, slander"), and Malone ("So viperous slander") and admitting that "we can never know what Shakespeare wrote here," makes a strong case for "So envious slander" (adopted here), giving analogous passages: *1 Henry VI* III.i.26, III.iv.33, IV.i.90, *2 Henry VI* III.i.157, *Richard III* I.iii.26, *Richard II* I.i.171, *Troilus and Cressida* III.iii.174, *Cymbeline* III.iv.33–35, *Winter's Tale* II.iii.86–87, and *Henry VIII* III.ii.446 (Jenkins LN). Other conjectures in Furness include "rumour" (Theobald), "malice" or "envy" (Cambridge), "suspicion" (Tschischwitz), and "calumny" (Staunton). "Munro uniquely, and oddly, supposes no words lost" (Jenkins LN), no doubt reading "Whose whisper" in line 41 as referring back to "what's untimely done," but the clause "As level ... poisoned shot" seems to require a different noun.
diameter: "whole extent from side to side or from end to end" (OED 2.g.).

Whose whisper o'er the world's diameter,

As level as the cannon to his blank,
Transports his poisoned shot, may miss our name

As level ... blank: "as straight as the cannon to its mark. The blank ... is ... a target in the line of direct, or *level*, aim (i.e. point-blank, which is thus distinguished from the angled sight-line requisite at longer range). Properly *blank* refers to the line or range of fire, as in *Winter's Tale* II.iii.5, *Othello* III.iv.[128] ... , but it is also used (as here) for the object aimed at. Cf. *King Lear* I.i.[159]" (Jenkins).

And hit the woundless air. O come away.
My soul is full of discord and dismay.   45

                                                    Exeunt.

                        Act IV, Scene ii

                        Enter Hamlet.

HAMLET
  Safely stowed. [*Calling within.*] But soft, what
  noise? Who calls on Hamlet? O, here they come.

          Enter Rosencrantz, Guildenstern, and others.

ROSENCRANTZ
  What have you done, my lord, with the dead body?   5

HAMLET
  Compounded it with dust, whereto 'tis kin.

ROSENCRANTZ
  Tell us where 'tis that we may take it thence
  And bear it to the chapel.
HAMLET
                        Do not believe it.
ROSENCRANTZ
  Believe what?   10
HAMLET
  That I can keep your counsel and not mine own.

  Besides, to be demanded of a sponge, what replication
  should be made by the son of a king?
ROSENCRANTZ
  Take you me for a sponge, my lord?

---

woundless: "incapable of being hurt" (Riverside), "invulnerable" (Jenkins), not in the sense of being protected but rather by its very nature, cf., I.i.145, *King John* II.i.251–52, and *Tempest* III.iii.61–66.

Act IV, Scene ii: Another room in the castle.

Safely stowed ... here they come: Q2, F has "*Ham.* Safely stowed. *Gentlemen within*: Hamlet, Lord Hamlet. *Ham.* What noise? Who calls on Hamlet? O, here they come." "The words supplied in F are evidently a playhouse addition suggested by line 2, not part of Shakespeare's text. Note that they replace Hamlet's 'But soft', which they make redundant" (Jenkins). It is possible that even lines 1–2 in Q2 are playhouse additions and that Shakespeare meant the scene to begin at line 3, since Q2 has "*Enter Hamlet, Rosencrantz, and others*" before Hamlet speaks and Hamlet's lines add nothing of substance. Riverside includes F's lines with Q2's, hence the discrepancy in line numbering here. **stowed:** bestowed, put away. **soft:** hush, be quiet, spoken to himself.

Compounded it with dust: buried it, cf., *2 Henry IV* IV.v.115. **whereto 'tis kin:** cf., Genesis 3:19. ● Hamlet is playing at melancholy madness. He has not actually buried the body, cf., IV.iii.36–37.

Tell us ... chapel: ● Rosencrantz recognizes that Hamlet's statement is not true, though he does not recognize it as playacting.

keep your counsel: keep your secrets, "An adaptation of the proverb that a man who cannot keep his own secrets is unlikely to keep another's. Tilley C 682" (Jenkins).

Besides ... king?: Though Rosencrantz began the scene in verse (lines 7–8), Hamlet here draws him into prose. **to be demanded:** for the infinitive used indefinitely, see Abbott §356. **of:** by (Abbott §170), cf., I.iv.18. **sponge:** "what the sponge soaks up can be just as easily squeezed out of it. This goes back to Suetonius, who tells how it was said of the emperor Vespasian that he used rapacious officials like sponges, advancing them to high position so that they would be richer when he came to condemn them (*Lives of the Caesars*: Vesp. 16). This story continued to be attached to Vespasian (as by B. Riche, *Faults, Faults*, 1606, page 44) but was also adapted by Raleigh, again with the sponge metaphor, to an account of Henry III (*Prerogative of Parliaments*, *Works*, Oxford, 1829, vii.165); and the same image to describe extortioners and acquirers of wealth in general is found in emblem-book ... satire ... and sermon ... as well as in

HAMLET

Ay, sir, that soaks up the King's countenance, his   15
rewards, his authorities. But such officers do the

King best service in the end: he keeps them, like
an ape, in the corner of his jaw—first mouthed, to be
last swallowed. When he needs what you have

gleaned, it is but squeezing you, and, sponge,   20
you shall be dry again.

ROSENCRANTZ

I understand you not, my lord.

HAMLET

I am glad of it. A knavish speech sleeps in a
foolish ear.

ROSENCRANTZ

My lord, you must tell us where the body is and   25
go with us to the King.

HAMLET

The body is with the King, but the King is not with
the body. The King is a thing—

GUILDENSTERN

A thing, my lord?

---

the drama.... Shakespeare is thus in the tradition here, while adapting the image from extortioners to obsequious hangers-on" (Jenkins LN). **replication:** reply, answer (OED 2.).

countenance: favor, patronage (OED 8.).

authorities: authorizations (OED 2.). ● "The sycophant sponge profits from the king's powers rather than, as Dover Wilson's note suggests, appropriates them" (Jenkins), cf., the places where the King authorizes Rosencrantz and Guildenstern to spy on or govern Hamlet in some way (II.ii.15–18, III.i.26–27, III.ii.312, IV.i.36–37, and below lines 54–55), see Introduction, pages 13–14.

like an ape: as an ape does, with the implied insult to the King. F corrects Q2's misreading of "apple" for "ape," an error that also appears in the Quarto of Peele's *Arraignment of Paris*, IV.ii.6 (Jenkins substantially).

squeezing you: ● "Hamlet threatens the pair that they are playing a dangerous game" (Jenkins).

knavish speech ... foolish ear: ● To the ("knavish") insult of calling him a sponge, Hamlet adds the insult that Rosencrantz is a fool ("foolish ear"). **knavish:** nasty, insulting. **sleeps in:** conveys no meaning to.

The body ... with the body: ● Hamlet is playing on multiple layers of meaning, which depend on the Renaissance idea of the two bodies of the king, the natural body of the man and the body politic (state, government) represented in him, symbolized in the use of the royal plural: 1) The dead body of Polonius is in the King's castle, but the King (Claudius) doesn't know where it is, 2) the body of Polonius is with the last rightful king, Hamlet Senior (i.e., dead), but the usurping king, Claudius, is not yet dead like Polonius, and 3) in principle, the body politic (Denmark, the government) is with whoever is king (perhaps also is in the hands of God), but paradoxically there is no rightful king with the body politic (Hamlet Senior being dead, Claudius being a usurper, and Hamlet himself not having inherited). That the two bodies of the king may be separated is one way of expressing Hamlet's anguish over the death of his father, whose natural body was wrongly separated from the body politic, and at the same time conveying a veiled threat against Claudius. Cf., Plowden, pages 212a–213, "For the King has in him two Bodies, *viz.* a Body natural, and a Body politic. His Body natural (if it be considered in itself) is a Body mortal, subject to all Infirmities that come by Nature or Accident .... But his Body politic is a Body that cannot be seen or handled, consisting of Policy and Government, and constituted for the Direction of the People, and the Management of the public-weal, and this Body is utterly

HAMLET

Of nothing. Bring me to him. 30

Exeunt.

void of ... natural Defects ... which the Body natural is subject to, and for this Cause, what the King does in his Body politic, cannot be invalidated or frustrated by any Disability in his natural Body," cf., I.ii.1 note.

thing: • Hamlet pauses here before his final phrase, suggesting that the word has its own contemptuous significance, perhaps that Claudius is soon to be a dead body, a merely material object, nothing but a thing, having forfeited his right to kingship and to life.

of nothing: • This phrase shifts the implication of the pause (see previous note) to a complex pun, arising from the pronunciation of *nothing* as *noting*. In the word *nothing*, Hamlet is referring to a) mortality, cf., Coverdale's translation of Psalm 144:4 in the Anglican Prayer Book ("Man is like a thing of nought; his time passeth away like a shadow") and b) "the common phrase, ... a thing of no account. Thus a metaphysical profundity is turned into a deliberate anticlimax" (Jenkins). "Hamlet's jibe may also hint that the King's days are numbered (Dover Wilson)" (Jenkins LN). In the word *noting*, Hamlet intends the senses a) publicly recognized, b) worthy of close attention, and c) deserving of public denunciation, as with similar punning in *Much Ado about Nothing*.

[Hide fox, and all after]: Only in F. "Balance of probability suggests that F's added words are a stage accretion" (Jenkins), therefore not included here. It is probably a reference to a game like hide and seek, but Hamlet's challenge to such a game would be incongruous after "Bring me to him," and the tone of Hamlet's playacted mad speech throughout this scene has been dark rather than manic.

Act IV, Scene iii

Enter King, and two or three [Lords].

KING

I have sent to seek him and to find the body.
How dangerous is it that this man goes loose!
Yet must not we put the strong law on him.
He's loved of the distracted multitude,
Who like not in their judgment but their eyes, 5

And where 'tis so, th' offender's scourge is weighed,

But never the offence. To bear all smooth and even,

Act IV, Scene iii: Another room in the castle.

S.D. *two or three:* "Presumably the 'wisest friends' of IV.i.38" (Jenkins).

body: of Polonius.

we: the royal plural.

distracted: misdirected, with only an overtone of irrationality. The primary meaning is closer to "drawn aside from proper direction" (OED *distract v.* 3.), with overtones of perplexity (OED 4.) as at I.v.97, than to actual irrationality or madness (OED 5.) as at III.i.5, IV.v.2, and V.ii.230.

scourge ... offense: • The King is politicking here, asserting that in their superficial love of Hamlet, liking him based on their eyes, the common people are wrongly pulled away ("distracted") from proper judgment and would therefore exhibit more disapproval of the offender's being punished than of his crime. **scourge:** punishment. **weighed:** taken into consideration.

never: probably elided to "ne'er" for the pentameter, cf., Abbott §466. **bear:** carry, manage, keep. **smooth and even:** i.e., without upset to the running of the state.

This sudden sending him away must seem
Deliberate pause. Diseases desperate grown
By desperate appliance are relieved,   10
Or not at all.

Enter Rosencrantz [and Guildenstern].

How now! what hath befall'n?

ROSENCRANTZ
Where the dead body is bestowed, my lord,
We cannot get from him.

KING
                    But where is he?

ROSENCRANTZ
Without, my lord, guarded, to know your pleasure.

KING
Bring him before us.

ROSENCRANTZ
                    Ho! Bring in the lord.   15

Enter Hamlet [with Guards].

KING
Now, Hamlet, where's Polonius?

HAMLET
                                At supper.

KING
At supper? Where?

must seem / Deliberate pause: must be made to seem the result of our having paused to deliberate carefully. **Diseases … not at all:** The idea is proverbial. "A desperate disease must have a desperate cure" (Tilley D 357). Jenkins also cites Cheke, Lyly, Nashe, and Chapman. The extreme degree of the King's planned remedy is seen later at line 65. **desperate:** extreme. **appliance:** remedy, treatment, cf., *Pericles* III.ii.86, *Henry VIII* I.i.124.

S.D.: Q2 has "Enter Rosencrans and all the rest," F has "Enter Rosincrans." "In leaving Rosencrantz unaccompanied and reducing Hamlet's escort to Guildenstern alone, F's economy is at its most ruthless; and its division of this pair … cannot be what Shakespeare envisaged. The pair are never otherwise separated on stage[,] and although only one speaks here, his *we* in line 13 shows that there are as usual two bodies with one voice. The pair enter together to report, while their assistants, in charge of Hamlet, wait without till called for" (Jenkins LN). ● Are their "two bodies with one voice" a subtle reflection of and antithesis to the "two bodies" of a king?
befall'n: happened.

bestowed: put, stowed, cf., IV.ii.1.

Without: outside (of this room).

S.D.: Q2 has "They enter" and F "Enter Hamlet and Guildenstern." See line 11 S.D. note above.

Now, Hamlet … Go seek him there: ● NOTE TO ACTORS: There is an interesting play with meter in lines 16-38. The King keeps speaking in verse half-lines, implying an attempt to draw Hamlet into verse and by implication into rationality. At least after line 16 Hamlet will not play along and resists by refusing to complete the King's pentameter lines, instead persistently responding in prose, to apparently mad effect. Thereupon the King in effect completes his own half lines: "Now, Hamlet, where's Polonius? /… At supper? Where?" (lines 16, 17), "Alas, alas. /… What dost thou mean by this?" (lines 26, 29), "What dost thou mean by this? /… Where is Polonius?" (lines 29, 32), and (making "Polonius" four syllables) "Where is Polonius? /… Go seek him there" (lines 32, 38).

HAMLET

Not where he eats, but where a is eaten. A certain
convocation of politic worms are e'en at him.   20

Your worm is your only emperor for diet: we fat all
creatures else to fat us, and we fat ourselves for
maggots. Your fat king and your lean beggar is

but variable service: two dishes, but to one table—
that's the end.   25

KING

Alas, alas.

HAMLET

A man may fish with the worm that hath eat of a
king, and eat of the fish that hath fed of that worm.

KING

What dost thou mean by this?

HAMLET

Nothing but to show you how a king may go a   30
progress through the guts of a beggar.

KING

Where is Polonius?

HAMLET

In heaven. Send thither to see. If your messenger
find him not there, seek him i' th' other place yourself.
But if indeed you find him not within this month,   35
you shall nose him as you go up the stairs into
the lobby.

KING

[*To Attendants*] Go seek him there.

HAMLET

A will stay till you come.

[*Exeunt Attendants.*]

KING

Hamlet, this deed, for thine especial safety—   40

---

a: he, as often in the play, cf., I.i.43 note.

politic: good at "policy" (political cunning), shrewd, crafty, alluding to Polonius's own craft, "but, *convocation* recalling the literal sense, also … busy at statecraft" (Jenkins). **e'en:** even = even now (Abbott §38). **at him:** at the business of eating him, we still say one is "at it" when in the act of doing something.

Your: "The fourfold *your* gives a classic illustration of the indefinite use. Cf. I.i.[138], and note" (Jenkins), cf., Abbott §221. **Your worm … for diet:** ● "Wittily improving on the usual aphorism, in which an emperor is the food of worms (e.g. Florio's Montaigne, II.12, 'The heart and life of a mighty and triumphant emperor, is but the breakfast of a seely little worm')" (Jenkins). Hamlet is also playing on the sense of "diet" meaning council, referring to the Diet of Worms, a council of the Holy Roman Empire held in the German city of Worms and presided over by the "emperor" Charles V between January 28 and May 26, 1521, before which Martin Luther appeared and refused to recant his writings, whereupon the emperor issued the Edict of Worms (May 26) decreeing that Luther be "apprehended and punished as a notorious heretic" (Jenkins, Braunmuller substantially). **only:** above all, surpassing, cf., III.ii.125 and Abbott §58. **we fat:** we fatten.

variable: different kinds of. **service:** food to be served (OED Service¹ 27.b.), cf., *Macbeth* I.vii s.d.

hath eat: has eaten, the past perfect tense. ● NOTE TO ACTORS: pronounced ĕt. **and eat:** the present tense ● NOTE TO ACTORS: with the usual pronunciation.

progress: a public ceremonial journey by a monarch from estate to estate, "as made famous by Elizabeth" (Jenkins).

seek him i' th' other place yourself: ● Hamlet's darkly bitter reference to hell reminds us of the purpose still on his mind, to effect the damnation of the King.

A: He. **stay:** remain, wait.

Which we do tender, as we dearly grieve
For that which thou hast done—must send thee hence

With fiery quickness. Therefore prepare thyself.
The bark is ready, and the wind at help,

Th' associates tend, and every thing is bent   45

For England.

HAMLET
      For England.
KING
           Ay, Hamlet.
HAMLET
                 Good.
KING
So is it, if thou knew'st our purposes.

HAMLET
I see a cherub that sees them. But come,
for England. Farewell, dear mother.
KING
Thy loving father, Hamlet.   50
HAMLET
My mother. Father and mother is man and wife;
Man and wife is one flesh—so, my mother.
Come, for England.
                 Exit with Guards.

KING
Follow him at foot; tempt him with speed aboard.
Delay it not—I'll have him hence tonight.   55

Away, for everything is sealed and done
That else leans on th' affair. Pray you make haste.
             Exeunt all but the King.

---

tender: hold dear, cf., I.iii.107. **dearly:** intensely.
● The King must publicly show himself to care both for Hamlet and for Polonius, for the reasons given above in lines 3–9.

With fiery quickness: F, not in Q2.

bark: ship. **at:** Shakespeare's usage for the older *a* as in *asleep*, *alive* (Abbott §143). **at help:** blowing, making sailing possible or favorable, i.e., blowing from a helpful direction or quarter of the compass (OED help *sb.* 1.c.). **Th':** probably for *thy* (Riverside) rather than *the*. **tend:** attend, await, cf., I.iii.83. **bent:** like a bow, made ready (Riverside).

For England: Q2 has a period, F a question mark, but Hamlet already knows about the King's plan to send him to England (III.iv.200).

So is it ... so, my mother. / Come, for England:
● The King is still in verse and Hamlet still in prose, cf., line 16 NOTE TO ACTORS.
a cherub that sees them: "Cherubim had the gift to 'see truly'" (Jenkins, who cites *Troilus and Cressida* III.ii.69–70 and *Macbeth* I.vii.22–24), but the line is not only a "hint that Hamlet perceives more than the King supposes" (Jenkins), which he does, and a suggestion that nothing is hidden from God (Riverside), but also a suggestion to the audience that Hamlet is here facetiously pretending to a kind of knowledge unavailable to mortals to which in III.iii he has aspired in earnest. **Farewell, dear mother ... so, my mother:** ● The King is not misunderstanding that Hamlet has "naturally" thought of his mother (as Jenkins suggests). Rather Hamlet is sarcastically needling the King by pretending to a mad identification of mother and father in keeping with his playacting of the sexual preoccupation mania we saw him performing in III.i.102ff. Here the point is his bitterly ironic reference to the sacramental union of his real father and mother and to the sinful pretense of that sacrament in the marriage of Claudius to his murdered brother's wife. **one flesh:** cf., Genesis 2:24 and, more pointedly, Matthew 19:5–9 and Mark 10:8–12, which focus on adultery.

at foot: closely, at his heels (Abbott §143). **tempt:** induce, persuade (OED 5.). **I'll have:** I intend to have, I purpose to have (Abbott §319).

everything ... That else leans: everything else that pertains is sealed and done. **sealed:** with the royal stamp. ● Though the King may also be using "sealed" metaphorically, at least one crucial document has been literally sealed, and at V.ii.17 Hamlet will report his having unsealed it. **leans:** touches, bears, appertains. **affair:** the business at hand.

And England, if my love thou hold'st at aught—

England: the King of England, as "Denmark" at I.i.48 and I.ii.59 and "Norway" at I.ii.28, 35.
my love: my good will, peaceful friendship.
hold'st at aught: hold to be worth anything at all, value at anything (Abbott §143).

As my great power thereof may give thee sense,

As ... sense: either a) Being that my power may well give you a feeling of the value of my good will, or b) And my power ought to make you sensible about valuing my good will.

Since yet thy cicatrice looks raw and red   60
After the Danish sword, and thy free awe
Pays homage to us—thou mayst not coldly set

yet: still now. **cicatrice:** scar.
free: voluntary. **awe:** reverential fear (Schmidt).
homage: perhaps in the form of the "neglected tribute" of III.i.170. **coldly set:** value lightly (OED set *v.* 89. c.), cf., I.iv.65.

Our sovereign process, which imports at full,

process: order, command, mandate, "Though a *process* is often an actual document, I take the word to refer here to the order which the *letters* contain" (Jenkins).
imports at full: fully implies, directs.

By letters cóngruing to that effect,
The present death of Hamlet. Do it, England,   65
For like the hectic in my blood he rages,
And thou must cure me. Till I know 'tis done,

cóngruing to that effect: according with that outcome. ● NOTE TO ACTORS: stress the first syllable of "congruing." **present:** immediate. **England:** the King of England. **hectic:** "continuous fever" (Riverside).

Howe'er my haps, my joys were ne'er begun.

                                                    Exit.

haps: fortunes. **were ne'er begun:** F, "will nere begin" Q2, "The rhyme seems to authenticate F's otherwise inferior reading" (Jenkins), or perhaps not inferior since in conditional sentences, "the consequent does not always answer to the antecedent in mood or tense. Frequently ... explained by a change of thought," here from "Till I know" to "[haps] (might be)" (Abbott §371).

Act IV, Scene iv

Enter Fortinbras with his army marching over the stage.

FORTINBRAS
Go, captain, from me greet the Danish king.

Act IV, Scene iv: The coast of Denmark.

Setting Note: "[I]t is not profitable to seek geographical precision for what Shakespeare is content to leave vague. The play is consistent with itself in making Fortinbras plan an invasion of Denmark (I.i.[95]ff., I.ii.17ff.), switch his troops [to fight] against Poland (II.ii.64ff.), proceed there by way of Denmark, and return by the same route (V.ii.[350]). The shipbuilding of I.i.[75] acknowledges that a Norwegian invasion would be by sea, and if we think of Fortinbras now as having just disembarked, a meeting between him and Hamlet, who is about to put to sea (IV.iii. [53–55]), is plausible enough" (Jenkins LN).
by his license: cf., II.ii.77–80.
conveyance of: "escort for" (Riverside).

Tell him that by his license Fortinbras
Craves the conveyance of a promised march
Over his kingdom. You know the rendezvous.
If that his Majesty would aught with us,   5
We shall express our duty in his eye,

his Majesty: the Danish king, Claudius. **would aught:** purposes to have anything to do. **us ... We ... our:** ● Fortinbras is apparently using the royal plural, a foreshadow of his future position as king and perhaps indicating a habit of mind fitting him for that position, cf., III.ii.334 note. **express our duty:** "pay our respects" (Jenkins). **in his eye:** in person in his presence, cf., I.ii.116 note and IV.vii.45.

And let him know so.

let: "imperative, parallel with *tell* (line2)" (Jenkins).

CAPTAIN

        I will do't, my lord.

FORTINBRAS

Go softly on.

                      Exeunt all but the Captain.

   Enter Hamlet, Rosencrantz, Guildenstern, and others.

HAMLET

        Good sir, whose powers are these?

CAPTAIN

They are of Norway, sir.   10

HAMLET

           How purposed, sir, I pray you?

CAPTAIN

Against some part of Poland.

HAMLET

              Who commands them, sir?

CAPTAIN

The nephew to old Norway, Fortinbras.

HAMLET

Goes it against the main of Poland, sir,   15

Or for some fróntier?

CAPTAIN

Truly to speak, and with no addition,

We go to gain a little patch of ground

That hath in it no profit but the name.

To pay five ducats—five—I would not farm it;   20

Nor will it yield to Norway or the Pole

---

softly: slowly, easily, leisurely (OED soft *a.* 5., softly *adv.* 3.). ● Perhaps intending both absence of warlike intentions toward Denmark and confidence about not being obstructed.

● **TEXT NOTE:** The rest of this scene (lines 9-66) is omitted in F. Riverside treats lines 9-13 as prose, hence the inconsistency in line numbering.

powers: military forces.

They are … commands them, sir?: These four lines can be read as two hexameters, as trimeter couplets with an additional isolated foot (Abbott §499, §500), as prose, as they are printed in Q2, or perhaps as pentameters if "They are" and "Who com-" are elided into one unstressed syllable each. **How purposed:** What is their intention?

main: principal domain.

Or … fróntier?: a half-line now that both the Captain and Hamlet are back in pentameters, perhaps indicating a pause before the Captain speaks—as if he hesitates to speak against the motives of his commander. **fróntier:** ● NOTE TO ACTORS: stressed on the first syllable.

speak, and: probably both words are stressed, with the missing unaccented syllable between them accounted for by the long vowel in "speak" or a pause after it (Abbott §484), cf., line 31.

addition: augmentation of its qualities.

We go … the name: "Similar reflections occur more than once in Montaigne [e.g., II.23, III.10]" (Jenkins LN). **name:** not the name of the place but the repute or fame to be gained by conquering it (OED 6.c., 8.), cf., lines 49 and 56 below and *Measure for Measure* I.ii.169, 171.

To pay … farm it: I would not pay as little as five ducats to lease it either for an annual or a one-time fee, the verb *farm* not having the sense of tilling or cultivating land until at least the 18th c. (OED). **—five—:** The second "five" is "Usually taken as derisory repetition, … Theobald … conjectured a misreading of 'fine' …. In the sense of a contractual payment on admission to a lease or tenancy, the emendation would be almost irresistible if it could be shown (as it has not been) that *fine* without any preposition was as idiomatic then as it would be now" (Jenkins). **ducat:** see II.ii.366 note.

Norway: The King of Norway. **the Pole:** the King of Poland.

A ranker rate should it be sold in fee.

HAMLET

Why then the Polack never will defend it.

CAPTAIN

Yes, it is already garrisoned.

HAMLET

Two thousand souls and twenty thousand ducats   25
Will not debate the question of this straw.

This is th' impóstume of much wealth and peace,
That inward breaks and shows no cause without
Why the man dies. I humbly thank you, sir.

CAPTAIN

God buy you, sir.

                                                          Exit.

ROSENCRANTZ

          Will't please you go, my lord?   30

HAMLET

I'll be with you straight. Go a little before.
                              Exeunt all but Hamlet.

How all occasions do inform against me,

And spur my dull revenge. What is a man

If his chief good and market of his time
Be but to sleep and feed? A beast, no more.   35

---

ranker rate: higher, richer price (than five ducats).
in fee: as a purchase, as opposed to merely leased.

the Polack: the King of Poland, like "the Pole" in line 21, cf., I.i.63 and II.ii.63 and 75.

garrisoned: stationed with troops to defend it.

souls: of soldiers.
Will not debate: "will scarcely be enough to fight out" (Riverside). **question of:** controversy over. **straw:** i.e., valueless thing.

impóstume: abscess, festering swelling or sore (from Greek *aposteme*). It may be external and visible or, more dangerously, internal and invisible, and it may be physical or (metaphorically) moral or political (Jenkins LN substantially), as here. ● NOTE TO ACTORS: stressed on the second syllable

buy: see II.i.66 n.

I'll be ... before: ● NOTE TO ACTORS: scan (following Abbott §484) thus: "I'll bé with you stráight. Gó a líttle befóre," cf., line 17. **straight:** right away.

occasions: circumstances (Crystal), incidental occurrences (Schmidt). **inform against:** bring incriminating information against, accuse (OED 5.b, 7.b).

spur ... revenge: in the metaphor revenge is the horse on which Hamlet wishes to ride if it were not so dull a horse. This sets up the theme of the soliloquy: his self-recrimination for not yet having taken vengeful action against the King.

good and market: probably a hendiadys, the noun "good" used in place of an implied adjective for "market," the price earned by sale at market, hence value, worth, or use (Wright, page 187, Jenkins), hence "advantage gained from the disposal of" (Jenkins), "the best use he makes of his time" (Onions). ● It is possible that Hamlet is referring to two different concepts. If so, "good" would refer to the question of what is man's chief good, raised by Aristotle in the *Nichomachean Ethics* ("the good for man is an activity of soul in accordance with virtue," I.7) and by St. Augustine in *Of the Morals of the Catholic Church* ("Man's chief good is not the chief good of the body only, but the chief good of the soul," Chapter 5), and "market" would refer to the value or worth of his time, that is, use of the time he is given to live on earth. In any case, Hamlet is continuing the long tradition of arguing that the value of the soul and its rational faculty is greater than that of the body in order to build his case against inaction, not realizing that the real inaction that has stymied him is the refraining in III. iii from his duty as executioner because his mind has been tainted by the desire to damn the King.

Sure he that made us with such large discóurse,

he: God, not capitalized in Q2. **discóurse:**
● In the medieval understanding of the nature of man that Shakespeare and the Renaissance inherited via Cicero's *De Officiis* and that has its roots in Plato's image of the tripartite soul, plants have a vegetable soul, the "form" that causes them to grow; animals have that plus a sensible soul, the form that causes them to feel and be aware; and human beings have both those plus an intelligible soul, the form that causes them to reason. Angels are pure intelligences (intelligible souls), the difference between angelic and human intellect being that angels have intuitive reason, which perceives reality directly and immediately, and humans have discursive reason, which must reason from premises to conclusions. "Discourse" is then "The act of the understanding, by which it passes from premises to consequences" (Johnson's *Dictionary*, reference in Jenkins), premises including first principles or self-evident axioms, observations, and sensations. According to John Milton in *Paradise Lost* (V.490), the difference between intuitive and discursive reason is one of degree rather than kind. It is thus the discursive reason that, being god-like, distinguishes man from beast, cf., I.ii.150 note. ● NOTE TO ACTORS: stressed on the second syllable.

Looking before and after, gave us not

before and after: i.e., forward and backward in time, unlike animals, who live always in the present. "As Theobald notes, this is Homeric (*Iliad* III.109, XVIII.250). But the *locus classicus* is Cicero's *De Officiis* [I.4], which specifically links man's power to regard both past and future with his possession of the gift of reason. Among Shakespeare's contemporaries cf. Bright, pages 70–1" (Jenkins LN), cf., I.ii.150 note and Baldwin II.597–98.

That capability and god-like reason

capability and god-like reason: a hendiadys for "god-like capacity of reason" (Wright, page 187), cf., line 36 note above and I.ii.150 note.

To fust in us unused. Now whether it be

fust: become musty or moldy. **whether:** perhaps "softened" to "whe'er" (Abbott §466).

Bestial oblivion, or some craven scruple   40

Bestial oblivion: the obliviousness (lack of reasoning capacity) appropriate to a beast, see line 36 note and line 37 note. **craven:** cowardly. **scruple:** minute moral consideration.

Of thinking too precisely on th' event—

Of: resulting from (Abbott §168). **thinking too precisely ... wisdom:** "Cf. Florio's Montaigne (I.23)" (Jenkins). **event:** outcome, upshot, as also in line 50.

A thought which, quartered, hath but one part wisdom
And ever three parts coward—I do not know
Why yet I live to say this thing's to do,

quartered: divided into quarters.

I do not know / Why ... this thing's to do: i.e., why this killing of the King is yet to be accomplished.
● Hamlet remains in ignorance of his own error of will revealed in III.iii and named in his mother's case at III.iv.88 ("reason panders will"), where he failed to see that the phrase applied to himself as well as to Gertrude. But we the audience *do* know why the deed is yet to be accomplished because we have seen why it was not accomplished at the only moment it

would have been possible to accomplish it without plunging all of Denmark into danger and causing the deaths of all the members of its two leading families. The reason is Hamlet's refusal of his actual mission (killing the King) in favor of the satisfaction of his personal desire for revenge (causing the King to be damned) at III.ii.87. **to do:** to be done (Abbott §359). **Sith:** since.

Sith I have cause, and will, and strength, and means   45
To do't. Examples gross as earth exhort me:
Witness this army of such mass and charge,
Led by a delicate and tender prince,

mass and charge: size and cost, cf., line 25.
delicate and tender: refined and youthful
• "In marked contrast with I.i.[96]" (Jenkins), because then Fortinbras was in rebellion against the rightful authority of his uncle whereas here he is fulfilling his legitimate mission.

Whose spirit, with divine ambition puffed,
Makes mouths at the invisible event,   50
Exposing what is mortal and unsure
To all that fortune, death, and danger dare
Even for an egg-shell. Rightly to be great
Is not to stir without great argument,
But greatly to find quarrel in a straw   55
When honor's at the stake. How stand I then?—
That have a father killed, a mother stained,

puffed: inflated, picking up the root meaning of "spirit" (breath). **makes mouths:** makes faces at, defies, cf., II.ii.364. **invisible:** unable to be foreseen. **event:** outcome, upshot, as at line 41.

egg-shell: i.e., something of no value.
Is not to stir: a condensation in the text (by accident or for euphony, or both) of what must be meant, i.e., "is not not to stir." • Any attempt to save the appearance of the phrase as printed in Q2 either reduces the antithesis to nonsense or contradicts the theme of the speech. The point is that greatness lies not in waiting for a great argument to justify action, but in finding justification in the most trivial thing when honor is at stake. This is Hamlet's intended meaning (Jenkins LN substantially). But from the audience's viewpoint, Hamlet remains in error. His real trouble is not that he has hesitated to act for lack of sufficiently great argument, but just the reverse. He has hesitated to act (in III.iii) by seeking *too great* a role for himself, i.e., by seeking to play God. So his discursive reason here, while it does distinguish him from a beast in nature, is still pandering his beastlike will, his unreformed desire to see the King damned. His conclusion, the wish to have only bloody thoughts, confirms this discreditable will in him. Had he entertained such bloody thoughts at the right time, "this thing" would not be still "to do." **argument:** cause of conflict, reason for "stirring" or "finding quarrel."

Excitements of my reason and my blood,

Excitements: provocations. **blood:** figured as the seat of the passions, as at I.iii.6 and III.ii.69.

And let all sleep, while to my shame I see

all: his whole self: reason, passion, and physical body (in not having acted). • Hamlet forgets, as we should not, that he *did* act in III.iv, killing who he thought was the King. He has not yet discovered that his erroneous action there was a direct result of his evil motives for the erroneous inaction in III.iii.

The imminent death of twenty thousand men   60

twenty thousand: "Contrast line 25. I fear we must ascribe the confusion to Shakespeare, often lax with numbers, rather than ... to Hamlet" (Jenkins). In

That for a fantasy and trick of fame
Go to their graves like beds, fight for a plot

Whereon the numbers cannot try the cause,

Which is not tomb enough and continent
To hide the slain. O from this time forth   65

My thoughts be bloody or be nothing worth.

Exit.

Act IV, Scene v

Enter Queen, Horatio, and a Gentleman.

QUEEN
  I will not speak with her.

---

the theater, the actual number of soldiers here is irrelevant, as is its difference from the number in the earlier line, because the point here is hyperbole.

fantasy and trick: a hendiadys (Wright, page 187) implying a fantastical trick, combining several senses of each word, "fantasy" meaning both a mere illusory image in the mind and a caprice, and "trick" meaning both an insignificant trifle and a deceptive device. • The "fame" (cf., "name" line 19) to be gained from this worthless Polish "patch of ground" is a deceptive illusion, played upon those who go to gain it. There is irony brewing here, for despite Hamlet's assessment of the insignificance of this enterprise, Fortinbras, having won in Poland, will on his return find that he has been made king of Denmark, fame achieved after all, though not as he could have imagined it. As in Hamlet's journey so in that of Fortinbras, Providence is at work, by "indirections find[ing] directions out" (II.i.63), in ways that the self-confident Polonius of II.i and the deeper-plotting Hamlet of III.iii cannot know.

Whereon … cause: On which plot of land there is not room enough for the numbers of soldiers fighting for it to do the fighting. **try:** put to the test of battle, determine the rightness of the "cause" by fighting it out (OED 5.c., 6.a.). **cause:** the matter to be decided, cf., trying a "cause" (= case) in court.

tomb enough and continent: a hendiadys (Wright, page 187) for a sufficiently large plot of land in which to bury those who died fighting for it. **continent:** receptacle, space to contain.

My thoughts … nothing worth: • This conclusion confirms that Hamlet, unlike Fortinbras, whose chastening (by the King of Norway) has already taken place (cf., II.ii.68–71), remains unaware of the fact and character of his fall in III.iii and so is as yet impenitent. It will not be his bloodthirstiness that gives worth to Hamlet's thoughts in the final act but rather humility in the form of readiness.

Act IV, Scene v: A room in the castle.

s.d. *Horatio:* Q2 has Horatio enter and gives him a single speech, lines 14–16 (line 16 probably erroneously). F has him (but no Gentleman) enter and gives him the Gentleman's lines and gives the Gentleman's lines to the Queen (also erroneously). Neither indicates an exit for him. "[T]he dialogue requires a second speaker other than the Queen at lines 14–15. The role of attendant on or adviser to the Queen is, however, a strange one for Horatio" (Jenkins). We could presume that Shakespeare and the company in Q2 and more surely in F are trying to make do with the minimum number of actors and have put Horatio into this scene to "save cast." Nonetheless,

GENTLEMAN
  She is importunate, indeed distract.

  Her mood will needs be pitied.
QUEEN
                    What would she have?
GENTLEMAN
  She speaks much of her father, says she hears
  There's tricks i' th' world, and hems, and beats her heart,   5

  Spurns enviously at straws, speaks things in doubt

  That carry but half sense. Her speech is nothing,
  Yet the unshapèd use of it doth move

  The hearers to collection. They aim at it

  And botch the words up fit to their own thoughts,   10

  Which, as her winks and nods and gestures yield them,

  Indeed would make one think there might be thought,
  Though nothing sure, yet much unhappily.

---

the speech at lines 14–15 and the presumed exit at line 74 are consistent with Horatio's character as the rational and balanced man, here a foil for Ophelia as well as in general for Hamlet. To ask why Horatio did not return to Wittenberg when Hamlet left for England is to belabor the irrelevant question of biography to the detriment of focus on the actual concerns of the play. See Introduction, page 6, note 13.
importunate: urgently demanding. **distract:** mad, cf., III.i.5, V.ii.230.
mood: mental state. **will needs:** must, demands to be.

would she have: does she wish to have (Abbott §329).

There's: for the singular before plural subject see Abbott §335. **tricks:** deceits, frauds. **hems:** makes the throat-clearing sound expressing doubt, disapproval, or the attempt to clear away painful emotion, cf., *Much Ado* V.i.16, *As You Like It* I.iii.18–19.
Spurns: rejects (lit., kicks) with scorn. **enviously:** with ill-will, grudgingly, spitefully. **straws:** trifles, nothings, cf., IV.iv.26. **in doubt:** the phrase modifies "things" adjectivally (rather than "speaks" adverbially), she says things that are unclear, obscure, semi-nonsensical.
Her speech is nothing: what she says is nonsense.
Yet the: ● NOTE TO ACTORS: a trochee rather than an iamb, throwing the more stress onto "shape-" and "use". **unshapèd:** shapeless, confused. **use of it:** her speaking, her employment of the capacity to speak.
collection: attempt to find coherence, "putting together (of the 'unshaped' fragments), gathering by inference. Cf. *Cym*[*beline*] V.v.431–2" (Jenkins).
aim: F, guess, try to comprehend, Q2 yawn = "gape eagerly (as if to swallow)" (Riverside), or "gape in wonderment" cf., *Othello* V.ii.101, *Coriolanus* III. ii.11, "But the sense there is of stupefaction, here of movement in an effort to gather or grasp something. Hence *yawn* is more probably a misreading" (Jenkins).
botch ... up: patch or stitch together clumsily (OED 3.). **fit to:** suiting to, tallying with (from OED fit *a.* 3.).
Which ... them: Both pronouns refer to her words. **yield:** express, report, deliver, represent (OED 12.a. and b., and cf., 13.d.), cf., *Antony and Cleopatra* II.v.28, "Ophelia's gestures seem to give her words more meaning than in themselves they have" (Jenkins).
there might be thought ... much unhappily: ● The repetition of "thoughts ... think ... thought" in lines 10 and 12 suggests the strain in those trying to make sense of Ophelia's seemingly nonsensical words and suggestive gestures. Here the grammar requires us to see "nothing" and "much" in line 13 as deferred subjects of the passive past participle "thought": Her words, as her gestures hint, would make one

think that in Ophelia's mind nothing is being thought that is certain ("sure"), yet much is being thought troublesomely, unfavorably, regrettably. This meaning comes clear, however, only after the audience hears "thought" in line 12 as a noun, "there might be thought" implying that Ophelia's words might express a mental intention the hearers can only guess at. Both impressions prepare the audience to hear Ophelia's words as both mad and potentially significant.

HORATIO
'Twere good she were spoken with, for she may strew

'Twere: It were, i.e., It would be. **she were:** that she were, contracted to one syllable ("sh'were") to preserve the pentameter (Abbott §461).
strew: spread.

Dangerous conjectures in ill-breeding minds. 15

ill-breeding: trouble-making.

QUEEN
Let her come in.

Exit Gentleman.

Let her come in: Q2 gives the line to Horatio, but in him it would be uncharacteristic pleading, if directed to Gertrude, and as an imperative "Only the Queen can give this order" (Jenkins). In F Horatio's lines as well as this one are given to Gertrude.

[*Aside.*] To my sick soul, as sin's true nature is,

my sick soul: "Hamlet's reproaches of III.iv have a lasting effect" (Jenkins). **To my sick soul ... spilt:** Before each of these lines Q2 has a single opening quotation mark, cf., I.iii.36 note, to indicate sententious sayings (Jenkins substantially).

Each toy seems prologue to some great amiss.
So full of artless jealousy is guilt,

toy: trifle. **amiss:** calamity (Riverside).

artless: unskilled, ignorant. **jealousy:** suspicion, mistrust, apprehension of evil (OED 5.).

It spills itself in fearing to be spilt. 20

It: the guilt as a synecdoche for the guilty person or soul. **spills:** ruins, destroys. ● The guilty soul, fearing punishment for guilt, suffers as much from the fear as from the eventual punishment it fears. In this Gertrude's words offer a parallel to the self-incriminating soliloquy of the King at III.iii.36ff. Her fear may also be a prophetic intuition, like Hamlet's at V.ii.212–216, and is certainly foreshadowing.

S.D.: Q2, F has "*Enter Ophelia distracted,*" i.e., mad, cf., line 2.

Enter Ophelia.

OPHELIA
Where is the beauteous majesty of Denmark?

QUEEN
How now, Ophelia!

How now: elliptical for "how is it now?" meaning "what is going on?" or "what's up?" ● SPEECH NOTE: Ophelia's songs (italicized in F) most probably are based on popular ballads familiar to Shakespeare's audience (versions of lines 23–24, 171–72, and 187 being still extant). All are about love lost, chastity kept or lost, or death, or a combination of them. From her own viewpoint, Ophelia's situation is this: Her brother is abroad. Her father demands that she drop her lover to protect her virginity and reputation. She does so. As a result her lover goes mad and kills her father, leaving her alone and forsaken. The agony of loss brought about by the conflict between the two most significant men in her life drives her into a madness that expresses itself in songs suggestive both psychologically and thematically. The Gentleman in lines 9–13 has described and so prepared us for the experience of trying to infer meaning in Ophelia's inexplicit words. Shakespeare here shows his immense skill in giving us an example of real madness contrasted with Hamlet's playacted madness. Whereas Hamlet intentionally played at two forms of madness, Ophelia's latently significant expressions are uncalculated. In her case the mania attendant on thwarted sexual love that Hamlet has performed (described by Ophelia at II.i.72ff. and observed by us at III.i.102ff) produces images of sexual betrayal that figure the actual betrayals as perceived by Ophelia, namely her father's betrayal in breaking off her relations with Hamlet and her lover's betrayal in killing her father. In addition Shakespeare uses Ophelia's mad perceptions to convey various thematic identifications for the benefit of the audience. "Coleridge observed (i.30) 'the conjunction here of these two thoughts that had never subsisted in disjunction, the love for Hamlet and her filial love'. The appropriateness of the person to whom the songs are sung may also be more than coincidence (cf., Long, *Shakespeare's Use of Music*, iii.115): the first, about a dead but unmourned lover, is sung to Gertrude; the second, a song of seduction, to the seducer Claudius; the third, a funeral elegy, to the son of the man just buried" (Jenkins LN). Works in which the musical tunes are given include Furness; Sternfeld, *Music in Shakespearean Tragedy*, 1964, pages 60–78 ("with the most authoritative discussion"); and Sternfeld, *Songs from Shakespeare's Tragedies*, 1964 ("arranged for modern performance") (Jenkins LN).

How should I ... sandal shoon: ● Ophelia responds to the Queen's "How now" with a "how" of her own, a quoted ballad in three sections about a maiden whose lover is gone. Ophelia begins in the middle of the song. In lines 23–26 the lover has left to become a pilgrim. In lines 29–32 and 36–40 he is dead. The maiden has asked a wayfarer whether he has seen her lover. Ophelia begins with the wayfarer's question how he could distinguish her lover from any other, to which the maiden replies with three distinguishing marks of a pilgrim: cockle hat, staff, and sandals. *cockle hat:* a pilgrim to the shrine of Santiago (St. James the Great) de Compostela in northwestern Spain would sew a cockle or scallop shell to his hat, a "practice [that] appears to have derived from the use of the scallop-shell in baptism" (Jenkins). *shoon:* shoes, "The ballad retains the archaic plural" (Jenkins), already "archaic in Shakespeare's time" (Delius in Furness). ● In this song, called from her memory by her sense of abandonment, Ophelia not only transposes the male and female roles of the likely original (a male seeking his female beloved), but reverses the usual trope of the lover's pursuit of his lady being figured as a pilgrim's journey to a holy shrine, cf., *Merchant of Venice* I.i.120 and II.vii.40, and

OPHELIA
(*Sings.*)
> How should I your true love know
> From another one?
> By his cockle hat and staff,
> And his sandal shoon.

25

the one full sonnet and first quatrain of another in which the lovers first speak to one another in *Romeo and Juliet* I.v.93–110, cf., Rappaport *N&Q*. The song signifies to us Ophelia's double loss, of the father who came between her and her lover, and of the lover who came between her and her father. It also implies her quandary. Was her true love Polonius or Hamlet, the one who claimed he loved her, or the one who claimed that her lover's love was a lie? The idea of the lover as pilgrim may be an echo in Ophelia's mind of Hamlet's playacted anti-marriage religious mania of III.i.102ff. "There is also, as well shown by [P. J.] Seng, [*The Vocal Songs in the Plays of Shakespeare*, 1967] (pp.133–4), an ironic application to … the Queen, to whom the song is pointedly directed (ll. 28, 35) and who herself has failed to distinguish her 'true love … from another one' and to lament him 'with true-love showers'" (Jenkins LN).

imports: signifies.

mark: listen, pay attention.

He is … gone: ● Ophelia continues the ballad, which shifts into a lament for the dead, which the audience must hear as a reference to her father. *At his head … a stone:* ● Ophelia seems ironically to reverse the normal form of burial (the stone at the head), in order to signify her awareness of the unorthodox speed and lack of ceremony in her father's interment, cf., lines 84 and 214–16. Though possibly the line "a large flint-stone weighs upon my feet" in Keats' *Isabella* (st. 38) justifies the idea that Ophelia's lines represent "Traditional burial-customs referred to in ballad and folklore" (Jenkins), because "At his heels" is not the same as "on his feet," the ironic interpretation seems preferable.

O ho: Q2, not in F, "A deep sigh" (Parrott-Craig in Jenkins) or cry of anguish or pain, cf., *Troilus and Cressida* III.i 121–26 (Schmidt substantially).

shroud: burial or winding sheet, from which modern Halloween costumes and cartoon images of ghosts derive.

Larded: decorated, adorned. "The culinary verb for inserting strips of fat [to dress meat] extended its range till it came to mean 'enrich' or 'garnish' in a general sense and so 'intersperse or sprinkle with ornaments'. Cf. V.ii.20, and for the practice of strewing flowers on the dead V.i.[243–46]" (Jenkins).

QUEEN
Alas, sweet lady, what imports this song?

OPHELIA
Say you? Nay, pray you mark.
(*Sings.*)
    He is dead and gone, lady,
        He is dead and gone,   30
    At his head a grass-green turf,
        At his heels a stone.

O ho.

QUEEN
Nay, but Ophelia—

OPHELIA
                    Pray you mark. [*Sings.*]   35
White his shroud as the mountain snow—

                    Enter King.

QUEEN
Alas, look here, my lord.

OPHELIA
(*Sings.*)
    Larded with sweet flowers

Which bewept to the grave did not go
*   With true-love showers.*   40

KING

How do you, pretty lady?

OPHELIA

Well, good dild you. They say the owl was a baker's
daughter. Lord, we know what we are, but know not
what we may be. God be at your table!

---

bewept: wept over. *grave*: F and Q1, Q2 ground.
did not go: ● The unmetrical "*not*" is Ophelia's
addition to the ballad to indicate her sense of the
inappropriateness of the funeral rites of Polonius
and to remind us of the profound error behind
Hamlet's inadvertent killing of him. In addition,
she was not permitted to mourn her own sudden
abandonment of Hamlet, effected in obedience to her
father, an abandonment that she feels has led to both
her lover's madness and her father's death. *true-love
showers*: i.e., tears.

good dild you: Q2, God dil'd you F, God yeeld you Q1,
God reward you for your compliment and kindness
in asking, "A corruption of God yield (i.e. requite)
you … (OED yield *v*. 7; God 8). Q2, with the *good* of
colloquial speech (cf. 'good-bye'), probably gives the
authentic reading" (Jenkins), cf., *Macbeth* I.vi.13.
owl … daughter: The reference is to a legend recorded
by Douce (1757–1834, quoted in Furness) as told
by "the vulgar in Gloucestershire," according to
which when Jesus asks a baker's wife for bread
and she prepares the dough, the baker's daughter
(stingy and not recognizing her guest) reduces the
amount. The loaf nonetheless swells to hugeness
in the oven and the daughter is turned into an owl.
Additional possible implications of the owl include
its mournfulness, its wintry singing signifying
loss of love (as contrasted with the sweetness of
the nightingale and cuckoo, whose spring singing
signifies love), and its betokening of death, disaster,
or loss of chastity (Jenkins LN substantially).
● Ophelia's observation suggests that she cannot
but feel that in obeying her father and withholding
her love from Hamlet she has been responsible for
Hamlet's madness, her father's death, and her own
abandonment. Thus to Ophelia the main relevance
of the reference to the baker's daughter is that like
the baker's daughter by her stinginess toward Jesus,
Ophelia has been suddenly ruined (as she thinks)
by her rejection of Hamlet. This leads to what she
herself observes in the next sentence. **Lord, we
know … may be:** Because of our choices and deeds,
we may instantly become something we cannot
foresee. ● If this is indeed "An ironic echo" (Jenkins)
of 1 John 3:2, "now are we the sons of God, but yet it
is not made manifest what we shall be, and we know
that when he shall be made manifest, we shall be like
him, for we shall see him as he is" (Geneva Bible),
to the irony may be added a plea for forgiveness for
not recognizing Jesus. The baker's daughter knew
not what she did, just as Ophelia did not know
what would seem to be the result of her obeying
her father and rejecting Hamlet's love. In fact, of
course, Hamlet's supposed madness was playacting
in response to Hamlet's charge from the Ghost,
and his killing of Polonius had nothing to do with
Ophelia's rejection. Hence Ophelia's sense of her
own responsibility is a sinless foil for Hamlet's sinful
error in taking the King's damnation into his own

KING

Conceit upon her father.   45

OPHELIA

Pray let's have no words of this, but when they ask you
what it means, say you this.
(*Sings.*)
    Tomorrow is Saint Valentine's day,
        All in the morning betime,
    And I a maid at your window,   50
        To be your Valentine.
    Then up he rose, and donned his clo'es,
        And dupped the chamber door,
    Let in the maid that out a maid
        Never departed more.   55

KING

Pretty Ophelia—

OPHELIA

Indeed without an oath I'll make an end on't.
[*Sings.*]

    By Gis and by Saint Charity,

hands at III.iii. **God be at your table:** • "A sentiment contrasting with that of the baker's daughter (who grudged Christ bread)?" (Jenkins), and perhaps also a prayer that God may be made manifest to the Queen, or to both Queen and King, so that they may avoid the fate of the baker's daughter, with which Ophelia identifies her own.

Conceit: image, fancy (OED 7., from OED conceive *v.* 8.). • The King is partly correct. Ophelia is conceiving fantastical images resulting from her father's death, but in her mind that death is connected to her own imagined responsibility for it.

Pray: i.e., I pray you. **have no words of:** not talk about, perhaps not argue about.

Tomorrow is ... come to my bed: A song about the loss of chastity. • Ophelia's perception that her rejection of Hamlet caused his madness of thwarted love and then his killing of her father leads Ophelia to the image of the unacceptable contrary choice that her father had laid out for her, namely loss of her virginity to Hamlet. Would it have been better for Ophelia to have lost her virginity to Hamlet (as her brother and father feared might happen) and thereby to have avoided his madness and her father's death? In the agony of the paradoxical conflict between her own thwarted love and the obedient chastity that she imagines has led to her lover's madness and her father's death, she has gone mad. Her songs of the loss of love and life both precede and follow this song about the loss of virginity. *St. Valentine's day*: Feb. 14, on which custom held that the first member of the opposite sex seen that day would be one's "Valentine." The custom is possibly rooted in the similar *Lupercalia* of ancient Rome, celebrated on Feb. 15, cf., *Julius Caesar*, I.i.67. • The events in the song ironically tell of the betrayal of love as a function of the betrayal of virtue. *betime*: early. *maid*: a) young woman, b) virgin. *Valentine*: beloved, true love. *donned*: put on (contraction from "do on"). *clo'es*: clothes. *dupped*: opened (contraction from "do up"). *maid ... maid*: young woman ... virgin, i.e., she departed no longer a virgin.

Pretty Ophelia: "Comparison with lines 34, 41, suggests that this, though almost always rendered as an exclamation, is addressed to Ophelia, in a vain attempt to divert the flow" (Jenkins).

Indeed ... oath: Ophelia substitutes "indeed" for an oath to avoid taking the Lord's name in vain and perhaps also ironically to deny the intention to blaspheme in the two oaths she is about to quote in song in the next line. **on't:** of it (the song).

Gis: a shortened form of "Jesus." • NOTE TO ACTORS: pronounced with a soft G. *Saint Charity*: holy charity. Charity is the greatest of the theological virtues, also translated "love," from the Greek *agape*, cf., I Corinthians 13:13. The phrase is a common oath, cf., *Shepheardes Calender*, May, line 247 and gloss, which ascribes it to Catholics, who wish to seem to have charity "always in their mouth, and sometime in their outward Actions, but neuer inwardly in fayth and godly zeale." Hence perhaps here it is a confession of bad faith in the maiden-speaker of the song whose own unchastity the song blames for the young man's infidelity. Ophelia's singing of this inappropriately bawdy song is then an ironic play on her madness, for it has been her chastity and obedience that, as she must feel, have resulted in disaster.

Alack and fie for shame,

Young men will do't, if they come to't—   60

By Cock they are to blame.

Quoth she, 'Before you tumbled me,
   You promised me to wed.'
He answers,

'So would I 'a' done, by yonder sun,   65
   And thou hadst not come to my bed.'

KING
How long hath she been thus?

OPHELIA
I hope all will be well. We must be patient. But I cannot choose but weep to think they would lay him i' th' cold ground. My brother shall know of it, and so I thank you   70 for your good counsel. Come, my coach.

Good night, ladies, good night.
Sweet ladies, good night, good night.
                                                   Exit.

KING
Follow her close; give her good watch, I pray you.
                                          [*Exit Horatio.*]
O, this is the poison of deep grief; it springs   75

Alack: see III.iv.200 note. *fie for shame*: see I.ii.101 note and OED *fie int.* 1.

do't: do it, behave this way, engage in sexual intercourse, cf., *Timon of Athens* IV.i.8. *if they come to't*: if they have the opportunity.

Cock: common corruption of "God," with a possible pun on the metaphor for penis (though OED lists this sense not earlier than the 18th c.).

tumbled: handled roughly, disordered (OED) with a pun on the sense "caused to fall down" with its sexual implication. **He answers:** cf., *Troilus and Cressida*, IV.iv.18, where a speaker similarly interrupts a song with dialogue.

'a': have. *by yonder sun*: an oath, sworn on a visibly obvious reality. *And*: If.

counsel: advice. **Come, my coach:** "Cf., *1 Tamburlaine*, V.i.315, where the mad Zabina calls for her coach in order to join her dead husband" (Jenkins).

Good night ... / ... good night: F prints these two lines as prose, but Q2 starts a new line with the capitalized "Sweet," which supports the supposition that Ophelia is singing, or at least speaking in trimeters.

S.D. *Exit Horatio*: see S.D. and note before line 1.

O, this is ... Gertrude, Gertrude: In Q2 these lines read "O this is the poison of deepe griefe, it springs all from her Fathers / death, and now behold, ô Gertrard, Gertrard." Perhaps "O Gertrude, Gertrude" was meant to replace "and now behold" in the ms. copy (Jenkins substantially), but though that would correct the meter, it removes the King's final observation of Ophelia's condition that seems to serve as a springboard for his following list of woes. F regularizes the meter by omitting "and now behold." **this is:** contracted to one syllable ("this'") (Abbott §461) to preserve the pentameter.

All from her father's death—and now behold.
O Gertrude, Gertrude,

All: entirely. ● a dramatic irony, for we know that it springs as much from Ophelia's sense of her own imagined part in driving her lover to cause that death, and more fundamentally, from the King's own crime.

When sorrows come, they come not single spies
But in battalions. First, her father slain;

When sorrows ... battalions: "An elegant variation on a familiar proverb. Tilley M 1012, 1013, 1004" (Jenkins). ● Gertrude expresses a similar sentiment at IV.vii.163–64, suggesting the piling up of the effects of their respective sins. **spies:** scouts.

Next, your son gone, and he most violent author   80
Of his own just remove; the people muddied,
Thick and unwholesome in their thoughts and whispers

author: cause.

just remove: rightful removal. **muddied, / Thick:** stirred or churned up, like a pool or fountain, hence cloudy-minded, confused, cf., *Taming of the Shrew*, V.ii.141–43. **unwholesome:** corrupted (by incipient disloyalty) and hence potentially corrupting to others.

For good Polonius' death—and we have done but greenly

For good ... greenly: a trimeter couplet (Abbott §501), stressing the antithesis between "Polonius" and "we," though "and we have" could be elided to count as a single unstressed syllable (*'n' we've*) to preserve the pentameter. **we:** the royal plural. **greenly:** unwisely, foolishly, cf., I.iii.101 and *Antony and Cleopatra* I.v.74.

In hugger-mugger to inter him; poor Ophelia

In hugger-mugger: secretly, clandestinely, in concealment, cf., line 31 note and lines 214–16. "The phrase was common but may here echo North's *Plutarch* (Life of Brutus) ... Cf. *Revenger's Trag*[edy], V.i.19" (Jenkins). ● NOTE TO ACTORS: The pentameter is preserved if "to inter" is elided as "t'inter" (Abbott §497) and "Ophelia" is given only one stress on the *e*, as with other "polysyllabic names ... at the end of the line" (Abbott §469).

Divided from herself and her fair judgment,   85

Divided ... judgment: mad, cf., V.ii.234, where Hamlet uses similar terms in offering the excuse of madness to Laertes. Wright finds "herself and her fair judgment" a hendiadys for "her own fair judgment" (pages 187 and 188 note 2).

Without the which we are pictures, or mere beasts;

we are: ● NOTE TO ACTORS: elide to *we're*. **pictures:** merely pictures, not living beings. **beasts:** i.e., lacking judgment, reason, cf., I.ii.150 note, I.iv.41 note, IV.iv.35 note.

as much containing: holding as much significance.

Last, and as much containing as all these,
Her brother is in secret come from France,
Feeds on his wonder, keeps himself in clouds,

Feeds on his wonder: is fed in his imagination not by facts but by his own astonishment or "bewilderment" (Jenkins) at his father's death. **Feeds on his:** Q2 Feeds on this (cf., line 94), but I accept Jenkins' suggestion that "this" may be an error "as at V.ii. [141 and] *Mer*[*chant of*] *V*[*enice*] IV.i.30" and follow the F reading. **keeps himself in clouds:** remains in confusion, uncertainty (Jenkins), in suspicions (Raffel).

And wants not buzzers to infect his ear   90
With pestilent speeches of his father's death,
Wherein necessity, of matter beggared,

wants: lacks. **buzzers:** "rumor-mongers" (Jenkins).

Wherein: i.e., in the poisonous speeches of rumor-mongers. **necessity:** the need to find a culprit. **of matter beggared:** poor in the possession of substantive facts.

Will nothing stick our person to arraign

Will nothing stick: will not scruple, hesitate. **our:** the royal plural. **our person to arraign:** to accuse me personally.

In ear and ear. O my dear Gertrude, this,

In ear and ear: to this person and that (the multitude, the mob soon to appear), or possibly in both of Laertes ears (Kittredge substantially in Jenkins) ● Using the abstraction "necessity," the King avoids accusing any one person of accusing him, but he seems to know that he is being accused, and we soon find that he is correct. **this:** i.e., these "battalions" (line 79) of troubles.

Like to a murdering-piece, in many places   95

murdering-piece: "a kind of cannon (also called a 'murderer') which by the scatter of its case-shot could hit many men at once. Cf. Fletcher, *Double Marriage*, IV.ii.6" (Jenkins).

Gives me superfluous death.

A noise within.

superfluous: because any one piece of shot (item on the list) would be enough to kill me.

Attend!

Enter a Messenger.

Attend!: listen! The word may complete a pentameter if the "noise within" counts as an iamb. But see next note. "F substitutes an exclamation from the Queen ['Alack, what noise is this?']. Most modern editors illogically include both" (Jenkins), as Riverside does, hence the discrepancy in line numbering here.

Where is my Switzers? Let them guard the door.
What is the matter?
MESSENGER

Save yourself, my lord.

Where is my Switzers: may "amphibiously" serve as both the completion of line 96, discounting the interjection "Attend!" and the beginning of line 97 (Abbott §513). **is:** the singular verb is often used when a plural subject follows or is deferred by "there," "where," etc. (Abbott §335). **Switzers:** Swiss guards, mercenaries who served as bodyguards of royalty, like those of the Pope, though "The bodyguard of the Danish kings were in fact not Swiss though sometimes thought to be so, probably because their red and yellow uniform resembled that of the Pope's Swiss guard" (Jenkins).

The ocean, overpeering of his list,   100

overpeering: rising above, derived by OED from "peer" both verb (to look) and substantive (an equal) ● "This comparison of a rebellious people to waters overflowing their banks is, significantly, a recurrent one with Shakespeare. Cf. *Troil*[*us and Cressida*] I.iii.111–13, *Cor*[*iolanus*] III.i.[247–49], *Sir Thomas More*, Addn II, 162–3" (Jenkins, and see *STM* in List of Bibliographical References). **overpeering of:** i.e., in the overpeering of. The *of* introduces the object of a gerund, which is here missing the preposition (*in*) before it, because of which omission we tend to read the gerund as a participle (Abbott §178). **his:** the common genitive of "it" (Abbott §228). **list:** border, limit, boundary (OED *sb.*³ 1. and 8.), here the shoreline.

Eats not the flats with more impetuous haste

Eats ... the flats: devours by inundating the land. **impetuous:** forceful, violent, unrestrained, and perhaps, given the spelling in Q2 ("impitious") and F ("impittious"), which are older spellings of the same word (OED), there is some influence from the sense pitiless, ruthless.

Than young Laertes, in a riotous head,

O'erbears your officers. The rabble call him lord,

And, as the world were now but to begin,
Antiquity forgot, custom not known—   105
The ratifiers and props of every word—
They cry, "Choose we! Laertes shall be king."
Caps, hands, and tongues applaud it to the clouds,
"Laertes shall be king, Laertes king!"

QUEEN
How cheerfully on the false trail they cry.   110

                    A noise within.

O, this is counter, you false Danish dogs!
KING
The doors are broke.

         Enter Laertes with Followers.

LAERTES
Where is this king?—Sirs, stand you all without.
DANES
No, let's come in.
LAERTES
         I pray you give me leave.
DANES
We will, we will.   115
LAERTES
I thank you: keep the door.

        [Exeunt Followers.]
      O thou vile king,
Give me my father!
QUEEN
          Calmly, good Laertes.
LAERTES
That drop of blood that's calm proclaims me bastard,

---

head: insurrection (OED *sb.* 30, 52), "Not merely an armed force, as usually explained, but its forward movement. Cf. *Cor*[*iolanus*] II.ii.[88], *Oth*[*ello*] I.iii.274" (Jenkins).

O'erbears: overwhelms, prevails over. **officers:** those who hold office under (and therefore are loyal to) you, or possibly military officers, not merely their men, hence implying how far the uprising may go.
● NOTE TO ACTORS: The word takes only one stress, on the first syllable (Abbott §495). **rabble:** mob.

as: as if.

ratifiers and props ... word: ● Antiquity and custom (line 105) are what sustain (ratify, prop up) every true statement ("word"), whether in the sense of "pledge, promise" (Riverside) or "motto, maxim" (Jenkins), in contrast to the "word" proclaimed in the next line ("Laertes shall be king"), which has neither antiquity nor custom to support it. ● The mob is behaving as if they could create the world anew by their proclamation, which implies political and social chaos, the overthrow not only of the present king but of the elective monarchy itself, traditional in Denmark.

cry: bay like hunting dogs chasing game, "hounds following a scent" (Jenkins), cf., *Merry Wives* IV.ii.196–97. **false trail:** like hunting dogs following a false scent.

counter: contrary, following the scent backwards toward where the game animal has come from, cf., *2 Henry IV* I.ii.90. ● Gertrude implies first that it is a "false trail" to follow Laertes rather than the King, and second that any uprising of a mob against a king goes contrary to the hierarchical order of things.

give me leave: permit me to handle this, let me deal with it, combined with a "formula of dismissal" (Jenkins), cf., II.ii.170 and note.

keep: guard.

blood: the seat of the passions, as at I.iii.6, 116, III.ii.69, and IV.iv.58. **proclaims me bastard:** to be calm in the face of the killing of my father would imply that not he but someone else was my father.

Cries cuckold to my father, brands the harlot
Even here between the chaste unsmirchèd brow   120

Of my true mother.
KING
                        What is the cause, Laertes,
That thy rebellion looks so giant-like?—

Let him go, Gertrude. Do not fear our person;

There's such divinity doth hedge a king
That treason can but peep to what it would,   125
Acts little of his will.—Tell me, Laertes,
Why thou art thus incensed.—Let him go, Gertrude.
Speak, man.

brands the harlot: see III.iv.42–43 note.

between ... the brow: (thus in Q2 and F) upon the brow or between the brows. **unsmirchèd:** stainless **true:** faithful, chaste.

cause: purpose, goal, mission. • the question is not "what causes your rebellion to look so giant-like" but "what can be the motive for this rebellion that looks so giant-like." **giant-like:** not only huge but also like the rebellion of the giants against the gods in Ovid (*Metamorphoses*, I.152ff., *Fasti* V.31–45), cf., V.i.252–54 note. • another image of the attempt to overturn the hierarchal order of the universe.

fear: "fear for, as at I.iii.51" (Jenkins). **our person:** my physical safety, with the royal plural.

such divinity: the divine right of kings to rule and the divine protection of them attendant upon it, cf., *Richard II* III.ii.47–57, Beaumont and Fletcher, *The Maid's Tragedy* III.i.233–41. The manuscript of physician Sir Hans Sloane records the report that Queen Elizabeth, during the Essex rebellion, said, "'He that had placed her in that seat [i.e., on the throne] would preserve her in it' (MS Sloane 718, fol. 26). For the political theory see J.N. Figgis, *The Divine Right of Kings* (1896)" (Jenkins LN). **hedge:** surround with protection. **treason can but peep to what it would:** either a) treason can only glimpse (through a narrow aperture or nearly closed eye) what it desires, not see it clearly or fully, or b) "treason can do nothing more than peep in comparison with what it wishes to do" (Abbott §187). **Acts little of his will:** accomplishes little of what it intends. **his:** its, cf., line 100 note and Abbott §228. • The sentence is fraught with irony. It was a standard shared belief that kings ruled by divine right and were protected in their office by God from harm at the hands of their subjects. But since Claudius succeeded in breaking through the divine hedge protecting his brother, his own claim of divine protection now rings false. In claiming it he is being both courageous before Laertes and brazen before God (and the audience). We are also reminded of the King's having remained unharmed by Hamlet in III.iii, of which the true cause, we know, was the spiritual ambition of Hamlet. If the King was under the divine protection at that moment, it was only in being spared for further opportunity either to repent or to confirm his damnation. Yet the maxim holds true in a broader sense, for any breach of the divinity that hedges a king (and God) is only apparent. In reality the divinity will reassert itself in the form of divine vengeance, demonstrating that the maxim is truer than either Claudius in his cynicism or Hamlet in his spiritual pride can foresee. Unlike Claudius, Hamlet will later understand the principle in larger terms as the "divinity that shapes our ends" (V.ii.10) and the "special providence in the fall of a sparrow" (V.ii.219–20). And, unlike Claudius, Hamlet will bring his own will into harmony with that "divinity."

LAERTES
Where is my father?

KING
     Dead.

QUEEN
      But not by him.

KING
Let him demand his fill.   130

LAERTES
How came he dead? I'll not be juggled with.
To hell, allegiance! Vows to the blackest devil!
Conscience and grace, to the profoundest pit!

I dare damnation. To this point I stand,
That both the worlds I give to negligence, 135
Let come what comes, only I'll be revenged
Most throughly for my father.

Where ... by him: ● If these three phrases were meant to make a pentameter, as indicated here and in most editions, supported by the presumed speed with which Gertrude completes the line, the half-lines before and after (lines 128 and 130) may indicate that after each of the King's speeches Laertes pauses before speaking, a hint of the diffidence in the face of the King's divine right, a foreshadow of the pull of conscience he expresses in the aside at V.ii.296, and a foil for Hamlet's hesitation (for a different reason) in III.iii. It is also possible that the five phrases in lines 128–30, printed on separate lines in Q2 and F, are to be read either as half-lines with pauses before or after to fill out the meter, or as a kind of truncated stichomythia for dramatic effect in which pentameters have been suspended altogether, or, with line 131, as some combination of "amphibious" lines described by Abbott (§513). ● NOTE TO ACTORS AND DIRECTORS: The actor or director is free to choose one or another of these ways of reading the lines since in this place the printed texts are an opaque veil between us and the way the lines were originally spoken on the stage. **by him:** If Abbott is right that "by" here means not "by means of" but "as a consequence of" (§146), then Gertrude is both right and wrong. The King was not the direct cause of the death of Polonius, but he was certainly the indirect cause because if not for the King's crimes, Hamlet would not have killed Polonius.

juggled with: tricked, beguiled, deceived.

Vows: of loyalty to the king.

Conscience: ● Here at least two senses of the word distinguished by C. S. Lewis (*Studies in Words*, Chapter 8) are conflated, the lawgiver and that "fear of Hell" that makes a man a coward (III.i.82 note). Hence Laertes is here renouncing, along with "allegiance," "vows," and "grace," both the awareness of the difference between right and wrong and the fear of the consequences of doing wrong, either of which might prevent his taking revenge, cf., II.ii.605 note. **grace:** the divine gift that makes salvation possible, "the rejection of which here leads on to the next line" (Jenkins). **profoundest pit:** hell, "the 'bottomless pit' of Revelation (ix.1, etc.)" (Jenkins).

I dare damnation: ● Compare this passionate outburst to Hamlet's rational concern in the two soliloquies at II.ii.598–603 and III.i.55–87. Laertes here represents the danger of unchecked passion, for the King is (like) a devil in pleasing shape whose abuse (i.e., deception) could well lead to the damnation Laertes passionately claims to dare. Laertes also presents a foil for Hamlet's failure in III.iii to fly into a passion and kill the King when doing so was called for. **To this point I stand:** I will go so far as and rest at the following point (Abbott §187). **both the worlds:** this world and the next, this life and the afterlife: **give to negligence:** cease to care about. **throughly:** thoroughly. ● Laertes exhibits both a contrast to Hamlet's rational limits on passion (I.v.i, II.ii.588–605)

KING

> Who shall stay you?

LAERTES

My will, not all the world's.
And for my means, I'll husband them so well,
They shall go far with little.

KING

> Good Laertes,   140
If you desire to know the certainty
Of your dear father, is't writ in your revenge

That swoopstake you will draw both friend and foe,
Winner and loser?

LAERTES

> None but his enemies.

KING

Will you know them then?   145

LAERTES

To his good friends thus wide I'll ope my arms

And like the kind life-rendering pelican

---

and a passionate parallel to Hamlet's rational but perverse overreaching (III.iii.73–96).
stay: stop, prevent.

all the world's: i.e., the will of all the world.
husband: preserve, use, marshal, govern.

Of your … revenge: either a trimeter couplet (Abbott §501) or the *-er* in "father" and "is't" are elided into one unstressed syllable, cf., Abbott §465 and §456. **writ in:** written down in your purpose, essential to.
swoopstake: "alternative form of *sweepstake*, the act of taking all the stakes in a game, or the person who does so. *OED* takes this to be a unique adverbial use (= indiscriminately. cf. Q1, *Swoop-stake-like*), but it might be regarded as an interjection. Cf. Heywood, 2 *Ed*[*ward*] IV, i.116, 'to cry swoop-stake'. This is what the King represents Laertes as doing when, pursuing revenge against guilty and innocent alike, he *draws* all the stakes and not only the winnings he is entitled to" (Jenkins). The comma after the word in Q2, absent in F, may suggest that the word is intended as the substantive referring to Laertes himself, but whether substantive, adverb, or interjection, the sense, given by Jenkins, is clear. **draw:** take up, pull in, as one's winnings from the pot or kitty in a betting game.
None but his enemies: "amphibious," completing the previous half-line and initiating the following (Abbott §513).

thus wide: ● NOTE TO ACTORS: he gestures by spreading his arms. **ope:** open.
kind: not only compassionate but akin, behaving (to its offspring) kindly as kin behaves, cf., I.ii.65 note. **life-rendering pelican:** the medieval fable of the pelican (see Isidore of Seville *Etymologies*, Bk. 12, 7:26, quoted at http://bestiary.ca/beasts/beast244.htm), which feeds and thereby revives its young with blood from its own breast, was a symbol of Christ's redemption of mankind from sin and death through his sacrifice and the gift of his blood in the Eucharist.
● Laertes is using hyperbole about his intended self-sacrifice as he used it about his desire for revenge. The difference between Hamlet's actual exaggeration of his function in III.iii and Laertes' verbal exaggerations here is just the difference between the internal spiritual drama unfolding in Hamlet and the external drama unfolding in the foil character of Laertes that sets it off. Both overstep the boundaries, failing to heed the strictures of the Ghost at I.v.85 and the "golden mean" advice of Aristotle via Polonius at I.iii.59ff., respectively.

Repast them with my blood.
KING
                        Why, now you speak
Like a good child and a true gentleman.
That I am guiltless of your father's death   150
And am most sensibly in grief for it
It shall as level to your judgment 'pear
As day does to your eye.
                              A noise within.
            Let her come in.
LAERTES
How now, what noise is that?
                    Enter Ophelia.

O heat, dry up my brains! Tears seven times salt   155
Burn out the sense and virtue of mine eye!

By heaven, thy madness shall be paid with weight
Till our scale turn the beam. O rose of May,
Dear maid, kind sister, sweet Ophelia—

O heavens, is't possible a young maid's wits   160
Should be as mortal as an old man's life?
Nature is fine in love, and where 'tis fine
It sends some precious instance of itself
After the thing it loves.

OPHELIA
(Sings.)
    They bore him barefaced on the bier,   165
        [*Hey non nonny, nonny, hey nonny,*]
    And in his grave rained many a tear—
        Fare you well, my dove.

Repast: feed.

sensibly: feelingly.
level: directly (OED *a.*, and *adv.* B.), cf., IV.i.42 note.
'pear: appear, related to *peer*, become visible (OED *v.*² 3.).

Let her come in: Q2 assigns this line to Laertes, F to S.D. "Cf. for a similarly misplaced speech-prefix III.iv.52–3" (Jenkins). In Q2 it is an "amphibious" line, completing the previous half-line and initiating the following (Abbott §513).

O heat ... eye: ● In medieval physiology, each of the four humors, characterized by four pairs of qualities, was thought to originate in one of four organs of the body, phlegm, which was cold and wet, from either the lungs or, as here, the brain. The opposite qualities, hot and dry, would be inimical to the brain, and hence to thought. Laertes, again in a hyperbolical passion, is calling upon nature to reverse itself so that he need not witness the condition of his sister. Tears so salty that they destroy the eyes' inherent capacity ("virtue") to see turn the theme of disnatured nature from the destructive effect of contraries to that of an excess. Natural saltiness of the tears being healthful to sight, seven-fold saltiness is inimical to it. **sense and virtue:** a hendiadys, "capacity to see" (Wright, page 187).
paid: repaid, avenged. **with:** Q2, by F. **weight / ...beam:** the image is of the scales of justice weighing out so much revenge that it overweighs Ophelia's madness and tilts the balance beam the other way. ● cf., Hamlet's weighing the value of his revenge at III.iii.84.
wits: reason.

Nature ... it loves: F, not in Q2. ● Human nature is so refined and sensitized by love that it sends after the thing it loves a token in proof of itself ("instance" = example, specimen). Normally what it sends is thoughts or prayers, but in Ophelia's case, so great is her love, it has sent her reason itself. Laertes hyperbolically ascribes this phenomenon in his sister to the degree of her love for her father, but the audience knows that the cause is rather the exquisite agony of a tragic conflict of loves. Ophelia's mad grief always reflects the complex impression, which we know to be inaccurate, that her father's death has been caused by the madness of her lover resulting from her rejection of him under her father's orders.
[*Hey non ... nonny,*]: Only in F, taken by Jenkins to be a stage addition. *rained many a tear:* ironic in light of line 39 and lines 214–16. **Fare you well, my dove:** "an endearment added by Ophelia to [the song]" (Jenkins), where F makes it part of the song and Q2 is ambiguous.

LAERTES

Hadst thou thy wits, and didst persuade revenge,

It could not move thus.   170

OPHELIA

You must sing *"A-down a-down,"* and you *"call*

him a-down-a." O, how the wheel becomes it!

It is the false steward that stole his master's daughter.

LAERTES

This nothing's more than matter.

Hadst ... and didst: If you had ... and if you did.
persuade: argue rationally for.
It could not move thus: It could not so move one (to revenge as her mad singing does).

A-down a-down: common refrain for songs.
● Ophelia is stirring the company to join in her grief by distributing the parts of the refrain, "You ... and you" presumably referring to Laertes and to the others respectively, cf., "a ballad of King Edgar in Deloney's *Garden of Goodwill* (Song 3): ... 'call him down a'" (Jenkins LN).

wheel: probably a term meaning the song refrain (supported by Guest, *A History of English Rhythms*, ii.290, 324, and Saintsbury, *A History of English Prosody*, i.428) (refs. in Jenkins LN), possibly "spinning-wheel, at which women sang ballads (?)" (Riverside).
becomes: fits.

false steward ... daughter: ● Whatever the source for this image (none yet convincingly found), in it Ophelia's madness is inverting and recombining elements from her own life. By forbidding Ophelia to see Hamlet, Polonius in a sense stole his own daughter from his true master, i.e., Hamlet, his rightful king. At the same time Polonius had feared that his young master would prove false in stealing his daughter from him, metaphorically the "steward." Ophelia touches on the theme in a way that both indicates her irrationality and reveals the inner logic of her pain.

This nothing's more than matter: this irrational nonsense is more (i.e., weightier, more moving, more laden with meaning) than rational sense or "lucid speech" (Riverside) would be, cf., *King Lear* IV.vi.174–75 ("matter and impertinency mix'd, / Reason in madness") (Jenkins substantially).
nothing's: nothing is.
● SPEECH NOTE: Ophelia's following distribution of flowers is laden with significance. As always in the play, madness, real or playacted, has a kind of logical significance at which we are expected to "aim," as predicted in lines 6–10. Here, however, that significance must be reconstructed from what we can discover of the commonplace Renaissance significations of particular flowers, with which Shakespeare's audience would have been familiar, and from the applicability of each to the individuals to whom she gives them. J. V. Cunningham's dictum that "in Shakespeare foreground is background" holds good here for "rosemary" and "pansies" but does not help us with the other flowers. Nor does the text tell us precisely to whom Ophelia gives each flower. We are thus left to speculate about which character is given which flower and what that gift means based on what we know of the characters in the rest of the play and on what we can discern about the flowers' significations in early works like Robert Greene's *A Quip for an Upstart Courtier* (1592) and "A

OPHELIA

There's rosemary, that's for remembrance—   175
pray you, love, remember. And there is pansies,
that's for thoughts.

LAERTES

A document in madness, thoughts and remembrance
fitted.

OPHELIA

There's fennel for you, and columbines. There's   180

rue for you, and here's some for me; we may
call it herb of grace a Sundays. You must wear
your rue with a difference. There's a daisy.

Nosegay always sweet, for Lovers to send for Tokens"
in Clement Robinson's *A Handful of Pleasant Delights*
(1584), "the two [sources] most often cited, because
of the number of relevant flowers they include"
(Jenkins LN).

Rosemary ... thoughts: Rosemary, "popularly
supposed to strengthen the memory," cf., *Romeo and
Juliet* IV.v.79, and pansies, "'for thoughts' because
of their name (Fr. *pensées*)," are given to Laertes
to keep him in mind of his father and of revenge,
cf., I.v.91 ("Remember me"). Both flowers are also
love tokens, rosemary to assure the beloved's
remembrance of the lover (cf., Drayton's *Pastorals*,
IX) and pansies, also called heartsease and love-
in-idleness (OED heartsease 2.), implying "lover's
thoughts" (Chapman, *All Fools* II.i.234) (Jenkins LN
substantially). ● There is irony in Ophelia's giving
these flowers to Laertes. He is, so far as she knows,
the only intact male left in her life to love, though she
does not acknowledge recognizing him. He is also
one who warned her against Hamlet, to whom in a
similar gesture she has "redelivered" gifts that have
lost their perfume (III.i.92–101).

A document in madness: a lesson, warning,
instruction in the form of madness. **fitted:**
appropriately bestowed (upon the right person).
● Laertes accepts his duty to remember his father and
his pledge to be revenged.

Fennel ... columbines: Fennel symbolizes flattery, cf.,
Jonson, *The Case Is Altered* I.vii.9, James Yates, *The
Caste of Courtesy*, 1582, fol. 47, Turbervile, "Of Certain
Flowers" in *Epitaphs*, 1570, folio 42ᵛ and fol. 43, and
Greene *Quip*, page 9. Columbine symbolizes
cuckoldry because of "the horned shape of its
nectaries," cf., Thomas Cutwode's *Caltha Poetarum*,
1599, stanza 16, Chapman, *All Fools* II.i.243–36, and
Love's Labor's Lost V.ii.655. ● These are given to
Gertrude to suggest respectively her succumbing to
the flatteries of Claudius and her betrayal of her first
husband (Jenkins LN substantially).

rue: also called "herb of grace," symbolizes regret,
sorrow, and repentance and was popularly thought to
have the power to reduce carnal lust, cf., Cogan,
Haven of Health, 1584, page 40, "citing the authority of
Galen." Rue is given to Claudius, suggesting the
repentance he failed to achieve in III.iii and his lust
for "my crown, mine own ambition, and my queen"
(III.iii.55) (Jenkins LN substantially). ● Ophelia keeps
some rue for herself, reinforcing the regret that has
come from her forced rejection of Hamlet's supposed
lust and her own thwarted-love sex mania expressed
in her song at line 48ff. **must:** F, may Q2. **with a
difference:** in heraldry the distinction made in coats
of arms to indicate the distinction between the ranks
of chief line and junior lines within a family (OED
4.b.). ● The implication here is the difference in the
quality of regret between the guilty king and his
innocent subject. **daisy:** representing both

constancy in love, cf., Chaucer, *Legend of Good Women*,
G Text, line 196, and the possibility, likelihood, or folly
of being forsaken or betrayed in love, cf., Greene, *Quip*,
page 10, or both together, cf., Turbervile, "Of Certain
Flowers sent him by his Love upon suspicion of
change" and "The Answer to the Same" in *Epitaphs*.
These are probably given to the King, no other "you"
being named, to signify ironically his breach of the
marital fidelity between Hamlet Senior and Gertrude
(Jenkins LN substantially).

I would give you some violets, but they withered

violets: another symbol of faithfulness in love.
● Ophelia gives two kinds of flower to each recipient
and would give the King a third, as befits his higher
rank, but cannot because faithfulness in love
represented by the violet has died in various ways. The
withering of all violets on the death of her father, cf.,
I.iii.7–9 and III.i.92–102, implies Polonius's prediction
of Hamlet's lack of faith, Ophelia's rejection of Hamlet
on those grounds, Hamlet's resulting madness (as she
thinks it), and the killing of Polonius by Hamlet.
Ophelia cannot know that all these betrayals of love
have resulted in fact from the King's betrayal of his
brother and the kingdom out of his own love for power
and for Gertrude.

all when my father died. They say a made   185
a good end.
[*Sings.*]
  For bonny sweet Robin is all my joy.

a: he. **made a good end:** died well. ● another irony,
since he died spying on the Queen and Prince for an
immoral king.

LAERTES
  Thought and afflictions, passion, hell itself,

For bonny ... joy: A line from a popular song whose
words are not known. **bonny:** good-looking, possibly
also glad, cf., *Much Ado* II.iii.67 ("blithe and bonny").

  She turns to favor and to prettiness.

Thought: i.e., sad thought, hence sorrow, cf., *Antony
and Cleopatra* IV.vi.34–35. **passion:** suffering (from
Latin *patior*, to bear or suffer).
favor: attractiveness, charm.

OPHELIA
  (*Sings.*)
    And will a not come again?   190
    And will a not come again?
      No, no, he is dead,
      Go to thy death-bed,
    He never will come again.

And will a not come again: a song about an old man's
death. ● It is colored by our knowledge that Ophelia
must link her father's death to her lover's madness
and to her own (erroneous) sense of responsibility for
both. *a*: he.

    His beard was as white as snow,   195
    All flaxen was his poll.
      He is gone, he is gone,
      And we cast away moan.
    God 'a' mercy on his soul.

flaxen: of the color of dressed flax, hence white. *Flaxen-
haired*, meaning blond, is presumably a hyperbolic
compliment, cf., OED 2.b. 1616 quotation ("... being
as white or whiter than the finest Flax"). *poll*: head.
● NOTE TO ACTORS: pronounced with a long *o* to
rhyme with "soul" in line 199. *cast away*: throw away,
i.e., waste. *moan*: moaning, grief. *'a'*: have.

And of all Christian souls. God buy   200
you.

                                    [*Exit.*]

of: parallel to "on" in the previous line (Abbott §181).
God buy you: see II.i.66 note. Because Riverside
includes "[I pray God]" from F before this phrase, it
runs onto the next line (201 in that edition), hence the
discrepancy in line numbering between lines 200 and
205 here.

LAERTES
  Do you see this, O God?

KING

Laertes, I must cómmune with your grief,

Or you deny me right. Go but apart,
Make choice of whom your wisest friends you will,   205

And they shall hear and judge 'twixt you and me.
If by direct or by collateral hand

They find us touched, we will our kingdom give,
Our crown, our life, and all that we call ours
To you in satisfaction; but if not,   210
Be you content to lend your patience to us,
And we shall jointly labor with your soul
To give it due content.

LAERTES

                                Let this be so;

His means of death, his óbscure funeral—

No trophy, sword, nor hatchment o'er his bones,   215

No noble rite, nor formal ostentation—
Cry to be heard, as 'twere from heaven to earth,

That I must call't in question.

KING

                                So you shall,

And where the offence is, let the great axe fall.
I pray you go with me.   220

                                Exeunt.

---

cómmune with: share in, have a role in your dealing with. ● NOTE TO ACTORS: stressed on the first syllable.

Go but apart: only go (with me) out of the public eye.

Make choice ... you will: choose whom you will of your wisest friends. **wisest:** most mature and sound in judgment.

'twixt: between.

by direct or by collateral hand: by my own hand or by my use of someone else's as an agent.

us: the royal plural. **touched:** implicated, touched with guilt (Jenkins).

satisfaction: repayment, requital ● i.e., satisfaction refers not to Laertes' personal feelings but to the repayment of a debt, in a sense akin to the third of the four parts of repentance in the Christian tradition, namely confession, contrition, satisfaction (= penance, repayment of spiritual debt), and absolution, cf., III.iii.65 note.

this: the King's proposal that Laertes' friends "hear and judge" his claim against the King.

His means of death: The means of his death, for the transposition see Abbott §423. **óbscure:** stressed on the first syllable (Abbott §492).

trophy ... bones: "It was an ancient custom ... that when a knight was buried, his helmet, sword, and coat-of-arms were hung over his tomb" (Jenkins). **trophy:** memorial, from the earlier form of celebrating a victory by setting up as trophies the arms taken in battle (Jenkins substantially). **hatchment:** "a tablet or painting displaying the coat-of-arms of the deceased" (Jenkins).

ostentation: ceremony (Jenkins).

Cry: cry out, demand. **as 'twere from heaven:** as if it were a voice crying out from heaven. ● yet another example of Laertes' hyperbolical treatment of the cause of his sorrow.

That: "so that, as at IV.vii.[147] (Abbott [§]283)" (Jenkins). **I must call't in question:** I am forced to call Polonius's death generally, together with the items listed above in lines 214–16, into question, i.e., to raise it in a debate between you and me to be judged by my "wisest friends." ● The willingness of the King to put the matter before Laertes' "wisest friends" justifies for Laertes his agreement at line 213. **call't:** call it.

great axe: generally the axe was used to execute a guilty nobleman by beheading, in contrast to the hanging used to execute a guilty commoner. ● The reference of the King is apparently to no particular earlier image but metaphorically implies the judgment and punishment of God. He means to put in the service of Laertes' revenge the state's most extreme form of execution. In doing so he is ironically, and unbeknownst to all but the audience, calling the ultimate justice of God upon himself and forgoing the "divinity [that] doth hedge a king," which he had hypocritically claimed for himself at lines 124–26.

Act IV, Scene vi: A room in the castle.

Act IV, Scene vi

Enter Horatio and others.

HORATIO
What are they that would speak with me?

What: i.e., of what sort or rank (OED what A. 2.).

GENTLEMAN
Seafaring men, sir. They say they have
letters for you.

letters: Although *letters* might mean letters on a page making up a single message, because "The plural (following Latin *litterae*) is common in a singular sense" (Jenkins), cf., II.ii.113 note, here probably multiple missives are intended (Hamlet's letter to Horatio, Hamlet's letter to the King, Hamlet's letter to the Queen, and possibly a letter to the King from the Pirates), especially if we follow F at IV.vii.36–37 (see note there).

HORATIO
Let them come in.

Exit Gentleman.
I do not know from what part of the world   5

should: would be likely to be (Abbott §325).

I should be greeted, if not from Lord Hamlet.

Enter Sailors.

FIRST SAILOR
God bless you, sir.

God bless ... please him:—The repetition of the idea of God's blessing and his will in these three lines may be to emphasize the Sailor's particular need of blessing (Jenkins following Kittredge), partly because, as we soon find out, he may be a pirate (lines 17–23). More important, however, is that it orients us to the implications about divine providence in the revelations of Hamlet to Horatio in the letter about to be read and later in the final scene (V.ii.4–55 and 219–24). Even a pirate sailor may know conventionally about the "divinity that shapes our ends" that we will soon see Hamlet having learned in deepest wisdom.

HORATIO
Let him bless thee too.

FIRST SAILOR
A shall, sir, and please him. There's a letter for you,

A: he. **and:** if (it), Q2, where "the suppression of the pronoun is colloquially idiomatic" (Jenkins), F "and 't".

sir—it came from th' ambassador that was bound for   10

ambassador: i.e., Hamlet, who has presumably concealed his identity from the pirate sailors (Jenkins substantially).

England—if your name be Horatio, as I am let to know
it is.

let to know: told, caused to know (*OED* let *v.*¹ 13.), for the infinitive particle "to" see Abbott §349.

HORATIO [*Reads.*]
"Horatio, when thou shalt have overlooked this,

overlooked: i.e., looked over, read, perused. **this:** i.e., this letter.

give these fellows some means to the King. They have

means to: way of gaining access to, cf., line 32 and Abbott §405.

letters for him. Ere we were two days old at sea, a pirate   15
of very warlike appointment gave us chase. Finding

pirate: pirate ship.

appointment: furnishing, equipage. **gave us chase:** pursued us, chased us.

ourselves too slow of sail, we put on a compelled valor,
and in the grapple I boarded them.

put on a compelled valor: were forced to fight.

I boarded them: i.e., boarded their ship. ● Here is the second disproof of Hamlet's own earlier rhetorical

and theoretical self-accusations of cowardice (II.
ii.571–78, III.i.82, IV.iv.43), the first proof being his
killing of who he *thought* was the King (III.iv.26, 32)
and this proof being that he was the first to leap
aboard the pirate ship to do battle, confirming that
his earlier hesitation to kill the King was not ever
about physical fear but only about what he then said
it was, fear of his own damnation (up until III.iii) and
then desire for the damnation of Claudius.

On the instant they got clear of our ship, so I alone
became their prisoner. They have dealt with   20

On the instant: at that instant. **got clear … ship:** the
pirate ship drifted away from the Danish ship.
I alone … prisoner: • This apparently accidental
event Hamlet later recognizes to be providential, like
his sleeplessness, his having been trained in formal
handwriting, his having the King's signet ring with
him, etc., cf., V.ii.48 and note.

me like thieves of mercy, but they knew what they
did: I am to do a turn for them. Let the King have

thieves of mercy, but they knew what they did:
merciful thieves, a seeming paradox, perhaps
intending a contrast to "angels of mercy" (Jenkins)
or alluding to "the thieves crucified next to Christ
… and [to] Christ's plea of forgiveness [mercy] for
those who 'know not what they do'" for "They have
been merciful, but with the expectation of a return"
(Greenblatt, referring to Luke 23:34). • However far
we wish to take the allusion, the phrase fits not only
with the Sailor's earlier mention of God's blessing
(line 9) but with the providential quality of the entire
sea voyage, in which the pirates indeed play the role
of angels (messengers) of mercy, for though they
help knowingly in "expectation of a return," they are
unknowingly an instrument of Hamlet's conversion
to humility and of his being restored to the path of
his duty as imposed by the Ghost. **turn:** a service,
recompense (OED turn *sb.* 23.) or possibly "an act
duly … following a similar act on the part of another"
(OED 28.b.[*c*]) (Jenkins).

the letters I have sent, and repair thou to me with as
much speed as thou wouldest fly death. I have

repair thou to me: come to me. • another of the
many imperatives in the play, charging that a thing be
done and stipulating how it should be done ("with as
much speed …").

words to speak in thine ear will make thee dumb,   25

will: i.e., that will. • for omission of the relative
pronoun see Abbott §244. **dumb:** speechless.

yet are they much too light for the bore of the matter.

too light … matter: the metaphor is of shot too small
for the caliber ("bore") of a gun, the size implying
seriousness and the "matter" (the implied gun)
being the subject matter to be reported, the fact of
the King's plot against Hamlet. I.e., the words heavy
enough to make you speechless are yet not heavy
enough to correspond with the degree of iniquity of
the King's deadly plot.

These good fellows will bring thee where I am.
Rosencrantz and Guildenstern hold their course for
England; of them I have much to tell thee. Farewell.
He that thou knowest thine,   30
                 Hamlet."
Come, I will give you way for these your letters,

where: to where.

hold their course for: continue on course toward.

give you way: provide access, free passage, cf., line 14
and 2 *Henry IV* V.ii.82, *Tempest* I.ii.186.

And do't the speedier that you may direct me
To him from whom you brought them.

Exeunt.

Act IV, Scene vii

Enter King and Laertes.

KING

Now must your conscience my acquittance seal,
And you must put me in your heart for friend,

Sith you have heard, and with a knowing ear,
That he which hath your noble father slain
Pursued my life.

LAERTES

           It well appears. But tell me   5

And do't: And I'll do it. **that:** in order that.
To him ... brought them: i.e., to Hamlet.

Act IV, Scene vii: A room in the castle.

conscience: Unlike the uses at II.ii.605, III.i.49 and 82, and V.ii.58, where the sense was awareness of having done wrong, or "fear of hell," here the meaning is the inner lawgiver conflated with the laws it gives, as in V.ii.67, and implying, more or less, one's judgment of right and wrong, one of the "Ramifications of the sense 'synteresis'" conjectured by C. S. Lewis (*Studies*, pages 208–210). **acquittance:** acquittal (in the matter of the death of Polonius). **seal:** ratify, confirm.
Sith: since. **knowing:** knowledgeable, well-informed, acute. **which:** = who (Abbott §265).

● SPEECH NOTE: **Pursued my life ... where I had aimed them** (lines 5–24): Though the audience knows that Hamlet means to kill the King, the King himself does not know it. There is no evidence that the Queen, who preserves from the King the secret that Hamlet is not in fact mad (IV.i.7–12), has reported Hamlet's words at III.iv.26 and 32, and the King's realization at IV.i.13 that he might have been killed if he had been spying where Polonius stood is not necessarily evidence of Hamlet's intention to kill him. So this claim is actually a lie. The astute king, however, does think that Hamlet is dangerous (IV.i.14–15), perceives Hamlet's antagonism (e.g., IV.iii.30–35), feels the threat "like the hectic in my blood" (IV.iii.66), and finds it expedient to interpret Hamlet's actions to Laertes as involving murderous intent, thereby to enlist the latter in his attempt to be rid of Hamlet. Laertes, impassioned by the desire for revenge and spurred by the madness of his sister, is convinced. The elaborate length of the following seduction of Laertes to commit murder authorized by the King serves the dramaturgical function of keeping Hamlet off the stage for a significant span of time and contributes to our feeling that there has been time for the various events of the sea voyage, recounted by Hamlet in his letter (IV.vi) and in person (V.ii), to have taken place. Of this the point is our *sensation* of the passage of time, not the intention of literal accuracy. More importantly, the elaboration of the King's persuasion forms a weighty parallel to the speech of the Ghost to Hamlet in I.v and contrasts with it in being the kind of demonic "abuse" that Hamlet feared at II.ii.603, though the purpose here is not Laertes' damnation but only the King's villainous self-interest. Though Laertes is less disposed to question the moral validity of the King's arguments than Hamlet was to question those of the Ghost (II.ii.598ff.), he will have a moment of doing so at V.ii.296.

Why you proceeded not against these feats

So criminal and so capital in nature,

As by your safety, greatness, wisdom, all things else,

You mainly were stirred up.
KING
                  O for two special reasons,

Which may to you perhaps seem much unsinewed,   10

But yet to me th' are strong: The Queen his mother
Lives almost by his looks, and for myself—

My virtue or my plague, be it either which—

She is so conjunctive to my life and soul

That, as the star moves not but in his sphere,   15

I could not but by her. The other motive
Why to a public count I might not go

Is the great love the general gender bear him,
Who, dipping all his faults in their affection,

---

proceeded: i.e., legally. **feats:** deeds, but possibly also evil deeds or crimes, cf., OED feat *sb.* 4.

criminal: Q2 (and Riverside), "crimeful" F (and Jenkins). **capital:** punishable by death, with the additional senses of deadly (imperiling the loss of a man's head, from Latin *caput*, *capitis*) and deadly to the head of state, cf., *Coriolanus* III.iii.80–82. Wright finds the phrase a hendiadys, "so capitally criminal" (page 187). Cf., also III.ii.105 note.

As by ... else: a hexameter line in Q2 which F regularizes by deleting "greatness." Jenkins accepts the change, taking the Q2 line to be "a rejected first thought." ● However, the first words of the King's response in both Q2 and F make a hexameter of the next line as well, as if Claudius were conforming to the unmetrical length of Laertes' line as he is seeming to conform to Laertes' unchristian desire for revenge.

mainly: powerfully. **were:** would have been, ought to have been, a subjunctive. ● Laertes wonders why the King has not been stirred up by that which ought to (and normally would) have stirred him to legal proceedings against Hamlet.

unsinewed: weak, feeble, without strength, as in Q2, F has "unsinnowed," a variant spelling.

th': they.

Lives almost by his looks: almost depends for life on the sight of him.

be it either which: whichever of the two it may be (Abbott §273).

conjunctive: closely joined, as in astrology two planets may be in conjunction in one house or adjoining houses of the zodiac, resulting in a particular influence (cf., I.i.119 note) affecting the lives of men.

star ... sphere: in the Ptolemaic astronomy the non-planetary stars were all fixed in their places on the eighth concentric sphere, which, with the other spheres, revolved around the earth in perfect (i.e., circular) motion at varying speeds, moved by the ninth and largest sphere, the Primum Mobile, itself moved by the will of God. In these two astronomical images, the King is saying that he is utterly dependent upon Gertrude as he has said Gertrude is dependent upon Hamlet, statements that, unlike Laertes, we know to be only partly true, for the King has confessed in soliloquy that Gertrude is only one of three motives in his life, the others being his crown and his ambition (III.iii.55). **his:** its, cf., I.i.37 note.

by: nearby and hence according to (Abbott §145).

count: accounting, reckoning; for the dropped prefix see Abbott §460.

general gender: the public, the people, "gender" = kind, sort, class, hence "the common sort (of people)" (OED gender *sb.* 1, quoting this line), cf., "general" at I.iv.35, II.ii.437, 563, and III.iii.23.

Work like the spring that turneth wood to stone,　20

spring ... stone: "Several British springs will petrify [wood] with lime deposits" (Mack/Boynton), "including one at King's Newnham in Shakespeare's county of Warwickshire" (Jenkins, citing Harrison's *Description of England*, the preface to Holinshed's *Chronicles* 1587, the edition Shakespeare used, pages 129–30, 215).

Convert his gyves to graces, so that my arrows,

gyves: leg irons, shackles, fetters, as a metaphor for "disabilities, deformities" (Jenkins), "handicaps, defects" (Crystal), ●NOTE TO ACTORS: usually pronounced with a soft *g* but in ME the *g* was hard, based on the spelling *guive* (OED), so here possibly alliterative with "graces."

Too slightly timbered for so loud a wind,

Too slightly timbered: of too light a wooden shaft. **loud:** powerful, strong. **wind:** "i.e. the powerful gust of popular feeling" (Jenkins). ● In this series of metaphors the King's point is that as a certain spring transformed the very nature of wood to that of stone, so the great affection of the people for Hamlet converts his faults to positive qualities, so that any attempt of the King to attack Hamlet would recoil against himself.

Would have reverted to my bow again,
But not where I had aimed them.

my bow... I had aimed them: cf., the King's concern for himself at IV.i.17 and 43. It is normally part of the proper duty of a king to keep himself safe in both his body natural and his body politic for the good of the commonwealth (cf., III.iii.1–2 note), but once we know that Claudius has taken the throne wrongly, any concern for the body politic that he may intend to imply, both in IV.i and here, rings hollow, as is now reinforced by his speaking in the singular rather than in the royal plural.

LAERTES
And so have I a noble father lost,　25
A sister driven into desperate terms,

have I ... terms: for the transposition of subject and verb for emphasis see Abbott §425. **desperate terms:** hopeless state, condition, circumstances, with the additional and foreshadowing theological sense of "desperate" implying the spiritual condition of despair, which leads to suicide. Whether Ophelia is literally in that spiritual condition will be debated comically by the gravediggers at V.i.1–29 and seriously by Laertes and the Priest at V.i.225–42.

Whose worth, if praises may go back again,
Stood challenger on mount of all the age

may go back again: may be applied to what Ophelia was before she was driven to madness. **worth ... For her perfections::** Ophelia's worth did stand (if "Stood" is indicative) or would have stood (if "Stood" is subjunctive) as challenger (asserter of the right to the top position against all comers, cf., *As You Like It* I.ii.168-72) of any contender living in that age in defense of the superiority of her qualities ("perfections"), "of all the age" modifying "challenger" not "mount" (Furness, Jenkins, Matthews). **on mount:** as if towering above, visible to anyone, for *the* omitted before a noun modified by a prepositional phrase see Abbott §89. There is no support either in Shakespeare or in OED (before the 19th c.) for the sense "mounted upon a horse" ("like a mounted knight"—Mack/Boynton). The likelier metaphor is that her worth might stand atop a military breastwork or a hill to defend the claim of her excellent qualities against all comers. C. E. Moberly, quoted in Furness, suggested an allusion to the traditional coronation rite of the King of Hungary, who would challenge the world to dispute his right to the throne by brandishing his sword toward the four compass points from atop the Mount of Defiance at Pressburg, an action said to have been repeated by the Empress Maria Theresa in 1740. That the allusion was intended by Shakespeare is unsubstantiated and unlikely, but it "gives the idea" (Jenkins).

For her perfections. But my revenge will come.

revenge: ● Laertes' desire for revenge continues his role as foil for Hamlet. The father of each has been murdered, and each seeks revenge. Further, as the Ghost has been the catalyst to Hamlet's action, so the King is the catalyst for that of Laertes. In Hamlet's case the tempter to the inappropriate revenge of seeking to damn the King rather than merely to execute him was internal, Hamlet's own proud will. With Laertes the tempter is external, the villainous King. For both good and ill, Laertes is less careful than Hamlet in considering the consequences of an act of revenge. His revenge is less justified than Hamlet's because, unlike the murder of Hamlet Senior, the killing of Polonius was unintentional. But both Hamlet and Laertes fall to the temptation of the personal desire for revenge. Hamlet obeys the arguments of his own will-pandering reason and Laertes obeys the arguments of the hypocritically passion-fueling King.

KING

Break not your sleeps for that. You must not think 30

That we are made of stuff so flat and dull

That we can let our beard be shook with danger

And think it pastime. You shortly shall hear more.

I loved your father, and we love ourself,

And that, I hope, will teach you to imagine— 35

Enter a Messenger with letters.

How now, what news?

MESSENGER

Letters, my lord, from Hamlet:
This to your Majesty, this to the Queen.

KING

From Hamlet? Who brought them?

Break … for that: Don't lose sleep worrying about whether your revenge will come, see line 33 note.

we: the royal plural. **stuff:** mettle, substance. **flat:** spiritless. **dull:** insensible, obtuse.

beard be shook: "To ruffle or tweak a man's beard was an act of insolent defiance that he could not disregard without loss of honor. Cf., II.ii.573" (Riverside).

You … hear more: "Presumably a reference to expected news from England [of Hamlet's death at the hands of England's king—see IV.iii.65]—which gives ironic impact to what immediately comes instead" (Jenkins).

ourself: a shift from singular to royal plural that deftly expresses the concept of the two bodies of the king, cf., lines 23–24 note, I.ii.1 note, and IV.ii.27 note.

imagine—: The King is interrupted by the entrance of the Messenger.

Enter a Messenger … Who brought them?: F, Q2 has "*Enter a Messenger with Letters. / Messen.* These to your Maiestie, this to the Queene. / *King.* From Hamlet, who brought them?" Jenkins argues that the F reading is a "theatrical elaboration," since from IV.vi.10–11 "it does not appear that the bearer of the letters knew the identity of their sender, and it is arguably better if the King is not thus forewarned." However, in Q2 the word "letter(s)" is never spoken, and the Messenger interrupts the King

MESSENGER

Sailors, my lord, they say; I saw them not.
They were given me by Claudio; he received them   40
Of him that brought them.

KING

                                        Laertes, you shall hear them—
Leave us.

Exit Messenger.

[*Reads.*] "High and mighty, you shall know I am set
naked on your kingdom. Tomorrow shall I beg

leave to see your kingly eyes, when I shall, first asking   45
you pardon, thereunto recount the occasion of my
sudden and more strange return.

                                        Hamlet."

What should this mean? Are all the rest come back?

and surprisingly speaks to him before he is spoken to, which would be a breach of protocol. Both texts may be corrupted in different ways, but the abruptness of the Messenger's words to the King in Q2 seeming the more untenable, I follow the F reading here on the supposition that the Sailor's ignorance of the identity of the sender was relevant in IV.vi, the Messenger's knowledge of it is relevant here, and the inconsistency, which would go unnoticed in the theater, is not out of keeping with Shakespeare's practice. The King's surprise at finding that the letter is from Hamlet, and hence that Hamlet is not dead, would seem to be equal whether his response is to the Messenger's statement or to the signature. *letters ... they* [line 40] *... them* [line 40] *... them* [line 41]: the plural letters here, one or (if we follow Q2) more to the King and one to the Queen, reinforce the plural sense of "letters" at IV.vi.2. **Claudio:** not elsewhere mentioned in the play, no doubt a lower ranking court official. There seems to be no particular significance to the similarity of the names Claudio and Claudius, the latter appearing in Q2 only in the s.d. and first speech heading of I.ii, and in F only in the s.d. of I.ii.

them: Here the plural may refer to one letter each to the King and Queen, to two letters to the King (one from Hamlet and one from the pirates), or to Hamlet's one letter to the King referred to in the plural because "The plural (following Latin *litterae*) is common in a singular sense" (Jenkins), cf., IV.vi.2 note .

naked: without possessions, which were left on board the ship bound for England when Hamlet leapt aboard the pirate ship, cf., IV.vi.18–19, and forming an antithesis to the flattering "High and mighty" addressed to the King.

your kingly eyes: your royal presence, cf., I.ii.116 note and IV.iv.6. **pardon:** indulgence, possibly forgiveness for Hamlet's unsanctioned return. **thereunto:** Q2's punctuation makes "thereunto" refer to "your kingly eyes," which, in the sense of "your royal presence" (cf., *Troilus and Cressida* I.iii.219) is likely correct (Jenkins substantially). F's punctuation, "(first asking your pardon thereunto)," is defensible if "thereunto" refers forward to "my ... return" and if "pardon to" or "unto" can be used not only of a person (e.g., "My high-repented blames ... pardon to me," *All's Well* V.iii.36–37) but of a deed, of which the only other instance I find in Shakespeare is "Give pardon to my speech," *Troilus and Cressida* I.iii.356. Riverside's "permission to do so" seems less persuasive because more vague. **occasion of:** circumstance that has brought about. **and more strange:** in F only, meaning "even more strange than sudden" (Abbott §6). **Hamlet:** in F only.

What should this mean?: What is this likely or intended to mean (Abbott §325). **all the rest:** i.e., Rosencrantz and Guildenstern and those who accompanied them and Hamlet to England.

Or is it some abuse, and no such thing?   50

LAERTES

Know you the hand?

KING

'Tis Hamlet's character. "Naked"—
And in a postscript here, he says "alone."
Can you devise me?

LAERTES

I am lost in it, my lord. But let him come.
It warms the very sickness in my heart   55

That I shall live and tell him to his teeth,
"Thus didst thou."

KING

If it be so, Laertes—

As how should it be so, how otherwise?—
Will you be ruled by me?

---

abuse: trick, deception, cf., I.v.38, II.ii.603. **no such thing:** i.e., as what is claimed in the letter.

hand: handwriting.

character: handwriting.

devise me: explain to or for me, *me* being in the ethical dative case.

lost in: perplexed by.

warms: heats, excites. **sickness in my heart:** heartsickness over his father's death, but the implication is also of the passion for revenge, which is a sickness in two senses, a) a distemperature or imbalance of humors, in this case excess of choler (yellow bile), and b) the moral sickness of any Christian's desire for revenge.

to his teeth: as we would say, to his face.

didst: Q2, probably disyllabic, F "diddest." Q1's "thus he dies" influences Jenkins to assume "a misreading of *e* as *d* in Q2" and to emend to "diest," arguing that it "provides the antithesis giving point to *I shall live* and calls forth the fatal stratagem on which the catastrophe depends." However, Laertes' intention to kill expressed here would a) weaken the point of the King's later question at lines 124–26, and b) preempt the climax of the King's careful temptation of Laertes. Neither in IV.v nor earlier in this scene does Laertes use a concrete image of killing. What he seems to have in mind is a challenge to Hamlet to confess or fight. At line 70 the abstraction continues with his wish to be the "organ" of what the King has called Hamlet's "fall." Only after the King challenges Laertes' sincerity (lines 107–109), recommends swift action (lines 110–23), and asks "What would you undertake … ?" (lines 124–26) does Laertes express readiness for shocking concrete action (line 126). And only once a specific plan is outlined by the King does Laertes commit to a specific deed. It is the serpent-tempter Claudius who channels Laertes' passion for revenge toward concrete action and calculated murder, as it is Hamlet's own will-pandering reason that tempts Hamlet toward the calculated damnation of the King at III.iii.87–95. Cf., Iago's temptation to murder in *Othello* III.iii.

it: i.e., that Hamlet is returned, reinforced by line 61.
• To take "it" to refer to Laertes' determination to kill Hamlet, as Jenkins does (assuming "diest" in line 57), renders incoherent the next line, in which the King introduces a line of argument meant to persuade Laertes to be the instrument of murdering Hamlet. Such a line would be unnecessary had Laertes already expressed the intention to kill the Prince.

As: though, or as regards which (Abbott §111). **how should it be so:** i.e., how can Hamlet have returned? **how otherwise?:** how (should it be) otherwise? How can Hamlet not have returned given that I have this letter from him?

LAERTES

Ay, my lord,

So you will not o'errule me to a peace.   60

KING

To thine own peace. If he be now returned,

As checking at his voyage, and that he means

No more to undertake it, I will work him
To an exploit, now ripe in my device,
Under the which he shall not choose but fall;   65

And for his death no wind of blame shall breathe,

But even his mother shall uncharge the practice
And call it accident.

LAERTES

My lord, I will be ruled,
The rather if you could devise it so
That I might be the organ.

KING

It falls right.   70
You have been talked of since your travel much,
And that in Hamlet's hearing, for a quality
Wherein they say you shine. Your sum of parts
Did not together pluck such envy from him
As did that one, and that, in my regard,   75
Of the unworthiest siege.

LAERTES

What part is that, my lord?

KING

A very ribbon in the cap of youth,

Yet needful too, for youth no less becomes
The light and careless livery that it wears
Than settled age his sables and his weeds   80
Importing health and graveness. Two months since
Here was a gentleman of Normandy.
I have seen myself, and served against, the French,

Ay: ●NOTE TO ACTORS: either the exclamation, though monosyllabic, counts as a full foot (Abbott §482) or it follows a pause the equivalent of one unstressed syllable.

So: so long as, provided that (Abbott §133). **o'errule me to a peace:** force me under obedience to make peace with Hamlet.

peace: i.e., peace of mind, with ironic foreshadowing of the peace of death, cf., II.ii.156.

As: either "inasmuch as he is" (Abbott §115) or perhaps "as if he were." **checking at:** balking at, diverted from, shying "like a falcon diverted from its quarry by other prey" (Riverside). **that:** for *that* omitted in the previous line but inserted here see Abbott §285.

it: the voyage to England. **work:** manipulate. **device:** devising.

Under the which: under which (exploit). **shall not choose but fall:** will not be able to avoid dying.

no wind … breathe: no one will even whisper an accusation (of foul play).

uncharge: refrain from charging or accusing. **practice:** plot, stratagem, cf., V.ii.317.

organ: agent, instrument.

It falls right: it fits well, is appropriate.

quality: attribute, skill.
parts: abilities, skills, accomplishments.

that one: that one ability, skill.
unworthiest: least significant. **siege:** rank, status (from Latin *sedes*, seat, bench), cf., *Othello* I.ii.22.

A very: nothing else but a, essentially a (OED A.9.b.). **ribbon:** "a mere decoration" (Jenkins). Q2 "ribaud" is a typesetting error for "riband," an old alternative spelling of *ribbon*.

needful: necessary, unavoidable. **for youth … graveness:** The mere frill ("ribbon in the cap of youth") that is the art of fencing (cf., II.ii.25 note) is also necessary because the young fit with "light and careless" clothes no less than the old fit with the dark or mourning clothes that imply seriousness and gravity ● As part of his flattering seduction of Laertes to his own purposes, the King shifts the image of fencing, from treating it as a youthful self-indulgence (as Polonius also does at II.i.25 and as perhaps Lamord did in describing Laertes to the King) to

And they can well on horseback, but this gallant

Had witchcraft in't. He grew unto his seat,   85
And to such wondrous doing brought his horse
As he had been incorpsed and demi-natured
With the brave beast. So far he topped my thought,

That I in forgery of shapes and tricks
Come short of what he did.

LAERTES
        A Norman was't?   90

KING
  A Norman.

LAERTES
  Upon my life, Lamord.

KING
      The very same.

LAERTES
  I know him well. He is the brooch indeed
And gem of all the nation.

KING
  He made confession of you,   95

---

treating it as an appropriate and admirable art.
light: trivial, frivolous. **careless:** trifling, unserious.
livery: dress, clothing. **sables:** dark rich clothing
or robes, cf., III.ii.130 note. **his:** its, cf., I.i.37 note.
weeds: clothes, garments, especially for age or
mourning, cf., Sonnet 2.1–4, *Titus Andronicus* V.iii.196,
Coriolanus II.iii.221, etc. **importing:** signifying.
health: well-being, a function of the well-ordered
humors and balanced temperament and hence
appropriate to age, cf., "health" at I.iii.21 and Hamlet's
image of the balanced man at III.ii.68–74. **graveness:**
gravity, seriousness. **since:** ago.

can: have knowledge or skill, from the early form
of the word meaning to know (Abbott §307), cf.,
"cunnings" line 155. **gallant:** i.e., gallant young man.
in't: i.e., in his horseback riding skill. **seat:** both his
posture on the horse and the horse itself.

As: as if. **As he ... brave beast:** "Cf. Sidney, *Arcadia*
(II.v.3), 'as if Centaur-like he had been one piece with
the horse'" (Jenkins). **incorpsed:** made into a single
body (with the horse). **demi-natured:** endowed
with half the nature of the horse and half of man, or
made such that man and horse were each half of one
whole being. ● This description "seems to make of
him an emblematic figure. One can hardly help being
reminded of the comparison of Claudius to a satyr
(I.ii.140)" (Jenkins LN), or of the simile of "Pyrrhus,
like th' Hyrcanian beast" (II.ii.450), or of other
allusions to man's being tempted by his own semi-
bestial nature, e.g., I.ii.150, I.v.42, and IV.iv.35. **brave:**
handsome, splendid (Raffel). **topped:** exceeded.

forgery: imagining, fabrication, cf., I.v.37, II.i.20.
● NOTE TO ACTORS: The antithesis to be brought
out here is between "forgery" (images in the mind)
and "did" (actual deeds) in the next line. **shapes and
tricks:** possibly a hendiadys for "imaginary tricks"
(Wright, page 187) if "shapes" in itself implies shaped
by imagination, but since "forgery" already implies
imagination, probably "shapes" = "forms, figures,
postures" and "tricks" = "feats of skill" (Jenkins).
Upon my life: an oath (I swear on my life).
Lamord: the name unites the French *la mort* (death)
with the Old English *morðor* (murder). ● The name
thus bestows upon the dialogue overtones of both
death and murder and foreshadows the catastrophe
being set in motion here.
The very same: he is the one I mean.

brooch ... gem: decorative ornament ... precious
jewel ●cf., Osric's imitation of such courtly diction at
V.ii.106ff.

made confession of you: a) acknowledged that he
knew you, in response to "I know him well" in line 93,
and b) testified to your qualities (as follows).

And gave you such a masterly report
For art and exercise in your defense,

And for your rapier most especial,
That he cried out 'twould be a sight indeed

If one could match you. The scrimers of their nation   100

He swore had neither motion, guard, nor eye

If you opposed them. Sir, this report of his
Did Hamlet so envenom with his envy
That he could nothing do but wish and beg

Your sudden coming o'er to play with you.   105
Now out of this—
LAERTES
                    What out of this, my lord?
KING
Laertes, was your father dear to you?

Or are you like the painting of a sorrow,
A face without a heart?
LAERTES
                    Why ask you this?

masterly report ... defense: report of your master-like ability in the practice of the art of fencing. **art and exercise:** a hendiadys for practice of the art. "Claudius praising Laertes for exercising the art of self-defense, for being so skillful (*art*) a practitioner (*exercise*) of it," not implying theory vs. practice "as some editors haplessly suggest" (Wright, page 192).

rapier: i.e., skill in using the rapier, the fashionable light thrusting sword, usually used with the dagger or poniard in the left hand for defense, which supplanted but did not entirely replace the medieval cutting sword and buckler, a small shield with a central boss or ornamental button.

one: anyone. **match you:** "encounter as an adversary ... with equal power" (OED *v.*¹3.) or "provide with an adversary or competitor of equal power" (OED *v.*¹4.). **scrimers:** fencers (from French *escrimeurs*, relate to *skirmish* and *scrimmage*).

motion: "a step, gesture, or other movement acquired by drill and training (e.g., in *Fencing* ...)" (OED *sb.*3.c.), cf., *Twelfth Night* III.iv.274–76. **guard:** defensive posture (OED *sb.*3.). **eye:** ability to gauge range or movement (cf., OED *sb.*7.), i.e., if opposed by Laertes, opponents would be as if without any skill in fencing.

this report ... play with you: "Note how the King first awakens Laertes's vanity by praising the reporter [lines 84–89], and then gratifies it by the report itself [lines 95–102], and finally points [sharpens, emphasizes] it by these lines [lines 102–105]" (Coleridge in Furness). ● Note too the repetition of sounds in "envenom" and "envy" and the introduction of the idea of poison, essential to the coming stratagem. The claim of envy in Hamlet is a mere fabrication by the King for the manipulation of Laertes, for Hamlet has expressed no ill-will toward Laertes, cf., V.i.224 and 290.

sudden coming o'er: speedy return (from France). **play:** i.e., have a fencing bout. ● The King's description of Lamord, flattery of Laertes, and imputation of envy to Hamlet are both his own crafty effort to seduce Laertes to an ignoble course of vengeful murder and Shakespeare's artful reinforcement of the themes of man-as-beast and the threat of seduction by a devil in disguise, cf., II.ii.598–603. Laertes is a foil for Hamlet in being given a charge not by a ghost who *may* be a devil, but by a flattering metaphorical devil disguised as a king. And the King's use of reason here becomes an external foil for the will-pandering reason within Hamlet's own mind revealed in the soliloquy at III.iii.73–96 and named in Hamlet's accusation of his mother at III.iv.88.

painting: mere image, cf., II.ii.480 ("painted tyrant").

KING

Not that I think you did not love your father,   110

you did not love your father: ● echoing the Ghost at I.v.23.

● **SPEECH NOTE: But that I know... hurts by easing:** The following disquisition by the King, exhorting Laertes to action on the grounds that his love for his father might cool in time, is a direct contrast to the sentiment of Hamlet expressed sarcastically at III.ii.130ff., implying that true love is constant and unchanging (cf., Sonnet 116) and a parallel to the speech of the Player King (II.ii.186ff. and note). The King's calculated cynicism here, hinting at his own thought process in his plot to murder his brother, further confirms the words of the Ghost at I.v.43–45 about the King's "wicked wit." "The similarity of these reflections to those of the Player King (III. ii.[187–99]) must be given a dramatic rather than a psychological explanation. It is not so much that 'Claudius cannot get "The Mousetrap" out of his head' (Kittredge) as that the dramatist reiterates a dominant motif" (Jenkins). In all who articulate this motif it exists to characterize the threat to virtuous constancy.

But that I know love is begun by time,

begun by time: brought into being in temporal circumstances and hence subject to the alteration of circumstances, cf., John Lyly, *Euphues and his England*: "Love which by time and fancy is bred in an idle head, is by time and fancy banished from the heart" (quoted in Jenkins).

And that I see in passages of proof

passages of proof: actual experience, "well-attested instances" (Jenkins), literally, instances or happenings (OED passage *sb*. 13.) that prove a point or in which people are tested and proven (OED proof *sb*. 4.).

Time qualifies the spark and fire of it.
There lives within the very flame of love
A kind of wick or snuff that will abate it,   115

qualifies: modifies, reduces. **it:** i.e., love.

wick: Jenkins, Q2 "weeke," a variant spelling. **snuff:** the part of the candle wick blackened by the flame, which the snuff in turn reduces. **abate:** dim, lessen ● The point is that love is altered not only by time but by an internal principle of self-destruction, a further denial of the constant love of Sonnet 116 in keeping with the King's seduction of Gertrude away from Hamlet Senior and of his own desire, in his final moments (V.ii.308 and 324), to protect himself and save his life despite the death of the queen he has claimed to be "so conjunctive to my life and soul" (lines 14–16).

And nothing is at a like goodness still,

nothing ... still: nothing remains always ("still") at the same degree of goodness.

For goodness, growing to a plurisy,

plurisy: Q2, not in F, a disease of excess. This variant spelling of *pleurisy* (inflammation of the pleura) is based on the false derivation from Latin *plus, pluris* (more) implying that the disease resulted from an excess of one or another humor in the body (OED pleurisy).

Dies in his own too much. That we would do
We should do when we would, for this "would" changes

too much: excess. ● The idea that there can be too much goodness, while true of merely natural goods (cf., *1 Henry IV* III.ii.71–73), is demonic when applied to love, cf., I.v.55–57 and *Othello* II.i.190–95. **That we would do … changes:** that which we intend to do we ought to do when we intend it, for the intention alters. ● Cf., the words of the Player King at III.ii.187ff. and Hamlet's climactic choice in III.iii to delay for evil reasons. **should:** ought to (Abbott §323). **would:** wish to, intend to (Abbott §329).

And hath abatements and delays as many   120
As there are tongues, are hands, are accidents,

abatements: decreases (of the will).

tongues … hands: the words and the deeds of others that might cause us to desist, "of those who would dissuade or prevent" (Jenkins). **accidents:** external events or circumstances.

And then this "should" is like a spendthrift sigh
That hurts by easing. But to the quick of th' ulcer:
Hamlet comes back. What would you undertake

spendthrift sigh … easing: The sigh, which relieves the emotions, was thought to draw blood from the heart to the detriment of life, hence a spendthrift of life's blood, the point being that in the absence of action, with "this 'should'" (= the sigh) we ease (and so harm by abating) our obligation (in this case, to revenge), cf., *2 Henry VI* III.ii.61,63, *3 Henry VI* IV.iv.22, *Midsummer Night's Dream* III.ii.97 (Jenkins substantially). **spendthrift:** Q5, spend thrifts Q2, spendthrift's Riverside following Pope, not in F. **quick of th' ulcer:** the sensitive (because living, blood-fed) heart of the sore, cf., II.ii.597.

To show yourself indeed your father's son   125
More than in words?

LAERTES
                    To cut his throat i'th' church.

indeed: intended both figuratively (= really) and literally in action, the antithesis being "indeed" and "in words" in the next line.

To cut … church: ● Compare Laertes' shocking statement, which arises not only from his own feelings but from the manipulation of them by the King, to Hamlet's decision *not* to kill the King in prayer lest the King go to heaven. The two avengers are foils. Laertes enacts in the more visible, practical realm the desire for revenge that Hamlet enacts in the more invisible, spiritual realm. Each, demonically tempted (Laertes by the King, Hamlet by his own will), intends the worst act of vengeance he can imagine. The contrast is pointed. Hamlet does not deserve what Laertes sinfully plans for him (at least not at Laertes' hands, even if he does deserve it at the hands of Providence), and the King deserves at Hamlet's hands precisely what Hamlet sinfully refrains from doing to him. Laertes sins by choosing to act, Hamlet by choosing not to act.

KING
No place indeed should murder sanctuarize;

No place … sanctuarize: no location should offer sanctuary, protection from requital, to the murderer for his murder. ● Ironically, the "place" that has provided sanctuary to the murderer Claudius is the kingship itself, though Providence has sent the Ghost, and the Ghost Hamlet, to fulfill the principle that he disingenuously expresses here.

Revenge should have no bounds. But good Laertes,

Revenge … no bounds: ● The King feeds the same passion in Laertes that in Hamlet sought the King's damnation. In fact the personal desire for revenge must have bounds, as the Ghost has hinted in "Taint not thy mind" at I.v.85. Personal vengeance that is not in the service of God's vengeance (cf., Romans 12:19), would indeed be beyond the bounds of justice, inordinate, in contrast with the ordination of events by Providence that Hamlet learns on the sea voyage and then expresses to Horatio (V.ii.10–11, 48, 219–20).

Will you do this, keep close within your chamber.

Will you do this: Though many editors punctuate with a question mark (= "Are you willing to do the following?"), the Q2 punctuation suggests a conditional: "if you are willing to do this" (i.e., "To cut his throat i'th' church"), then "Keep close … . [etc.]" (Jenkins substantially) ● Having found Laertes willing to serve as his instrument of revenge, the King begins to give orders, cf., Hamlet's willingness at I.v.29–31. **keep close:** remain secluded, "so there will be no chance for a meeting of Laertes and Hamlet, which might turn to the King's discredit" (Mack/Boynton).

Hamlet returned shall know you are come home.   130

returned: having returned—the line reinforces the parallelism of the foils, Hamlet returned and Laertes come home. ● NOTE TO ACTORS: The antithesis is not between "returned" and "come home," which are synonyms, but between "Hamlet" and "you."

We'll put on those shall praise your excellence

put on: incite (Riverside), appoint (Jenkins). **those shall:** those who shall; for omission of the relative pronoun see Abbott §244.

And set a double varnish on the fame
The Frenchman gave you, bring you in fine together
And wager o'er your heads. He, being remiss,

double varnish: a second coat of brightening varnish. **in fine:** finally, at last, cf., II.ii.69, V.ii.15. **wager o'er your heads:** bet on you respectively, "This metonymic use of 'head' was common in betting parlance. Cf. V.ii.[102–103], 2 *Henry IV* III.ii.[45]" (Jenkins). **remiss:** negligent, inattentive.

Most generous and free from all contriving,   135

generous: magnanimous, noble in nature, cf., I.iii.74, V.ii.242, where Hamlet expects similar magnanimity from Laertes. **free from all contriving:** innocent of any scheming. ● Hamlet will not suspect any threat because he himself is not a plotting sort. The comment is an ironic compliment to the contriver of the "Mousetrap" in III.ii and the "deep plot" (V.ii.9) of the plan in III.iii to damn the King, though the description would be generally accurate about Hamlet but for the extreme circumstances revealed by the Ghost. The phrase also carries the self-incriminating implication for us that the King, being himself a plotter, lacks the magnanimity of Hamlet.

Will not peruse the foils, so that with ease,

peruse: examine closely, cf., II.i.87. **foils:** fencing swords blunted at the tip with buttons for sporting bouts, cf., line 99 note and *Much Ado* V.ii.13–14.

Or with a little shuffling, you may choose

shuffling: trickery, cf., III.iii.61 ● "the King's own word condemns him" (Jenkins).

A sword unbated, and in a pass of practice

unbated: unblunted (see OED *abate v.*[1] III.8 and *bate v.*[2] 3), i.e., lacking the button at the tip that a foil used in sport would normally have, cf., *Love's Labor's Lost* I.i.6. **pass of practice:** The phrase equivocally means both a bout held according to customary manner and a cunning and treacherous sword thrust (cf., OED

 Requite him for your father.
LAERTES
                    I will do't,

And for that purpose I'll anoint my sword.   140

I bought an unction of a mountebank

So mortal that, but dip a knife in it,
Where it draws blood, no cataplasm so rare,

Collected from all simples that have virtue

Under the moon, can save the thing from death   145

practice *sb.*¹ 5., line 66 above, V.ii.317, and *King Lear* V.iii.152). ● The King either means to characterize equivocally how it will appear to the crowd and Gertrude (the first sense) and to himself and Laertes (the second), or perhaps "feeling Laertes out, insinuates the second meaning under cover of the first" (Mack/Boynton).
Requite: repay.

I will do't: ● By his assent Laertes unites his will to the evil will of the King in a moment parallel to Hamlet's pivotal evil choice at III.iii.87, and the bad will choices of the other foils, Fortinbras (I.ii.22–25), Horatio (V.ii.340–42), Pyrrhus (II.ii.472 and 488–92), and Lucianus (III.ii.257–60). Claudius remains evil-willed throughout, even in his attempt to repent (III.iii.97–98) and even at the point of death (V.ii.308, 324).

anoint: (from Latin *in* + *unctum*, ppl. of *in* + *unguere*) to rub with oil or ointment, cf., "unction" in the next line. "'Some barbarous nations there are who use to poison their swords' (Plutarch, *Moralia* trans. Holland, Everyman, page 117). A precedent in the drama is a Roman referred to in [Thomas Kyd (?),] *Soliman and Perseda* who fought with 'his weapon's point empoisoned' (I.iii.32)" (Jenkins). ● The overtone ("anoint") of the ritual by which kings are consecrated is not accidental. In IV.v Laertes entered to shouts of "Laertes shall be king," and now, by means of an unction that will work too quickly to permit Hamlet to receive the church's last rites of extreme unction, Laertes is plotting to prevent the rightful heir from living to be anointed king. In an even broader implication, the sword of revenge is being (temporarily) anointed king over Laertes as the illusory sword of justice in the judgment of souls became king over Hamlet in III.iii. The play illustrates the tragic consequences of making revenge, poison, and sword king in the place of God, and also (in Act V) the providential conversions effected before it is too late.

unction: ointment, see line 140 note. **mountebank:** "an itinerant quack who, as the name implies, mounted a bench [Old English *benc*] or platform to prate his wares. See [Ben Jonson,] *Volpone*, II.ii" (Jenkins).
mortal: deadly.
cataplasm: poultice or plaster, treatment for sores or wounds which are "plastered over" with medicated cloth.
simples: elements or herbs, in contrast with compounds. **virtue:** power or influence, hence healing power.
Under the moon: anywhere beneath the sphere of the moon, i.e., in this world. ● The heavenly sphere on which the moon circled the earth, since the moon was both constant and changing, was considered

the border between the fallen and hence mutable world and the perfect and constant heavens, so that Laertes' phrase means there is no substance in all this world of mutability beneath the perfect heavens that can counteract this poison. The less emphatic, more technical implication that "To gather simples by moonlight was supposed to add to their medicinal power or 'virtue'" (Furness) requires that the phrase modify "Collected" and seems less plausible.

withal: with which, with it, therewith, used at the end of a clause. ● NOTE TO ACTORS: Not stressed (stress "scratched" instead).

contagion: poison that infects the blood (OED 3.b., from the abstract idea of the power or principle by which corrupting or destructive influence is transmitted). **gall:** rub sore, chafe (the skin) so as to break the surface, here to graze or scratch.
● "So fabulous a thing is obviously not to be identified with any known poison. But cf. Gerard on a kind of aconite (wolfsbane): 'If a man ... be wounded with an arrow or other instrument dipped in the juice hereof, [he] doth die within half an hour remediless' (*Herbal*, 1597, page 818). Cf. V.ii.315" (Jenkins).

think of: think about.

That is but scratched withal. I'll touch my point

With this contagion, that if I gall him slightly,
It may be death.

KING
       Let's further think of this,
Weigh what convenience both of time and means
May fit us to our shape. If this should fail,   150

And that our drift look through our bad performance,

'Twere better not assayed; therefore this project
Should have a back or second that might hold

If this should blast in proof. Soft, let me see.

We'll make a solemn wager on your cunnings—   155

I ha't!
When in your motion you are hot and dry—

---

fit us to: adapt us to, prepare us for. **our shape:** our role, the part we are to play (OED *sb.* 8), cf., "performance" in the next line, with the possible additional implication of disguise (OED *sb.* 7), cf., "shuffling," line 137.

that: for *that* omitted and then inserted see Abbott §285. **drift:** intention, purpose, cf., II.i.37. **look through:** be visible through (OED *sb.* 20.b). **our bad performance:** i.e., in case the performing of our plan goes awry, with the overtone of playing a role; see "shape" in line 150.

'Twere: it were, i.e., it would be: **assayed:** attempted.
back: back-up plan, from backing, supporters (OED *sb.*¹ 12). **second:** support, assistance (OED second *sb.*² 8.).

this: like "this" in line 150 and "this project" in line 152, a reference to Laertes' plan for poisoning the unbated sword. **blast in proof:** blow up in being tried, "A metaphor taken from the trying or proving of fire-arms or cannon, which blast or burst in the proof [testing]" (Steevens in Furness), though "contemporary evidence of the phrase is lacking" (Jenkins). **Soft:** an imperative interjection calling for patience or deliberation, the equivalent of "just a minute" or "hold on."

cunnings: i.e., your and Hamlet's respective skills in fencing, cf., "can" line 84.

ha't: have it (an idea).
motion: physical exertion. **dry:** thirsty.

As make your bouts more violent to that end—

And that he calls for drink, I'll have prepared him

A chalice for the nonce, whereon but sipping,   160

If he by chance escape your venomed stuck,

Our purpose may hold there. But stay, what noise?

Enter Queen.

QUEEN
One woe doth tread upon another's heel,
So fast they follow. Your sister's drowned, Laertes.

LAERTES
Drowned! O where?   165
QUEEN
There is a willow grows askant the brook

That shows his hoary leaves in the glassy stream.

Therewith fantastic garlands did she make

Of crow-flowers, nettles, daisies, and long purples
That liberal shepherds give a grosser name,   170

As: as regards which (Abbott §III rather than §110). **bouts:** set of fencing attacks, cf., V.ii.165 note. **violent:** physically taxing, intense.

that: for *that* omitted and then inserted see Abbott §285. **prepared:** F, Q2's "prefard" may be a misprint for "prepared" but also possibly for "preferred" (cf., OED *prefer v.* 3. and 4.).

chalice: goblet. **for the nonce:** for the occasion, for the particular purpose. **whereon:** on which.

stuck: thrust or lunge with a pointed weapon, variant of *stock* (OED *sb.*³ 2.) from *stoccado* (It. *stoccata*, *stoccado*).

Our purpose may hold there: we will achieve our goal in that way. ● This elaborate murder plot is a foil for what Philip Thompson called Hamlet's own writing of the ultimate revenge play (see Introduction, page 9, note 19), Hamlet's "deep plot" of refraining from killing the King in III.iii in order to be certain he would be damned, and like Hamlet's plot, this too will "pall," the words Hamlet uses at V.ii.9 when he has realized that only the rough-hewing, not the shaping, of human ends lies in human hands. **stay:** stop, wait, hold on.

tread upon … heel: cf., IV.v.78–79 note. ● The announcement of the death of Ophelia follows upon Laertes' resolve to murder Hamlet, as the death of Polonius follows upon (and more directly from) Hamlet's resolve to damn the soul of the King.

Drowned!: Drown'd! F, Drown'd, Q2.

willow: symbol of unrequited or forsaken love, cf., *Merchant of Venice* V.i.10, *Much Ado* II.i.187–92, *Twelfth Night* I.v.268, *3 Henry VI* III.iii.228 and IV.i.100, *Othello* IV.iii.28ff., *Two Noble Kinsmen* IV.i.80 (lines probably by Fletcher), and "a sad tree, whereof such who have lost their love make their mourning garlands," Thomas Fuller, *History of the Worthies of England*, 1662 (quoted in Jenkins LN, who adds "which they then wear or hang up like a trophy" as at line 173). **grows:** i.e., that grows. **askant:** ascaunt Q2, aslant F, slanting or sideways over, a variation of *askance*, this being its only recorded use as a preposition.

shows: i.e., reflected. **his:** its, cf., I.i.37 note. **hoary:** "The common 'white' willow (*salix alba*), when precariously rooted in a riverbank, often leans across the stream (l. [166]); and its leaves are *hoary* (silver-grey) on the underside, which it *shows* when reflected in the water" (Jenkins LN).

Therewith: with the willow twigs. **fantastic:** fanciful, capricious, odd, i.e., not the sorts of garlands normally made by even lovelorn maidens who are sane.

crow-flowers: probably ragged robin, or *Lychnis flos-cuculi*, "perhaps a symbol of dejection" (Jenkins LN). **nettles:** weeds (*Urtica dioica*) that sting and irritate the skin, cf., *Winter's Tale* I.ii.329, *Richard II* III.ii.18, and especially *King Lear* IV.iv.4, where they make part of the mad king's crown of weeds. **daisies:** symbol of love and perhaps of love deceived, cf., IV.v.184 note. **long purples:** "Usually identified, more or less confidently, with a kind of wild orchis which suits the name by the purple spike of its inflorescence and is said to have been known as *dead men's fingers* (l. [171])" (Jenkins); "Among the various species the favoured candidate is *orchis mascula*" (Jenkins LN). **liberal:** free-speaking, hence indecorous in speech, licentious. **grosser:** coarser, ruder.

But our cold maids do dead men's fingers call them.

cold: F, Q2's "cull-cold" may be "a false start in the ms. (a deletion-stroke perhaps giving rise to the hyphen)" (Jenkins), chaste, modest, antithesis to "liberal" in the previous line. **dead men's fingers:** cf., line 170 note, a phrase suggesting to some a phallic shape, but "recorded names for the orchis, derived (like the term *orchis* itself [from the Greek for testicle]) from the testicle-like tubers of most species, include dogstones (L[atin] *testiculus canis*), dog's cods, cullions, fool's ballocks, and many variations on these" (Jenkins). ● Whether the flower is phallic or testicular in shape, Ophelia's madness continues the melding of maidenly and lewd images arising from her chaste love and its tragic frustration.

There on the pendant boughs her crownet weeds

pendant: overhanging. **crownet:** variant of "coronet," small crown, the shape into which Ophelia has woven the garland of weeds.

Clambering to hang, an envious sliver broke,

Clambering: climbing, see line 166 note. **envious:** ill-willed, spiteful. **sliver:** branch.

When down her weedy trophies and herself

trophies: memorial tokens, originally of victory in battle, here the coronet of weeds symbolizing Ophelia's lost loves, in one sense Polonius and in another Hamlet.

Fell in the weeping brook. Her clothes spread wide,   175

weeping: wet, as if with tears, and sad, perhaps with the sense that the sounds of the brook resembled those of weeping.

And mermaid-like awhile they bore her up,

mermaid-like: modifying "her" rather than the clothes, so that like a mermaid Ophelia is half in and half out of the water, with the additional ironic reference to the singing of mermaids, which Shakespeare regularly conflates with the sirens of Homer's *Odyssey* Book 12, cf., *Venus and Adonis* lines 429, 777, *Rape of Lucrece* line 1411, *3 Henry VI* III.ii.186, and *Comedy of Errors* III.ii.45–51. ● Unlike the singing of the mermaids or sirens, which leads to the destruction of others, Ophelia's chanting of divine songs accompanies the destruction of herself, as befits her form of madness.

Which time she chanted snatches of old lauds,

Which time: during which time (Abbott §202). **snatches:** short bits. **lauds:** songs or hymns of praise. ● cf., Ophelia's mixing of sexually explicit popular songs with prayers in IV.v.

As one incapable of her own distress,

incapable of: unable to comprehend, unaware of, insensible to, "Cf. *capable*, III.ii.[11], III.iv.127" (Jenkins).

Or like a creature native and indued
Unto that element. But long it could not be   180
Till that her garments, heavy with their drink,

native and indued / Unto: born in and endowed with the ability to live in, possibly a hendiadys (Wright, page 187). **that element:** i.e., water, one of the four elements, the other three being earth, air, and fire. ●NOTE TO ACTORS: The word *element* may be counted as a single stressed syllable with its last two unstressed syllables elided (Abbott §495), otherwise the line becomes a hexameter.

●SPEECH NOTE: lines 166–83: It is dramatically appropriate (as Jenkins' LN suggests) that the Queen, who has contributed to the unfolding tragedy by her own betrayal of love, be "the messenger of Ophelia's lovelorn death." The speech is characterized by combinations of innocence with madness, chaste maidenhood with vulgar sexual innuendo, youth and beauty with sorrow and dejection, and love with death. It opens but intentionally does not resolve the question of whether or not Ophelia is guilty of suicide in the eyes of God. Critics have tried to resolve this question based on clues in Gertrude's lyrical speech, in which the free will and madness of Ophelia, like her love and her death, are inextricably intertwined. Is she "incapable of her own distress" or only "As one" who is (line 178)? Like that phrase, the entire speech distances us from certainty. In the climactic scene, III.iii, Hamlet assumes he can see the state of the soul of the King when the audience, granted the divine perspective, know that he cannot. In this speech the audience is granted only the mortal perspective, which leaves us in ignorance of the true condition of Ophelia's will at the moment of her death, and hence of the eternal fate of her soul, the play's central concern in relation to death, cf., especially II.ii.598–603, III.i.55ff., III.iii.80–95. This human incapacity to judge Ophelia's, and hence anyone's, true spiritual condition, is made explicit in the next scene in the comic debate between the gravedigger and his assistant (V.i.1–29) and in the serious debate between Laertes and the Priest (V.i.223–42). Conclusion is not possible, and our ignorance of the eternal fate of Ophelia's soul serves as a foil for both Hamlet's attempt to arrogate divine power in III.iii and his renunciation of that power in the final scene in the recognition that human beings "defy augury" (V.ii.219), and cf., V.i.116–17. Our future, here and hereafter, is beyond human "augury" (V.ii.219), not to be predicted or foreknown by mortal men.

Pulled the poor wretch from her melodious lay
To muddy death.

LAERTES

　　　　　Alas, then she is drowned.

QUEEN

Drowned, drowned.

wretch: miserable, unfortunate person, cf., II.ii.168 and V.ii.333. **lay:** song.

LAERTES

Too much of water hast thou, poor Ophelia,   185
And therefore I forbid my tears. But yet
It is our trick; nature her custom holds,
Let shame say what it will. When these are gone,

The woman will be out. Adieu, my lord.

Too much ... tears: cf., *Twelfth Night* II.i.30–32.
our: that of human beings in general.

trick: natural behavior, characteristic. **nature ... what it will:** nature keeps to her custom of causing us to weep when we are in grief, however ashamed we may be (as men) to do so. **these:** i.e., his tears.

the woman ... out: the feminine characteristics (weeping and pity) inappropriate to men will be out of my system and I'll again be a man (i.e., ready to fight). ●Laertes' confession of this particular human limitation intensifies our awareness of general human fallibility. As it is impossible for the brave Laertes to keep from weeping like a woman at his sister's death, so it is impossible for the King and Laertes to get away with murder, or for Hamlet to get away with playing God, as he tried to do in III.iii. As we cannot avoid the custom to which "nature" holds in the matter of tears, so we cannot avoid the custom of that larger structure of reality that governs the invisible moral realm.

I have a speech a' fire that fain would blaze   190
But that this folly douts it.
                                                            Exit.

a': Riverside, a Q2, of F, o' Jenkins. **fain would:** much desires to, would prefer to. **this folly:** i.e., his tears. **douts:** drownes Q2, doubts F (which, allowing for the interchangeable spelling [see OED doubt *v.* and dout *v.*], supports the Cunningham emendation at I.iv.37, see note there), does out, extinguishes.

KING

                    Let's follow, Gertrude:
How much I had to do to calm his rage.
Now fear I this will give it start again.
Therefore let's follow.
                                                            Exeunt

give it start: set (his rage) in motion, with perhaps some influence from the sense "sudden fit of passion ... outburst" (OED start *sb.*² 5.d. and 4.d.).

Act V, Scene i

Enter two Clowns.

Act V, Scene i: A graveyard.

S.D.: Q2 and F. ●"*Clowns*" are country fellows, rustics, the first being a grave-digger. A later Quarto edition (1676) adds "with Spades and Mattocks," a mattock being a digging tool whose metal head has a pick on one side and an adze blade on the other.

CLOWN

Is she to be buried in Christian burial when she
willfully seeks her own salvation?

she: Ophelia (see line 241). **in Christian burial:** in consecrated ground with the church funeral rites usually denied to suicides, whose burial is described at lines 229–31. **willfully seeks her own salvation:** intentionally commits suicide, with the irony that, whether or not the Clown in his pretension is mistaking the word "salvation" for "damnation" (Jenkins), the suicide who seeks relief (salvation) from the agonies of life (cf., III.i.62–63) must according to Christian doctrine in fact find damnation. ●The word "willfully" reinforces the play's emphasis on the central Christian idea that damnation is a consequence of the free will's evil choice and that salvation depends upon the conversion of the will in repentance. Ophelia's hypothetically willful attempt to "seek her own salvation" is a foil for Hamlet's willful attempt to seek the damnation of the King.

OTHER

I tell thee she is, therefore make her grave straight.

The crowner hath sat on her and finds it Christian burial.   5

CLOWN

How can that be, unless she drowned herself in her own defense?

OTHER

Why, 'tis found so.

CLOWN

It must be *se offendendo*, it cannot be else. For here lies the point: if I drown myself wittingly, it argues   10 an act, and an act hath three branches—it is to act, to do, to perform. Argal, she drowned herself wittingly.

straight: immediately, straight away, as at II.ii.431 and III.iv.1, "with a play on *strait*, confined" (Jenkins).

crowner: coroner, the officer charged with investigating suspicious or violent deaths, originally an officer of the king "charged with maintaining the rights of the private property of the crown" (OED coroner). **sat on her:** judged her case. **finds it:** concludes that it calls for. • The coroner has concluded that Ophelia was not guilty of suicide, but whether his finding was based on the facts (Jenkins) or on the influence of the King (as implied in lines 23–25) we do not know. In any case, as we shall see at lines 219 and 226–34, Ophelia is afforded "Christian burial" but with significant limitation of the ceremonies because her death was "doubtful," i.e., *possibly* a suicide.

in her own defense: • In this phrase and the following discussion, the Clown is attempting to sound more knowledgeable than he is by using a pastiche of the legal and theological vocabulary that Shakespeare and many in his audience would have learned, as Baldwin shows, in grammar school studies of Latin, specifically Cicero's *Topica* and Cooper's *Thesaurus*, "the standard dictionary of the time for Latin, and hence for English" (Baldwin, II.121–22). Through the Clown's pretense Shakespeare is raising the serious question of whether or not Ophelia's death resulted from an act of her own will, which would be damnable theologically, and demonstrating, as again at lines 227–42, that no human being but only God can know the answer to that question. Self-defense in the case of murder is some justification in a court of law, but the outward absurdity of the Clown's blunder about killing oneself in one's own defense hints at the idea that the death of Ophelia might be a release from tragic suffering, whether by her own will or not.

found: concluded (by the coroner). **so:** that she merits Christian burial.

se offendendo: Latin for "in self-offense," the Clown's blunder for *se defendendo*, "in self-defense." • The Clown's choice of the antithetically incorrect Latin word here is comically pretentious ignorance, as confirmed by Hamlet in lines 137–41. As such it is "An instance, among many in this scene, of Shakespeare's delight in 'the uneducated mind, and its tendency to express a sound meaning in an absurd form' (Bradley on *Cor*[*iolanus*])" (Jenkins). But the Clown's verbal error in judging the state of Ophelia's soul is also a foil for wiser men's similarly pretentious spiritual ignorance of the states of others' souls, in particular of Hamlet's climactic assumption of such knowledge about the King's soul in III.iii. It also echoes Polonius's admonition at I.iii.78–80 to be true to oneself. In being a comical instance of the same human pride that forms the crux of the tragedy, it illustrates Shakespeare's characteristic use of what is often called "comic relief" to serve the serious dramatic purposes of analogy to the main plot and intensification of main themes. **wittingly:** knowingly, intentionally. **three branches:** more pseudo-logic. The formal division into three parts was a rule of rhetoric that Shakespeare, in grammar school, would have found promoted in Cicero's *Ad Herennium* and criticized in Quintilian. The Clown's "absurdity is in [his] ludicrous misapplication of a time-honored rhetorical rule, not in [his] ignorance of the rule itself. This is a usual situation with Shakspere's clowns" (Baldwin II.91–92). There may also be an allusion to the famous lawsuit over the estate of the suicide Sir James Hales, who in 1554 had drowned himself in the river at Canterbury, in the form of "a recognizable caricature of the argument of the defending counsel that the act of self-destruction 'consists of three parts[:] ... Imagination... Resolution ... Perfection'" (Jenkins LN). • The Clown's three parts, however, are not divisions but synonyms, perhaps under the influence of the synonyms for *actus* in Cooper's *Thesaurus* (Baldwin II.121–22). From them his conclusion that Ophelia drowned herself intentionally is absurd. The folly of pretending to know more than one does about grammar, logic, and rhetoric becomes an analogous example of the folly of man's pretending to know what he cannot know about souls and the afterlife, the Clown thus becoming yet another foil for Hamlet. **argal:** a blunder for the Latin *ergo* = therefore, with a pun on the name of the Elizabethan logician John Argall (d. 1606) (Jenkins), as at lines 19 and 48. • Of the whole discussion Baldwin writes, "The First Clown is thoroughly correct in his fundamental procedure, however ludicrously he may have expressed it," for it is based on the discussion of causes in the *Topica* of Cicero (§§63–64), which Shakespeare would have known "in Stratford grammar school" (Baldwin II.120–21).

goodman delver: = mister digger; "The prefix *Goodman* was especially used when designating a man by his occupation," and from its use here, despite stage tradition, it seems that "Shakespeare does not think of the second man as a grave-digger" (Jenkins).

leave: permission. **Here lies the water ... drowns not himself:** • more absurd comical parody of the legal arguments in the Hales case (see line 11 note), and further focusing of the audience's attention on the matter of the human being's free will. **will he, nill he:** whether he wills or not (*nill* = will not, from *ne* + *will*), from which *willy nilly*, a hilarious absurdity given that the whole subject is precisely whether he does or does not will it. **Argal:** see line 12 note. **not guilty ... his own life:** the Clown's literal tautology again inadvertently makes the point that guilt lies in the will as opposed to the physical action, reinforcing that it is the will's motive for non-action in III.iii that constitutes Hamlet's own great guilt there.

OTHER

Nay, but hear you, goodman delver—

CLOWN

Give me leave. Here lies the water—good. Here stands   15
the man—good. If the man go to this water and drown
himself, it is—will he, nill he—he goes, mark you
that. But if the water come to him and drown him, he
drowns not himself. Argal, he that is not guilty of his
own death shortens not his own life.   20

OTHER

But is this law?

CLOWN

Ay marry is't—crowner's quest law.

OTHER

Will you ha' the truth an't? If this had not been a
gentlewoman, she should have been buried out a
Christian burial.   25

CLOWN

Why, there thou say'st, and the more pity that great
folk should have countenance in this world to drown

or hang themselves more than their even-Christen.

Come, my spade. There is no ancient gentlemen but
gardeners, ditchers, and grave-makers; they hold up   30

Adam's profession.

OTHER

Was he a gentleman?

CLOWZN

A was the first that ever bore arms.

OTHER

Why, he had none.

---

marry: an oath, originally "by the Virgin Mary."
crowner's quest: coroner's inquest.

ha': have. **an't:** on it = of it, cf., I.v.19 note.
gentlewoman: i.e., of the gentility, the upper class.
out a Christian burial: see line 1 note. **a:** of (Abbott
§24 and §140). ● NOTE TO ACTORS: the stress
needs to be on the phrase "out a" as opposed to "in
Christian burial" (lines 1 and 4–5).

great folk: the higher classes, namely gentility,
nobility, and royalty. **countenance:** sanction,
privilege, from that bearing or facial expression in a
superior which indicates acceptance or approval.

even-Christen: fellow-Christians (OED Christen
a. 3.b.), cf., Chaucer, *Canterbury Tales*, Parson's Tale,
lines 395, 805, and examples from Thomas More and
Langland's *Piers Plowman* cited in Furness. ● The
irony is that he is implying it would be a privilege to
be able to commit suicide without the disapproval of
the gentry, comically ignoring the question of divine
disapproval.

Come, my spade: F, i.e., hand me my spade, Q2
"Come my spade," the absence of the comma perhaps
implying direct address (vocative) to the spade.
There is no ... grave-makers: No members of the
gentility can trace their lineage further back than can
diggers in the earth. **is ... gentlemen:** for the singular
verb with plural deferred subject see Abbott §335.
hold up: uphold, sustain, continue.

Adam's profession: Adam was set by God to "dress"
the Garden of Eden (Genesis 2:5, 15, cf., OED *dress*
13.c.) and later "to till the earth" (Genesis 3:23), so that
Adam's role as gardener and his being therefore not of
the gentility was proverbial, cf., *2 Henry VI* IV.ii.134
and the rhyming proverb "When Adam delved [=
dug] and Eve span [past tense of *to spin* (flax or
wool)] / Who was then the gentleman?" (Tilley
A 30 and cited in Thomas Walsingham, *Historia
Anglicana*) (Raffel), "the text on which John Ball
preached during the Peasants' Revolt (Holinshed,
1587, III.437)" (Jenkins), implying that in the
beginning there were no gentlemen or any other class
distinctions, the parents of the human race and first
human rulers of the world not being above physical
labor. ● In contrast to the humbling of class pride
intended by the proverb, the Clown instead ennobles
his trade by implying that he can trace his lineage
back further than any member of the gentility
can — that is, to Adam.

A: he. **bore arms:** a triple pun: a) carried weapons,
therefore merited to have b) been granted a family
crest or coat of arms, c) had two physical arms, as
four lines below.

had none: had no coat of arms, and perhaps no
weapons of war.

CLOWN

What, art a heathen? How dost thou understand the   35
Scripture? The Scripture says Adam digged. Could he
dig without arms? I'll put another question to thee.

If thou answerest me not to the purpose, confess
thyself—

OTHER

Go to.   40

CLOWN

What is he that builds stronger than either the mason,
the shipwright, or the carpenter?

OTHER

The gallows-maker, for that frame outlives a thousand
tenants.

CLOWN

I like thy wit well, in good faith; the gallows does well.   45
But how does it well? It does well to those that do ill.
Now thou dost ill to say the gallows is built stronger

than the church. Argal, the gallows may do well to thee.
To't again, come.

OTHER

Who builds stronger than a mason, a shipwright, or a   50
carpenter?

CLOWN

Ay, tell me that and unyoke.

OTHER

Marry, now I can tell.

CLOWN

To't.

OTHER

Mass, I cannot tell.   55

CLOWN

Cudgel thy brains no more about it, for your dull ass
will not mend his pace with beating, and when you
are asked this question next, say a grave-maker. The
houses he makes lasts till doomsday. Go, get thee in,
and fetch me a stoup of liquor.   60

[Exit Other.]

digged: his (traditional) version of "dress," "till," or "work" the ground, cf., line 31 note. **without arms:** the third layer of the pun in line 33.

to the purpose: on point, correctly. **confess thyself—:** admit it. ● The Other interrupts the Clown in the middle of the proverb "Confess and be hanged" (Tilley C587). Cf., Marlowe's *Jew of Malta*, IV.i.149–50. The phrase is played on in *Othello* IV.i.39 and possibly in *1 Henry IV*, II.ii.4. The unspoken conclusion perhaps predisposes the Other to give the answer he offers at line 43.

Go to: Come, come (Raffel), perhaps implying "no need to finish with an insult."

frame: F, not in Q2, a pun on a) a gallows, and b) the wooden structure of a house.

does well: is a decent answer.
does well to: works effectively on. **do ill:** do evil.
dost ill: do badly (in terms of wit) and do evil (in terms of morality).
Argal: see line 12 note.
To't: To it, try.

unyoke: like oxen at the end of the day's labor, unburden, be done with it, call it a day (Jenkins substantially).
Marry: a mild oath, formerly "by the Virgin Mary."

To't: (get) to it.

Mass: short for the oath "by the mass" (i.e., the church service of the Eucharist).

Cudgel: beat as with a cudgel (a short heavy club), i.e., trouble. **your:** the colloquial indefinite use = one's, see I.i.138 note. **ass:** donkey.

lasts: Shakespeare often uses the now only singular verb inflection (-s) with plural subjects, cf., Abbott §333, *Richard III* II.iii.35, *Macbeth* II.i.61, etc.. **doomsday:** the day of final judgment (*doom* = decision, judgment) that marks the end of time and the resurrection of all souls from their graves (hence houses they will need no longer) to face God and be judged for eternal salvation or damnation, cf., I.iv.35 note. **in, and:** Q2, F has "to *Yaughan*," leading to much conjecture and no certainty. Though the Q2 reading (which offers no difficulties in meaning)

[*Clown sings as he digs.*]
   In youth when I did love, did love,
   Methought it was very sweet;
   To contract—O—the time for—a—my behove—
   O methought there—a—was nothing—a—meet.

   Enter Hamlet and Horatio [while the Clown sings.]

HAMLET
   Has this fellow no feeling of his business? a sings   65
   in grave-making.

HORATIO
   Custom hath made it in him a property of
   easiness.

HAMLET
   'Tis e'en so, the hand of little employment hath
   the daintier sense.   70

may be a compositor's misreading of the ms., F may
preserve a non-authoritative actor's gag in the form
of a topical allusion, perhaps to a local ale-house
keeper (Jenkins). Without some new discovery, "It
is impossible to detect the meaning which lies
under this corruption" (Clarendon). **stoup:** F, Q1
(Q2 soope, hence Riverside's "sup"), a tankard or
flagon, a pottery or pewter mug with one handle and
sometimes a lid.

In youth ... meet: The Clown's words are a corruption
of a poem (reprinted in Furness) by Thomas Lord
Vaux, "The Aged Lover Renounceth Love," which
was printed in *Tottel's Miscellany* (1557) and later
became a popular song. ● To an audience member
who knew the song, the Clown's transpositions
and alterations would evoke both humor at his bad
memory and again a deepening of the themes of
thwarted love and mortality. *Methought:* it seemed
to me. *To contract ... meet:* To make a contract for
marriage (OED contract *sb.* 3.b.) for my benefit
("*behove*" = behoof) seemed not at all appropriate
("meet"), comically echoing from the boy's viewpoint
the theme of Ophelia's song at IV.v.48ff. "To contract"
may also mean to shorten, but it is not clear how
it would be "nothing ... meet" either to shorten the
time or, if this is another "instance of his penchant
for replacing the required sense with its opposite"
(Jenkins), to lengthen it. ● NOTE TO ACTORS:
The *o*'s and *a*'s in Roman type within the lines of the
song are the Clown's grunts as he digs.

business? a sings in grave-making: Q2, business,
that he sings at Grave-making? F, business a sings in
grave-making? Jenkins. The "a," colloquial for "he,"
probably here implies "that he" but was confusing
to typesetters, so that Q2 clarifies it in one way and F
in another. Jenkins may be right, but the copy text is
followed here. See line 69 note.

Custom ... easiness: the precise sense may be either
a) custom (habit) has given grave-making for him an
easy quality, or b) custom has made of grave-making
for him an appurtenance to ease. ● "For the proverb
that custom makes all things easy, see Tilley C 933,
and cf. *Oth*[*ello*] I.iii.229–31, *A*[*s*] *Y*[*ou*] *L*[*ike It*] II.i.2"
(Jenkins).

'Tis: It is. **e'en:** even. **so, the:** Q2, which may imply
an understood "that" as in line 65 above, F has a
semicolon. ● As at lines 65–66, F makes the sense
more explicit, but here it may be eliminating an
understood "that" where above it provides one.
Since Q2 and F differ in opposite ways in these
two instances, it is not certain whether Hamlet is
speaking in simple sentences ("Has he no feeling?
He sings at grave-making" and "What you say is
true; the hand of little employment has the daintier
sense") or in elliptical complex sentences ("Has he
no feeling that he sings at grave-making?" and "It

CLOWN

[*Sings.*]

> But age with his stealing steps
> Hath clawed me in his clutch,
> And hath shipped me into the land
> As if I had never been such.

[*Clown throws up a skull.*]

HAMLET

That skull had a tongue in it and could sing once.   75

How the knave jowls it to the ground as if 'twere

Cain's jawbone, that did the first murder. This

---

is true that the hand of little employment has the daintier sense") or in a combination of both. Here Q2 is followed in both cases, with acknowledgment of Jenkins' strong argument for the understood "that." **little employment:** less use. **daintier sense:** greater sensitivity, more delicate feeling. ● As the less used hand feels things more sensitively, so the familiarity of his work has hardened the Clown's feelings so that he can sing while digging a grave. The implied analogy is to the soul, like that of the King, that may harden through familiarity with sin.

into the land: back toward earth from which man was first taken (cf., Genesis 3:19), as in the original poem, see line 61 note, F intill the land, *till = to*, (Abbott §184). *such*: i.e., young and in love, referring to line 61.

● **SPEECH NOTE:** Here begins Hamlet's meditation on the humbling of human ambitions that must attend the contemplation of physical death, Shakespeare's visual and verbal *memento mori* (Latin for "remember that you die," often applied to the death's head itself). In medieval and Renaissance art, saints, monks, and by the 15th and 16th centuries portrait subjects, were often depicted contemplating a human skull as a reminder of their mortality and an invitation to humility. Jenkins notes "the indignities suffered by the dead" at the hands of gravediggers, as exemplified in Luis de Granada's *Of Prayer and Meditation*, trans. Hopkins, 1582 (fols. 202–4) (Jenkins LN). This contemplation of Hamlet reinforces in him the wisdom of submitting the individual will to God, a wisdom that he has gained during his eventful sea voyage, as we will learn in the next scene. Hamlet imagines that the two or three skulls successively thrown up by the Clown are those of various kinds of pretentious men, a politician (meaning a schemer or plotter), a flattering courtier, a lawyer, and one who buys lands to raise his status, all of whose aspirations in life are now reduced to dust. The implication is that not only the political ambition and lust of the King, but also Hamlet's own effort to play God in the matter of damning him, must come to dust.

jowls: strikes, knocks, "with a play on *jowl*, jawbone" (Jenkins).

Cain's jawbone: Medieval tradition in literature (e.g., Wakefield Mystery Cycle "Killing of Abel" [Towneley 2.324]) and art (see Barb) has Cain killing Abel with a jawbone, usually that of an ass, which ties the story to that of Samson (Judges 15:15–17). ● Hamlet implies that it is as if the Clown were repaying Cain for committing the "first murder" by knocking Cain's own jawbone, or the jawbone of the ass that Cain used, to the ground. There is also "the justice of Cain's being in his turn jowled by an *ass* (line 77)" (Jenkins). **that:** referring to Cain (for *that* separated from its antecedent see Abbott §262). **first murder:** "Cain's crime, not merely murder but fratricide, is the

might be the pate of a politician, which this ass

now o'er-offices; one that would circumvent God,
might it not?   80

HORATIO

It might, my lord.

HAMLET

Or of a courtier, which could say, "Good morrow,
sweet lord. How dost thou, sweet lord?" This

might be my Lord Such-a-one, that praised my
Lord Such-a-one's horse when a meant to beg it,   85
might it not?

HORATIO

Ay, my lord.

HAMLET

Why, e'en so, and now my Lady Worm's, chopless,

and knocked about the mazard with a sexton's spade.

Here's fine revolution and we had the trick to see't.   90

Did these bones cost no more the breeding
but to play at loggets with 'em? Mine ache to think
on't.

CLOWN

[*Sings.*]

> *A pickaxe and a spade, a spade,*
> *For and a shrouding sheet,*   95
> *O a pit of clay for to be made*
> *For such a guest is meet.*

[*Clown throws up another skull.*]

HAMLET

There's another. Why may not that be the skull of a

---

prototype of Claudius's, as we were reminded at III.
iii.37" (Jenkins), see Genesis 4.

pate: head. **politician:** schemer, plotter, one who uses
"policy," meaning cunning, intrigue (Crystal).

o'er-offices: F, "lords it over (by virtue of his office). Cf.
Cor[iolanus] V.ii.60, ... Note the irony of over-officing
an intriguer for office" (Jenkins, who disparages "The
preference of editors and bibliographers for Q2's *o'er-
reaches*"). ● Hamlet too has tried to "o'eroffice" God by
usurping the role of the judge of souls. **would:** wished
to (Abbott §329). **circumvent God:** as Cain tried to do
in Genesis 4:9 (Jenkins substantially), as Hamlet has
chosen to try to do in III.iii, and as the King continues
trying to do.

my Lord Such-a-one ... meant to beg it: cf., *Timon of
Athens*, I.ii.210–212. **a:** he.

e'en so: even so, exactly. **my Lady Worm's:** belonging
to the ironically titled courtly mistress, the worm,
i.e., dead and eaten by worms, cf., IV.iii.20. **chopless:**
missing the lower jaw, continuing the jawbone imagery
of lines 76–77, cf., line 192 ("chop-fallen").

mazard: head, from "mazer," a drinking cup or bowl
and the hard wood from which it was made (OED *sb.¹*
2.). **sexton's:** of a grave-digger or the bell-ringer of a
church, from a popular O.Fr. version of *sacristan*.

revolution: of Fortune's wheel, reversing the worldly
condition of lord and sexton, see II.ii.229 note, "or
the whirligig of time" (Jenkins), cf., *Twelfth Night*
V.i.376–77 ("And thus the whirligig of time brings in his
revenges"). **trick:** knack, skill.

the breeding: for *the* with the gerund see Abbott §93.

loggets: a game of throwing or tossing pieces of wood
(loggets or loggats) at a stake, cf., Jonson, *Tale of a Tub*,
IV.vi.69. **Mine:** i.e., my own bones.

For and: plus, and also (OED For *conj.* 5). *shrouding
sheet:* winding sheet, the cloth in which the dead were
traditionally wrapped for burial, from which derive the
white sheet with eye holes as the costume for a ghost
on Halloween and in popular culture. *for to:* to, as a
sign of the infinitive, see Abbott §152 and cf., I.ii.175 (Q2)
and III.i.167. *meet:* fitting, appropriate.

Why: As at III.i.120, Jenkins argues that the word is an
interjection, rather than a question, despite lack of the
comma in both Q2 and F, so that the question would be
not "*why* may not that be?" but "*may* not that be?" line
101 giving support to the former even as line 88 gives
support to the latter. The effects of both rhetorical
questions are similar, but to my ear, in the context the
former sounds more Hamlet-like.

lawyer? Where be his quiddities now, his quillities,

his cases, his tenures, and his tricks? Why does he   100

suffer this mad knave now to knock him about the
sconce with a dirty shovel, and will not tell him of his

action of battery? Hum. This fellow might be

in's time a great buyer of land, with his statutes, his
recognizances, his fines, his double vouchers, his   105
recoveries. Is this the fine of his fines, and the

● NOTE TO ACTORS: Either reading can be justified, but probably the same choice should be made here and at line 203 at least, if not also at III.i.120.

Where be … : "The traditional *ubi sunt* motif, as at line [189]" (Jenkins), which derives from medieval Latin poems with *Ubi sunt qui ante nos fuerunt* ("where are those who have been before us") as first line or refrain, appears often in medieval and Renaissance literature, and can be thought of as an emotional and sentimental version of the more theologically rooted *memento mori* theme, cf., line 75 note. For the use of *be* in questions of appeal, see Abbott §299. **quiddities… quillities:** niceties or refinements of argument, quibbles ● Hamlet is imitating the speech of lawyers in terms derived from the schoolmen, the medieval scholastic philosophers and their students, among whose intellectual heirs Hamlet has been a student at Wittenberg. *Quiddities* from the Latin *quidditas*, the abstract essence of something, its "whatness," and *quillities* (Q3–4, or quillites Q2, or quillets F) either from the same word or possibly from Latin *qualitas* (quality) or *quodlibet*, literally, "what you will," applied to a topic for scholastic debate set as an exercise (cf., *1 Henry IV* II.iv.17). Hamlet questions what, when the lawyer is dead, becomes of the subtle distinctions on which in life he may have spent much energy.

cases: citations of court case precedents (Raffel).
tenures: real estate holdings or the titles to them.
tricks: skills or artifices.

mad: wild, irrepressible (Jenkins).

sconce: head, probably colloquial, possibly from the name for a shielded candlestick or lantern, or from the name of a small defensive fort or a protective screen or shelter, cf., OED sconce *sb.*² and *Comedy of Errors* II.ii.34–38.

action of battery: court suit for illegal beating, cf., *Twelfth Night* IV.i.34. ● Hamlet wonders why this dead lawyer does not sue the Clown for beating him about the head with a shovel, i.e., what good is a court of law when one is dead? **Hum:** the early texts' indication of the sound of human pondering, which we would spell "Hmmm."

in's: in his. **great buyer of land:** "Like many who aspired to become landed gentry. The practice had long been notorious among lawyers, who were accused of using their legal expertise to their own advantage. Cf. Chaucer, *Prologue*, lines 318–20; Wyclif, *Three Things*, Eng. Works (EETS), pages 182–83" (Jenkins).
statutes … recognizances: "Often coupled together, the *recognizance* being a bond acknowledging a debt or obligation, the *statute* (statute merchant or statute staple, according to the manner of record) securing the debt upon the debtor's lands" (Jenkins, following Ritson in Furness). **fines … recoveries:** "A *fine* (an action leading to an agreement calling itself *finalis concordia* [final agreement]) and a *recovery* (a suit for obtaining possession) were procedures for effecting

recovery of his recoveries, to have his fine pate full of

fine dirt? Will his vouchers vouch him no more of his

purchases, and double ones too, than the length and
breadth of a pair of indentures? The very   110

conveyances of his lands will scarcely lie in this box,

and must th' inheritor himself have no more, ha?

HORATIO
    Not a jot more, my lord.

HAMLET
    Is not parchment made of sheep-skins?

HORATIO
    Ay, my lord, and of calve-skins too.   115

HAMLET
    They are sheep and calves which seek out assurance in
    that. I will speak to this fellow. Whose grave's

this, sirrah?

CLOWN
    Mine, sir.
    [Sings.]
        O a pit of clay for to be made   120

---

the transfer of estates when an entail or other obstacle prevented simple sale. A *voucher* in a recovery suit was the process of summoning a third party to warrant the holder's title, and the customary *double voucher* involved a second warrantor" (Jenkins, following Ritson in Furness). ● Shakespeare no doubt knew these meanings from his business dealings, and Hamlet has heard them bandied about by lawyers. **fine of his fines:** end result of his legal agreements, the first two of the four senses of the word *fine* on which Hamlet plays (see notes to the next two lines).

recovery: the sum of what he regains. **fine pate:** handsome or well-groomed head, the third sense of *fine*.

fine dirt: powdered soil, the fourth sense. **vouch him:** guarantee him.

length and breadth of a pair of indentures: the "pair of indentures" was "a deed duplicated on a single sheet which was then divided by a zigzag (indented) cut so that the fitting together of the two parts would prove their genuineness" (Jenkins). ● The point is that all the land he purchased in life could guarantee him no more land in death than a grave, whose length and breadth was about that of the two sheets of parchment on which his land-ownership was recorded.

conveyances ... this box: all the man's documents by which title to property was transferred might barely have fit into this grave.

inheritor: owner, acquirer.

jot: least bit, from Greek *iota*.

parchment: scraped and stretched skin of sheep, goat, or calf prepared for writing on.

sheep and calves: i.e., fools. **assurance:** a) legal deed of possession, b) certainty. ● As parchments are made of the skins of flayed sheep and calves, so the documents written on them are made by fools, who, presuming that the possession of documents offers "assurance" of protection, will nevertheless inevitably be flayed (like sheep and calves) by death. ● The implication again is that human pride is a form of folly when seen in the light of inevitable death, the *memento mori* theme, cf., line 75 note.

sirrah: from "sir," used only with those of inferior status. ● NOTE TO ACTORS: stressed on the first syllable. ● Hamlet speaks to him as to an inferior (thou) and Clown replies as to a superior (you).

O a pit ... made: repeating the line of the song from line 96, F adds "*For such a guest is meet*" from line 97, "evidently an actor's addition" (Jenkins), cf., IV.v.165 note, and for "*meet*" see line 97 note. Riverside follows F, hence the anomaly in line numbering.

HAMLET

I think it be thine indeed, for thou liest in't.

CLOWN

You lie out on't, sir, and therefore 'tis not

yours. For my part, I do not lie in't, yet it is mine.

HAMLET

Thou dost lie in't, to be in't and say it is thine.   125
'Tis for the dead, not for the quick; therefore
thou liest.

CLOWN

'Tis a quick lie, sir; 'twill away again from me
to you.

HAMLET

What man dost thou dig it for?   130

CLOWN

For no man, sir.

HAMLET

What woman then?

CLOWN

For none neither.

HAMLET

Who is to be buried in't?

CLOWN

One that was a woman, sir; but, rest her soul, she's   135
dead.

HAMLET [*Aside to Horatio.*]

How absolute the knave is. We must speak by the card

or equivocation will undo us. By the Lord, Horatio,

these three years I have took note of it: the age is grown

so picked that the toe of the peasant comes so near the   140
heel of the courtier he galls his kibe.—[*To the Clown.*]
How long hast thou been grave-maker?

---

be: for *be* after verbs of thinking see Abbott §299.
liest: a) are physically in it, and b) are telling lies (by saying it was his grave).

lie out on't: a) are physically outside of it, hence it is not yours to be buried in, and b) are telling lies (which can be done only by someone living) by saying I am a) lying dead in it, and b) telling lies in it. • The accusation of telling a lie, outside of jesting, is dangerous to be said directly, especially to a superior.

I do not lie in't: I am not a) lying dead in it, and b) telling lies in it.

lie in it: are telling lies in it.

the quick: the living. **liest:** tell lies.

quick lie: a) a living lie, despite being spoken in a grave, and b) a nimble lie. • with the additional implication that the word "lie," having been used in three senses, is swift and changeable, like quicksilver, cf., I.v.66, or more likely wanton, like "the kind of woman with whom one could have a quick sexual encounter (whence the name Mistress Quickly [Quick-lie] ... in [*1 and 2 Henry IV*])" (Andrews). In addition to answering one accusation of lying with another as in courtly insults, cf., II.ii.574–75 and *As You Like It* V.iv.68–97, the Clown is implying that the lying down in death comes quickly and that before long Hamlet will himself inevitably be lying in a grave prepared by some gravedigger if not by this one. To us this is a bit of foreshadowing. The Clown intends it to be homiletically applicable to anyone, not prophetically to Hamlet in particular, whom in any case the Clown does not recognize as Hamlet, cf., lines 147–48.

rest her soul: i.e., God rest her soul.

absolute: precise, strict in his use of words. **knave:** a male of low status, a menial. **by the card:** precisely, punctiliously, by the shipman's chart or "the card on which the 32 points of the compass were marked" (Jenkins).

equivocation: double-meanings, ambiguity, with a possible reference to the technique of deceiving one's accusers, particularly when on trial for heresy, cf., *Macbeth*, II.iii.8, V.v.42.

these three years: possibly a topical allusion, but not one yet argued for persuasively. **took:** "This use of the past tense for the participle ... is common in Shakespeare" (Jenkins), cf., lines 173 and 186, *Julius Caesar* II.i.50, and Abbott §343.

picked: ornate, refined, fastidious, finicky.

galls his kibe: irritates or rubs the blister or chilblain on his heel, "to judge from frequent allusion, a

CLOWN

Of all the days i' the year, I came to't that day that our
last king Hamlet overcame Fortinbras.

prevalent affliction" (Jenkins), cf., *Merry Wives of
Windsor* I.iii.31–32, *King Lear* I.v.9, *Tempest* II.i.276.
 ● Hamlet is mocking the Clown's pretention to verbal
wit by observing that peasants are behaving so
pretentiously like courtiers that the distance between
them seems to disappear, much to the discomfort of
the latter.

 ● SPEECH NOTE: **Of all the days … three and twenty
years:** Lines 143–47, 161–62, and 173–74 have occasioned
much debate on Hamlet's age, since through most of
the play, like Fortinbras and Laertes, he is referred to
as a young man, e.g., I.i.170, I.ii.113, I.iii.7, 124, I.v.16, 38,
II.i.113, III.i.159, IV.i.19. Here, if the terms are taken
literally, the arithmetic would make him thirty years
old. However, we are not to suppose that the timeline
of the play covers over a decade or that Shakespeare
blundered in his counting. Here, as elsewhere (most
notably in *Othello*, where, depending on which lines
we focus on, the span of time of the play is both
several days and several months), the discrepancy is
apparent only to scholars in the study. In the theater,
such references to time serve the purposes of the
immediate impression and are not to be taken, as they
would be in a novel, for consistent signposts. The
numbers here "are not in fact precise and … they are not
attached to Hamlet." They are round numbers intended
thematically. Twenty-three is a general figure, in this
case for the number of "years that separate Hamlet from
his boyhood" as Leontes from his (*Winter's Tale* I.ii.155),
and cf., *Winter's Tale* III.iii.59–60, *Troilus and Cressida*
I.ii.235, *1 Henry VI* I.i.113. Thirty years is "a traditional
formula for a stretch of time covering most of a man's
life," cf., III.ii.155, 157, *Romeo and Juliet* I.v.33–40, *1 Henry
IV* III.iii.47–48, where Falstaff's exaggeration of "two
and thirty" means a lifetime plus two, just as he adds
"two or three" to the "fifty of them" he supposedly
fought with at II.iv.186–87, and, outside of Shakespeare,
Marlowe's *Doctor Faustus* V.ii.42 and *Jew of Malta* I.ii.305,
Lyly's *Mother Bombie* V.iii.16, and the old *King Leir* line
2442. "The gravedigger's numbers are less important
for themselves than for the pattern of a life which they
evoke…. [The point of the reference to] King Hamlet's
victory over Fortinbras … was to link the end with the
beginning, so that the activity of the grave-digger … is
found to span the whole play and with it the whole
career of Hamlet" (Jenkins LN). That career has been the
equivalent of a lifetime's internal spiritual struggle, akin
both to Hamlet Senior's external battle with Fortinbras
and to the Clown's life of grave-digging, and tied by both
to the meditation on mortality and the fundamental
question of the play, namely considering the ends of
our bodies in the grave, what are the implications of our
choices in life for the state of our souls after death?

since: used adverbially for "ago" (Abbott §62).

HAMLET

How long is that since?   145

CLOWN

Cannot you tell that? Every fool can tell that. It was
that very day that young Hamlet was born—he that is
mad and sent into England.

HAMLET

Ay, marry, why was he sent into England?

CLOWN

Why, because a was mad. A shall recover his   150
wits there; or if a do not, 'tis no great matter
there.

HAMLET

Why?

CLOWN

'Twill not be seen in him there; there the men are as
mad as he.   155

HAMLET

How came he mad?

CLOWN

Very strangely they say.

HAMLET

How strangely?

CLOWN

Faith, e'en with losing his wits.

HAMLET

Upon what ground?   160

CLOWN

Why, here in Denmark. I have been sexton here, man
and boy, thirty years.

HAMLET

How long will a man lie i' th' earth ere he
rot?

CLOWN

Faith, if a be not rotten before a die—as we have many   165
pocky corses nowadays that will scarce hold the laying
in—a will last you some eight year or nine year. A
tanner will last you nine year.

HAMLET

Why he more than another?

CLOWN

Why, sir, his hide is so tanned with his trade that   170
a will keep out water a great while, and your water
is a sore decayer of your whoreson dead body.

Here's a skull now hath lien you i' th' earth

three and twenty years.

---

marry: a mild interjection here akin to "oh really?" or "you don't say," derived from "By the Virgin Mary".

a...A...a: he...He...he

'Twill: It will. **there ... as mad as he:** an obvious irony for the sake of Shakespeare's London audience, "presently [to become], if it was not already, a stock joke (as in Marston, *Malcontent*, III.i.95; Massinger, *A Very Woman*, III.i.119–22)" (Jenkins), but also ironically its own opposite, for the audience knows that Hamlet is not in fact mad. Baldwin (II.515) cites a parallel that Steevens finds in Horace (*Sermonum* II.2.3.120–21).

How came he: how did he become.

How: in what way (not to what degree).

Faith: In faith, a mild oath. **e'en:** even, here the equivalent of "precisely" or "namely" ● another example of the Clown's false and hence tautological distinctions among synonyms, cf., lines 11–12.

Upon what ground: i.e., by what cause. ● in the next line the Clown takes it literally.

sexton: see line 90 note.

thirty years: see line 143 note.

How long ... he rot?: "Note the ... variation[s] on the theme of how long a man is remembered after his death (I.ii.87–108, 145–57; III.ii.124–33)" (Jenkins). ● The theme, that the fact of physical death humbles the will, will reach its pitch in Hamlet's rhymes in lines 213–216. **i' th':** in the. **ere:** before.

a ... a: he ... he.

pocky corses: pox-ridden (i.e., syphilitic) corpses. **scarce hold the laying in:** barely hold together enough to be buried in the ground, being so rotten already, cf., *Coriolanus* III.ii.80, *Timon of Athens* I.ii.154.

your ... your: the colloquial indefinite use, one's, see I.i.138 note. **whoreson:** literally, son of a whore, often used as a general term of disapproval, here of "contemptuous familiarity" (Jenkins).

hath lien: has lain, see line 139 note to "took."
you: the ethical dative.

three and twenty: see line 143 note.

HAMLET

Whose was it?   175

CLOWN

A whoreson mad fellow's it was. Whose do you think it
was?

HAMLET

Nay, I know not.

CLOWN

A pestilence on him for a mad rogue! A poured a
flagon of Rhenish on my head once. This same skull,   180
sir, was, sir, Yorick's skull, the King's jester.

HAMLET

This? [*Takes the skull.*]

CLOWN

E'en that.

HAMLET

Alas, poor Yorick. I knew him, Horatio—a fellow

of infinite jest, of most excellent fancy. He hath bore   185

me on his back a thousand times, and now how
abhorred in my imagination it is. My gorge rises at it.
Here hung those lips that I have kissed I know not

how oft. Where be your gibes now, your gambols, your

songs, your flashes of merriment that were wont to   190
set the table on a roar? Not one now to mock your own
grinning? Quite chop-fallen? Now get you

to my lady's chamber and tell her, let her paint an inch
thick, to this favor she must come; make her laugh at
that. Prithee, Horatio, tell me one thing.   195

HORATIO

What's that, my lord?

---

mad: mad, irrepressible, as at line 101.

A: He.
Rhenish: Rhine wine, as at I.iv.10.
Yorick's: The name Yorick is variously accounted for
as an English spelling of the Danish form of George
(Jörg) (*Y* representing *J*), or of Eric (the king in *Der
Bestrafte Brüdermord*), or as a corruption of Rorik
(the Queen's father in both Saxo Grammaticus and
Belleforest), and "Jerick" is the name of a character in
a contemporary play called *Alphonsus of Germany*.
E'en that: that very one.

Alas, poor Yorick: To entertain Jenkins' question
whether "Alas, poor Yorick" in line 184 may be an
echo in Shakespeare's mind of "Alas, poor York" in *3
Henry VI* (I.iv.84) is to invite madness.

fancy: the imaginative faculty of inventing images or
concepts not occurring in reality or available to the
senses. ● Yorick was highly imaginative, whimsical,
entertaining. **hath bore:** has borne, carried; for the
curtailed form of the past participle see Abbott §343.
a thousand times: a hyperbole for many times. **now
how abhorred in my imagination:** how horrifying
and disgusting being imagined now (with the dead
man's skull in his hands). **gorge rises:** the sickening
feeling of being about to vomit (OED gorge *sb.*¹ 5.b.).
gibes: satirical jokes. ● NOTE TO ACTORS:
pronounced with a soft *g* (as *jibes*). **gambols:** dancing,
leaping.
were wont: were used to, in the habit of.
on a roar: roaring with laughter. **Not one now ...
grinning?:** Are you not now going to mock your own
(skull's) grinning as in life you mocked the grinning
of others? **chop-fallen:** depressed, with a play on the
skull's now being literally without a lower jaw (OED
chop *sb.*²), cf., line 89.
paint an inch thick: put on heavy makeup.
● "A common motif in the tradition of the *danse
macabre*, in which a skull appears beside a woman at
her toilet, here makes use of a hyperbole which seems
to have been current in the satire of women. Queen
Elizabeth herself was reported by the Jesuit priest
Anthony Rivers at Christmas 1600 to have been
painted 'in some places near half an inch thick' (Foley,
Records of the Society of Jesus, i.8); and Nashe in the
1594 Preface to *Christ's Tears*, ridiculing Gabriel
Harvey's style, had compared his vainglory to a
mistress 'new painted over an inch thick' (Nash,
II.180)" (Jenkins LN). From this motif descends that

HAMLET

Dost thou think Alexander looked a this fashion i' th'
earth?

HORATIO

E'en so.

HAMLET

And smelt so? Pah!   200

[*Puts down the skull.*]

HORATIO

E'en so, my lord.

HAMLET

To what base uses we may return, Horatio. Why may
not imagination trace the noble dust of Alexander till a
find it stopping a bung-hole?

HORATIO

'Twere to consider too curiously to   205
consider so.

HAMLET

No, faith, not a jot, but to follow him thither with

modesty enough, and likelihood to lead it:
Alexander died, Alexander was buried, Alexander
returneth to dust, the dust is earth, of earth we make   210

---

of "Death and the Maiden," in which a corpse appears to a beautiful maiden (in some images seducing or embracing her) to remind her of, or threaten her with, her own mortality, or at least that of her youthful beauty. **favor:** appearance, look of the face. **make her laugh at that:** • In Hamlet's sarcasm here the antithesis of corpse and maiden is extended to include the contrast of horror with jesting and laughter.

Alexander: Alexander the Great, ancient conqueror of the known world from the Mediterranean to India. "From ancient times Alexander was regularly cited in meditations on Death the leveller. See, e.g., Lucian's *Dialogues of the Dead*, XII–XIV. Marcus Aurelius (VI.24) comments on the sameness of the dust of Alexander and his groom" (Jenkins), cf., Baldwin I.733–34. **a:** Q2, a contraction of OE *on* or *an* (cf., Abbott §140), possibly a variant form of *in* (cf., Crystal), or, since F has o', possibly a contraction of *of*.

E'en: even, exactly.

And smelt so: "Alexander in life was noted for his 'very fair white colour' and a body of 'so sweet a smell' that his apparel 'took thereof a passing delightful savour, as if it had been perfumed' (North's Plutarch, Tudor Trans. iv.301)" (Jenkins). • The emphasis in this implied contrast of Alexander's physical sweetness with mortal corruption is on the humbling of his greatness, as of Caesar's at line 213.

uses: functions for which to be employed, services to be put to. **Why:** Here again, as at III.i.120 and line 98, Jenkins argues, despite absence of the comma in Q2 and F, for the interjection sense (OED IV.7.b.) rather than the interrogative, so that the question would be not "why may not imagination trace?" but "may not imagination trace?" As above, to my ear the former question sounds more Hamlet-like. • NOTE TO ACTORS: Either reading can be justified, but probably the same choice should be made here and at line 98, if not also at III.i.120. **trace:** track, follow the trail of. **a:** he, the one whose imagination is doing the tracing, or possibly it (imagination itself) (OED A *pron*. 3.). **stopping a bung-hole:** serving as the stopper or cork for the hole in the bulge of a cask of beer or wine.

curiously: precisely, minutely, and possibly also inquisitively.

faith: in faith or by my faith, a mild oath. **jot:** least bit, as at line 113. **him:** Alexander. **thither:** to (toward) there, i.e., to the notion of his "stopping a bung-hole". **modesty:** propriety, moderation, lack of excessive "curiosity" in the sense of line 205, and also, as a secondary sense, humility, cf., II.ii.440, III.ii.19. **it:** either "modesty" (likelihood leads and so justifies the propriety of the idea), or "imagination" of line 203 (likelihood leads the imagination to the idea), or perhaps both.

loam, and why of that loam whereto he was converted

might they not stop a beer-barrel?
Imperious Caesar, dead and turned to clay,
Might stop a hole to keep the wind away.

O that that earth which kept the world in awe   215

Should patch a wall t' expel the winter's flaw.

But soft, but soft awhile. Here comes the King,
The Queen, the courtiers.

Enter King, Queen, Laertes, [Priest,] and the corse
[with Lords attendant.]

                    Who is this they follow?
And with such maimèd rites? This doth betoken

The corse they follow did with desperate hand   220

Fordo it own life. 'Twas of some estate.

Couch we awhile and mark.

LAERTES
What ceremony else?

---

loam: moistened clay, or a paste of moistened clay, sand, and humus, that can be molded into various shapes and then dried for various purposes (OED 2.).

stop: use as a stopper to plug (the bung-hole) of.

Imperious: The usual form for "imperial," which F uses, but both qualities are relevant here. Both Caesar's rank ("imperial") and his attitude ("imperious") are humbled by death. **Caesar:** "The citation of *Caesar* along with Alexander was traditional" (Jenkins). ● Hamlet shifts into rhymed couplets, and he keeps to the tradition in his two couplets by joining the all-conquering Roman to the all-conquering Greek to sum up the idea that even the greatest men of the greatest ages must come to dust.

that earth: i.e., the body of Caesar, since "thou art dust" (Genesis 3:19) and "the dust is earth" (line 210).

patch a wall: "Caldecott cites ... Harrison's *Description of England* [1577, published as part of Holinshed's *Chronicles*:] '[Builders in open country] cast [a cottage] all ouer with claie to keepe out the wind, which otherwise would annoie them" (Furness).

flaw: gust of wind, squall, spell of rough weather (OED *sb.*²).

soft: hush, just a minute, cf., III.i.87 note.

s.d.: Q2 Enter K., Q., Laertes and the corse [= corpse], F Enter King, Queen, Laertes, and a coffin, with Lords attendant, Q1 Enter King and Queen, Laertes, and other lords, with a Priest after the coffin. Probably Shakespeare originally intended a shrouded body with no coffin but F and Q1 suggest staging with a coffin, which then would have been open, considering lines 249–51 below, cf., *Romeo and Juliet* IV.i.110, "the common if not the usual practice of the time" (Dover Wilson, quoted in Jenkins).

maimèd rites: reduced, incomplete ceremonies, "Contrast above lines 4–5 and note. This is not so much an inconsistency as a balancing of what is essential to Christian burial against what is usual but is here withheld. See lines [229–38]" (Jenkins).

betoken: signify.

corse: corpse. **desperate hand:** i.e., suicidally. Theologically, despair is the conviction that one is certainly damned and cannot be saved even by God. Psychologically, that conviction leads to suicide.

Fordo: kill, destroy, variant spellings in Q2 (Foredoo) and F (Fore do). **it:** Q2 and F, for *its* (Q5, it's F3) about an unknown person (Abbott §228), cf., I.ii.216 and note. **'Twas:** It was. **estate:** status, rank.

Couch we ... mark: imperatives, let us conceal ourselves and observe. **mark:** observe, pay attention, as in line 222.

What ceremony else?: ● The space between Laertes' two iterations of his question gives time for Hamlet's line to Horatio and increases the audience's suspense before Hamlet's discovery that it is Ophelia who has

HAMLET [*Aside to Horatio.*]
   That is Laertes, a very noble youth. Mark.
LAERTES
   What ceremony else?   225
PRIEST
   Her obsequies have been as far enlarged

   As we have warranty. Her death was doubtful,

   And but that great command o'ersways the order,

   She should in ground unsanctified been lodged

   Till the last trumpet. For charitable prayers,   230

   Shards, flints, and pebbles should be thrown on her.

   Yet here she is allowed her virgin crants,

died. The repetition itself may also suggest the Priest's hesitation to answer in the face of Laertes' passionate intensity.

s.h. Priest: F, Q2 has "Doctor," i.e., of the church, "Doctor of Divinity" (Riverside). **obsequies:** funeral rites.

warranty: authorization, "This must refer to the Church's sanction of its own offices, as distinct from the coroner's warrant for burial (lines 4–5). The prohibition of the burial service for suicides (on which see Blunt, *Book of Church Law*, 1921 edn, pages 182–3) became explicit in the Prayerbook of 1662. Discretion was allowed in *doubtful* cases (which are provided for in the Roman *Codex Iuris Canonici*, 1240 §2)" (Jenkins). **doubtful:** • The question of whether Ophelia's death was intentional suicide or not remains unsettled. That question is the point of the comical debate of the gravediggers in lines 1–29 and of the serious debate here, both of which illustrate the impossibility of our knowing the eternal fate of any other person's soul and cast light back upon Hamlet's pretending to know just that about the King's soul in III.iii.

but: except. **great command:** the command of the great (i.e., the King), confirming the Clown's comical version of this idea at lines 23–29. **o'ersways:** overrules. **order:** the church's normal procedure.

should: would, rather than ought to be (Abbott §322). **been lodged:** Q2, *have* before "been" being understood, F substitutes "have lodged," making the verb active instead of passive, "a manifest attempt at 'improvement,'" but "the omission of *have* … when other words intervene is idiomatic" (Jenkins), cf., *Coriolanus* IV.vi.34–35, *Henry V* III.ii.118–19. **lodged:** placed.

last trumpet: doomsday, the Last Judgment, when the dead shall be raised for final judgment by God, see 1 Corinthians 15:52. **For:** in place of (Abbott §148).

Shards, flints, and pebbles: symbolic of brokenness (shards being broken pieces of pottery) and hardness (flints and pebbles) in contrast to "charitable prayers" in the previous line and "crants" (soft flowers) in the next. **should:** would, rather than ought to be (Abbott §322) as at line 229.

crants: garland, also spelled *cranse* and *crance*, from the German *kranz* and Danish *krans*, meaning wreath, garland, chaplet, and hence singular. "The original floral wreath for the burial of a maiden came to be replaced by a less perishable artificial structure. For women of rank this might be a chaplet of pearl or gold and silver filigree, but surviving and recorded examples show characteristically a frame of wood shaped like a crown twelve or more inches high, covered with cloth or paper, adorned with artificial flowers (or occasionally black rosettes), and hanging

Her maiden strewments, and the bringing home

Of bell and burial.

LAERTES

Must there no more be done?

PRIEST

No more be done: 235

We should profane the service of the dead

To sing sage requiem and such rest to her

As to peace-parted souls.

LAERTES

Lay her i' th' earth,

And from her fair and unpolluted flesh

May violets spring. I tell thee, churlish priest,   240

A minist'ring angel shall my sister be

When thou liest howling.

---

from it ribbons, a pair of gloves, and sometimes a collar or kerchief. The practice of bearing such a symbol of virginity before the coffin and then hanging it in the church seems to have extended throughout northern Europe (see *Edin. Rev.* cxxx, 96–7), in parts of which examples can still be seen.... [T]he practice was certainly widespread in Elizabethan England and in various parts continued through the 18th century" (Jenkins LN).

strewments: flowers strewn on the grave of a virgin, as on the marriage bed, as a symbol and celebration of her chastity, cf., lines 243–46, *Romeo and Juliet* IV.v.79, 89, V.iii.12–17, 281, *Cymbeline* IV.ii.218–21, 283–87, *Winter's Tale* IV.iv.128–31, *Henry VIII* IV.ii.167–70, and Spenser's "Epithalamion" line 302. **bringing home:** traditional phrase for proper ritual burial, "home" = to the grave (OED home *adv.* 1.c.) and cf., Ecclesiastes 12:5 (King James) and *Titus Andronicus* I.i.83. "In these words reference is still made to the marriage rites, which in the case of maidens are sadly parodied in the funeral rites. See *Ro[meo] and Jul[iet]* IV.v.[84–90]. As the bride was brought home to her husband's house with bell and wedding festivity, so the dead maiden is brought to her last home 'with bell and burial'" (Clarendon in Furness).

Of: as regards, as relates to (Abbott §173) or with respect to (Abbott §174). **bell and burial:** formal funeral rites, involving the tolling of the church bells and burial in consecrated ground, possibly a hendiadys for "religious burial" (Wright, page 187).

profane ... requiem: "Psalms and masses for suicides were explicitly forbidden in the canon law" (Jenkins). **sage:** F, solemn (OED sage *adj.* A.3.), Q2 a, "Presumably the word ['sage'] defeated the Q2 compositor" (Jenkins). **requiem:** a chant, service, or mass said or sung for the repose of the dead (from the line *requies, -ētis*, rest).

peace-parted: departing life peacefully because repentant before death, which is impossible in the case of successful suicide. For the compound see Abbott §430.

unpolluted: both sinless (generally) and virginal (specifically), in contrast with the fears of Laertes and Polonius in I.iii and Hamlet's sarcasm about them at II.ii.184–86, and making more pointed the thwarted-love madness expressed in the lewdness of Ophelia's song at IV.v.48ff.

May violets spring: Baldwin cites Steevens' note of a parallel in Persius (Satire I, 39–40) and adds his own parallel from Mantuan's Eclogues (in *Adulescenta*), adding that "Badius [the editor of the Renaissance edition of Mantuan and Perseus] pointed out that this was an ancient superstition, and quoted in full the passage from Persius, together with others from Juvenal, Martial, Ovid, and Tibullus in illustration. After he had mastered this passage and the notes, Shakspere should have known how to conduct a Renaissance, classical-pastoral funeral. So, like that of Mantuan's heroine, Ophelia's grave is strewn with flowers" (Baldwin I.649–50, II.543), cf., lines 243–46, line 233 note. **violets:** symbolic of faithful love, cf., IV.v.184–85 and note, and of chastity (cf., Lydgate, *Troy Book*, III.4380, reference in Jenkins).

• contrasting with Laertes' use of the violet to represent fleeting love at I.iii.7–9 and reinforcing our conviction that Ophelia never lost her virginity to Hamlet. Any argument that she did arises from an utter misreading of both Hamlet's character and everything in the play related to Ophelia. **churlish:** low-bred, boorish, here specifically ungracious. **howling:** i.e., in hell, cf., Matthew 13:42, 25:30, *Romeo and Juliet* III.iii.48, *2 Henry IV* II.iv.345, *Measure for Measure* III.i.127, *Two Noble Kinsmen* IV.iii.33.

• In passionate hyperbole, Laertes pretends to know of the soul of the priest that it will be damned, as in equal hyperbole he asserts that Ophelia will be saved and made an angel. (This metaphor, erroneously taken literally, has drawn many people and much popular entertainment into a sentimental form of theological nonsense, namely that good human beings become angels in death, a doctrine not known to Christianity before Swedenborg [1688–1772]). Laertes' claims here are in direct parallel to Hamlet's more rational but damnable pretension to knowledge and control of the eternal fate of the King (III.iii). The argument between Laertes and the Priest about the fate of Ophelia's soul, parallel to the comical debate between the two Clowns at lines 1–29, reinforces the fact of the unalterable human ignorance of eternal consequences for anyone's soul, one's own or another's, and is especially pointed after Hamlet's humbling meditation on the universal consequences of the death of the body. The Christian context of the play assumes the universal belief, based on divine revelation, that in death human souls undergo divine judgment and consequent reward or punishment (see Introduction, page 7, Thompson, page 223). But the fate of any particular soul cannot be known by living men. What we know about physical death is a reminder that humility is the proper relation to the mystery of the implications for the soul of the fact that the human being dies. Instead, Laertes is in a state of passionate pride, driven by grief, akin to Hamlet's various outbursts of passion earlier and to the one we are about to witness. Out of that passion Laertes has resolved on a course of vengeful villainy plotted against Hamlet that mirrors Hamlet's deepest plot of all (cf., V.ii.9) against the King, his "ultimate revenge play" (see Introduction, page 9, note 19). Laertes' choice to take Hamlet's life is an outward parallel (foil) to Hamlet's inward choice to damn the soul of Claudius.

HAMLET

What, the fair Ophelia!

What, … Ophelia!: It is Laertes' phrase "my sister" at line 241 that first informs Hamlet of Ophelia's death. **Ophelia:** shortened to one stress, on the middle syllable (Abbott §469).

QUEEN [*scattering flowers.*]
   Sweets to the sweet. Farewell.
   I hoped thou shouldst have been my Hamlet's wife;
   I thought thy bride-bed to have decked, sweet maid,   245
   And not have strewed thy grave.

LAERTES
                      O treble woe
   Fall ten times treble on that cursèd head
   Whose wicked deed thy most ingenious sense
   Deprived thee of!—Hold off the earth awhile,

   Till I have caught her once more in mine arms.   250

         [*Leaps into the grave.*]

   Now pile your dust upon the quick and dead
   Till of this flat a mountain you have made
   T' o'ertop old Pelion or the skyish head

   Of blue Olympus.
HAMLET [*advancing.*]
              What is he whose grief

   Bears such an emphasis, whose phrase of sorrow   255

   Conjures the wand'ring stars and makes them stand
   Like wonder-wounded hearers? This is I,

Sweets: i.e., flowers, see line 233 note, line 240 note.

bride-bed ... grave: see above line 233 note, line 240 note. **decked:** bedecked, decorated. **strewed:** cf., line 233. • Gertrude here reinforces what we know from Hamlet's character, that Laertes' worries about Hamlet's intentions (I.iii.5–44), though reasonable, and Polonius's overreaching accusations about them (I.iii.105–131) did not correspond to reality. Gertrude at least has thought that the match between Hamlet and Ophelia would have been appropriate and desirable.

O treble woe ... Deprived thee of: May a triple curse of misery fall thirty times on the head of him whose wicked deed deprived you of your rational wits. **treble:** triple. **that ... head:** i.e., Hamlet's. **wicked deed:** Hamlet's killing of Polonius, which has "Deprived" Ophelia of her wits. **ingenious sense:** intellectual capacity, ability to reason aptly, cf., *Richard III* III.i.155, *King Lear* IV.vi.280. **Hold off the earth:** do not begin filling the grave.

caught ... in mine arms: see line 218 S.D. note.

S.D.: only in F ("*Leaps in the grave*").

the quick: the living, i.e., upon himself as well as upon his dead sister. **flat:** level ground (Raffel).

T' o'ertop: To overtop, to rise higher than. **Pelion:** "A mountain famed through the Greek myth in which the giants in their war with the gods piled [Mount] Pelion on the neighbouring [Mount] Ossa [line 283] in order to scale [Mount] Olympus [line 254] ... a lofty mountain in Greece, fabled home of the gods" (Jenkins), cf., Tilley O 81 ("To heap Ossa upon Pelion"). **skyish:** high.

blue: i.e., as high as the sky. • Laertes is again engaging in extreme hyperbole to express extreme passion, here the combination of grief and wrath, like the passions Hamlet has previously expressed, which are always evoked by some external cause. Hamlet will again fly into such a passion here and will do so twice more in the final scene.

emphasis: rhetorical term meaning "the enforcement of the sense 'by a word of more than ordinary efficacy' (Puttenham, *Art of Eng. Poesy*, III.17), hence excessive or violent language. Cf. *rant* (line [284]), *bravery* (v.ii.79)" (Jenkins). **phrase:** phrasing, expression, with the possible sense of exaggeration, outburst (OED *sb*. 4, where, however, the first example comes from 1725).

Conjures: invokes or influences by magical incantation, casts a charm upon. **wand'ring stars:** the planets, including sun and moon, as opposed to the fixed stars. **and makes them stand ... hearers:** i.e., stand still, as if stunned by wonder at Laertes' speech. • Hamlet is, by even greater hyperbole, at once returning to his public pretense of being mad and parodying Laertes' exaggeration by out-

Hamlet the Dane.

LAERTES [*grappling with him.*]
        The devil take thy soul!

exaggerating him. **This is I:** "Cf. 'What is he', line [254]" (Jenkins). ● Hamlet has asked of Laertes what rank or status permits him to speak thus and justifies his own outdoing Laertes' hyperbole with the statement of his own proclaimed rank.

Hamlet the Dane: meaning the king of Denmark, cf., I.i.15, I.ii.44. ● *Pace* Jenkins, Hamlet is not actually assuming his title as if Claudius weren't standing nearby. Rather, through this hyperbole (which we know to be the literal truth if every man had his rights), Hamlet is publicly pretending to the kind of false madness previously enacted for the sake of the King, Rosencrantz, and Guildenstern, namely that of thwarted ambition, even as he has emotionally entered a "towering passion," cf., V.ii.80, fueled by the shock and grief of his having just now learned of Ophelia's death. The passion continues through lines 266–83. We must not mistake Hamlet's words for either actual madness or direct public proclamation of his rivalry with Claudius, in contrast to Laertes' own passion at IV.v.116–40. As at III.i.102ff., Hamlet's expression of his passion is again being directed by art in the form of pretended madness. This is confirmed when, as with each previous flight of passion, Hamlet waxes rational and calm in lines 259–63, 283–84, and 288–92. These passages are crucial in revealing that the change that has taken place within Hamlet's soul in the course of the sea voyage, a change that we will be shown explicitly in the next scene, has not altered his personality. He remains a man who flies into passions under provocation, as earlier in the play (I.iv.82–85, I.v.92–109, II.ii.550–81, III.i.102–149, and III.iv.23–24), and then becomes reasonable again (I.v.1–2, 165–90, II.ii.582, III.iv.31–33). It is not a change in personality that Hamlet has undergone. He has not ceased to be himself or become a Horatio. It is a spiritual transformation. It is his will that has been altered by the sea voyage and the *memento mori* meditation we have just witnessed. The demonstration of that change will come in his dialogue with Horatio (V.ii.4–48 and 219–24), in his acting in "readiness" rather than in evil calculation when he kills the King, and in his forgiveness of Laertes (V.ii.332) in direct contrast to his predisposition expressed at I.ii.182–83.

s.d.: Despite Q1's marginal s.d., "Hamlet leaps in after Leartes," there is no evidence for such a gesture in either Q2 or F, and since the text implies that Laertes is the aggressor, tells us that Laertes has his hands on Hamlet's throat, tells us that the King orders them to be plucked apart, and implies that they are in fact plucked apart, Laertes must jump out of the grave to grapple with Hamlet rather than Hamlet into the grave to grapple with him (Granville-Barker substantially, reference in Jenkins). ● As confirmed in his next speech, Hamlet is in a wiser state of mind than Laertes at present and is not about to profane the dead by his actions, though for his own purposes he will reach extremes of hyperbole in speech.

HAMLET

                                Thou pray'st not well.

I prithee take thy fingers from my throat,   260

For though I am not splenative and rash,

Yet have I in me something dangerous,

Which let thy wisdom fear. Hold off thy hand.

KING

Pluck them asunder.

QUEEN

             Hamlet! Hamlet!

ALL

                    Gentlemen!

                [*Attendants part them.*]

HORATIO

Good my lord, be quiet.   265

HAMLET

Why, I will fight with him upon this theme

Until my eyelids will no longer wag.

QUEEN

O my son, what theme?

HAMLET

I loved Ophelia. Forty thousand brothers

The devil take thy soul: an "amphibious" half line, completing the previous phrase and completed by the following (Abbott §513). • Laertes' passionate curse is akin to Hamlet's calm expression of the same negative idea, as a tendency expressed at I.ii.182–83 (and see note) and as an actual choice made when Hamlet chooses at III.iii.87ff. to attempt to effect the King's damnation.

Thou pray'st ... wisdom fear: • Hamlet's response to Laertes' curse hints at a newfound attitude whose full expression will come in the final scene. **splenative:** Q2, F *spleenative*, subject to excessive influence of spleen, seat of the choleric humor; hence, depending on the context, liable to changeable temper, outbursts of passion, caprice, laughter, impetuosity, rage, violence, etc., here specifically implying proud-tempered, hot-headed, and violent. • cf., Hotspur in *1 Henry IV* I.iii.200–238, II.iii.77–79, and V.ii.19, Tybalt in *Romeo and Juliet* III.i.157–60, Richard III in *Richard III* II.iv.63–64, and Cassius in *Julius Caesar* IV.iii.47. **something dangerous:** • This "something" is the capacity to act extremely, *like* someone who is characteristically "splenative and rash." Also implied is the danger to one of lower rank like Laertes in threatening one of Hamlet's rank, whether we think of him as prince or as rightful king. It may also imply Hamlet's capacity (which we will learn in the next scene) to remove threats to his life and his mission from men like Rosencrantz and Guildenstern. **wisdom:** Q2 and Q1, F wiseness. Though Jenkins chooses the latter reading on the grounds that it is rarer and hence the likelier to be authentic, adding "Possibly there is a distinction to be made between *wisdom*, sagacity in general, and *wiseness*, the exercise of it on a particular occasion," the argument seems not to warrant departure from Q2. **Hold off:** remove.

quiet: i.e., calm (not silent).

eyelids ... wag: "The stirring of the eyelids is thought of as the smallest sign of life" (Jenkins).

I loved Ophelia: • That this statement is true we believe on grounds of Ophelia's words at I.iii.99–114, Hamlet's honest letter read aloud in II.ii.109–124, and his passionate rage at finding Ophelia, like Gertrude, being corrupted by the court at III.i.102ff. At the same time, Hamlet has earlier set up thwarted love, alongside thwarted ambition, as one of the pseudo-causes of his pretended madness. As in line 258 above he reverts to the ambition theme, so in the exaggerations following this true declaration, which do express his passion of grief, he reverts to the thwarted love theme in seeming to be mad. That the ploy works we see in the King's public statement at line 272.

Could not with all their quantity of love   270

Make up my sum. What wilt thou do for her?

KING

O he is mad, Laertes.

QUEEN

For love of God forbear him.

HAMLET

'Swounds, show me what thou't do.

Woo't weep, woo't fight, woo't fast, woo't tear thyself,   275

Woo't drink up eisel, eat a crocodile?

---

quantity: possibly "small fragment" (OED quantity II.8.b.) as opposed to the neutral "portion or amount" (OED quantity II.8.a.), hence "depreciatory" (Clarendon in Furness) or "contemptuous" (Jenkins), but I take the neutral sense to be likelier since Hamlet's hyperbole seems to imply that though the amount of love of forty thousand brothers might be great, Hamlet's love is greater, cf., III.ii.41, III.iv.75. **Make up:** add up to. **my sum:** the amount of my love for her.

For love of God: for *the* omitted before a noun modified by a prepositional phrase see Abbott §89. **forbear him:** leave him alone, bear with him. • spoken with passion to Laertes in fear for her son (whose "madness," though not this passion, she knows to be playacting).

'Swounds: by his (i.e., Christ's) wounds, literally the five wounds of Christ on the cross, to hands, feet, and side, and figuratively the vehicles of man's salvation through Christ's sacrifice. • evidence itself that Hamlet is in a "towering passion," cf., V.ii.80. **thou't:** thou wilt, echoing line 271.

Woo't: "colloquial for Wilt [and short for Wilt thou = will you] (OED will *v*.¹ A.3.δ), perhaps also conflated with "wouldst thou" (Abbott §241). • Clarendon suggests that the colloquialism implies Hamlet's contempt for Laertes but that it can also indicate "affectionate familiarity," as in *Antony and Cleopatra* IV.ii.7 ("Woo't thou fight well") and IV.xv.59 ("Woo't die?"). The phrase seems highly rhetorical, Hamlet adopting, for the purpose of out-ranting Laertes, the tone of familiar boys in passionate competition. Given Hamlet's intellect and the meditation in which we have just seen him, we must not mistake either his hyperbole or his tone for thoroughly genuine, though it is certainly fueled by passionate grief at Ophelia's death and frustration at being accused and attacked by her brother, whom he respects and admires, cf., line 224 and V.ii.75ff.

drink up: "drink avidly or unhesitatingly," cf., Sonnet 114:2 (Jenkins following the long discussion in Furness). **eisel:** Q2 Esill, F Esile, as Theobald recognized (quoted in Furness), is an old word for vinegar (Old French *aisil*, late Latin *acetillum*, diminutive of Latin *acetum*, vinegar), not merely unpleasant but "a bitter drink *par excellence*," the forced drink of Christ on the cross and linked with gall, as in Sonnet 111:10. Hence "To *drink up easel* is ... something humanly possible which yet inspires extreme repugnance." Some examples among many include Chaucer *Romaunt of the Rose* (line 217), Lydgate *Troy Book* II.62, Wyclif Bible (Matthew 27:48), *Cursor Mundi* line 24400, *Castle of Perseverance* lines 3137, 3355, Thomas More *Twelve Rules of John Picus*

I'll do't. Dost come here to whine,

To outface me with leaping in her grave?
Be buried quick with her, and so will I.
And if thou prate of mountains, let them throw   280

Millions of acres on us, till our ground,
Singeing his pate against the burning zone,

Make Ossa like a wart! Nay, and thou'lt mouth,
I'll rant as well as thou.

line 35, Skelton *Now Synge We* lines 39–40 (Jenkins
LN substantially and citations), cf., *eager* at I.v.69
and note. **eat a crocodile:** like "drinking up eisel," a
repulsive, outrageous, almost impossible thing to do.
• conveying at the same time both Hamlet's genuine
passion at the death of Ophelia and his pretended
madness expressed in hyperbolical challenges to his
competitor in grief.

I'll do't … whine: a line of only three feet. • NOTE
TO ACTORS: The stresses are on "do't," "come,"
and "whine," and the two empty feet should perhaps
come after "I'll do't" and before "Dost come" to indicate
Hamlet's need to take a breath after the last list of
challenges to Laertes and before the next list.
Dost: "After a verb ending with the second person
singular inflection, the *thou* is sometimes omitted in
questions" (Abbott §241), cf., V.ii.82.

outface: brave, defy.

quick: alive.

prate of mountains: referring to lines 251–54.
prate: chatter, with the additional sense of boasting.
ground: burial-ground.

Singeing his pate: rising high enough above the
earth to burn its head. **the burning zone:** This
phrase was used to refer to either of two ancient
images, or to a confusion of both: a) According
to the Ptolemaic astronomy following Aristotle,
between the sphere of air (surrounding the earth
and seas) and the sphere of the moon was a sphere
of fire. Through it Dante and Beatrice pass in their
upward journey (*Paradiso* I.76–93) and to it ("*dal cielo
del fuoco*") the howl of Cellini reached (Benvenuto
Cellini *Autobiography*, translated by George Bull,
Penguin 1956, reprinted 1973, page 345), b) According
to Virgil, the celestial sphere is divided into five *zones*
(from the Latin and Greek words for girdle) or wide
rings or belts surrounding the sphere of the earth,
"whereof [the central] one is ever glowing with the
flashing sun, ever scorched by his flames" (Virgil
Georgics, I.233–34) and lies above the equatorial
and tropical regions of the earth. At the extreme
north and south are the dark and frozen zones, and
between the burning zone of the sun and each frozen
zone is a temperate zone in which alone human
beings can live. The phrase was also used of the
corresponding earthly (i.e., the equatorial) region,
as in Robert Recorde, *The Castle of Knowledge* (1556)
64: "The olde Cosmographers … called all that space
betweene the twoo Tropykes, the Burnynge Zone"
(cited in OED zone *sb.* 1.), but here the reference is to
the celestial zone.

Ossa like a wart: Out-exaggerating Laertes in lines 251–
54, Hamlet's imagery picks a mountain near Pelion and
Olympus, namely Mount Ossa, and claims the amount
of dirt under which he will be buried with Ophelia
will make Ossa seem no bigger than a wart, "Echoing
Erasmus, *Colloquia*, [XXIV:] *Naufragium*, which
describes a tempest with huge waves in comparison

QUEEN

      This is mere madness,
And thus awhile the fit will work on him.   285

Anon, as patient as the female dove

When that her golden couplets are disclosed,

His silence will sit drooping.

HAMLET

       Hear you, sir,

What is the reason that you use me thus?
I loved you ever. But it is no matter.   290
Let Hercules himself do what he may,
The cat will mew, and dog will have his day.

             Exit.

KING

I pray you, good Horatio, wait upon him.

           Exit Horatio.

---

with which the Alps are warts (*verrucae*)" (Jenkins), cf., lines 253–54 note and Ovid *Metamorphoses* I.154–55. **and:** if. **thou'lt:** thou wilt. **mouth:** declaim pompously, with exaggerated rhetoric, cf., III.ii.2. ● Hamlet recognizes the absurdity of the image contest of words and here suddenly waxes reasonable again, as he has after all previous bursts of passion, cf., particularly I.ii.159 and II.ii.582. In his next speech, recovered from the "towering passion," he expresses his true relation to Laertes. He does not know that the King has poisoned Laertes against him, which (to us) has added fury to Laertes' cursing of Hamlet for the death of Polonius. In the next scene Hamlet will sympathize with Laertes' condition as being parallel to his own.

mere: entirely, only. Though F gives this speech to the King, Q2 must be correct. Not only does the image not fit the King's character, but Gertrude is explicitly remaining true to her word to Hamlet at III.iv.197–99, reinforcing the fiction that Hamlet is "essentially [= merely] in madness" and not "mad in craft," cf., III.iv.187–88.

Anon: soon, presently. **patient:** calm, meek. **dove:** "Proverbial for meekness. Cf. Tilley D 573" (Jenkins).

golden couplets: yellow pair of young chicks, "The dove lays two eggs and the new-hatched birds have yellow (*golden*) down" (Jenkins). **disclosed:** hatched, cf., III.i.166 and note.

His silence ... drooping: an elliptical metaphor, meaning that as the dove falls to quiet patience when her chicks hatch, so will Hamlet's silence, a metonymy for Hamlet himself, become calm and focused downward ("drooping") instead of outward at Laertes.

use me: treat me.

ever: always.

Hercules: proverbial image of strength, particularly in accomplishing impossible tasks, and in Shakespeare's time characteristically played on the stage in loud, ranting style, cf., *Midsummer Night's Dream* I.ii.29 and 40 and Robert Greene, *Greene's Groats-Worth of Wit* (1592), in which the wandering player says, "The twelve labors of *Hercules* have I terribly thundered on the Stage." **Let Hercules ... have his day:** No strength can prevent the cat from following its nature, which is to "mew," or Laertes from doing what his nature compels him to do, i.e., to rant and to "use me thus." Likewise no strength can prevent the dog from having his day, i.e., coming into his own, or Hamlet from doing what his nature and mission compel him to do. For the proverb "Every dog has his day" see Tilley D 464, especially "A dog hath a day. There is none so vile nor simple a person but at one time or other may avenge himself of wrongs done unto him" (Richard Taverner, translator, *Proverbes or Adagies gathered out of Erasmus*, f. 63, 1552), and Ben Jonson *A Tale of a Tub* (1633 but set in the 1550's) II.i.4, "vor [= for] a Man ha' [= hath, has] his

[*To Laertes.*]
Strengthen your patience in our last night's speech.

We'll put the matter to the present push.—   295
[*To Gertrude.*]
Good Gertrude, set some watch over your son.—
[*To All.*]
This grave shall have a living monument.

[*To Laertes.*]
An hour of quiet shortly shall we see.

Till then in patience our proceeding be.

                                          Exeunt.

Act V, Scene ii

Enter Hamlet and Horatio.

HAMLET
So much for this, sir. Now shall you see the other.

---

hour, and a Dog his day." ● Hamlet, implying that his own day will come, is hinting at his new-found patience, his acceptance of the shaping of things by Providence that he will fully reveal in dialogue with Horatio in the final scene. This suggests that Gertrude's description of him (lines 284–88) is an apt précis of Hamlet's life if we substitute the phrase "moral error" for "madness," though Gertrude cannot intend it as such. Hamlet's fit of pride, chosen in III.iii and acted on in III.iv, has been chastened by his closeness to death, which was providentially prevented on the sea voyage, and by the *memento mori* of V.i. What follows is patience in the deepest spiritual sense.

Strengthen your patience: ● The theme of patience is echoed by the villain, for what is being awaited here is the right time for committing a murder.
in: "in the thought of" (Abbott §162), in consideration of (what we have planned). **last night's speech:** i.e., IV.vii.129–62.

present push: immediate attempt, trial, effort, thrust, cf., *Macbeth* V.iii.20.

watch: guard.

living: a) lasting, enduring, or b) life-like, cf., *Romeo and Juliet* V.iii.299 and Tourneur's *Atheist's Tragedy* III.i.2–4 ("But she shall bear a living monument / To let succeeding ages truly know / That she [the body] is [= has] satisfied, what he [the dead man] did owe") (reference in Jenkins, who suggests that "A second meaning, for Laertes' ear, may hint at the memorial the life [i.e., the murder] of Hamlet will provide."
quiet: calm, peace, meaning for Laertes the satisfaction of revenge and for himself freedom from the fear of Hamlet's threats to him, cf., IV.i.14–15.
in patience: calmly, without further passionate demonstration of rage, cf., line 294 note. **our proceeding be:** imperative, let us proceed.

Act V, Scene ii: A hall in the castle.

So much ... sir. ● Hamlet and Horatio are entering in the midst of a conversation of which the immediately previous topic is not relevant or we would have been told what it was, cf., III.ii.141–42.
● SPEECH NOTE: **see the other:** Hamlet now shares with Horatio not only "the words [that] will make thee dumb" promised in his letter at IV.vi.24–25, but the spiritual fruits of his journey. Why this conversation has not taken place earlier is another question that would not arise in the theater. One might say that this is the first moment since the sea voyage that Hamlet and Horatio have been alone in private. More importantly, the thematic focus

on *memento mori* of the graveyard scene (V.i) had to
precede the readiness theme of this scene because
any earlier the education of Hamlet exhibited in this
conversation would not yet have been complete.
Hamlet must first contemplate philosophically the
physical aspect of "being dead," the dead Yorick,
Alexander, Caesar, and finally Ophelia. Only after
such contemplation, coming immediately after
his own providential escape from death, is Hamlet
capable of realizing and expressing, and the audience
capable of appreciating, the spiritual resolution of
Hamlet's dilemma, and of man's. The events of the
sea voyage, which we are about to learn, preceded the
graveyard contemplation chronologically, but only
in the light of that meditation can their meaning be
properly appreciated. Hamlet's inner conflict is over,
and hence so are his soliloquies. Now, in dialogue
with his trusted friend, Hamlet articulates the fruits
of his experience.

You do remember all the circumstance?

circumstance: the subordinate or non-essential facts
of the situation (OED 9.), as for example his being
aboard the ship bound for England.

HORATIO
Remember it, my lord—

my lord—: Lord. Q2, Lord? F, which implies that
Horatio is asking for clarification, which makes
him sound not like himself and too much like Osric,
Rosencrantz, or Guildenstern. Q2 may imply the
assertion, perhaps with surprise, that Horatio
certainly does remember the facts. There may be an
ellipsis of the nominative "I" (cf., Abbott §401), in
which case Horatio is making a simple statement of
fact, "I remember it, my lord," in keeping with his
character throughout, cf., e.g., I.ii.239 and note.

HAMLET
Sir, in my heart there was a kind of fighting
That would not let me sleep. Methought I lay   5

Methought: It seemed to me, past tense of *methinks*,
cf., III.ii.230 note. **lay:** remained captive, as if in
prison (OED lie v.¹ 3.).

Worse than the mutines in the bilboes. Rashly—
And praised be rashness for it; let us know

Worse: feeling more confined, restless. **mutines:**
mutineers, rebels. **bilboes:** "A long iron bar,
furnished with sliding shackles to confine the ankles
of prisoners and a lock by which to fix one end of the
bar to the floor or ground" (OED). ● Hamlet's feeling
like a mutineer at that point is apt, since within his
own will he was in a state of mutiny against God's will
(Mulgrew), precisely until he gave in to the rashness
he now praises for saving him in the moment and
revealing to him the lesson in divinity he is about
to report. **Rashly ... rashness:** ● In a parenthetical
comment Hamlet now recognizes that man's
rashness, including that caused by the passionate
aspect of his own character, may at times be what
is called for by Providence when man's reasoning
("deep plots") goes astray. Had Hamlet been rash
rather than willfully calculating in III.iii, the
complete disaster toward which all are moving would
have been avoided. There is humility in recognizing
that there is a place in the divine plan even for those
qualities of one's self that are felt to be negative, and

Hamlet is about to voice that lesson and have it confirmed by Horatio. **for it:** i.e., for those actions for which "rashness" (line 7) is responsible, and which he will narrate below (lines 12ff.) after these parenthetical comments. **let us know:** "that is, take notice and remember" (Johnson in Furness).

Our indiscretion sometime serves us well

indiscretion: a synonym for rashness, impulsiveness, a movement of the will without rational forethought. **sometime:** occasionally, sometimes.

When our deep plots do pall, and that should learn us

deep plots: The deepest plot of all has been Hamlet's plot to make certain of the King's damnation (cf., Thompson's "ultimate revenge play," see Introduction, page 9, note 19). **pall:** fail, become faint, weaken (OED *v.*¹ 2.). **learn:** teach (OED 4.c.), cf., *Tempest* I.ii.365.

There's a divinity that shapes our ends,   10
Rough-hew them how we will—

There's a divinity: ● Hamlet is not here asserting the existence of God (OED divinity 1. and 2.), his belief in whom has never been in question (cf., I.ii.131–32, 195, I.v.186, IV.iv.36, etc.). Nor has he doubted the existence of angels and devils (cf., I.iv.39 and II.ii.598–603), or the immortality of the soul (cf., I.iv.66–67). Hamlet is a Christian prince. Rather he is asserting the newly discovered *relation* between God and man. God shapes men's "ends" no matter how men themselves exercise their free will. That is, there is divineness (OED 3.) in the shaping. Cf., the "divinity that doth hedge a king" at IV.v.124. In reality the two meanings, God and divineness, here are one, but in Hamlet's use of the more abstract term Shakespeare unites both the mystery and the factual reality of the divine shaping in a phrase that is both abstract, like God to the rational intellect, and empathically immediate, like the physical shaping of wood or stone. In this union of abstract idea and concrete language in the phrase "There is a divinity that shapes," Shakespeare articulates the mystery of the interpenetration of spirit and body, and of divine and human will, operating in man. The general sentiment is familiar to Shakespeare's audience from Psalms (33:10, 15), Proverbs (16:9, 19:21), and Montaigne, who uses the same metaphor of hewing in *Essays* III.8: "My consultation doth somewhat roughly hew the matter, and by its first show, lightly consider the same: the main and chief point of the work, I am wont to resign to heaven" (translated by Florio, quoted in Jenkins LN). But the crucial point is not merely the general one, that Hamlet, in his frustration with his mother and later his suspicions about his uncle, has lost sight of the divine significance in the created world and man (cf., I.ii.132–34, II.ii.298–303). The crucial specific point is that Hamlet has thought that ultimate matters, like the damnation of the King and the satisfaction of his own desire for ultimate revenge, could be achieved as a function of his own will. Hamlet here conveys what he has learned on the sea voyage, namely that his own will is not absolute but is subject to God's will. We learn that had Hamlet's will been submitted to God's from the start, Hamlet would have permitted God to use him for His own purposes, namely cleansing Denmark of the sins of Claudius, and not gotten in the way of them. This recognition, combined with the humility exhibited in the previous *memento mori* scene, brings Hamlet to the "readiness" that he "espouses" (cf., Thompson, see Introduction, page 5) and voices to Horatio in line 222 and that he enacts in the final gestures of killing the King in a passion and of forgiving Laertes. **shapes … rough-hew:** the metaphor is from wood or stone work. Rough-hewing is the initial carving of the general form in broad strokes, and shaping is the subtle finish work of sculpting. **ends:** three senses are combined here: a) aims, goals, purposes, b) deaths, completions of our missions and life spans, and c) ultimate eternal destinations, either hell or heaven. **how:** however. **will:** three senses are combined here: a) the future tense (however we actually will rough-hew our ends), b) choose by exercising our God-given power of free will (however we freely decide to rough-hew our ends), and c) engage in willfulness (however willfully in pride we stray from the divine will). ● NOTE TO ACTORS: The antithesis here is both between "shapes" and "rough-hew" and between "divinity" and the spondee "we will."

HORATIO

That is most certain.

That is most certain: Q2, F. Probably Horatio's line does not interfere with Hamlet's verse line (Abbott §514, whose quotation of Horatio's "interruption," however, is the emendation "That's certain").
● Horatio, the supremely balanced man in Hamlet's and our own estimation (cf., III.ii.63–74) and the man who from the beginning was aware of Heaven's direction of events (cf., I.iv.91) confirms Hamlet's insight.

HAMLET

          Up from my cabin,

Up from my cabin: probably the completion of Hamlet's own verse line at line 11 (see previous note), though possibly empty feet are intended after Horatio's line, implying a pause during which a) Horatio's line sinks in, and b) Hamlet returns from his digression to the thread of his description. There is good authority for either reading.

My sea-gown scarfed about me, in the dark

sea-gown: "a coarse, high-collared, and short-sleeved gown, reaching down to the mid-leg, and used most by seamen and sailors" (Cotgrave, under *esclavine*, quoted in Furness and Jenkins, cf., OED sea *sb.* 18.j.).
scarfed: wrapped about like a scarf rather than worn normally, reinforcing Hamlet's impulsiveness in the moment.

Groped I to find out them, had my desire,

to find out them: to find where Rosencrantz and Guildenstern were sleeping. **had my desire:** i.e., did find them.

Fingered their packet, and in fine withdrew   15
To mine own room again, making so bold,

Fingered: lifted, pinched, stole. **packet:** parcel of state letters or dispatches (OED *sb.* 1.). **in fine:** in the end, finally, cf., II.ii.69, IV.vii.133.

My fears forgetting manners, to unseal
Their grand commission; where I found, Horatio—

Ah royal knavery!—an exact command,

Larded with many several sorts of reasons   20

Importing Denmark's health, and England's too,

With ho! such bugs and goblins in my life,

That on the supervise, no leisure bated,

No, not to stay the grinding of the axe,

My head should be struck off.

HORATIO
                        Is't possible?   25

HAMLET
Here's the commission; read it at more leisure.

But wilt thou hear now how I did proceed?

HORATIO
I beseech you.

HAMLET
Being thus benetted round with villainies—

Or I could make a prologue to my brains,   30
They had begun the play—I sat me down,

My fears forgetting manners: Fear of what the letter might contain overcoming the customary resistance to opening the royal mail. **unseal:** break the wax seal stamped with the royal signet.

Ah: (Dover Wilson, Riverside, Jenkins, Braunmuller, Hoy, etc.), A Q2, Oh F.

Larded: decorated, adorned, from the use of strips of fat inserted in meat to dress it, cf., IV.v.38 note.

Importing: concerning, of importance to, cf., I.ii.23. **Denmark's ... England's:** the health of the two kings, secondarily of the two nations, with whom the kings are identified.

ho!: here an exclamation of "scornful astonishment" (Jenkins). **bugs and goblins in my life:** "bugs" are imaginary causes of terror (bugaboos, bugbears, bogeys, boogeymen), and "goblins" are mischievous demons, both constituting the supposed threats to be feared in Hamlet's remaining alive, hence arguments for his being put to death, cf., *Taming of the Shrew* I.ii.210, *Troilus and Cressida* V.x.29.

on the supervise: immediately upon the looking over of the letter, another instance of a verb (OED supervise *v.* 1., to read through, peruse) used as a noun, cf., *avouch* I.i.57, *inquire* II.i.4, *disclose* III.i.166 (Abbott §451). **no leisure bated:** no unoccupied or in-between time "deducted (from the stipulated speediness)" (Riverside), "no time lost" (Jenkins).

not to stay: not even to wait for. **grinding:** sharpening.

struck: F, strooke Q2, an old form of the same word.

leisure: ● This repetition of the word used three lines earlier suggests that Hamlet too, answering the King's haste, feels the pressure of time in wanting to inform Horatio of his experience and to win Horatio's approval of his recent actions (lines 27–62) and his plans (lines 63–74).

now: Q2, an antithesis to "leisure" in the previous line (see previous note), F me, quoted in Abbott's note on the redundant object (§414).

beseech: beg, earnestly request; for the interspersed short line see Abbott §511.

benetted round: entirely ensnared, entangled; for the prefix *be-* see Abbott §438.

Or I could ... begun the play: Before I could form the idea of what to do, my brains had begun the action. A prologue would give the essentials of the story about to be enacted in a play. His brains are the actors, who begin the action ("the play") even before the prologue is spoken. **Or:** before, a form of *ere* from OE *aer*, cf., I.ii.147 note, I.ii.183 (Abbott §131). **to:** ahead of, as a prologue is spoken before the actors begin to enact the play.

Devised a new commission, wrote it fair—

Devised: thought up. **fair:** in final-copy form as a professional scribe would write it, "clean, clear" (Raffel).

I once did hold it, as our statists do,
A baseness to write fair and labored much
How to forget that learning, but, sir, now   35

I once did hold it ... forget that learning: Baldwin (I.729) finds a parallel in Ioannes Lodovicus (Juan Luis) Vives, *De Conscribendis Epistolis* (1534), with whom Shakespeare would have been familiar in grammar school. **did hold it:** believed it to be. **statists:** those skilled in state affairs, statesmen. **baseness:** "a skill befitting men of low rank" (Riverside).

It did me yeoman's service. Wilt thou know

yeoman's service: "good, efficient, or useful service, such as is rendered by a faithful servant of good standing" (OED yeoman I.1.c.).

Th' effect of what I wrote?

effect: purport, drift, tenor (OED *sb.* 2.b.).

HORATIO
                          Ay, good my lord.
HAMLET
An earnest conjuration from the King,

conjuration: solemn appeal, entreaty (OED II.2.), cf., *Romeo and Juliet* V.iii.68.

As England was his faithful tributary,

England: the king of England. **tributary:** payer of tribute, cf., III.i.170, IV.iii.61–62.

As love between them like the palm might flourish,   40

palm might flourish: cf., Psalm 92:12.

As peace should still her wheaten garland wear

still: always, continuously. **wheaten:** of wheat, symbol of peace, "since agriculture can flourish only in time of peace" (Kittredge).

And stand a comma 'tween their amities,

comma: Q2 and F, a much debated crux. ● Without addressing all the far-fetched emendations and interpretations, the following may be offered: Jenkins calls it the "type of something small and insignificant," Hamlet's bathetic satire of a fulsome image of peace standing between amities in preparation for the "open contempt" of the next line. Against this argument is that it is the next line, not this, that is meant to break the effect of the list of *as*'s. Baldwin argues that Shakespeare is using the term in the sense given it in Lily's *Brevissima Institutio* (*A Shorte Introduction of Grammar*, 1542, ascribed to John Colet and William Lily), which R.R. translates in *An English Grammar* (1641) as "a note of silence, or rather a place of breathing; as whereby the term of pronunciation, the sence still remaining, is so suspended: as that that which followeth ought presently to succeed," in other words, "If the King of England observes the condition which now suspends Peace, then Peace shall be only a comma continuing to join their amities as before. Shakespeare was thinking in the very phraseology of Lily, which he had been forced to master, and which any learned grammarian of his time should have understood. What a solemn farce would the pages of comment which have been expended on his comma appear to him!" (Baldwin I.574). Against this interpretation is that nothing in Hamlet's letter implies any suspension of peace in Denmark's relation to England since England has been defeated by

Denmark and pays tribute to it (cf., IV.iii.60–62) and "still … wear / And stand" implies the opposite, a continuation of peaceful amity. Though I have not found numismatic evidence of such an image, Theobald attributed to Warburton that "The poet without doubt wrote '… *Commere*,' i.e. a guarantee, a common mother. Nothing can be more picturesque than this image of Peace's standing, drest in her wheaten garland, between the two Princes, and extending a hand to each. We thus frequently see her on Roman coins" and then added "But Warburton, in his ed., goes further, and says that *commere* here means 'a trafficker in love, one who brings people together, a procuress'" (quoted in Furness). Riverside gives the sense "connective, link," following Johnson's gloss: "The *comma* is the note of *connection* and continuity of sentences; the *period* is the note of *abruption* and disjunction. Sh[akespeare] had it perhaps in his mind to write,—That unless England complied with the mandate, war should put a *period* to their amity; he altered his mode of diction, and thought that, in an opposite sense, he might put, that peace should stand a *comma* between their amities" (quoted in Furness). Riverside's and Johnson's readings seem to offer the most sense with the least reaching.

And many such-like *as*'s of great charge,

as's: as sir Q2, Assis F. ● referring to the three clauses in the previous lines beginning with the word *as*, with a pun on *asses*, the animals burdened with heavy or important loads ("great charge"). Malone notes that "the letter *s* in the particle *as* in the midland counties is usually pronounced … as in the pronoun *us* [i.e., as *s* rather than *z*]. Dr. Johnson himself always pronounced the particle [so] and so I have no doubt did Sh[akespeare]. It is so pronounced in Warwickshire at this day" (in Furness), cf., *Twelfth Night*, II.iii.170.

That on the view and knowing of these conténts,

That on … contents: ● NOTE TO ACTORS: The stresses should fall on "That," "view," "know-," "these," and "-ténts," "knowing" being "Contracted, or slurred in pronunciation, into a monosyllable" (Furness, referring to Abbott §470).

Without debatement further more or less,   45

Without debatement further more or less: without further discussion or deliberation about either extending or reducing the instructions.

He should the bearers put to sudden death,

bearers: i.e., Rosencrantz and Guildenstern. ● NOTE TO ACTORS: stress should fall on this word as an antithesis to "my head" in line 25, contrasting this command with Claudius's actual command that Hamlet be put to death.

Not shriving time allowed.
HORATIO
              How was this sealed?

shriving time: time for formal confession and absolution. ● The point is the requested speed, matching that of Claudius's instructions (lines 23–24), rather than the withholding of the possibility of repentance, which can be accomplished in an instant by the turning of the will to God even at the point of death (*in articulo mortis*). With his new awareness of the "divinity that shapes our ends," Hamlet knows (at this time of speaking with Horatio) that the eternal fates of Rosencrantz and Guildenstern are not in the hands of men, himself or anyone else. The disposition of their souls, however soon or late they are put to death, remains up to God. This awareness is reinforced by the contrast between the abstraction of "not shriving time allowed" here and the real savagery of Hamlet's desire for revenge in the form of damnation at III.iii.84–95. It is inaccurate to suggest that Hamlet is in vengeance cruelly enacting upon Rosencrantz and Guildenstern a death parallel to that of his father. The Ghost has reported having been killed while asleep, hence unable to repent *in articulo mortis*, unlike Rosencrantz and Guildenstern, who will be awake and aware of what is happening to them and hence able to repent, even without official church "shriving."

HAMLET
Why, even in that was heaven ordinant.

ordinant: ordering, arranging, directing (OED A.), in other words, providential, cf., the "divinity that shapes" (line 10 above). • With the phrase "even in that" Hamlet shows how thorough-going is his recognition of the hand of Providence in the entire experience of the sea voyage. His restlessness, his success in stealing the written commission, his early training in "writing fair," his rewriting and replacing the commission without the forgery's being discovered (lines 4–55), the attack of the pirate ship, his courageous impulse in boarding it, the separation of the two ships, the kindness of the pirates (IV.vi.15–29)—all these Hamlet has come to see as arranged not by himself but by Providence. In a series of what some might call accidents, including Hamlet's happening to have his father's signet ring with him, Hamlet sees the shaping hand of God, compared with which all human will is merely rough-hewing. This lesson in humility and that of the graveyard scene have led Hamlet to a revised and penitent relation to the world, his mission, and his mortality. His desire for revenge, and his conviction of the justice of his being the instrument of that revenge, have both come under the government of God's will. The King's damnation (III.iii.87–95) is no longer Hamlet's goal, and his own thoughts are no longer merely bloody (IV.iv.66).

I had my father's signet in my purse,
Which was the model of that Danish seal,   50

signet: a small seal often set into a ring.

model: smaller replica. **that:** "Indicating a person or thing assumed to be known" (OED that II. Demonstrative Adjective 1.b.)

Folded the writ up in the form of th' other,

writ: work of writing, the new commission. **in the:** Q2, F in, for the absent *the* in F see Abbott §89. **other:** Claudius's original commission.

Subscribed it, gave't th' impression, placed it safely,

Subscribed: F, Subscribe Q2, signed at the bottom, obviously with the King's name. **impression:** i.e., of the seal ring.

The changeling never known. Now the next day

changeling: Hamlet's new commission. The metaphor is of a child secretly exchanged by fairies for a real child they have stolen, applied (affectionately or hurtfully) to one seeming to be alien to a family in looks or behavior. **never known:** in this case the changeling

Was our sea fight, and what to this was sequent
Thou knowest already.   55

HORATIO

So Guildenstern and Rosencrantz go to't.

HAMLET

[Why, man, they did make love to this employment.]

They are not near my conscience. Their defeat
Does by their own insinuation grow.

'Tis dangerous when the baser nature comes   60

Between the pass and fell incensèd points
Of mighty opposites.

---

was like enough to the original not to be recognized
as a substitution.
sea fight: cf., Hamlet's letter to Horatio at IV.vi.15ff.
sequent: following.

to't: i.e., to death, cf., *Two Gentlemen* IV.iv.3–4.

[Why … employment]: in F only—i.e., they were
asking for such treatment. **employment:** usage.
● Rosencrantz and Guildenstern have been willing
to be used as the King's spies and are being treated
as such by Hamlet, cf., III.iv.202–209. We are not
told whether Rosencrantz and Guildenstern knew
their commission was to convey Hamlet to death,
but Hamlet has reason to think they did, and we
are meant "to accept the poetic justice of their end"
(Jenkins); see next note.
conscience: awareness of having done wrong,
see II.ii.605 note. ● Hamlet's statement is not a
confession of depravity, cruelty, or heartlessness. It
is a statement of perfectly justifiable fact, for already
suspecting them (cf., III.iv.203 and note), and then
having seen the King's writ on his life, he saw that
Rosencrantz and Guildenstern might be in on the
plot against him and in any case were willing and
flattering executors of the evil king's intentions.
Since this took place before the pirate ship appeared,
Hamlet could only assume that all three would soon
be before the English king and either he or they must
be put to death, for Rosencrantz and Guildenstern
might be personal carriers of the King's intention
as well as bearers of his written "commission."
Hamlet's only self-defense was this, and it fulfilled
his intention expressed at III.iv.202–209. In addition,
he has now got beyond imagining in his pride that
the disposition of the souls of Rosencrantz and
Guildenstern are in his hands. Their eternal fates
will be determined by God, not by Hamlet, as a
result of their own wills as God alone judges them,
and "suffering that punishment is not inconsistent
with redemption, a theme later central to *King Lear*"
(Spencer). Only their temporal fate can be influenced
by Hamlet. Therefore, since he has good cause to
defend himself against their service to Claudius,
and since by rights he is their king and may dispose
of their earthly existences, his conscience is in the
right not to be troubled by their ends, cf., *Henry V*
IV.i.176–77. **defeat:** ruin, undoing, cf., I.ii.10, II.ii.571.
insinuation: winding themselves in, stealing
covertly into the King's favor and thereby out of
Hamlet's.

'Tis dangerous … opposites: It is dangerous for
inferior men to come between the dueling swords of
mighty opponents. **baser:** inferior, lower ranking.
Between the pass and … points: a hendiadys
(Wright, page 187), between the sword points of
two enraged fencers. **pass:** a fencing attack, see

HORATIO

Why, what a king is this!

HAMLET

Does it not, think thee, stand me now upon—

He that hath killed my king and whored my mother,

Popped in between the election and my hopes,   65

Thrown out his angle for my proper life,

And with such coz'nage—is't not perfect conscience

To quit him with this arm? And is't not to be damned,

To let this canker of our nature come
In further evil?   70

---

line 147 note. **fell:** fiercely. **incensèd:** enraged or burning. **points:** sword points. **opposites:** enemies, opponents.

Does it not … stand me now upon: Is it not imperative to me, am I not obliged, for clarification of the idiom see Abbott §204, of the impersonal verb §297. **think thee:** consider, think (to yourself) about it, bethink you, said parenthetically, cf., *Measure for Measure* II.ii.143 ("I will bethink me"), rather than either "do you think" (which would be "thinkest thou" as F tries to make it without, however, altering "thee" to "thou"), or "does it seem to you" (OED think *v.*[1] with the dative, which would be "thinks thee" as in "methinks," unless Clarendon [quoted in Furness] is right that the *e* in Q2's "thinke" was a compositor's error for *s*). Jenkins argues for a loosely grammatical interrogative sense ("don't you think?"), but Hamlet does not actually seem to expect an answer to his larger question, nor does Horatio give one.

He: Claudius, for use of the subjective case because it is distant from the object "him" in line 68 see Abbott §216. **whored:** I.v.45–46, III.iv.40ff.

Popped … hopes: ● Hamlet here very reasonably assumes his own right to the crown. That simple assumption is not here motivated by the thwarted ambition to which he pretended for the ears of Rosencrantz and Guildenstern when he picked up their cue at II.ii.252 and reflected it to them at II.ii.269, 272, and to the King at III.ii.94. See I.ii.16 note and lines 355–56. It is true that Claudius has been duly elected to the crown by the electors, but the fact that he has murdered his brother and king to make such an election possible delegitimizes that election, and as soon as Hamlet is certain that the Ghost has spoken truly (III.ii.286–90), he is justified in thinking of himself as the rightful heir to his father. Among the list of Claudius's crimes, this usurpation from Hamlet is given its proper weight.

angle: fish hook, used also for fishing tackle in general, including rod and line (OED *sb.*[1] 1.), cf., *Antony and Cleopatra* II.v.10. **proper:** own (OED 1.), very (OED 4.b.).

coz'nage: trickery, falsehood "with the common word-play on *cousinage*, kinship" (Jenkins), cf., I.ii.64–65, 117. **perfect:** complete, unmarred. **conscience:** "conformity to what is right" (OED 6.) with the conflation of additional senses, as at IV.vii.1, implying both the inner lawgiver and the laws given, "what any sound synteresis would approve" (Lewis *Studies*, page 209), cf., II.ii.605 note and lines 68–80.

To quit him … who comes here? (lines 68–80): only in F. "The absence of these lines from Q2 is difficult to explain except as an accidental omission" (Jenkins). **quit:** requite, pay back.

canker of our nature: "canker" is literally a) a spreading sore or ulcer, or gangrene (Jenkins substantially), or b) a canker-worm, which destroys

HORATIO

It must be shortly known to him from England
What is the issue of the business there.

HAMLET

It will be short. The interim is mine,

And a man's life's no more than to say "One."
But I am very sorry, good Horatio,   75

That to Laertes I forgot myself,

For by the image of my cause I see
The portraiture of his. I'll court his favors.

---

plant buds (often from within) or leaves (Schmidt).
Hence the phrase refers to Claudius either as a
spreading sore who by participating in human nature
(being a member of the human race) corrupts it, or as
a human caterpillar secretly destroying the kingdom
from within (Schmidt substantially). **come / In
further evil:** either (as the King) enter into further
evil (actions, behavior) or (as spreading sore or
canker-worm) spread further corruption into the
yet uncorrupted parts of the body politic. For "in"
as "into" see Abbott §159 and cf., V.i.278, *Richard III*
V.iii.228, *Richard II* II.iii.160.

shortly: soon. **England:** probably the nation rather
than the king of England because of "there" in the
next line. **issue:** outcome.

It: i.e., the time it will take for the news to arrive.
short: brief. **interim is:** Jenkins following Hanmer, F
interim's leaves an awkward empty foot.

'One': one sword thrust (Dover Wilson, cited in
Jenkins), cf., line 280, or perhaps merely the first
number in counting, implying the brevity of life
(Jenkins substantially).

forgot myself: lost my temper, flew into a passion—
not that he forgot any item of knowledge.

● **SPEECH NOTE: For by the image...portraiture of
his:** Hamlet is making explicit, as he will again at
lines 255–57 (see note there), that Laertes and he are
foils for one another, each having to avenge a father's
death. "The irony, which Hamlet does not remark on
but which we can hardly miss, is that the *image* which
shows Laertes as a revenger like Hamlet must also
show Hamlet as revenge's object" (Jenkins). This is
so, but the parallel is yet more significant. The King's
murder of Hamlet Senior was explicit and intentional,
the outgrowth of Claudius's sinful ambition to be
king and to possess the Queen, whereas Hamlet's
killing of Polonius was not intentional, though it was
the outgrowth of the worse sin of Hamlet's even
higher ambition to play God by trying to damn the
King. In this way, even as the two young men are
parallel as revengers in externals, Laertes' passion of
revenge and plot to kill take place on the literal and
emotional plane of society, honor, and feelings,
whereas Hamlet's passion of revenge and his act of
killing unfold on the spiritual plane of the soul's
relation to God and eternity. (Compare this parallel
to that between Gloucester and Lear in *King Lear*.)
Both reveal themselves to have been chastened by
the workings of providence and the experience of
mortality. Laertes' simple conversion is revealed in
his final three lines of forgiveness offered and sought,
brought about by his death wound (lines 329–31).
Hamlet's subtler and more profound conversion is
revealed in his speeches to Horatio in this scene
(lines 6–11 and 219–24), in his killing of the King in a
sudden passion without calculation, and in his own
forgiveness of Laertes (line 332). The Laertes story, as

But sure the bravery of his grief did put me
Into a towering passion.

HORATIO

                Peace, who comes here?   80

          Enter Osric, a courtier.

OSRIC

Your lordship is right welcome back to Denmark.

HAMLET

I humbly thank you, sir.
[*To Horatio.*]   —Dost know this waterfly?

HORATIO

No, my good lord.

HAMLET

Thy state is the more gracious, for 'tis a vice to know

him. He hath much land and fertile. Let a beast be lord   85
of beasts and his crib shall stand at the King's mess.

'Tis a chough, but, as I say, spacious in the possession
of dirt.

Hamlet tells us here, is a version of the Hamlet story.
For: The following sentence explains not why he forgot himself but why he is now sorry that he did. **by:** a) according to, in light of, or possibly b) next to. If sense a) is meant, as is most probable, Hamlet sees in his mind's eye a picture of Laertes' situation set in relief by contrast with his image of his own situation ("I understand him in light of my own case"). If less probably sense b) is meant, Hamlet is seeing two images placed side by side for comparison like two portraits in the gallery of his mind ("we are both in a similar condition"). **image:** likeness, imaginary picture. **portraiture:** picture, image. **cause:** mission, purpose, motive, case. **court his favors:** invite his good will.
● For the audience this is ironic because they know that Laertes is plotting Hamlet's murder, yet with his last breath Laertes will bestow a form of "favor" on Hamlet and ask for the same in return.
bravery: bravado, extravagance, i.e., at V.i.251–54.
a towering passion: a passion "rising [as a tower rises above other things] to a high pitch of violence or intensity" (OED *ppl. a.* 4.), i.e., at V.i.254–83.
Peace: hush, stop talking.

S.D.: *Enter a Courtier* Q2, *Enter young Osric* F, *Enter a braggart gentleman* Q1.

right: very, thoroughly.

Dost: for the omission of "thou" see Abbott §241.
waterfly: "A water-fly skips up and down upon the surface of the water without any apparent purpose or reason, and is thence the proper emblem of a busy trifler" (Johnson in Furness). Here and in the passages where Thersites uses the word about Patroclus in *Troilus and Cressida* (V.i.30–34) and Mercutio uses "flies" about Tybalt in *Romeo and Juliet* (II.iv.28–35) "There are obvious hints for a costume-designer" (Jenkins LN), cf., Nashe *Pierce Penniless* i.177–78 (reference in Jenkins).
state: condition. **gracious:** blessed (Jenkins), graced, and also within God's grace, hence virtuous (Riverside), an antithesis to "vice."

much land and fertile: if the "and" is not for emphasis, the phrase may be a hendiadys for much fertile land (not listed in Wright). **Let a beast ... king's mess:** "A man of large possessions is received at court though himself no better than the cattle he owns" (Jenkins). **crib:** manger for feeding animals, "continues the beast metaphor" (Jenkins). **mess:** large gathering of people at a meal.
chough: Q2, chowgh F, both pronounced "chuff," a jackdaw or other chattering bird that can be taught to speak, hence an empty-headed talker, which Hamlet must already know Osric to be and which Osric proves himself to be beginning at line 90, with a pun on "chuff," a rustic or boor, often "a country fellow of more wealth than worth ... always implicit in the word is the

OSRIC

Sweet lord, if your lordship were at leisure, I should
impart a thing to you from his Majesty.   90

HAMLET

I will receive it, sir, with all diligence of spirit.
Put your bonnet to his right use; 'tis for the
head.

paradox of riches possessed by one unfit to have
them" (Jenkins), as in *1 Henry IV* II.ii.89, cf., Cotgrave
under "*Maschefouyn*" and "*Franc-gontier*," Marlowe
Ovid's Elegies III.vi.50, III.vii.9, the character Chough
in Middleton and Rowley *A Fair Quarrel* (II.ii), etc.
(all cited in Jenkins LN). ● In Osric Shakespeare has
combined the two stock character types, chattering
jackdaw and wealthy boor, both of which are relevant
to his function as a foil for Hamlet (see line 92 note).
Sweet: "common in courtly address" (Jenkins), cf.,
III.ii.53 note. **impart:** tell, relate. ● Osric here begins
a series of passages of pretentiously inflated diction
which he takes to be courtly and which Hamlet will
satirize, subtly in the next line and extravagantly at
lines 112–20. **a:** a particular, an important, "some, a
certain" (Abbott §81).

diligence of spirit: attentiveness, determination
to serve and please (the King). **Put your bonnet ...
head:** ● Here Hamlet begins to test Osric's devotion
to himself in the matter of the hat. Hamlet is
asking Osric to put on his hat when Osric, as was
customary, has removed it in the presence of the
Prince and is waving it about for courtly effect. The
request confronts Osric with a painful dilemma.
The Prince, who is known to be mad and in need of
humoring, is telling him to behave in a way insulting
to a prince and contrary to court fashion. Will Osric
obey the custom or obey the Prince himself? Is the
Prince mad or not? Osric's dilemma thus becomes
a comical foil to Hamlet's dilemma about revenge.
Scripture forbids but the Ghost has demanded
revenge, see I.v.85 note. Is the Ghost from hell or
heaven? Unlike Hamlet before III.iii but like him *in*
III.iii, Osric gets it wrong here by putting his own
desire to follow polite custom and fashion, devised to
honor princes, ahead of his obedience to the Prince
himself. Similarly Hamlet has put his own desire for
personal revenge and the King's damnation above
the Ghost's command. As Hamlet gives Osric several
different opportunities to change his mind and obey
the Prince, so has Providence given Hamlet several
opportunities to change his mind and submit to the
"divinity that shapes our ends" (line 10). The whole
passage thus becomes a gloss on the folly of Hamlet's
pride before his enlightenment and conversion. As
foolish as Osric appears to Hamlet, Horatio, and the
audience, so foolish does Hamlet's attempt to play
God in the matter of the damnation of a soul appear
to God and, because of the play, also to the audience.
This reading of the scene gives point to the otherwise
frivolous interruption of the action, which no appeal
to the value of mere "comic relief" can justify. In his
tragedies Shakespeare almost never engages in comic
relief for its own sake alone, however theatrically
useful, but always in what might be called comic
reiteration of or foil to the central thematic concerns
of the play. This reading is not altered by Jenkins'
description of it as "An adaptation of an old joke"
involving the two kinds of reason for donning and

OSRIC

I thank your lordship, it is very hot.

HAMLET

No, believe me, 'tis very cold; the wind is   95
northerly.

OSRIC

It is indifferent cold, my lord, indeed.

HAMLET

But yet methinks it is very sultry and hot for my
complexion.

OSRIC

Exceedingly, my lord; it is very sultry—as 'twere—   100
I cannot tell how. My lord, his Majesty bade me

signify to you that a has laid a great wager on your
head. Sir, this is the matter—

HAMLET [*Gesturing to him to put on his hat.*]
I beseech you remember—

OSRIC

Nay, good my lord, for my ease, in good faith.   105

Sir, here is newly come to court Laertes—believe me,

---

doffing a hat: politeness and comfort (= "ease"), cf.,
line 105. **Put your:** F, Your Q2. **bonnet:** hat, cf., II.i.76
note and *Venus and Adonis* lines 339 and 351. **his:** its
(Abbott §228).

hot ... cold: Theobald finds Shakespeare deriving
this exchange from a passage in Juvenal that satirizes
flatterers: "if you request a little fire in winter time,
he puts on his coat. if you say 'I'm hot,' he sweats"
(*Satires* III.100–103), and cf., Baldwin II.531.

indifferent: moderately, cf., III.i.121, III.ii.36.

methinks: it seems to me, cf., III.ii.230 note.
for: F, or Q2. **complexion:** one's natural makeup or
particular temperament (along with skin quality), cf.,
I.iv.27 note.

as 'twere: as it were.
I cannot tell how: "For Hamlet's mockery of the
obsequious who will agree to contrary propositions,
cf. III.ii.[376–83]" (Jenkins) and note there.
a has: he has. **laid ... head:** bet on you. The phrase
does not mean and need not imply that the King has
bet on Hamlet's death (= having his head), and Osric
certainly does not intend it. The overtone may be
there for the audience. **matter:** the substance of the
wager.

remember: ● This may be short for the formula
"remember your courtesy" meaning "cover your
head" (so OED remember *v.* 1.d. and Grant White in
Furness) on the presumption that "the demands of
courtesy are now satisfied (and that the hat should
therefore be resumed)" (Jenkins), cf., *Love's Labor's
Lost* V.i.98–99. Whether or not that formula is
intended, Osric remains caught between contrary
demands, the desire to keep his hat off for courtesy's
sake in the presence of royalty and the direct
instruction to put it on by a possibly mad prince.

good my lord: for the transposition of the possessive
adjective, see Abbott §13. **for my ease:** a conventional
phrase, "a polite insistence on maintaining ceremony"
(Riverside), with possible reference to "an old joke"
(Jenkins) referring to two reasons for removing the
hat, politeness and comfort, cf., Florio *Second Fruits*
1591, page 111, and *The Malcontent* Ind. 37–39 (cited in
Jenkins), and see lines 91–92 note.

here is newly come ... unfellowed (lines 106–143):
● "This praise of Laertes fulfils IV.vii.[130–33]"
(Jenkins). Baldwin says that Osric has "begun to
deliver a formal oration of praise *a la* Aphthonius... .
If Hamlet had permitted him to develop the body
of his oration, Osric might have betrayed the
tutelage of [Cicero's] *Ad Herennium* also. For Hamlet
immediately recognizes the symptoms, and cuts
Osric off before he gets under full sail, thereby
robbing him of all his 'golden words.' An audience
reared on Aphthonius would have enjoyed this bit of
rhetorical fencing hugely" (II.329–30).

an absolute gentleman, full of most excellent
differences, of very soft society and great showing.

absolute: perfect, complete.

differences: distinctions, distinctive qualities, a
technical term, appropriate to Osric's formal oration
of praise, derived from Cicero's *Topica*, cf., Baldwin
II.114. **soft society:** pleasant manners. **great
showing:** impressive appearance.

Indeed, to speak feelingly of him, he is the card or
calendar of gentry, for you shall find in him the   110
continent of what part a gentleman would see.

feelingly: Q3, sellingly Q2 (uncorrected), fellingly
Q2 (corrected), not in F, precisely, accurately,
pointedly, "so as to hit home" (Schmidt), cf., *Twelfth
Night* II.iii.159, *Measure for Measure* I.ii.34. **card or
calendar of gentry:** "model or paradigm. Two words
for the same thing" (Jenkins). A "card" is a map or
chart, i.e., that by which one navigates, cf., V.i.138,
and a "calendar" is either a list or register (OED *sb.*
4. [a.]), another guide to behavior, or more likely an
outward sign or index (OED *sb.* 5. b.), in this case
of "gentry" which means the behavior proper to a
gentleman, cf., II.ii.22. • Osric is saying that Laertes
is the paragon of gentility by whose example others
may guide their own behavior. **continent:** container,
the whole of which Osric is delineating the various
parts, cf., IV.iv.64 and Baldwin II.114. **what part …
see:** whatever quality a gentleman would wish to
see in another gentleman, with a pun on whatever
part of the world, each known for its particular
good qualities, a traveler would wish to discover,
"sustaining the metaphor of *card*, *continent*" (Jenkins).

HAMLET
Sir, his definement suffers no perdition in you,
though I know to divide him inventorially would

• **SPEECH NOTE: Sir, his … nothing more** (lines
112–20): Hamlet now extravagantly and satirically
outdoes Osric in inflated courtly diction, weaving
a spell of exaggeration throughout the speech.
definement: description. **perdition:** loss (from the
literal sense of Latin *perdo*). **to divide him … quick
sail:** To list Laertes' qualities one by one would daze
the memory's capacity to count things, and even at
that the dividing and counting would lag clumsily
behind the reality, like a ship wavering in its course,
by comparison with (or perhaps because of) the
speedy sailing of Laertes' qualities themselves.
In short, "the excellences of Laertes elude any
attempt to catalogue them" (Jenkins). **divide him
inventorially:** list his qualities individually, as Cicero
in *Topica* instructs, cf., Baldwin II.114.

dozy th'arithmetic of memory and yet but yaw

dozy: dosie Q2 (uncorrected), dazzie Q2 (corrected),
dizzie Q3, daze. **arithmetic of memory:** the
memory's ability to keep count. **but:** only, nothing
except (Abbott §128). **yaw:** said of a ship, literally "to
deviate temporarily from a straight course" but here
to move unsteadily or clumsily (OED *sb.*¹ 1., 2.).

neither in respect of his quick sail. But in the   115

neither: even at that, for all that (Riverside), either
(Abbott §128). **in respect of:** either in comparison
with or possibly because of. **quick:** lively, alive, cf.,
V.i.126–28. **sail:** the action of sailing.

verity of extolment, I take him to be a soul of
great article and his infusion of such dearth and

verity of extolment: truth of praise, i.e., to praise him
truly. **of great article:** of extreme significance (OED
article *sb.* IV.10.) or "theme; matter for an inventory"
(Jenkins). **infusion:** i.e., that which has been infused
into him, the sum of his qualities. **dearth and**

rareness as, to make true diction of him, his
semblable is his mirror and who else would trace
him his umbrage, nothing more.   120

OSRIC

Your lordship speaks most infallibly of him.

HAMLET

The concernancy, sir? Why do we wrap the gentleman
in our more rawer breath?

OSRIC

Sir?

HORATIO

Is't not possible to understand in another tongue?   125
You will to't, sir, really.

rareness: both words mean rarity. **to make true diction:** to speak accurately. **his semblable is his mirror:** what is like him is his own image in a mirror only, i.e., nothing else could approach being anything like him. **who else:** whoever else. **would trace him:** might wish to imitate him or follow in his track. **his umbrage ... more:** nothing more than his mere shadow, "he himself being the substance" (Jenkins).

most infallibly: ● Osric's reply is both comically exaggerated in itself and ironic in that he does not observe that Hamlet has been satirizing him with the very diction that Osric calls "infallible."

concernancy: the subject of our concern, the point, still in inflated diction. **Why ... breath?:** Why are we encasing Laertes in our more uncultivated speech, i.e., speaking about Laertes in terms that are more unskilled, uncultivated, crude ("rawer") than the fancier terms that he deserves? i.e., why are we discussing Laertes? ● The language Hamlet and Osric have been using being the opposite of raw, being in fact overripe, Hamlet is continuing the satire by implying that even such words are crude by comparison with the supposed merits of Laertes (Jenkins substantially), and perhaps by comparison with the finer language of which Laertes himself would be master.

Sir?: ● Osric, taken aback by hearing their previous speeches described as "raw" and not expecting Hamlet's return to relatively plain speaking, fails to comprehend Hamlet's question.

Is't not possible ... sir, really?: ● This passage is debated: Should "another tongue" be emended to "a mother tongue" (Johnson) or "to't" to "do't" (Q2 corrector)? I take both emendations to be uncalled for. More importantly, are the lines spoken to Osric (most eds.) or to Hamlet (Jenkins)? The tone of the lines seems inappropriate for and uncharacteristic of Horatio if read as directed to Hamlet. And "in another tongue" must mean "in a language different from the one you are using" (Jenkins) and not "when someone else is the speaker" (Riverside), because Osric has presumably understood his own stylized speech coming from Hamlet at line 121. I conclude that the debate is unnecessary. Hamlet's question (lines 122–23), despite its metaphor and irony, is a plain question spoken in plain language. Osric is dumbfounded by Hamlet's sudden departure from inflated courtly diction, to which Osric is accustomed at court. Horatio, seeing Osric's mystification, challenges him to get to the point in plain speech. **possible to understand in another tongue:** possible to learn in plain language what you are trying to tell us. **You will to't:** Please get to (or come to) the business of making your point. The phrase is "thoroughly idiomatic" (Jenkins), the pronoun reference depending on the context, cf., II.ii.429, V.i.49, 54, *Two Gentlemen* II.vii.89, *Romeo and Juliet* III.i.172, *Measure for Measure* II.i.233, *Timon of Athens*

HAMLET

What imports the nomination of this
gentleman?

OSRIC

Of Laertes?

HORATIO

His purse is empty already; all's golden words are   130
spent.

HAMLET

Of him, sir.

OSRIC

I know you are not ignorant—

HAMLET

I would you did, sir. Yet in faith if you did, it would not
much approve me. Well, sir?   135

OSRIC

You are not ignorant of what excellence
Laertes is—

HAMLET

I dare not confess that, lest I should compare with
him in excellence; but to know a man well were to
know himself.   140

III.vi.35, etc.. **really:** indeed, in actuality (instead of ineffectively in your inflated diction).

imports the nomination: signifies the naming, another version of "why are we talking about Laertes?" • That Osric does not respond to Horatio's exhortation, a simple request in plain language, causes Hamlet to return to the inflated language to get an answer out of him.

all's: all his. **spent:** used up, with a pun on expending coin money from a purse.

not ignorant—: Hamlet interrupts him, turning the implication of the phrase from knowledge of Laertes to knowledge in general.

I would you did: I wish that you did (know that I am not ignorant in general), i.e., I would certainly want to be truly known not to be ignorant, especially in the sense of line 139–40 below. **not much approve:** not say much to my credit. • Hamlet is insulting Osric, whose opinion of Hamlet is not to be valued. To be thought wise by a fool is not necessarily to be wise. **Laertes is—:** again, Hamlet interrupts him.

I dare not ... know himself: "Implying that only the excellent can appreciate excellence and that only through self-knowledge can a man thoroughly know another. The first proposition, however, does not entail the second, which exceeds it. Hence *but*" (Jenkins). **confess:** admit. **that:** i.e., that I know how excellent Laertes is in general. **lest I should ... excellence:** to avoid judging myself to be comparable to him in excellence, i.e., to avoid being guilty of pride: "I dare not pretend to know him, lest I should pretend to an equality" (Johnson in Furness). **to know a man ... himself:** "no man can completely know another but by knowing himself, which is the utmost extent of human wisdom" (Johnson in Furness). • The reference is to the Greek phrase *gnothi seauton* (Latin, *nosce te ipsum*) "know thyself," said by Pausanias to have been inscribed upon the temple of Apollo at Delphi, the seat of the Delphic oracle. Taken up by Socrates, it came to mean not only "know that you are merely mortal and not a god" but an extension of the Socratic dictum that "the unexamined life is not worth living," something like "learn who and what you are, what is true and what is not about your own nature and hence the nature of reality." Thence the phrase became a foundation proverb of Western thought, as Johnson exemplifies, and Hamlet presents it as such. Thematically, it is central to the play in both its senses, for Hamlet both forgets that he is not God (in III.iii) and must go through a process of learning who and what he is, the instrument, not the master, of God's justice, cf.,

OSRIC

I mean, sir, for his weapon; but in the
imputation laid on him, by them in his meed,
he's unfellowed.

HAMLET

What's his weapon?

OSRIC

Rapier and dagger.   145

HAMLET

That's two of his weapons. But well.

OSRIC

The King, sir, hath wagered with him six Barbary
horses, against the which he has impawned, as I take it,
six French rapiers and poniards, with their assigns,
as girdle, hanger, and so. Three of the carriages, in   150

faith, are very dear to fancy, very responsive to
the hilts, most delicate carriages, and of very

liberal conceit.

HAMLET

What call you the carriages?

I.iii.78 ("to thine own self be true") and note. **were:** would be. **himself:** oneself.

for his weapon: continuing the thought of line 137. **but:** even only. **imputation laid on him:** estimation, reputation, or prestige ascribed to him. **by them in his meed:** by those who serve him, receive of his bounty, "meed" = wages, pay, recompense (OED 1.), "So Dover Wilson in accord with Q2 punctuation and the plain sense. To take *in his meed* (= merit) with *unfollowed*, as usually done, is, after stress on *excellence*, tautological and leaves *them* unidentified" (Jenkins). **unfellowed:** peerless. • Osric asserts that Laertes is unequaled for his skill in fencing even if one goes not by direct knowledge but only by the high estimation of him given by those who serve him, presumably those with whom Osric would be in communication about Laertes, as he would not be with Laertes himself or someone of similar rank.

Rapier and dagger: The rapier is a light thrusting sword, cf., IV.vii.98 note, and the dagger here is a short "blunt blade with a basket hilt used for defence" (Schmidt). The rapier and dagger in Shakespeare's own time became for the upper classes "The fashionable mode, *c.* 1600, displacing sword and buckler … . With the dagger (or *poniard*, as line [149]) in the left hand, one warded off the opponent's rapier while thrusting with one's own. Cf. *Rom[eo and Juliet]* III.i.[159–64]" (Jenkins). The sword and buckler were "used only by the lowest class of soldiers" (Riverside at *1 Henry IV* I.iii.230 note).

The King, sir, … and so: The King is betting the six horses against Laertes' rapiers, poniards, and accessories, no doubt bought in France. **with him:** i.e., with Laertes. **Barbary horses:** Arab horses, "A much-prized breed, noted for their swiftness" (Jenkins). **he:** i.e., Laertes. **impawned:** impaund Q2, impon'd F, bet, staked, cf., line 164. **poniards:** a poniard is a slender dagger usually with a triangular or square blade in cross-section. **their assigns:** their accessories, that which is assigned to or connected with them. **girdle:** belt. **hanger:** "Attached to a man's girdle was the hanger, which consisted of one or two straps and a plate or pad to which was buckled the scabbard of the sword" (Linthicum, page 265, quoted in Jenkins). **hanger, and so:** hanger and so Q2, Hangers or so F. **and so:** and so on. **carriages:** see lines 154–57. • This and the following phrases are examples of Osric's continuing to use inflated diction.

dear to fancy: precious, valuable in (anyone's) estimation, judgment, appreciation. **very responsive to the hilts:** thoroughly corresponding to the highly ornamented sword hilts. **delicate:** subtly and finely made.

liberal conceit: elaborate in conception, highly wrought.

What call you: What are you calling, i.e., what do you mean by the term "carriages"?

HORATIO

I knew you must be edified by the margent ere you   155
had done.

OSRIC

The carriages, sir, are the hangers.

HAMLET

The phrase would be more german to the matter
if we could carry a cannon by our sides. I would it
might be hangers till then. But on. Six Barbary horses   160
against six French swords, their assigns, and three

liberal-conceited carriages—that's the French bet
against the Danish. Why is this impawned, as you
call it?

OSRIC

The King, sir, hath laid, sir, that in a dozen passes   165
between yourself and him, he shall not exceed you
three hits. He hath laid on twelve for nine. And

must: would have to, were destined to (Abbott §314).
edified by the margent: enlightened by marginal
notes or glosses. • Horatio is satirizing Osric's
inflated diction, cf., line 160 note.

german: Ierman Q2, Germaine F, germane, relevant.
a cannon: Q2, Cannon F, the carts upon which
cannon were mounted were called carriages, cf.,
Henry V III.Prol.26. **I would it might be hangers till
then:** I wish you would use the term *hangers* until
that (impossible) time. • Osric has used the inflated
term "carriages" (meaning things that carry) for the
common term "hanger," and Hamlet is playing on the
contrast between small and large weapons. Baldwin
notes Quintilian's discussion of rhetorical obscurity,
with which Shakespeare was familiar in grammar
school. "[A] book with obscure passages annotated
in the margin … was regular in Shakspere's day"
and Osric's "carriages" gives "this figure a specific
rhetorical application…. Hamlet objects that the
proper term for the support of a rapier is hanger, that
for a cannon, carriage. He has, therefore, been obliged
to have recourse to the margin of Osric to explain
this improper and translated use of the term carriage
which has resulted in obscurity" (Baldwin II.222–23).
But on: But go on.

liberal-conceited: extravagantly conceived.
• Picking up Osric's phrase from line 153, Hamlet
turns its application from the making of the hangers
to Osric's excessively extravagant ("liberal")
imaginative flights ("conceits" = conceptions) in his
use of language. **French bet … Danish:** "What the
Frenchified Laertes has brought back with him is
set against the home product. Danish horses were
esteemed and exported (Dollerup, pages 118–19)"
(Jenkins). **impawned, as:** Malone, all Q2, impon'd as
F. Malone corrects Q2's probable error based on F (see
Jenkins LN), cf., line 148. • Whether Osric's word is
impawned or *imponed*, Hamlet is still satirizing Osric's
diction, which exhibits the vice of speech called
cacozelia ("affected diction, especially the coining of
fine words out of Latin" SMJ *Lang.*, page 72).

laid: wagered. • SPEECH NOTE: **that in a
dozen … twelve for nine:** The apparent
contradiction between the two statements of
the wager (lines 165–67), much belabored with
commentary, lies not in the text or in Shakespeare's
confusion of intention but in our misunderstanding
of the meaning of the words as applied to fencing,
which leads to our false assumptions that a) "in a
dozen passes" states a total limit and b) the "twelve"
refers to passes again rather than to hits. If "a
dozen passes" means "any set of a dozen passes"
and "twelve" refers to hits rather than passes, the
apparent contradiction disappears. In fencing a
"pass" is not synonymous with a "bout" (*pace* Jenkins

and Riverside) but refers to that motion called an "attack," a movement that puts one fencer's "point in line," creating a "right of way" and requiring a parry (block) and potentially a riposte (counter-attack) from the other fencer. In this period an attack or pass was a running rather than a lunging motion, in which the initiator attacked in the course of running at and passing by the defender (see OED pass *sb.*[2] 9. and quotation of 1692, Sir Walter Hope, *Fencing Master*, 2nd ed., page 79). The pass may result in a hit scored by either fencer or in no hit at all. Cf., line 61 ("pass and fell incensèd points"), IV.vii.138 ("in a pass of practice" = a deceptive attack), and *Twelfth Night* III.i.42 ("Nay, an thou pass upon me" = make a fencing attack on me with words) and III.iv.274 ("I had a pass with him" = one exchange of attack and parry). By contrast, a "bout" consists of some number of passes (a set of attacks), in this case a dozen, until an agreed-on number of hits or "touches" is reached (as in F at line 286). Cf., IV.vii.158 ("make your bouts more violent") and below line 284 ("I'll play this bout first" = play out this dozen, *not* this next individual pass). The apparent contradiction between Osric's two statements therefore may be resolved as follows: The King has bet that 1) in any one bout of twelve passes, Laertes will not score above three hits more than Hamlet scores, and 2) that for every twelve hits scored by Laertes in any number of bouts, Hamlet will score at least nine.

trial: testing, putting to proof the bet that will be resolved in the fencing match. **vouchsafe:** grant, be willing to provide. **answer … answer no:** ● Osric, as he explains in his next speech, means by "vouchsafe the answer" the act of answering the challenger with his "person" (i.e., his body) in the act of fencing, cf., *Troilus and Cressida* I.iii.332. Hamlet plays with him by asking, "What if I give the answer 'no' to the question whether I will play?" cf., III.ii.313 note.

breathing: exercising, exertion (which speeds up the breath) cf., *All's Well* I.ii.17, *Pericles* II.iii.100. **foils:** a foil is a light, flexible fencing sword, rectangular in cross-section and either pointed for dueling or blunted ("bated," meaning with the point covered with a "button") for sporting matches.

The gentleman … purpose: If the gentleman (Laertes) be willing and if the King keep to his intention. **will win:** intend, desire to win. **and I can:** if I can. **will gain:** am willing, consent to gain (Abbott §319). ● Though it is hard not to feel that the sense is shading into a simple future tense (which, as Jenkins points out, would normally require "shall"), the use of "will" in line 180 in the sense of desire and choice reinforces that sense here. **odd hits:** any hits Laertes may score that would lose Hamlet the match and the King his bet "at the odds," cf., line 165 note.

it would come to immediate trial if your lordship would vouchsafe the answer.

HAMLET

How if I answer no?   170

OSRIC

I mean, my lord, the opposition of your person in trial.

HAMLET

Sir, I will walk here in the hall. If it please his Majesty—it is the breathing time of day with me—let the foils be brought. The gentleman willing and the King   175 hold his purpose, I will win for him and I can. If not, I will gain nothing but my shame and the odd hits.

OSRIC

Shall I deliver you so?

HAMLET

To this effect sir, after what flourish your   180
nature will.

OSRIC

I commend my duty to your lordship.

HAMLET

                    Yours.

                        Exit Osric.

A does well to commend it himself; there are no
tongues else for's turn.

HORATIO

This lapwing runs away with the shell on   185
his head.

HAMLET

A did comply with his dug before a sucked it.

---

deliver you: report your answer. **so:** in this way.

effect: point, substance of the answer. **after what flourish your nature will:** with whatever decoration of speech and gesture your natural impulses (perhaps as opposed to your relatively meager rational gift) might desire or choose (of your free will).

● **SPEECH NOTE:** In this comical context Hamlet is giving voice to a major theme of the play, for nearly every imperative has been made with a stipulation about how it is to be done, specifically to avoid going too far or falling short. The central instance is the Ghost's charge to Hamlet to "revenge my foul and most unnatural murder" but "taint not thy mind" (I.v.25, 81–86). Other instances range from the important to the pedestrian. Among the important are the King to Cornelius and Voltemand at I.ii.34–38, Laertes to Ophelia at I.iii.5–44, Polonius to Laertes at I.iii.58–80 (with its many forms of the Aristotelian principle of the golden mean that underlies all the examples), Hamlet to Polonius at II.ii.522–32, Hamlet to Horatio at III.ii.78–87, and Hamlet to the Queen at III.iv.144–96. Among the pedestrian instances are Hamlet to Horatio at IV.vi.23–24 and Hamlet to Osric here. The most thematically essential instance is Hamlet to the Players at III.ii.1–45 (see note there).

commend my duty: offer my respects, no doubt in the form of a bow, cf., line 195.

Yours: Hamlet returns the salutation though without the bow.

A: he, Riverside after a Parrott-Craig conjecture, not in Q2, hee F. **commend it:** Hamlet plays on Osric's word in the sense "praise," as if Osric were praising his own manner of bowing (Riverside). **no tongues else for's turn:** no other people to serve his purpose, i.e., to pay him compliments, cf., OED turn *sb.* 30. b. (*g*). **for's:** for his.

lapwing: a foolish bird, that "runneth away with the shell on her head as soon as she is hatched" (Meres's *Wit's Treasury*, 1598, quoted by Malone in Furness), echoed in Robert Greene's *Never Too Late* (Greene, viii.35) (quoted by Steevens in Furness and Jenkins), based on the fact that "the lapwing is ornithologically remarkable for leaving the nest within a few hours of [hatching] and hence became the proverbial type of juvenile pretension" (Jenkins), with the added implication that Osric has at last put on his hat (Riverside following Dover Wilson).

A did comply ... sucked it: He paid courtesies (as an infant) to the nipple before sucking milk from it, i.e., he has been a timepleaser from birth. **A ... a:** He ... he. **comply with:** "pay courtesies to" (Jenkins), cf., II.ii.372, Complie F, sir Q2 [uncorrected], so sir Q2 [corrected]. **his dug:** his mother's or wet-nurse's nipple.

Thus has he—and many more of the same breed that

I know the drossy age dotes on—only got the tune of
the time, and out of an habit of encounter, a kind   190

of yeasty collection, which carries them through and
through the most fanned and winnowed opinions;

and do but blow them to their trial, the bubbles
are out.

Enter a Lord.

Thus has he … bubbles are out: Osric—and others
like him that the bad times dote on—have caught
only the outward form of the manners of the time,
and merely out of superficial familiarity with them,
a collection of mere frothy words, which causes
them to pass muster in the opinion of even the most
discriminating; but when they are put to a real test,
these bubbles pop. **breed:** Q2, Beauy F (for bevy), "a
word used of birds, perhaps suggested by *lapwing*"
(Jenkins, who prefers the F reading).

drossy age: inferior, worthless period of history,
from *dross*, the waste scum that forms on the surface
of molten metal. **dotes on:** is enamored of and
depends on. ● There is a significant distinction to be
made between a) Hamlet's genuine feeling (here as at
III.iv.153 and V.i.139–40) of the moral and social
decline of the world, and b) Hamlet's calculated
building upon this feeling to serve the purposes
of his play-acted madness to mislead Polonius
(II.ii.192–217) and Rosencrantz and Guildenstern
(II.ii.293–310, 363–68). The former is consistent with
medieval and Renaissance conceptions of the world
derived from the fall story in Genesis, the decline of
the ages in the book of Daniel (2:32–45), and the four
declining ages of man from the Golden Age to the
Silver, Brass, and Iron in Ovid's *Metamorphoses*
(I.89–150), cf., Dante's *Inferno* XVI:103–115.

only got the tune of the time: caught only the style
or outward form of the present times, i.e., without
real substance, "the cant of the day" (Johnson quoted
in Jenkins). **and out of:** i.e., and (got the "tune") only
out of. **a habit of encounter:** "habitual intercourse"
(Jenkins), a superficial familiarity with social
situations (OED habit 10.).

yeasty collection: yesty F, histy Q2, frothy gathering,
i.e., of phrases, "fashionable prattle" (Johnson in
Jenkins), in apposition to "tune." **carries them …
opinions:** stands them in good stead even in the
opinions of the most discriminating judges, like grain
that survives the sifting out of chaff (fanning and
winnowing). **fanned and winnowed:** prophane and
trennowed Q2, fond and winnowed F. With Jenkins
I accept Warburton's emendation of "fond" to
"fanned" (probably "fand" in the ms., as in *Midsummer
Night's Dream* Q1 III.ii.142) and F's winnowed in place
of Q2's trennowed, a non-word with no meaning,
"fan" being an instrument for winnowing grain and
the phrase "fanned and winnowed" being common
at the time, cf., *Troilus and Cressida* I.iii.26–30 (and see
Jenkins LN for other examples).

do but blow … bubbles are out: "This continues the
metaphor of *yeasty* [line 191]: when you put Osric and
his like to the test by as much as blowing on them,
the bubbles burst, i.e. when you try to converse with
them their fine phrases are shown to be empty of
substance or thought" (Jenkins).

LORD

My lord, his Majesty commended him to you by   195

young Osric, who brings back to him that you attend

him in the hall. He sends to know if your pleasure
hold to play with Laertes, or that you will take
longer time.

HAMLET

I am constant to my purposes; they follow the King's   200
pleasure. If his fitness speaks, mine is ready, now or

whensoever, provided I be so able as now.

LORD

The King and Queen and all are coming
down.

HAMLET

In happy time.   205

LORD

The Queen desires you to use some gentle
entertainment to Laertes before you fall to play.

HAMLET

She well instructs me.

Exit Lord.

---

commended him to you: asked to be kindly remembered to you (OED 5.), sends his regards. **him:** himself. **by:** through, by means of.

who: i.e., Osric. **attend:** await, wait upon (in a courtly sense).

pleasure hold: intention or preference remains. **play:** compete. **that:** for *that* omitted and then inserted see Abbott §285. **take longer time:** postpone the match for a time. • The speech of this Lord is simple and direct, a complete contrast with the "yeasty" speech of Osric. We may gather that the King has had to send this follow-up messenger because he could not discern the meaning of Osric's report through all the inflated diction.

I am constant … King's pleasure: • Hamlet speaks in a double sense, a) as the Lord will understand his words, and b) as the audience will: sense a) I am faithful to my public intentions, which are to fence with Laertes as expressed to Osric, in accordance with the King's wishes, and sense b) I remain committed to my private intentions to fulfill my mission of killing the King as an instrument of justice, which intentions are the consequence of ("follow") the King's ambition and lust that led to his crimes ("pleasure"). As he does often, Shakespeare is conveying to the audience two entirely different levels of meaning in one sentence, one level being the normal civil formality of the court, the other the profound intention of Hamlet's soul to greet, now with untainted mind, the demand of the hour. **If his fitness … ready:** If he is ready, I am ready, cf., III.ii.45 and the final transfiguration of the word "ready" at line 222 below. **If his fitness speaks:** if his inclination or state of readiness (Crystal) or convenience (Jenkins) or aptness expresses itself, with a possible irony in Hamlet's calling the King "His Fitness," akin to "His Majesty."

whensoever: whenever. **provided … as now:** so long as, at some other time, I be as able to fence as I am now.

In happy time: • both a) a conventional phrase of politeness meaning at an opportune moment, good timing, cf., *All's Well* V.i.6 and *Othello* III.i.30, and b) a pregnant note to the tense audience, who know the treacherous plans of the King and Laertes, implying at a time full of "hap," fateful, and perhaps (either ironically or, in light of the divine shaping implied at lines 10 and 48, genuinely) at a propitious, fortunate, felicitous time, cf., OED happy 2.a. and 5.b.

gentle entertainment: gentlemanly courtesy.

fall to play: • another double implication, only one sense intended by the speaker, a) begin to play (i.e., to fence) and b) be destroyed by the playing. In addition, Hamlet will soon engage in a profound courtesy

HORATIO

You will lose, my lord.

HAMLET

I do not think so. Since he went into France, I have   210
been in continual practice. I shall win at the odds.

Thou wouldst not think how ill all's here about my
heart. But it is no matter.

HORATIO

Nay, good my lord.

HAMLET

It is but foolery, but it is such a kind of gaingiving as   215
would perhaps trouble a woman.

HORATIO

If your mind dislike anything, obey it. I will forestall
their repair hither and say you are not fit.

HAMLET

Not a whit. We defy augury. There is special
providence in the fall of a sparrow. If it be now, 'tis   220
not to come; if it be not to come, it will be now; if it
be not now, yet it will come. The readiness is all.

toward Laertes of eternal import to himself before his fall into death, see line 332 and note.

I have been in continual practice: ● Though Jenkins points out that this contradicts "foregone all custom of exercises" at II.ii.296–97, Hamlet's previous statement was part of his effort to persuade Rosencrantz and Guildenstern of his melancholy madness and is not there meant to be taken by us as true, just as Hamlet's "man delights not me" at II.ii.309, the conclusion of his self-portrait to the spies, is refuted in reality by his genuinely self-revealing words to Horatio at III.ii.54–74. **at the odds:** i.e., the three-hit handicap, cf., line 165 note.

Thou: Q2, But thou F. **Thou wouldst not think:** You cannot imagine. **how ill all's here about my heart:** what a bad feeling I have about this. ● This speech is a powerful example of a common convention in Shakespeare's drama, the emotional premonition of disaster or death felt but not comprehended by a character, or seen and reported by some oracle, cf., *Richard III* II.iii.32–43 ("By a divine instinct men's minds mistrust / Ensuing danger," reference in Jenkins), *Merchant of Venice* I.i.1ff., the cause of Antonio's "sadness" (= heaviness or depressed spirits) being his premonition of the life-threatening danger into which he will soon run and not any of the myriad causes invented by critics, *Romeo and Juliet* I.iv.106–111, *Julius Caesar* II.ii, *Othello* IV.iii.23ff. including Desdemona's "Willow" song, etc.

Nay: a polite rejection of Hamlet's own denial of the significance of his feeling.

foolery: nonsense. **gaingiving:** "The same as *mis-giving*. We thus use *gainsay* [= contradict]" (Theobald in Furness), *gain-* from *against*; for the dropped prefix (*a-*) see Abbott §460.

dislike: feel an aversion to. **it:** your mind, i.e., follow your intuition or feeling about this matter. **forestall:** intercept, obstruct. **repair:** coming, cf., IV.vi.23, another instance of a verb used as a noun, cf., *avouch* I.i.57, *inquire* II.i.4, *disclose* III.i.166, and *supervise* above line 23, and Abbott §451. **fit:** cf., line 201 note.

whit: least bit. **We defy augury:** we human beings cannot be successfully predicted ("augured") about, "defy" as in something defies description (OED 4.b.), rather than as in Romeo's "I defy you stars" in *Romeo and Juliet* [Q1] V.i.24 (OED 4.[a.] or 5.) ● Whatever choices we make, to obey or to ignore premonition, our ends are shaped (as opposed to rough-hewn) not by ourselves but by divinity, cf., lines 10–11 and 48 and next note. **special providence:** ● divine providence is understood in two categories, a) "general providence," God's care of the world as a whole exercised through the operation of universal natural law, and b) "special providence," the direct care exercised by God on each individual creature in any particular moment. The Stoics (e.g., Epictetus) espoused the former. To it the latter was added by St.

Augustine and St. Thomas Aquinas and was particularly emphasized by John Calvin (*Institutes* I.16–17). Hamlet here finds the doctrine explicit in the passages in Matthew and Luke to which he refers (see next note), and from it he gathers patience in the matter of the timing of death, which any man must know to be coming, and in particular his own death, which he intuits to be near, and which we know to be hastening toward him with the sword and poison of Laertes incited by the King. **fall of a sparrow:** a reference to Matthew 10:29–31, and cf., Luke 12:6–7 ("Are not two sparrows sold for a farthing? and one of them shall not fall on the ground without your Father.... Fear ye not therefore, ye are of more value than many sparrows"). • The passage has particular resonance for the play because the previous verse in Matthew (and in Luke) distinguishes between "them which kill the body, but are not able to kill the soul" and "him, which is able to destroy both soul and body in hell," precisely the distinction Hamlet had failed to make in III.iii (Spencer). **If it be now ... let be:** Though J. Dover Wilson thought the passage "a distillation of Montaigne" in the essay "That to Philosophise is to learn how to die" (quoted in Harmon, page 998, cf., Florio's translation of Montaigne's *Essays* I.xix), Harmon argues that much of Montaigne's essay consists "of adaptations of Latin—chiefly Senecan—aphorisms" which "were probably familiar to Shakespeare in the original [and of which] variants ... are to be found among the commonplaces in Nicholas Ling's *Politeuphuia, or Wits Commonwealth* (1597), William Baldwin's *Treatise of Moral Philosophy* (1547), Thomas Elyot's *Bankette of Sapience* (1534), and elsewhere," including a translation of Philippe de Mornay's *Excellent Discours de la Vie et de la Mort* (London, 1577) by E.A. (Edward Addis) called *The Defense of Death* (Harmon, pages 998–99, with examples). **The readiness is all:** • Whether or not the reference is to Matthew 24:44 ("Therefore be ye also ready; for in the hour that ye think not, will the Son of man come") or Luke 12:40 (Geneva "prepared," King James "ready"), the word "readiness" resonates back through the play to Hamlet's "Go make you ready" (III.ii.45), with which he completes his charge to the players to fulfill their mission without getting in the way of higher purposes about which they can know nothing, and to Hamlet's own fatal lack of moral and spiritual readiness in III.iii. As Philip Thompson writes about that scene, "At his one 'ready' moment, in terms of the success of his cause, Hamlet is (literally) damnably unready. In explicit renunciation of that 'readiness' he later [i.e., here] espouses, he declares himself unsatisfied by the mere 'hire and salary' of killing the body and leaving the soul to God, and demands the eternal damnation of Claudius as the only possible means of relief for his personal shame and suffering. This is the Hamlet that must be transformed" (Thompson, page 186, see Introduction,

Since no man, of aught he leaves, knows what is't to leave betimes, let be.

page 5). By virtue of his experience of Heaven's "special providence" in the events of the sea voyage (cf., line 48), and of the humbling of the *memento mori* experience in the graveyard (V.i), Hamlet is indeed transformed, and his transformation is now complete, as will be confirmed at line 332 when Hamlet forgives even his own murderer. The readiness that is all is the readiness a) to recognize that human beings but rough-hew their ends, whose shaping is done only by God, and b) to submit to that shaping, as Hamlet here explicitly does, even if the "end" is death, the ultimate surrender of the will, if that is what is willed by that "special providence" in the fall of even a sparrow.

Since … let be: Thus Riverside (following Dover Wilson) punctuates a notorious crux: since no man of ought he leaues, knowes what ist to leaue betimes, let be. Q2, since no man ha's ought of what he leaues. What is't to leaue betimes? F, Since no man, of aught he leaves, knows, what is't to leave betimes? Let be. Warburton (followed by Furness). Because that dangling "knows" makes for an awkwardness "harsh and strained" (Jenkins LN), Jenkins adds the word "aught" and changes the punctuation ("Since no man, of aught he leaves, knows aught, what is't to leave betimes? Let be."), picking up Johnson's emendation to "Since no man knows aught of what he leaves," and arguing that "what is't" must be a question and cannot mean "what it is," a point refuted by IV.iii.2 and *Cymbeline* IV.ii.141 and IV.iv.35. Jenkins adds that "Let be" is merely an attempt to break off the conversation because of the entry of other people, with which point Cunningham agreed. C. S. Lewis notes about the F version: "I think the last clause is best explained by the assumption that Shakespeare had come across Seneca's *Nihil perdis ex tuo tempore, nam quod relinquis alienum est* ["You are throwing away none of your own time; for what you leave behind does not belong to you"—trans. Gummere] (Epist. lxix)" (Lewis P/P, page 99 note). Other traditional statements of which this passage is a descendant appear in Montaigne's *Essays* (Florio), I.19, "What matter is it when it cometh, since it is unavoidable? … No man dies before his hour. The time you leave behind was no more yours, than that which was before your birth, and concerneth you no more" (quoted in Jenkins V.ii.218–20 LN), and the Dedication to Giordano Bruno's *Candelajo*, "whatsoever may be the appointed hour of that evening which I am awaiting, when the change will take place, I, who am in the night, await the day, and those who are in the day await the night. Everything that exists is either at hand or at a distance, near or far, now or later, instantly or hereafter" (quoted in Furness). Since F introduces a question mark after "betimes," the key conflict becomes whether Hamlet means to drive to the question "since no man knows anything, what difference does it make to leave (life) early?" (F) or whether he means to drive to the statement "Since no man knows what it means to leave (life) early, let be." (Q2). Even at his lowest, Hamlet had asserted that man is given the gift of "That capability and godlike reason" (IV. iv.38), suggesting that in his enlightenment here he cannot be expressing despair of all knowledge, as if in the voice of a modern existentialist. The trajectory of his spiritual journey, along with the examples from Seneca, Bruno, and Montaigne quoted above, suggests that Hamlet is far likelier to mean that it is specifically the point of his departure (from life) that man cannot control and whose ultimate significance he cannot know. This meaning comports with the greater authority of Q2 than F, in which even Jenkins finds "an attempt to tidy and make sense of what was found awkward and obscure" (Jenkins). But we need not take F's question mark to confirm that what we have in Q2 is in fact awkward and obscure, only that the editors of F may have thought it so. I take the Q2 reading to be the closest thing we have to Shakespeare's actual intention, and hence adopt the Riverside punctuation of Q2, concluding that Hamlet is not asking the equivalent of "what difference does it make?" but rather driving logically to the imperative to Horatio to "let be" (see Introduction, page 13ff., "Imperatives."). • In this statement, Shakespeare has transfigured whatever stoical or other secular rational influences stand behind it into an expression of the fruits of the complex spiritual journey of Hamlet that the play as a whole depicts. Hamlet is not here worried about possessions (F's "ha's") or even about mere quantity of time. He is recognizing, and helping Horatio to see, that man cannot know the full meaning of things in their eternal or divine context, and therefore fear of death's coming sooner ("betimes") rather than later is misplaced. "We defy augury" (line 219) means we cannot be augured about, hence we cannot know whether it is better to die now or later, precisely the kind of knowledge Hamlet erroneously pretended to have about Claudius. The whole speech is an exact repudiation of Hamlet's pride in III.iii. In classical terms, his hubris is gone. And, as Shakespeare is fond of doing at heightened moments, its conclusion, "Let be," has a fully double sense. It may well mean "break off the conversation because others are coming," just as Lear really wants his physical button undone (*King Lear* V.iii.310). At the same time and in the same words, Hamlet also means "let Providence shape our ends (cf., line 10), let us submit our individual will to God's will, trusting in that special providence that governs even the fall of a sparrow (cf., line 220)." It is difficult to imagine that at this moment in the play Shakespeare would not intend us to feel the spiritual implications of such a phrase, and only a resolute ignoring of the trajectory of the spiritual drama could reduce the phrase to the merely practical level of discourse. Like Lear's button, which fastens not only his shirt but his eternal soul to his physical time-and-space-bound body, this imperative to Horatio in the context demands to be read poetically.

S.D.: Q2 substantially. *all the state:* the nobility, or perhaps the council of state, cf., *Troilus and Cressida* IV.ii.67, IV.v.264, *Timon of Athens* I.ii.1, *Cymbeline* III. iv.38.

A table prepared, trumpets, drums, and officers with cushions. [Enter] King, Queen, Laertes, [Osric], and all the state, [Attendants with] foils [and] daggers.

KING

Come, Hamlet, come and take this hand from me.   225

[King puts Laertes' hand into Hamlet's.]

HAMLET

Give me your pardon, sir. I have done you wrong,

But pardon't as you are a gentleman.

This presence knows, and you must needs have heard,

How I am punished with a sore distraction.

Give me … wrong: Hamlet is penitent about the death of Polonius, cf., III.iv.172–73, 176–77, and is also fulfilling his mother's request at lines 206–207 and his approval of it at line 208.

pardon't: pardon it.

This presence: those in the presence of the King, as with "audience" in line 240.

punished: "afflicted" (Riverside). **sore distraction:** serious madness, cf., III.i.5, IV.v.2.

● **SPEECH NOTE: What I have done … my brother:** Johnson finds the falsehood in Hamlet's claiming madness "unsuitable to the character of a brave or a good man," and Seymour finds it ignoble (both quoted in Furness). Both misunderstand the import of the speech. Hamlet is justified by the facts that he must keep up the pretense of suffering from madness until his mission is complete and that he had in truth no intention to kill Polonius. What led to the death of Polonius was the villainy of the King and the pride of Hamlet, a pride which Hamlet now realizes to have been a kind of madness of the will though not of the intellect, matters of which Laertes can and need have no knowledge. Hamlet is about to suffer the consequence of his earlier error, but he is not adding to his sins that of lying here, for he is the rightful king of Denmark at the moment, and state matters require him to do so, as they required him to swear the guards and Horatio to secrecy, to play at madness for the court, to add lines to the play within the play, to write a false commission to the King of England, and so on. Hamlet loses no virtue in asking genuine pardon for a genuine error even though the true cause of the error remains hidden from the pardoner. His "disclaiming from a purposed evil" (denying that his killing of Polonius was intentional) is no lie, cf., line 382 note. The only significant lie in this exchange, as we see in the next speech, is that of Laertes.

What I have done   230

What I have done: The lineation in both Q2 and F being irregular and differing from one another, I follow Jenkins in setting these two feet as a separate line, with the implied pause of the empty feet before rather than after the words. Following F, where "distraction" comes in the middle of a line, Abbott notes that it has four syllables (§479).

That might your nature, honor, and exception

nature, honor, and exception: a hendiadys implying objection for reasons of nature and honor. Wright (pages 192–93) correctly rejects treating "exception" as a third parallel term. Laertes' response addresses nature (line 244) and honor (line 246) but not "exception" as a third term, and OED cites only this use as evidence for the sense "dislike, dissatisfaction." It is Laertes' filial nature and sense of honor that take exception to Hamlet's killing of Polonius and therefore stir him to violent action. **nature:** filial feelings, cf., I.v.81, III.ii.393. **honor:** the aristocratic duty to preserve one's family honor by redressing injury. **exception:** objection, complaint (OED 6.a.).

Roughly awake I here proclaim was madness.
Was't Hamlet wronged Laertes? Never Hamlet.
If Hamlet from himself be ta'en away,
And when he's not himself does wrong Laertes, 235
Then Hamlet does it not; Hamlet denies it.
Who does it then? His madness. If't be so,
Hamlet is of the faction that is wronged;
His madness is poor Hamlet's enemy.

Roughly awake: stir to violence, harshness, or severity.

from himself be ta'en away: be out of his mind. Though Abbott suggests "be" is indicative, parallel to "does wrong" in the next line (§298), Hamlet does not mean that he is out of his mind now but only at times. Hence "be" is probably subjunctive, implying "if he be out of his mind at certain times." Only the verbs of the *when* clause (*is* and *does wrong*) are indicative, "Cf. 'Ophelia divided from herself and her fair judgment' (IV.v.84–5)" (Jenkins). ● Unlike Ophelia's madness there, Hamlet's madness is a fiction, but we know that in a moral sense Hamlet too had been taken from himself and divided from his better judgment by the succumbing of his will to the personal desire for revenge in the form of willing the damnation of the King, cf., SPEECH NOTE after line 229.

Sir, in this audience, 240

Sir, in this audience: i.e., publicly, in F only, cf., line 228 note.

Let my disclaiming from a purposed evil

my disclaiming from a purposed evil: my claiming not to have intended harm (to Polonius).

Free me so far in your most generous thoughts

Free: absolve (Riverside). **so far … that:** such that it be as if.

That I have shot mine arrow o'er the house
And hurt my brother.

I have shot … brother: ● This phrase may owe something to the common "figure of the arrow that, once released, may go farther than one meant" (Jenkins), but the point here is not the distance but the obstruction of the house, which prevents seeing where and therefore on whom the arrow will land, as in III.iv the arras prevented Hamlet's seeing who was behind it. In short, it was an accident. **my brother:** a reinforcement of Laertes' role as foil for Hamlet, "both his foe and his second self" (Jenkins).

● SPEECH NOTE: **I am satisfied … wrong it:** From his plotting with the King in IV.vii we know that Laertes is lying here, for it is precisely for reasons of "nature" (cf., line 231 note and next note) that he desires his revenge, nor has he any intention of actually demanding "reconcilement" by the mediation of honorable masters, for he expects Hamlet to be dead momentarily. Even as he is saying that he accepts Hamlet's love, i.e., Hamlet's humble confession, request for forgiveness, and brotherhood, and that he will not wrong it, Laertes is planning to murder Hamlet. The intentional lie of this speech is, in terms of Laertes' purpose of revenge, a parallel to Hamlet's playacted madness, for each is a calculated falsehood to keep the avenger's true intentions hidden. At a deeper level, it is a spiritual fall, the refusal of divinely ordained forgiveness of one's (in this case penitent) enemy, which makes a parallel to Hamlet's refusal of his own divine mission in his soliloquy of III.iii.

LAERTES

I am satisfied in nature,
Whose motive in this case should stir me most   245
To my revenge, but in my terms of honor

I am satisfied ... terms of honor: The antithesis is between "nature" and "honor," the motive of nature being to preserve his self-respect as a man, an honorable man, and a son, and the motive of honor being his care for his public name in the eyes of others.

I stand aloof and will no reconcilement
Till by some elder masters of known honor

stand aloof: keep myself apart. **will no:** choose not to accept any. For *will* without another verb here see Abbott §316. **reconcilement:** reconciliation. ● Laertes rejects reconciliation with his "brother" of line 244.

I have a voice and precedent of peace

voice and precedent: "authoritative pronouncement [cf., *voice* at lines 356 and 392 and at I.iii.28], justified by precedent" (Dowden quoted in Jenkins), perhaps a hendiadys, "an opinion that will serve as a precedent" (Wright, page 187). **precedent:** Jenkins following Johnson, president Q2 and F. **of peace:** formal reconcilement.

To keep my name ungored. But till that time   250

name: reputation. **ungored:** unwounded, cf., line 344 and *Troilus and Cressida* III.iii.228. **till:** all F, Q2.

I do receive your offered love like love

love like love: gesture of kindness, i.e., lines 226–44 as the honestly intended kindness it appears to be.

And will not wrong it.

And will not wrong it: Essentially a lie, for he intends to murder Hamlet in a moment.

HAMLET

                I embrace it freely

it: the reception of his apology, or perhaps Laertes' implied love and forgiveness. **freely:** without reservations, like those we know to be in Laertes' mind.

And will this brother's wager frankly play.

this brother's wager: Editors are fairly equally divided between amending Q2 brothers and F Brothers to "brother's" (= this brother-like match") or to "brothers'" (the match between two brothers), cf., line 244 note. ● In either case, Hamlet is treating Laertes as his metaphorical brother not only as a form of courtly kindness but in recognition that Laertes' situation is akin to his own, cf., lines 77–78. **frankly:** openly, genuinely.

Give us the foils.

foils: cf., line 175 note.

LAERTES

          Come, one for me.

HAMLET

I'll be your foil, Laertes. In mine ignorance   255
Your skill shall like a star i' th' darkest night

foil: Hamlet is playing on a second sense of the word in the previous line, namely the thin metal background that enhances by contrast the luminosity of jewels set against it. That sense is applied to a character in a play whose similarity to another character brings out their differences by contrast.
● Hamlet means that his own relatively poor fencing skill will make that of Laertes look the better, but

Stick fiery off indeed.

LAERTES

You mock me, sir.

HAMLET

No, by this hand.

KING

Give them the foils, young Osric. Cousin Hamlet,
You know the wager?

HAMLET

Very well, my lord.   260
Your Grace has laid the odds a th' weaker side.

KING

I do not fear it; I have seen you both.
But since he is bettered, we have therefore odds.

LAERTES

This is too heavy. Let me see another.

HAMLET

This likes me well. These foils have all a length?   265

OSRIC

Ay, my good lord.

KING

Set me the stoups of wine upon that table.

If Hamlet give the first or second hit,

Or quit in answer of the third exchange,

Let all the battlements their ordnance fire.   270
The King shall drink to Hamlet's better breath,

And in the cup an union shall he throw
Richer than that which four successive kings
In Denmark's crown have worn. Give me the cups,

Shakespeare means, and we hear, the witty implication of Laertes' dramatic function as foil character, and perhaps also a subtle hint that Hamlet will become, though unintentionally, the deadly means of Laertes' death when the foils in the other sense are exchanged (lines 302–303). **ignorance:** relative lack of fencing skill, ● NOTE TO ACTORS: the last two syllables slurred (*ig-n'rance*), preserving the pentameter (Abbott §494). **Stick fiery off:** stand out brightly, cf., *Coriolanus* V.iii.73.

by this hand: an oath, I swear by this (my) hand.

Give them … Osric: an "amphibious" phrase, completing the previous line and beginning its own (Abbott §513). **young:** cf., line 185 note. **Cousin:** relative, here nephew, as at I.ii.64.

Your Grace: an honorific title for the King, as for the Queen at III.iv.3, cf., *your Majesty*. **laid the odds a:** bet on, cf., *2 Henry IV* V.v.105. About *a* for *on*, see Abbott §140.

it: the consequences of having bet on the weaker fencer.

bettered: F, judged to be better at fencing, better Q2.

odds: the three-hit handicap, cf., line 165 note and line 211.

This … another: referring to the foils.

likes me: pleases me, agrees with me, cf., II.ii.80. For the impersonal verb see Abbott §297. **all a length:** all one length (Abbott §81).

me: for me, the ethical dative, see Abbott §220 and Webster's 2nd. **stoups:** drinking vessel, cup, flagon, or tankard (OED 2.), cf., V.i.60.

If Hamlet give … drinks to Hamlet": I follow Jenkins in taking this whole speech to image what the King will do on fulfillment of the *if*-clause of lines 268–69, with the parenthetical interruption to have the "cups" "placed by him in readiness" and ignoring Q2's marginal S.D. at line 278 ("*Trumpets the while*"), which "may be a bookkeeper's misunderstanding" (Jenkins).

quit: requite, i.e., pay back a third hit of Laertes with a hit of his own, assuming Hamlet does not make either of the first two hits. ● the King is looking for the quickest way for Hamlet to drink the poison.

ordnance: cannons, cf., line 275 note.

better breath: freer and easier breathing, i.e., increased energy. ● the King is covering his plot of murder by pretending to be Hamlet's cheering section.

union: vnion F, Vnice Q2 (uncorrected), Onixe Q2 (corrected). ● "A pearl [cf., line 282] of large size, good quality, and great value, esp. one which is supposed to occur singly" (OED sb.², cf., the origin of *onion*), from the report of Pliny the Elder in his *Natural History*

that "no two pearls are ever found perfectly alike;
and it was from this circumstance, no doubt, that
our Roman luxury first gave them the name of *unio*,
or the unique gem" (IX.56), and that "it was in the
time of the Jugurthine war [110–107 BC], that the
name of *unio* was first given to pearls of remarkable
size" (IX.59). "Drinking a pearl" became an image of
luxury and extravagance, as illustrated by an incident
reported by Pliny in which Cleopatra, to win a wager,
dissolves a rare pearl in vinegar and drinks it (IX.58).
Horace reports a similar story (*Satires* II.3.239–42):
"The son of Aesopus, [the actor] (that he might,
forsooth, swallow a million of sesterces at a draught),
dissolved in vinegar a precious pearl, which he had
taken from the ear of Metella: how much wiser was
he [in doing this] than if he had thrown the same into
a rapid river, or the common sewer?" "Shakespeare
presumably [also] knew ... that ... Sir Thomas
Gresham ... was fabled to have crushed a pearl in wine
to drink the Queen's health when she visited the new
Exchange in 1571" (Jenkins LN).

And let the kettle to the trumpet speak,	275
The trumpet to the cannoneer without,	
The cannons to the heavens, the heaven to earth,	

let the kettle ... drinks to Hamlet": ● "This resumes
and expands line [270]" (Jenkins). ● Cf., I.ii.125–28
and especially I.iv.10–38, where Hamlet, objecting
to the custom, ties it to the danger of the individual
soul's corruption from "one particular fault." The
hypocritical public glorification of Hamlet with
a custom of which he disapproves reinforces our
awareness of the King's arrogant self-indulgence. In
symbolically commanding the heavens into his own
service ("respeaking earthly thunder"), the King
makes both a parallel to Hamlet's attempt to play
God in III.iii and a contrast with Hamlet's newfound
humility after the sea voyage and graveyard scene.
kettle: kettle drum. **the heaven:** Q2 and F, "Later Qq
and some eds. regularize to *heavens*, but 17th-century
usage permits either and the singular occurs in the
corresponding I.ii.127" (Jenkins).

"Now the king drinks to Hamlet." Come, begin.
And you, the judges, bear a wary eye.

"Now the king drinks to Hamlet": Not an indication
of what he is doing at this moment but of what
he will be saying and doing in fulfillment of the *if*-
clause of lines 268–69, as he does at lines 282–83, cf.,
line 268 note.

HAMLET
Come on, sir.
LAERTES
　　　　　Come, my lord. [*They play.*]

s.d.: only in F. ● i.e., they begin fencing.

HAMLET
　　　　　　　One.
LAERTES
　　　　　　　　No.

One: one hit, for Hamlet against Laertes.

HAMLET
　　　　　　　　　Judgment.   280
OSRIC
A hit, a very palpable hit.

Judgment: ● Hamlet calls for a judgment about the
hit from Osric, the referee.

LAERTES
　　　　　Well, again.

again: begin fencing again.

KING

   Stay. Give me drink. Hamlet, this pearl is thine.
   Here's to thy health.

Drum, trumpets, and shot.

Give him the cup.

HAMLET

   I'll play this bout first. Set it by awhile.
   Come.

[They play again.]

   Another hit; what say you?   285

LAERTES

   I do confess't.

KING

   Our son shall win.

QUEEN

                 He's fat, and scant of breath.
   Here, Hamlet, take my napkin, rub thy brows.
   The Queen carouses to thy fortune, Hamlet.

HAMLET

   Good madam.

KING

                Gertrude, do not drink.   290

QUEEN

   I will, my lord, I pray you pardon me.

Stay: stop, pause. **Give me drink:** • Fulfilling the promise of line 268, Hamlet having given the first hit, the King drinks, which sets the drum, trumpets, and cannon to sound successively, as instructed at lines 268–71, 275–78. **this pearl is thine. / Here's to thy health:** • NOTE TO DIRECTORS: The text does not make explicit whether the King drinks first and then puts the pearl in the cup to be handed to Hamlet, or puts the pearl in the cup and then drinks (or pretends to drink) and then hands it to Hamlet, or whether "Here's to thy health" is intended to introduce the King's drinking or the King's handing the cup over to Hamlet, or whether the pearl itself bears the poison or the poison is already in the cup meant for Hamlet. Any of these possibilities fits the text, which leaves the director at liberty here.

S.D.: Q2 has "Drum, trumpets and shot. / Florish, a peece goes off" set inappropriately in the margin several lines too early and is in itself redundant, since "*Flourish*" means a blare of "*trumpets*," and "*a piece goes off*" is synonymous with "*shot*." F has *Trumpets sound, and shot goes off*. • These directions are in accordance with the King's promise of lines 268–78 and with the Danish custom that Hamlet repudiates at I.iv.15–16.

bout: group of a dozen passes or attacks, cf., line 165 note.

Another hit: "There is no need for the second hit to be celebrated like the first, and the opportunity afforded by 'the first *or* second' (line [268]) has been taken already" (Jenkins).

son: recalling I.ii.64, 65, 67, and 117.

fat: moistened with sweat.
napkin: handkerchief. **rub:** wipe, cf., 2 *Henry IV* II.iv.217.
carouses: drinks. **to thy fortune:** • in honor of your past (good) fortune, in having made two hits, and implying your future (good) fortune, in winning the match, with weighty irony to the audience, who understand that "fortune" without the word *good* can imply the bad fortune we know the King wishes on Hamlet.

I will ... pardon me: • Directors have sometimes caused Gertrude to indicate by her expression and gesture that she is aware that the cup is poisoned and is choosing to commit suicide, whether out of a guilty conscience or an effort to forestall Hamlet's being poisoned or both. There is absolutely no textual evidence for such a reading, and Shakespeare's method being what it is, if the audience were meant to think that Gertrude knowingly drinks poison, the text would somewhere have said so. As Hamlet observes, "The players cannot keep counsel, they'll tell all," cf., III.ii.141–42 and note. In fact the evidence of lines 309–10 is that Gertrude is surprised by finding the drink poisoned. More importantly, it is heaven, not Gertrude, who is "ordinant" here. The Ghost had said "Leave her to heaven" (I.v.86), and Gertrude, having continued in her penitent loyalty to Hamlet, now dies as penance by the divine shaping expressed in Hamlet's newfound insight at lines 10–11. There is no evidence for the guilt of suicide upon Gertrude's soul, and to depict her as intending to drink poison is entirely to disrupt the significance of the trajectory of her role in the drama and to introduce a distraction from the point of Hamlet's revelation as it applies to her.

KING [*Aside.*]
  It is the poisoned cup; it is too late.

It is the poisoned ... too late: ● NOTE TO DIRECTORS AND ACTORS: While in the context of modern, more literal forms of drama it may be hard to imagine executing this aside persuasively, there being so many people onstage within earshot of the King, the stage convention in Shakespeare's time was so strong that delivering this aside seriously posed no significant difficulty. Even audiences whose experience is mostly of modern drama can recognize the expectation of Shakespeare's style that they should willingly suspend their disbelief here. In practice, if no one onstage titters, neither will the audience.

HAMLET
  I dare not drink yet, madam—by and by.
QUEEN
  Come, let me wipe thy face.
LAERTES [*Aside to the King.*]
  My lord, I'll hit him now.
KING [*Aside to Laertes.*]
                I do not think't.   295

dare not: perhaps because the alcohol might affect his fencing. **by and by:** soon.

Come ... face: cf., line 288 note.

s.d. [*Aside to the King.... Aside to Laertes.*]: cf., line 292 note.

think't: think so. ● Perhaps the King thinks that Laertes means he will win the next fencing pass with a hit, though Laertes' aside suggests that he means he will hit Hamlet "now," outside the bounds of the sporting match when Hamlet is not prepared.

LAERTES [*Aside.*]
  And yet it is almost against my conscience.

And yet it ... conscience: cf., line 292 note. **conscience:** the inner lawgiver and the laws it gives, cf., line 67 note. ● Whether what is against Laertes' conscience is specifically hitting Hamlet when he is unprepared or hitting him at all with the unbated and poisoned foil, the point is that Laertes is experiencing a questioning of his own will to commit the sinful act of betraying the Prince, whose "love" he has just promised not to wrong. In keeping with Laertes' role as foil, his aside here is a short outward parallel to the inner debate of Hamlet at III.iii.73ff. Hamlet had accepted the duty to revenge the murder of his father but with evil will chose not to do so, and Laertes has announced that he would not wrong Hamlet's love (lines 251–52) and is now about to do so. Each has a moment of self-questioning before making the evil choice, Hamlet's choice being *not* killing the King in III.iii, Laertes' choice being killing Hamlet at line 302.

HAMLET
  Come for the third, Laertes. You do but dally.

third: third pass or attack. **but dally:** are only toying with me, not taking the contest seriously.

I pray you pass with your best violence.

I am afeard you make a wanton of me.
LAERTES
Say you so? Come on.   300

They play.

OSRIC
Nothing, neither way.
LAERTES
                    Have at you now!

[Laertes wounds Hamlet; then] in scuffling,
they change rapiers.

KING
Part them; they are incensed.
HAMLET
Nay, come again.

      [Hamlet wounds Laertes; the Queen falls.]

OSRIC
               Look to the Queen there, ho!

pass: attack, cf., line 165 note. **best violence:** most serious effort and force, for the *io* in "violence" as two syllables, see Abbott §479.

afeard: afraid, affear'd F, sure Q2. **make a wanton of:** are treating me like a spoiled child, whom you are allowing to win. ● "Laer[tes] is not playing his best, and it is the conscience [consciousness? burdened conscience?] of what is at the point of his foil that keeps him from doing so; and the effects are perceptible to Ham[let], though he dreams not of the reason" (Hudson quoted in Furness).
s.d. *They play.*: F, not in Q2.

Nothing, neither way: In this pass neither has scored a hit.

Have at: I will attack. **now:** before Hamlet is ready, outside the rules of the match. In all previous passes at least one or both of them have said "Come" to indicate readiness for the pass. Here Laertes has not said or waited for Hamlet to say "Come."

s.d. *they change rapiers*: "An exchange of weapons as a result of disarming was not uncommon in Elizabethan fencing ... Yet the imperious gesture [sometimes enacted on the stage] is the reverse of what is called for by *scuffling* and *incensed*. Nor is there anything in the confession of Laertes (lines [313–320]) to imply that Hamlet has deliberately sought to punish his 'foul practice'. What kills Laertes is not Hamlet's will but his 'own treachery' ([line 307]) when it has 'turn'd itself' ([line 318]) against him, and fallen on the inventor's head ([line 385]). To see in the exchange of weapons a human rather than a providential design goes against both the text and the spirit of the play. A distinction between the hero's treatment of the man on whom he must exact revenge and the man from whom he must suffer it is consistently maintained" (Jenkins LN).
incensed: enraged.

come again: an invitation to fence again, now formally invited by Hamlet's word "come" but no longer within the formal rules of fencing, both of them being "incensed," Laertes in vengeance, Hamlet because he has been wounded. Now that the unbated and poisoned weapon is in Hamlet's hands, Laertes knows that he is fencing for his life, whereas Hamlet is fencing only to repay what he thinks is a minor wound. In this last pass Hamlet fulfills the King's *if*-clause at lines 268–69, not only having made the first two hits but, in wounding Laertes, "quitting in answer of the third exchange" (or rather the fourth, since the third led to no hit on either side). The full dimensions of the requital, life for life, are known to Laertes and to us at this point and will become known to Hamlet only at lines 315–319.

ho!: The word may be "A call to stop the combat, as in Chaucer, *Knight's T[ale]*, lines 1706, 2656" (Jenkins), cf., Staunton in Furness and OED (*int.*², *sb.*³,

HORATIO

They bleed on both sides. How is it, my lord?

OSRIC

How is't, Laertes? 305

LAERTES

Why, as a woodcock to mine own springe, Osric;

I am justly killed with mine own treachery.

HAMLET

How does the Queen?

KING

She sounds to see them bleed.

QUEEN

No, no, the drink, the drink—O my dear Hamlet—

The drink, the drink; I am poisoned. 310

Dies.

HAMLET

O villainy! Ho!

Let the door be locked. Treachery! Seek it out.

[*Exit Osric.*]

LAERTES

It is here, Hamlet. Hamlet, thou art slain.

No medicine in the world can do thee good;

In thee there is not half an hour's life. 315

The treacherous instrument is in thy hand,

Unbated and envenomed. The foul practice

and *v.*²), but could also serve to call for attention to the Queen, as at line 311.

How is't, Laertes?: Horatio tends to Hamlet, Osric to Laertes.

as a woodcock … springe: as a fool caught in my own trap. The "woodcock" is a proverbially silly or foolish bird, and a "springe" is a snare. ● Laertes' line combines "two proverbs (Tilley F 626 ['The fowler is caught (taken) in his own net (snare)'], S 788 ['A springe to catch a woodcock']), so that the man who is caught in his own snare becomes the foolish bird who is easily caught" (Jenkins). And cf., "a woodcock is trained to decoy other birds into a springe… . while strutting about just outside the springe, … the woodcock incautiously places his foot in or on the springe, and so is caught" (F.J.V., *Notes & Queries*, 8 Aug. 1874, page 103, reference in Furness).

I am justly … treachery: ● Deathbed clarity about one's life, like deathbed prophecy, is a standard trope in Shakespeare's drama. Laertes, knowing he is on the point of death, can now see his choice and the justice of its consequences with perfect clarity. It was under the influence of the malicious King that Laertes did not honestly accept Hamlet's repentance of line 226ff. Now, about to die, Laertes recognizes his own fault in succumbing to the temptation of the King and expresses his penitence here. He will forgive Hamlet and ask for his forgiveness at line 329.

sounds: swoons, faints.

O my dear Hamlet: ● There are no textual grounds for imagining (as some have done) that Gertrude is addressing the Prince's father rather than the Prince himself.

O villainy … art slaine: Line breaks, regularized here, are inconsistent in Q2 and F, any of their half-lines being potentially "amphibious" in the sense used by Abbott (§513). **Ho!:** A call for attention, presumably from attendants or guards (OED *int.*¹ 2.a.,), cf., line 303.

Treachery: treason against a sovereign (OED b.) as well as other forms of betrayal. ● Laertes uses the word at line 307 and "treacherous" at line 316.

s.d. *Exit Osric*: Not in Q2 or F, but "Necessary for the entry before l. [351], which most eds. delete. But if an editor is to help Shakespeare out, he should not remove a clearly purposed entry but contrive an unobtrusive exit… . it may occur … plausibly in the general commotion here" (Jenkins). ● NOTE TO DIRECTORS: Osric may be seen as leaving to obey the order to have the doors locked, or as perhaps running in fear from danger and returning only under the safety he feels in the presence of Fortinbras.

treacherous: see line 312 note.

Unbated and envenomed: unblunted (by the usual button or knob used in fencing for sport) and poisoned,

Hath turned itself on me. Lo, here I lie,
Never to rise again. Thy mother's poisoned.

I can no more. The King—the King's to blame.   320

HAMLET
The point envenomed too! Then, venom, to thy work.

[Hurts the King.]

cf., IV.vii.138, 140–48. **foul practice:** vile plot, trick, deception, cf., IV.vii.67, 138.

Lo: behold. **here I lie:** ● "Emphasizing Nemesis" (Jenkins), or rather God's retributive justice, cf., I.v.110, where Hamlet intends to be the instrument of that justice, *King Lear* V.iii.171, 175, where Edmund, agreeing with Edgar that "the gods are just" and recognizing that "The wheel is come full circle, I am here," chooses to do some good as Laertes does here, and *Macbeth* V.ix.20–21, the justice of whose end is recognized only by others, as with the King here. Cf., also Hamlet's "Here" about the potion at line 325.

can no more: i.e., can speak no more. ● except that Laertes is able to add a final accusation of the King, which serves as the crucial spur to Hamlet's passionate rage and consequent action. **the King's to blame:** ● Laertes is correct in many senses. The King has not only unintentionally caused the death of the Queen and seduced Laertes into the evil plot against Hamlet, whom, if Laertes could see from our perspective, he would recognize as his rightful king. The original crimes of the King and his compounding of them by plotting against Hamlet are the source of all the tragic disaster and the cause of all the deaths. Had the King not killed his brother, Polonius and Ophelia would be alive and Laertes, like Hamlet, would not have been tempted to revenge.

The point … work: Q2 sets as one line, F as two. Riverside as two, hence the discrepancy in line numbering. The line may be read as a pentameter (rather than a hexameter) if the syllables "-om to thy" are elided and counted as a single unstressed syllable, cf., Abbott §503, or it may be a trimeter couplet, cf., Abbott §500.

s.d. [*Hurts the King.*]: F, not in Q2, *Wounds the King* Jenkins. ● Hamlet acts now in a sudden passionate fury, with the intention of causing not the damnation but only the death of the King, his passion now the very instrument of divine justice that it would have been (as it ought to have been) in III.iii had not Hamlet's perverse will then got in the way of the divine shaping. Having learned his lesson of humility from the providential events of the sea voyage and from the *memento mori* of the graveyard scene, Hamlet has espoused "readiness" (line 222) in place of "deep plots" (line 9). The result is that, having got his own will out of the way, he is now a pure instrument of the divine will, and the mission laid upon him by the Ghost is at last accomplished. His action also resolves the question of revenge upon which the play turns. Vengeance remains God's, not man's, but God can use any man, and any of the qualities of that man (as passionate rage or right reason in Hamlet), to effect the divine revenge, as God uses Hamlet's passion here. Laertes too has performed the divine will in being the instrument of justice executed upon Hamlet. Though Laertes *thought* he was punishing the crime of killing Polonius, in fact Hamlet's crime was the choice *not* to kill the King in III.iii. In all three punishments, of Laertes for treachery, of Hamlet for pride, and of the King for all his crimes, the instrument is the same envenomed sword. In the case of Claudius, the poisoned drink prepared by himself is added as an ironic "back or second" (IV.vii.153). There remains one additional task necessary to the completion of Hamlet's spiritual journey, namely the forgiveness of Laertes. And two tasks remain to him in his function as rightful king: the preservation of the life and soul of Horatio, in order that he might tell Hamlet's story and avoid damnation for suicide, and the naming of Fortinbras as legitimate successor to the throne for the sake of the kingdom.

Treason!: ● It is this reaction from the court that was always to be feared, hence Hamlet's playacted madness, his requirement of four witnesses to testify to the reality of the Ghost, cf., I.i.29 note, and his confiding in Horatio and specifically charging him to observe the King's reaction to the "Murder of Gonzago" at III.ii.78–87, all for potential defenses against the charge of treason. The request that Horatio live and tell his story (lines 344–49) similarly protects Hamlet's posthumous reputation.

I am but hurt: ● Even at the point of death, the King, grasping at false hopes, refuses, unlike Laertes, to repent, recalling his own words about his soul "that struggling to be free / Art more engaged" (III.iii.68–69).

damnèd: ● Hamlet is in a passionate rage, not engaging in the calculating and sinful intellection of his soliloquy in III.iii. Here he is not willing the King's damnation but only in a passion condemning the King's villainy.

Drink off this potion: Finish this cup of poison. ● Hamlet forces Claudius to drink the poison that was meant to kill Hamlet and did kill Gertrude. "[T]reachery falls on the inventor's head [cf., lines 307, 328, and 385]" (Jenkins). **thy union:** F, the Onixe Q2. ● the pearl of lines 272 and 282, see line 272 note, and possibly also "the King's marriage, of which the poisoned cup thus becomes the symbol" (Jenkins). Hamlet's question is bitter sarcasm: Is this the supposed rich gift ("union") you publicly offered me? Here, have it (i.e., the poison) yourself.

Follow my mother: i.e., to death. ● The desire of Claudius to follow Gertrude and to be king led him to the crimes for which he is now punished. Now divine justice, with Hamlet as its instrument, ironically punishes Claudius with following Gertrude where, in his treachery though unintentionally, he has sent her, so that as the death of Hamlet Senior joined Claudius and Gertrude in a false life, it now joins them in death. It does not join them in the afterlife, however, for Gertrude has repented and Claudius has not. Love and ambition, the two motives that led Claudius into sin, are also the two motives that, when thwarted, were thought to cause the two forms of madness

ALL
Treason! treason!

KING
O yet defend me, friends; I am but hurt.

HAMLET
Here, thou incestuous, murderous, damnèd Dane,   325

Drink off this potion! Is thy union here?

Follow my mother!

King dies.

LAERTES

He is justly served.
It is a poison tempered by himself.

Exchange forgiveness with me, noble Hamlet.

Mine and my father's death come not upon thee,   330
Nor thine on me.

Dies.

HAMLET
Heaven make thee free of it. I follow thee.

---

from which Hamlet pretended to suffer. Thus all the elements of the main plot come full circle.

served: a) fed (on the drink), and b) requited, paid back

tempered: "mixed, concocted. Cf. *Cym[beline]* V.v.250, *Rom[eo and Juliet]* III.v.97, *[Much] Ado* II.ii.[19]" (Jenkins).

Exchange forgiveness with me: • Here Laertes, having seen his evil plan trumped by a higher power and now knowing he is dying, turns his will toward repentance and the desire to be forgiven, absolving Hamlet too of guilt for the death of Polonius. On a more obvious, less profound level, Laertes thus fulfills his function as Hamlet's foil. His will, like Hamlet's, is now corrected by the recognition of the divinity that shapes our ends and of the humbling fact of death. Asking forgiveness, and giving it, he goes to death as a Christian penitent.

Mine and my father's death come not: subjunctive, i.e., let them not come. His last words may be compared with Ophelia's (IV.v.200–201). **Mine:** my, "often used by Shakespeare where we should say *my*" (Abbott §238)

Heaven make thee free of it: i.e., may Heaven absolve you of any guilt in relation to my death. For *of = from* see Abbott §166, and for the "amphibious" quality of the phrase, see Abbott §513. • If we compare this statement of Hamlet's complete Christian forgiveness of Laertes, the man immediately responsible for his death, with the expression of Hamlet's feeling that the redemption of his "dearest enemy" would be the next-to-last thing desirable, only just better than seeing his mother marry his uncle (I.ii.182–83), we see the great trajectory of Hamlet's spiritual development. From that dram of evil with the potential to corrupt his soul and risk its damnation in the judgment of God, cf., I.iv.23–38, Hamlet fell into corruption itself through pride and evil will, embodied in his decision to cause the damnation of the King in order to satisfy his desire for revenge (III.iii.73–96). Thereupon he committed the violent deed that confirmed his evil will, namely the killing of Polonius under the presumption that it was the King he was killing, which act led inevitably to this penalty of death. But the events of the sea voyage by the grace of Providence afforded Hamlet a second chance, akin to the second chance for honor afforded Fortinbras by his uncle (II.ii.61–80), to that afforded Gertrude by Hamlet's chastisement (III.iv), to that afforded Laertes in his having the time and impulse to beg Hamlet's forgiveness (lines 329–31), to that afforded Horatio by Hamlet's wrenching the cup from his hand (lines 342–49), and even to that afforded Osric to put on his hat (line 104). Thanks to that second chance, Hamlet has grown into the condition of humility in the face of human mortality (V.i.75–217), to a completely chastened will and spiritual readiness expressed above (lines 7–11 and 219–24), and finally to this pinnacle of Christian moral achievement, the forgiveness of his enemy. Attending that arc of character development is the elucidation of the true nature of revenge and the profound apotheosis of the revenge play form, namely the experience of the Christian truth that revenge against a man, even if accomplished by the hand of a man, belongs to God, and that only the man whose will is subordinated to God's may justly serve as God's instrument. It is this trajectory of character and theme that forms the essential story of Hamlet, and not any morally irrelevant excess of thought or incapacity to make up his mind or Oedipal love of his mother or other of the modern concerns foisted upon this play by later Romantic, Freudian, Existentialist, and other critics. Hamlet's essential heroism consists not in his intellectuality or melancholy or dreary situation or wit or magnanimity, though he has all these. His heroism consists in his representing the Christian ideal of the transformation of the human will through submission to the divine, even as the play at the same time confirms the Christian doctrine that nothing happens outside the divine will.

I am dead, Horatio. Wretched queen, adieu.

Wretched: miserable, unfortunate, cf., II.ii.168 and IV.vii.182. **adieu:** literally (I commend you) to God, French for "good-bye" in both the common meaning and the original sense "God be with you." ● yet another fulfillment of the Ghost's charge at I.v.86 ("leave her to heaven").

You that look pale and tremble at this chance,

You: at the literal level, those standing around on stage having seen the havoc unfold. The play-watching audience of course already know "what I could tell you," but see line 335 note below. **look pale and tremble:** are filled with fear ("pale") and awe ("tremble"), according to Aristotle the two essential effects of tragedy upon an audience, see line 363 note. **this chance:** this event or happening, this tragic catastrophe. ● "chance" "concentrates in a word the two main aspects of [the central Elizabethan conception of tragedy], aspects that had long been fused in the Latin equivalent, *casus* ... the fall and death of a great figure ... and ... the external cause of such a fall, the operation of that agency which to man seems Chance or Fortune, but which from a true and theological point of view is to be regarded as the unfolding of Divine Providence.... [T]he display on the stage of [that] operation ... strikes the witnesses with fear and terror when the case is notable, for it illuminates the disparity between the relative world of man and the absoluteness of the Eternal Cause" (Cunningham, *W/W*, page 17).

That are but mutes or audience to this act,   335

mutes or audience: ● The phrase figures the events on the stage as if they were happening in a play. The people on the stage are like mutes, i.e., non-speaking actors, or audience, i.e., non-speaking observers. The obvious implication of making characters in a play into "mutes" and "audience" is that the actual audience of *Hamlet* become, correspondingly, "mutes" and "audience" not only of *Hamlet* but of the universal drama of salvation, though mute ones for the duration of the play. Once again, as with the speech to the actors in III.ii and the "Murder of

Had I but time—as this fell sergeant Death

Is strict in his arrest—O, I could tell you—

But let it be. Horatio, I am dead,

Thou livest. Report me and my cause aright

To the unsatisfied.

HORATIO
          Never believe it.   340
I am more an antique Roman than a Dane.

Here's yet some liquor left.

HAMLET
          As th'art a man
Give me the cup. Let go! By heaven I'll have't!
[*Hamlet wrests the cup from Horatio's hand.*]
O God, Horatio, what a wounded name,

Gonzago," the implication is that "all the world's a stage" (*As You Like It* II.vii.139) and that the mute observers of this play are also players in the drama of life. **act:** this action, this conclusion of the play, this real performance of living parts.

as: which I have not because (Abbott §110).
fell: terrible, cruel. **sergeant:** "an officer of the courts whose duties included the making of arrests. Death as a 'fell arrest' occurs also in *Sonn.* LXXIV. The metaphor was traditional" (Jenkins LN, where examples are cited).

strict: precise (OED 8.), rigorous (OED 11., 14.a. and b.). **arrest:** both legal (performing the office as the sergeant of the divine judge) and "stopping of things in motion" (Raffel).

But let it be: cf., line 224 and note. ● Here at least no one could argue that Hamlet intends to suspend the conversation because of being interrupted by the entrance of other characters. He is being interrupted by death, but his phrase is clearly a resignation, a letting go of the will to report on his life and motives, though he has still several charges to give. His self-regard is surrendered in the face of the humbling by death.

cause: specifically his legal case against the King, in general his mission, purpose. **aright:** rightly, justly.

unsatisfied: i.e., because lacking knowledge of the facts, uninformed, cf., "unknowing" at line 379.

Never believe it: i.e., that I will live on.

I am more … a Dane: I am more an ancient ("antique") Roman stoic, capable of honorable suicide, than a Christian Dane, for whom suicide is forbidden, cf., I.ii.131–32, *Julius Caesar* V.iii.89 and V.v.51, *Antony and Cleopatra* IV.xv.86–87, and *Macbeth* V.viii.1.

Here's yet … left: ● Horatio tries to drink the remaining poison in a gesture which ties his own story as foil to those of Fortinbras, Laertes, and Hamlet, for even the balanced and rational man, as Hamlet and we see Horatio to be, cf., I.i.19 note, is driven at last by the passion of grief to a desperate choice, a potential fall resulting from the refusal of his will to obey both the charge of his friend and prince, who is theoretically at the moment his rightful king, and the "canon" of the "Everlasting" (I.ii.131–32), who forbids suicide. As with the others, however, Providence, here using the instrument of Hamlet's corrected will, prevents him, giving him a second chance to obey, as it did to Hamlet with the sea voyage, and to both Fortinbras and Laertes, see line 329 note.

As th'art a man … cup: ● Hamlet appeals to the most fundamental quality he can think of to reverse Horatio's decision to die with and because of him. He appeals to the fact of his being a man and hence a responsible moral being. Hamlet's demand then echoes and reverses Christ's prayer to have the cup of his sacrifice removed from him (Matthew 26:39,42,

Mark 14.36, Luke 22:42, and cf., John 18:11). Horatio's calling by a higher authority is precisely *not* to die, but his sacrifice must be to live in pain and to speak, and he will fulfill this charge. **th'art:** thou art. **Let go ... I'll ha't:** ● Hamlet then swears "by heaven" that his authoritative will that Horatio live, and not Horatio's will perverted by passion, shall be done, and Hamlet prevails by virtue of grace above all, of his rank, of his strength of purpose, of his love toward his friend, and, in the only plea sure to work on Horatio hereafter, of his appeal to Horatio's love and duty. **I'll:** I will, in the sense of am determined to. **ha't:** have it, take it from you.

Things standing thus unknown, shall I leave behind
                                        [me.   345

Things standing ... behind me: Q2, (Things standing thus unknown) shall live behind me F, the apparently unmetrical "shall I leave" and F's metrical regularity have led some to suspect both corruption in Q2 here and false correction in F (Jenkins substantially). Q2 being our best authority, the line can be made both grammatical and metrical if the words "shall I" are elided ("sh'll'I") and the stress placed on "leave."

If thou didst ever hold me in thy heart,

If thou ... heart: bringing the relationship to bear to enforce the following imperative, cf., I.v.23 and III.ii.72–74.

Absént thee from felicity awhile
And in this harsh world draw thy breath in pain
To tell my story.

Absént: ● NOTE TO ACTORS: stress on the second syllable, cf., *Taming of the Shrew* Induction ii.123 (Schmidt). **felicity:** joy (in heaven).

A march afar off, and shot within.

s.d. *shot within:* firing of cannon offstage.

What warlike noise is this?

Enter Osric.

s.d. *Enter Osric:* cf., line 312 note.

OSRIC
Young Fortinbras, with conquest come from Poland,   350

with conquest ... Poland: ● Fortinbras has triumphed in battle and won the honor he wanted to achieve originally by fighting for the portion of Denmark lost by his father (I.i.95–104, I.ii.17–25) and then, once his will was chastened, by fighting for land in Poland under rightful commission from Old Norway (II.ii.72–75).

To the ambassadors of England gives

ambassadors of England: bringing news to the Danish king that his supposed request has been fulfilled (lines 370–71).

This warlike volley.
HAMLET
          O, I die, Horatio.
The potent poison quite o'ercrows my spirit.
I cannot live to hear the news from England,

volley: simultaneous firing of cannon, salvo.

potent: powerful. **o'ercrows:** overcrows, triumphs over, as the victor in a cockfight (cf., instances in Chapman, Nashe, and Spenser quoted in Furness).

But I do prophesy the election lights   355
On Fortinbras. He has my dying voice.

But I do prophesy ... dying voice: ● To the dying Shakespeare ascribes authoritative spiritual insight as well as truthfulness, cf., line 307 note, *Merchant of Venice* I.ii.27–28, *Richard II* II.i.5–6 and 31, and *1 Henry IV* V.iv.83. Thus Hamlet both predicts that the election of the next king of Denmark, cf., line 65 note and I.ii.6 note, will land or settle, or perhaps "shine" (Raffel), on Fortinbras and supports Fortinbras' succession with his own will and vote, cf., "voice" at III.ii.341–42. "The importance naturally attaching to a monarch's own view of his successor is reflected here, as in the concern for Elizabeth [I]'s deathbed nomination of James [VI of Scotland to become King James I of England]" (Jenkins). Hamlet's approval, weighted by his being the rightful king, joins his foresight, weighted by his dying, in confirming the succession. As we know from I.i.80ff., and as Fortinbras reminds us at line 389, he has some "rights ... in this kingdom" and is now the only Denmark-related man of royalty left alive. Thus the very Denmark that Fortinbras at first willfully and wrongly would have attacked now falls providentially into his lap, the reward of his true obedience (II.ii.68–70), and the career of Fortinbras is finally seen as a complete parallel and foil to that of Hamlet, whose own true obedience to God, expressed at lines 10–11, 48, and 219–24, is also to be rewarded when he himself, as we are left hoping and as Horatio believes, falls into the lap of that kingdom of Heaven in which all men, even kings, are servants.

So tell him, with th' occurrents more and less

So tell him: i.e., tell him as much (that "He has my dying voice"), "so" = thus. **occurrents:** occurrences (OED B. *sb.* 1). **more and less:** greater and lesser, both major and minor, cf., Abbott §17.

Which have solicited—The rest is silence.

Dies.

solicited—: incited, urged (with the possible sense of disturbed, troubled). • If the sentence is complete, Hamlet is charging Horatio to tell Fortinbras all the events, great and small, that have impelled him (or them). If it is incomplete, shortened by his dying, he may mean impelled me (or us) to do what I (or we) have done, or perhaps "urged (me to give it him)" (Jenkins), i.e., to name Fortinbras heir to the throne. **The rest is silence:** i.e., what is left, all I have left to speak, is silence, with the possible sense of "eternal rest" and the final confirmation that barring some special revelation like that performed by the Ghost, the living cannot know the state of the dead, cf., Psalm 115:17 in context and 2 Esdras 7:32.

HORATIO

Now cracks a noble heart. Good night, sweet prince,

cracks: breaks, cf., *King Lear* II.i.90, *Coriolanus* V.iii.9, *Pericles* III.ii.77. **sweet:** common courtly epithet of affection or compliment, cf., III.ii.53 note.

And flights of angels sing thee to thy rest.   360

And flights of angels ... rest: i.e., may they do so (optative mood). • Though, as with Ophelia, human beings cannot know the particular judgment that God will pass on any soul, Horatio prays not only for Hamlet's rest but, by the implication of the reference to angels, for his salvation. "No specific source can be alleged or should be sought for so traditional a conception. But cf. e.g. the antiphon of the old Latin burial service, 'In paradisum deducant te angeli ... Chorus angelorum te suscipiat ... aeternam habeas requiem'; *Everyman*, lines 891–3, 'Methinketh that I hear angels sing ... where Everyman's soul received shall be'. See R.M. Frye, *Sh. and Christian Doctrine*, pages 135–6" (Jenkins). Horatio's use of the word "rest" echoes Hamlet's last line, but here the "silence" on this side of the line that divides life from death becomes the imagined music of angels on the other side of that line, so that Horatio's response to the death of his beloved friend becomes a chiasmus: "rest … silence … sing … rest," the echo enacting the whole play's juxtaposition of this-worldly and other-worldly viewpoints, the errors of the former, now successfully expiated, yielding to the joy of redemption in the latter.

S.D. *within*: i.e., offstage.

S.D. *colors*: flags, ensigns.

[March within.]

Why does the drum come hither?

Enter Fortinbras with the English Ambassadors, [Soldiers,] and Attendants with drum and colors.

FORTINBRAS

Where is this sight?

HORATIO

What is it ye would see?

If aught of woe or wonder, cease your search.

this sight: • Fortinbras, like Hamlet the son of a king and now having won honor in battle, naturally takes charge of the situation and asks to see the scene of which he has just heard.

aught: anything. **woe or wonder:** • Along with the fear exhibited by the bystanders at line 334 above, these words name the traditional response to the experience of tragedy, descending from the "pity and fear" of Aristotle's *Poetics* (1452a) through a long literary tradition, highly influenced by the fourth-century Roman grammarian Donatus. "Pity [*misericordia* or *commiseratio*] … denotes precisely the relationship of the spectator to the catastrophe; but the nature of the catastrophe itself is woeful [woe = *dolor* or *tristitia*]…. [The catastrophe] is also sudden, surprising, on a large scale, and involves great persons; hence it evokes wonder [*admiratio*] … that state of overpowering surprise, the shocked limit of feeling, which represents either the extreme of joy or, as in this case, the extreme of fear. Indeed, in the medieval tradition of psychological analysis it is defined as a species of fear … and thus the relation of wonder to fear is similar to that of pity to sorrow" (Cunningham, *W/W*, page 20–21). Horatio is naming precisely the essential qualities of tragedy as elaborated in the literary tradition stretching from Plato and Aristotle through the Medieval grammarians down to Shakespeare and his contemporaries. Cf., the phrase "woe and wonder" in the ballad "Northumberland Betrayed by Douglas" 2.2 (Child III.vi.411).

FORTINBRAS

This quarry cries on havoc. O proud death,

quarry: pile of dead bodies, from the word for the heap of dead deer killed in a hunt. **cries on:** cries out, shouts, cf., *Richard III* V.iii.231, *Othello* V.i.48. **havoc:** battle cry used to exhort soldiers to kill and plunder, cf., *King John* II.i.357, *Julius Caesar* III.i.273, *Coriolanus* III.i.273.
• Fortinbras says that the heap of corpses proclaims that Death has ordered a general spoliation and plunder of human beings. "The peculiarly Shakespearean use of a hunting metaphor (cf. *quarry*), as also in [*Julius*] *Caes*[*ar*] and *Cor*[*iolanus*], by imaging soldiers as hounds, intensifies the savagery. The word for the signal came to be used for the consequent devastation, so that … it is not here a call for further slaughter or vengeance but a description of the scene with which Fortinbras is confronted" (Jenkins). **proud:** because of the high rank

What feast is toward in thine eternal cell   365

That thou so many princes at a shot
So bloodily hast struck?

FIRST AMBASSADOR
                              The sight is dismal,

And our affairs from England come too late.
The ears are senseless that should give us hearing
To tell him his commandment is fulfilled,   370
That Rosencrantz and Guildenstern are dead.
Where should we have our thanks?

HORATIO
                              Not from his mouth,
Had it the ability of life to thank you.
He never gave commandment for their death.
But since, so jump upon this bloody question,   375
You from the Polack wars and you from England
Are here arrived, give order that these bodies
High on a stage be placèd to the view,

And let me speak to the yet unknowing world
How these things came about. So shall you hear   380

Of carnal, bloody, and unnatural acts,

Of accidental judgments, casual slaughters,

---

of all those here killed in addition to Death's general pride of triumph over all men.

feast: that of Death personified devouring those killed along with the literal devouring of bodies in the grave, cf., *1 Henry VI* IV.v.7, *King John*, II.i.350–55. **toward:** imminent, about to happen, cf., I.i.77 and *As You Like It* V.iv.35.

at a shot: at once (Abbott §81).

dismal: miserable, dreadful (OED B. 4.), "much stronger in meaning than now. Literally, characteristic of the *dies mali*, days of ill omen; hence calamitous" (Jenkins at II.ii.452), cf., II.ii.456.

affairs: business, undertaking.

The ears ... hearing: Those ears that ought to have heard our message, namely those of the King, lack the sense of hearing because he's dead.

Where should we have: From whom might we expect to have.

his: that of Claudius.

jump upon: precisely at the moment of, cf., I.i.65.
question: matter, subject for discussion or explanation, cf., III.i.55 note.

stage: platform, with the implication that Horatio's words will recreate the story we have seen as a tragedy performed on a stage, cf., line 380 note.

unknowing: cf., line 345.

So shall you hear ... inventors' heads: ● Horatio, the supremely rational man, gives a prologue to the events he is about to recount, namely those which we have just seen, as if in reality, on the "stage" where *Hamlet* is being performed. His list of plural general terms, each of which corresponds to one or more particular events we have witnessed, is meant to announce that what he is about to recount is a tragedy. See Cunningham *W/W*, pages 26–35.

carnal: the adultery (at least in the will) of Claudius with Gertrude. **bloody:** the murder of Hamlet Senior. **unnatural:** the fratricide and the incest committed by Claudius.

accidental judgments, casual slaughters: The former refers to "Hamlet's mistaking Polonius for the King, a judgment based upon misconstrued signs and hence not a true or substantial judgment. This is clear to anyone who is familiar with the scholastic discussion of manslaughter, or casual homicide [in which the example is given of one who commits manslaughter under the influence of alcohol: he is held responsible for the drunkenness that might lead to such an act but not for intentional murder, cf., Hamlet's distinction at lines 230–44]. To employ the Latin terminology which Shakespeare uses in its anglicized form, this judgment *per accidens* leads to a slaughter which is *praeter intentionem*, and so casual, not causal [like the unintentional killing of Gertrude by the King] (S[umma] T[heologica], 2–2. 64. 8)" (Cunningham *W/W*, page 32). • The full implication includes the idea of divine judgment or retribution taking the form of what appears to be accidental.

Of deaths put on by cunning and forced cause,

deaths put on by cunning and forced cause: those of Rosencrantz and Guildenstern, instigated ("put on") by Hamlet in cunning because he was enforced by circumstances (not naturally disposed) to cause them. **forced:** a) enforced or constrained and b) contrived, unnatural, not spontaneous (OED 2.), F, for no Q2.

And, in this upshot, purposes mistook

upshot: final outcome, conclusion. **purposes mistook:** Two senses may be at work here: Sense a) erroneous or transgressing intentions, specifically the evilly-conceived intentions of Claudius in murdering his brother and of Claudius and Laertes in seeking to murder Hamlet, but also applicable to the entire play. The central instance is Hamlet's mistaken purpose of seeking the damnation rather than merely the death of Claudius. Other instances are the mistaken purpose of Polonius in forbidding his daughter to speak with Hamlet, of Rosencrantz and Guildenstern in serving an evil king, of Fortinbras in initially seeking to attack Denmark, and of Horatio in seeking to commit suicide. The last two, like that of Hamlet, were forestalled by providential grace. Sense b) intentions that mistakenly land on unintended victims, like Polonius's on Ophelia, Hamlet's on Polonius, the King's on Gertrude, and Laertes' on himself, cf., III.ii.252 note (on "mistake").

Fall'n on the inventors' heads. All this can I   385
Truly deliver.

Fall'n on th'inventors' heads: the plans backfired, hurting those who made them. • In the immediate instance, the King sees Gertrude die from the cup he has prepared for Hamlet, and then he and Laertes die from the unbated and poisoned sword and the poisoned cup intended for Hamlet. But the idea is "a dominant motif of the play" (Jenkins), as seen in the spying on Hamlet by Polonius, which led to his own demise; the original murder and usurpation of Claudius; and Hamlet's plot to damn Claudius, which led to his own death because of the unintentional killing of Polonius, cf., III.ii.211–212 and III.iv.206–207. **Truly deliver:** correctly and faithfully report.

FORTINBRAS
        Let us haste to hear it,
And call the noblest to the audience.
For me, with sorrow I embrace my fortune.

to the audience: a) to the hearing of the tragedy Horatio is about to tell, and b) into the presence of Fortinbras, already feeling himself to be in the role of king.

I have some rights of memory in this kingdom,
Which now to claim my vantage doth invite me.   390

of memory: remembered, unforgotten.

vantage: both a) advantageous position, "favourable opportunity" (Jenkins), and b) advantage, self-advancement. **invite me:** i.e., to claim my rights.

HORATIO
Of that I shall have also cause to speak,
And from his mouth whose voice will draw on more.

Of that … draw on more: "that" is Fortinbras's claim to the throne in the previous two lines. Horatio is saying that he has reason to speak of Fortinbras's claim, referring to Hamlet's "prophecy" and "dying voice" in lines 355–56. • Hamlet's authority and vote will draw

But let this same be presently performed

Even while men's minds are wild, lest more
                                    [mischance

On plots and errors happen.

FORTINBRAS

                    Let four captains   395
Bear Hamlet like a soldier to the stage,

For he was likely, had he been put on,

To have proved most royal; and for his passage

The soldier's music and the rite of war
Speak loudly for him.   400

Take up the bodies. Such a sight as this
Becomes the field, but here shows much amiss.
Go bid the soldiers shoot.

          Exeunt marching, [bearing off the bodies,]
          after which a peal of ordnance is shot off.

---

other electors to vote in favor of making Fortinbras king of Denmark, cf., line 355 note. **his mouth:** i.e., Hamlet's. **more:** more voices, i.e., electors' votes.

this same: i.e., the placing of the bodies on a platform (line 378), the calling of the "noblest to the audience" (line 387), and Horatio's retelling (lines 379, 391). **presently:** immediately.

Even: ● NOTE TO ACTORS: elided into one syllable (*ev'n*) to preserve the pentameter. **wild:** agitated by fear and amazement.

On: in consequence of (Abbott §180).

captains: high ranking officers rather than common soldiers, as a sign of honor to a commanding officer, cf., *Coriolanus* V.vi.147–48. **stage:** the platform of line 378.

had he been put on: if he had been put to the test. ● As we know, but as Fortinbras does not yet know, Hamlet has indeed been put to the test of a kingship unrevealed to Denmark and of an obedience to God revealed only to Horatio and to us, a greater test than that which Fortinbras himself has faced. Like Fortinbras his foil, but at a profounder level, Hamlet has at first balked and then triumphed in a war, not only against the external foe but against the potential for evil within.

To have ... passage: ● NOTE TO ACTORS: the line appears to be a tetrameter, assuming "To have" to be elided to "T'have," but the pentameter may be preserved if "and" is treated as emphatic (cf., Abbott §481) with stresses on both "and" and "for." **To have proved:** to have been proven to be. For the use of the infinitive see Abbott §360. **royal:** kingly in both nature and art, i.e., worthy to be king. **passage:** passing to judgment and the next life, cf., III.iii.86.

soldier's: or possibly "soldiers'" (cf., line 253 note).

Speak: i.e., let the music and rite of war speak, an optative subjunctive mood (Abbott §364). ● Hamlet has triumphed in the most profound of human battles, that against the self in favor of God. Hence the soldier's music is even more appropriate for him than Fortinbras realizes.

this: this "quarry" or heap of dead bodies, cf., line 364.

Becomes the field: is appropriate to a battlefield.

shows much amiss: appears out of place if "shows" is intransitive, and perhaps also demonstrates that much has gone wrong if "shows" is transitive.

S.D. Jenkins, *Exeunt Marching: after the which, a Peal of Ordenance are shot off* F, *Exeunt.* Q2; **peal of ordnance:** loud volley or discharge of cannon fire, here appropriate, unlike at I.iv, cf., I.iv.15–16.

Printed in the USA
CPSIA information can be obtained
at www.ICGtesting.com
LVHW061213070124
768335LV00014B/163